11 Years
CBSE
Class 12
Mathematics

Previous Year-wise Solved Papers

(2013 - 2023) Powered with Concept Notes

DISHA ™
Publication Inc

DISHA Publication Inc.

45, 2nd Floor, Maharishi Dayanand Marg,
Corner Market, Malviya Nagar, new Delhi –110017
Tel: 49842349/ 49842350

By:

Raghvendra Kumar Sinha

Dileep Singh

Jitesh Acharya

Typeset By

DISHA DTP Team

Buying books from DISHA

Just Got A Lot More Rewarding!!!

We at DISHA Publication, value your feedback immensely and to show our apperciation of our reviewers, we have launched a review contest.

To participate in this reward scheme, just follow these quick and simple steps:
- Write a review of the product you purchase on Amazon/Flipkart.
- Take a screenshot/photo of your review.
- Mail it to *disha-rewards@aiets.co.in*, along with all your details.

Each month, selected reviewers will win exciting gifts from DISHA Publication. Note that the rewards for each month will be declared in the first week of next month on our website.

https://bit.ly/review-reward-disha.

Write To Us At

feedback_disha@aiets.co.in

CONTENTS

Chapterwise Division of Questions

The table below presents the chapter-wise division of the questions of the 19 papers. So this book can be put to dual usage-yearwise as well as chapter-wise. To find questions of a chapter just follow the question numbers in its row against the 19 papers. This table also depicts the Trend Analysis of 2023-2013 papers.

Ch. No.	Chapter Name	Year of Examination								
		2023		2022		2021	2020		2019	
		All India	Delhi	Term-I	Term-II		All India	Delhi	All India	Delhi
1.	Relations and Functions	35 & OR	2, 37	10, 15, 27, 37		Exam not held in 2021 due to Covid-19 pandemic	11, 21 (OR), 27	5, 7, 30	6, 15 & OR	7, 15 & OR
2.	Inverse Trigonometric Functions	20, 22, & OR	1, 21	7, 19, 23, 31, 34			3, 21	2, 14 & OR, 30 (OR)	18	14
3.	Matrices	1, 4, 5, 6	3, 4	2, 9, 18, 20, 24, 26			2, 13 & OR	22	8, 26	1, 8, 25 (OR)
4.	Determinants	2, 33	5, 26, 36	6, 13, 16, 30, 32, 36, 39, 44			1, 16, 33 & OR	9, 12, 35 & OR	2, 13, 26 (OR)	13, 25
5.	Continuity and Differentiability	3, 15, 21, 37	3, 7, 9, 23 & OR, 27 & OR	1, 4, 8, 12, 22, 25, 33			12, 22, 28	4, 18, 20 & OR, 23 & OR, 32 & OR	4, 17 & OR, 19	3, 17 & OR, 18
6.	Application of Derivatives	24, 38	8, 33 & OR	3, 5, 14, 17, 21, 29, 35, 40, 41, 43, 46, 47, 48, 49, 50			14 & OR, 23, 35	3, 11, 33	22	16, 24
7.	Integrals	9, 12, 26, 27 & OR, 31 & OR	10, 11, 19, 28 & OR, 32		1, 7. 12 & OR		7, 17 & OR, 18, 20, 29	16, 24, 29	5, 12 & OR, 16, 20	5, 6 & OR, 19, 20
8.	Application of Integrals	34	24, 29		11		34	34 & OR	24, 27 & OR	26 & OR
9.	Differential Equations	11, 18, 30 & OR	12, 38		2, 8 & OR		6, 30 & OR	19, 27	1, 11, 14 & OR	2, 10, 21 & OR
10.	Vector Algebra	10, 13, 19, 23	13, 14, 22 & OR, 31 (OR)		3, 9 & OR		4, 15, 24 & OR	1, 8, 10	7 & OR, 21	12 & OR, 22
11.	Three Dimensional Geometry	7, 16, 25 & OR, 32 & OR	15, 16, 25, 30, 31		4, 10, 13		5, 8, 25, 36 & OR	6, 15 & OR, 17, 21 & OR, 25, 31	3 & OR, 23, 29 & OR	4 & OR, 23, 28 & OR
12.	Linear Programming	8, 14, 28	35	11, 28, 38, 42, 45			10, 31	13, 28	28	27
13.	Probability	17, 29, 36	17, 18, 20, 34 & OR		5, 6 & OR, 14 (case study)		9, 19, 26, 32 & OR	26, 36	9, 10 & OR, 25	11 & OR, 9, 29
	Total	**38**	**38**	**50**	**14**		**36**	**36**	**29**	**29**

Chapterwise Division of Questions

Chapter Number	Chapter Name	Year of Examination		
		2018	2017	
		All India	All India	Delhi
1.	Relations and Functions	1, 26 & OR	25 & OR	25 & OR
2.	Inverse Trigonometric Functions	4, 8	13	13
3.	Matrices	3, 28 (OR)	14 (OR)	1, 5
4.	Determinants	7, 17, 28	1, 5, 14, 24	14 & OR, 24
5.	Continuity and Differentiability	6, 13, 23 & OR	2, 6, 15 & OR	2, 6, 15 & OR
6.	Application of Derivatives	5, 18 & OR, 22	7, 8, 26	7, 8, 26
7.	Integrals	12, 19, 24 & OR	3, 12, 16, 17 & OR	3, 12, 16, 17 & OR
8.	Application of Integrals	27	27 & OR	27 & OR
9.	Differential Equations	11, 14 & OR	18, 28	18, 28
10.	Vector Algebra	2, 10, 21	19, 20	4, 19, 20
11.	Three Dimensional Geometry	15, 29	4, 9, 29 & OR	9, 29 & OR
12.	Linear Programming	25	11, 23	11,23
13.	Probability	9, 16, 20	10, 21, 22	10, 21, 22
	Total	**29**	**29**	**29**

Chapterwise Division of Questions

Chapter Number	Chapter Name	Year of Examination			
		2016		2015	
		All India	Delhi	All India	Delhi
1.	Relations and Functions	23	25	23 & OR	20
2.	Inverse Trigonometric Functions	11 & OR	16 & OR	13 & OR	14 & OR
3.	Matrices	4, 5	1, 6	12, 14	4, 19
4.	Determinants	3, 12, 24 & OR	5, 17, 26 & OR	4, 7	7 & OR, 8
5.	Continuity and Differentiability	13 & OR, 14	18 & OR, 19	8, 9, 10	15, 16
6.	Application of Derivatives	15, 25 & OR	7, 20 & OR	24	17, 25
7.	Integrals	16 & OR, 17, 18	8 & OR, 9, 10	11 & OR, 18, 19	9 & OR, 10, 18
8.	Application of Integrals	26	21	20	21 & OR
9.	Differential Equations	7, 19	11, 12	5, 6, 21 & OR	5, 6, 22 & OR
10.	Vector Algebra	1, 6, 8	2, 3, 13	1, 2, 15	1, 2, 12
11.	Three Dimensional Geometry	2, 9, 20	4, 14, 22	3, 16 & OR, 22	3, 13, 23
12.	Linear Programming	22	24	25	26
13.	Probability	10 & OR, 21	15 & OR, 23	17 & OR, 26	11 & OR, 24
	Total	**26**	**26**	**26**	**26**

Chapterwise Division of Questions

Chapter Number	Chapter Name	Year of Examination			
		2014		2013	
		All India	Delhi	All India	Delhi
1.	Relations and Functions	1, 11	1, 11	11	11
2.	Inverse Trigonometric Functions	2, 12 & OR	2, 12 & OR	1, 2, 12 & OR	1, 2, 12 & OR
3.	Matrices	3, 4	3, 4	3, 4	3, 5
4.	Determinants	5, 13, 23	5, 13, 23	6, 13, 29	4, 13, 23
5.	Continuity and Differentiability	14, 15	14, 15	14, 15, 16 & OR	14, 15, 16 & OR
6.	Application of Derivatives	16 & OR, 24	16 & OR, 24	10, 23 & OR	10, 24 & OR
7.	Integrals	6, 7, 17 & OR, 25	6, 7, 17 & OR, 25	17 & OR, 18, 19	17 & OR, 18, 19
8.	Application of Integrals	26	26	24	25 & OR
9.	Differential Equations	18, 19	18, 19	5, 25	6, 26
10.	Vector Algebra	8, 9, 20 & OR	8, 9, 20 & OR	7, 8, 20	7, 8, 20
11.	Three Dimensional Geometry	10, 21, 27 & OR	10, 21, 27 & OR	9, 21 & OR, 26 & OR	9, 21 & OR, 27
12.	Linear Programming	28	28	28	28
13.	Probability	22, 29 & OR	22, 29 & OR	22, 27	22, 29
	Total	29	29	29	29

A Unique Exhaustive Collection for CUET
(Central Universities Entrance Test)

Section II

Domain Specific Books

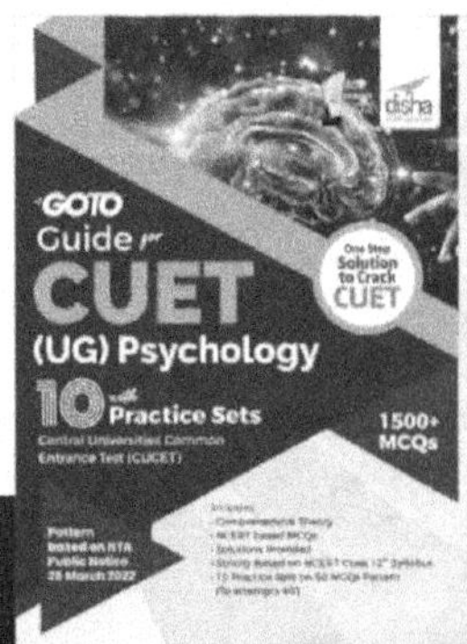

A Collection as RARE as it Gets!!

Must have Books for CUET

All India *2023*
CBSE Board Solved Paper

Time Allowed : 3 Hours   *Maximum Marks : 100*

General Instructions:

(i)   This question paper contains **38** questions. **All** questions are compulsory.

(ii)   Question paper is divided into **Five** Sections - Sections **A, B, C, D** and **E**.

(iii) In Section **A** - Question Number **1** to **18** are Multiple Choise Questions (MCQ) type and Question Number **19 & 20** are Assertion-Reason based questions of **1** mark each.

(iv) In Section **B** - Question Number **21** to **25** are Very Short Answer (VSA) type questions of **2** marks each.

(v)   In Section **C** - Question Number **26** to **31** are Short Answer (SA) type questions, carrying **3** marks each.

(vi) In Section **D** - Question Number **32** to **35** are Long Answer (LA) type questions carrying **5** marks each.

(vii) In Section **E** - Question Number **36** to **38** are case study based questions carrying **4** marks each where **2 VSA** type questions are of **1** mark each and **1 SA** type question is of **2** marks. Internal choice is provided in **2** marks question in each case study.

(viii) There is no overall choice. However, an internal choice has been provided in **2** questions in Section - **B, 3** questions in Section - **C, 2** questions in Section - **D** and **2** questions in Section - **E**.

(ix) Use of calculators is **NOT** allowed.

SECTION - A

Select the correct option out of the four given options:

1. If A is a 3 × 4 matrix and B is a matrix such that A'B and AB' are both defined, then the order of the matrix B is:

(a) 3 × 4   (b) 3 × 3   (c) 4 × 4   (d) 4 × 3

2. If the area of a triangle with vertices $(2, -6)$, $(5, 4)$ and $(k, 4)$ is 35 sq. units, then k is:

(a) 12   (b) –2   (c) –12, –2 (d) 12, –2

3. If $f(x) = 2|x| + 3|\sin x| + 6$, then the right hand derivative of $f(x)$ at $x = 0$ is:

(a) 6   (b) 5   (c) 3   (d) 2

4. If $x\begin{bmatrix} 1 \\ 2 \end{bmatrix} + y\begin{bmatrix} 2 \\ 5 \end{bmatrix} = \begin{bmatrix} 4 \\ 9 \end{bmatrix}$, then :

(a) $x = 1, y = 2$ (b) $x = 2, y = 1$

(c) $x = 1, y = -1$ (d) $x = 3, y = 2$

5. If a matrix $A = [1\ 2\ 3]$, then the matrix AA' (where A' is the transpose of A) is:

(a) 14   (b) $\begin{bmatrix} 1 & 0 & 0 \\ 0 & 2 & 0 \\ 0 & 0 & 3 \end{bmatrix}$

(c) $\begin{bmatrix} 1 & 2 & 3 \\ 2 & 3 & 1 \\ 3 & 1 & 2 \end{bmatrix}$ (d) [14]

6. The product $\begin{bmatrix} a & b \\ -b & a \end{bmatrix}\begin{bmatrix} a & -b \\ b & a \end{bmatrix}$ is equal to:

(a) $\begin{bmatrix} a^2 + b^2 & 0 \\ 0 & a^2 + b^2 \end{bmatrix}$ (b) $\begin{bmatrix} (a+b)^2 & 0 \\ (a+b)^2 & 0 \end{bmatrix}$

(c) $\begin{bmatrix} a^2 + b^2 & 0 \\ a^2 + b^2 & 0 \end{bmatrix}$ (d) $\begin{bmatrix} a & 0 \\ 0 & b \end{bmatrix}$

7. Distance of the point (p, q, r) from y-axis is :

(a) q   (b) |q| (c) |q| + |r| (d) $\sqrt{p^2 + r^2}$

8. The solution set of the inequation $3x + 5y < 7$ is:

(a) whole xy-plane except the points lying on the line $3x + 5y = 7$.

(b) whole xy-plane along with the points lying on the line $3x + 5y = 7$.

(c) open half plane containing the origin except the points of line $3x + 5y = 7$.

(d) open half plane not containing the origin.

9. If $\int\limits_{0}^{a} 3x^2 dx = 8$, then the value of 'a' is:

(a) 2   (b) 4   (c) 8   (d) 10

10. The sine of the angle between the vectors
$\vec{a} = 3\hat{i} + \hat{j} + 2\hat{k}$ and $\vec{b} = \hat{i} + \hat{j} + 2\hat{k}$ is:

(a) $\sqrt{\dfrac{5}{21}}$ (b) $\dfrac{5}{\sqrt{21}}$ (c) $\sqrt{\dfrac{3}{21}}$ (d) $\dfrac{4}{\sqrt{21}}$

11. The order and degree (if defined) of the differential equation,
$$\left(\dfrac{d^2 y}{dx^2}\right)^2 + \left(\dfrac{dy}{dx}\right)^3 = x \sin\left(\dfrac{dy}{dx}\right) \text{ respectively are:}$$

(a) $2, 2$ (b) $1, 3$

(c) $2, 3$ (d) 2, degree not defined

12. $\int e^{5 \log x} dx$ is equal to:

(a) $\dfrac{x^5}{5} + C$ (b) $\dfrac{x^6}{6} + C$

(c) $5x^4 + C$ (d) $6x^5 + C$

13. A unit vector along the vetor $4\hat{i} - 3\hat{k}$ is:

(a) $\dfrac{1}{7}(4\hat{i} - 3\hat{k})$ (b) $\dfrac{1}{5}(4\hat{i} - 3\hat{k})$

(c) $\dfrac{1}{\sqrt{7}}(4\hat{i} - 3\hat{k})$ (d) $\dfrac{1}{\sqrt{5}}(4\hat{i} - 3\hat{k})$

14. Which of the following points satisfies both the inequations $2x + y \le 10$ and $x + 2y \ge 8$?

(a) $(-2, 4)$ (b) $(3, 2)$ (c) $(-5, 6)$ (d) $(4, 2)$

15. If $y = \sin^2 (x^3)$, then $\dfrac{dy}{dx}$ is equal to:

(a) $2 \sin x^3 \cos x^3$ (b) $3x^3 \sin x^3 \cos x^3$

(c) $6x^2 \sin x^3 \cos x^3$ (d) $2x^2 \sin^2(x^3)$

16. The point (x, y, 0) on the xy-plane divides the line segment joining the points (1, 2, 3) and (3, 2, 1) in the ratio:

(a) 1 : 2 internally   (b) 2 : 1 internally

(c) 3 : 1 internally   (d) 3 : 1 externally

17. The events E and F independent. If $P(E) = 0.3$ and $P(E \cup F) = 0.5$, then $P(E/F) - P(F/E)$:

(a) $\dfrac{1}{7}$ (b) $\dfrac{2}{7}$ (c) $\dfrac{3}{35}$ (d) $\dfrac{1}{70}$

18. The integrating factor for solving the differential equation
$x\dfrac{dy}{dx} - y = 2x^2$ is:

(a) e^{-y} (b) e^{-x} (c) x (d) $\dfrac{1}{x}$

Questions number 19 and 20 are Assertion and Reason based questions carrying 1 mark each. Two statements are given, one labelled Assertion (A) and the other labelled Reason (R). Select the correct answer from the codes (a), (b), (c) and (d) as given below.

(a) Both Assertion (A) and Reason (R) are true and Reason (R) is the correct explanation of Assertion (A).

(b) Both Assertion (A) and Reason (R) are true but Reason (R) is not the correct explanation of Assertion (A)

(c) Assertion (A) is true and Reason (R) is false.

(d) Assertion (A) is false and Reason (R) is true.

19. **Assertion (A):** The lines $\vec{r} = \vec{a_1} + \lambda \vec{b_1}$ and $\vec{r} = \vec{a_2} + \mu \vec{b_2}$ are perpendicular, when $\vec{b_1} . \vec{b_2} = 0$.

Reason (R): The angle θ between the lines $\vec{r} = \vec{a_1} + \lambda \vec{b_1}$ and $\vec{r} = \vec{a_2} + \mu \vec{b_2}$ is given by $\cos\theta = \dfrac{\vec{b_1} . \vec{b_2}}{|\vec{b_1}||\vec{b_2}|}$.

20. **Assertion (A):** All trigonometric functions have their inverses over their respective domains.

Reason (R): The inverse of $\tan^{-1}x$ exists for some $x \in R$.

SECTION - B

This section comprises of Very Short Answer (VSA) type questions of 2 marks each.

21. If $xy = e^{x-y}$, then show that $\dfrac{dy}{dx} = \dfrac{y(x-1)}{x(y+1)}$

22. (a) Find the domain of $y = \sin^{-1}(x^2 - 4)$.

OR

(b) Evaluate:
$$\cos^{-1}\left[\cos\left(-\dfrac{7\pi}{3}\right)\right]$$

23. If the projection of the vector $\hat{i} + \hat{j} + \hat{k}$ on the vector $p\hat{i} + \hat{j} - 2\hat{k}$ is $\dfrac{1}{3}$, then find the value(s) of p.

24. Find the point on the curve $y^2 = 8x$ for which the abscissa and ordinate change at the same rate.

25. (a) Find the vector equation of the line passing through the point (2, 1, 3) and perpendicular to both the lines.
$$\dfrac{x-1}{1} = \dfrac{y-2}{2} = \dfrac{z-3}{3} ; \dfrac{x}{-3} = \dfrac{y}{2} = \dfrac{z}{5}.$$

OR

(b) The equations of a line are $5x - 3 = 15y + 7 = 3 - 10z$. Write the direction cosines of the line and find the coordinates of a point through which it passes.

SECTION - C

The section comprises of Short Answer (SA) type questions of 3 marks each.

26. Find $\displaystyle\int \frac{2}{(1-x)(1+x^2)}dx$.

27. (a) Evaluate $\displaystyle\int_{1/3}^{1} \frac{\left(x-x^3\right)^{1/3}}{x^4}dx$.

OR

(b) Evaluate: $\displaystyle\int_{1}^{3} \left\{ |(x-1)| + |(x-2)| \right\}dx$

28. Solve the following linear programming problem graphically:

Maximise $z = 5x + 3y$

subject to the constraints

$3x + 5y \le 15,$

$5x + 2y \le 10,$

$x, y \ge 0.$

29. From a lot of 30 bulbs which include 6 defective bulbs, a sample of 2 bulbs is drawn at random one by one with replacement. Find the probability distribution of the number of defective bulbs and hence find the mean number of defective bulbs.

30. (a) Find the particular solution of the differential equation

$$\frac{dy}{dx} = \frac{x+y}{x}, \quad y(1) = 0$$

OR

(b) Find the general solution of the differntial equation

$$e^x \tan y\, dx + (1 - e^x)\sec^2 y\, dy = 0$$

31. (a) Evaluate: $\displaystyle\int_{\pi/4}^{\pi/2} e^{2x}\left(\frac{1-\sin 2x}{1-\cos 2x}\right)dx$

OR

(b) Evaluate $\displaystyle\int_{-2}^{2} \frac{x^2}{1+5^x}dx$

SECTION - D

This section comprises of Long Answer (LA) type questions of 5 marks each.

32. (a) Find the image of the point $(2, -1, 5)$ in the line

$$\frac{x-11}{10} = \frac{y+2}{-4} = \frac{z+8}{-11}$$

OR

(b) Vertices B and C of $\triangle ABC$ lie on the line $\dfrac{x+2}{2} = \dfrac{y-1}{1} = \dfrac{z}{4}$. Find the area of $\triangle ABC$ given that point A has coordinates $(1, -1, 2)$ and the line segment BC has length of 5 units.

33. Find the inverse of the matrix $A = \begin{bmatrix} 1 & -1 & 2 \\ 0 & 2 & -3 \\ 3 & -2 & 4 \end{bmatrix}$. Using the inverse, A^{-1}, solve the sysyem of linear equations

$x - y + 2z - 1;\ 2y - 3z = 1;\ 3x - 2y + 4z = 3$

34. Using integration, find the area of the region bounded by the parabola $y^2 = 4ax$ and its latus rectum.

35. (a) If N denotes the set of all natural numbers and R is the relation on $N \times N$ defined by $(a,b,) R (c,d)$, if $ad(b+c) = bc(a + d)$. Show that R is an equivalence relation.

OR

(b) Let $f: R - \left\{ -\dfrac{4}{3} \right\} \to R$ be a function defined as

$f(x) = \dfrac{4x}{3x+4}$. Show that f is one-one function. Also, check whether f is an onto function or not.

SECTION - E

This section comprises of 3 Case Study/Passage-Bassed questions of 4 marks each with two sub-parts. First two case study questions have three sub-parts (I), (II), (III) of marks 1, 1, 2 respectively. The third case study question has two sub – parts (I) and (II) of marks 2 each.

Case Study-I

36. A building contractor undertakes a job to construct 4 flats on a plot along with parking area. Due to strike the probability of many construction workers not being present for the job is 0.65. The probability that many are not present and still the work gets completed on time is 0.35. The probability that work will be completed on time when all workers are present is 0.80.

Let: E_1 : represent the events when many workers were not present for the job;

E_2 : represent the events when all workers were present; and

E : represent completing the condtruction work on time.

Based on the above information, answer the following questions:

(i)   What is the probability that all the workers are present for the job ?

(ii) What is the probability that construction will be completed on time?

(iii) (a) What is the probability that many workers are not present given that the costruction work is completed on time ?

OR

(IV) (b) What is the probability that all workers were present given that the construction job was completed on time?

Case Study - II

37. Let f(x) be a real valued function. Then its
   * Left Hand Derivative (L.H.D.) :

$$Lf'(a) = \lim_{h \to 0} \frac{f(a-h) - f(a)}{-h}$$

   * Right Hand Derivative (R.H.D) :

$$Rf'(a) = \lim_{h \to 0} \frac{f(a+b) - f(a)}{h}$$

Also, a function f(x) is said to be differentiable at x = a if its L.H.D. and R.H.D. at x = a exist and both are equal.

For the function $f(x) = \begin{cases} |x-3|, x \geq 1 \\ \dfrac{x^2}{4} - \dfrac{3x}{2} + \dfrac{13}{4}, x < 1 \end{cases}$

answer the following questions:

(i)   What is R.H.D. of f(x) at x = 1

(ii) What is L.H.D. of f(x) at x = 1

(iii) (a) Check if the function f(x) is differentiable at x =1

OR

(iii) (b) Find the f'(2) and f'(-1)

Case Study-III

38. Sooraj's father wants to construct a rectangular garden using a brick wall on one side of the garden and wire fencing for the other three sides as shown in the figure. He has 200 meters of fencing wire.

Based on the above information, answer the following questions;

(i)   Let 'x' meters denote the length of the side of the garden perpendicular to the brick wall and 'y' metres denote the length of the side parallel to the brick wall. Determine the relation representing the total length of fencing wire and also write A(x) the area of the garden.

(ii) Determine the maximum value of A(x)

Solutions

1. **(a)** Order of matrix A is 3×4
Let order of B is $m \times n$ them B′ is $n \times m$ and A′ is 4×3
$\Rightarrow$ Number of columns of A′ must equal number of rows of B, because A′ B is defined, so m = 3
Also (B A′) is defined that is 2 why n = 4   **(1 mark)**

2. **(d)** Area of triangle having vertices $(2, -6)$, $(5, 4)$,
$(k, 4)$ is $A = \dfrac{1}{2}\begin{vmatrix} 2 & -6 & 1 \\ 5 & 4 & 1 \\ k & 4 & 1 \end{vmatrix} = 35$

$\Rightarrow A = \dfrac{1}{2}\big[\,2(4-4)+6(5-k)+20-4k\,\big] = 35$

$\Rightarrow |30 - 6k + 20 - 4k| = 70$

$\Rightarrow 50 - 10k = \pm 70$

$\Rightarrow 50 - 10k = -70\,;\, 50 - 10\,k = 70$

$\Rightarrow k = \dfrac{-20}{10} = -2\,,\, k = \dfrac{120}{10} = 12$ **(1 mark)**

3. **(b)** Let $x = 0 + h$, where $h \to 0$

$\Rightarrow f'(x) = \lim\limits_{h \to 0} \dfrac{f(0+h) - f(0)}{h}$

$\Rightarrow f'(x) = \lim\limits_{h \to 0} \dfrac{2|h| + 3|\sin h| + 6 - 6}{h}$
for $h > 0$

$\Rightarrow f'(x) = \lim\limits_{h \to 0}\left(\dfrac{2h}{h} + \dfrac{3\sin h}{h}\right) = 5$ **(1 mark)**

4. **(b)** Given, $x\begin{bmatrix} 1 \\ 2 \end{bmatrix} + y\begin{bmatrix} 2 \\ 5 \end{bmatrix} = \begin{bmatrix} 4 \\ 9 \end{bmatrix}$

We can write given equation as,
$\Rightarrow x + 2y = 4$ (1)
and, $2x + 5y = 9$ (2)
By multiplying 2 in equation (1)

$\quad 2x + 4y = 8$
$\quad 2x + 5y = 9$
$\Rightarrow \quad \underline{\;-\;\;-\;\;\;-\;}$
$\quad -y = -1 \;\Rightarrow y = 1$
Put y = 1 in equation (i)
$\Rightarrow x + 2 = 4 \qquad \Rightarrow x = 2$ **(1 mark)**

5. **(a)** Given, $A = \begin{bmatrix} 1 & 2 & 3 \end{bmatrix}$

Then, $A' = \begin{bmatrix} 1 \\ 2 \\ 3 \end{bmatrix}$

$\Rightarrow AA' = \begin{bmatrix} 1 & 2 & 3 \end{bmatrix}\begin{bmatrix} 1 \\ 2 \\ 3 \end{bmatrix}$

$\Rightarrow AA' = \begin{bmatrix} 1 + 4 + 9 \end{bmatrix} = 14$ **(1 mark)**

6. **(a)** Product of given matrix define as.

$\Rightarrow \begin{bmatrix} a & b \\ -b & a \end{bmatrix}\begin{bmatrix} a & -b \\ b & a \end{bmatrix} = \begin{bmatrix} a^2 + b^2 & -ab + ab \\ -ab + ab & b^2 + a^2 \end{bmatrix}$

$\Rightarrow \begin{bmatrix} a^2 + b^2 & 0 \\ 0 & a^2 + b^2 \end{bmatrix}$ **(1 mark)**

7. **(d)** Let point on y-axis is $(0, q, 0)$ that is nearest from $(p. q, r)$

Distance $(d) = \sqrt{p^2 + (q-q)^2 + r^2} = \sqrt{p^2 + r^2}$ **(1 mark)**

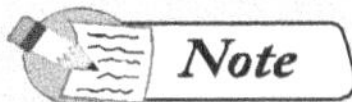

> **Note**
> If $A \equiv (x_1, y_1, z_1)$ and $B \equiv (x_2, y_2, z_2)$
> then $AB = \sqrt{(x_2 - x_1)^2 + (y_2 - y_1)^2 + (z_2 - z_1)^2}$

8. **(c)** Given inequation, $3x + 5y < 7$
solution defines in open half plane containing the origin except the points of line
$3x + 5y = 7$

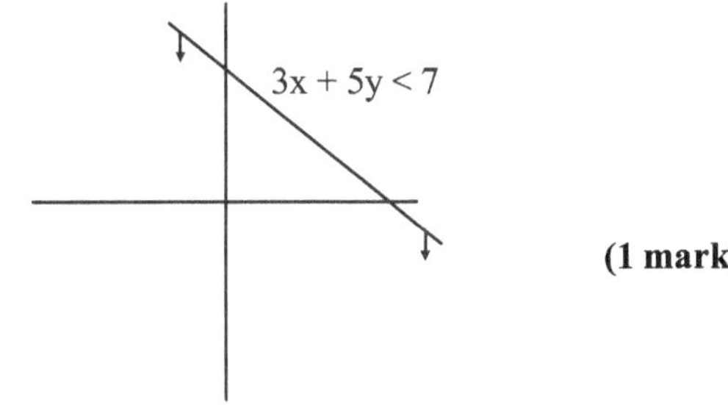

   (1 mark)

9. **(a)** Given, $\displaystyle\int_0^a 3x^2 dx = 8$

By integrating the equation,

$\Rightarrow 3\left[\dfrac{x^3}{3}\right]_0^a = 8$

$\Rightarrow a^3 = 8 \;\Rightarrow a = 2$ **(1 mark)**

10. **(a)** Let Angle between $\vec{a}$ and $\vec{b}$ is θ

Then, $\cos\theta = \dfrac{\vec{a}.\vec{b}}{|\vec{a}||\vec{b}|} = \dfrac{\left(3\hat{i} + \hat{j} + 2\hat{k}\right)\left(\hat{i} + \hat{j} + 2\hat{k}\right)}{\sqrt{3^2 + 1^2 + 2^2}\,\sqrt{1^2 + 1^2 + 2^2}}$

$$\Rightarrow \cos\theta = \frac{3+1+4}{\sqrt{14}\sqrt{6}} = \frac{8}{\sqrt{7}\sqrt{2}\sqrt{3}\sqrt{2}} = \frac{4}{\sqrt{21}}$$

$$\Rightarrow \sin\theta = \sqrt{1-\cos^2\theta} = \sqrt{1-\frac{16}{21}} = \sqrt{\frac{5}{21}} \qquad \textbf{(1 mark)}$$

11. (d) Given differential equation is not in polynomial form
Order = 2, but degree is not defined **(1 mark)**

12. (b) Given, $\int e^{5\log x}dx$

where, $e^{5\log x} = e^{\log x^5} = x^5 \qquad \left[\because e^{\log_e^x} = x\right]$

Now, $\int e^{5\log x}dx = \int x^5 dx$

By integrating the given equation.

$$\Rightarrow \frac{x^6}{6}+C \qquad \textbf{(1 mark)}$$

13. (b) Given, $4\hat{i}-3\hat{k}$

Unit vector $= \dfrac{4\hat{i}-3\hat{k}}{\sqrt{4^2+3^2}}$

$$\Rightarrow \frac{4\hat{i}}{5}-\frac{3\hat{k}}{5} = \frac{1}{5}(4\hat{i}-3\hat{k}) \qquad \textbf{(1 mark)}$$

14. (d) At $(-2,4)$
$\Rightarrow\ 2x+y \le 10 \Rightarrow -4+4 \le 10 \Rightarrow \qquad 0 \le 10$
$\Rightarrow\ x+2y \ge 8 \Rightarrow -2+8 \ge 8 \Rightarrow 6 \not\ge 8$
At $(3,2)$
$\Rightarrow\ 2x+y \le 10 \Rightarrow 6+2 \le 10 \Rightarrow \qquad 8 \le 10$
$\Rightarrow\ x+2y \ge 10 \Rightarrow 3+4 \ge 10 \Rightarrow 7 \not\ge 10$
At $(-5,6)$
$\Rightarrow\ 2x+y \le 10 \Rightarrow -10+6 \le 10 \Rightarrow -4 \le 10$
$\Rightarrow\ x+2y \ge 8 \Rightarrow -5+12 \ge 8 \Rightarrow 7 \not\ge 8$
At $(4,2)$
$\Rightarrow\ 2x+y \le 10 \Rightarrow 8+2 \le 10$
$\Rightarrow\ 10 \le 10 \Rightarrow x+2y \ge 8$
$\Rightarrow\ 4+4 \ge 8 \Rightarrow 8 \ge 8 \qquad \textbf{(1 mark)}$

15. (c) Given, $y = \sin^2(x^3)$
By Chain Rule differentiation the above equation

$$\Rightarrow \frac{dy}{dx} = 2\sin(x^3)\frac{d}{dx}\left(\sin(x^3)\right)$$

$$\Rightarrow \frac{dy}{dx} = 2\sin(x^3)\frac{d}{dx}(x^3)$$

$$\Rightarrow \frac{dy}{dx} = 2\sin(x^3)\ \cos(x^3)\cdot(3x^2)$$

$$= 6x^2\sin x^3\cdot\cos x^3 \qquad \textbf{(1 mark)}$$

16. (c) Let $(x, y, 0)$ divides the point in $k:1$

Then, $x = \dfrac{3k-1}{k+1}, y = \dfrac{2k-2}{k+1}, z = \dfrac{k-3}{k+1}$

In $(x, y, 0), z = 0$

$$\Rightarrow \frac{k-3}{k+1} = 0 \Rightarrow k = 3$$

So, $(x, y, 0)$ divides the line segment in ratio
$3:1$ internally. **(1 mark)**

17. (d) The events E and F are independent

so, $P(E \cap F) = P(E)\cdot P(F) = (0.3)(P(F))$

We know, $P(E \cup F) = P(E)+P(F)-P(E \cap F)$

$\Rightarrow\ 0.5 = 0.3+P(F)-(0.3)(P(F))$

$\Rightarrow\ (0.7)P(F) = 0.2 \Rightarrow P(F) = \dfrac{2}{7}$

Now $P\left(\dfrac{E}{F}\right) = P(E)$ and $P\left(\dfrac{F}{E}\right) = P(E)$ because

E & F are independent.

$$\Rightarrow\ P(E)-P(F) = 0.3-\frac{2}{7} = \frac{1}{70} \qquad \textbf{(1 mark)}$$

Note

If E_1 & E_2 are independent events then
$P(E_1 \cap E_2) = P(E_1)\cdot P(E_2)$

18. (d) Given, $x\dfrac{dy}{dx}-y = 2x^2$

or, $\dfrac{dy}{dx}-\dfrac{y}{x} = 2x$

Integrating factor $= e^{-\int\frac{1}{x}dx}$

$$\Rightarrow\ e^{-(\log x)} = e^{\log\frac{1}{x}} = \frac{1}{x} \qquad \textbf{(1 mark)}$$

19. (a) Given Asseration is true and Reason is correct explanation of Asseration.

$$\Rightarrow \cos\theta = \frac{\vec{b}_1\cdot\vec{b}_2}{|\vec{b}_1||\vec{b}_2|}$$

If $\vec{b}_1$ and $\vec{b}_2$ are perpendicular then

$$\Rightarrow \cos 90° = \frac{\vec{b}_1\cdot\vec{b}_2}{|\vec{b}_1||\vec{b}_2|} = 0 \Rightarrow \vec{b}_1\cdot\vec{b}_2 = 0 \qquad \textbf{(1 mark)}$$

20. (d) Assertion is not true for all trigonometric function.
Domain of $\sin x$ is R but $\sin^{-1}x$ is not define on R
$\Rightarrow$ Reason is true $\tan^{-1}x$ inverse exist for some $x \in R$
(1 mark)

21. Given, $xy = e^{x-y} = e^x \cdot e^{-y}$
Differentiate above function w.r.t. x

$$\Rightarrow x\frac{dy}{dx} + y = e^x \frac{d}{dx}e^{-y} + e^{-y}\frac{d}{dx}e^x$$

$$\Rightarrow x\frac{dy}{dx} + y = -e^x e^{-y}\frac{dy}{dx} + e^x e^{-y}$$

$$\Rightarrow x\frac{dy}{dx} + y = -xy\frac{dy}{dx} + xy \qquad \textbf{(1 mark)}$$

$$\Rightarrow (x+xy)\frac{dy}{dx} = -y + xy$$

$$\Rightarrow \frac{dy}{dx} = \frac{y(x-1)}{x(y+1)} \qquad \textbf{(1 mark)}$$

22. (a) Domain of $\sin^{-1}x$ is $[-1, 1]$
So, domain of $\sin^{-1}(x^2 - 4)$ is $\qquad \textbf{(1 mark)}$

$$\Rightarrow -1 \le x^2 - 4 \le 1$$

$$\Rightarrow 3 \le x^2 \le 5$$

$$\Rightarrow \sqrt{3} \le |x| \le \sqrt{5} \qquad \textbf{(1 mark)}$$

OR

(b) $\cos^{-1}\left[\cos\left(-\frac{7\pi}{3}\right)\right]$

$$\Rightarrow \cos^{-1}\left[\cos\left(-2\pi - \frac{\pi}{3}\right)\right] \qquad \textbf{(1 mark)}$$

$$= \cos^{-1}\cos\left(\frac{\pi}{3}\right) = \frac{\pi}{3} \qquad \textbf{(1 mark)}$$

23. Let $\vec{a} = \hat{i} + \hat{j} + \hat{k}$ and $\vec{b} = P\hat{i} + \hat{j} - 2\hat{k}$

Then projection of $\vec{a}$ on $\vec{b}$ is $\dfrac{\vec{a}\cdot\vec{b}}{|\vec{b}|}$

$$\Rightarrow \frac{\vec{a}\cdot\vec{b}}{|\vec{b}|} = \frac{\left(\hat{i}+\hat{j}+\hat{k}\right)\left(P\hat{i}+\hat{j}-2\hat{k}\right)}{\sqrt{P^2+1^2+2^2}} = \frac{1}{3} \qquad \textbf{(1 mark)}$$

$$\Rightarrow \frac{P+1-2}{\sqrt{P^2+5}} = \frac{1}{3}$$

$$\Rightarrow P = 2 \qquad \textbf{(1 mark)}$$

> **Note**
>
> If $\vec{a} = a_1\hat{i} + a_2\hat{j} + a_3\hat{k}$ and $\vec{b} = b_1\hat{i} + b_2\hat{j} + b_3\hat{k}$
>
> then $\vec{a}\cdot\vec{b} = (a_1\hat{i} + a_2\hat{j} + a_3\hat{k})\cdot(b_1\hat{i} + b_2\hat{j} + b_3\hat{k})$
> $= a_1 b_1 + a_2 b_2 + a_3 b_3$

24. Given, $y^2 = 8x$
Derivative of given equation, w.r.t. x

$$\Rightarrow 2y\frac{dy}{dx} = 8 \Rightarrow \frac{dy}{dx} = \frac{8}{2y} = 1$$

$$\Rightarrow 2y = 8 \Rightarrow y = 4 \qquad \textbf{(1 mark)}$$
or derivative w.r.t. y is

$$2y = 8\frac{dx}{dy} \Rightarrow 2y = 8 \Rightarrow y = 4$$

At $y = 4$, $16 = 8x \Rightarrow x = 2 \qquad \textbf{(1 mark)}$

25. (a) Let the required line Parallel to the vector $\vec{b}$

$$\vec{b}, \vec{b} = b_1\hat{i} + b_2\hat{j} + b_3\hat{k}$$

The position vector of $(2, 1, 3)$ & parallel to $\vec{b}$ is $\vec{r} = \vec{a} + \lambda\vec{b}$

$$\Rightarrow \vec{r}(2\hat{i} + \hat{j} + 3\hat{k}) + \lambda(b_1\hat{i} + b_2\hat{j} + b_3\hat{k}) \qquad \text{...(i)}$$

Given line $\dfrac{x-1}{1} = \dfrac{y-2}{2} = \dfrac{z-3}{3} \qquad \text{...(ii)}$

$$\Rightarrow \frac{x}{-3} = \frac{y}{2} = \frac{z}{5} \qquad \text{...(iii)}$$

are $\perp$ to each other
$\therefore \ b_1 + 2b_2 + 3b_3 = 0 \qquad \text{...(iv)}$
$\qquad\qquad\qquad\qquad\qquad \textbf{(1 mark)}$

lines (i) and (iii) are $\perp$ to each other
$\therefore \ -3b_1 + 2b_2 + 5b_3 = 0 \qquad \text{...(v)}$
Then

$$\frac{b_1}{2(5)-3(2)} = \frac{b_2}{5-3(-3)} = \frac{b_3}{2-2(-3)}$$

$$\Rightarrow \frac{b_1}{2} = \frac{-b_2}{7} = \frac{b_3}{4}$$

Direction ratios of $\vec{b}$ are $2, -7, 4$
Then required equation is

$$\vec{r}(2\hat{i} + \hat{j} + 3\hat{k}) + \lambda(2\hat{i} - 7\hat{j} + 4\hat{k}) \qquad \textbf{(1 mark)}$$
OR

(b) Given, $5x - 3 = 15y + 7 = 3 - 10z$

$$\Rightarrow \frac{x - \dfrac{3}{5}}{\dfrac{1}{5}} = \frac{y - \left(-\dfrac{7}{15}\right)}{\dfrac{1}{15}} = \frac{z - \dfrac{3}{10}}{-\dfrac{1}{10}}$$

Compare to $\dfrac{x - a_1}{b_1} = \dfrac{y - a_2}{b_2} = \dfrac{z - a_3}{b_3}$

Then, $b_1 = \dfrac{1}{5}, b_2 = \dfrac{1}{15}, b_3 = \dfrac{-1}{10} \qquad \textbf{(1 mark)}$

The direction cosines are the components of unit vector

$$\hat{b} = \frac{b_1\hat{i} + b_2\hat{j} + b_3\hat{k}}{\sqrt{b_1^2 + b_2^2 + b_3^2}} = \frac{\dfrac{1}{5}\hat{i} + \dfrac{1}{15}\hat{j} - \dfrac{1}{10}\hat{k}}{\dfrac{7}{30}}$$

$$\Rightarrow \frac{6}{7}\hat{i}+\frac{2}{7}\hat{j}-\frac{3}{7}\hat{k}$$

Direction cosines are $\dfrac{6}{7},\dfrac{2}{7},-\dfrac{3}{7}$　　**(1 mark)**

26. Let $I=\displaystyle\int \frac{2}{(1-x)(1+x^2)}\,dx$

$$\Rightarrow \frac{-2}{(x-1)(1+x^2)}=\frac{A}{(x-1)}+\frac{Bx+C}{1+x^2}$$

$$\Rightarrow -2=A(1+x^2)+(Bx+C)(x-1)\qquad\textbf{(1 mark)}$$

On comparing, we get

$A+B=0$　　　　　　　　　　　　　　　...(i)
$-B+C=0$　　　　　　　　　　　　　　...(ii)
$A-C=-2$　　　　　　　　　　　　　　...(iii)

On solving equations (i), (ii) and (iii), we get
$A=-1,\ B=1,\ C=1$

So, $\displaystyle\int \frac{-2dx}{(x-1)(1+x^2)}=\int\frac{-1}{x-1}dx+\int\frac{x+1}{x^2+1}dx$　　**(1 mark)**

$$\Rightarrow -\log|x-1|+\frac{1}{2}\int\frac{2xdx}{x^2+1}+\int\frac{dx}{x^2+1}$$

$$I=-\log|x-1|+\frac{1}{2}\log(x^2+1)+\tan^{-1}x+C\qquad\textbf{(1 mark)}$$

$$\left[\because \int\frac{f'(x)}{f(x)}dx=\log f(x)\right]$$

Note

$\dfrac{px^2+qx+r}{(x-a)(x^2+bx+c)}$ *can be written as*

$\dfrac{A}{x-a}+\dfrac{Bx+C}{x^2+bx+C}$

27. (a) Let $I=\displaystyle\int_{1/3}^{1}\frac{(x-x^3)^{1/3}}{x^4}\,dx$

$$\Rightarrow \int_{1/3}^{1}\frac{x\left(\frac{1}{x^2}-1\right)^{1/3}}{x^4}\,dx=\int_{1/3}^{1}\frac{\left(\frac{1}{x^2}-1\right)^{1/3}}{x^3}\,dx\qquad\textbf{(1 mark)}$$

Let $\left(\dfrac{1}{x^2}-1\right)=t$, then, $-\dfrac{2}{x^3}dx=dt$

$$\Rightarrow \frac{1}{2}\int -t^{1/3}dt=\frac{-3t^{4/3}}{4}\times\frac{1}{2}$$

$$\Rightarrow I=\frac{-3}{8}\left[\left(\frac{1}{x^2}-1\right)^{4/3}\right]_{1/3}^{1}\qquad\textbf{(1 mark)}$$

$$\text{or } I=\frac{-3}{8}\left[0-(8)^{4/3}\right]=\frac{3}{8}\left(2^3\right)^{4/3}$$

$$\Rightarrow I=\frac{3}{8}\times16=6\qquad\textbf{(1 mark)}$$

OR

(b) $I=\displaystyle\int_{1}^{3}\{|x-1|+|x-2|\}\,dx$

In given limit $|x-1|=(x-1)$

And, $|x-2|=\begin{cases}-(x-2) & ,\ x<2\\ x-2 & ,\ x>2\end{cases}$　　**(1 mark)**

$$\Rightarrow I=\int_{1}^{2}\left[(x-1)-(x-2)\right]dx+\int_{2}^{3}\left[(x-1)+(x-2)\right]dx$$

$$\Rightarrow I=\int_{1}^{2}dx+\int_{2}^{3}(2x-3)\,dx\qquad\textbf{(1 mark)}$$

$$\Rightarrow I=\left[x\right]_{1}^{2}+\left[x^2-3x\right]_{2}^{3}$$

$$\Rightarrow I=(2-1)+[0-(4-6)]$$
$$\Rightarrow I=1+2=3\qquad\textbf{(1 mark)}$$

28. Let $3x+5y\le15$
　　　　$5x+2y\le10$

By solving both equation we get $(0,3),(2,0)$

$$\left(\frac{20}{19},\frac{45}{19}\right)\qquad\textbf{(1 mark)}$$

Corner points are

$(0,3),(2,0),\left(\dfrac{20}{19},\dfrac{45}{19}\right)$　　**(1 mark)**

and value of z are $9,\dfrac{235}{19},10$

Maximum value is $\dfrac{235}{19}=12.36$

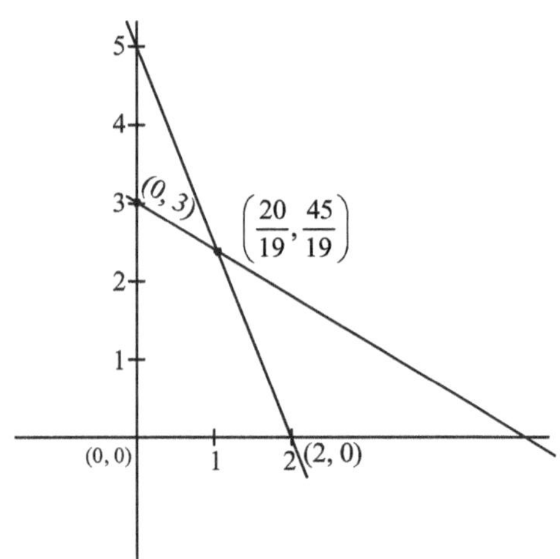

(1 mark)

29. Non-defective bulbs $= 30 - 6 = 24$

Let X be the random variable that denotes the number of defective bulbs.

$P(X = 0) = P(2 \text{ non-defective and 0 defective})$

$= {}^2C_0 \cdot \dfrac{24}{30} \cdot \dfrac{24}{30} = \dfrac{16}{25}$ **(1 mark)**

$P(X = 1) = {}^2C_1 \cdot \dfrac{24}{30} \cdot \dfrac{6}{30} = \dfrac{8}{25}$ **(1 mark)**

$P(X = 2) = {}^2C_2 \cdot \dfrac{6}{30} \cdot \dfrac{6}{30} = \dfrac{1}{25}$ **(1 mark)**

Required Probability distribution is,

X	0	1	2
P(x)	$\dfrac{16}{25}$	$\dfrac{8}{25}$	$\dfrac{1}{25}$

30. **(a)** Given, $\dfrac{dy}{dx} = \dfrac{x+y}{x}$, $y(1) = 0$ (1)

Let $y = vx$ **(1 mark)**

then, $\dfrac{dy}{dx} = v + x\dfrac{dv}{dx}$

$\Rightarrow \quad v + x\dfrac{dv}{dx} = \dfrac{x + vx}{x}$

$\Rightarrow \quad v + x\dfrac{dv}{dx} = 1 + v \Rightarrow \dfrac{dv}{dx} = \dfrac{1}{x}$ **(1 mark)**

$\Rightarrow \quad \int dv = \int \dfrac{dx}{x}$

$\Rightarrow \quad v = \log x + c$

$\Rightarrow \quad \dfrac{y}{x} = \log x + c$

At $x = 1, y = 0$

$\Rightarrow \quad 0 + c \Rightarrow c = 0$

Then, $y = x \log x$ **(1 mark)**

OR

(b) Given, $e^x \tan y\, dx + (1 - e^x)\sec^2 y\, dy = 0$

or $\dfrac{e^x}{1 - e^x} dx + \dfrac{\sec^2 y}{\tan y} dy = 0$ **(1 mark)**

$\Rightarrow \quad \int \dfrac{\sec^2 y}{\tan y} dy = \int \dfrac{e^x dx}{(e^x - 1)}$ **(1 mark)**

$\Rightarrow \quad \log|\tan y| = \log|e^x - 1| + c$ **(1 mark)**

$$\left[\because \int \dfrac{f^1(x)}{f(x)} dy = \log f(x) \right]$$

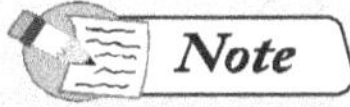 *Note*

For homogeneous function, power of x & y (should be) same in given function. Then put y = vx

31. **(a)** Let $I = \displaystyle\int_{\pi/4}^{\pi/2} e^{2x}\left(\dfrac{1 - \sin 2x}{1 - \cos 2x} \right) dx$

$\Rightarrow \quad I = \displaystyle\int_{\pi/4}^{\pi/2} e^{2x}\left[\dfrac{1}{1 - \cos 2x} - \dfrac{\sin 2x}{1 - \cos 2x} \right] dx$

$\Rightarrow \quad I = \displaystyle\int_{\pi/4}^{\pi/2} e^{2x}\left[\dfrac{1}{2\sin^2 x} - \dfrac{2\sin x \cos x}{2\sin^2 x} \right] dx$

$\Rightarrow \quad I = \displaystyle\int_{\pi/4}^{\pi/2} e^{2x}\left[\dfrac{\cos ec^2 x}{2} - \cot x \right] dx$ **(1 mark)**

Put $2x = t$

$\Rightarrow \quad x = t/2 \Rightarrow dx = \dfrac{dt}{2}$

$\therefore \quad I = -\int e^t \left(\cot\dfrac{t}{2} - \dfrac{1}{2}\cos ec^2\dfrac{t}{2} \right)\dfrac{dt}{2}$

$$\left[\because \int e^t\left(f(t) + f^1(t) \right) dt = e^t f(t) + c \right]$$

$\Rightarrow \quad I = -\dfrac{1}{2}\left(e^t \cot\dfrac{t}{2} \right)$ **(1 mark)**

$\Rightarrow \quad I = \left[-\dfrac{1}{2}e^{2x}\cot x \right]_{\pi/4}^{\pi/2}$

$\Rightarrow \quad I = -\left[0 - \dfrac{1}{2}e^{\pi/2} \right] = \dfrac{e^{\pi/2}}{2}$ **(1 mark)**

OR

(b) Let $I = \displaystyle\int_{-2}^{2} \dfrac{x^2 dx}{1 + 5^x}$ ...(i)

$$\left[\because \int_a^b f(x)dx = f(a + b - x)dx \right]$$

$\Rightarrow \quad I = \displaystyle\int_{-2}^{2} \dfrac{(-x)^2}{1 + 5^{-x}} dx$ ...(ii)   **(1½ marks)**

Add equations (i) and (ii)

$\Rightarrow \quad 2I = \displaystyle\int_{-2}^{2}\left[\dfrac{5^x x^2}{1 + 5^x} + \dfrac{x^2}{1 + 5^x} \right] dx = \displaystyle\int_{-2}^{2} x^2 dx$

$I = \dfrac{1}{2}\left[\dfrac{x^3}{3} \right]_{-2}^{2} = \dfrac{1}{2} \times \dfrac{16}{3} = 8/3$ **(1½ marks)**

32. Let N is foot of perpendicular drawn from the point
P(2, –1, 5)
Any point on line is N (11 + 10t, –2–4t, –8–11t)
Now, direction ratio of NP is

$\langle 9 + 10t, -1 - 4t, -13 - 11t \rangle$ **(2 marks)**

Direction ratio of line is $\langle 10, -4, -11 \rangle$

$\Rightarrow 10(9 + 10t) + 4(1 + 4t) + 11(13 + 11t) = 0$
$\Rightarrow 237t + 237 = 0$
$\Rightarrow t = -1$

Now, $(1, 2, 3) = \left(\dfrac{2+x}{2}, \dfrac{-1+y}{2}, \dfrac{5+z}{2} \right)$

$\Rightarrow \dfrac{x+2}{2} = 1 \Rightarrow x = 0$

$\Rightarrow \dfrac{y-1}{2} = 2 \Rightarrow y = 5$ **(2 marks)**

$\Rightarrow \dfrac{z+5}{2} = 3 \Rightarrow z = 1$

So image is (0, 5, 1) **(1 mark)**

OR

(b) BC lie on $\dfrac{x+2}{2} = \dfrac{y-1}{1} = \dfrac{z}{4}$

Coordinates of D can be
expressed as,
$(2\lambda - 2, \lambda + 1, 4\lambda)$
Dr's of AD are $(2\lambda - 3, \lambda + 2, 4\lambda - 2)$
AD is perpendicular to BC
So, $2(2\lambda - 3) + (\lambda + 2)$
$+ 4(4\lambda - 2) = 0$

$\Rightarrow \lambda = \dfrac{12}{21} \Rightarrow z = 1$

A (1, –1, 2)

B   D   C
$(2\lambda -, \lambda + 1, 4\lambda)$

(3 marks)

$|AD| = \sqrt{(2\lambda - 3)^2 + (\lambda + 2)^2 + (4\lambda - 2)^2}$

$= \sqrt{\left(\dfrac{39}{21}\right)^2 + \left(\dfrac{54}{21}\right)^2 + \left(\dfrac{6}{21}\right)^2} = \sqrt{\dfrac{4473}{441}}$

$\text{Area} = \dfrac{1}{2} \times 5 \times \sqrt{\dfrac{4473}{441}} = \sqrt{\dfrac{1775}{28}}$ **(2 marks)**

33. Given, $A = \begin{bmatrix} 1 & -1 & 2 \\ 0 & 2 & -3 \\ 3 & -2 & 4 \end{bmatrix}$

$\Rightarrow |A| = 1(8 - 6) + (0 + 9) - 2(0 - 6) = -1$ **(1 mark)**
On finding adjoint of A

$\Rightarrow F_{11} = \begin{vmatrix} 2 & -3 \\ -2 & 4 \end{vmatrix} = 2, \; F_{12} = \begin{vmatrix} 0 & -3 \\ 3 & 4 \end{vmatrix} = -9$

$\Rightarrow F_{13} = \begin{vmatrix} 0 & 2 \\ 3 & -2 \end{vmatrix} = -6, \; F_{21} = \begin{vmatrix} -1 & 2 \\ -2 & 4 \end{vmatrix} = 0$

$\Rightarrow F_{22} = \begin{vmatrix} 1 & 2 \\ 3 & 4 \end{vmatrix} = -2, \; F_{23} = -\begin{vmatrix} 1 & -1 \\ 3 & -2 \end{vmatrix} = 1$

$\Rightarrow F_{31} = \begin{vmatrix} -1 & 2 \\ 2 & -3 \end{vmatrix} = -1, \; F_{32} = -\begin{vmatrix} 1 & 2 \\ 0 & -3 \end{vmatrix} = 3$

$\Rightarrow F_{33} = \begin{vmatrix} 1 & -1 \\ 0 & 2 \end{vmatrix} = 2$

Matrix formed by adjoint of A is

$\Rightarrow \text{adj } A = B^T = \begin{bmatrix} 2 & 0 & -1 \\ -9 & -2 & -3 \\ -6 & -1 & 2 \end{bmatrix}$

Then, $A^{-1} = \begin{bmatrix} 2 & -9 & -6 \\ 0 & -2 & -1 \\ -1 & 3 & 2 \end{bmatrix}$ **(2 marks)**

$\Rightarrow = \dfrac{1}{-1} \begin{bmatrix} 2 & 0 & -1 \\ -9 & -2 & 3 \\ -6 & -1 & 2 \end{bmatrix}$

Now, AX = B
Then X = A⁻¹B

$\Rightarrow \begin{bmatrix} x \\ y \\ z \end{bmatrix} = \dfrac{1}{(-1)} \begin{bmatrix} 2 & 0 & -1 \\ -9 & -2 & 3 \\ -6 & -1 & 2 \end{bmatrix} \begin{bmatrix} 1 \\ 1 \\ 3 \end{bmatrix} = \dfrac{1}{(-1)} \begin{bmatrix} -1 \\ -2 \\ -1 \end{bmatrix}$

$\Rightarrow \begin{bmatrix} x \\ y \\ z \end{bmatrix} = \begin{bmatrix} 1 \\ 2 \\ 1 \end{bmatrix}$

$x = 1, y = 2, z = 1$ **(2 marks)**

34. Given, $y^2 = 4ax$
Then the equation of latus rectum is x = a
Required area = 2(area of AOL) **(1 mark)**

$= 2 \int_0^a y \, dx = 2 \int_0^a 2\sqrt{a} \sqrt{x} \, dx$

$= 4\sqrt{a} \int_0^a \sqrt{x} \, dx$ **(2 marks)**

$= 4\sqrt{a} \left[\dfrac{2x^{3/2}}{3} \right]_0^a$

$= 4\sqrt{a} \times \dfrac{2}{3} \left[a^{3/2} - 0 \right]$

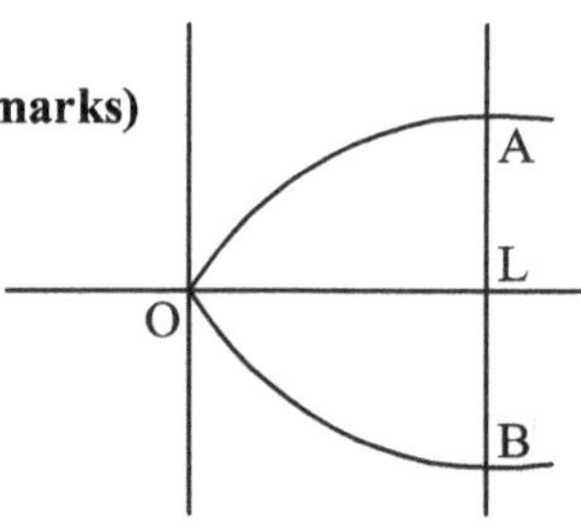

$= \dfrac{8}{3}a^2$ sq units. **(2 marks)**

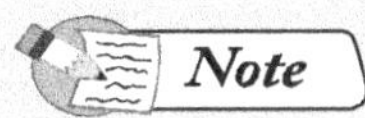

ar. AOL = ar. BOL
because both are symmetric figure

35. (a) Let R be defined on N × N
Reflexivity: Sum and product of natural numbers obeys commutative property
$(a, b)\, R\,(c, d) \Leftrightarrow ad\,(b+c) = bc(a+d)$
Hence, R is reflexive. **(1½ marks)**
Symmetry: Let $(a, b)\, R(c, d)$
$\Rightarrow\quad ad(b+c) = bc(a+d)$
$\Rightarrow\quad da(c+b) = cb(d+a)$
$\Rightarrow\quad (c, d) = R(a, b)$ **(1½ marks)**
So, R is symmetric.
Transitivity: Let $(a, b), (c, d), (e, f) \in$ N × N
$(a, b)\, R(c, d)$ and $(c, d)\, R\,(e, f)$
$ad(b+c) = bc(a+d)$ and $cf(d+e) = de\,(c+f)$

$\Rightarrow\quad \dfrac{ab}{a-b} = \dfrac{cd}{c-d}, \dfrac{cd}{c-d} = \dfrac{ef}{e-f}$

$\Rightarrow\quad \dfrac{ab}{a-b} = \dfrac{ef}{e-f} \Rightarrow (a, b)\, R(e, f)$

Hence, R is transitive.

OR

(b) Given, $f(x) = \dfrac{4x}{3x+4} \Rightarrow f(x) = f(y)$

$\Rightarrow\quad \dfrac{4x}{3x+4} = \dfrac{4y}{3y+4} \Rightarrow 12xy + 16x = 12xy + 16y$
$\Rightarrow\quad 16x = 16y \Rightarrow x = y$

$\therefore\quad$ f is one-one $\Rightarrow f(x) = \dfrac{4x}{3x+4}$ **(2½ marks)**

$\Rightarrow\quad 4x = 3xy + 4y \Rightarrow x = \dfrac{4y}{4-3y}$

So $\quad y \in R - \left\{\dfrac{4}{3}\right\}$

So, every element in $R - \left\{\dfrac{4}{3}\right\}$ has pre-image in $R - \left\{-\dfrac{4}{3}\right\}$

Hence, f is onto. **(2½ marks)**

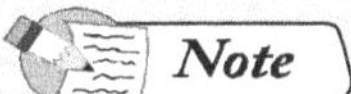

If f(x) = f(y) $\Rightarrow$ x = y for one-one function & for onto x = f⁻¹(y)
exists i.e. Range = codomain.

36. Given that
E_1 = Represent the event when many workers where not present
E_2 = Represent the event when all workers where present

E = Represent completing the construction work on time.
$\therefore\quad P(E_1) = 0.65,\ P(E/E_1) = 0.35$
and $P(E/E_2) = 0.80$
(i) P(All workers are present for the job)
$\quad = P(E_2) = 1 - 0.65 = 0.35$ **(1 mark)**
(ii) P(Construction will be completed on time)
$\quad = P(E) = P(E_1) \cdot P(E/E_1) + P(E_2) \cdot P(E/E_2)$
$\quad = 0.65 \times 0.35 + 0.35 \times 0.80$

$\quad = \dfrac{13}{20} \times \dfrac{7}{20} + \dfrac{7}{20} \times \dfrac{16}{20} = \dfrac{91}{400} + \dfrac{112}{400}$

$\quad = \dfrac{203}{400} = 0.51$ **(1 mark)**

(iii) (a) P(Many workers are not present given that construction work is completed on time)

$= P(E_1/E) = \dfrac{P(E/E_1) \cdot P(E_1)}{P(E/E_1)\,P(E_1) + P(E/E\,2) \cdot P(E_2)}$ **(1 mark)**

$= \dfrac{\dfrac{13}{20} \times \dfrac{7}{20}}{\dfrac{203}{400}} = \dfrac{\dfrac{91}{400}}{\dfrac{203}{400}}$

$= \dfrac{91}{203} = 0.45$ **(1 mark)**

OR

(b) P(all workers were present given that the construction job was completed on time)

$= P(E_2/E) = \dfrac{P(E/E_2) \cdot P(E_2)}{P(E/E_1)\,P(E_1) + P(E/E_2) \cdot P(E_2)}$

$= \dfrac{112}{203} = 0.55$ **(2 marks)**

37. (i) Given, $f(x) = \begin{cases} |x-3|,\ x \geq 1 \\ \dfrac{x^2}{4} - \dfrac{3x}{2} + \dfrac{13}{4},\ x < 1 \end{cases}$

RHD of f(x) at x = 1 is define as $\lim\limits_{x \to 1^+} f(1^+)$

$|x-3| = \begin{cases} -(x-3),\ x < 3 \\ (x-3),\ x > 3 \end{cases}$

$\Rightarrow\quad \lim\limits_{x \to 1^+} |x-3| = \lim\limits_{x \to 1^+} (3-x) = 3-1 = 2$ **(1 mark)**

(ii) LHD of f(x) at x = 1 is define as $\lim\limits_{x \to 1^-} f(1^-)$

At $x \to 1^-$, $f(x) = \dfrac{x^2}{4} - \dfrac{3x}{2} + \dfrac{13}{4}$

$\Rightarrow\quad \lim\limits_{x \to 1^-} f(1^-) = \dfrac{1}{4} - \dfrac{3}{2} + \dfrac{13}{4} = \dfrac{1}{4} - \dfrac{3}{4} + \dfrac{13}{4}$

$\Rightarrow\quad \dfrac{11}{4}$ **(1 mark)**

(iii) (a) $f'(x) = \lim\limits_{h \to 0} \dfrac{f(x+h) - f(x)}{h}$

LHS

At $x \to 1 + h$, where $h \to 0$

$f'(x) = \lim\limits_{h \to 0} \dfrac{f(1+h) - f(1)}{h} = \dfrac{-(1+h-3) - 2}{h}$

$\qquad = \dfrac{-h + 2 - 2}{h} = -1$ **(1 mark)**

RHS

At $x \to 1 - h$, where $h \to 0$

$f'(x) = \lim\limits_{h \to 0} \dfrac{f(1-h) - f(1)}{h}$

$= \dfrac{\dfrac{(1-h)^2}{4} - \dfrac{6(1-h)}{4} + \dfrac{13}{4} - \left(\dfrac{1}{4} - \dfrac{6}{4} + \dfrac{13}{4}\right)}{h}$

$\Rightarrow \dfrac{h^2 - 2h + 6h}{4h} = \dfrac{h - 2 + 6}{4} = 1$ **(1 mark)**

So given function is not differentiable at $x = 1$ RHS $\neq$ LHS

OR

(b)   At $x = 2$, $f(x) = -(x-3)$

Then, $f'(x) = -1$

so, $f'(2) = -1$

And, at $x = -1$, $f(x) = \dfrac{x^2}{4} - \dfrac{3x}{2} + \dfrac{13}{4}$

$\Rightarrow \quad f'(x) = \dfrac{2x}{4} - \dfrac{3}{2}$

$\Rightarrow \quad f'(x) = -\dfrac{1}{2} - \dfrac{3}{2} = -2$ **(2 marks)**

38. (i)   Three sides are wire fencing
So $2x + y = 200$ ...(i)
Area of rectangular garden is,
$A = xy$
Put value of y from equation (i)
$A(x) = x(200 - 2x)$
$A(x) = 200x - 2x^2$ **(2 marks)**
(ii)   For maximum area
$\qquad A'(x) = 200 - 4x = 0$
$\Rightarrow \quad 4x = 200 \Rightarrow x = 50$
Put value of x in equation (i)
$\Rightarrow 100 + y = 200 \Rightarrow y = 100$
So area $= xy = 100 \times 50 = 5000$ **(2 marks)**

Note

To find maximum or minimum area put $\dfrac{dy}{dx} = 0$ *for finding the values of x.*

Delhi *2023*

CBSE Board Solved Paper

Time Allowed : 3 Hours   *Maximum Marks : 100*

General Instructions:
(i)   This question paper contains **38** questions. **All** questions are compulsory.
(ii) Question paper is divided into **Five** Sections - Sections **A, B, C, D** and **E**.
(iii) In Section **A** - Question Number **1** to **18** are Multiple Choise Questions (MCQ) type and Question Number **19 & 20** are Assertion-Reason based questions of **1** mark each.
(iv) In Section **B** - Question Number **21** to **25** are Very Short Answer (VSA) type questions of **2** marks each.
(v)   In Section **C** - Question Number **26** to **31** are Short Answer (SA) type questions, carrying **3** marks each.
(vi) In Section **D** - Question Number **32** to **35** are Long Answer (LA) type questions carrying **5** marks each.
(vii) In Section **E** - Question Number **36** to **38** are case study based questions carrying **4** marks each where **2** VSA type questions are of **1** mark each and **1** SA type question is of **2** marks. Internal choice is provided in **2** marks question in each case study.
(viii) There is no overall choice. However, an internal choice has been provided in **2** questions in Section - **B**, **3** questions in Section - **C**, **2** questions in Section - **D** and **2** questions in Section - **E**.
(ix) Use of calculators is NOT allowed.

SECTION - A

Select the correct option out of the four given options:

1. $\sin\left[\dfrac{\pi}{3} + \sin^{-1}\left(\dfrac{1}{2}\right)\right]$ is equal to

(a) 1

(b) $\dfrac{1}{2}$

(c) $\dfrac{1}{3}$

(d) $\dfrac{1}{4}$

2. Let A = {3, 5}. Then number of reflexive relations on A is

(a) 2

(b) 4

(c) 0

(d) 8

3. If $A = \begin{bmatrix} 1 & 0 \\ 2 & 1 \end{bmatrix}$, $B = \begin{bmatrix} x & 0 \\ 1 & 1 \end{bmatrix}$ and $A = B^2$, then equals

(a) ± 1

(b) −1

(c) 1

(d) 2

4. If $A = [a_{ij}]$ is a square matrix of order 2 such that

$$a_{ij} = \begin{cases} 1, & \text{when } i \neq j \\ 0, & \text{when } i = j \end{cases}, \text{ then } A^2 \text{ is}$$

(a) $\begin{bmatrix} 1 & 0 \\ 1 & 0 \end{bmatrix}$

(b) $\begin{bmatrix} 1 & 1 \\ 0 & 0 \end{bmatrix}$

(c) $\begin{bmatrix} 1 & 1 \\ 1 & 0 \end{bmatrix}$

(d) $\begin{bmatrix} 1 & 0 \\ 0 & 1 \end{bmatrix}$

5. The value of the determinant $\begin{vmatrix} 6 & 0 & -1 \\ 2 & 1 & 4 \\ 1 & 1 & 3 \end{vmatrix}$ is

(a) 10

(b) 8

(c) 7

(d) −7

6. The function f(x) =[x], where [x] denotes the greatest integer less than or equal to x, is continuous at

(a) x = 1

(b) x = 1. 5

(c) x = −2

(d) x = 4

7. The derivative of x^{2x} w.r.t. x is

(a) x^{2x-1}

(b) $2x^{2x}\log x$

(c) $2x^{2x}\left(1+\log x\right)$

(d) $2x^{2x}\left(1-\log x\right)$

8. The interval in which the function $f(x) = 2x^3 + 9x^2 + 12x - 1$ is decreasing, is

(a) $(-1, \infty)$ (b) $(-2, -1)$

(c) $(-\infty, -2)$ (d) $[-1, 1]$

9. The function $f(x) = x|x|, x \in R$ is differentiable

(a) only at $x = 0$ (b) only at $x = 1$

(c) in R (d) in $R - \{0\}$

10. $\int \dfrac{\sec x}{\sec x - \tan x}\, dx$ equals

(a) $\sec x - \tan x + c$ (b) $\sec x + \tan x + c$

(c) $\tan x - \sec x + c$ (d) $-(\sec x + \tan x) + c$

11. The value of $\displaystyle\int_{0}^{\frac{\pi}{4}} (\sin 2x)\, dx$ is

(a) 0 (b) 1

(c) $\dfrac{1}{2}$ (d) $-\dfrac{1}{2}$

12. The sum of the order and the degree of the differential equation $\dfrac{d}{dx}\left(\left(\dfrac{dy}{dx}\right)^3\right)$ is

(a) 2 (b) 3

(c) 5 (d) 0

13. Two vectors $\vec{a} = a_1\hat{i} + a_2\hat{j} + a_3\hat{k}$ and $\vec{b} = b_1\hat{i} + b_2\hat{j} + b_3\hat{k}$ are collinear if

(a) $a_1 b_1 + a_2 b_2 + a_3 b_3 = 0$

(b) $\dfrac{a_1}{b_1} = \dfrac{a_2}{b_2} = \dfrac{a_3}{b_3}$

(c) $a_1 = b_1, a_2 = b_2, a_3 = b_3$

(d) $a_1 + a_2 + a_3 = b_1 + b_2 + b_3$

14. A unit vector $\hat{a}$ makes equal but acute angles on the co-ordinate axes. The projection of the vector $\hat{a}$ on the vector $\vec{b} = 5\hat{i} + 7\hat{j} - \hat{k}$ is

(a) $\dfrac{11}{15}$ (b) $\dfrac{11}{5\sqrt{3}}$

(c) $\dfrac{4}{5}$ (d) $\dfrac{3}{5\sqrt{3}}$

15. The angle between the lines $2x = 3y = -z$ and $6x = -y = -4z$ is

(a) $0°$ (b) $30°$

(c) $45°$ (d) $90°$

16. If a line makes angles of $90°$, $135°$ and $45°$ with the x, y and z axes respectively, then its direction cosines are

(a) $0, -\dfrac{1}{\sqrt{2}}, \dfrac{1}{\sqrt{2}}$ (b) $-\dfrac{1}{\sqrt{2}}, 0, \dfrac{1}{\sqrt{2}}$

(c) $\dfrac{1}{\sqrt{2}}, 0, -\dfrac{1}{\sqrt{2}}$ (d) $0, \dfrac{1}{\sqrt{2}}, \dfrac{1}{\sqrt{2}}$

17. If for any two events A and B, $P(A) = \dfrac{4}{5}$ and $P(A \cap B) = \dfrac{7}{10}$, then $P(B/A)$ is equal to

(a) $\dfrac{1}{10}$ (b) $\dfrac{1}{8}$

(c) $\dfrac{7}{8}$ (d) $\dfrac{17}{20}$

18. If A and B are two independent events such that $P(A) = \dfrac{1}{3}$ and $P(B) = \dfrac{1}{4}$, then $P(B'/A)$ is

(a) $\dfrac{1}{4}$ (b) $\dfrac{1}{8}$

(c) $\dfrac{3}{4}$ (d) 1

Assertion – Reason Based Questions

In the following questions 19 and 20, a statement of Assertion (A) is followed by a statement of Reason (R). Choose the correct answer out of the following choices:

(a) Both (A) and (R) are true and (R) is the correct explanation of (A).

(b) Both (A) and (R) are true but (R) is not the correct explanation of (A).

(c) (A) is true and (R) is false.

(d) (A) is false, but (R) is true.

19. Assertion (A): $\displaystyle\int_{2}^{8} \dfrac{\sqrt{10-x}}{\sqrt{x} + \sqrt{10-x}}\, dx = 3$

Reason (R): $\displaystyle\int_{a}^{b} f(x)\, dx = \int_{a}^{b} f(a + b - x)\, dx$

20. **Assertion (A):** Two coins are tossed simultaneously. The probability of getting two heads, if it is known that at least one head comes up, is $\dfrac{1}{3}$.

Reason (R): Let E and F be two events with a random experiment, then $P(F/E) = \dfrac{P(E \cap F)}{P(E)}$.

SECTION - B

This section comprises of **Very Short Answer (VSA) type** questions of 2 marks each.

21. Draw the graph of the principal branch of the function $f(x) = \cos^{-1} x$.

22. (a) If the vectors $\vec{a}$ and $\vec{b}$ are such that $|\vec{a}| = 3, |\vec{b}| = \dfrac{2}{3}$ and $\vec{a} \times \vec{b}$ is a unit vector, then find the angle between $\vec{a}$ and $\vec{b}$.

OR

(b) Find the area of a parallelogram whose adjacent sides are determined by the vectors
$$\vec{a} = \hat{i} - \hat{j} + 3\hat{k} \text{ and } \vec{b} = 2\hat{i} - 7\hat{j} + \hat{k}.$$

23. (a) If $f(x) = \begin{cases} x^2, & \text{if } x \geq 1 \\ x, & \text{if } x < 1 \end{cases}$, then show that f is not differentiable at $x = 1$.

OR

(b) Find the value(s) of 'λ', if the function
$$f(x) = \begin{cases} \dfrac{\sin^2 \lambda x}{x^2}, & \text{if } x \neq 0 \\ 1, & \text{if } x = 0 \end{cases}$$
is continuous at $x = 0$.

24. Sketch the region bounded by the lines $2x + y = 8$, $y = 2$, $y = 4$ and the y-axis. Hence, obtain its area using integration.

25. Find the angle between the following two lines:
$$\vec{r} = 2\hat{i} - 5\hat{j} + \hat{k} + \lambda(3\hat{i} + 2\hat{j} + 6\hat{k});$$
$$\vec{r} = 7\hat{i} - 6\hat{k} + \mu(\hat{i} + 2\hat{j} + 2\hat{k})$$

SECTION - C

The section comprises of **Short Answer (SA) type** questions of 3 marks each.

26. Using determinants, find the area of ΔPQR with vertices $P(3, 1)$, $Q(9, 3)$ and $R(5, 7)$. Also, find the equation of line PQ using determinants.

27. (a) Differentiate $\sec^{-1}\left(\dfrac{1}{\sqrt{1-x^2}}\right)$ w.r.t. $\sin^{-1}(2x\sqrt{1-x^2})$.

OR

(b) If $y = \tan x + \sec x$, then prove that $\dfrac{d^2 y}{dx^2} = \dfrac{\cos x}{(1-\sin x)^2}$.

28. (a) Evaluate: $\displaystyle\int_{\frac{-\pi}{4}}^{\frac{\pi}{4}} \dfrac{\cos 2x}{1 + \cos 2x}\,dx$

OR

(b) Find: $\displaystyle\int e^{x^2}(x^5 + 2x^3)dx$

29. Find the area of the minor segment of the circle $x^2 + y^2 = 4$ cut off by the line $x = 1$, using integration.

30. Find the distance between the lines:
$$\vec{r} = (\hat{i} + 2\hat{j} - 4\hat{k}) + \lambda(2\hat{i} + 3\hat{j} + 6\hat{k});$$
$$\vec{r} = (3\hat{i} + 3\hat{j} - 5\hat{k}) + \mu(4\hat{i} + 6\hat{j} + 12\hat{k})$$

31. (a) Find the coordinates of the foot of the perpendicular drawn from the point $P(0, 2, 3)$ to the line $\dfrac{x+3}{5} = \dfrac{y-1}{2} = \dfrac{z+4}{3}$.

OR

(b) Three vectors $\vec{a}, \vec{b}$ and $\vec{c}$ satisfy the condition $\vec{a} + \vec{b} + \vec{c} = \vec{0}$. Evaluate the quantity $\mu = \vec{a}.\vec{b} + \vec{b}.\vec{c} + \vec{c}.\vec{a}$, if $|\vec{a}| = 3, |\vec{b}| = 4$ and $|\vec{c}| = 2$.

SECTION - D

This section comprises of **Long Answer (LA) type** questions of 5 marks each.

32. Evaluate: $\displaystyle\int_0^{} \dfrac{x}{1 + \sin x}\,dx$

33. (a) The median of an equilateral triangle is increasing at the rate of $2\sqrt{3}$ cm/s. Find the rate at which its side is increasing.

OR

(b) Sum of two numbers is 5. If the sum of the cubes of these numbers is least, then find the sum of the squares of these numbers.

34. (a) In answering a question on a multiple choice test, a student either knows the answer or guesses. Let $\dfrac{3}{5}$ be the probability that he knows the answer and $\dfrac{2}{5}$ be the probability that he guesses. Assuming that a student who guesses at the answer will be correct with probability $\dfrac{1}{3}$.

What is the probability that the student knows the answer, given that he answered it correctly?

OR

(b)　A box contains 10 tickets, 2 of which carry a prize of ₹ 8 each, 5 of which carry a prize of ₹ 4 each, and remaining 3 carrry a prize of ₹ 2 each. If one ticket is drawn at random, find the mean value of the prize.

35.　Solve the following Linear Programming Problem graphically:

Maximize: $P = 70x + 40y$

subject to: $3x + 2y \leq 9$,

$3x + y \leq 9$,

$x \geq 0, y \geq 0$

SECTION - E

This section comprises of 3 Case Study/Passage-Bassed questions of 4 marks each with two sub-parts. First two case study questions have three sub-parts (I), (II), (III) of marks 1, 1, 2 respectively. The third case study question has two sub – parts (I) and (II) of marks 2 each.

Case Study-I

36.　Gautam buys 5 pens, 3 bags and 1 instrument box and pays a sum of ₹ 160. From the same shop, Vikram buys 2 pens, 1 bag and 3 instrument boxes and pays a sum of ₹ 190. Also Ankur buys 1 pen, 2 bags and 4 instrument boxes and pays a sum of ₹ 250.

Based on the above information, answer the following questions:

(I)　Convert the given above situation into a matrix equation of the form AX = B.

(II)　Find $|A|$.

(III)　Find A^{-1}.

OR

Determine $P = A^2 - 5A$.

Case Study - II

37.　An organization conducted bike race under two different categories – Boys and Girls. There were 28 participants in all. Among all of them, finally three from category 1 and two from category 2 were selected for the final race. Ravi forms two sets B and G with these participants for his college project.

Let $B = \{b_1, b_2, b_3\}$ and $G = \{g_1, g_2\}$, where B represents the set of Boys selected and G the set of Girls selected for the final race.

Based on the above information, answer the following question:

(I)　How many relations are possible from B to G?

(II)　Among all the possible relations from B to G, how many functions can be formed from B to G?

(III)　Let R: B $\rightarrow$ B be defined by R = {(x, y) : x and y are students of the same sex}. Check if R is an equivalence relation.

OR

A function f : B $\rightarrow$ G be defined by f = {(b_1, g_1), (b_2, g_2), (b_3, g_1)}.

check if is bijective. Justify your answer.

Case Study-III

38.　An equation involving derivatives of the dependent variable with respect to the independent variables is called a differential equation. A differential equation of the form

$\dfrac{dy}{dx} = F(x, y)$　is said to be homogeneous if F(x, y) is a

homogeneous function of degree zero, whereas a function F(x, y) is a homogenous function of degree n if

$F(\lambda x, \lambda y) = \lambda^n\, F(x, y)$.　To　solve　a　homogeneous

differential equation of the type $\dfrac{dy}{dx} = F(x, y) = g\left(\dfrac{y}{x}\right)$, we

make the substitution y = vx and then separate the variables. Based on the above information, answer the following questions:

(I)　Show that $(x^2 - y^2)dx + 2xy\, dy = 0$ is a differential equation

of the type $\dfrac{dy}{dx} = g\left(\dfrac{y}{x}\right)$.

(II)　Solve the above equation to find its general solution.

Solutions

1. **(a)** $\sin\left[\dfrac{\pi}{3} + \sin^{-1}\left(\dfrac{1}{2}\right)\right] = \sin\left[\dfrac{\pi}{3} + \dfrac{\pi}{6}\right] = \sin\left(\dfrac{2\pi + \pi}{6}\right)$

$= \sin\left(\dfrac{3\pi}{6}\right) = \sin\left(\dfrac{\pi}{2}\right) = 1$ **(1 Mark)**

> **Note**
>
> $-\dfrac{\pi}{2} \le \sin^{-1} x \le \dfrac{\pi}{2}$

2. **(b)** Given set $A = \{3,5\} \Rightarrow n(A) = 2$

Now number of reflexive relation on A

$= 2^{(n^2 - n)} = 2^{(2^2 - 2)} = 2^{(4-2)} = 2^2 = 4$ **(1 Mark)**

3. **(c)** Given, $A = \begin{bmatrix} 1 & 0 \\ 2 & 1 \end{bmatrix}$ and $B = \begin{bmatrix} x & 0 \\ 1 & 1 \end{bmatrix}$

Since, given $A = B^2$

$\Rightarrow \begin{bmatrix} 1 & 0 \\ 2 & 1 \end{bmatrix} = \begin{bmatrix} x \cdot x + 0 \cdot 1 & x \cdot 0 + 0 \cdot 1 \\ x \cdot 1 + 1 \cdot 1 & 1 \cdot 0 + 1 \cdot 1 \end{bmatrix}$

$\Rightarrow \begin{bmatrix} 1 & 0 \\ 2 & 1 \end{bmatrix} = \begin{bmatrix} x^2 & 0 \\ x+1 & 1 \end{bmatrix}$

If $x^2 = 1 \Rightarrow x = \pm 1$

If $x + 1 = 2 \Rightarrow x = 1$

So $x = 1$ only   **(1 Mark)**

4. **(d)** Given, $A = \left[a_{i,j}\right]_{2\times 2}$

Such that $a_{ij} = \begin{cases} 1 & \text{when } i \ne j \\ 0 & \text{when } i = j \end{cases}$

So, $A = \begin{bmatrix} a_{11} & a_{12} \\ a_{21} & a_{22} \end{bmatrix} = \begin{bmatrix} 0 & 1 \\ 1 & 0 \end{bmatrix}$

Now, $A^2 = \begin{bmatrix} 0 & 1 \\ 1 & 0 \end{bmatrix}\begin{bmatrix} 0 & 1 \\ 1 & 0 \end{bmatrix} \Rightarrow A^2 = \begin{bmatrix} 1 & 0 \\ 0 & 1 \end{bmatrix}$ **(1 Mark)**

5. **(d)** Since,

$\begin{vmatrix} 6 & 0 & -1 \\ 2 & 1 & 4 \\ 1 & 1 & 3 \end{vmatrix} = 6(3-4) - 0(6-4) - 1(2-1)$

$= 6 \times (-1) - 0 - 1 \times 1 = -6 - 1 = -7$ **(1 Mark)**

6. **(b)** Given the function $f(x) = [x]$

$\Rightarrow [x] = \begin{cases} -2 & \text{If } -2 \le x < -1 \\ -1 & \text{If } -1 \le x < 0 \\ 0 & \text{If } 0 \le x < 1 \\ 1 & \text{If } 1 \le x < 2 \\ 2 & \text{If } 2 \le x < 3 \end{cases}$

We can see easily $f(x) = [x]$ is not continuous at all integer. So $f(x) = [x]$ is continuous at $x = 1.5$ **(1 Mark)**

7. **(c)** Let $y = x^{2x}$

Since $y = x^{2x} = e^{\ln(x^{2x})} = e^{2x \ln(x)}$

Now,

$\dfrac{dy}{dx} = \dfrac{d(e^{2x \ln(x)})}{dx} = e^{2x\ln(x)}\left(\dfrac{d(2x \ln(x))}{dx}\right)$

$= y\left(2x\dfrac{d}{dx}\big(\ln(x)\big) + 2\ln(x)\dfrac{d(x)}{dx}\right) = y\left(\dfrac{2x}{x} + 2\ln x\right)$

$x^{2x}(2 + 2\ln x) = 2x^{2x}(1 + \ln x)$ **(1 Mark)**

8. **(b)** Given the function

$f(x) = 2x^3 + 9x^2 + 12x - 1$

Now, $f'(x) = \dfrac{d}{dx}\left(2x^3 + 9x^2 + 12x - 1\right)$

$\Rightarrow f'(x) = 6x^2 + 18x + 12$

Since, the interval for which the given function is dicreasing

$f'(x) < 0$

$\Rightarrow (x + 2)(x + 1) < 0$

So $x \in (-2, -1)$ **(1 Mark)**

> **Note**
>
> If $(x - a)(x - b) < 0$ then $(x - a) < 0$ and $(x - b) > 0$ or $(x - a) > 0$ and $(x - b) < 0$

9. **(c)** Given the fucntion $f(x) = x \mid x \mid$, $x \in R$

$f(x) = \begin{cases} -x^2 & \text{If } x < 0 \\ x^2 & \text{If } x \ge 0 \end{cases} \Rightarrow f'(x) = \begin{cases} -2x & \text{If } x < 0 \\ 2x & \text{If } x \ge 0 \end{cases}$

at $x = 0$,

$f(0) = 0 \Rightarrow f(x)$ is differentiable at $x = 0$

So $f(x)$ is differentiable $\forall x \in R$ **(1 Mark)**

10. **(b)** Let $I = \displaystyle\int \dfrac{\sec x}{\sec x - \tan x}\,dx$

$\Rightarrow I = \displaystyle\int \dfrac{(\sec^2 x - \tan^2 x)\sec x}{\sec x - \tan x}\,dx$

$= \displaystyle\int \dfrac{(\sec x - \tan x)(\sec x + \tan x)\sec x}{\sec x - \tan x}\,dx$

$= \displaystyle\int (\sec x + \tan x)\sec x\,dx \int \sec^2 x\,dx + \int \sec x \tan x\,dx$

$= \tan x + \sec x + c$ **(1 Mark)**

11. **(c)** Let $I = \displaystyle\int_0^{\pi/4} (\sin 2x)\,dx$

$= \left(\dfrac{-\cos 2x}{2}\right)_0^{\pi/4} = -\dfrac{1}{2}\left\{\cos\left(2\times\dfrac{\pi}{4}\right) - \cos(2\times 0)\right\}$

$= -\dfrac{1}{2}\left\{\cos\left(\dfrac{\pi}{2}\right) - \cos(0)\right\} = -\dfrac{1}{2}(0-1) = \dfrac{1}{2}$ **(1 Mark)**

12. (b) Since, $\dfrac{d}{dx}\left(\left(\dfrac{dy}{dx}\right)^3\right)$

$$= 3\left(\dfrac{dy}{dx}\right)^2\cdot\dfrac{d}{dx}\left(\dfrac{dy}{dx}\right) = 3\left(\dfrac{dy}{dx}\right)^2\cdot\dfrac{d^2y}{dx^2}$$

Now, order = 2, degree = 1
So, order + degree = 2 + 1 = 3   **(1 Mark)**

13. (b) Given the vectors are

$$\vec{a} = a_1\hat{i} + a_2\hat{j} + a_3\hat{k},\ \vec{b} = b_1\hat{i} + b_2\hat{j} + b_3\hat{k}$$

For collinear of vector $\vec{a}$ and $\vec{b}$ = $\dfrac{a_1}{b_1} = \dfrac{a_2}{b_2} = \dfrac{a_3}{b_3}$ **(1 Mark)**

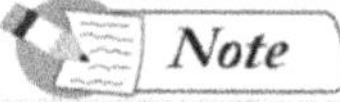

$\vec{a}$ and $\vec{b}$ are collinear if $\vec{a} = \lambda\,\vec{b}$.

14. (a) Given $|\hat{a}| = 1$
Since, $\ell = \cos\alpha = m = n$
Now, $\ell^2 + m^2 + n^2$
$\Rightarrow\quad \cos^2\alpha + \cos^2\alpha + \cos^2\alpha = 1 \Rightarrow 3\cos^2\alpha = 1$

$\Rightarrow\quad \cos\alpha = \dfrac{1}{\sqrt{3}}$ So, $\hat{a} = \dfrac{1}{\sqrt{3}}\hat{i} + \dfrac{1}{\sqrt{3}}\hat{j} + \dfrac{1}{\sqrt{3}}\hat{k}$

Now, projection of the vector $\hat{a}$ on the vector
$\vec{b} = 5\hat{i} + 7\hat{j} - \hat{k}$ is

$$\dfrac{\hat{a}\cdot\vec{b}}{|\vec{b}|} = \dfrac{\left(\dfrac{1}{\sqrt{3}}\hat{i} + \dfrac{1}{\sqrt{3}}\hat{j} + \dfrac{1}{\sqrt{3}}\hat{k}\right)\cdot\left(5\hat{i} + 7\hat{j} - \hat{k}\right)}{\sqrt{5^2 + 7^2 + (-1)^2}}$$

$$= \dfrac{\dfrac{5}{\sqrt{3}} + \dfrac{7}{\sqrt{3}} + \dfrac{-1}{\sqrt{3}}}{\sqrt{25 + 49 + 1}} = \dfrac{5 + 7 - 1}{\sqrt{75}\cdot\sqrt{3}} = \dfrac{11}{5\sqrt{3}\cdot\sqrt{3}} = \dfrac{11}{15}$$ **(1 Mark)**

15. (d) Given the lines
$2x = 3y = -z$ and $6x = -y = -4z$

$$\dfrac{x}{\dfrac{1}{2}} = \dfrac{y}{\dfrac{1}{3}} = \dfrac{z}{-1} \text{ and } \dfrac{x}{\dfrac{1}{6}} = \dfrac{y}{-1} = \dfrac{z}{-\dfrac{1}{4}}$$

Now, $a_1a_2 + b_1b_2 + c_1c_2 = \dfrac{1}{2}\times\dfrac{1}{6} + \dfrac{1}{3}\times(-1) + (-1)\times\left(\dfrac{-1}{4}\right)$

$$\dfrac{1}{12} - \dfrac{1}{3} + \dfrac{1}{4} = \dfrac{1}{12} - \dfrac{1}{12} = 0$$

So, angle between the given lines is 90°   **(1 Mark)**

16. (a) Let $\alpha = 90°$, $\beta = 135°$, $\gamma = 45°$
Now $\cos\alpha = \cos(90°) = 0$
$\cos\beta = \cos(135°) = \cos(90° + 45°)$

$$= -\sin(45°) = -\dfrac{1}{\sqrt{2}} \Rightarrow \text{ and } \cos\gamma = \cos(45°) = \dfrac{1}{\sqrt{2}}$$

So, direction cosines are $0, -\dfrac{1}{\sqrt{2}}, \dfrac{1}{\sqrt{2}}$ **(1 Mark)**

17. (c) Given $P(A) = \dfrac{4}{5}$, $P(A\cap B) = \dfrac{7}{10}$

Now, $P\left(\dfrac{B}{A}\right) = \dfrac{P(A\cap B)}{P(A)} = \dfrac{\dfrac{7}{10}}{\dfrac{4}{5}} = \dfrac{7\times5}{10\times4} = \dfrac{7}{8}$ **(1 Mark)**

18. (c) Given $P(A) = \dfrac{1}{3}$, $P(B) = \dfrac{1}{4}$ and
A and B are independent event.

Now, $P\left(\dfrac{B'}{A}\right) = 1 - P\left(\dfrac{B}{A}\right) = 1 - \dfrac{P(A\cap B)}{P(A)}$

$$= 1 - \dfrac{P(A)\cdot P(B)}{P(A)} = 1 - P(B) = 1 - \dfrac{1}{4} = \dfrac{3}{4}$$ **(1 Mark)**

19. (a) Let $I = \displaystyle\int_2^8 \dfrac{\sqrt{10-x}}{\sqrt{x}+\sqrt{10-x}}\,dx$ ...(i)

$$\Rightarrow\ I = \int_2^8 \dfrac{\sqrt{10-10+x}}{\sqrt{10-x}+\sqrt{10-10+x}}\,dx$$

$$\Rightarrow\ I = \int_2^8 \dfrac{\sqrt{x}}{\sqrt{10-x}+\sqrt{x}}\,dx$$ ...(ii)

By adding (i) and (ii), we get

$$\Rightarrow\ 2I = \int_2^8 \dfrac{\sqrt{10-x}}{\sqrt{x}+\sqrt{10-x}}\,dx + \int_2^8 \dfrac{\sqrt{x}}{\sqrt{10-x}+\sqrt{x}}\,dx$$

$$\Rightarrow\ 2I = \int_2^8 dx \Rightarrow 2I = (x)_2^8 = 8 - 2 \Rightarrow 2I = 6 \Rightarrow I = 3$$

and $\displaystyle\int_a^b f(x)\,dx = \int_a^b f(a+b-x)\,dx$

So, both A and R are correct and R is correct explanation of A.   **(1 Mark)**

20. (a) Let E_1 = getting two head
E_2 = at least one head
and sample space = $\{(HH), (HT), (TH), (TT)\}$

So, $P(E_1) = \dfrac{1}{4}$, $P(E_2) = \dfrac{3}{4}$, $P(E_1\cap E_2) = \dfrac{1}{4}$

Now, $P\left(\dfrac{E_1}{E_2}\right) = \dfrac{P(E_1\cap E_2)}{P(E_2)} = \dfrac{\dfrac{1}{4}}{\dfrac{3}{4}} = \dfrac{1}{3}$ **(1 Mark)**

So, Both A and R is correct and R is correct explanation of A.

21. Given the function $f(x) = \cos^{-1}x$
Since, $-1 \le x \le 1$ and $0 \le f(x) \le \pi$ **(1 Mark)**

So, 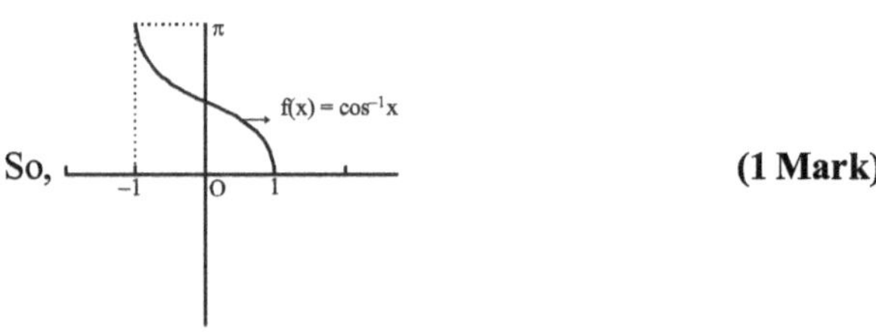

   (1 Mark)

22. (a) Given, $|\vec{a}| = 3, |\vec{b}| = \dfrac{2}{3}$ and $|\vec{a} \times \vec{b}| = 1$

Since, $|\vec{a} \times \vec{b}| = |\vec{a}| \times |\vec{b}| \sin\theta = 3 \times \dfrac{2}{3} \sin\theta$ **(1 Mark)**

$\Rightarrow 1 = 2\sin\theta \Rightarrow \sin\theta = \dfrac{1}{2} \Rightarrow \theta = \dfrac{\pi}{6}$

So, angle between $\vec{a}$ and $\vec{b}$ is $\dfrac{\pi}{6}$ **(1 Mark)**

OR

(b) Given the adjacent sides of parallelogram are
$\hat{a} = \hat{i} - \hat{j} + 3\hat{k}$ and $\hat{b} = 2\hat{i} - 7\hat{j} + \hat{k}$
Since, we know that
Area of parrallogram = $|\vec{a} \times \vec{b}|$

Now, $\vec{a} \times \vec{b} = \begin{vmatrix} \hat{i} & \hat{j} & \hat{k} \\ 1 & -1 & 3 \\ 2 & -7 & 1 \end{vmatrix} = 20\hat{i} + 5\hat{j} - 5\hat{k}$ **(1 Mark)**

So, Area of Parallelogram = $|\vec{a} \times \vec{b}|$

$= \left|20\hat{i} + 5\hat{j} - 5\hat{k}\right| = \sqrt{20^2 + 5^2 + (-5)^2}$

$= \sqrt{400 + 25 + 25} = \sqrt{450} \qquad = 15\sqrt{2}$ sq unit. **(1 Mark)**

23. (a) Given the function $f(x) = \begin{cases} x^2 & \text{if } x \geq 1 \\ x & \text{if } x < 1 \end{cases}$

at $x = 1$, Left hand derivative (L.H.D)

$f'_-(1) = \lim\limits_{h \to 0} \dfrac{f(1-h) - f(1)}{-h}$

$\lim\limits_{h \to 0} \dfrac{1 - h - 1^2}{-h} = \lim\limits_{h \to 0} \dfrac{-h}{-h} = 1$ **(1 Mark)**

at $x = 1$, Right hand derivative (R.H.D)

$f^1_+(1) = \lim\limits_{h \to 0} \dfrac{f(1+h) - f(1)}{+h}$

$= \lim\limits_{h \to 0} \dfrac{(1+h)^2 - 1}{h} = \lim\limits_{h \to 0} \dfrac{1 + h^2 + 2h - 1}{h}$

$= \lim\limits_{h \to 0} \dfrac{h(h+2)}{h} = \lim\limits_{h \to 0}(h+2) = 0 + 2 = 2$

Since L.H.D. $\neq$ R.H.D.
so, $f(x)$ is not differentiable at $x = 1$ **(1 Mark)**

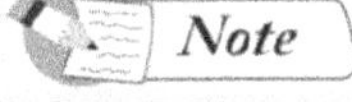

Note

For differentiable function L.H.D = R.H.D

(b) Given the function $f(x) = \begin{cases} \dfrac{\sin^2 \lambda x}{x^2} & \text{if } x \neq 0 \\ 1 & \text{if } x = 0 \end{cases}$

at $x = 0$, Left hand limit (L.H.L.)

$\lim\limits_{h \to 0^-} f(x) = \lim\limits_{h \to 0^-} \dfrac{\sin^2 \lambda x}{x^2}$

$\lim\limits_{x \to 0^-} \left(\dfrac{\sin \lambda x}{\lambda x}\right)^2 \times \lambda^2 = \lambda^2$ **(½ Mark)**

at $x = 0$, Right hand limit (R.H.L)

$\lim\limits_{x \to 0^+} f(x) = \lim\limits_{x \to 0^+} \dfrac{\sin^2 \lambda x}{x^2} = \lim\limits_{x \to 0^+} \dfrac{(\sin\lambda x)^2}{(\lambda x)^2} \times \lambda^2$

$= 1 \times \lambda^2 = \lambda^2$ **(½ Mark)**

Since, $f(x)$ is continuous at $x = 0$

So, $\lim\limits_{x \to 0^-} f(x) = \lim\limits_{x \to 0^+} f(x) = f(0)$

$\Rightarrow \lambda^2 = \lambda^2 = 1 \Rightarrow \lambda = \pm 1$ **(1 Mark)**

24. Given the lines $2x + y = 8$, $y = 2$, $y = 4$
Now, graph of the given lines are

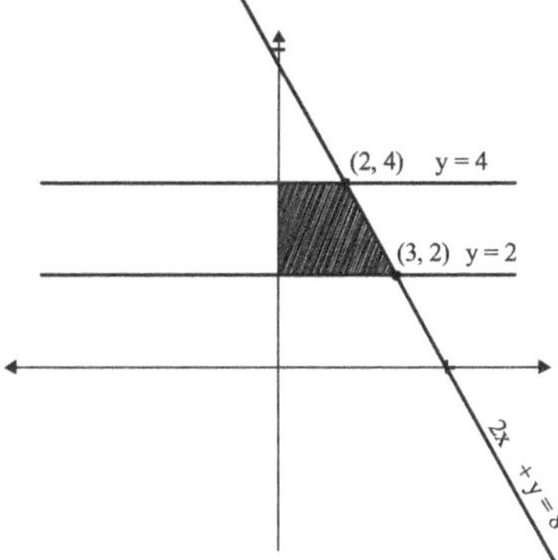

Since, $2x + y = 8 \Rightarrow 2x = 8 - y$ **(1 Mark)**

$\Rightarrow x = 4 - \dfrac{y}{2}$

So, required area $= \int_2^4 x\,dy = \int_2^4 \left(4 - \dfrac{y}{2}\right) dy$

$= \left(4y - \dfrac{y^2}{4}\right)_2^4 = \left(4 \times 4 - \dfrac{4^2}{4}\right) - \left(4 \times 2 - \dfrac{2^2}{4}\right)$

$(16 - 4) - (8 - 1) = 12 - 7 = 5$ **(1 Mark)**

25. Given the lines $\vec{r} = 2\hat{i} - 5\hat{j} + \hat{k} + \lambda\left(3\hat{i} + 2\hat{j} + 6\hat{k}\right)$ and

$\vec{r} = 7\hat{i} - 6\hat{k} + \mu\left(\hat{i} + 2\hat{j} + 2\hat{k}\right)$

Let $\vec{a}_1 = (2, -5, 1), \vec{b}_1 = (3, 2, 6)$ and $a_2 = (7, 0, -6), b_2 = (1, 2, 2)$

Now, angle between these two lines is given by.

$\cos\theta = \dfrac{\vec{b}_1 \cdot \vec{b}_2}{|\vec{b}_1| \cdot |\vec{b}_1|} = \dfrac{(3, 2, 6) \cdot (1, 2, 2)}{\sqrt{3^2 + 2^2 + 6^2} \cdot \sqrt{1^2 + 2^2 + 2^2}}$ **(1 Mark)**

$= \dfrac{3 + 4 + 12}{\sqrt{9 + 4 + 36} \cdot \sqrt{1 + 4 + 4}} = \dfrac{19}{\sqrt{49} \cdot \sqrt{9}} = \dfrac{19}{7 \times 3} = \dfrac{19}{21}$

$\Rightarrow \cos\theta = \dfrac{19}{21} \Rightarrow \theta = \cos^{-1}\left(\dfrac{19}{21}\right)$ **(1 Mark)**

26. Given the vertices of the Δ PQR
P(3, 1), Q(9 ,3) and R (5, 7)

Now, area of Δ PQR $= \dfrac{1}{2}\begin{vmatrix} x_1 & y_1 & 1 \\ x_2 & y_2 & 1 \\ x_3 & y_3 & 1 \end{vmatrix} = \dfrac{1}{2}\begin{vmatrix} 3 & 1 & 1 \\ 9 & 3 & 1 \\ 5 & 7 & 1 \end{vmatrix}$

$= \dfrac{1}{2}\{3(3-7)-1(9-5)+1(63-15)\}$ **(1 Mark)**

$= \dfrac{1}{2}(-12-4+48) = \dfrac{1}{2}\times 32 = 16$ **(1 Mark)**

$\Rightarrow$ Area of ΔPQR= 16 sq. units

Now, equation of line PQ is given by $\dfrac{1}{2}\begin{vmatrix} 3 & 1 & 1 \\ 9 & 3 & 1 \\ x & y & 1 \end{vmatrix} = 0$

$\Rightarrow \begin{vmatrix} 3 & 1 & 1 \\ 9 & 3 & 1 \\ x & y & 1 \end{vmatrix} = 0 \Rightarrow 3(3-y)-1(9-x)+(9y-3x) = 0$

$\Rightarrow \quad -2x + 6y = 0 \Rightarrow x - 3y = 0$
It is equation of line PQ.   **(1 Mark)**

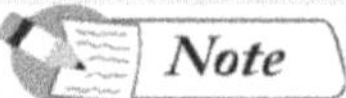
Note

Area of ΔPQR $= \begin{vmatrix} x_1 & y_1 & 1 \\ x_2 & y_2 & 1 \\ x_3 & y_3 & 1 \end{vmatrix}$ where $(x_1, y_1), (x_2, y_2)$ and

(x_3, y_3) are given coordinates.

27. (a) Let $y = \sec^{-1}\left(\dfrac{1}{\sqrt{1-x^2}}\right)$

$z = \sin^{-1}\left(2x\sqrt{1-x^2}\right)$ and $x = \sin\theta$

So, $y = \sec^{-1}\left(\dfrac{1}{\sqrt{1-\sin^2\theta}}\right) = \sec^{-1}\left(\dfrac{1}{\sqrt{\cos^2\theta}}\right)$

$\Rightarrow \quad \sec^{-1}\left(\dfrac{1}{\cos\theta}\right) = \sec^{-1}(\sec\theta) = \theta \Rightarrow y = \sin^{-1}x$

and $\mu = \sin^{-1}\left(2\sin\theta \cdot \sqrt{1-\sin^2\theta}\right)$

$= \sin^{-1}\left(2\sin\theta \cdot \sqrt{\cos^2\theta}\right) = \sin^{-1}(2\sin\theta\,\cos\theta)$
$= z = \sin^{-1}(\sin 2\theta) = 2\theta = 2\sin^{-1}x$ **(1 Mark)**

Now, $\dfrac{dy}{dx} = \dfrac{d\left(\sin^{-1}x\right)}{dx} = \dfrac{1}{\sqrt{1-x^2}}$

and $\dfrac{dz}{dx} = \dfrac{d\left(2\sin^{-1}x\right)}{dx} = \dfrac{2}{\sqrt{1-x^2}}$ **(1 Mark)**

Since, $\dfrac{dy}{dz} = \dfrac{\dfrac{dy}{dx}}{\dfrac{dz}{dx}} = \dfrac{\dfrac{1}{\sqrt{1-x^2}}}{\dfrac{2}{\sqrt{1-x^2}}} = \dfrac{1}{2}$ **(1 Mark)**

Note

$\sin 2\theta = 2\sin\theta\cos\theta$ and $\sin^2\theta + \cos^2\theta = 1$

OR

(b) Given $y = \tan x + \sec x$

Now $\dfrac{dy}{dx} = \dfrac{d}{dx}(\tan x + \sec x) = \dfrac{d(\tan x)}{dx} + \dfrac{d(\sec x)}{dx}$

$\Rightarrow \dfrac{dy}{dx} = \sec^2 x + \sec x \cdot \tan x = \dfrac{1}{\cos^2 x} + \dfrac{1}{\cos x}\times\dfrac{\sin x}{\cos x}$

$= \dfrac{1}{\cos^2 x} + \dfrac{\sin x}{\cos^2 x} = \dfrac{1+\sin x}{\cos^2 x}$ **(1 Mark)**

$= \dfrac{1+\sin x}{1-\sin^2 x} = \dfrac{1+\sin x}{(1+\sin x)(1-\sin x)}$

$\Rightarrow \dfrac{dy}{dx} = \dfrac{1}{1-\sin x}$ **(1 Mark)**

Since, $\dfrac{d^2y}{dx^2} = \dfrac{d}{dx}\left(\dfrac{dy}{dx}\right) = \dfrac{d}{dx}\left(\dfrac{1}{1-\sin x}\right)$

$\Rightarrow \dfrac{dy}{dx} = \dfrac{\cos x}{(1-\sin x)^2}$ **(1 Mark)**

28. (a) Let $I = \displaystyle\int_{-\frac{\pi}{4}}^{\pi/4} \dfrac{\cos 2x}{1+\cos 2x}dx \Rightarrow I = \displaystyle\int_{-\frac{\pi}{4}}^{\pi/4} \dfrac{2\cos^2 x - 1}{2\cos^2 x}dx$

$I = \displaystyle\int_{-\frac{\pi}{4}}^{\pi/4}\left(1 - \dfrac{1}{2\cos^2 x}\right)dx$ **(1 Mark)**

$= \displaystyle\int_{-\frac{\pi}{4}}^{\pi/4}\left(1 - \dfrac{\sec^2 x}{2}\right)dx = \displaystyle\int_{-\frac{\pi}{4}}^{-\pi/4} 1\,dx - \dfrac{1}{2}\displaystyle\int_{-\frac{\pi}{4}}^{\pi/4}\sec^2 x\,dx$

$= (x)_{-\pi 4}^{\pi/4} - \dfrac{1}{2}(\tan x)_{-\pi/4}^{\pi/4}$ **(1 Mark)**

$= \dfrac{\pi}{4} - \left(\dfrac{-\pi}{4}\right) - \dfrac{1}{2}\{\tan(\pi/4) - \tan(-\pi/4)\}$

$= \dfrac{\pi}{4} + \dfrac{\pi}{4} - \dfrac{1}{2}\{1-(-1)\} = \dfrac{2\pi}{4} - \dfrac{(1+1)}{2} = \dfrac{\pi}{2} - 1$

$= \displaystyle\int_{-\frac{\pi}{4}}^{\pi/4}\dfrac{\cos 2x}{1+\cos 2x}dx = \dfrac{\pi}{2} - 1$ **(1 Mark)**

OR

(b) Let $I = \int e^{x^2}\left(x^5 + 2x^3\right)dx = \int e^{x^2}(x^4 + 2x^2)\,x\,dx$

$= \int e^{x^2}((x^2)^2 + 2x^2)x\,dx$ **(1 Mark)**

Let $x^2 = t \Rightarrow 2x\,dx = dt \Rightarrow x\,dx = \dfrac{1}{2}dt$

Now $I = \dfrac{1}{2}\int e^t \left(t^2 + 2t\right)dt$ **(1 Mark)**

$= \left(\text{Since}\int e^x \left(f(x) + f'(x)\right)dx = e^x f(x) + c\right)$

$I = \dfrac{1}{2}e^t t^2 + c = \dfrac{x^4 e^{x^2}}{2} + c$ **(1 Mark)**

29. Given equation of circle $x^2 + y^2 = 4$ and lines $x = 1$
Now, graph of given curves are

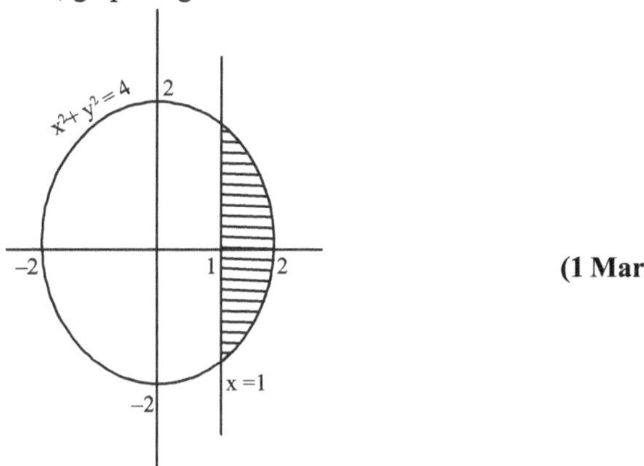

(1 Mark)

Now, $x^2 + y^2 = 4 \Rightarrow y^2 = 4 - x^2 \Rightarrow y = \sqrt{4 - x^2}$

So, Requaired area $= 2\int_1^2 y\,dx = 2\int_1^2 \sqrt{4 - x^2}\,dx$ **(1 Mark)**

$= 2\int_1^2 \sqrt{2^2 - x^2}\,dx = 2\left\{\dfrac{x}{2}\sqrt{2^2 - x^2} + \dfrac{2^2}{2}\sin^{-1}\left(\dfrac{x}{2}\right)\right\}_1^2$

$= \left(x\sqrt{4 - x^2} + 4\sin^{-1}\left(\dfrac{x}{2}\right)\right)_1^2$

$= \left[2\sqrt{4 - 4} + 4\sin^{-1}\left(\dfrac{2}{2}\right)\right] - \left[1\sqrt{4 - 1} + 4\sin^{-1}\left(\dfrac{1}{2}\right)\right]$

$= 4 \times \dfrac{\pi}{2} - \sqrt{3} - 4 \times \dfrac{\pi}{6} = 2\pi - \dfrac{2\pi}{3} - \sqrt{3} = \dfrac{4\pi}{3} = -\sqrt{3}$

Required area $= \dfrac{4\pi}{3} - \sqrt{3}$ sq. unit **(1 Mark)**

30. Given the lines $\vec{r} = \left(\hat{i} + 2\hat{j} - 4\hat{k}\right) + \lambda\left(2\hat{i} + 3\hat{j} + 6\hat{k}\right)$

$\vec{r} = \left(3\hat{i} + 3\hat{j} - 5\hat{k}\right) + \mu\left(4\hat{i} + 6\hat{j} + 12\hat{k}\right)$

$= \left(3\hat{i} + 3\hat{j} - 5\hat{k}\right) + 2\hat{j}\left(2\hat{i} + 3\hat{j} + 6\hat{k}\right)$ **(1 Mark)**

Since the given both lines are parallel.

Let $\vec{a}_1 = \left(\hat{i} + 2\hat{j} - 4\hat{k}\right), \vec{a}_2 = 3\hat{i} + 3\hat{j} - 5\hat{k}$

and $\vec{b} = 2\hat{i} + 3\hat{i} + 6\hat{k}$

Now, distance between these two parallel lines is given by

$d = \dfrac{\left|\left(\vec{a}_2 - \vec{a}_1\right) \times \vec{b}\right|}{\left|\vec{b}\right|}$ **(½ Mark)**

Now $\vec{a}_2 - \vec{a}_1 = \left(3\hat{i} + 3\hat{j} - 5\hat{k}\right) - \left(\hat{i} + 2\hat{j} - 4\hat{k}\right) = 2\hat{i} + \hat{j} - \hat{k}$

and, $\left(\vec{a}_2 - \vec{a}_1\right) \times \vec{b} = \begin{vmatrix} \hat{i} & \hat{i} & \hat{k} \\ 2 & 1 & -1 \\ 2 & 3 & 6 \end{vmatrix}$

$= (6 + 3)\,\hat{i} - (12 + 2)\,\hat{j} + (6 - 2)\,\hat{k}$ **(½ Mark)**

$\Rightarrow \left(\vec{a}_2 - \vec{a}_1\right) \times \vec{b} = 9\hat{i} - 14\hat{j} + 4\hat{k}$

So, required distance $= \dfrac{\left|\left(\vec{a}_2 - \vec{a}_1\right) \times \vec{b}\right|}{\left|\vec{b}\right|} = \dfrac{\left|9\hat{i} - 14\hat{j} + 4\hat{k}\right|}{\left|2\hat{i} + 3\hat{j} + 6\hat{k}\right|}$

$= \dfrac{\sqrt{9^2 + (-14)^2 + 4^2}}{\sqrt{2^2 + 3^2 + 6^2}} = \dfrac{\sqrt{81 + 196 + 16}}{\sqrt{4 + 9 + 36}} = \dfrac{\sqrt{293}}{7}$ units **(1 Mark)**

Note

If $\vec{r} = x\,\hat{i} + y\hat{j} + z\hat{k}$

$(\vec{r}) = \sqrt{x^2 + y^2 + z^2}$

31. (a) Given the line $\dfrac{x+3}{5} = \dfrac{y-1}{2} = \dfrac{z+4}{3}$

Let $\dfrac{x+3}{5} = \dfrac{y-1}{2} = \dfrac{z+4}{3} = t$

$\Rightarrow \quad x = 5t - 3,\; y = 2t + 1,\; z = 3t - 4$ **(1 Mark)**

So the point $(5t - 3, 2t + 1, 3t - 4)$ on the given line
Now, the point $(5t - 3, 2t + 1, 3t - 4)$ is foot of perpendicular from $P(0, 2, 3)$
So $(5t - 3, 2t - 1, 3t - 7)$ is perpendicular to $(5, 2, 3)$
So $(5t - 3, 2t - 3t - 7).\,(5, 2, 3) = 0$ **(1 Mark)**
$\Rightarrow 5(5t - 3) + 2(2t - 1) + 3(3t - 7) = 0$
$\Rightarrow 25t - 15 + 4t - 2 + 9t - 21 = 0$
$\Rightarrow 48t - 48 \Rightarrow 48t = 48 \Rightarrow t = 1$
So foot of perpendiculars $= (5 - 3, 2 + 1, 3 - 4)$
$= (2, 3, -1)$ **(1 Mark)**

OR

(b) Given the vector $\vec{a}, \vec{b}$ and $\vec{c}$ such that $\vec{a} + \vec{b} + \vec{c} = 0$ and $|\vec{a}| = 3, |\vec{b}| = 4, |\vec{c}| = 2$

Since, given $\vec{a} + \vec{b} + \vec{c} = 0 \Rightarrow \left|\vec{a} + \vec{b} + \vec{c}\right|^2 = 0$

$\left(\vec{a} + \vec{b} + \vec{c}\right).\left(\vec{a} + \vec{b} + \vec{c}.\right) = 0$ **(1 Mark)**

$$\Rightarrow |\vec{a}|^2 + |\vec{b}|^2 + |\vec{c}|^2 + 2\left(\vec{a}.\vec{b} + \vec{b}.\vec{c} + \vec{c}.\vec{a}\right) = 0$$

$$\Rightarrow 3^2 + 4^2 + 2^2 + 2\left(\vec{a}.\vec{b} + \vec{b}.\vec{c} + \vec{c}.\vec{a}\right) = 0 \qquad \textbf{(1 Mark)}$$

$$\Rightarrow 9 + 16 + 4 + 2\left(\vec{a}.\vec{b} + \vec{b}.\vec{c} + \vec{c}.\vec{a}\right) = 0$$

$$\Rightarrow 29 + 2\left(\vec{a}.\vec{b} + \vec{b}.\vec{c} + \vec{c}.\vec{a}\right) = 0$$

$$\Rightarrow \left(\vec{a}.\vec{b} + \vec{b}.\vec{c} + \vec{c}.\vec{a}\right) = -\frac{29}{2} \qquad \textbf{(1 Mark)}$$

32. Let $I = \int_0^{\pi} \dfrac{x}{1+\sin x}\,dx \qquad \ldots(i)$

$$= \left(\because \int_a^b f(x)\,dx = \int_a^b f(a+b-x)\,dx\right)$$

So $I = \int_0^{\pi} \dfrac{\pi - x}{1 + \sin(\pi - x)}\,dx = \int_0^{\pi} \dfrac{\pi - x}{1 + \sin}\,dx \quad \ldots(ii)$ **(1 Mark)**

Adding (i) and (ii), we get.

$$2I = \int_0^{\pi} \frac{\pi}{1+\sin x}\,dx + \int_0^{\pi} \frac{\pi - x}{1+\sin x}\,dx \qquad \textbf{(1 Mark)}$$

$$\Rightarrow 2I = \int_0^{\pi} \frac{\pi}{1+\sin x}\,dx$$

$$\Rightarrow 2I = \frac{1}{2}\int_0^{\pi} \frac{\pi(1-\sin x)}{(1+\sin x)(1-\sin x)}\,dx = \frac{1}{2}\int_0^{\pi} \frac{\pi(1-\sin x)}{1-\sin^2 x}\,dx$$

$$\Rightarrow \frac{\pi}{2}\int_0^{\pi} \frac{1-\sin x}{\cos^2 x}\,dx = \frac{\pi}{2}\int\left(\frac{1}{\cos^2 x} - \frac{\sin x}{\cos^2 x}\right)dx \qquad \textbf{(1 Mark)}$$

$$= \frac{\pi}{2}\left\{\int_0^{\pi} \sec^2 x\,dx - \int_0^{\pi} \sec x \cdot \tan x\,dx\right\}$$

$$= \frac{\pi}{2}\left\{(\tan x)_0^{\pi} - (\sec x)_0^{\pi}\right\} \qquad \textbf{(1 Mark)}$$

$$= \frac{\pi}{2}\left\{(\tan(\pi) - \tan(0)) - (\sec \pi - \sec(0))\right\}$$

$$= \frac{\pi}{2}\left\{(0-0) - (-1-1)\right\} = \frac{\pi}{2}(0+1+1) = \frac{2\pi}{2}$$

$$= \int_0^{\pi} \frac{x}{1+\sin x}\,dx = \pi \qquad \textbf{(1 Mark)}$$

33. (a) Let ABC be an equilateral triangle in which AD is a median.

Let side of triangle be a **(1 Mark)**

Since, $\angle ADC = 90°$

So, In ADC, $AD^2 = AC^2 - CD^2$

$$\Rightarrow AD^2 = a^2 - \left(\frac{a}{2}\right)^2 = a^2 - \frac{a^2}{4} = \frac{3a^2}{4}$$

$$\Rightarrow AD = \frac{\sqrt{3}a}{2}$$

Since, given $\dfrac{d}{dt}(AD) = 2\sqrt{3}$ cm/s

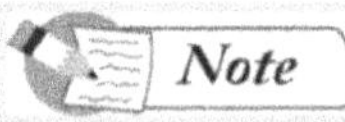

$$\Rightarrow \frac{d\left(\frac{\sqrt{3}}{2}a\right)}{dt} = 2\sqrt{3}\ \text{cm/s} \qquad \textbf{(2 Marks)}$$

$$\Rightarrow \frac{\sqrt{3}}{2}\frac{d(a)}{dt} = 2\sqrt{3}\ \text{cm/s} \Rightarrow \frac{d(a)}{dt} = 2\sqrt{3} \times \frac{2}{\sqrt{3}}\ \text{cm/s}$$

$$\Rightarrow \frac{d(a)}{dt} = 4\ \text{cm/s} \qquad \textbf{(2 Marks)}$$

OR

(b) Let first number be x, then second number be $5 - x$

Let $y = x^3 + (5 - x)^3$

Now, $\dfrac{dy}{dx} = \dfrac{d(x^3 + (5-x)^3)}{dx} = \dfrac{d\left(x^3\right)}{dx} + \dfrac{d(5-x)^3}{dx}$

$= 3x^2 + 3(5-x)^2\,(0 - 1)$

$$\Rightarrow \frac{dy}{dx} = 3x^2 - 3(5-x)^2 \qquad \textbf{(1 Mark)}$$

For least of y, $\dfrac{dy}{dx} = 0 \Rightarrow 3x^2 - 3(5-x)^2 = 0$

$\Rightarrow x^2 - (5 - x^2) = 0$

$$\Rightarrow 10x = 25 \Rightarrow x = \frac{5}{2} \qquad \textbf{(1 Mark)}$$

Now, $\dfrac{d^2 y}{dx^2} = \dfrac{d}{dx}(3x^2 - 3(5-x)^2)$

$$= \frac{3d}{dx}(x)^2 - \frac{3d}{dx}(5-x)^2$$

$$= 3 \times 2x - 3 \times 2(5-x)\left(\frac{d(5)}{dx} - \frac{d(x)}{dx}\right)$$

$= 6x - 6(5-x)(0-1) = 6x + 6(5-x)$

$= 6x + 30 - 6x = 30$ **(1 Mark)**

At $x = \dfrac{5}{2} \Rightarrow \dfrac{d^2 y}{dx^2} = 30 > 0$

So, y has least at $x = \dfrac{5}{2}$

So, first number $= \dfrac{5}{2}$, second number $= 5 - \dfrac{5}{2} = \dfrac{5}{2}$

Now, required number $= \left(\dfrac{5}{2}\right)^2 + \left(\dfrac{5}{2}\right)^2$

$$= \frac{25}{4} + \frac{25}{4} = \frac{50}{4} = \frac{25}{2} \qquad \textbf{(2 Marks)}$$

Note

$\dfrac{d^2 y}{dx^2} > 0$ at any point then that point is point of minima.

34. (a) Let the event E_1 = Student knows the answer.

Event E_2 = Student guesses the answer

Since, $P(E_1) = \dfrac{3}{5}$, $P(E_2) = \dfrac{2}{5}$ **(1 Mark)**

Let A is the event that answer is correct, if the student knows the answer.

Now, $P\left(\dfrac{A}{E_1}\right) = 1$, $P\left(\dfrac{A}{E_2}\right) = \dfrac{1}{3}$ **(1 Mark)**

So, probability that the student knows the number, given that answer is correct

$$P\left(\dfrac{E_1}{A}\right) = \dfrac{P(E_1)\,P\left(\dfrac{A}{E_1}\right)}{P(E_1)P\left(\dfrac{A}{E_1}\right)+P(E_2)P\left(\dfrac{A}{E_2}\right)}$$ **(1 Mark)**

$$= \dfrac{\dfrac{3}{5}\times 1}{\dfrac{3}{5}\times 1+\dfrac{2}{5}\times\dfrac{1}{3}} = \dfrac{\dfrac{3}{5}}{\dfrac{3}{5}+\dfrac{2}{15}} = \dfrac{\dfrac{3}{5}}{\dfrac{9+2}{15}} = \dfrac{3}{5}\times\dfrac{15}{11} = \dfrac{9}{11}$$ **(2 Marks)**

OR

(b) Since, 2 tickets carry a prize of E 8 each 5 tickets carry a prize of E 4 each 3 tickets carry a prize E 2 each.

X	2	4	8	Total	
P(X)	$\dfrac{3}{10}$	$\dfrac{5}{10}$	$\dfrac{2}{10}$	1	**(2 Marks)**
XP(X)	$\dfrac{6}{10}$	$\dfrac{20}{10}$	$\dfrac{16}{10}$	$\dfrac{42}{10}$	**(2 Marks)**

Mean $= \dfrac{42}{10} = 4.2$ **(1 Mark)**

35. Given P = 70x + 40y

and Subject to $3x + 2y \le 9$

$$3x + y \le 9$$

$$x \ge 0,\ y \ge 0$$

Now graph of the given constraints

Let (0, 0) **[2 Marks]**

$B\,(3, 0),\ C\left(0, \dfrac{9}{2}\right)$

For maximize of P

$P_{(0,0)} = 0 + 0 = 0$

$P_{(3,0)}$
$= 70 \times 3 + 40 \times 0 = 210$ **[2 Marks]**

$P\left(0, \dfrac{9}{2}\right) = 70 \times 0 + 40 \times \dfrac{9}{2} = 20 \times 9 = 180$

$\Rightarrow\ P_{max} = 210$ at (3, 0) **(1 Mark)**

36. Let cost of a pen, a bag and an instrument box be ₹ x, y and z respectively.

given, $5x + 3y + z = 160$

$$2x + y + 3z = 190$$

$$x + 2y + 4z = 250$$

(I) Now, above system of equation can be represented into matrix form

$$\begin{bmatrix} 5 & 3 & 1 \\ 2 & 1 & 3 \\ 1 & 2 & 4 \end{bmatrix} \begin{bmatrix} x \\ y \\ z \end{bmatrix} = \begin{bmatrix} 160 \\ 190 \\ 250 \end{bmatrix}$$

Where $A = \begin{bmatrix} 5 & 3 & 1 \\ 2 & 1 & 3 \\ 1 & 2 & 4 \end{bmatrix}$, $X = \begin{bmatrix} x \\ y \\ z \end{bmatrix}$, $B = \begin{bmatrix} 160 \\ 190 \\ 250 \end{bmatrix}$ **(1 Mark)**

(II) Now $|A| = \begin{vmatrix} 5 & 3 & 1 \\ 2 & 1 & 3 \\ 1 & 2 & 4 \end{vmatrix}$

$= 5\,(4 - 6) - 3\,(8 - 3) + 1\,(4 - 1)$
$= 5 \times (-2) - 3 \times 5 + 1 \times 3 = -10 - 15 + 3 = -22$

$\Rightarrow\ |A| = -22$ **(1 Mark)**

(III) Since $|A| = -22 \ne 0$

So A^{-1} exist

Now $C_{11} = (-1)^{1+1}\,(4 - 6) = -2$
$C_{12} = (-1)^{1+2}\,(8 - 3) = -5$
$C_{13} = (-1)^{1+3}\,(4 - 1) = 3$
$C_{21} = (-1)^{2+1}\,(12 - 2) = -10$
$C_{22} = (-1)^{2+2}\,(20 - 1) = 19$
$C_{23} = (-1)^{2+3}\,(10 - 3) = -7$
$C_{31} = (-1)^{3+1}\,(9 - 1) = 8$
$C_{32} = (-1)^{3+2}\,(15 - 2) = -13$
$C_{33} = (-1)^{3+3}\,(5 - 6) = -1$

So $\text{adj}(A) = \begin{bmatrix} -2 & -5 & 3 \\ -10 & 19 & -7 \\ 8 & -13 & -1 \end{bmatrix} = \begin{bmatrix} -2 & -10 & 8 \\ -5 & 19 & -13 \\ 3 & -7 & -1 \end{bmatrix}$

Now, $A^{-1} = \dfrac{\text{adj}(A)}{|A|} = -\dfrac{1}{22}\begin{bmatrix} -2 & -10 & 8 \\ -5 & 19 & -13 \\ 3 & -7 & -1 \end{bmatrix}$

$\Rightarrow A^{-1} = \dfrac{1}{22}\begin{bmatrix} 2 & 10 & -8 \\ 5 & -19 & 13 \\ -3 & 7 & 1 \end{bmatrix}$ **(2 Marks)**

📝 *Note*

If $|A| = 0$, then matrix is singular and if $|A| \ne 0$, then matrix is not singular then A^{-1} exists.

OR

Now, $P = A^2 - 5A$

$= \begin{bmatrix} 5 & 3 & 1 \\ 2 & 1 & 3 \\ 1 & 2 & 4 \end{bmatrix}\begin{bmatrix} 5 & 3 & 1 \\ 2 & 1 & 3 \\ 1 & 2 & 4 \end{bmatrix} - 5\begin{bmatrix} 5 & 3 & 1 \\ 2 & 1 & 3 \\ 1 & 2 & 4 \end{bmatrix}$

$= \begin{bmatrix} 25+6+1 & 15+3+2 & 5+9+4 \\ 10+2+3 & 6+1+6 & 2+3+12 \\ 5+4+4 & 3+2+8 & 1+6+16 \end{bmatrix} - \begin{bmatrix} 25 & 15 & 5 \\ 10 & 5 & 15 \\ 5 & 10 & 20 \end{bmatrix}$

$$= \begin{bmatrix} 32 & 20 & 18 \\ 15 & 13 & 17 \\ 13 & 13 & 23 \end{bmatrix} - \begin{bmatrix} 25 & 15 & 5 \\ 10 & 5 & 15 \\ 5 & 10 & 20 \end{bmatrix}$$

$$= \begin{bmatrix} 32-25 & 20-15 & 18-5 \\ 15-10 & 13-5 & 17-15 \\ 13-5 & 13-10 & 23-20 \end{bmatrix} = \begin{bmatrix} 7 & 5 & 13 \\ 5 & 8 & 2 \\ 8 & 3 & 3 \end{bmatrix}$$

(2 Marks)

37. Let B = $\{b_1, b_2, b_3\}$ and G = $\{g_1, g_2\}$

(i) n (B) = 3 and n (G) = 2

∴   n (B × G) = 3 × 2 = 6

Now, number of relations from B to G   **(1 Mark)**

   = 2^6 = 64

(ii) we know that, a relation 'f' is said to be function, if every elements of a non-empty set B has only one image on set G.

∴   Number of choice of b_1 = 2

   Number of choice of b_2 = 2

   Number of choice of b_3 = 2

So, number of functions = 2 × 2 × 2 = 8.   **(1 Mark)**

(iii) Let R : B → B

   R = {(x,y) : x and y are students of the same sex}.

   Let x, y, z ∈ B

   For reflexive

   ∴   x and x are students of the same sex

   ∴   (B, B) ∈R

       So, R is reflexive.

For symmetric

   Let (x, y) ∈R

   ⇒ x and y are students of the same sex.

   ⇒ y and x are students of the same sex.

   ⇒ (y, x) ∈R

   So, R is symmetric

For transitive

   Let (x, y) ∈R

   ⇒ x and y are students of same sex   …(i)

       and (y, z) ∈R

   ⇒ y and z are students of the same sex   …(ii)

       from (i) and (ii)

       x and z are students of same sex

   ⇒ (x, z) ∈R

   So, R is transitive

Hence, R is an equivalence relation.   **(2 Marks)**

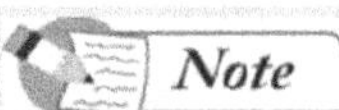

For equivalence relation, function should be reflexive, symmetric as well as transitive.

OR

f : B → G

f = {(b_1, g_1), (b_2, g_2), (b_3, g_1)}

Since $f(b_1) = g_1$ and $f(b_3) = g_1$

So f is not one-one.

Range of f = {g_1, g_2} = G = codomain

So f is onto function

Hensce f is not bijective.   **(2 Marks)**

38. (I) Given differential equation is

   $(x^2 - y^2)\, dx + 2xy\, dy = 0$

   $\Rightarrow 2xy\, dy = -(x^2 - y^2)\, dx$

   $\Rightarrow \dfrac{dy}{dx} = \dfrac{(y^2 - x^2)}{2xy} = \dfrac{1}{2}\left(\dfrac{y}{x} - \dfrac{1}{y/x}\right) = g\left(\dfrac{y}{x}\right)$ **(1 Mark)**

Put $x = \lambda x$, $y = \lambda y$

$$f(\lambda x, \lambda y) = \dfrac{1}{2}\left(\dfrac{\lambda y}{\lambda x} - \dfrac{1}{\lambda y / \lambda x}\right)$$

$$= \dfrac{1}{2}\left(\dfrac{y}{x} - \dfrac{1}{y/x}\right) = f(x, y)$$

So, given differential equation has type

$$\dfrac{dy}{dx} = g\left(\dfrac{y}{x}\right)$$ **(1 Mark)**

(II) $\dfrac{dy}{dx} = \dfrac{1}{2}\left(\dfrac{y}{x} - \dfrac{1}{y/x}\right)$

Let $\dfrac{y}{x} = v$ i.e $y = vx \Rightarrow \dfrac{dy}{dx} = v + x\,\dfrac{dv}{dx}$

$v + x\,\dfrac{dv}{dx} = \dfrac{v^2 - 1}{2v} \Rightarrow x\,\dfrac{dv}{dx} = \dfrac{v^2 - 1}{2v} - v = \dfrac{v^2 - 1 - 2v^2}{2v}$

$x\,\dfrac{dv}{dx} = -\dfrac{(1 + v^2)}{v}$ **(1 Mark)**

$\displaystyle\int \dfrac{2v}{1 + v^2}\, dv = -\int \dfrac{1}{x}\, dx \Rightarrow \log_e(1 + v^2) = \log_e\left(\dfrac{c}{x}\right)$

$\Rightarrow 1 + v^2 = \dfrac{c}{x} \Rightarrow 1 + \dfrac{y^2}{x^2} = \dfrac{c}{x} \Rightarrow \dfrac{x^2 + y^2}{x^2} = \dfrac{c}{x}$

$\Rightarrow x^2 + y^2 = cx$ **(1 Mark)**

All India *2022*

CBSE Board Solved Paper Term-II

Time Allowed : 2 Hours   *Maximum Marks : 40*

General Instructions:

(i) This question paper contains **three** Sections – Section **A**, **B** and **C**.

(ii) Each Section is compulsory.

(iii) Section-**A** has **6** short answer type-I questions of **2** marks each.

(iv) Section-**B** has **4** short answer type-II questions of **3** marks each.

(v) Section-**C** has **3** long answer type questions of **4** marks each.

(vi) There is an internal choice in some questions.

(vii) Question **14** is a Case Study based problem with **2** sub-parts of **2** marks each.

SECTION - A

Question Nos. 1 to 6 carry 2 marks each.

1. Find : $\displaystyle\int \frac{dx}{x^2 - 6x + 13}$

2. Find the general solution of the differential equation : $e^{dy/dx} = x^2$.

3. Write the projection of the vector $(\vec{b} + \vec{c})$ on the vector $\vec{a}$, where $\vec{a} = 2\hat{i} - 2\hat{j} + \hat{k}, \vec{b} = \hat{i} + 2\hat{j} - 2\hat{k}$ and $\vec{c} = 2\hat{i} - \hat{j} + 4\hat{k}$.

4. If the distance of the point $(1, 1, 1)$ from the plane $x - y + z + \lambda = 0$ is $\dfrac{5}{\sqrt{3}}$, find the value (s) of λ.

5. Two cards are drawn successively with replacement from a well shuffled pack of 52 cards. Find the probability distribution of the number of spade cards.

6. A pair of dice is thrown and the sum of the numbers appearing on the dice is observed to be 7. Find the probability that the number 5 has appeared on atleast one die.

OR

The probability that A hits the target is $\dfrac{1}{3}$ and the probability that B hits it, is $\dfrac{2}{5}$. If both try to hit the target independently, find the probability that the target is hit.

SECTION - B

Question Nos. 7 to 10 carry 3 marks each.

7. Evaluate : $\displaystyle\int_{0}^{2\pi} \frac{dx}{1 + e^{\sin x}}$

8. Find the particular solution of the differential equation $x\dfrac{dy}{dx} - y = x^2 \cdot e^x$, given $y(1) = 0$.

OR

Find the general solution of the differential equation $x\dfrac{dy}{dx} = y(\log y - \log x + 1)$.

9. The two adjacent sides of a parallelogram are represented by vectors $2\hat{i} - 4\hat{j} + 5\hat{k}$ and $\hat{i} - 2\hat{j} - 3\hat{k}$. Find the unit vector parallel to one of its diagonals. Also, find the area of the parallelogram.

OR

If $\vec{a} = 2\hat{i} + 2\hat{j} + 3\hat{k}, \ \vec{b} = -\hat{i} + 2\hat{j} + \hat{k}$ and $\vec{c} = 3\hat{i} + \hat{j}$ are such that the vector $(\vec{a} + \lambda\vec{b})$ is perpendicular to vector $\vec{c}$, then find the value of λ.

10. Show that the lines :

$\dfrac{1-x}{2} = \dfrac{y-3}{4} = \dfrac{z}{-1}$ and $\dfrac{x-4}{3} = \dfrac{2y-2}{-4} = z-1$ are coplanar.

SECTION - C

Question Nos. 11 to 14 carry 4 marks each.

11. Find the area of the region bounded by curve $4x^2 = y$ and the line $y = 8x + 12$, using integration.

12. Find : $\int \dfrac{x^2}{(x^2+1)(3x^2+4)}\,dx$

OR

Evaluate : $\displaystyle\int_{-2}^{1} \sqrt{5-4x-x^2}\,dx$

13. Find the distance of the point $(1, -2, 9)$ from the point of intersection of the line $\vec{r} = 4\hat{i} + 2\hat{j} + 7\hat{k} + \lambda(3\hat{i} + 4\hat{j} + 2\hat{k})$ and the plane $\vec{r} \cdot (\hat{i} - \hat{j} + \hat{k}) = 10$.

Case Study Problem:

14. A shopkeeper sells three types of flower seeds A1, A2, A3. They are sold in the form of a mixture, where the proportions of these seeds are 4 : 4 : 2, respectively. The germination rates of the three types of seeds are 45% , 60% and 35% respectively.

Based on the above information:

(a) Calculate the probability that a randomly chosen seed will germinate;

(b) Calculate the probability that the seed is of type A2, given that a randomly chosed seed germinates.

Solutions

1. $\displaystyle \int \frac{dx}{x^2 - 6x + 13}\,dx$

$\displaystyle = \int \frac{dx}{x^2 - 6x + 9 - 9 + 13}$ [by completing the square method.]

$\displaystyle = \int \frac{dx}{(x-3)^2 + (2)^2}$ **(1 Mark)**

Let $t = x - 3$

$\displaystyle \frac{dt}{dx} = 1 \Rightarrow dx = dt$

$\displaystyle = \int \frac{dt}{t^2 - (2)^2} \left(\because \int \frac{dx}{x^2 - a^2} = \frac{1}{2a} \log \left| \frac{x-a}{x+a} \right| + c \right)$

$\displaystyle = \frac{1}{4} \log \left| \frac{t-2}{t+2} \right| + c$

$\displaystyle = \frac{1}{4} \log \left| \frac{x-3-2}{x-3+2} \right| = \frac{1}{4} \log \left| \frac{x-5}{x-1} \right| + c$ **(1 Mark)**

2. $\displaystyle e^{\frac{dy}{dx}} = x^2 \qquad\qquad \left(\begin{array}{l} \because \quad e^y = x \\ \quad\quad y = \log x \end{array} \right)$

$\displaystyle \frac{dy}{dx} = \log x^2$

$\displaystyle \int dy = 2 \int \log x\, dx$

$\displaystyle y = 2 \int 1 \cdot \log x\, dx$ **(1 Mark)**
$\qquad\quad$ II $\quad$ I

$\displaystyle = 2 \left[\log x \int 1.dx - \int \left(\frac{d \log x}{dx} \int 1.dx \right) dx \right]$

$\displaystyle = 2 \left[x \log x - \int \frac{1}{x} \cdot x\, dx \right]$

$\displaystyle = 2 \left[x \log x - \int 1\, dx \right]$

$\displaystyle = 2 \left[x \log x - x \right] + c$

$\displaystyle = 2x \left[\log x - 1 \right] + c$ **(1 Mark)**

Note

If $x > 0$, then $\log x^2 = 2 \log x$ should be written. If $x < 0$ then $\log (x)$ is not defined.

3. $\displaystyle \therefore \ \vec{b} + \vec{c} = \left(\hat{i} + 2\hat{j} - 2\hat{k} \right) + \left(2\hat{i} - \hat{j} + 4\hat{k} \right)$

$\displaystyle = 3\hat{i} + \hat{j} + 2\hat{k}$ **(1 Mark)**

$\therefore$ Projection of $\left(\vec{b} + \vec{c} \right)$ on $\vec{a}$

$\displaystyle = \frac{\left(\vec{b} + \vec{c} \right) . \vec{a}}{\left| \vec{a} \right|}$

$\displaystyle = \frac{\left(3\hat{i} + \hat{j} + 2\hat{k} \right) . \left(2\hat{i} - 2\hat{j} + \hat{k} \right)}{\sqrt{2^2 + (-2)^2 + (1)^2}}$

$\displaystyle = \frac{(6 - 2 + 2)}{\sqrt{9}} = \frac{6}{3} = 2$ **(1 Mark)**

4. Given : point $= (1, 1, 1)$, equation of plane $= x - y + z + \lambda = 0$ and

Distance $= \dfrac{5}{\sqrt{3}}$

We have,

$\displaystyle D = \frac{\left| ax_1 + by_1 + cz_1 + d \right|}{\sqrt{a^2 + b^2 + c^2}}$ **(1 Mark)**

$\displaystyle \frac{5}{\sqrt{3}} = \frac{\left| 1 \times 1 + (-1) \times 1 + 1 \times 1 + \lambda \right|}{\sqrt{1^2 + (-1)^2 + 1^2}}$

$\displaystyle \frac{5}{\sqrt{3}} = \frac{\left| 1 - 1 + 1 + \lambda \right|}{\sqrt{3}}$

$\qquad\qquad 5 = 1 + \lambda$

$\Rightarrow \qquad \lambda = 4$

or $\qquad -5 = 1 + \lambda$

$\Rightarrow \qquad \lambda = -6$ **(1 Mark)**

5. Number of drawn cards n $= 2$

Let X : Number of spades cards $= 0, 1, 2$

Probability of success i.e.

Probability of a spade card $= \dfrac{13}{52} = \dfrac{1}{4}$

Probability of failure $= \left(1 - \dfrac{1}{4} \right) = \dfrac{3}{4}$

Since, X follow the binomial distribution $\left(2, \dfrac{1}{4} \right)$ **(1 Mark)**

Therefore binomial distribution.

x	0	1	2	Total
$P(x)$	$\dfrac{9}{16}$	$\dfrac{6}{16}$	$\dfrac{1}{16}$	1

(1 Mark)

6. Event A (sum is 7) $= \{(1,6),(6,1),(2,5),(5,2),(3,4),(4,3)\}$

$n(\text{A}) = 6$ **(1 Mark)**

Event B (5 has appeared atleast one die) $= \{(5,1),(5,2),$
$(5,3),(5,4),(5,5),(5,6),(1,5),(2,5),(3,5),(4,5),(6,5)\}$

$A \cap B = \{(2,5),(5,2)\}$

Therefore, required probability

$$= P(B/A) = \frac{P(A \cap B)}{P(A)} = \frac{2}{6} = \frac{1}{3}$$ **(1 Mark)**

OR

There are three ways that the target can hit

A hit and B does not hit $= \dfrac{1}{3} \times \dfrac{3}{5}$

A does not hit and B hit $= \dfrac{2}{3} \times \dfrac{2}{5}$ **(1 Mark)**

A hit and B hit $= \dfrac{1}{3} \times \dfrac{2}{5}$

Therefore probability of hit the target

$$= \frac{1}{3} \times \frac{3}{5} + \frac{2}{3} \times \frac{2}{5} + \frac{1}{3} \times \frac{2}{5}$$

$$= \frac{3}{15} + \frac{4}{15} + \frac{2}{15} = \frac{9}{15} = \frac{3}{5}$$ **(1 Mark)**

7. Let $I = \displaystyle\int_{0}^{2\pi} \frac{1}{1+e^{\sin x}}dx$

$$I = \int_{0}^{\pi}\left(\frac{1}{1+e^{\sin x}} + \frac{1}{1+e^{\sin(2\pi-x)}}\right)dx$$ **(1 Mark)**

$$\left[\begin{array}{l}\text{by property}\\[4pt]\displaystyle\int_{0}^{2a} f(x)\,dx = \int_{0}^{a} f(x)+f(2a-x)\,dx\end{array}\right]$$

$$I = \int_{0}^{\pi}\left(\frac{1}{1+e^{\sin x}} + \frac{1}{1+e^{-\sin x}}\right)dx$$

$$= \int_{0}^{\pi}\left(\frac{1}{1+e^{\sin x}} + \frac{1}{1+\dfrac{1}{e^{\sin x}}}\right)dx$$ **(1 Mark)**

$$= \int_{0}^{\pi}\left(\frac{1}{1+e^{\sin x}} + \frac{e^{\sin x}}{e^{\sin x}+1}\right)dx$$

$$= \int_{0}^{\pi}\left(\frac{1+e^{\sin x}}{1+e^{\sin x}}\right)dx$$

$$I = \int_{0}^{\pi} 1\,dx = \left[\pi - 0\right]$$

$I = \pi$ **(1 Mark)**

8. $x\dfrac{dy}{dx} - y = x^2.e^x$

$$\Rightarrow \quad \frac{dy}{dx} - \frac{1}{x.}y = x.e^x$$

We have

$$\frac{dy}{dx} + Py = Q$$ **(1 Mark)**

Here $P = -\dfrac{1}{x}$ and $Q = x.\,e^x$

$$I.F. = e^{\int -\frac{1}{x}dx} = e^{-\log x} = e^{\log x^{-1}} = \frac{1}{x}\left[\because e^{\log x} = x\right]$$

Now

$$y(IF) = \int Q.(IF)\,dx + c$$ **(1 Mark)**

$$\Rightarrow \quad y.\frac{1}{x} = \int\left(x.e^x.\frac{1}{x}\right)dx + c$$

$$\Rightarrow \quad y.\frac{1}{x} = \int e^x dx + c$$

$$\Rightarrow \quad y.\frac{1}{x} = e^x + c \ \text{ or } \ y = e^x x + c.x$$

Substituting $x = 1$ and $y = 0$

$0 = e + c$ or $c = -e$

Therefore particular solution,

$y = e^x x - ex$ or $y = x(e^x - e)$ **(1 Mark)**

OR

$$x\frac{dy}{dx} = y(\log y - \log x + 1)$$

$$\Rightarrow \quad \frac{dy}{dx} = \frac{y}{x}(\log y - \log x + 1)$$

$$\Rightarrow \quad \frac{dy}{dx} = \frac{y}{x}\left(\log\frac{y}{x} + 1\right) \quad ...(i) \quad \left[\because \log a - \log b = \log\frac{a}{b}\right]$$

Put $y = vx \Rightarrow v = \dfrac{y}{x}$ **(1 Mark)**

Differentiating both side w.r.t x

$$\frac{dy}{dx} = v + x\frac{dv}{dx} \quad ...(ii)$$

From (i) and (ii), we have

$$v + x\frac{dv}{dx} = v(\log v + 1)$$

$$\Rightarrow \quad v + x\frac{dv}{dx} = v\log v + v$$

$$\Rightarrow \quad x\frac{dv}{dx} = v\log v \qquad \textbf{(1 Mark)}$$

$$\Rightarrow \quad \frac{dv}{v\log v} = \frac{dx}{x}$$

Apply integration on both side

$$\int\frac{1}{v\log v}dv = \int\frac{1}{x}dx$$

$$\log(\log v) = \log x + \log c$$
$$\Rightarrow \quad \log(\log v) = \log x \cdot c$$
$$\Rightarrow \quad \log v = xc \qquad \textbf{(1 Mark)}$$

$$\Rightarrow \quad \log\left(\frac{y}{x}\right) = xc\left(\because v = \frac{y}{x}\right)$$

9. Given, adjacent sides

$$\vec{a} = 2\hat{i} - 4\hat{j} + 5\hat{k}$$

$$\hat{b} = \hat{i} - 2\hat{j} - 3\hat{k}$$

Let one of its diagonal is $\vec{p}$

So, $\vec{p} = \vec{a} + \vec{b}$

$$= \left(2\hat{i} - 4\hat{j} + 5\hat{k}\right) + \left(\hat{i} - 2\hat{j} - 3\hat{k}\right)$$

$$= 3\hat{i} - 6\hat{j} + 2\hat{k} \qquad \textbf{(1 Mark)}$$

Therefore,
Unit vector $\parallel$ to one of its diagonal, p

$$\hat{p} = \frac{\vec{p}}{|p|}$$

$$= \frac{3\hat{i} - 6\hat{j} + 2\hat{k}}{\sqrt{9 + 36 + 4}}$$

$$= \frac{3\hat{i} - 6\hat{j} + 2\hat{k}}{7}$$

$$= \frac{3}{7}\hat{i} - \frac{6}{7}\hat{j} + \frac{2}{7}\hat{k} \qquad \textbf{(1 Mark)}$$

Now area of $\parallel$ gram $= \left|\vec{a} \times \vec{b}\right|$

$$\therefore \quad \vec{a} \times \vec{b} = \begin{vmatrix} \hat{i} & \hat{j} & \hat{k} \\ 2 & -4 & 5 \\ 1 & -2 & -3 \end{vmatrix}$$

$$= i(12 + 10) - \hat{j}(-6 - 5) + \hat{k}(-4 + 4)$$

$$= 22\hat{i} + 11\hat{j} + 0\hat{k}$$

$$\therefore \quad \left|\vec{a} \times \vec{b}\right| = \sqrt{(22)^2 + (11)^2 + (0)^2}$$

$$= \sqrt{605} \text{ sq unit} \qquad \textbf{(1 Mark)}$$

OR

Given that

$$(\vec{a} + \lambda\vec{b}) \perp \vec{c}$$

$$\Rightarrow \quad (\vec{a} + \lambda\vec{b}) \cdot \vec{c} = 0 \qquad (\because \ \vec{a} \perp \vec{c} \text{ then } \vec{a}.\vec{c} = 0)$$

$$\vec{a} \cdot \vec{c} + \lambda\vec{b} \cdot \vec{c} = 0$$

$$\lambda = -\frac{\vec{a} \cdot \vec{c}}{\vec{b} \cdot \vec{c}} \qquad \textbf{(1 Mark)}$$

$$= -\frac{(2\hat{i} + 2\hat{j} + 3\hat{k}) \cdot (3\hat{i} + \hat{j})}{(-\hat{i} + 2\hat{j} + \hat{k}) \cdot (3\hat{i} + \hat{j})}$$

$$= \frac{-(6 + 2)}{-3 + 2} = \frac{-8}{-1} = 8$$

$$\lambda = 8 \qquad \textbf{(2 Marks)}$$

10. $\dfrac{1-x}{2} = \dfrac{y-3}{4} = \dfrac{z}{-1} \Rightarrow -\dfrac{(x-1)}{-2} = \dfrac{y-3}{4} = \dfrac{z-0}{-1}$ and

$$\frac{x-4}{3} = \frac{2y-2}{-4} = z - 1 \Rightarrow \frac{x-4}{3} = \frac{y-1}{-2} = \frac{z-1}{1}$$

(1 Mark)

Comparing given equations with standard form.

$$x_1 = 1, y_1 = 3, z_1 = 0 \qquad ; \qquad x_2 = 4, y_2 = 1, z_2 = 1$$
$$a_1 = -2, b_1 = 4, c_1 = -1 \quad \text{and } a_2 = 3, b_2 = -2, c_2 = 1$$

Lines are coplaner if

$$\begin{vmatrix} x_2 - x_1 & y_2 - y_1 & z_2 - z_1 \\ a_1 & b_1 & c_1 \\ a_2 & b_2 & c_2 \end{vmatrix} = 0$$

LHS

$$= \begin{vmatrix} 4-1 & 1-3 & 1-0 \\ -2 & 4 & -1 \\ 3 & -2 & 1 \end{vmatrix} \qquad \textbf{(1 Mark)}$$

$$= \begin{vmatrix} 3 & -2 & 1 \\ -2 & 4 & -1 \\ 3 & -2 & 1 \end{vmatrix}$$

Expanding along R_1

$$= 3(4 - 2) + 2(-2 + 3) + 1(4 - 12)$$
$$= 3 \times 2 + 2 \times 1 + 1(-8)$$
$$= 6 + 2 - 8 = 0$$

Therfore both line are coplaner. **(1 Mark)**

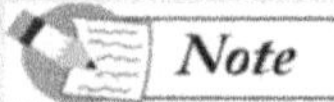

Note

Three or more non-zero vectors are coplanar if they lie in the same plane.

11. Given equations

$$y = 4x^2 \qquad \text{...(i)}$$
$$y = 8x + 12 \qquad \text{...(ii)}$$

Eliminating y from eqn. (ii)

$$4x^2 = 8x + 12$$
$$4x^2 - 8x - 12 = 0$$
$$4x^2 - 12x + 4x - 12 = 0$$
$$4x(x-3) + 4(x-3) = 0$$
$$(x-3)(4x+4) = 0 \qquad \textbf{(1 Mark)}$$
$$\therefore \quad x = 3 \text{ and } x = -1$$

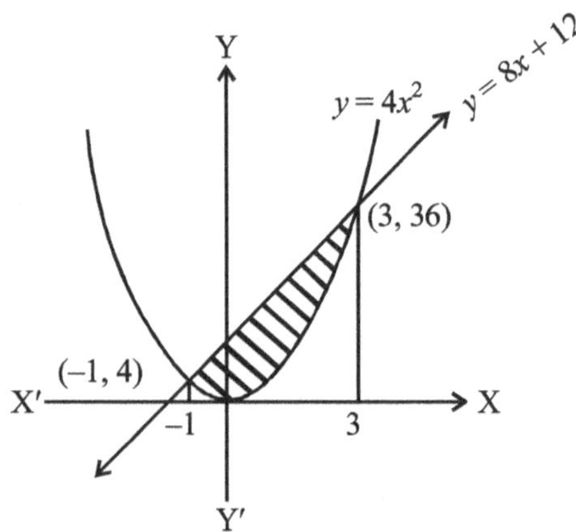

From eqn (ii), we have

When $\quad x = 3, y = 36$
$$x = -1, y = 4$$

Area of region bounded by curve

$$= \int_{-1}^{3} (y_1 - y_2)\, dx \qquad \textbf{(2 Marks)}$$

$$= \int_{-1}^{3} \left\{ (8x+12) - 4x^2 \right\} dx$$

$$= \left[\frac{8x^2}{2} + 12x - 4 \cdot \frac{x^3}{3} \right]_{-1}^{3}$$

$$= \left[4x^2 + 12x - \frac{4}{3}x^3 \right]_{-1}^{3}$$

$$\left[\left\{ 4(3)^2 + 12(3) - \frac{4}{3}(3)^3 \right\} - \left\{ 4(-1)^2 + 12(-1) - \frac{4}{3}(-1)^3 \right\} \right]$$

$$\{36 + 36 - 36\} - \left\{ 4 - 12 + \frac{4}{3} \right\}$$

$$36 - \left\{ \frac{12 - 36 + 4}{3} \right\}$$

$$36 - \left(-\frac{20}{3} \right)$$

$$36 + \frac{20}{3}$$

$$\frac{128}{3} \text{ sq. units} \qquad \textbf{(1 Mark)}$$

Note

Area of bounded region is obtained only by use of integration not by area formula.

12. $\displaystyle \int \frac{x^2}{(x^2+1)(3x^2+4)}\, dx$

Put $x^2 = y$

Let $\dfrac{y}{(y+1)(3y+4)} = \dfrac{A}{(y+1)} + \dfrac{B}{(3y+4)}$ **(1 Mark)**

$$y = A(3y+4) + B(y+1)$$

Comparing coefficient of y & constant term from both side

$$1 = 3A + B \qquad \text{...(i)}$$
$$\text{and } 0 = 4A + B \qquad \text{...(ii)}$$

From eqns. (i) and (ii)

$$A = -1 \text{ and } B = 4 \qquad \textbf{(1 Mark)}$$

$$\int \frac{y}{(y+1)(3y+1)}\, dx = -\int \frac{1}{y+1}\, dx + \int \frac{4}{3y+4}\, dx$$

$$= -\int \frac{1}{x^2+1}\, dx + \int \frac{4}{3x^2+4}\, dx$$

$$= -[\tan^{-1} x] + 4\int \frac{1}{3x^2+4}\, dx - [\tan^{-1}x] + 4\int \frac{1}{3\left(x^2+\frac{4}{3}\right)}\, dx$$

$$= -\tan^{-1} x + \frac{4}{3}\int \frac{1}{x^2 + \left(\frac{2}{\sqrt{3}}\right)^2}\, dx \qquad \textbf{(1 Mark)}$$

$$= -\tan^{-1} x + \frac{4}{3}\left[\frac{1}{\left(\frac{2}{\sqrt{3}}\right)} \tan^{-1} \frac{x}{\frac{2}{\sqrt{3}}} \right] + c$$

$$= -\tan^{-1} x + \frac{4}{3} \times \frac{\sqrt{3}}{2} \tan^{-1} \frac{\sqrt{3}x}{2} + c$$

$$= -\tan^{-1} x + \frac{2}{\sqrt{3}} \tan^{-1} \frac{(\sqrt{3}x)}{2} + c$$

$$= \frac{2}{\sqrt{3}} \tan^{-1} \frac{(\sqrt{3}x)}{2} - \tan^{-1} x + c \qquad \textbf{(1 Mark)}$$

OR

$$\int_{-2}^{1} \sqrt{5-4x-x^2}\ dx$$

$$= \int_{-2}^{1} \sqrt{-(x^2+4x-5)}\ dx \qquad \textbf{(1 Mark)}$$

$$= \int_{-2}^{1} \sqrt{-\left(x^2+4x+4-4-5\right)}\ dx$$

$$= \int_{-2}^{1} \sqrt{-\left((x+2)^2-9\right)}\ dx$$

$$= \int_{-2}^{1} \sqrt{9-(x+2)^2}\ dx \qquad \textbf{(1 Mark)}$$

Let $t = x+2$ Limit when $x=-2$

$\dfrac{dt}{dx}=1$ $t=0$

$dx = dt$ when $x=1$

                                 $t=3$

$$\int_{0}^{3} \sqrt{9-t^2}\, dt = \int_{0}^{3} \sqrt{(3)^2-(t)^2}\ dt$$

$$= \left[\frac{t}{2}\sqrt{3^2-t^2} + \frac{9}{2}\sin^{-1}\frac{t}{3}\right]_0^3$$

$$= \left[0 + \frac{9}{2}\sin^{-1}\left(\frac{3}{3}\right)\right] - [0+0]$$

$$= \frac{9}{2}\sin^{-1}(1)$$

$$= \frac{9}{2}\sin^{-1}\left(\sin\frac{\pi}{2}\right) \quad \left[\because \frac{\pi}{2} \in \left[-\frac{\pi}{2}, \frac{\pi}{2}\right]\right]$$

or $\dfrac{9}{2}\left(\dfrac{\pi}{2}\right) = \dfrac{9\pi}{4}$ **(2 Marks)**

13. Given line $\vec{r} = 4\hat{i}+2\hat{j}+7\hat{k}+\lambda(3\hat{i}+4\hat{j}+2\hat{k})$ ...(i)

and plane $\vec{r}\cdot(\hat{i}-\hat{j}+\hat{k})=10$ ...(ii)

From eqns. (i) and (ii)

$\left[4\hat{i}+2\hat{j}+7\hat{k}+\lambda(3\hat{i}+4\hat{j}+2\hat{k})\right]\cdot(\hat{i}-\hat{j}+\hat{k})=10$ **(1 Mark)**

or $\left[(4\hat{i}+2\hat{j}+7\hat{k})(\hat{i}-\hat{j}+\hat{k})+\lambda(3\hat{i}+4\hat{j}+2\hat{k})\cdot(\hat{i}-\hat{j}+\hat{k})\right]=10$

$(4-2+7)+\lambda(3-4+2)=10$

$9+\lambda(1)=10$

or $\lambda=1$ **(1 Mark)**

$\therefore$ The point of intersection of line and plane is

$$4\hat{i}+2\hat{j}+7\hat{k}+1(3\hat{i}+4\hat{j}+2\hat{k})$$

$$= 4\hat{i}+2\hat{j}+7\hat{k}+3\hat{i}+4\hat{j}+2\hat{k}$$

$$= 7\hat{i}+6\hat{j}+9\hat{k} \Rightarrow (7,6,9)$$

Other given point is $(1,-2,9)$

Therefore distance between the two point

$$= \sqrt{(x_2-x_1)^2+(y_2-y_1)^2+(z_2-z_1)^2}$$

$$= \sqrt{(7-1)^2+(6-(-2))^2+(9-9)^2}$$

$$= \sqrt{36+64+0}$$

$$= \sqrt{100} = 10 \text{ units} \qquad \textbf{(2 Marks)}$$

14. We have

$A_1 : A_2 : A_3 = 4:4:2$

$$\therefore P(A_1) = \frac{4}{10}$$

$$P(A_2) = \frac{4}{10}$$

and $P(A_3) = \dfrac{2}{10}$

Let E be event that a seed germinates and $\vec{E}$ be the event that a seed does not germinate.

Then $P\left(\dfrac{E}{A_1}\right) = \dfrac{45}{100}$ and $P\left(\dfrac{\overline{E}}{A_1}\right) = \dfrac{55}{100}$

$$P\left(\frac{E}{A_2}\right) = \frac{60}{100} \text{ and } P\left(\frac{\overline{E}}{A_2}\right) = \frac{40}{100}$$

$$P\left(\frac{E}{A_3}\right) = \frac{35}{100} \text{ and } P\left(\frac{\overline{E}}{A_3}\right) = \frac{65}{100}$$

(a) Probability that a randomly chosen seed to germinate

$$P(E) = P(A_1).P\left(\frac{E}{A_1}\right) + P(A_2).P\left(\frac{E}{A_2}\right) + P(A_3).P\left(\frac{E}{A_3}\right)$$

$$= \frac{4}{10}\times\frac{45}{100} + \frac{4}{10}\times\frac{60}{100} + \frac{2}{10}\times\frac{35}{100}$$

$$= \frac{180}{1000} + \frac{240}{1000} + \frac{70}{1000}$$

$$= \frac{490}{1000} = 0.49 \qquad \textbf{(2 Marks)}$$

(b) $P\left(\dfrac{A_2}{E}\right) = \dfrac{P(A_2).P\left(\dfrac{E}{A_2}\right)}{P(A_1).P\left(\dfrac{E}{A_1}\right) + P(A_2).P\left(\dfrac{E}{A_2}\right) + P(A_3).P\left(\dfrac{E}{A_3}\right)}$

$$= \dfrac{\dfrac{4}{10} \times \dfrac{60}{100}}{\dfrac{4}{10} \times \dfrac{45}{100} + \dfrac{4}{10} \times \dfrac{60}{100} + \dfrac{2}{10} \times \dfrac{35}{100}}$$

$$= \dfrac{\dfrac{240}{1000}}{\dfrac{180}{1000} + \dfrac{240}{1000} + \dfrac{70}{1000}}$$

$$\dfrac{\dfrac{240}{1000}}{\dfrac{490}{1000}} = \dfrac{240}{490} = \dfrac{24}{49} = 0.48 \qquad \textbf{(2 Marks)}$$

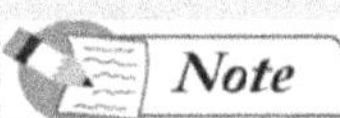

Conditional probability $P(B/A)$ applied when probability of occurence of event B is under the condition that A has already occured and $P(B) \neq 0$

All India *2022*

CBSE Board Solved Paper Term-I

Time Allowed : 90 Minutes *Maximum Marks : 40*

General Instructions:

(i) This question paper comprises **50** questions out of which **40** questions are to be attempted as per instructions. All questions carry equal marks.

(ii) The question paper consists of **three** Sections – Section **A**, **B** and **C**.

(iii) Section **A** contains **20** questions Attempt any **16** questions from Q. No. **1** to **20**.

(iv) Section **B** also contains **20** questions. Attempt any **16** questions from Q. No. **21** to **40**.

(v) Section **C** contains **10** questions including one Case Study. Attempt any **8** from Q. No. **41** to **50**.

(vi) There is only one correct option for every Multiple Choice Question (MCQ). Marks will not be awarded for answering more than one option.

(vii) There is no negative marking.

SECTION - A

In this section, attempt any 16 questions out of questions 1–20. Each question is of one mark.

1. Differential of $\log [\log(\log x^5)]$ w.r.t. x is

   (a) $\dfrac{5}{x\log\left(x^5\right)\log\left(\log x^5\right)}$
   (b) $\dfrac{5}{x\log\left(\log x^5\right)}$

   (c) $\dfrac{5x^4}{\log\left(x^5\right)\log\left(\log x^5\right)}$
   (d) $\dfrac{5x^4}{\log x^5\log\left(\log x^5\right)}$

2. The number of all possible matrices of order 2×3 with each entry 1 or 2 is

   (a) 16   (b) 6   (c) 64   (d) 24

3. A function $f : R \to R$ is defined as $f(x) = x^3 + 1$. Then the function has
   (a) on minimum value
   (b) no maximum value
   (c) both maximum and minimum values
   (d) neither maximum value nor minimum value

4. If $\sin y = x \cos (a + y)$, then $\dfrac{dx}{dy}$ is

   (a) $\dfrac{\cos a}{\cos^2\left(a+y\right)}$
   (b) $\dfrac{-\cos a}{\cos^2\left(a+y\right)}$

   (c) $\dfrac{\cos a}{\sin^2 y}$
   (d) $\dfrac{-\cos a}{\sin^2 y}$

5. The points on the curve $\dfrac{x^2}{9}+\dfrac{y^2}{25}=1$, where tangent is parallel to x-axis are

   (a) $(\pm 5, 0)$ (b) $(0, \pm 5)$ (c) $(0, \pm 3)$ (d) $(\pm 3, 0)$

6. Three points $P(2x, x + 3)$, $Q(0, x)$ and $R(x + 3, x + 6)$ are collinear, then x is equal to

   (a) 0   (b) 2   (c) 3   (d) 1

7. The principal value of $\cos^{-1}\left(\dfrac{1}{2}\right)+\sin^{-1}\left(-\dfrac{1}{\sqrt{2}}\right)$ is

   (a) $\dfrac{\pi}{12}$ (b) π (c) $\dfrac{\pi}{3}$ (d) $\dfrac{\pi}{6}$

8. If $(x^2 + y^2)^2 = xy$, then $\dfrac{dy}{dx}$ is

   (a) $\dfrac{y+4x\left(x^2+y^2\right)}{4y\left(x^2+y^2\right)-x}$
   (b) $\dfrac{y-4x\left(x^2+y^2\right)}{x+4\left(x^2+y^2\right)}$

   (c) $\dfrac{y-4x\left(x^2+y^2\right)}{4y\left(x^2+y^2\right)-x}$
   (d) $\dfrac{4y\left(x^2+y^2\right)-x}{y-4x\left(x^2+y^2\right)}$

9. If a matrix A is both symmetric and skew symmetric, then A is necessarily a
   (a) Diagonal matrix   (b) Zero square matrix
   (c) Square matrix   (d) Identity matrix

10. Let set $X = \{1, 2, 3\}$ and a relation R is defined in X as : R $= \{(1, 3), (2, 2), (3, 2)\}$, then minimum ordered pairs which should be added in relation R to make it reflexive and symmetric are
(a) $\{(1,1), (2, 3), (1, 2)\}$
(b) $\{(3, 3), (3, 1), (1, 2)\}$
(c) $\{(1, 1), (3, 3), (3, 1), (2, 3)\}$
(d) $\{(1, 1), (3, 3), (3, 1), (1, 2)\}$

11. A linear programming problem is as follows:
Minimise $\qquad Z = 2x + y$
Subject to the constraints $\quad x \geq 3, x \leq 9, y \geq 0$
$\qquad\qquad\qquad\qquad\quad x - y \geq 0, x + y \leq 14$
The feasible region has
(a) 5 corner points including $(0, 0)$ and $(9, 5)$
(b) 5 corner points including $(7, 7)$ and $(3, 3)$
(c) 5 corner points including $(14, 0)$ and $(9, 0)$
(d) 5 corner points including $(3, 6)$ and $(9, 5)$

12. The function $f(x) = \begin{cases} \dfrac{e^{3x} - e^{-5x}}{x}, & \text{if } x \neq 0 \\ k, & \text{if } x = 0 \end{cases}$

is continuous at $x = 0$ for the value of k, is
(a) 3 $\qquad$ (b) 5 $\qquad$ (c) 2 $\qquad$ (d) 8

13. If C_{ij} denotes the cofactor of element p_{ij} of the matrix
$P = \begin{bmatrix} 1 & -1 & 2 \\ 0 & 2 & -3 \\ 3 & 2 & 4 \end{bmatrix}$, then the value of $C_{31}.C_{23}$ is

(a) 5 $\qquad$ (b) 24 $\qquad$ (c) -24 $\qquad$ (d) -5

14. The function $y = x^2 e^{-x}$ is decreasing in the interval
(a) $(0, 2)$ $\qquad\qquad$ (b) $(2, \infty)$
(c) $(-\infty, 0)$ $\qquad\quad$ (d) $(-\infty, 0) \cup (2, \infty)$

15. If $R = \{(x, y): x, y \in Z, x^2 + y^2 \leq 4\}$ is a relation in set Z, then domain of R is
(a) $\{0, 1, 2\}$ $\qquad\qquad$ (b) $\{-2, -1, 0, 1, 2\}$
(c) $\{0, -1, -2\}$ $\qquad\quad$ (d) $\{-1, 0, 1\}$

16. The system of linear equations
$5x + ky = 5, 3x + 3y = 5$
will be consistant
(a) $k \neq -3$ $\qquad\qquad$ (b) $k = -5$
(c) $k = 5$ $\qquad\qquad$ (d) $k \neq 5$

17. The equation of the tangent to the curve $y(1 + x^2) = 2 - x$, where it crosses the x-axis is
(a) $x - 5y = 2$ $\qquad\qquad$ (b) $5x - y = 2$
(c) $x + 5y = 2$ $\qquad\qquad$ (d) $5x + y = 2$

18. If $\begin{bmatrix} 3c + 6 & a - d \\ a + d & 2 - 3b \end{bmatrix} = \begin{bmatrix} 12 & 2 \\ -8 & -4 \end{bmatrix}$ are equal, then value of $ab - cd$ is
(a) 4 $\qquad\qquad\qquad$ (b) 16
(c) -4 $\qquad\qquad\qquad$ (d) -16

19. The principal value of $\tan^{-1}\left(\tan\dfrac{9\pi}{8}\right)$ is

(a) $\dfrac{\pi}{8}$ $\quad$ (b) $\dfrac{3\pi}{8}$ $\quad$ (c) $-\dfrac{\pi}{8}$ $\quad$ (d) $-\dfrac{3\pi}{8}$

20. For two matrices $P = \begin{bmatrix} 3 & 4 \\ -1 & 2 \\ 0 & 1 \end{bmatrix}$ and $Q^T = \begin{bmatrix} -1 & 2 & 1 \\ 1 & 2 & 3 \end{bmatrix}$

$P - Q$ is

(a) $\begin{bmatrix} 2 & 3 \\ -3 & 0 \\ 0 & -3 \end{bmatrix}$ $\qquad$ (b) $\begin{bmatrix} 4 & 3 \\ -3 & 0 \\ -1 & -2 \end{bmatrix}$

(c) $\begin{bmatrix} 4 & 3 \\ 0 & -3 \\ -1 & -2 \end{bmatrix}$ $\qquad$ (d) $\begin{bmatrix} 2 & 3 \\ 0 & -3 \\ 0 & -3 \end{bmatrix}$

SECTION - B

In this section, attempt any 16 questions out of questions 21–40. Each question is of one mark.

21. The function $f(x) = 2x^3 - 15x^2 + 36x + 6$ is increasing in the interval
(a) $(-\infty, 2) \cup (3, \infty)$ $\qquad$ (b) $(-\infty, 2)$
(c) $(-\infty, 2] \cup [3, \infty)$ $\qquad$ (d) $[3, \infty)$

22. If $x = 2\cos\theta - \cos 2\theta$ and $y = 2\sin\theta - \sin 2\theta$, then $\dfrac{dy}{dx}$ is

(a) $\dfrac{\cos\theta + \cos 2\theta}{\sin\theta - \sin 2\theta}$ $\qquad$ (b) $\dfrac{\cos\theta - \cos 2\theta}{\sin 2\theta - \sin\theta}$

(c) $\dfrac{\cos\theta - \cos 2\theta}{\sin\theta - \sin 2\theta}$ $\qquad$ (d) $\dfrac{\cos 2\theta - \cos\theta}{\sin 2\theta + \sin\theta}$

23. What is the domain of the function $\cos^{-1}(2x - 3)$?
(a) $[-1, 1]$ $\quad$ (b) $(1, 2)$ $\quad$ (c) $(-1, 1)$ $\quad$ (d) $[1, 2]$

24. A matrix $A = [a_{ij}]_{3 \times 3}$ is defined by

$$a_{ij} = \begin{cases} 2i + 3j & , i < j \\ 5 & , i = j \\ 3i - 2j & , i > j \end{cases}$$

The number of elements in A which are more than 5, is
(a) 3 $\qquad$ (b) 4 $\qquad$ (c) 5 $\qquad$ (d) 6

25. If a function f defined by

$$f(x) = \begin{cases} \dfrac{k\cos x}{\pi - 2x} & , \text{if } x \neq \dfrac{\pi}{2} \\ 3 & , \text{if } x = \dfrac{\pi}{2} \end{cases}$$

is continuous at $x = \dfrac{\pi}{2}$, then the value of k, is
(a) 2 $\qquad$ (b) 3 $\qquad$ (c) 6 $\qquad$ (d) -6

26. For the matrix $X = \begin{bmatrix} 0 & 1 & 1 \\ 1 & 0 & 1 \\ 1 & 1 & 0 \end{bmatrix}$, $(X^2 - X)$ is

 (a) $2I$ (b) $3I$ (c) I (d) $5I$

27. Let $X = \{x^2 : x \in N\}$ and the function $f : N \to X$ is defined by $f(x) = x^2, x \in N$. Then this function is
 (a) injective only   (b) not bijective
 (c) surjective only   (d) bijective

28. The corner points of the feasible region for a linear programming problem are $P(0, 5)$, $Q(1, 5)$, $R(4, 2)$ and $S(12, 0)$. The minimum value of the objective function $Z = 2x + 5y$ is at the point
 (a) P (b) Q
 (c) R (d) S

29. The equation of the normal to the curve $ay^2 = x^3$ at the point (am^2, am^3) is
 (a) $2y - 3mx + am^3 = 0$
 (b) $2x + 3my - 3am^4 - am^2 = 0$
 (c) $2x + 3my + 3am^4 - 2am^2 = 0$
 (d) $2x + 3my - 3am^4 - 2am^2 = 0$

30. If A is a square matrix of order 3 and $|A| = -5$, then $|\text{adj } A|$ is
 (a) 125   (b) -25 (c) 25   (d) ± 25

31. The simplest form of $\tan^{-1}\left[\dfrac{\sqrt{1+x} - \sqrt{1-x}}{\sqrt{1+x} + \sqrt{1-x}}\right]$ is

 (a) $\dfrac{\pi}{4} - \dfrac{x}{2}$ (b) $\dfrac{\pi}{4} + \dfrac{x}{2}$

 (c) $\dfrac{\pi}{4} - \dfrac{1}{2}\cos^{-1}x$ (d) $\dfrac{\pi}{4} + \dfrac{1}{2}\cos^{-1}x$

32. If for the matrix $A = \begin{bmatrix} \alpha & -2 \\ -2 & \alpha \end{bmatrix}$, $|A^3| = 125$, then the value of α is
 (a) ± 3 (b) -3 (c) ± 1 (d) 1

33. If $y = \sin(m \sin^{-1} x)$, then which one of the following equations is true?

 (a) $(1 - x^2)\dfrac{d^2y}{dx^2} + x\dfrac{dy}{dx} + m^2 y = 0$

 (b) $(1 - x^2)\dfrac{d^2y}{dx^2} - x\dfrac{dy}{dx} + m^2 y = 0$

 (c) $(1 + x^2)\dfrac{d^2y}{dx^2} - x\dfrac{dy}{dx} - m^2 y = 0$

 (d) $(1 + x^2)\dfrac{d^2y}{dx^2} + x\dfrac{dy}{dx} - m^2 x = 0$

34. The principal value of $[\tan^{-1}\sqrt{3} - \cot^{-1}(-\sqrt{3})]$ is

 (a) π (b) $-\dfrac{\pi}{2}$ (c) 0   (d) $2\sqrt{3}$

35. The maximum value of $\left(\dfrac{1}{x}\right)^x$ is

 (a) $e^{1/e}$ (b) e (c) $\left(\dfrac{1}{e}\right)^{1/e}$ (d) e^e

36. Let matrix $X = [x_{ij}]$ is given by $X = \begin{bmatrix} 1 & -1 & 2 \\ 3 & 4 & -5 \\ 2 & -1 & 3 \end{bmatrix}$. Then the matrix $Y = [m_{ij}]$, where $m_{ij} = $ Minor of x_{ij}, is

 (a) $\begin{bmatrix} 7 & -5 & -3 \\ 19 & 1 & -11 \\ -11 & 1 & 7 \end{bmatrix}$ (b) $\begin{bmatrix} 7 & -19 & -11 \\ 5 & -1 & -1 \\ 3 & 11 & 7 \end{bmatrix}$

 (c) $\begin{bmatrix} 7 & 19 & -11 \\ -3 & 11 & 7 \\ -5 & -1 & -1 \end{bmatrix}$ (d) $\begin{bmatrix} 7 & 19 & -11 \\ -1 & -1 & 1 \\ -3 & -11 & 7 \end{bmatrix}$

37. A function $f : R \to R$ defined by $f(x) = 2 + x^2$ is
 (a) not one-one
 (b) one-one
 (c) not onto
 (d) neither one-one nor onto

38. A linear programming problem is as follow:
 maximise / minimise objective function $Z = 2x - y + 5$
 Subject to the constraints
 $3x + 4y \le 60$
 $x + 3y \le 30$
 $x \ge 0, y \ge 0$
 If the corner points of the feasible region are $A(0, 10)$, $B(12, 6)$, $C(20, 0)$ and $O(0, 0)$, then which of the following is true?
 (a) Maximum value of Z is 40
 (b) Minimum value of Z is -5
 (c) Difference of maximum and minimum values of Z is 35
 (d) At two corner points, value of Z are equal

39. If $x = -4$ is a root of $\begin{vmatrix} x & 2 & 3 \\ 1 & x & 1 \\ 3 & 2 & x \end{vmatrix} = 0$, then the sum of the other two roots is
 (a) 4   (b) -3
 (c) 2   (d) 5

40. The absolute maximum value of the function $f(x) = 4x - \dfrac{1}{2}x^2$ in the interval $\left[-2, \dfrac{9}{2}\right]$ is
 (a) 8   (b) 9
 (c) 6   (d) 10

SECTION - C

Attempt any 8 questions out of the questions 41-50. Each question is of one mark.

41. In a sphere of radius r, a right circular cone of height h, having maximum curved surface area is inscribed. The expression for the square of curved surface of cone is

(a) $2\pi^2 rh\,(2rh + h^2)$ (b) $\pi^2 hr\,(2rh + h^2)$

(c) $2\pi^2 r\,(2rh^2 - h^3)$ (d) $2\pi^2 r^2\,(2rh - h^2)$

42. The corner points of the feasible region determined by a set of constraints (linear inequalities) are P(0, 5), Q(3, 5), R(5, 0) and S(4, 1) and the objective function is $Z = ax + 2by$ where $a, b > 0$. The condition on a and b such that the maximum Z occurs at Q and S is

(a) $a - 5b = 0$ (b) $a - 3b = 0$

(c) $a - 2b = 0$ (d) $a - 8b = 0$

43. If curves $y^2 = 4x$ and $xy = c$ cut at right angles, then the value of c is

(a) $4\sqrt{2}$ (b) 8

(c) $2\sqrt{2}$ (d) $-4\sqrt{2}$

44. The inverse of the matrix $X = \begin{bmatrix} 2 & 0 & 0 \\ 0 & 3 & 0 \\ 0 & 0 & 4 \end{bmatrix}$ is

(a) $24\begin{bmatrix} 1/2 & 0 & 0 \\ 0 & 1/3 & 0 \\ 0 & 0 & 1/4 \end{bmatrix}$ (b) $\dfrac{1}{24}\begin{bmatrix} 1 & 0 & 0 \\ 0 & 1 & 0 \\ 0 & 0 & 1 \end{bmatrix}$

(c) $\dfrac{1}{24}\begin{bmatrix} 2 & 0 & 0 \\ 0 & 3 & 0 \\ 0 & 0 & 4 \end{bmatrix}$ (d) $\begin{bmatrix} 1/2 & 0 & 0 \\ 0 & 1/3 & 0 \\ 0 & 0 & 1/4 \end{bmatrix}$

45. For an L.P.P. the objective function is $Z = 4x + 3y$ and the feasible region determined by a set of constraints (linear inequations) is shown in the graph.

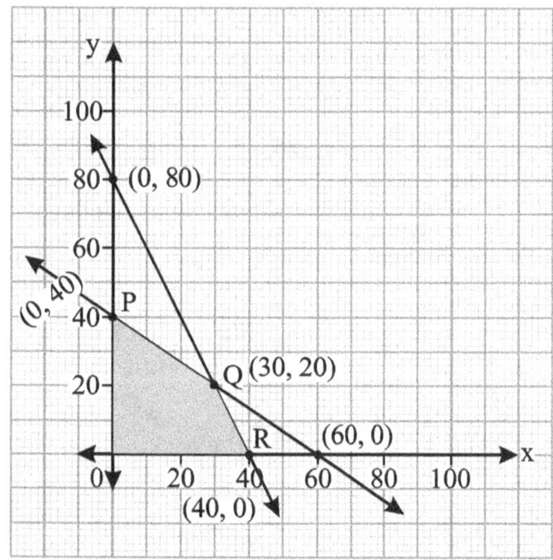

Which one of the following statements is true?

(a) Maximum value of Z is at R.

(b) Maximum value of Z is at Q.

(c) Value of Z at R is less than the value at P.

(d) Value of Z at Q is less than the value at R.

Case Study

In a residential society comprising of 100 houses, there were 60 children between the ages of 10-15 years. They were inspired by their teachers to start composting to ensure that biodegradable waste is recycled. For this purpose, instead of each child doing it for only his/her house, children convinced the Residents Welfare Association to do it as a society initiative. For this they identified a square area in the local park. Local authorities charged amount of ₹ 50 per square metre for space so that there is no misuse of the space and Resident Welfare Association takes it seriously. Association hired a labourer for digging out 250 m³ and he charged ₹ 400 ×(depth)². Association will like to have minimum cost.

Based on this information, answer the any 4 of the following questions.

46. Let side of square plot is x m and its depth is h metres, then cost c for the pit is

(a) $\dfrac{50}{h} + 400\,h^2$ (b) $\dfrac{12500}{h} + 400\,h^2$

(c) $\dfrac{250}{h} + h^2$ (d) $\dfrac{250}{h} + 400\,h^2$

47. Value of h (in m) for which $\dfrac{dc}{dh} = 0$ is

(a) 1.5   (b) 2

(c) 2.5   (d) 3

48. $\dfrac{d^2 c}{dh^2}$ is given by

(a) $\dfrac{25000}{h^3} + 800$ (b) $\dfrac{500}{h^3} + 800$

(c) $\dfrac{100}{h^3} + 800$ (d) $\dfrac{500}{h^3} + 2$

49. Value of x (in m) for minimum cost is

(a) 5 (b) $10\sqrt{\dfrac{5}{3}}$

(c) $5\sqrt{5}$ (d) 10

50. Total minimum cost of digging the pit (in ₹) is

(a) 4100   (b) 7500

(c) 7850   (d) 3220

Solutions

1. (a) Let $y = \log[\log(\log x^5)]$
Differentiate w.r.t x.

$$\frac{dy}{dx} = \frac{1}{\log(\log x^5)} \times \frac{dy}{dx}\log(\log x^5) \qquad \text{[by chain rule]}$$

$$= \frac{1}{\log(\log x^5)} \times \frac{1}{\log(x^5)} \times \frac{dy}{dx}\log x^5$$

$$= \frac{1}{\log(\log x^5)} \times \frac{1}{\log(x^5)} \times 5\frac{dy}{dx}\log x$$

$$= \frac{1}{\log(\log x^5)} \times \frac{1}{\log(x^5)} \times \frac{5}{x}$$

$$= \frac{5}{x\log(x^5)\log(\log x^5)} \qquad \textbf{(1 Mark)}$$

2. (c) Let the matrix is $\begin{bmatrix} a_{11} & a_{12} & a_{13} \\ a_{21} & a_{22} & a_{23} \end{bmatrix}_{2\times3}$

The given matrix of the order 2×3 has 6 elements and each of these element can be either 1 or 2.
Then the 6 elements can be filled in two possible ways.
Therefore by multiplication principle
No. of possible matrices $2^{2\times3} = 2^6 = 64$ **(1 Mark)**

3. (d) Given that $f(x) = x^3 + 1$
Then $f'(x) = 3x^2$
For critical point, we have
$3x^2 = 0 \Rightarrow x = 0$
Now IInd derivative test at point $x = 0$, we have
$f''(x) = 6x$

$$f''(x)]_{x=0} = 6 \times 0 = 0$$

Note

If $f'(c) = 0$ and $f''(c) = 0$ in this case, we go to the first derivative test to check whether c is a point of local maxima, local minima or a point of inflexion.

Zero is neither positive nor negative. Therefore function has neither maximum value nor minimum value. **(1 Mark)**

4. (a) $\sin y = x\cos(a+y)$

or $\quad x = \dfrac{\sin y}{\cos(a+y)}$

Differentiate both side w.r.t. y, we have

$$\frac{dx}{dy} = \frac{\cos(a+y)\dfrac{d}{dy}\sin y - \sin y\dfrac{d}{dy}\cos(a+y)}{[\cos(a+y)]^2}$$

$$= \frac{\cos(a+y)\cos y - \sin y[-\sin(a+y)]}{\cos^2(a+y)}$$

$$= \frac{\cos(a+y)\cos y + \sin(a+y)\sin y}{\cos^2(a+y)}$$

$$= \frac{\cos\{a+y-y\}}{\cos^2(a+y)}$$
$$[\because \cos(a-b) = \cos a\cdot\cos b + \sin a\cdot\sin b]$$

$$= \frac{\cos a}{\cos^2(a+y)} \qquad \textbf{(1 Mark)}$$

5. (b) Given curve

$$\frac{x^2}{9} + \frac{y^2}{25} = 1 \qquad \text{...(i)}$$

or $\dfrac{y^2}{25} = 1 - \dfrac{x^2}{9}$

Differentiate both side, we have

$$\frac{1}{25}\cdot2y\frac{dy}{dx} = -\frac{2x}{9} \Rightarrow \frac{dy}{dx} = -\frac{2x}{9}\times\frac{25}{2y} = -\frac{25x}{9y}$$

Since tangent is $\parallel$ to x-axis i.e.

$$\frac{dy}{dx} = 0 \Rightarrow -\frac{25x}{9y} = 0 \Rightarrow x = 0$$

Putting $x = 0$ in eqn. (i), we have

$$\frac{y^2}{25} = 1 \Rightarrow y^2 = 25 \text{ or } y = \pm5$$

Therefore the required points are $(0, 5)$ and $(0, -5)$. **(1 Mark)**

6. (c) If $P(2x, x+3)$, $Q(0, x)$ and $R(x+3, x+6)$ are collinear then the area of Δ will be zero
We have

$$\text{Area of }\Delta = \frac{1}{2}\left|x_1(y_2 - y_3) + x_2(y_3 - y_1) + x_3(y_1 - y_2)\right|$$

$$= \frac{1}{2}\left|2x(x - x - 3) + 0(x + 6 - x - 3) + (x + 3)(x + 3 - x)\right| = 0$$

$$= \frac{1}{2}\left|2x(-3) + 0 + (x+3)3\right| = 0 = \frac{1}{2}\left|-6x + 3x + 9\right| = 0$$

$$-3x + 9 = 0 \Rightarrow x = 3 \qquad \textbf{(1 Mark)}$$

7. (a) $\quad \cos^{-1}\left(\dfrac{1}{2}\right) + \sin^{-1}\left(-\dfrac{1}{\sqrt{2}}\right)$

$$\cos^{-1}\left(\cos\frac{\pi}{3}\right) - \sin^{-1}\left(\frac{1}{\sqrt{2}}\right) \quad [\because \sin^{-1}(-\theta) = -\sin^{-1}\theta]$$

$$\cos^{-1}\left(\cos\frac{\pi}{3}\right) - \sin^{-1}\left(\sin\frac{\pi}{4}\right)$$

$$\frac{\pi}{3} - \frac{\pi}{4} \Rightarrow \frac{\pi}{12} \qquad \textbf{(1 Mark)}$$

Note

$$\sin^{-1}(\sin x) = x; \qquad x \in \left[\frac{-\pi}{2}, \frac{\pi}{2}\right]$$

$$\cos^{-1}(\cos x) = x; \qquad x \in [0, \pi]$$

8. **(c)** $(x^2 + y^2)^2 = xy$
$x^4 + y^4 + 2x^2y^2 = xy$
Differentiating both side w.r.t. x

$$4x^3 + 4y^3\frac{dy}{dx} + 2\left[x^2 \cdot 2y\frac{dy}{dx} + y^2 \cdot 2x\right] = x\frac{dy}{dx} + y$$

$$4x^3 + 4y^3\frac{dy}{dx} + 4x^2y\frac{dy}{dx} + 4xy^2 = x\frac{dy}{dx} + y$$

$$\frac{dy}{dx}(4y^3 + 4x^2y - x) = y - 4x^3 - 4xy^2$$

$$\frac{dy}{dx} = \frac{y - 4x^3 - 4xy^2}{4y^3 + 4x^2y - x}$$

or $\dfrac{dy}{dx} = \dfrac{y - 4x(x^2 + y^2)}{4y(y^2 + x^2) - x}$ **(1 Mark)**

9. **(b)** Given that A is both symmetric and skew symmetric
i.e. $A' = A$ ...(i)
and $A' = -A$ ...(ii)
From (i) and (ii)
$\quad A = -A$
or $A + A = 0$
$\quad 2A = 0$
$\Rightarrow\ A = 0$
Therefore A is a zero matrix.   **(1 Mark)**

10. **(c)** Given that set $X = \{1, 2, 3\}$
R is reflexive since $(1, 1), (2, 2)$ and $(3, 3)$ lie in R.
Also,
R is symmetric if
$(1, 3) \in X \Rightarrow (3, 1) \in X \Rightarrow (3, 2) \in X \Rightarrow (2, 3) \in X$
Therefore
$R = \{(1, 1), (2, 2), (3, 3), (1, 3), (3, 1), (3, 2), (2, 3)\}$ **(1 Mark)**

11. **(b)** Objective function $Z = 2x + y$
Constraints: $x \geq 3, x \leq 9, y \geq 0$
$x - y \geq 0, x + y \leq 14$

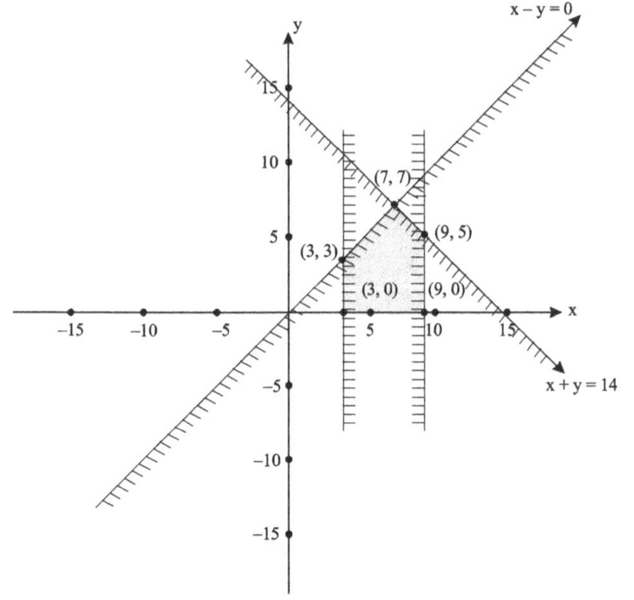

Consider the line
$x - y = 0$ ...(i) $x + y = 14$ ...(ii)

x	0	1	2
y	0	1	2

x	0	14
y	14	0

From eqns. (i) and (ii)
$x = 7$ and $y = 7$
Therefore feasible region has five corner, respectively
$(3, 0), (9, 0), (9, 5), (7, 7)$ and $(3, 3)$ **(1 Mark)**

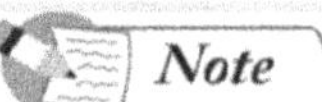
Note

Objective function is a linear function which is to be optimized in LPP.

12. **(d)** $f(x) = \begin{cases} \dfrac{e^{3x} - e^{-5x}}{x}, & \text{if } x \neq 0 \\ k, & \text{if } x = 0 \end{cases}$

Given that $f(0) = k$ ...(i)
Also given that function is continous at $x = 0$
Therefore, RHL $=$ LHL $= f(0)$ ...(ii)

Since, RHL $= f(0)^+ \Rightarrow \displaystyle\lim_{x \to 0^+}\frac{e^{3x} - e^{-5x}}{x} \Rightarrow \frac{1-1}{0} = \frac{0}{0}$

$\displaystyle\lim_{x \to 0^+}\frac{e^{3x} - 1}{3x} \cdot 3 + \frac{e^{-5x} - 1}{(-5x)} \cdot 5$ $\quad\left[\because \displaystyle\lim_{x \to 0}\frac{e^x - 1}{x} = 1\right]$

$= 3 \times 1 + 5 \times 1 = 8$
From (i) and (ii)
$k = 8$ **(1 Mark)**

13. **(a)** Given matrix, $P = \begin{bmatrix} 1 & -1 & 2 \\ 0 & 2 & -3 \\ 3 & 2 & 4 \end{bmatrix}$

Now cofactor, $C_{31} = (-1)^{3+1}\begin{vmatrix} -1 & 2 \\ 2 & -3 \end{vmatrix}$

$= 1(3 - 4) = -1$

and cofactor, $C_{23} = (-1)^{2+3}\begin{vmatrix} 1 & -1 \\ 3 & 2 \end{vmatrix}$

$= -1(2 + 3) = -5$
Therefore, $C_{31} \times C_{23} = (-1) \times (-5) = 5$ **(1 Mark)**

14. **(d)** $y = x^2e^{-x}$

$$\frac{dy}{dx} = x^2(-e^{-x}) + e^{-x}(2x)$$

$$= -x^2e^{-x} + 2xe^{-x}$$

$$\frac{dy}{dx} = e^{-x}x(2 - x)$$

For decreasing

$$\frac{dy}{dx} < 0$$

$$e^{-x}x(2 - x) < 0$$

e^{-x} is always positive for $\forall\, x \in R$
For $x(2-x)=0$
or $x=0$ and $x=2$
Therefore the point $x=0$ and $x=2$ divide the real line into three disjoint intervals.

For $-\infty < x < 0$, $\dfrac{dy}{dx}=(-)(+)=(-)ve$

For $0 < x < 2$, $\dfrac{dy}{dx}=(+)(+)=(+)ve$

For $2 < x < \infty$, $\dfrac{dy}{dx}=(+)(-)=(-)ve$

Therefore function is decreasing in interval
$(-\infty,0)\cup(2,\infty)$ **(1 Mark)**

Note

A function is strictly decreasing in interval I if $f'(x)<0\ \forall\, x \in I$

15.   (b)   We have $R=\{(x,y): x,y \in Z, x^2+y^2 \le 4\}$
When $x=0$
$x^2+y^2 \le 4 \Rightarrow y^2 \le 4 \Rightarrow y=0,\pm 1,\pm 2$
When $x=\pm 1$
$x^2+y^2 \le 4 \Rightarrow 1+y^2 \le 4 \Rightarrow y^2 \le 3 \Rightarrow y=0,\pm 1$
When $x=\pm 2$
$x^2+y^2 \le 4 \Rightarrow 4+y^2 \le 4 \Rightarrow y^2 \le 0 \Rightarrow y=0$
Therefore, $R=\{(0,0),(0,-1),(0,1),(0,-2),(0,2),$
$(-1,0),(1,0),(1,1),(1,-1),(-1,1),(-1,-1),(2,0),(-2,0)\}$
Hence,
Domain of $R=\{x:(x,y)\in R\}$
$=\{0,-1,1,-2,2\}$ **(1 Mark)**

16.   (d) $5x+ky-5=0$ ...(i)
$3x+3y-5=0$ ...(ii)
By the rule of consistancy
$\dfrac{5}{3}\ne\dfrac{k}{3}\quad\left(\because\ \dfrac{a_1}{a_2}\ne\dfrac{b_1}{b_2}\right)$
$3k \ne 15 \Rightarrow k \ne 5$ **(1 Mark)**

17.   (c)   Equation of the curve
$(1+x^2)y=2-x$
Curve crosses the x-axis which means y-coordinate is 0.
So $(1+x^2)\times 0=2-x$
$\quad 0=2-x$
or $x=2$
Therefore the curve passes through the point $(2,0)$.
Equation of the curve,
$y(1+x^2)=2-x$
$y+yx^2=2-x$

$\dfrac{dy}{dx}+x^2\dfrac{dy}{dx}+y\cdot 2x=-1$

$\dfrac{dy}{dx}(1+x^2)=-(1+2xy)\Rightarrow\dfrac{dy}{dx}=\dfrac{-(1+2xy)}{1+x^2}$

Slope at point $(2,0)$

$\dfrac{dy}{dx}\Big]_{(2,0)}=\dfrac{-(1+2\times 2\times 0)}{1+(2)^2}\Rightarrow\ -\dfrac{1}{1+4}$

or $\dfrac{dy}{dx}\Big]_{(2,0)}=-\dfrac{1}{5}$

Equation of tangent

$y-y_1=\dfrac{dy}{dx}\Big]_{(2,0)}(x-x_1)\Rightarrow y-0=-\dfrac{1}{5}(x-2)$

$5y=-x+2$
or $x+5y=2$ **(1 Mark)**

18.   (a) $\begin{bmatrix}3c+6 & a-d \\ a+d & 2-3b\end{bmatrix}=\begin{bmatrix}12 & 2 \\ -8 & -4\end{bmatrix}$

$3c+6=12$ ...(i)
$a-d=2$ ...(ii)   (by equality of property of matrix)
$a+d=-8$ ...(iii)
$2-3b=-4$ ...(iv)
From eqn (i)
$c=2$
From eqns. (ii) and (iii)
$a=-3$ and $d=-5$
From eqn. (iv)
$b=2$
Therefore, $ab-cd=(-3)(2)-(2)(-5)$
$=-6+10=4$ **(1 Mark)**

19.   (a) $\tan^{-1}\left[\tan\dfrac{9\pi}{8}\right]\quad\left(\because\ \dfrac{9\pi}{8}\notin\left(-\dfrac{\pi}{2},\dfrac{\pi}{2}\right)\right)$

$\tan^{-1}\left[\tan\left(\pi+\dfrac{\pi}{8}\right)\right]\quad\left(\because\ \dfrac{\pi}{8}\in\left(-\dfrac{\pi}{2},\dfrac{\pi}{2}\right)\right)$

$\tan^{-1}\left[\tan\dfrac{\pi}{8}\right]\qquad\qquad(\because\ \tan(\pi+\theta)=\tan\theta)$

$=\dfrac{\pi}{8}$ **(1 Mark)**

20.   (b)   Transpose of $(Q^T)=\begin{bmatrix}-1 & 2 & 1 \\ 1 & 2 & 3\end{bmatrix}^T$

$\therefore\ Q=\begin{bmatrix}-1 & 1 \\ 2 & 2 \\ 1 & 3\end{bmatrix}\qquad\qquad[\because\ (Q^T)^T=Q]$

Therefore $P-Q$

$\begin{bmatrix}3 & 4 \\ -1 & 2 \\ 0 & 1\end{bmatrix}-\begin{bmatrix}-1 & 1 \\ 2 & 2 \\ 1 & 3\end{bmatrix}\Rightarrow\begin{bmatrix}4 & 3 \\ -3 & 0 \\ -1 & -2\end{bmatrix}$ **(1 Mark)**

21. **(c)** $f(x) = 2x^3 - 15x^2 + 36x + 6$

$f'(x) = 6x^2 - 30x + 36$

For increasing

$\quad f'(x) \geq 0$

$6x^2 - 30x + 36 \geq 0 \Rightarrow 6[x^2 - 5x + 6] \geq 0$

$6[x^2 - 3x - 2x + 6] \geq 0 \Rightarrow 6[x(x-3) - 2(x-3)] \geq 0$

$6[(x-2)(x-3)] \geq 0$

when $x \leq 2, f'(x)$ is (+)ve

when $x \geq 3, f'(x)$ is (+)ve

therefore for increasing. Interval is $(-\infty, 2] \cup [3, \infty)$

$$(-\infty) \xrightarrow{\quad + \quad \underset{2}{|} \quad - \quad \underset{3}{|} \quad + \quad} (+\infty)$$ **(1 Mark)**

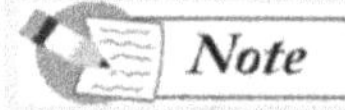 **Note**

A function is increasing in interval I if $f'(x) \geq 0, \forall x \in$ I

22. **(b)** $x = 2\cos\theta - \cos 2\theta$

Differentiating both side w.r.t θ

$$\frac{dx}{d\theta} = 2(-\sin\theta) - (-\sin 2\theta \cdot 2)$$

$= -2\sin\theta + 2\sin 2\theta$ or $2\sin 2\theta - 2\sin\theta$

Now, $y = 2\sin\theta - \sin 2\theta$

Differentiating both side w.r.t. θ

$$\frac{dy}{d\theta} = 2\cos\theta - \cos 2\theta \cdot 2$$

$= 2\cos\theta - 2\cos 2\theta$

Therefore, $\dfrac{dy}{dx} = \dfrac{dy}{d\theta} \Big/ \dfrac{dx}{d\theta}$

$$= \frac{2\cos\theta - 2\cos 2\theta}{2\sin 2\theta - 2\sin\theta} = \frac{2(\cos\theta - \cos 2\theta)}{2(\sin 2\theta - \sin\theta)}$$

$$\frac{dy}{dx} = \frac{\cos\theta - \cos 2\theta}{\sin 2\theta - \sin\theta}$$ **(1 Mark)**

23. **(d)** We know that domain of $\cos^{-1} x$ is $[-1, 1]$

for domain of $\cos^{-1}(2x - 3)$ is the set of all values of x which satisfying

$-1 \leq 2x - 3 \leq 1$

$-1 + 3 \leq 2x - 3 + 3 \leq 1 + 3$

add 3 in equality

$2 \leq 2x \leq 4$

or $1 \leq x \leq 2$

Hence the domain of $\cos^{-1}(2x - 3)$ is $[1, 2]$ **(1 Mark)**

24. **(b)** Given $A = [a_{ij}]_{3\times 3} \Rightarrow \begin{bmatrix} a_{11} & a_{12} & a_{13} \\ a_{21} & a_{22} & a_{23} \\ a_{31} & a_{32} & a_{33} \end{bmatrix}$

Given, $a_{ij} = \begin{cases} 2i + 3j, & i < j \\ 5, & i = j \\ 3i - 2j, & i > j \end{cases}$

From the defined condition for elements, we have

$a_{11} \ (i=j) \quad \Rightarrow \quad a_{11} = 5$

$a_{12} \ (i<j) \quad \Rightarrow \quad a_{12} = 2 \times 1 + 3 \times 2 = 8$

$a_{13} \ (i<j) \quad \Rightarrow \quad a_{13} = 2 \times 1 + 3 \times 3 = 11$

$a_{21} \ (i>j) \quad \Rightarrow \quad a_{21} = 3 \times 2 - 2 \times 1 = 4$

$a_{22} \ (i=j) \quad \Rightarrow \quad a_{22} = 5$

$a_{23} \ (i<j) \quad \Rightarrow \quad a_{23} = 2 \times 2 + 3 \times 3 = 13$

$a_{31} \ (i>j) \quad \Rightarrow \quad a_{31} = 3 \times 3 - 2 \times 1 = 7$

$a_{32} \ (i>j) \quad \Rightarrow \quad a_{32} = 3 \times 3 - 2 \times 2 = 5$

$a_{33} \ (i=j) \quad \Rightarrow \quad a_{33} = 5$

Therefore $A = \begin{bmatrix} 5 & 8 & 11 \\ 4 & 5 & 13 \\ 7 & 5 & 5 \end{bmatrix}$

Hence, 4 elements are in A which are more than 5. **(1 Mark)**

25. **(c)** $f(x) = \begin{cases} \dfrac{k\cos x}{\pi - 2x}, & \text{if } x \neq \dfrac{\pi}{2} \\ 3, & \text{if } x = \dfrac{\pi}{2} \end{cases}$

Given: $f\left(\dfrac{\pi}{2}\right) = 3$

Function is continuous at $x = \dfrac{\pi}{2}$, so

$$\text{LHL} = \text{RHL} = f\left(\frac{\pi}{2}\right)$$ ...(i)

Now, LHL $\Rightarrow \lim\limits_{x \to \frac{\pi^-}{2}} \dfrac{k\cos x}{\pi - 2x}$

Put $x = \dfrac{\pi}{2} - h$

$$\lim\limits_{h \to 0} \frac{k\cos\left(\dfrac{\pi}{2} - h\right)}{\pi - 2\left(\dfrac{\pi}{2} - h\right)} \Rightarrow \lim\limits_{h \to 0} \frac{k\sin h}{\pi - \pi + 2h}$$

$$\lim\limits_{h \to 0} \frac{k}{2} \frac{\sin h}{h} \qquad \left(\because \lim\limits_{h \to 0} \frac{\sin h}{h} = 1\right)$$

$$= \frac{k}{2}$$

RHL $\Rightarrow \lim\limits_{x \to \frac{\pi^+}{2}} \dfrac{k\cos x}{\pi - 2x}$, put $x = \dfrac{\pi}{2} + h$

$$\lim\limits_{h \to 0} \frac{k\cos\left(\dfrac{\pi}{2} + h\right)}{\pi - 2\left(\dfrac{\pi}{2} + h\right)} \Rightarrow \lim\limits_{h \to 0} \frac{k\sin h}{-2h} = \frac{k}{2}$$

From eqn (i), we have

$k/2 = 3$ or $k = 6$ **(1 Mark)**

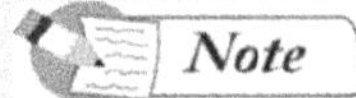 **Note**

If a function $f(x)$ takes the form $\dfrac{0}{0}$ or $\dfrac{\infty}{\infty}$ at $x = a$, then we say that $f(x)$ is indeterminate or meaning less at $x = a$.

26. (a) $X = \begin{bmatrix} 0 & 1 & 1 \\ 1 & 0 & 1 \\ 1 & 1 & 0 \end{bmatrix}$

$X^2 = X \cdot X$

$= \begin{bmatrix} 0 & 1 & 1 \\ 1 & 0 & 1 \\ 1 & 1 & 0 \end{bmatrix} \begin{bmatrix} 0 & 1 & 1 \\ 1 & 0 & 1 \\ 1 & 1 & 0 \end{bmatrix}$

$= \begin{bmatrix} 0+1+1 & 0+0+1 & 0+1+0 \\ 0+0+1 & 1+0+1 & 1+0+0 \\ 0+1+0 & 1+0+0 & 1+1+0 \end{bmatrix} \Rightarrow \begin{bmatrix} 2 & 1 & 1 \\ 1 & 2 & 1 \\ 1 & 1 & 2 \end{bmatrix}$

Now, $X^2 - X \Rightarrow \begin{bmatrix} 2 & 1 & 1 \\ 1 & 2 & 1 \\ 1 & 1 & 2 \end{bmatrix} - \begin{bmatrix} 0 & 1 & 1 \\ 1 & 0 & 1 \\ 1 & 1 & 0 \end{bmatrix}$

$= \begin{bmatrix} 2 & 0 & 0 \\ 0 & 2 & 0 \\ 0 & 0 & 2 \end{bmatrix}$ or $2 \begin{bmatrix} 1 & 0 & 0 \\ 0 & 1 & 0 \\ 0 & 0 & 1 \end{bmatrix} = 2I$ **(1 Mark)**

27. (d) Let $f(x_1) = f(x_2)$
$\Rightarrow x_1^2 = x_2^2$
$\Rightarrow x_1 = x_2$ $\qquad [\because x \in N]$
$\therefore$ $f(x)$ is injective
$\because$ $f : N \to X$
Angle range of
$f(x) = x^2, x \in N$ is X
$\therefore$ Range = codomain
So, it is surjective also
Hence, it is bijective. **(1 Mark)**

28. (c)

Corner points	Objective function $Z = 2x + 5y$
$P(0, 5)$	$Z = 2 \times 0 + 5 \times 5 = 0 + 25 = 25$
$Q(1, 5)$	$Z = 2 \times 1 + 5 \times 5 = 2 + 25 = 27$
$R(4, 2)$	$Z = 2 \times 4 + 5 \times 2 = 8 + 10 = 18(\text{min})$
$S(12, 0)$	$Z = 2 \times 12 + 5 \times 0 = 24 + 0 = 24$

Therefore minimum value will be at point R. **(1 Mark)**

29. (d) Equation of curve
$ay^2 = x^3$

$a \cdot 2y \dfrac{dy}{dx} = 3x^2 \Rightarrow \dfrac{dy}{dx} = \dfrac{3x^2}{2ay}$

Slope of tangent at point (am^2, am^3)

$\dfrac{dy}{dx}\Big]_{(am^2, am^3)} = \dfrac{3(am^2)^2}{2a(am^3)} \Rightarrow \dfrac{3m}{2}$

Slope of normal $= -\dfrac{1}{\text{Slope of tangent}}$

$= -\dfrac{1}{\dfrac{3m}{2}} \Rightarrow -\dfrac{2}{3m}$

Therefore, equation of normal

$(y - am^3) = -\dfrac{2}{3m}(x - am^2)$

$3my - 3am^4 = -2x + 2am^2$
$2x + 3my - 3am^4 - 2am^2 = 0$ **(1 Mark)**

30. (c) Given, $n = 3, |A| = -5$
We know that
$|\text{Adj } A| = |A|^{n-1}$, where n is order of matrix
$= (-5)^{3-1}$
$= (-5)^2 = 25$
Therefore, $|\text{Adj } A| = 25$ **(1 Mark)**

31. (c) $\tan^{-1}\left[\dfrac{\sqrt{1+x} - \sqrt{1-x}}{\sqrt{1+x} + \sqrt{1-x}}\right]$

Let $x = \cos 2\theta \Rightarrow 2\theta = \cos^{-1}x$

$\theta = \dfrac{1}{2} \cos^{-1}x$

$\tan^{-1}\left[\dfrac{\sqrt{1+\cos 2\theta} - \sqrt{1-\cos 2\theta}}{\sqrt{1+\cos 2\theta} + \sqrt{1-\cos 2\theta}}\right]$

$\tan^{-1}\left[\dfrac{\sqrt{1+2\cos^2\theta - 1} - \sqrt{1 - 1 + 2\sin^2\theta}}{\sqrt{1+2\cos^2\theta - 1} + \sqrt{1 - 1 + 2\sin^2\theta}}\right]$

$\tan^{-1}\left[\dfrac{\sqrt{2}\left(\sqrt{\cos^2\theta} - \sqrt{\sin^2\theta}\right)}{\sqrt{2}\left(\sqrt{\cos^2\theta} + \sqrt{\sin^2\theta}\right)}\right]$

$\tan^{-1}\left[\dfrac{\cos\theta - \sin\theta}{\cos\theta + \sin\theta}\right]$

$\tan^{-1}\left[\dfrac{\cos(1 - \tan\theta)}{\cos(1 + \tan\theta)}\right]$

$\tan^{-1}\left[\tan\left(\dfrac{\pi}{4} - \theta\right)\right] \quad \left(\because \tan(x - y) = \dfrac{\tan x - \tan y}{1 + \tan x \cdot \tan y}\right)$

$\dfrac{\pi}{4} - \theta$

$\dfrac{\pi}{4} - \dfrac{1}{2}\cos^{-1}x$ **(1 Mark)**

32. (a) Given $|A^3| = 125$
$|A|^3 = 125 \ (\because |A^n| = |A|^n)$
or $|A| = 5I$

$\begin{vmatrix} \alpha & -2 \\ -2 & \alpha \end{vmatrix} = 5\begin{vmatrix} 1 & 0 \\ 0 & 1 \end{vmatrix}$

$\alpha^2 - 4 = 5(1)$
$\alpha^2 - 9 = 0$
$\alpha = \pm 3$ **(1 Mark)**

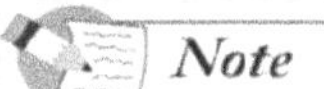 *Note*

A matrix is non-singular if and only if $|A| \neq 0$.

33. **(b)** $y = \sin(m\sin^{-1}x)$

Differentiating both side w.r.t x

$$\frac{dy}{dx} = \cos(m\sin^{-1}x) \times \frac{d}{dx} m\sin^{-1}x$$

$$\frac{dy}{dx} = \cos(m\sin^{-1}x) \times \frac{m}{\sqrt{1-x^2}}$$

$$\sqrt{1-x^2}\,\frac{dy}{dx} = m.\cos(m\sin^{-1}x)$$

Again differentiating both side

$$\sqrt{1-x^2}\,\frac{d^2y}{dx^2} + \frac{dy}{dx}\left[\frac{1}{2\sqrt{1-x^2}} \times (-2x)\right]$$

$$= -m\sin(m\sin^{-1}x) \times \frac{m}{\sqrt{1-x^2}}$$

$$\sqrt{1-x^2}\,\frac{d^2y}{dx^2} + \frac{dy}{dx}\left[\frac{-2x}{2\sqrt{1-x^2}}\right] = -\frac{m^2\sin(m\sin^{-1}x)}{\sqrt{1-x^2}}$$

$$(1-x^2)\frac{d^2y}{dx^2} - x\frac{dy}{dx} = -m^2y \quad (\because y = \sin(m\sin^{-1}x))$$

$$(1-x^2)\frac{d^2y}{dx^2} - x\frac{dy}{dx} + m^2y = 0 \qquad \textbf{(1 Mark)}$$

34. **(b)** $\tan^{-1}\sqrt{3} - \cot^{-1}\left(-\sqrt{3}\right)$

$$\tan^{-1}\left(\tan\frac{\pi}{3}\right) - \left[\pi - \cot^{-1}\left(\sqrt{3}\right)\right] (\because \cot^{-1}(-x) = \pi - \cot^{-1}x)$$

$$\frac{\pi}{3} - \left[\pi - \cot^{-1}\left(\cot\frac{\pi}{6}\right)\right] \Rightarrow \frac{\pi}{3} - \left[\pi - \frac{\pi}{6}\right]$$

$$\frac{\pi}{3} - \pi + \frac{\pi}{6} = -\frac{\pi}{2} \qquad \textbf{(1 Mark)}$$

35. **(a)** $y = \left(\dfrac{1}{x}\right)^x$

$$\log y = \log\left(\frac{1}{x}\right)^x \Rightarrow \log y = x \cdot \log\left(\frac{1}{x}\right)$$

$$\log y = x \cdot \log x^{-1}$$

$$\log y = -x\log x$$

$$\frac{1}{y} \times \frac{dy}{dx} = -\left[x \cdot \frac{1}{x} + \log x\right]$$

$$\frac{dy}{dx} = -y[1 + \log x] \Rightarrow \frac{dy}{dx} = -\left(\frac{1}{x}\right)^x [1 + \log x]$$

For critical point $\dfrac{dy}{dx} = 0$

$$\left(\frac{1}{x}\right)^x [1 + \log x] = 0$$

$$1 + \log x = 0 \Rightarrow \log x = -1$$

$$x = e^{-1} \Rightarrow \frac{1}{e}$$

$$\frac{d}{dx}\left(\frac{dy}{dx}\right) = -\frac{d}{dx}[y + y\log x]$$

$$\frac{d^2y}{dx^2} = -\left[\frac{dy}{dx} + y \cdot \frac{1}{x} + \log x \cdot \frac{dy}{dx}\right]$$

$$= -\left[\frac{dy}{dx}(1 + \log x) + \frac{y}{x}\right] < 0$$

Therefore $x = \dfrac{1}{e}$ is the point of maxima

and maximum value

$$y = \left(\frac{1}{x}\right)^x$$

$$= \left(\frac{1}{\frac{1}{e}}\right)^{\frac{1}{e}} \Rightarrow (e)^{\frac{1}{e}} \qquad \textbf{(1 Mark)}$$

> **Note**
>
> If function is in the form of variable to the power of variable then use log before differentiate.

36. **(d)** Given, $X = \begin{bmatrix} 1 & -1 & 2 \\ 3 & 4 & -5 \\ 2 & -1 & 3 \end{bmatrix}$

Given that minor of element x_{ij} is denoted by m_{ij}, so

$$m_{11} = \begin{vmatrix} 4 & -5 \\ -1 & 3 \end{vmatrix} \Rightarrow 12 - 5 = 7$$

$$m_{12} = \begin{vmatrix} 3 & -5 \\ 2 & 3 \end{vmatrix} \Rightarrow 9 + 10 = 19$$

$$m_{13} = \begin{vmatrix} 3 & 4 \\ 2 & -1 \end{vmatrix} \Rightarrow -3 - 8 = -11$$

$$m_{21} = \begin{vmatrix} -1 & 2 \\ -1 & 3 \end{vmatrix} \Rightarrow -3 + 2 = -1$$

$$m_{22} = \begin{vmatrix} 1 & 2 \\ 2 & 3 \end{vmatrix} \Rightarrow 3 - 4 = -1$$

$$m_{23} = \begin{vmatrix} 1 & -1 \\ 2 & -1 \end{vmatrix} \Rightarrow -1 + 2 = 1$$

$$m_{31} = \begin{vmatrix} -1 & 2 \\ 4 & -5 \end{vmatrix} \Rightarrow 5 - 8 = -3$$

$$m_{32} = \begin{vmatrix} 1 & 2 \\ 3 & -5 \end{vmatrix} \Rightarrow -5 - 6 = -11$$

$$m_{33} = \begin{vmatrix} 1 & -1 \\ 3 & 4 \end{vmatrix} \Rightarrow 4 + 3 = 7$$

Therefore,

$$Y = \begin{bmatrix} m_{11} & m_{12} & m_{13} \\ m_{21} & m_{22} & m_{23} \\ m_{31} & m_{32} & m_{33} \end{bmatrix} = \begin{bmatrix} 7 & 19 & -11 \\ -1 & -1 & 1 \\ -3 & -11 & 7 \end{bmatrix}$$ **(1 Mark)**

37. **(d)** Let $f(x_1) = f(x_2)$
$\Rightarrow \quad 2 + x_1^2 = 2 + x_2^2$
$\Rightarrow \quad x_1 = \pm x_2$
$\therefore \quad f(x)$ is not one-one
$\because \quad x^2 \geq 0 \Rightarrow 2 + x^2 \geq 2$
$\Rightarrow \quad f(x) \geq 2$
$\therefore \quad$ Range $= [2, \infty) \neq$ codomain
So, $f(x)$ is not onto.   **(1 Mark)**

38. **(b)**

Corner points	Objective function $Z = 2x - y + 5$
$A\,(0, 10)$	$Z = 2 \times 0 - 10 + 5 \Rightarrow -10 + 5 = -5$
$B\,(12, 6)$	$Z = 2 \times 12 - 6 + 5 \Rightarrow 24 - 6 + 5 = 23$
$C\,(20, 0)$	$Z = 2 \times 20 - 0 + 5 \Rightarrow 40 + 5 = 45$
$O\,(0, 0)$	$Z = 2 \times 0 - 0 + 5 \Rightarrow 5$

Therefore minimum value of $Z = -5$.   **(1 Mark)**

39. **(a)** $\begin{vmatrix} x & 2 & 3 \\ 1 & x & 1 \\ 3 & 2 & x \end{vmatrix} = 0$

Expanding along R_1, we have
$x(x^2 - 2) - 2(x - 3) + 3(2 - 3x) = 0$
$x^3 - 2x - 2x + 6 + 6 - 9x = 0$
$x^3 - 13x + 12 = 0$ ...(i)
$12 = 1 \times 3 \times 4$
if $x = -4$ is one root then it satisfy the equation (i)
$x(-4) = (-4)^3 - 13(-4) + 12$
$-64 + 52 + 12$
$-64 + 64 = 0$
Similarly, $x = 3$ and $x = 1$ satisfy the equation (i)
$x(3) = (3)^3 - 13(3) + 12 \Rightarrow 27 - 39 + 12 \Rightarrow 39 - 39 = 0$
$x(1) = (1)^3 - 13(1) + 12 \Rightarrow 1 - 13 + 12 \Rightarrow 13 - 13 = 0$
Both $x = 3$ and $x = 1$ satisfy the equation, so $x = 3$ and $x = 1$
are two other roots.
Therefore sum of other two root $= 3 + 1 = 4$ **(1 Mark)**

40. **(a)** $f(x) = 4x - \dfrac{1}{2}x^2$

$f(x) = 4 - \dfrac{1}{2}2x$

$f'(x) = 4 - x$
For critical point $f'(x) = 0$
$4 - x = 0 \Rightarrow x = 4$

Now, find the value of $f(x)$ at $x = -2, 4, \dfrac{9}{2}$

$f(-2) = 4(-2) - \dfrac{1}{2}(-2)^2 \Rightarrow -8 - 2 = -10$

$f(4) = 4(4) - \dfrac{1}{2}(4)^2 \Rightarrow 16 - 8 = 8$

$f\left(\dfrac{9}{2}\right) = 4\left(\dfrac{9}{2}\right) - \dfrac{1}{2} \times \dfrac{81}{4} \Rightarrow 18 - \dfrac{81}{8} = \dfrac{63}{8} = 7.875$

Therefore, absolute maximum value is 8.   **(1 Mark)**

41. **(c)** Given that:
Radius of sphere $= r$
Height of cone $= h$
Let radius of cone $= R$
Slant height of cone $= \ell$
Now, In $\triangle OPQ$
$OP^2 = PQ^2 + QO^2$ [by pythagoras theorem]
$r^2 = R^2 + (h - r)^2$
$r^2 = R^2 + h^2 + r^2 - 2hr$
$R^2 = r^2 - h^2 - r^2 + 2hr$
$R^2 = 2hr - h^2$

$R = \sqrt{2hr - h^2}$

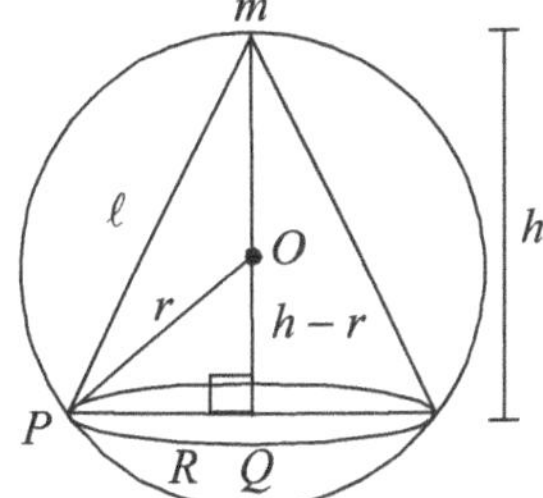

In $\triangle MPQ$,

$\ell^2 = R^2 + h^2$ [by pythagoras theorem]

$\ell^2 = (2hr - h^2) + h^2$

$\ell = \sqrt{2hr}$

C.S.A. of the cone $= \pi R \ell$

C.S.A. $= \pi(\sqrt{2hr - h^2})(\sqrt{2hr})$

Squaring both side, we have
$(CSA)^2 = \pi^2 (2hr - h^2)(2hr)$
$\qquad = 2\pi^2 hr\,(2hr - h^2)$
$\qquad = 2\pi^2 r\,(2h^2 r - h^3)$ **(1 Mark)**

42. **(d)** Objective function
$Z = ax + 2by$, where $a, b > 0$
Given: maximum Z occurs at $Q(3, 5)$ and $S(4, 1)$
Therefore,
max $Z(3, 5) =$ max. $Z(4, 1)$
$3a + 10b = 4a + 2b$
$4a - 3a + 2b - 10b = 0$
$a - 8b = 0$ **(1 Mark)**

43. **(a)** Given curves are
$y^2 = 4x$ ...(i)
and $xy = c$ ...(ii)
From (i)

$x = \dfrac{y^2}{4}$ put in eqn. (ii)

$\left(\dfrac{y^2}{4}\right)y = c \Rightarrow \dfrac{y^3}{4} = c$

$y^3 = 4c$ or $y = (4c)^{1/3}$
Put $y = (4c)^{1/3}$ in eqn. (i)

$$[(4c)^{1/3}]^2 = 4x \Rightarrow 4x = (4c)^{2/3} \Rightarrow x = \frac{(4c)^{2/3}}{4}$$

So both curves intersect at point $\left[\dfrac{(4c)^{2/3}}{4}, (4c)^{1/3}\right]$

Now, differentiating eqn. (i) w.r.t. x

$$2y\frac{dy}{dx} = 4 \Rightarrow \frac{dy}{dx} = \frac{4}{2y}$$

$$\left.\frac{dy}{dx}\right]_{\frac{(4c)^{2/3}}{4},\,(4c)^{1/3}} = \frac{4}{2(4c)^{1/3}} = \frac{2}{(4c)^{1/3}} \qquad \ldots(\text{say } m_1)$$

Differentiating eqn. (ii) w.r.t. x, we have

$$x\frac{dy}{dx} + y = 0 \Rightarrow \frac{dy}{dx} = \frac{-y}{x}$$

$$\left.\frac{dy}{dx}\right]_{\frac{(4c)^{2/3}}{4},\,(4c)^{1/3}} = \frac{-(4c)^{1/3}}{\dfrac{(4c)^{2/3}}{4}} = \frac{-4(4c)^{1/3}}{(4c)^{2/3}}$$

$$= -4(4c)^{1/3 - 2/3}$$

$$= -4(4c)^{-1/3} \text{ or } \frac{-4}{(4c)^{1/3}} \qquad \ldots(\text{say } m_2)$$

Curves (i) and (ii) cut at right angle
We must have

$$\frac{2}{(4c)^{1/3}} \times \frac{-4}{(4c)^{1/3}} = -1 \Rightarrow \frac{-8}{(4c)^{2/3}} = -1$$

$$\Rightarrow \quad 8 = (4c)^{2/3} \Rightarrow (4c)^{2/3} = 8 \Rightarrow 4c = 8^{3/2} \Rightarrow 4c = \sqrt{8 \times 8 \times 8}$$

$$\Rightarrow \quad 4c = 8\sqrt{8} \Rightarrow c = \frac{8\sqrt{8}}{4} \Rightarrow c = 2\sqrt{8}$$

$$\Rightarrow \quad c = 2 \times 2\sqrt{2} \Rightarrow c = 4\sqrt{2} \qquad \textbf{(1 Mark)}$$

44. **(d)** $X = \begin{bmatrix} 2 & 0 & 0 \\ 0 & 3 & 0 \\ 0 & 0 & 4 \end{bmatrix}$

$|X| = 2(12-0) + 0 + 0$
$= 24 \neq 0$ (This is singular matrix. So X^{-1} exist)

Now cofactor, $C = \begin{bmatrix} 12 & 0 & 0 \\ 0 & 8 & 0 \\ 0 & 0 & 6 \end{bmatrix}$

$$C^T = \begin{bmatrix} 12 & 0 & 0 \\ 0 & 8 & 0 \\ 0 & 0 & 6 \end{bmatrix}$$

$$\text{Adj } X \Rightarrow C^T = \begin{bmatrix} 12 & 0 & 0 \\ 0 & 8 & 0 \\ 0 & 0 & 6 \end{bmatrix}$$

Therefore,

$$X^{-1} = \frac{1}{|X|} \cdot \text{Adj } X$$

$$\frac{1}{24}\begin{bmatrix} 12 & 0 & 0 \\ 0 & 8 & 0 \\ 0 & 0 & 6 \end{bmatrix} \Rightarrow X^{-1} = \begin{bmatrix} 1/2 & 0 & 0 \\ 0 & 1/3 & 0 \\ 0 & 0 & 1/4 \end{bmatrix} \qquad \textbf{(1 Mark)}$$

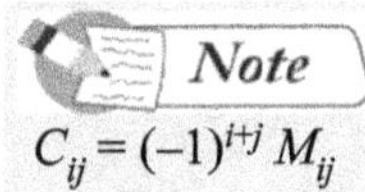

$C_{ij} = (-1)^{i+j} M_{ij}$

45. **(b)**

Corner points	Objective function $Z = 4x + 3y$
$O(0,0)$	$Z = 4 \times 0 + 3 \times 0 = 0$
$P(0,40)$	$Z = 4 \times 0 + 3 \times 40 \Rightarrow 0 + 120 = 120$
$Q(30,20)$	$Z = 4 \times 30 + 3 \times 20 \Rightarrow 120 + 60 = 180$
$R(40,0)$	$Z = 4 \times 40 + 3 \times 0 \Rightarrow 160 + 0 = 160$

Therefore for maximum value of $Z = 180$ at point $Q(30,20)$
(1 Mark)

46. **(b)** Total cost = Cost for space + Cost of digging
$C = \text{Area} \times \text{Rate} + 400 \times (\text{Depth})^2$

$$C = \frac{250}{h} \times 50 + 400 \times h^2$$

$$C = \frac{12500}{h} + 400h^2 \qquad \textbf{(1 Mark)}$$

47. **(c)** $\dfrac{dc}{dh} = \dfrac{-12500}{h^2} + 800h = 0$

$$\Rightarrow h^3 = \frac{125}{8} \Rightarrow h = \frac{5}{2} = 2.5 \text{ m} \qquad \textbf{(1 Mark)}$$

48. **(a)** $\dfrac{d^2c}{dh^2} = \dfrac{25000}{h^3} + 800$ **(1 Mark)**

49. **(d)** $\dfrac{d^2c}{dh^2} = \dfrac{25000 \times 8}{125} + 800 > 0$

$\therefore$ cost is minimum
Area of square plot

$$x^2 = \frac{250}{h} = \frac{250 \times 2}{5} = 100$$

$$x = 10 \text{ m} \qquad \textbf{(1 Mark)}$$

50. **(b)** Total minimum cost

$$= \frac{12500 \times 2}{5} + 400 \times \frac{25}{4}$$

$$= 5000 + 2500 = ₹ 7500 \qquad \textbf{(1 Mark)}$$

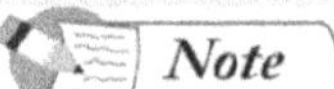

Constraints are the conditions of the problem expressed as simultaneous equations or inequalities.

CBSE Board Sample Paper Term-II

Time Allowed : 2 Hours   *Maximum Marks : 40*

General Instructions:

(i)   This question paper contains **three** sections – **A**, **B** and **C**. Each part is compulsory.

(ii) Section-**A** has **6** short answer type (SA1) questions of **2** marks each.

(iii) Section-**B** has **4** short answer type (SA2) questions of **3** marks each.

(iv) Section-**C** has **4** long answer type questions (LA) of **4** marks each.

(v)   There is an internal choice in some of the questions.

(vi) Question **14** is a case-based problem having **2** sub parts of **2** marks each.

SECTION - A

Question Nos. 1 to 6 carry 2 marks each.

1.   Find : $\int \dfrac{\log x}{(1 + \log x)^2}\, dx$

OR

Find : $\int \dfrac{\sin 2x}{\sqrt{9 - \cos^4 x}}\, dx$

2.   Write the sum of the order and the degree of the following differential equation:

$$\frac{d}{dx}\left(\frac{dy}{dx}\right) = 5$$

3.   If $\hat{a}$ and $\hat{b}$ are unit vectors, then prove that

$|\hat{a} + \hat{b}| = 2 \cos \dfrac{\theta}{2}$, where θ is the angle between them.

4.   Find the direction cosines of the following line:

$$\frac{3 - x}{-1} = \frac{2y - 1}{2} = \frac{z}{4}$$

5.   A bag contains 1 red and 3 white balls. Find the probability distribution of the number of red balls if 2 balls are drawn at random from the bag one-by-one without replacement.

6.   Two cards are drawn at random from a pack of 52 cards one-by-one without replacement. What is the probability of getting first card red and second card jack?

SECTION - B

Question Nos. 7 to 10 carry 3 marks each.

7.   Find : $\int \dfrac{x + 1}{(x^2 + 1)x}\, dx$

8.   Find the general solution of the following differential equation:

$$x\frac{dy}{dx} = y - x \sin\left(\frac{y}{x}\right)$$

OR

Find the particular solution of the following differential equation, given that $y = 0$ when $x = \dfrac{\pi}{4}$:

$$\frac{dy}{dx} + y \cot x = \frac{2}{1 + \sin x}$$

9.   If $\vec{a} \neq \vec{0}, \vec{a} \cdot \vec{b} = \vec{a} \cdot \vec{c}, \vec{a} \times \vec{b} = \vec{a} \times \vec{c}$, then show that $\vec{b} = \vec{c}$.

10. Find the shortest distance between the following lines:

$$\vec{r} = (\hat{i} + \hat{j} - \hat{k}) + s(2\hat{i} + \hat{j} + \hat{k})$$

$$\vec{r} = (\hat{i} + \hat{j} + 2\hat{k}) + t(4\hat{i} + 2\hat{j} + 2\hat{k})$$

OR

Find the vector and the cartesian equations of the plane containing the point $\hat{i} + 2\hat{j} - \hat{k}$ and parallel to the lines

$$\vec{r} = (\hat{i} + 2\hat{j} + 2\hat{k}) + s(2\hat{i} - 3\hat{j} + 2\hat{k}) \text{ and}$$

$$\vec{r} = (3\hat{i} + \hat{j} - 2\hat{k}) + t(\hat{i} - 3\hat{j} + \hat{k})$$

SECTION - C

Question Nos. 11 to 14 carry 4 marks each.

11. Evaluate: $\displaystyle\int_{-1}^{2} |x^3 - 3x^2 + 2x|\, dx$

12. Using integration, find the area of the region in the first quadrant enclosed by the line $x + y = 2$, the parabola $y^2 = x$ and the x-axis.

OR

Using integration, find the area of the region

$$\{(x, y) : 0 \le y \le \sqrt{3}x,\ x^2 + y^2 \le 4\}$$

13. Find the foot of the perpendicular from the point $(1, 2, 0)$ upon the plane $x - 3y + 2z = 9$. Hence, find the distance of the point $(1, 2, 0)$ from the given plane.

Case-Based/Data-Based:

14.

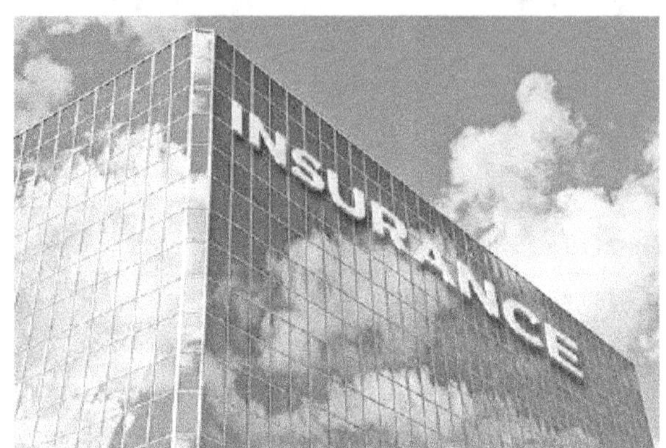

An insurance company believes that people can be divided into two classes: those who are accident prone and those who are not. The company's statistics show that an accident-prone person will have an accident at sometime within a fixed one-year period with probability 0.6, whereas this probability is 0.2 for a person who is not accident prone. The company knows that 20 percent of the population is accident prone.

Based on the above information, answer the following questions

(a) What is the probability that a new policyholder will have an accident within a year of purchasing a policy?

(b) Suppose that a new policyholder has an accident within a year of purchasing a policy. What is the probability that he or she is accident prone?

Solutions

1. $\int \dfrac{\log x}{(1+\log x)^2}\,dx = \int \dfrac{\log x + 1 - 1}{(1+\log x)^2}\,dx$

$= \int \dfrac{1}{1+\log x}\,dx - \int \dfrac{1}{(1+\log x)^2}\,dx$ **(½ Mark)**

By using by parts formula

$= \dfrac{1}{1+\log x}\times x - \int \dfrac{-1}{(1+\log x)^2}\times \dfrac{1}{x}\times x\,dx - \int \dfrac{1}{(1+\log x)^2}\,dx$

$= \dfrac{x}{1+\log x} + c$ **(1 + ½ Mark)**

OR

Put $\cos^2 x = t \Rightarrow -2\cos x \sin x\,dx = dt \Rightarrow \sin 2x\,dx = -dt$ **(1 Mark)**

The given integral

$= -\int \dfrac{dt}{\sqrt{3^2 - t^2}} = -\sin^{-1}\dfrac{t}{3} + c$

$= -\sin^{-1}\dfrac{\cos^2 x}{3} + c$ **(1 Mark)**

2. Order $= 2$ **(1 Mark)**
Degree $= 1$ **(½ Mark)**
Sum $= 3$ **(½ Mark)**

3. $(\hat{a}+\hat{b}).(\hat{a}+\hat{b}) = |\hat{a}|^2 + |\hat{b}|^2 + 2(\hat{a}.\hat{b})$ **(1 Mark)**

$|\hat{a}+\hat{b}|^2 = 1+1+2\cos\theta$

$= 2(1+\cos\theta) = 4\cos^2\dfrac{\theta}{2}$ **(½ Mark)**

$\therefore\ |\hat{a}+\hat{b}| = 2\cos\dfrac{\theta}{2}$ **(½ Mark)**

4. The given line is

$\Rightarrow \dfrac{x-3}{1} = \dfrac{y-\frac{1}{2}}{1} = \dfrac{z}{4}$ **(1 Mark)**

Its direction ratios are $<1, 1, 4>$ **(½ Mark)**
Its direction cosines are

$\Rightarrow \left(\dfrac{1}{3\sqrt{2}}, \dfrac{1}{3\sqrt{2}}, \dfrac{4}{3\sqrt{2}}\right)$ **(½ Mark)**

5. Let X be the random variable defined as the number of red balls.
Then $X = 0, 1$ **(½ Mark)**

$P(X=0) = \dfrac{3}{4}\times\dfrac{2}{3} = \dfrac{6}{12} = \dfrac{1}{2}$ **(½ Mark)**

$P(X=1) = \dfrac{1}{4}\times\dfrac{3}{3} + \dfrac{3}{4}\times\dfrac{1}{3} = \dfrac{6}{12} = \dfrac{1}{2}$ **(½ Mark)**

Probability distribution table :

X	0	1
$P(X)$	$\dfrac{1}{2}$	$\dfrac{1}{2}$

(½ Mark)

6. The required probability $=$ P((The first is a red jack card and the second is a jack card) or (The first is a red non-jack card and the second is a jack card)) **(1 Mark)**

$= \dfrac{2}{52}\times\dfrac{3}{51} + \dfrac{24}{52}\times\dfrac{4}{51} = \dfrac{1}{26}$ **(1 Mark)**

7. Let $\dfrac{x+1}{(x^2+1)x} = \dfrac{Ax+B}{x^2+1} + \dfrac{C}{x} = \dfrac{(Ax+B)x + C(x^2+1)}{(x^2+1)x}$ **(½ Mark)**

$\Rightarrow\ x+1 = (Ax+B)x + C(x^2+1)$ (An identity)

Equating the coefficients, we get
$B = 1, C = 1, A + C = 0$

Hence, $A = -1, B = 1, C = 1$ **(½ Mark)**

The given integral

$= \int \dfrac{-x+1}{x^2+1}\,dx + \int \dfrac{1}{x}\,dx$

$= \dfrac{-1}{2}\int \dfrac{2x-2}{x^2+1}\,dx + \int \dfrac{1}{x}\,dx$ **(½ Mark)**

$= \dfrac{-1}{2}\int \dfrac{2x}{x^2+1}\,dx + \int \dfrac{1}{x^2+1}\,dx + \int \dfrac{1}{x}\,dx$

$= \dfrac{-1}{2}\log(x^2+1) + \tan^{-1}x + \log|x| + c$ **(1 + ½ Mark)**

8. We have the differential equation :
$\dfrac{dy}{dx} = \dfrac{y}{x} - \sin\left(\dfrac{y}{x}\right)$

The equation is a homogeneous differential equation.

Putting $y = vx \Rightarrow \dfrac{dy}{dx} = v + x\dfrac{dv}{dx}$ **(1 Mark)**

The differential equation becomes $v + x\dfrac{dv}{dx} = v - \sin v$

$\Rightarrow\ \dfrac{dv}{\sin v} = -\dfrac{dx}{x} \Rightarrow\ \operatorname{cosec} v\,dv = -\dfrac{dx}{x}$ **(½ Mark)**

Integrating both sides, we get

$\Rightarrow\ \log|\operatorname{cosec} v - \cot v| = -\log|x| + \log K, K > 0$ **(1 Mark)**

(Here, $\log K$ is an arbitrary constant)

$\Rightarrow \quad \log\left|(\operatorname{cosec} v - \cot v)x\right| = \log K$

$\Rightarrow \quad \left|(\operatorname{cosec} v - \cot v)x\right| = K$

$\Rightarrow \quad (\operatorname{cosec} v - \cot v)x = \pm K$

$\Rightarrow \quad \left(\operatorname{cosec}\dfrac{y}{x} - \cot\dfrac{y}{x}\right)x = C,$ which is the rerquired

general solution.   **(½ Mark)**

OR

The differential equation is a linear differential equation

$IF = e^{\int \cot x\, dx} = e^{\log \sin x} = \sin x$ **(1 Mark)**

The general solution is given by

$y\sin x = \int 2\dfrac{\sin x}{1+\sin x}dx$ **(½ Mark)**

$\Rightarrow \quad y\sin x = 2\int \dfrac{\sin x+1-1}{1+\sin x}dx = 2\int\left[1-\dfrac{1}{1+\sin x}\right]dx$

$\Rightarrow \quad y\sin x = 2\int\left[1-\dfrac{1}{1+\cos\left(\dfrac{\pi}{2}-x\right)}\right]dx$

$\Rightarrow \quad y\sin x = 2\int\left[1-\dfrac{1}{2\cos^2\left(\dfrac{\pi}{4}-\dfrac{x}{2}\right)}\right]dx$

$\Rightarrow \quad y\sin x = 2\int\left[1-\dfrac{1}{2}\sec^2\left(\dfrac{\pi}{4}-\dfrac{x}{2}\right)\right]dx$

$\Rightarrow \quad y\sin x = 2\left[x+\tan\left(\dfrac{\pi}{4}-\dfrac{x}{2}\right)\right]+c$ **(1 Mark)**

Given that $y = 0$, when $x = \dfrac{\pi}{4}$,

Hence, $0 = 2\left[\dfrac{\pi}{4}+\tan\dfrac{\pi}{8}\right]+c$

$\Rightarrow \quad c = -\dfrac{\pi}{2} - 2\tan\dfrac{\pi}{8}$

Hence, the particular solution is

$y = \operatorname{cosec} x\left[2\left\{x+\tan\left(\dfrac{\pi}{4}-\dfrac{x}{2}\right)\right\}-\left(\dfrac{\pi}{2}+2\tan\dfrac{\pi}{8}\right)\right]$

(½ Mark)

9. We have $\vec{a}.(\vec{b}-\vec{c}) = 0$

$\Rightarrow \quad (\vec{b}-\vec{c}) = \vec{0}$ or $\vec{a} \perp (\vec{b}-\vec{c})$

$\Rightarrow \quad \vec{b} = \vec{c}$ or $\vec{a} \perp (\vec{b}-\vec{c})$ **(1 Mark)**

Also, $\vec{a} \times (\vec{b}-\vec{c}) = \vec{0}$

$\Rightarrow \quad (\vec{b}-\vec{c}) = \vec{0}$ or $\vec{a} \parallel (\vec{b}-\vec{c})$

$\Rightarrow \quad \vec{b} = \vec{c}$ or $\vec{a} \parallel (\vec{b}-\vec{c})$ **(1 Mark)**

$\vec{a}$ can not be both perpendicular to $(\vec{b}-\vec{c})$ and parallel to $(\vec{b}-\vec{c})$

Hence, $\vec{b} = \vec{c}$ **(1 Mark)**

10. Here, the lines are parallel. The shortest distance

$= \dfrac{\left|(\overrightarrow{a_2}-\overrightarrow{a_1})\times\vec{b}\right|}{\left|\vec{b}\right|}$

$= \dfrac{\left|(3\hat{k})\times(2\hat{i}+\hat{j}+\hat{k})\right|}{\sqrt{4+1+1}}$ **(1 + ½ Mark)**

$(3\vec{k})\times(2\hat{i}+\hat{j}+\hat{k}) = \begin{vmatrix} \hat{i} & \hat{j} & \hat{k} \\ 0 & 0 & 3 \\ 1 & 2 & 1 \end{vmatrix} = -3\hat{i}+6\hat{j}$ **(1 Mark)**

Hence, the required shortest distance $= \dfrac{3\sqrt{5}}{\sqrt{6}}$ units

(½ Mark)

OR

Since, the plane is parallel to the given lines, the cross product of the vectors $2\hat{i}-3\hat{j}+2\hat{k}$ and $\hat{i}-3\hat{j}+\hat{k}$ will be a normal to the plane

$(2\hat{i}-3\hat{j}+\hat{k})\times(\hat{i}-3\hat{j}+\hat{k}) = \begin{vmatrix} 1 & 1 & \hat{k} \\ 2 & -3 & 2 \\ 1 & -3 & 1 \end{vmatrix} = 3i-3\hat{k}$

(1 Mark)

The vector equation of the plane is

$\vec{r}.(3\hat{i}-3\hat{k}) = (i+2\hat{j}-\hat{k}).(3\hat{i}-3\hat{k})$

or $\quad \vec{r}.(\hat{i}-\hat{k}) = 2$ **(1 Mark)**

and the cartessian equation of the plane is $x - z - 2 = 0$

(1 Mark)

11. The given definite integral

$= \displaystyle\int_{-1}^{2} |x(x-1)(x-2)|\,dx$

$= \displaystyle\int_{-1}^{0} |x(x-1)(x-2)|dx + \int_{0}^{1} |x(x-1)(x-2)|dx$

$\qquad\qquad + \displaystyle\int_{1}^{2} |x(x-1)(x-2)|dx$ **(1 + ½ Mark)**

$= -\displaystyle\int_{-1}^{0} (x^3 - 3x^2 + 2x)dx + \int_{0}^{1}(x^3 - 3x^2 + 2x)dx$

$\qquad\qquad -\displaystyle\int_{1}^{2}(x^3 - 3x^2 + 2x)dx$ **(½ Mark)**

$= -\left[\dfrac{x^4}{4} - x^3 + x^2\right]_{-1}^{0} + \left[\dfrac{x^4}{4} - x^3 + x^2\right]_{0}^{1} - \left[\dfrac{x^4}{4} - x^3 + x^2\right]_{1}^{2}$

$= \dfrac{9}{4} + \dfrac{1}{4} + \dfrac{1}{4} = \dfrac{11}{4}$ **(2 Marks)**

12. Solving $x + y = 2$ and $y^2 = x$ simultaneously, we get the points of intersection as $(1, 1)$ and $(4, -2)$. **(1 Mark)**

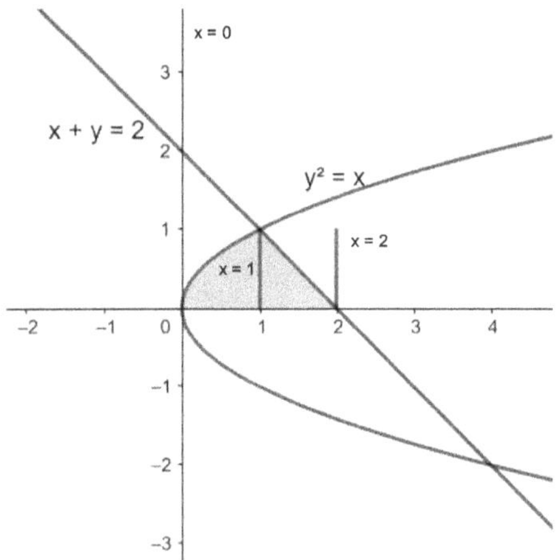

The required area = the shaded area

$$= \int_0^1 \sqrt{x}\, dx + \int_1^2 (2 - x)\, dx \qquad \textbf{(1 Mark)}$$

$$= \frac{2}{3}[x^{\frac{3}{2}}]_0^1 + \left[2x - \frac{x^2}{2} \right]_1^2 \qquad \textbf{(1 Mark)}$$

$$= \frac{2}{3} + \frac{1}{2} = \frac{7}{6} \text{ square units} \qquad \textbf{(1 Mark)}$$

OR

Solving $y = \sqrt{3}x$ and $x^2 + y^2 = 4$, we get the points of intersection as $(1, \sqrt{3})$ and $(-1, -\sqrt{3})$ **(1 Mark)**

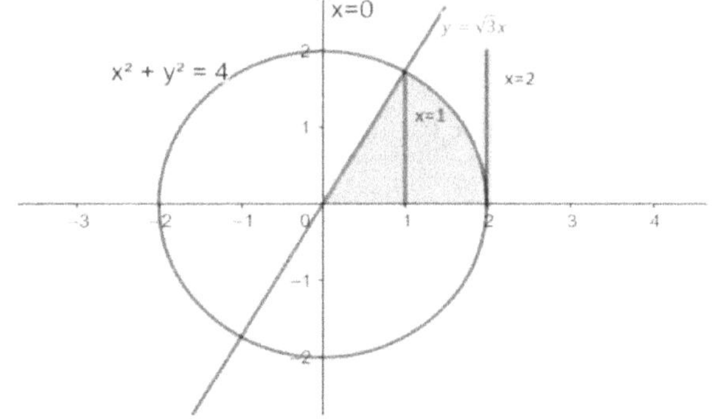

The required area = the shaded are

$$= \int_0^1 \sqrt{3}x\, dx + \int_1^2 \sqrt{4 - x^2}\, dx \qquad \textbf{(1 Mark)}$$

$$= \frac{\sqrt{3}}{2}[x^2]_0^1 + \frac{1}{2}\left[x\sqrt{4 - x^2} + 4\sin^{-1}\frac{x}{2} \right]_1^2 \qquad \textbf{(1 Mark)}$$

$$= \frac{\sqrt{3}}{2} + \frac{1}{2}\left[2\pi - \sqrt{3} - 2\frac{\pi}{3} \right]$$

$$= \frac{2\pi}{3} \text{ square units} \qquad \textbf{(1 Mark)}$$

13. The equation of the line perpendicular to the plane and passing through the point $(1, 2, 0)$ is

$$\frac{x - 1}{1} = \frac{y - 2}{-3} = \frac{z}{2} \qquad \textbf{(1 Mark)}$$

The coordinates of the foot of the perpendicular are $(\mu + 1, -3\mu + 2, 2\mu)$ for some μ

These coordinates will satisfy the equation of the plane.
Hence, we have $\mu + 1 - 3(-3\mu + 2) + 2(2\mu) = 9$
                                          (½ Mark)
$\Rightarrow \mu = 1$ **(1 Mark)**

The foot of the perpendicular is $(2, -1, 2)$. **(½ Mark)**
Hence, the required distance

$$= \sqrt{(1 - 2)^2 + (2 + 1)^2 + (0 - 2)^2} = \sqrt{14} \ units \qquad \textbf{(1 Mark)}$$

14. Let E_1 = The policy holder is accident prone.

E_2 = The policy holder is not accident prone.

E = The new policy holder has an accident within a year of purchasing a policy.

(i) $P(E) = P(E_1) \times P(E/E_1) + P(E_2) \times P(E/E_2)$ **(1 Mark)**

$$= \frac{20}{100} \times \frac{6}{10} + \frac{80}{100} \times \frac{2}{10} = \frac{7}{25} \qquad \textbf{(1 Mark)}$$

(ii) By Bayes' Theorem,

$$P(E_1/E) = \frac{P(E_1) \times P(E/E_1)}{P(E)} \qquad \textbf{(1 Mark)}$$

$$= \frac{\dfrac{20}{100} \times \dfrac{6}{10}}{\dfrac{280}{1000}} = \frac{3}{7} \qquad \textbf{(1 Mark)}$$

CBSE Board Sample Paper Term-I

Time Allowed : 90 Minutes   *Maximum Marks : 40*

General Instructions:

(i)   This question paper contains three sections – **A**, **B** and **C**. Each part is compulsory.

(ii) Section-**A** has **20** MCQs, attempt any **16** out of **20**.

(iii) Section-**B** has **20** MCQs, attempt any **16** out of **20**.

(iv) Section-**C** has **10** MCQs, attempt any **8** out of **10**.

(v)   All questions carry equal marks.

(vi) There is no negative marking.

SECTION - A

*In this section, attempt **any 16** questions out of questions 1-20. Each question is of 1 mark weightage.*

1. $\sin\left[\dfrac{\pi}{3} - \sin^{-1}\left(-\dfrac{1}{2}\right)\right]$ is equal to

(a) $\dfrac{1}{2}$ (b) $\dfrac{1}{3}$ (c) -1 (d) 1

2. The value of k ($k < 0$) for which the function f defined as

$$f(x) = \begin{cases} \dfrac{1-\cos kx}{x\sin x} & , x \neq 0 \\ \dfrac{1}{2} & , x = 0 \end{cases}$$

is continuous at $x = 0$ is:

(a) ± 1 (b) -1 (c) $\pm\dfrac{1}{2}$ (d) $\dfrac{1}{2}$

3. If $A = [a_{ij}]$ is a square matrix of order 2 such that $a_{ij} = \begin{cases} 1, & \text{when } i \neq j \\ 0, & \text{when } i = j \end{cases}$, then A^2 is:

(a) $\begin{bmatrix} 1 & 0 \\ 1 & 0 \end{bmatrix}$ (b) $\begin{bmatrix} 1 & 1 \\ 0 & 0 \end{bmatrix}$ (c) $\begin{bmatrix} 1 & 1 \\ 1 & 0 \end{bmatrix}$ (d) $\begin{bmatrix} 1 & 0 \\ 0 & 1 \end{bmatrix}$

4. Value of k, for which $A = \begin{bmatrix} k & 8 \\ 4 & 2k \end{bmatrix}$ is a singular matrix is:

(a) 4 (b) -4 (c) ± 4 (d) 0

5. Find the intervals in which the function f given by $f(x) = x^2 - 4x + 6$ is strictly increasing:

(a) $(-\infty, 2) \cup (2, \infty)$ (b) $(2, \infty)$
(c) $(-\infty, 2)$ (d) $(-\infty, 2] \cup (2, \infty)$

6. Given that A is a square matrix of order 3 and $|A| = -4$, then $|\text{adj } A|$ is equal to:

(a) -4 (b) 4 (c) -16 (d) 16

7. A relation R in set A = {1,2,3} is defined as R = {(1, 1), (1, 2), (2, 2), (3, 3)}. Which of the following ordered pair in R shall be removed to make it an equivalence relation in A?

(a) $(1,1)$ (b) $(1,2)$ (c) $(2,2)$ (d) $(3,3)$

8. If $\begin{bmatrix} 2a+b & a-2b \\ 5c-d & 4c+3d \end{bmatrix} = \begin{bmatrix} 4 & -3 \\ 11 & 24 \end{bmatrix}$, then value of $a + b - c + 2d$ is:

(a) 8 (b) 10 (c) 4 (d) -8

9. The point at which the normal to the curve $y = x + \dfrac{1}{x}, x > 0$ is perpendicular to the line $3x - 4y - 7 = 0$ is:

(a) $(2, 5/2)$ (b) $(\pm 2, 5/2)$
(c) $(-1/2, 5/2)$ (d) $(1/2, 5/2)$

10. $\sin(\tan^{-1}x)$, where $|x| < 1$, is equal to:

(a) $\dfrac{x}{\sqrt{1-x^2}}$ (b) $\dfrac{1}{\sqrt{1-x^2}}$

(c) $\dfrac{1}{\sqrt{1+x^2}}$ (d) $\dfrac{x}{\sqrt{1+x^2}}$

11. Let the relation R in the set A = {$x \in Z : 0 \leq x \leq 12$}, given by R = {(a, b) : |a – b| is a multiple of 4}. Then [1], the equivalence class containing 1, is:

(a) $\{1, 5, 9\}$ (b) $\{0, 1, 2, 5\}$
(c) ϕ (d) A

12. If $e^x + e^y = e^{x+y}$, then $\dfrac{dy}{dx}$ is:

  (a)　e^{y-x}　　(b)　e^{x+y}　　(c)　$-e^{y-x}$　　(d)　$2e^{x-y}$

13. Given that matrices A and B are of order $3 \times n$ and $m \times 5$ respectively, then the order of matrix $C = 5A + 3B$ is:

  (a)　3×5 and $m = n$　　　　(b)　3×5

  (c)　3×3　　　　　　　　　(d)　5×5

14. If $y = 5 \cos x - 3 \sin x$, then $\dfrac{d^2 y}{dx^2}$ is equal to:

  (a)　$-y$　　(b)　y　　(c)　$25\,y$　　(d)　$9\,y$

15. For matrix $A = \begin{bmatrix} 2 & 5 \\ -11 & 7 \end{bmatrix}$, $(adj\ A)'$ is equal to :

  (a)　$\begin{bmatrix} -2 & -5 \\ 11 & -7 \end{bmatrix}$　　　　(b)　$\begin{bmatrix} 7 & 5 \\ 11 & 2 \end{bmatrix}$

  (c)　$\begin{bmatrix} 7 & 11 \\ -5 & 2 \end{bmatrix}$　　　　(d)　$\begin{bmatrix} 7 & -5 \\ 11 & 2 \end{bmatrix}$

16. The points on the curve $\dfrac{x^2}{9} + \dfrac{y^2}{16} = 1$ at which the tangents are parallel to y-axis are:

  (a)　$(0, \pm 4)$　(b)　$(\pm 4, 0)$　(c)　$(\pm 3, 0)$　(d)　$(0, \pm 3)$

17. Given that $A = [a_{ij}]$ is a square matrix of order 3×3 and $|A| = -7$, then the value of $\sum_{i=1}^{3} a_{i2} A_{i2}$, where A_{ij} denotes the cofactor of element a_{ij} is:

  (a)　7　　(b)　-7　　(c)　0　　(d)　49

18. If $y = \log(\cos e^x)$, then $\dfrac{dy}{dx}$ is :

  (a)　$\cos e^{x-1}$　　　　　　(b)　$e^{-x} \cos e^x$

  (c)　$e^x \sin e^x$　　　　　　(d)　$-e^x \tan e^x$

19. Based on the given shaded region as the feasible region in the graph, at which point(s) is the objective function $Z = 3x + 9y$ maximum?

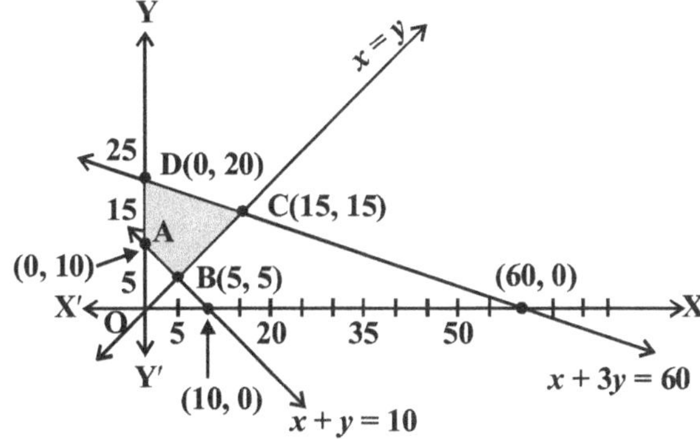

  (a)　Point B

  (b)　Point C

  (c)　Point D

  (d)　every point on the line segment CD

20. The least value of the function $f(x) = 2\cos x + x$ in the closed interval $\left[0, \dfrac{\pi}{2}\right]$ is :

  (a)　2　　　　　(b)　$\dfrac{\pi}{6} + \sqrt{3}$

  (c)　$\dfrac{\pi}{2}$　　　　　(d)　The least value does not exist.

SECTION - B

*In this section, attempt **any 16** questions out of the questions 21-40. Each question is of 1 mark weightage.*

21. The function $f : R \to R$ defined as $f(x) = x^3$ is:

  (a)　One-one but not onto

  (b)　Not one-one but onto

  (c)　Neither one-one nor onto

  (d)　One-one and onto

22. If $x = a \sec \theta$, $y = b \tan \theta$, then $\dfrac{d^2 y}{dx^2}$ at $\theta = \dfrac{\pi}{6}$ is :

  (a)　$\dfrac{-3\sqrt{3}b}{a^2}$　(b)　$\dfrac{-2\sqrt{3}b}{a}$　(c)　$\dfrac{-3\sqrt{3}b}{a}$　(d)　$\dfrac{-b}{3\sqrt{3}a^2}$

23. In the given graph, the feasible region for a LPP is shaded. The objective function $Z = 2x - 3y$, will be minimum at:

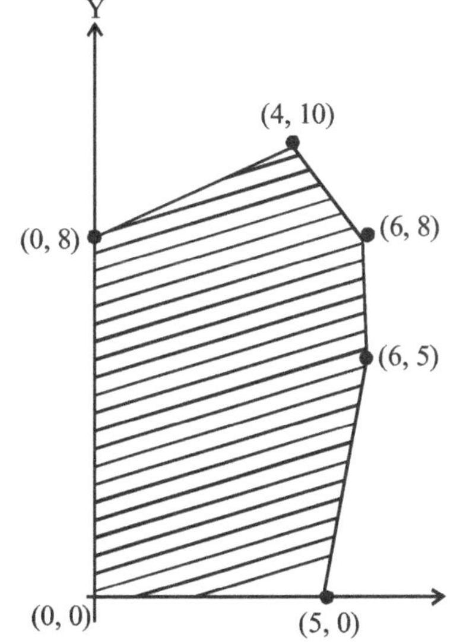

  (a)　(4, 10)　　　　　　(b)　(6, 8)

  (c)　(0, 8)　　　　　　(d)　(6, 5)

24. The derivative of $\sin^{-1}(2x\sqrt{1-x^2})$ w.r.t $\sin^{-1} x$, $\dfrac{1}{\sqrt{2}} < x < 1$, is

  (a)　2　　(b)　$\dfrac{\pi}{2} - 2$　　(c)　$\dfrac{\pi}{2}$　　(d)　-2

25. If $A = \begin{bmatrix} 1 & -1 & 0 \\ 2 & 3 & 4 \\ 0 & 1 & 2 \end{bmatrix}$ and $B = \begin{bmatrix} 2 & 2 & -4 \\ -4 & 2 & -4 \\ 2 & -1 & 5 \end{bmatrix}$, then :

  (a) $A^{-1} = B$ (b) $A^{-1} = 6B$

  (c) $B^{-1} = B$ (d) $B^{-1} = \dfrac{1}{6}A$

26. The real function $f(x) = 2x^3 - 3x^2 - 36x + 7$ is:

  (a) Strictly increasing in $(-\infty, -2)$ and strictly decreasing in $(-2, \infty)$

  (b) Strictly decreasing in $(-2, 3)$

  (c) Strictly decreasing in $(-\infty, 3)$ and strictly increasing in $(3, \infty)$

  (d) Strictly decreasing in $(-\infty, -2) \cup (3, \infty)$

27. Simplest form of $\tan^{-1}\left(\dfrac{\sqrt{1+\cos x} + \sqrt{1-\cos x}}{\sqrt{1+\cos x} - \sqrt{1-\cos x}}\right)$,

$\pi < x < \dfrac{3\pi}{2}$ is

  (a) $\dfrac{\pi}{4} - \dfrac{x}{2}$ (b) $\dfrac{3\pi}{2} - \dfrac{x}{2}$

  (c) $-\dfrac{x}{2}$ (d) $\pi - \dfrac{x}{2}$

28. Given that A is a non-singular matrix of order 3 such that $A^2 = 2A$, then value of $|2A|$ is:

  (a) 4   (b) 8   (c) 64   (d) 16

29. The value of b for which the function $f(x) = x + \cos x + b$ is strictly decreasing over R is:

  (a) $b < 1$ (b) No value of b exists

  (c) $b \leq 1$ (d) $b \geq 1$

30. Let R be the relation in the set N given by $R = \{(a, b) : a = b - 2, b > 6\}$, then

  (a) $(2, 4) \in R$ (b) $(3, 8) \in R$

  (c) $(6, 8) \in R$ (d) $(8, 7) \in R$

31. The point(s), at which the function f given by

$$f(x) = \begin{cases} \dfrac{x}{|x|}, & x < 0 \\ -1, & x \geq 0 \end{cases}$$ is continuous, is/are :

  (a) $x \in R$ (b) $x = 0$

  (c) $x \in R - \{0\}$ (d) $x = -1$ and 1

32. If $A = \begin{bmatrix} 0 & 2 \\ 3 & -4 \end{bmatrix}$ and $kA = \begin{bmatrix} 0 & 3a \\ 2b & 24 \end{bmatrix}$, then the values of

k, a and b respectively are:

  (a) $-6, -12, -18$ (b) $-6, -4, -9$

  (c) $-6, 4, 9$ (d) $-6, 12, 18$

33. A linear programming problem is as follows:

  Minimize $Z = 30x + 50y$ subject to the constraints,

$$3x + 5y \geq 15$$
$$2x + 3y \leq 18$$
$$x \geq 0, y \geq 0$$

  In the feasible region, the minimum value of Z occurs at

  (a) a unique point   (b) no point

  (c) infinitely many points   (d) two points only

34. The area of a trapezium is defined by function f and given by $f(x) = (10 + x)\sqrt{100 - x^2}$, then the area when it is maximised is :

  (a) 75 cm^2 (b) $7\sqrt{3}$ cm^2

  (c) $75\sqrt{3}$ cm^2 (d) 5 cm^2

35. If A is square matrix such that $A^2 = A$, then $(I + A)^3 - 7A$ is equal to

  (a) A   (b) $I + A$ (c) $I - A$ (d) I

36. If $\tan^{-1} x = y$, then :

  (a) $-1 < y < 1$ (b) $\dfrac{-\pi}{2} \leq y \leq \dfrac{\pi}{2}$

  (c) $\dfrac{-\pi}{2} < y < \dfrac{\pi}{2}$ (d) $y \in \left\{\dfrac{-\pi}{2}, \dfrac{\pi}{2}\right\}$

37. Let $A = \{1, 2, 3\}$, $B = \{4, 5, 6, 7\}$ and let $f = \{(1, 4), (2, 5), (3, 6)\}$ be a function from A to B. Based on the given information, f is best defined as:

  (a) Surjective function   (b) Injective function

  (c) Bijective function   (d) Function

38. For $A = \begin{bmatrix} 3 & 1 \\ -1 & 2 \end{bmatrix}$, then $14\,A^{-1}$ is given by :

  (a) $14\begin{bmatrix} 2 & -1 \\ 1 & 3 \end{bmatrix}$ (b) $\begin{bmatrix} 4 & -2 \\ 2 & 6 \end{bmatrix}$

  (c) $2\begin{bmatrix} 2 & -1 \\ 1 & -3 \end{bmatrix}$ (d) $2\begin{bmatrix} -3 & -1 \\ 1 & -2 \end{bmatrix}$

39. The point(s) on the curve $y = x^3 - 11x + 5$ at which the tangent is $y = x - 11$ is/are:

  (a) $(-2, 19)$ (b) $(2, -9)$

  (c) $(\pm 2, 19)$ (d) $(-2, 19)$ and $(2, -9)$

40. Given that $A = \begin{bmatrix} \alpha & \beta \\ \gamma & -\alpha \end{bmatrix}$ and $A^2 = 3I$, then

  (a) $1 + \alpha^2 + \beta\gamma = 0$ (b) $1 - \alpha^2 - \beta\gamma = 0$

  (c) $3 - \alpha^2 - \beta\gamma = 0$ (d) $3 + \alpha^2 + \beta\gamma = 0$

SECTION - C

*In this section, attempt **any 8** questions. Each question is of 1 mark weightage. Questions 46-50 are based on a case-study.*

41. For an objective function $Z = ax + by$, where $a, b > 0$; the corner points of the feasible region determined by a set of constraints (linear inequalities) are $(0, 20)$, $(10, 10)$, $(30, 30)$ and $(0, 40)$. The condition on a and b such that the maximum Z occurs at both the points $(30, 30)$ and $(0, 40)$ is:

(a) $b - 3a = 0$ (b) $a = 3b$

(c) $a + 2b = 0$ (d) $2a - b = 0$

42. For which value of m is the line $y = mx + 1$ a tangent to the curve $y^2 = 4x$?

(a) $\dfrac{1}{2}$ (b) 1 (c) 2 (d) 3

43. The maximum value of $\left[x(x-1) + 1 \right]^{1/3}, 0 \le x \le 1$ is

(a) 0 (b) $\dfrac{1}{2}$ (c) 1 (d) $\sqrt[3]{\dfrac{1}{3}}$

44. In a linear programming problem, the constraints on the decision variables x and y are $x - 3y \ge 0$, $y \ge 0$, $0 \le x \le 3$. The feasible region

(a) is not in the first quadrant

(b) is bounded in the first quadrant

(c) is unbounded in the first quadrant

(d) does not exist

45. Let $A = \begin{bmatrix} 1 & \sin\alpha & 1 \\ -\sin\alpha & 1 & \sin\alpha \\ -1 & -\sin\alpha & 1 \end{bmatrix}$, where $0 \le \alpha \le 2\pi$, then

(a) $|A| = 0$ (b) $|A| \in (2, \infty)$

(c) $|A| \in (2, 4)$ (d) $|A| \in [2, 4]$

Case Study

The fuel cost per hour for running a train is proportional to the square of the speed it generates in km per hour. If the fuel costs ₹ 48 per hour at speed 16 km per hour and the fixed charges to run the train amount to ₹ 1200 per hour.
Assume the speed of the train as υ km/h.

Based on the given information, answer the following questions.

46. Given that the fuel cost per hour is k times the square of the speed the train generates in km/h, the value of k is:

(a) $\dfrac{16}{3}$ (b) $\dfrac{1}{3}$ (c) 3 (d) $\dfrac{3}{16}$

47. If the train has travelled a distance of 500 km, then the total cost of running the train is given by function:

(a) $\dfrac{15}{16}\upsilon + \dfrac{600000}{\upsilon}$ (b) $\dfrac{375}{4}\upsilon + \dfrac{600000}{\upsilon}$

(c) $\dfrac{5}{16}\upsilon^2 + \dfrac{150000}{\upsilon}$ (d) $\dfrac{3}{16}\upsilon + \dfrac{6000}{\upsilon}$

48. The most economical speed to run the train is:

(a) 18 km/h (b) 5 km/h (c) 80 km/h (d) 40 km/h

49. The fuel cost for the train to travel 500 km at the most economical speed is:

(a) ₹ 3750   (b) ₹ 750

(c) ₹ 7500   (d) ₹ 75000

50. The total cost of the train to travel 500 km at the most economical speed is:

(a) ₹ 3750   (b) ₹ 75000

(c) ₹ 7500   (d) ₹ 15000

Solutions

1. (d) $\sin\left(\dfrac{\pi}{3} - \left(\dfrac{-\pi}{6}\right)\right) = \sin\left(\dfrac{\pi}{2}\right) = 1$

2. (b) $\lim_{x\to 0} f(x) = \lim_{x\to 0}\left(\dfrac{1 - \cos kx}{x\sin x}\right) = \dfrac{1}{2}$

$\Rightarrow \lim_{x\to 0}\left(\dfrac{2\sin^2 \frac{kx}{2}}{x\sin x}\right) = \dfrac{1}{2}$

$\Rightarrow \lim_{x\to 0} 2\left(\dfrac{k}{2}\right)^2 \left(\dfrac{\sin\frac{kx}{2}}{\frac{kx}{2}}\right)^2 \left(\dfrac{x}{\sin x}\right) = \dfrac{k^2}{2}$

and $f(0) = \dfrac{1}{2}$

$\Rightarrow k^2 = 1 \Rightarrow k = \pm 1$ but $k < 0 \Rightarrow k = -1$

3. (d) $A = \begin{bmatrix} 1 & 0 \\ 0 & 1 \end{bmatrix} \Rightarrow A^2 = \begin{bmatrix} 1 & 0 \\ 0 & 1 \end{bmatrix}$

4. (c) Since A is singular matrix

$\Rightarrow |A| = 0$

$\Rightarrow 2k^2 - 32 = 0 \Rightarrow k = \pm 4$

5. (b) $f(x) = x^2 - 4x + 6$

$f'(x) = 2x - 4$

Let $f'(x) = 0 \Rightarrow x = 2$

(sign diagram: $-$ for $x < 2$, $+$ for $x > 2$; $-\infty \quad 2 \quad \infty$)

$\Rightarrow f(x)$ is strictly increasing in $(2, \infty)$

6. (d) We have $|adj\,A| = |A|^{n-1}$, where n is order of matrix A

$= (-4)^2 = 16$

7. (b) $(1, 2)$

8. (a) $2a + b = 4$ ..... (i)

$a - 2b = -3$ ..... (ii)

$5c - d = 11$ ..... (iii)

$4c + 3d = 24$ ..... (iv)

Solving equation (i), (ii), (iii) and (iv), we get

$a = 1,$

$b = 2,$

$c = 3,$

$d = 4$

$\therefore \ a + b - c + 2d = 8$

9. (a) $f(x) = x + \dfrac{1}{x}, x > 0$

$\Rightarrow f'(x) = 1 - \dfrac{1}{x^2} = \dfrac{x^2 - 1}{x^2}, x > 0$

Since normal to $f(x)$ is $\perp$ to given line $3x - 4y - 7 = 0$

$\Rightarrow \left(\dfrac{x^2}{1 - x^2}\right) \times \dfrac{3}{4} = -1 \quad (\because m_1 . m_2 = -1)$

$\Rightarrow x^2 = 4 \Rightarrow x = \pm 2$

But $x > 0, \quad \therefore \ x = 2$

Therefore point $= \left(2, \dfrac{5}{2}\right)$

10. (d) $\sin(\tan^{-1} x) = \sin\left(\sin^{-1}\left(\dfrac{x}{\sqrt{1 + x^2}}\right)\right) = \dfrac{x}{\sqrt{1 + x^2}}$

11. (a) $(1, 5, 9)$

12. (c) $e^x + e^y = e^{x+y}$

$\Rightarrow e^{-y} + e^{-x} = 1$

Differentiating w.r.t. x:

$\Rightarrow -e^{-y}\dfrac{dy}{dx} - e^{-x} = 0 \Rightarrow \dfrac{dy}{dx} = -e^{y-x}$

13. (b) 3×5 (Two matrices can be added when both have same order).

14. (a) $y = 5\cos x - 3\sin x \Rightarrow \dfrac{dy}{dx} = -5\sin x - 3\cos x$

$\Rightarrow \dfrac{d^2 y}{dx^2} = -5\cos x + 3\sin x = -y$

15. (c) $(adj\,A = \begin{bmatrix} 7 & -5 \\ 11 & 2 \end{bmatrix} \Rightarrow adj\,A = \begin{bmatrix} 7 & -5 \\ 11 & 2 \end{bmatrix}$

$\Rightarrow (adj\,A)' = \begin{bmatrix} 7 & 11 \\ -5 & 2 \end{bmatrix}$

16. (c) $\dfrac{x^2}{9}+\dfrac{y^2}{16}=1 \Rightarrow \dfrac{2x}{9}+\dfrac{2y}{16}\dfrac{dy}{dx}=0$

$\Rightarrow$ Slope of tangent $=\dfrac{dy}{dx}=-\dfrac{16x}{9y}$

Since tangent of curve is parallel to y-axis

$\Rightarrow \dfrac{9y}{16x}=0 \Rightarrow y=0$ and $x=\pm 3$

$\therefore$ points $=(\pm 3,\,0)$

17. (b) $|A|=-7$

$\therefore \sum_{i=1}^{3} a_{i2}A_{i2}=a_{12}A_{12}+a_{22}A_{22}+a_{32}A_{32}=|A|=-7$

18. (d) $y=\log(\cos e^x)$
Differentiating w.r.t. x:

$\dfrac{dy}{dx}=\dfrac{1}{\cos(e^x)}.(-\sin e^x)\,.e^x$ (by chain rule)

$\Rightarrow \dfrac{dy}{dx}=-e^x \tan e^x$

19. (d) Z is maximum 180 at points C (15,15) and D(0, 20).

$\Rightarrow$ Z is maximum at every point on the line segment CD

20. (c) Given that $f(x)=2\cos x+x,\ x\in\left[0,\dfrac{\pi}{2}\right]$

$\therefore \quad f'(x)=-2\sin x+1$

Let $f'(x)=0$

$\Rightarrow x=\dfrac{\pi}{6}\in\left[0,\dfrac{\pi}{2}\right]$

$f(0)=2$

$f\left(\dfrac{\pi}{6}\right)=\dfrac{\pi}{6}+\sqrt{3}$

$f\left(\dfrac{\pi}{2}\right)=\dfrac{\pi}{2} \Rightarrow$ least value of $f(x)$ is $\dfrac{\pi}{2}$ at $x=\dfrac{\pi}{2}$

21. (d)

Let $f(x_1)=f(x_2)\forall x_1 x_2\in R$	Let $f(x)=x^3=y$
$\Rightarrow x_1^3=x_2^3$	$\Rightarrow x=y^{\frac{1}{3}},\forall y\in R$
$\Rightarrow x_1=x_2$	every image $y\in R$ has a
So, $f(x)$ is one-one	unique pre image in R
	$\Rightarrow\ f$ is onto

$\therefore\ f$ is one-one and onto

22. (a) $\because\ x=a\sec\theta \Rightarrow \dfrac{dx}{d\theta}=a\tan\theta\sec\theta$

and $y=b\tan\theta \Rightarrow \dfrac{dy}{d\theta}=b\sec^2\theta$

$\therefore\quad \dfrac{dy}{dx}=\dfrac{dy}{d\theta}\bigg/\dfrac{dx}{d\theta}=\dfrac{b}{a}\cosec\theta$

$\Rightarrow \dfrac{d^2y}{dx^2}=\dfrac{-b}{a}\cosec\theta\cdot\cot\theta\cdot\dfrac{d\theta}{dx}=\dfrac{-b}{a^2}\cot^3\theta$

$\therefore\quad \dfrac{d^2y}{dx^2}\bigg]_{\theta=\frac{\pi}{6}}=\dfrac{-3\sqrt{3b}}{a^2}$

23. (c) Z is minimum -24 at $(0,8)$

24. (a) Let $u=\sin^{-1}(2x\sqrt{1-x^2})$

and $\sin^{-1}x=\theta,\ \dfrac{1}{\sqrt{2}}<x<1 \Rightarrow x=\sin\theta$

$\therefore\quad u=\sin^{-1}(2\sin\theta\cos\theta)$

$\Rightarrow\quad u=2\theta$

Differentiating with respect to θ, we get : $\dfrac{du}{d\theta}=2$

25. (d) $AB=6I \Rightarrow B^{-1}=\dfrac{1}{6}A$

26. (b) $f'(x)=6(x^2-x-6)=6(x-3)(x+2)$

$\quad\ (+)\qquad (-)\qquad (+)$

$\quad -\infty \quad -2 \qquad 3 \quad \infty$

$\Rightarrow\ f(x)$ is strictly decreasing in $(-2,3)$

27. (a) $\tan^{-1}\left(\dfrac{\sqrt{1+\cos x}+\sqrt{1-\cos x}}{\sqrt{1+\cos x}-\sqrt{1-\cos x}}\right)$

$=\tan^{-1}\left(\dfrac{-\sqrt{2}\cos\dfrac{x}{2}+\sqrt{2}\sin\dfrac{x}{2}}{-\sqrt{2}\cos-\sqrt{2}\sin\dfrac{x}{2}}\right),\ \pi<x<\dfrac{3\pi}{2}$

$=\tan^{-1}\left(\dfrac{\cos\dfrac{x}{2}-\sin\dfrac{x}{2}}{\cos\dfrac{x}{2}+\sin\dfrac{x}{2}}\right)=\tan^{-1}\left(\dfrac{1-\tan\dfrac{x}{2}}{1+\tan\dfrac{x}{2}}\right)$

$=\dfrac{\pi}{4}-\dfrac{x}{2}$

28. (c) $A^2=2A$

$\Rightarrow |A^2|=|2A|$

$\Rightarrow |A^2|=2^3|A|$

$\qquad\qquad [\because\ |kA|=k^n|A|$ for a matrix of order $n\,]$

$\Rightarrow$ either $|A|=0$ or $|A|=8$

But given that A is non-singular matrix

$\therefore\quad |A|=8^2=64$

29. **(b)** $f'(x) = 1 - \sin x = \left(\sin\dfrac{x}{2} - \cos\dfrac{x}{2}\right)^2$

$\Rightarrow$ $f'(x) > 0 \ \forall x \in R$

$\Rightarrow$ no value of b exists

30. **(c)** $a = b - 2$ and $b > 6$

$\Rightarrow$ $(6, 8) \in R$

31. **(a)** $f(x) = \begin{cases} \dfrac{x}{-x} = -1, & x < 0 \\ -1, & x \geq 0 \end{cases}$

$\Rightarrow$ $f(x) = -1 \ \forall \ x \in R$

$\Rightarrow$ $f(x)$ is continuous $\forall \ x \in R$ as it is a constant function.

32. **(b)** $kA = \begin{bmatrix} 0 & 2k \\ 3k & -4k \end{bmatrix} = \begin{bmatrix} 0 & 3a \\ 2b & 24 \end{bmatrix}$

$\Rightarrow$ $k = -6$, $a = -4$ and $b = -9$

33. **(d)** Corner points of feasible region　　　$Z = 30x + 50y$

$(5, 0)$	150
$(9, 0)$	270
$(0, 3)$	150
$(0, 6)$	300

Minimum value of Z occurs at two points

34. **(c)** $f'(x) = \dfrac{-2x^2 - 10x + 100}{\sqrt{100 - x^2}}$

$f'(x) = 0 \Rightarrow x = -10$ or 5, But $x > 0 \Rightarrow x = 5$

$f''(x) = \dfrac{2x^3 - 300x - 1000}{(100 - x)^{3/2}} \Rightarrow f''(5) = \dfrac{-30}{\sqrt{75}} < 0$

$\Rightarrow$ Maximum area of trapezium is $75\sqrt{3}$ cm^2 when $x = 5$

35. **(d)** $(I + A)^3 - 7A = I^3 + A^3 + 3A^2 + 3A - 7A$
$\qquad\qquad\qquad = I + A^2 + 3A + 3A - 7A = I$

36. **(c)** $\dfrac{-\pi}{2} < y < \dfrac{\pi}{2}$

37. **(b)** As every per-image $x \in A$ has a unique image $y \in B$ but range $= \{4, 5, 6\} \neq B$.
$\Rightarrow$ f is injective function

38. **(b)** $|A| = 7$, $adjA = \begin{bmatrix} 2 & -1 \\ 1 & 3 \end{bmatrix}$, $A^{-1} = \dfrac{1}{7}\begin{bmatrix} 2 & -1 \\ 1 & 3 \end{bmatrix}$

$\therefore$ $14A^{-1} = \begin{bmatrix} 4 & -2 \\ 2 & 6 \end{bmatrix}$

39. **(b)** $y = x^3 - 11x + 5 \Rightarrow \dfrac{dy}{dx} = 3x^2 - 11$

Slope of line $y = x - 11$ is $1 \Rightarrow 3x^2 - 11 = 1 \Rightarrow x = \pm 2$

$\therefore$ point is $(2, -9)$ as $(-2, 19)$ does not satisfy given line

40. **(c)** $A^2 = 3I$

$\Rightarrow$ $\begin{bmatrix} \alpha^2 + \beta r & 0 \\ 0 & \beta r + \alpha^2 \end{bmatrix} = \begin{bmatrix} 3 & 0 \\ 0 & 3 \end{bmatrix} \Rightarrow 3 - \alpha^2 - \beta r = 0$

41. **(a)** As Z is maximum at $(30, 30)$ and $(0, 40)$
$\Rightarrow$ $30a + 30b = 40b \Rightarrow b - 3a = 0$

42. **(b)** $y = mx + 1$ 　　　　　　　.....(1)
and $y^2 = 4x$ 　　　　　　　.....(2)
Substituting (1) in (2) : $(mx + 1)^2 = 4x$
$\Rightarrow$ $m^2x^2 + (2m - 4)x + 1 = 0$ 　　.....(3)
As line is tangent to the curve
$\Rightarrow$ line touches the curve at only one point
$\Rightarrow$ D $= 0 \ (2m - 4)^2 - 4m^2 = 0 \Rightarrow$ m $= 1$

43. **(c)** Let $f(x) = [x(x - 1) + 1]^{1/3}$, $0 \leq x \leq 1$

$f'(x) = \dfrac{2x - 1}{3(x^2 - x + 1)^{2/3}}$, Let $f'(x) = 0 \Rightarrow x = \dfrac{1}{2} \in [0, 1]$

$f(0) = 1$, $f\left(\dfrac{1}{2}\right) = \left(\dfrac{3}{4}\right)^{1/3}$ and $f(1) = 1$

$\therefore$ Maximum value of $f(x)$ is 1

44. **(b)** Feasible region is bounded in the first quadrant

45. **(d)** $|A| = 2 + 2\sin^2\theta$

We have $-1 \leq \sin\theta \leq 1$, $\forall \ 0 \leq \theta \leq 2\pi$

$\Rightarrow$ $2 \leq 2 + 2\sin^2\theta \leq 4 \Rightarrow |A| \in [2, 4]$

46. **(d)** Fuel cost $= k(\text{speed})^2$

$\Rightarrow$ $48 = k.16^2 \Rightarrow k = \dfrac{3}{16}$

47. **(b)** Let time taken be t hours

Total cost of running train $= \dfrac{3}{16}v^2 t + 1200t$

Distance covered $= 500$km $\Rightarrow$ time $= \dfrac{500}{v}$ hrs

Total cost of running train for 500 km

$= \dfrac{3}{16}v^2\left(\dfrac{500}{v}\right) + 1200\left(\dfrac{500}{v}\right) \quad = \dfrac{375}{4}v + \dfrac{600000}{v}$

48. **(c)** Let $C = \dfrac{375}{4}v + \dfrac{600000}{v}$

$\therefore$ $\dfrac{dC}{dv} = \dfrac{375}{4} + \dfrac{600000}{v^2}$

Let $\dfrac{dC}{dv} = 0 \Rightarrow v = 80$ km/h

49. **(c)** Fuel cost for running 500 km
$= \dfrac{375}{4}v = \dfrac{375}{4} \times 80 = ₹7500/-$

50. **(d)** Total cost for running 500 km $= \dfrac{375}{4}v + \dfrac{600000}{v}$

$= \dfrac{375 \times 80}{4} + \dfrac{600000}{80} = ₹15000/-$

All India *2020*

CBSE Board Solved Paper

Time Allowed : 3 Hours   *Maximum Marks : 80*

General Instructions:

Read the following instructions very carefully and strictly follow them:

(i)   This question paper comprises **four** Sections A, B, C and D. This question paper carries **36** questions. **All** questions are compulsory.

(ii) **Section A:** Questions no. **1** to **20** comprises of **20** questions of **1** mark each.

(iii) **Section B:** Questions no. **21** to **26** comprises of **6** questions of **2** marks each.

(iv) **Section C:** Questions no. **27** to **32** comprises of **6** questions of **4** marks each.

(v)   **Section D:** Questions no. **33** to **36** comprises of **4** questions of **6** marks each.

(vi) There is no overall choice in the question paper. However, an internal choice has been provided in **3** questions of **one** mark, **2** questions of **two** marks, **2** questions of **four** marks and **2** questions of **six** marks. Only one of the choices in such questions have to be attempted.

(vii) In addition to this, separate instructions are given with each section and question, wherever necessary.

(viii) Use of calculators is not permitted.

SECTION - A

Question numbers 1 to 20 carry 1 mark each.

Question numbers 1 to 10 are multiple choice type questions.
Select the correct option.

1. If A is a square matrix of order 3 and $|A| = 5$, then the value of $|2A'|$ is

   (a) -10 (b) 10

   (c) -40 (d) 40

2. If A is a square matrix such that $A^2 = A$, then $(I - A)^3 + A$ is equal to

   (a) I   (b) 0

   (c) $I - A$ (d) $I + A$

3. The principal value of $\tan^{-1} (\tan \frac{3\pi}{5})$ is

   (a) $\dfrac{2\pi}{5}$ (b) $\dfrac{-2\pi}{5}$

   (c) $\dfrac{3\pi}{5}$ (d) $\dfrac{-3\pi}{5}$

4. If the projection of $\vec{a} = \hat{i} - 2\hat{j} + 3\hat{k}$ on $\vec{b} = 2\hat{i} + \lambda\hat{k}$ is zero, then the value of λ is

   (a) 0   (b) 1

   (c) $\dfrac{-2}{3}$ (d) $\dfrac{-3}{2}$

5. The vector equation of the line passing through the point $(-1, 5, 4)$ and perpendicular to the plane $z = 0$ is

   (a) $\vec{r} = -\hat{i} + 5\hat{j} + 4\hat{k} + \lambda(\hat{i} + \hat{j})$

   (b) $\vec{r} = -\hat{i} + 5\hat{j} + (4 + \lambda)\hat{k}$

   (c) $\vec{r} = \hat{i} - 5\hat{j} - 4\hat{k} + \lambda\hat{k}$

   (d) $\vec{r} = \lambda\hat{k}$

6. The number of arbitrary constants in the particular solution of a differential equation of second order is (are)

   (a) 0   (b) 1

   (c) 2   (d) 3

7. $\displaystyle\int_{-\frac{\pi}{4}}^{\frac{\pi}{4}} \sec^2 x\, dx$ is equal to

   (a) -1 (b) 0

   (c) 1 (d) 2

8. The length of the perpendicular drawn from the point $(4, -7, 3)$ on the y-axis is

   (a) 3 units   (b) 4 units

   (c) 5 units   (d) 7 units

9. If A and B are two independent events with $P(A) = \dfrac{1}{3}$ and $P(B) = \dfrac{1}{4}$, then $P(B'|A)$ is equal to

   (a) $\dfrac{1}{4}$ (b) $\dfrac{1}{3}$

   (c) $\dfrac{3}{4}$ (d) 1

10. The corner points of the feasible region determined by the system of linear inequalities are $(0, 0)$, $(4, 0)$, $(2, 4)$ and $(0, 5)$. If the maximum value of $z = ax + by$, where $a, b > 0$ occurs at both $(2, 4)$ and $(4, 0)$, then

   (a) $a = 2b$ (b) $2a = b$

   (c) $a = b$ (d) $3a = b$

Fill in the blanks in question numbers 11 to 15.

11. A relation R in a set A is called _________, if $(a_1, a_2) \in R$ implies $(a_2, a_1) \in R$, for all $a_1, a_2 \in A$.

12. The greatest integer function defined by $f(x) = [x]$, $0 < x < 2$ is not differentiable at $x =$ _________.

13. If A is a matrix of order 3×2, then the order of the matrix A' is _________.

OR

A square matrix A is said to be skew-symmetric, if _________.

14. The equation of the normal to the curve $y^2 = 8x$ at the origin is _________.

OR

The radius of a circle is increasing at the uniform rate of 3 cm/sec. At the instant when the radius of the circle is 2 cm, its area increases at the rate of _________ cm²/s.

15. The position vectors of two points A and B are $\overrightarrow{OA} = 2\hat{i} - \hat{j} - \hat{k}$ and $\overrightarrow{OB} = 2\hat{i} - \hat{j} + 2\hat{k}$, respectively. The position vector of a point P which divides the line segment joining A and B in the ratio 2 : 1 is _________.

Question numbers 16 to 20 are very short answer type questions.

16. If $A = \begin{bmatrix} 2 & 0 & 0 \\ -1 & 2 & 3 \\ 3 & 3 & 5 \end{bmatrix}$, then find A (adj A).

17. Find : $\displaystyle\int x^4 \log x\, dx$

OR

Find: $\displaystyle\int \dfrac{2x}{\sqrt[3]{x^2 + 1}}\, dx$

18. Evaluate: $\displaystyle\int_1^3 |2x - 1|\, dx$

19. Two cards are drawn at random and one-by-one without replacement from a well-shuffled pack of 52 playing cards. Find the probability that one card is red and the other is black.

20. Find: $\displaystyle\int \dfrac{dx}{\sqrt{9 - 4x^2}}$

SECTION - B

Question numbers 21 to 26 carry 2 marks each.

21. Prove that $\sin^{-1}(2x\sqrt{1 - x^2}) = 2\cos^{-1}x$, $\dfrac{1}{\sqrt{2}} \le x \le 1$.

OR

Consider a bijective function $f = R_+ \to (7, \infty)$ given by $f(x) = 16x^2 + 24x + 7$, where R_+ is the set of all positive real numbers. Find the inverse function of f.

22. If $x = at^2$, $y = 2at$, then find $\dfrac{d^2y}{dx^2}$.

23. Find the points on the curve $y = x^3 - 3x^2 - 4x$ at which the tangent lines are parallel to the line $4x + y - 3 = 0$.

24. Find a unit vector perpendicular to each of the vectors $\vec{a}$ and $\vec{b}$ where $\vec{a} = 5\hat{i} + 6\hat{j} - 2\hat{k}$ and $\vec{b} = 7\hat{i} + 6\hat{j} + 2\hat{k}$.

OR

Find the volume of the parallelopiped whose adjacent edges are represented by $2\vec{a}$, $-\vec{b}$ and $3\vec{c}$, where

$$\vec{a} = \hat{i} - \hat{j} + 2\hat{k},\ \vec{b} = 3\hat{i} + 4\hat{j} - 5\hat{k},\ \text{and}\ \vec{c} = 2\hat{i} - \hat{j} + 3\hat{k}.$$

25. Find the value of k so that the lines $x = -y = kz$ and $x - 2 = 2y + 1 = -z + 1$ are perpendicular to each other.

26. The probability of finding a green signal on a busy crossing X is 30%. What is the probability of finding a green signal on X on two consecutive days out of three?

SECTION - C

Question number 27 to 32 carry 4 marks each.

27. Let N be the set of natural numbers and R be the relation on $N \times N$ defined by $(a, b)\, R\, (c, d)$ if $ad = bc$ for all $a, b, c, d \in N$. Show that R is an equivalence relation.

28. If $y = e^{x^2 \cos x} + (\cos x)^x$, then find $\dfrac{dy}{dx}$.

29. Find: $\int \sec^3 x\, dx$

30. Find the general solution of the differential equation
$$y\, e^y\, dx = (y^3 + 2x\, e^y)dy.$$

OR

Find the particular solution of the differential equation
$$x\frac{dy}{dx} = y - x\tan\left(\frac{y}{x}\right), \text{ given that } y = \frac{\pi}{4} \text{ at } x = 1.$$

31. A furniture trader deals in only two items – chairs and tables. He has ₹ 50,000 to invest and a space to store at most 35 items. A chair costs him ₹ 1000 and a table costs him ₹ 2000. The trader earns a profit of ₹ 150 and ₹ 250 on a chair and table, respectively. Formulate the above problem as an LPP to maximise the profit and solve it graphically.

32. There are two bags, I and II. Bag I contains 3 red and 5 black balls and Bag II contains 4 red and 3 black balls. One ball is transferred randomly from Bag I to Bag II and then a ball is drawn randomly from Bag II. If the ball so drawn is found to be black in colour, then find the probability that the transferred ball is also black.

OR

An urn contains 5 red, 2 white and 3 black balls. Three balls are drawn, one-by-one, at random without replacement. Find the probability distribution of the number of white balls. Also, find the mean and the variance of the number of white balls drawn.

SECTION - D

Question numbers 33 to 36 carry 6 marks each.

33. If $A = \begin{bmatrix} 1 & 2 & -3 \\ 3 & 2 & -2 \\ 2 & -1 & 1 \end{bmatrix}$, then find A^{-1} and use it to solve the following system of the equations:
$$x + 2y - 3z = 6$$
$$3x + 2y - 2z = 3$$
$$2x - y + z = 2$$

OR

Using properties of determinants, prove that
$$\begin{vmatrix} (b+c)^2 & a^2 & bc \\ (c+a)^2 & b^2 & ca \\ (a+b)^2 & c^2 & ab \end{vmatrix}$$
$$= (a-b)(b-c)(c-a)(a+b+c)(a^2 + b^2 + c^2).$$

34. Using integration, find the area of the region bounded by the triangle whose vertices are $(2, -2)$, $(4, 5)$ and $(6, 2)$.

35. Show that the height of the right circular cylinder of greatest volume which can be inscribed in a right circular cone of height h and radius r is one-third of the height of the cone, and the greatest volume of the cylinder is $\dfrac{4}{9}$ times the volume of the cone.

36. Find the equation of the plane that contains the point $A(2, 1, -1)$ and is perpendicular to the line of intersection of the planes $2x + y - z = 3$ and $x + 2y + z = 2$. Also find the angle between the plane thus obtained and the y-axis.

OR

Find the distance of the point $P(-2, -4, 7)$ from the point of intersection Q of the line $\vec{r} = (3\hat{i} - 2\hat{j} + 6\hat{k}) + \lambda(2\hat{i} - \hat{j} + 2\hat{k})$ and the plane $\vec{r}.(\hat{i} - \hat{j} + \hat{k}) = 6$. Also write the vector equation of the line PQ.

Solutions

1. **(d)** $|A| = 5$

We know that $|A| = |A|'$

$\therefore \quad |A|' = 5$

$|2A'| = 2^n |A|'$

$= 2^3 (5)$ $\hspace{2cm}$ $(n = 3)$

$= 8 \times 5 = 40$ $\hspace{2cm}$ **(1 Mark)**

2. **(a)** $A^2 = A$ $\hspace{3cm}$ (given)

$(I - A)^3 + A = I^3 - A^3 - 3IA(I - A) + A$

$\hspace{2cm} [\because (a - b)^3 = a^3 - b^3 - 3ab(a - b)]$

$= I - A^2 \cdot A - 3I^2 A + 3IA^2 + A$ $\hspace{1cm}$ $(\because I^3 = I)$

$= I - A \cdot A - 3IA + 3A^2 + A$

$\hspace{2cm} (\because I^2 = I \text{ and } IA = A)$

$= I - A^2 - 3A + 3A + A$ $\hspace{1cm}$ $(\because IA = A)$

$= I - A + A = I$ $\hspace{2cm}$ **(1 Mark)**

3. **(b)** Let $y = \tan^{-1}\left(\tan\dfrac{3\pi}{5}\right)$

$\Rightarrow \quad \tan y = \tan\dfrac{3\pi}{5}$

$\Rightarrow \quad \tan y = \tan\left(\pi - \dfrac{2\pi}{5}\right)$

$\Rightarrow \quad \tan y = -\tan\left(\dfrac{2\pi}{5}\right)$ $\hspace{1cm}$ $[\because \tan(\pi - \theta) = -\tan\theta]$

$\Rightarrow \quad \tan y = \tan\left(-\dfrac{2\pi}{5}\right)$ $\hspace{1cm}$ $[\because \tan(-\theta) = -\tan\theta]$

$\Rightarrow \quad y = -\dfrac{2\pi}{5}$ $\hspace{2cm}$ **(1 Mark)**

> **Note**
>
> *The principal value branch of $\tan^{-1}$ is $\left(\dfrac{-\pi}{2}, \dfrac{\pi}{2}\right)$. So, angle θ in $\tan^{-1}\theta$ must be such that $\dfrac{-\pi}{2} < \theta < \dfrac{\pi}{2}$.*

4. **(c)** Projection of $\vec{a}$ on $\vec{b} = 0$ $\hspace{2cm}$ (given)

Projection of $\vec{a}$ on $\vec{b} = \dfrac{\vec{a}.\vec{b}}{|\vec{b}|}$

$\therefore \quad \dfrac{\vec{a}.\vec{b}}{|\vec{b}|} = 0$

$\Rightarrow \quad \vec{a}.\vec{b} = 0$

$\Rightarrow \quad (\hat{i} - 2\hat{j} + 3\hat{k}).(2\hat{i} + \lambda\hat{k}) = 0$

$\Rightarrow \quad 2 - 2(0) + 3(\lambda) = 0$

$\Rightarrow \quad 2 + 3\lambda = 0$

$\Rightarrow \quad 3\lambda = -2$

$\Rightarrow \quad \lambda = \dfrac{-2}{3}$ $\hspace{2cm}$ **(1 Mark)**

5. **(b)** Line is perpendicular to $z = 0$ plane.

So it will be along $\hat{k}$ vector and also it passes through $(-1, 5, 4)$

$\therefore \quad \vec{r} = -\hat{i} + 5\hat{j} + 4\hat{k} + \lambda\hat{k}$

$\hspace{1cm} \vec{r} = -\hat{i} + 5\hat{j} + \hat{k}(4 + \lambda)$ $\hspace{1cm}$ **(1 Mark)**

6. **(a)** In particular solution of any differential equation, arbitrary constants have to be removed by substituting some particular values. So 0 is answer. $\hspace{0.3cm}$ **(1 Mark)**

> **Note**
>
> *Perticular solution of a differential equation does not contain any arbitrary constant.*

7. **(d)** $\displaystyle\int_{-\frac{\pi}{4}}^{\frac{\pi}{4}} \sec^2 x\, dx = [\tan x]_{-\frac{\pi}{4}}^{\frac{\pi}{4}}$ $\hspace{0.5cm}$ $\left[\because \int \sec^2\theta\, d\theta = \tan\theta\right]$

$= \tan\dfrac{\pi}{4} - \tan\left(-\dfrac{\pi}{4}\right)$

$= 1 - \left(-\tan\dfrac{\pi}{4}\right)$ $\hspace{1cm}$ $[\because \tan(-\theta) = -\tan\theta]$

$= 1 + 1 = 2$ $\hspace{2cm}$ **(1 Mark)**

8. **(c)** Let point on y-axis be A$(0, y, 0)$ and point B$(4, -7, 3)$

As the line is perpendicular from B to A.

So coordinate of y will be same $y = -7$

$\therefore$ A$(0, -7, 0)$

Distance $= \sqrt{(x_1 - x_2)^2 + (y_1 - y_2)^2 + (z_1 - z_2)^2}$

$\Rightarrow$ AB $= \sqrt{(0-4)^2 + (-7+7)^2 + (0-3)^2}$

$\Rightarrow$ AB $= \sqrt{16 + 0 + 9} = \sqrt{25} = 5$

$\Rightarrow$ AB = 5 units   **(1 Mark)**

9. **(c)** $P\left(\dfrac{B'}{A}\right) = \dfrac{P(B' \cap A)}{P(A)} = \dfrac{P(B')P(A)}{P(A)}$

$[\because$ A and B are independent elements$]$

$= P(B') = 1 - P(B)$

$= 1 - \dfrac{1}{4}$ $\qquad \left[\therefore P(B) = \dfrac{1}{4} \text{ (given)}\right]$

$= \dfrac{3}{4}$ **(1 Mark)**

10. **(a)** $Z = ax + by$

Maximum value at $(2, 4)$ is

$Z = a(2) + b(4) = 2a + 4b$ $\qquad$ ...(1)

Maximum value at $(4, 0)$

$Z = a(4) + b(0)$

$Z = 4a$ $\qquad$ ...(2)

Maximum value occur at both points.

So it should have equal value

$2a + 4b = 4a$ $\qquad$ [from (1) and (2)]

$\Rightarrow$ $4b = 4a - 2a$

$\Rightarrow$ $4b = 2a$

$\Rightarrow$ $2b = a$

$\Rightarrow$ $a = 2b$ **(1 Mark)**

Note

Let R be the feasible region for a linear programming problem, and let Z = ax + by be the objective function. If R is bounded, then the objective function Z has both a maximum and a minimum value on R and each of these occur at a corner point of R.

11. [Symmetric]   **(1 Mark)**

12. [1] At 1 L.H.D. $= \lim\limits_{h \to 0} \dfrac{f(x) - f(x-h)}{h}$

$= \lim\limits_{h \to 0} \dfrac{f(1) - f(1-h)}{h} = \lim\limits_{h \to 0} \dfrac{[1] - [(1-h)]}{h}$

$= \lim\limits_{h \to 0} \dfrac{1-0}{h} = \lim\limits_{h \to 0} \dfrac{1}{h} = \dfrac{1}{0}$, Not defined.

R.H.D. $= \lim\limits_{h \to 0} \dfrac{f(x+h) - f(x)}{h}$

$= \lim\limits_{h \to 0} \dfrac{f(1+h) - f(1)}{h} = \lim\limits_{h \to 0} \dfrac{[(1+h)] - [1]}{h}$

$= \lim\limits_{h \to 0} \dfrac{1-1}{h} = \lim\limits_{h \to 0} \dfrac{0}{h} = \lim\limits_{h \to 0} 0 = 0$

L.H.D. $\neq$ R.H.D

$\therefore f(x)$ is not differentiable at $x = 1$.   **(1 Mark)**

13. [2 × 3]   **(1 Mark)**

OR

$[A^T = -A]$ **(1 Mark)**

14. [y = 0] $y^2 = 8x$

Differentiating on both sides

$\dfrac{d}{dx}(y^2) = \dfrac{d}{dx}(8x)$

$2y\dfrac{dy}{dx} = 8(1)$

$\dfrac{dy}{dx} = \dfrac{8}{2y} = \dfrac{4}{y}$

Slope of normal $= \dfrac{-1}{\dfrac{dy}{dx}} = \dfrac{-1}{\dfrac{4}{y}} = \dfrac{-y}{4}$

at origin $(0, 0)$, slope of normal $= 0$

$\therefore$ Equation of normal

$\dfrac{y-0}{x-0} = 0$

$y = 0$ **(1 Mark)**

OR

$[12\pi]$

Area of circle $= \pi r^2$

$A = \pi r^2$

$\dfrac{dA}{dt} = \pi(2r)\dfrac{dr}{dt}$ $\qquad \left[\because \dfrac{dx^n}{dx} = nx^{n-1}\right]$

$$\frac{dA}{dt} = 2\pi r \frac{dr}{dt} \qquad \ldots(1)$$

As radius is increasing at uniform rate of 3 cm/sec.

$$\frac{dr}{dt} = 3 \text{ cm/sec} \qquad \text{[From (1)]}$$

$$\frac{dA}{dt} = 2\pi r(3) = 6\pi r$$

At $r = 2$,

$$\frac{dA}{dt} = 6\pi(2) = 12\pi \text{ cm}^2/\text{sec.} \qquad \text{(given)} \textbf{(1 Mark)}$$

15. $[2\hat{i} - \hat{j} + \hat{k}]$ Point A(2, −1, −1), Point B(2, −1, 2)

$$\overset{2}{\bullet} \qquad \overset{1}{\bullet} \qquad \bullet$$

A(2, −1, −1)   P   B(2, −1, 2)

By section formula

$$P = \left(\frac{mx_2 + nx_1}{m+n}, \frac{my_2 + ny_1}{m+n}, \frac{mz_2 + nz_1}{m+n} \right)$$

$$= \left(\frac{4+2}{2+1}, \frac{-2-1}{2+1}, \frac{4-1}{2+1} \right) = (2, -1, 1)$$

Position vector, $\overrightarrow{OP} = 2\hat{i} - \hat{j} + \hat{k}$ **(1 Mark)**

16. $A = \begin{bmatrix} 2 & 0 & 0 \\ -1 & 2 & 3 \\ 3 & 3 & 5 \end{bmatrix}$

$|A| = 2(10 - 9) = 2$

$$A^{-1} = \frac{1}{|A|} \text{adj}(A)$$

$$\Rightarrow \quad \text{adj}(A) = |A| A^{-1}$$

Multiplying both side by A

$A(\text{adj } A) = |A| AA^{-1}$

$$\Rightarrow \quad A(\text{adj } A) = |A| I \qquad [\because AA^{-1} = I]$$

$$= 2 \begin{bmatrix} 1 & 0 & 0 \\ 0 & 1 & 0 \\ 0 & 0 & 1 \end{bmatrix} = \begin{bmatrix} 2 & 0 & 0 \\ 0 & 2 & 0 \\ 0 & 0 & 2 \end{bmatrix} \qquad \textbf{(1 Mark)}$$

17. $\int x^4 \log x \, dx$

$$\because \quad \int u v \, dx = u \int v \, dx - \int \left[\frac{du}{dx} \int v \, dx \right] dx$$

$$\int \log x \cdot x^4 \, dx = \log x \int x^4 \, dx - \int \left[\frac{d}{dx} \log x \int x^4 \, dx \right] dx$$

$$= \log x \left(\frac{x^5}{5} \right) - \int \frac{1}{x} \frac{x^5}{5} \, dx \qquad \left[\because \frac{d}{dx} \log x = \frac{1}{x} \right]$$

$$\left[\because \int x^n \, dx = \frac{x^{n+1}}{n+1} + C \right]$$

$$= \frac{x^5}{5} \log x - \frac{1}{5} \int x^4 \, dx + C = \frac{x^5}{5} \log x - \frac{1}{5} \times \frac{x^5}{5} + C$$

$$= \frac{x^5}{5} \log x - \frac{x^5}{25} + C = \frac{x^5}{5} \left[\log x - \frac{1}{5} \right] + C \quad \textbf{(1 Mark)}$$

Note

If any integral is of the form $\int f(x) \log x \, dx$, then take log as the first function when $f(x)$ is any polynomial function.

OR

$$\int \frac{2x}{(x^2 + 1)^{3/2}} \, dx$$

Let $x^2 + 1 = t$

$$2x \, dx = dt$$

$$\int \frac{dt}{t^{3/2}} = \frac{t^{-3/2+1}}{-\frac{3}{2}+1} + C \qquad \left[\because \int x^n \, dx = \frac{x^{n+1}}{n+1} + C \right]$$

$$= \frac{t^{-1/2}}{-\frac{1}{2}} + C = \frac{-2}{t^{1/2}} + C = \frac{-2}{\sqrt{x^2 + 1}} + C \qquad \textbf{(1 Mark)}$$

18. $\displaystyle\int_1^3 |2x - 1| \, dx$

$2x - 1 > 0$ for $[1, 3]$

$$\therefore \quad \int_1^3 |2x - 1| \, dx = \int_1^3 (2x - 1) \, dx$$

$$= \left[\frac{2x^2}{2} - x \right]_1^3 \qquad \left[\because \int x^n \, dx = \frac{x^{n+1}}{n+1} \right]$$

$$= [x^2 - x]_1^3 = (9 - 3) - (1 - 1) = 6 \qquad \textbf{(1 Mark)}$$

19. 2 cards drawn one by one without replacement

Number of red cards = 26

Number of black cards = 26

Total number of cards = 52

P(RB) = Probability of drawn card is first red and then black

$$P(RB) = \frac{\text{Number of favourable outcomes}}{\text{Total number of outcomes}}$$

$$P(RB) = \frac{26}{52} \times \frac{26}{51}$$

$P(BR)$ = Probability when first card is black and second is red

$$P(BR) = \frac{26}{52} \times \frac{26}{51}$$

Hence $P(B \text{ or } R) = \dfrac{26 \times 26}{52 \times 51} + \dfrac{26 \times 26}{52 \times 51}$

$$= \frac{2 \times 26 \times 26}{52 \times 51} = \frac{26}{51} \qquad \textbf{(1 Mark)}$$

20. Let $I = \displaystyle\int \frac{dx}{\sqrt{9 - 4x^2}}$

$$I = \frac{1}{2}\int \frac{dx}{\sqrt{\left(\dfrac{3}{2}\right)^2 - x^2}}$$

$$\because \quad \int \frac{dx}{\sqrt{a^2 - x^2}} = \sin^{-1}\left(\frac{x}{a}\right) + C$$

$$\therefore \quad I = \frac{1}{2}\sin^{-1}\left(\frac{x}{3/2}\right) + C = \frac{1}{2}\sin^{-1}\left(\frac{2x}{3}\right) + C \quad \textbf{(1 Mark)}$$

SECTION - B

21. L.H.S. $= \sin^{-1}(2x\sqrt{1 - x^2})$, $\dfrac{1}{\sqrt{2}} \le x \le 1$

Let $x = \cos\theta \Rightarrow \theta = \cos^{-1}x$, $0 \le \theta \le \dfrac{\pi}{4}$ **(1 Mark)**

$$\therefore \quad \text{L.H.S.} = \sin^{-1}(2\sin\theta\sqrt{1 - \sin^2\theta})$$

$$= \sin^{-1}(2\sin\theta\cos\theta) \qquad [\because \sin^2\theta + \cos^2\theta = 1]$$

$$= \sin^{-1}(\sin 2\theta) \qquad [\because \sin 2\theta = 2\sin\theta.\cos\theta]$$

$$= 2\theta$$

$$= 2\cos^{-1}x = \text{R.H.S.} \qquad \textbf{(1 Mark)}$$

Note

If inverse trigonometric function contains $\sqrt{1 - x^2}$ then put $x = \sin\theta$ or $\cos\theta$, $\sqrt{x^2 - 1}$ then put $x = \sec\theta$ or $\csc\theta$ and $\sqrt{1 + x^2}$ then put $x = \tan\theta$ or $\cot\theta$.

OR

$f : R_+ \to (7, \infty)$

$f(x) = 16x^2 + 24x + 7$

$\qquad = 16x^2 + 24x + 7 + 9 - 9$

$\qquad = (4x)^2 + 2 \times 3 \times 4x + (3)^2 - 2$

$\qquad = (4x + 3)^2 - 2 > 0, \ \forall \ x \in R_+$

Then, function is strictly increasing in R_+

$\therefore \quad f(x)$ is injective   **(½ Mark)**

Now, $f(x) = (4x + 3)^2 - 2$

$\therefore \quad (4x + 3)^2 = f(x) + 2 \qquad [\because f(x) + 2 \in (9, \infty)]$

$\Rightarrow \quad 4x + 3 = \sqrt{f(x) + 2}$

$\Rightarrow \quad x = \dfrac{\sqrt{f(x) + 2} - 3}{4}$

For every $f(x) \in (7, \infty)$, there exist one $x \in R_+$.

$\therefore \quad f(x)$ is surjective   **(½ Mark)**

$\therefore \quad$ Function is bijective, so inverse of the function is

$$f^{-1}(x) = \frac{\sqrt{x + 2} - 3}{4} \qquad \textbf{(1 Mark)}$$

22. $x = at^2$

$$\frac{dx}{dt} = a(2t) = 2at \qquad \left[\because \frac{dx^n}{dx} = nx^{n-1}\right] \textbf{(½ Mark)}$$

$y = 2at$

$$\frac{dy}{dx} = \frac{\dfrac{dy}{dt}}{\dfrac{dx}{dt}} \quad \Rightarrow \quad \frac{dy}{dx} = \frac{2a}{2at} = \frac{1}{t}$$

$$\Rightarrow \quad \frac{dy}{dx} = \frac{1}{t} \qquad \textbf{(½ Mark)}$$

$$\frac{d^2y}{dx^2} = \frac{d}{dx}\left(\frac{dy}{dx}\right) = \frac{d}{dt}\left(\frac{dy}{dx}\right).\frac{dt}{dx}$$

$$= \frac{-\dfrac{1}{t^2}}{2at} = -\frac{1}{2at^3} \qquad \left[\because \frac{dx}{dt} = 2at\right]$$

$$= \left[\frac{-1}{2a\left(\dfrac{x}{a}\right)^{3/2}}\right] = \frac{-a^{1/2}}{2x^{3/2}} \qquad \left[\because t = \left(\frac{x}{a}\right)^{1/2}\right] \textbf{(1 Mark)}$$

23. $y = x^3 - 3x^2 - 4x$

$$\frac{dy}{dx} = 3x^2 - 6x - 4$$

Slope of tangent = $\dfrac{dy}{dx} = 3x^2 - 6x - 4$ ...(1) **(1 Mark)**

Given that tangent is parallel to $4x + y - 3 = 0$

$\qquad 4x + y - 3 = 0$

$\qquad y = -4x + 3$

Slope, $m = -4$ ....(2) $[\because y = mx + C]$

From (1) and (2),

$\qquad 3x^2 - 6x - 4 = -4$

(Slope of parallel lines are equal)

$\Rightarrow \quad 3x^2 - 6x = 0$

$\Rightarrow \quad 3x(x - 2) = 0$

$\Rightarrow \quad x = 0, 2$

$\Rightarrow \quad y = x^3 - 3x^2 - 4x$

when $x = 0$, $y = 0$, then the point is $(0, 0)$

when $x = 2$, $y = 2^3 - 3(2)^2 - 4(2) = -12$,

then the point is $(2, -12)$

$\therefore \quad$ Required points are $(0, 0)$ and $(2, -12)$ **(1 Mark)**

24. Let $\hat{C}$ be a vector perpendicular to $\vec{a}$ and $\vec{b}$

$\qquad \hat{C} = \vec{a} \times \vec{b}$

$\qquad \hat{C} = \begin{vmatrix} \hat{i} & \hat{j} & \hat{k} \\ 5 & 6 & -2 \\ 7 & 6 & 2 \end{vmatrix}$

$\qquad = \hat{i}(12 + 12) - \hat{j}(10 + 14) + \hat{k}(30 - 42)$

$\qquad = 24\hat{i} - 24\hat{j} - 12\hat{k} = 12(2\hat{i} - 2\hat{j} - \hat{k})$ **(1 Mark)**

Unit vector $\hat{C} = \dfrac{\vec{C}}{|\vec{C}|}$ **(½ Mark)**

$|\vec{C}| = \sqrt{(12)^2[2^2 + (-2)^2 + (-1)^2]}$

$\qquad = 12\sqrt{4 + 4 + 1} = 12\sqrt{9} = 36$

$\qquad \hat{C} = \dfrac{12}{36}(2\hat{i} - 2\hat{j} - \hat{k})$

$\Rightarrow \quad \hat{C} = \dfrac{1}{3}(2\hat{i} - 2\hat{j} - \hat{k})$

$\Rightarrow \quad \hat{C} = \dfrac{2}{3}\hat{i} - \dfrac{2}{3}\hat{j} - \dfrac{1}{3}\hat{k}$ **(½ Mark)**

OR

Vector length of sides of parallelopiped are

$\vec{l_1} = 2\vec{a} = 2(\hat{i} - \hat{j} + 2\hat{k}) = 2\hat{i} - 2\hat{j} + 4\hat{k}$

$\vec{l_2} = -\vec{b} = -(3\hat{i} + 4\hat{j} - 5\hat{k}) = -3\hat{i} - 4\hat{j} + 5\hat{k}$

$\vec{l_3} = 3\vec{c} = 3(2\hat{i} - \hat{j} + 3\hat{k}) = 6\hat{i} - 3\hat{j} + 9\hat{k}$

Volume = $\left| (\vec{l_1} \times \vec{l_2}) \cdot \vec{l_3} \right|$

$\vec{l_1} \times \vec{l_2} = \begin{vmatrix} \hat{i} & \hat{j} & \hat{k} \\ 2 & -2 & 4 \\ -3 & -4 & 5 \end{vmatrix}$

$\qquad = \hat{i}(-10 + 16) - \hat{j}(10 + 12) + \hat{k}(-8 - 6)$

$\qquad = 6\hat{i} - 22\hat{j} - 14\hat{k}$ **(1 Mark)**

$\left| (\vec{l_1} \times \vec{l_2}) \cdot \vec{l_3} \right| = \left| (6\hat{i} - 22\hat{j} - 14\hat{k}) \cdot (6\hat{i} - 3\hat{j} + 9\hat{k}) \right|$

$\Rightarrow \quad \left| (\vec{l_1} \times \vec{l_2}) \cdot \vec{l_3} \right| = |36 + 66 - 126| = 24$

Volume is 24 cubic units.   **(1 Mark)**

25. $x = -y = kz$

$\qquad \dfrac{x}{1} = \dfrac{y}{-1} = \dfrac{z}{\frac{1}{k}}$

Vector, $\vec{a} = \hat{i} - \hat{j} + \dfrac{1}{k}\hat{k}$ ...(1)

$x - 2 = 2y + 1 = -z + 1$

$\Rightarrow \quad \dfrac{x - 2}{1} = \dfrac{y + \frac{1}{2}}{\frac{1}{2}} = \dfrac{z - 1}{-1}$ **(1 Mark)**

Vector $\vec{b} = \hat{i} + \dfrac{1}{2}\hat{j} - \hat{k}$ ...(2)

For two lines to be perpendicular

$\qquad \vec{a} \cdot \vec{b} = 0$

$\Rightarrow \quad \left(\hat{i} - \hat{j} + \dfrac{1}{k}\hat{k} \right) \cdot \left(\hat{i} + \dfrac{1}{2}\hat{j} - \hat{k} \right) = 0$

$\Rightarrow \quad 1 - \dfrac{1}{2} - \dfrac{1}{k} = 0$

$\Rightarrow \quad \dfrac{1}{2} = \dfrac{1}{k} \Rightarrow k = 2$ **(1 Mark)**

26. Probability of green signal $= 30\% = \dfrac{30}{100}$

P(green signal) $= 0.3$

$\qquad \because$ P(G) $= 0.3$

Probability of other signals, P(other) $= 1 - 0.3 = 0.7$

P(X) = Probability of getting green signal on two consecutive days out of 3.

$$= P(G)\ P(G)\ P(Other) + P(Other)\ P(G)\ P(G)$$

$$= (0.3)(0.3)(0.7) + (0.7)(0.3)(0.3)$$

$$= 2(0.3)(0.3)(0.7)$$

$$= 2 \times 0.09 \times 0.7$$

$$= 0.126 \qquad \textbf{(2 Marks)}$$

SECTION - C

27. $(a, b)\ R(c, d) \Leftrightarrow ad = bc$ (given relation)

(i) Reflexivity:

Since $ab = ba$ $\because ab \in N$

$(a, b)\ R\ (a, b)$ is true

Relation R is reflexive.   **(1 Mark)**

(ii) Symmetry:

Let $(a, b)\ R\ (c, d)$

$$ad = bc$$

But $bc = cb$ and $ad = da$

$\because\quad cb = da \Rightarrow cb = ad$

$(c, d)\ R\ (a, b)$

$\therefore (a, b)\ R\ (c, d) \Leftrightarrow (c, d)\ R\ (a, b)$

Relation is symmetric.   **(1 Mark)**

(iii) Transitivity:

Let $(a, b)\ R\ (c, d)$ and $(c, d)\ R\ (e, f)$

$$ad = bc \text{ and } cf = de$$

$$(ad)\ (cf) = (bc)\ (de)$$

$$(af)\ (dc) = (be)\ (dc)$$

$$af = be$$

$$\Rightarrow (a, b)\ R\ (e, f)$$

$\therefore (a, b)\ R\ (c, d)$ and $(c, d)\ R\ (e, f)$

$\Rightarrow (a, b)\ R\ (e, f)$

$\Rightarrow$ Relation is transitive   **(1 Mark)**

Relation is symmetric, equivalence and transitive.

$\therefore$ Relation is equivalence relation.   **(1 Mark)**

28. $y = e^{x^2 \cos x} + (\cos x)^x$

$$y = e^{x^2 \cos x} + e^{\log(\cos x)^x}$$

$$y = e^{x^2 \cos x} + e^{x \log(\cos x)}$$

By chain rule

$$\frac{d}{dx} f(g(x)) = \frac{df}{dg} \frac{dg}{dx} \qquad \textbf{(1 Mark)}$$

$$\frac{dy}{dx} = \frac{d}{dx}(e^{x^2 \cos x}) + \frac{d}{dx}(e^{x \log \cos x})$$

$$= e^{x^2 \cos x}(2x \cos x - x^2 \sin x)$$

$$+ e^{x \log(\cos x)}\left[\log(\cos x) - \frac{x}{\cos x} \sin x \right] \qquad \textbf{(1 Mark)}$$

$$\left[\because \frac{d}{dx}e^x = e^x, \frac{d}{dx}\log x = \frac{1}{x}, \frac{d}{dx}\cos x = -\sin x \right]$$

$$= e^{x^2 \cos x}(2x \cos x - x^2 \sin x)$$

$$+ (\cos x)^x [\log \cos x - x \tan x] \qquad \textbf{(2 Marks)}$$

29. Let $I = \int \sec^3 x\, dx$

$$I = \int \sec x \sec^2 x\, dx$$

$$\int uv\, dx = u \int v\, dx - \int \left(\frac{du}{dx} \int v\, dx \right) dx$$

$$I = \sec x \int \sec^2 x\, dx - \int \left(\frac{d}{dx} \sec x \int \sec^2 x \right) dx$$

$$= \sec x \tan x - \int \sec x \tan x \tan x\, dx \qquad \textbf{(1 Mark)}$$

$$\left[\because \int \sec^2 x\, dx = \tan x + C, \frac{d}{dx} \sec x = \sec x \tan x \right]$$

$$= \sec x \tan x - \int \sec x \tan^2 x\, dx$$

$$= \sec x \tan x - \int \sec x(\sec^2 x - 1)dx$$

$$[\because \sec^2 \theta = 1 + \tan^2 \theta] \qquad \textbf{(1 Mark)}$$

$$I = \sec x \tan x - \int \sec^3 dx + \int \sec x\, dx$$

$$= \sec x \tan x - I + \log| \sec x + \tan x | + C$$

$$\left[\because \int \sec x = \log| \sec x + \tan x | + C \right]$$

$$2I = \sec x \tan x + \log | \sec x + \tan x | + C$$

$$\Rightarrow I = \frac{1}{2} \sec x.\tan x + \frac{1}{2} \log | \sec x + \tan x | + C \quad \textbf{(2 Marks)}$$

30. $ye^y\, dx = (y^3 + 2xe^y)dy$

$$\Rightarrow \frac{dx}{dy} = \frac{y^3 + 2xe^y}{ye^y}$$

$$\Rightarrow \frac{dx}{dy} = \frac{y^2}{e^y} + \frac{2x}{y}$$

$$\Rightarrow \frac{dx}{dy} - \frac{2}{y}x = y^2 e^{-y} \qquad \textbf{(1 Mark)}$$

This is a linear differential equation of the form

$$\frac{dx}{dy} + Px = Q$$

where $P = \dfrac{-2}{y}$, $Q = y^2 e^{-y}$

$$\therefore \text{I.F.} = e^{\int P\,dy} = e^{\int \frac{-2}{y}dy} = e^{-2\log y} \qquad \left[\because \int \frac{1}{y}dy = \log y\right]$$

$$\text{I.F.} = e^{\log y^{-2}} = y^{-2} = \frac{1}{y^2} \quad \left[\because e^{\log m^n} = m^n\right] \qquad \textbf{(1 Mark)}$$

$$x \cdot (\text{I.F.}) = \int \text{I.F.} \times Q\, dy + C$$

$$x \times \frac{1}{y^2} = \int \frac{1}{y^2}(y^2 e^{-y})dy + C$$

$$\Rightarrow \frac{x}{y^2} = \int e^{-y}dy + C$$

$$\Rightarrow \frac{x}{y^2} = -e^{-y} + C \qquad \left[\because \int e^{-y}dx = -e^{-y}\right]$$

$$\Rightarrow \frac{x}{y^2} + e^{-y} = C \qquad \textbf{(2 Marks)}$$

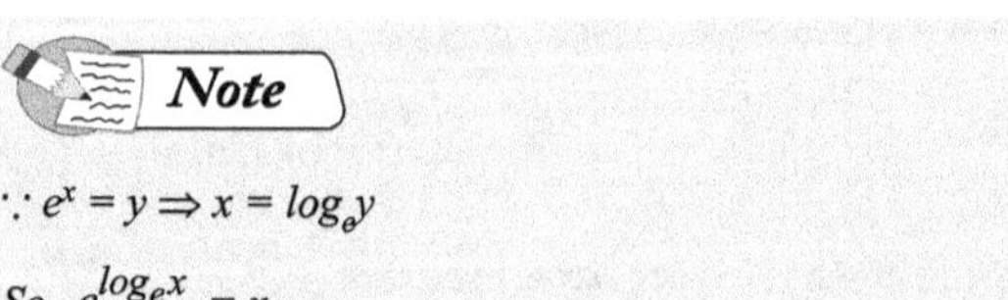

$\because e^x = y \Rightarrow x = \log_e y$

So, $e^{\log_e x} = x$

OR

$$x\frac{dy}{dx} = y - x\tan\left(\frac{y}{x}\right)$$

$$\Rightarrow \frac{dy}{dx} = \frac{y}{x} - \tan\left(\frac{y}{x}\right) \qquad \text{...(1)}$$

Let $z = \dfrac{y}{x}$

Given $y = \dfrac{\pi}{4}$ at $x = 1$

$$\therefore \qquad z = \frac{\pi}{4}$$

$z = \dfrac{y}{x}$, Differentiating w.r.t. x

$$\frac{dz}{dx} = \frac{1}{x}\frac{dy}{dx} + y\frac{d}{dx}\left(\frac{1}{x}\right) \qquad \textbf{(1 Mark)}$$

$$\Rightarrow \frac{dz}{dx} = \frac{1}{x}\frac{dy}{dx} - \frac{y}{x^2}$$

$$\Rightarrow \frac{dz}{dx} = \frac{1}{x}\left(\frac{dy}{dx} - \frac{y}{x}\right)$$

$$\Rightarrow \frac{dz}{dx} = \frac{1}{x}\left(-\tan\left(\frac{y}{x}\right)\right) \qquad \text{[from (1)]}$$

$$\Rightarrow \frac{dz}{dx} = \frac{-\tan z}{x}$$

$$\Rightarrow \frac{-dz}{\tan z} = \frac{dx}{x} \Rightarrow -\cot z\,dz = \frac{dx}{x} \qquad \textbf{(1 Mark)}$$

Integrating on both sides

$$\int \cot z\,dz = -\int \frac{1}{x}dx$$

$$\log|\sin z| = -\log|x| + \log|c| \quad \left[\because \int \cot x\,dx = \log|\sin x|\right]$$

$$\Rightarrow \log|\sin z| = \log\left|\frac{c}{x}\right|$$

$$\sin z = \frac{c}{x} \qquad \textbf{(1 Mark)}$$

Putting $x = 1$, $y = \dfrac{\pi}{4}$

$$\sin \frac{\pi}{4} = c$$

$$c = \frac{1}{\sqrt{2}}$$

$$\sin z = \frac{1}{\sqrt{2}x}$$

$$\Rightarrow z = \sin^{-1}\left(\frac{1}{\sqrt{2}x}\right)$$

$$\Rightarrow \frac{y}{x} = \sin^{-1}\left(\frac{1}{\sqrt{2}x}\right) \qquad \textbf{(1 Mark)}$$

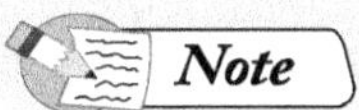

When the function in the form of $\dfrac{dy}{dx} = f\left(\dfrac{y}{x}\right)$ *then put y = vx and solve it.*

31. Let the number of chairs be x and the number of tables be y

Maximize profit $Z = 150x + 250y$

Subjected to: $1000x + 2000y \le 50000$

$x + 2y \le 50$

$x + y \le 35, x \ge 0, y \ge 0$ **(1 Mark)**

$x + y = 35$		
x	0	35
y	35	0

$x + 2y = 50$		
x	0	50
y	25	0

Intersecting point

$$
\begin{array}{ccccc}
x & + & y & = & 35 \\
x & + & 2y & = & 50 \\
- & & - & & - \\
\hline
& & -y & = & -15 \\
& & y & = & 15
\end{array}
$$

$x + 15 = 35$

$x = 20, B(20, 15)$

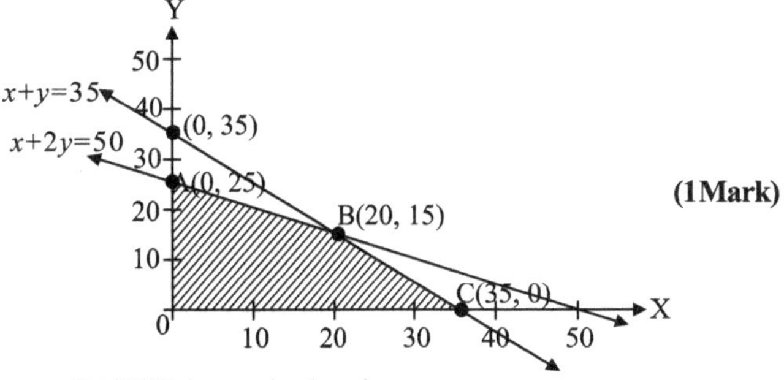

(1 Mark)

OABCO is required region

	x	y	z
O(0, 0)	0	0	0
A(0, 25)	0	25	6250
C(35, 0)	35	0	5250
B(20, 15)	20	15	6750 (Max.)

Maximum profit is ₹ 6750 when number of chairs are 20 and tables are 15.   **(2 Marks)**

The optimal solution of a linear programming problem with bounded region is achieved at any corner point of its region.

32.

Bag I
Red = 3
Black = 5

Bag II
Red = 4
Black = 3

1 ball is transferred randomly from bag I to bag II.

Let E_1: transferred ball is black

E_2: transferred ball in red

F: Ball drawn from bag II is black

$$P(E_1) = \frac{5}{8}, \qquad P(E_2) = \frac{3}{8}$$

$$P(F/E_1) = \frac{4}{8}, \qquad P(F/E_2) = \frac{3}{8} \qquad \textbf{(2 Marks)}$$

By Baye's theorem:

$$P(E_1/F) = \frac{P(F/E_1)\cdot P(E_1)}{P((F/E_1)\cdot P(E_1) + P(F/E_2)\cdot P(E_2)}$$ **(1 Mark)**

$$= \frac{\dfrac{5}{8}\times\dfrac{4}{8}}{\dfrac{5}{8}\times\dfrac{4}{8} + \dfrac{3}{8}\times\dfrac{3}{8}} = \frac{20}{29}$$ **(1 Mark)**

OR

Red = 5
White = 2
Black = 3

Let X denote the number of white balls when 3 balls are drawn one by one without replacement.

So, X can be 0, 1, 2

$P(X = 0)$ = Probability when none of the balls are white

$$P(X = 0) = \frac{{}^{8}C_3}{{}^{10}C_3}$$ **(1 Mark)**

$$\left[\because \text{Probability} = \frac{\text{Number of favourable outcomes}}{\text{Total number of outcomes}}\right]$$

$${}^{n}C_r = \frac{n!}{(n-r)!\,r!}$$

$$P(X=0) = \dfrac{\dfrac{8 \times 7 \times 6 \times 5!}{5! \; 3!}}{\dfrac{10 \times 9 \times 8 \times 7!}{3! \; 7!}}$$

$$= \dfrac{8 \times 7 \times 6}{10 \times 9 \times 8} = \dfrac{7}{15}$$

$P(X=1)$ = Probability when 1 of 3 balls in white

$$P(X=1) = \dfrac{{}^{8}C_2 \times {}^{2}C_1}{{}^{10}C_3}$$

$$= \dfrac{\dfrac{8 \times 7 \times 6!}{6! \times 2!} \times \dfrac{2!}{1! \, 1!}}{\dfrac{10 \times 9 \times 8 \times 7!}{7! \times 3!}} = \dfrac{7}{15}$$

$P(X=2)$ = Probability when two balls out of 3 are white

$$P(X=2) = \dfrac{{}^{8}C_1 \times {}^{2}C_2}{{}^{10}C_3}$$

$$= \dfrac{\dfrac{8 \times 7!}{1! \times 7!} \times \dfrac{2!}{0! \, 2!}}{\dfrac{10 \times 9 \times 8 \times 7!}{7! \, 3!}} = \dfrac{1}{15}$$

$\therefore$ Probability distribution of X is

X	0	1	2	Total
P(X)	$\dfrac{7}{15}$	$\dfrac{7}{15}$	$\dfrac{1}{15}$	1
XP(X)	0	$\dfrac{7}{15}$	$\dfrac{2}{15}$	$\dfrac{9}{15}$
X²P(X)	0	$\dfrac{7}{15}$	$\dfrac{4}{15}$	$\dfrac{11}{15}$

(1 Mark)

Mean $= \Sigma X \, P(X) = \dfrac{9}{15} = \dfrac{3}{5} = 0.6$ **(1 Mark)**

Variance $= \Sigma X^2 \, P(X) - [\Sigma X \, P(X)]^2$

$$= \dfrac{11}{15} - \dfrac{9}{25} = \dfrac{55-27}{75}$$

$$= \dfrac{28}{75} = 0.37.$$ **(1 Mark)**

33. $A = \begin{bmatrix} 1 & 2 & -3 \\ 3 & 2 & -2 \\ 2 & -1 & 1 \end{bmatrix}$

$|A| = 1(2-2) -2(3+4) -3(-3-4)$

$\quad = -14 + 21 = 7$ **(1 Mark)**

$\because \;\; |A| \neq 0, \, A^{-1}$ exist.

$A_{11} = (-1)^2 \begin{vmatrix} 2 & -2 \\ -1 & 1 \end{vmatrix} = 2-2 = 0$

$A_{12} = (-1)^3 \begin{vmatrix} 3 & -2 \\ 2 & 1 \end{vmatrix} = (-1)[3+4] = -7$

$A_{13} = (-1)^4 \begin{vmatrix} 3 & 2 \\ 2 & -1 \end{vmatrix} = [-3-4] = -7$

$A_{21} = (-1)^3 \begin{vmatrix} 2 & -3 \\ -1 & 1 \end{vmatrix} = (-1)[2-3] = 1$

$A_{22} = (-1)^4 \begin{vmatrix} 1 & -3 \\ 2 & 1 \end{vmatrix} = 1+6 = 7$

$A_{23} = (-1)^5 \begin{vmatrix} 1 & 2 \\ 2 & -1 \end{vmatrix} = (-1)[-1-4] = 5$

$A_{31} = (-1)^4 \begin{vmatrix} 2 & -3 \\ 2 & -2 \end{vmatrix} = -4+6 = 2$

$A_{32} = (-1)^5 \begin{vmatrix} 1 & -3 \\ 3 & -2 \end{vmatrix} = -1(-2+9) = -7$

$A_{33} = (-1)^6 \begin{vmatrix} 1 & 2 \\ 3 & 2 \end{vmatrix} = 2-6 = -4$

$$\text{adj } A = \begin{bmatrix} 0 & -7 & -7 \\ 1 & 7 & 5 \\ 2 & -7 & -4 \end{bmatrix}^{T}$$

$$= \begin{bmatrix} 0 & 1 & 2 \\ -7 & 7 & -7 \\ -7 & 5 & -4 \end{bmatrix}$$ **(1 Mark)**

$$A^{-1} = \dfrac{1}{|A|} \text{adj} A$$

$$= \dfrac{1}{7} \begin{bmatrix} 0 & 1 & 2 \\ -7 & 7 & -7 \\ 7 & 5 & -4 \end{bmatrix}$$

$$= \begin{bmatrix} 0 & \dfrac{1}{7} & \dfrac{2}{7} \\ -1 & 1 & -1 \\ 1 & \dfrac{5}{7} & -\dfrac{4}{7} \end{bmatrix}$$ **(1 Mark)**

Given equation:

$$x + 2y - 3z = 6$$
$$3x + 2y - 2z = 3$$
$$2x - y + z = 2$$

$$A = \begin{bmatrix} 1 & 2 & -3 \\ 3 & 2 & -2 \\ 2 & -1 & 1 \end{bmatrix},\ B = \begin{bmatrix} 6 \\ 3 \\ 2 \end{bmatrix},\ X = \begin{bmatrix} x \\ y \\ z \end{bmatrix}$$

$$AX = B$$

Multiply A^{-1} on both sides

$$(A^{-1}A)X = A^{-1}B$$

$$IX = A^{-1}B \qquad\qquad [\because A^{-1}A = I]$$

$$X = A^{-1}B \qquad\qquad \textbf{(1 Mark)}$$

$$X = \begin{bmatrix} 0 & \dfrac{1}{7} & \dfrac{2}{7} \\ -1 & 1 & -1 \\ 1 & \dfrac{5}{7} & -\dfrac{4}{7} \end{bmatrix}\begin{bmatrix} 6 \\ 3 \\ 2 \end{bmatrix}$$

$$X = \begin{bmatrix} \dfrac{3}{7}+\dfrac{4}{7} \\ -6+3-2 \\ 6+\dfrac{15}{7}-\dfrac{8}{7} \end{bmatrix}$$

$$X = \begin{bmatrix} 1 \\ -5 \\ 7 \end{bmatrix}$$

$$\therefore\quad \begin{bmatrix} x \\ y \\ z \end{bmatrix} = \begin{bmatrix} 1 \\ -5 \\ 7 \end{bmatrix}$$

$$\therefore\qquad x = 1,\, y = -5,\, z = 7 \qquad \textbf{(2 Marks)}$$

OR

L.H.S.

$$\Delta = \begin{vmatrix} (b+c)^2 & a^2 & bc \\ (c+a)^2 & b^2 & ca \\ (a+b)^2 & c^2 & ab \end{vmatrix}$$

$$R_1 \to R_1 - R_3,\ R_2 \to R_2 - R_3$$

$$\Delta = \begin{vmatrix} (b+c+a+b)(b+c-a-b) & (a+c)(a-c) & b(c-a) \\ (c+a+a+b)(c+a-a-b) & (b+c)(b-c) & a(c-b) \\ (a+b)^2 & c^2 & ab \end{vmatrix}$$

$$\Delta = \begin{vmatrix} (c-a)(2b+a+c) & (a+c)(a-c) & b(c-a) \\ (c-b)(2a+c+b) & (b+c)(b-c) & a(c-b) \\ (a+b)^2 & c^2 & ab \end{vmatrix}$$

$$\Delta = (c-a)(b-c)\begin{vmatrix} a+c+2b & -a-c & b \\ -2a-c-b & b+c & -a \\ (a+b)^2 & c^2 & ab \end{vmatrix} \qquad \textbf{(2 Marks)}$$

$$R_1 \to R_1 + R_2$$

$$\Delta = (c-a)(b-c)\begin{vmatrix} -a+b & b-a & b-a \\ -2a-b-c & b+c & -a \\ (a+b)^2 & c^2 & ab \end{vmatrix}$$

$$\Delta = (a-b)(c-a)(b-c)\begin{vmatrix} -1 & -1 & -1 \\ -2a-b-c & b+c & -a \\ (a+b)^2 & c^2 & ab \end{vmatrix} \qquad \textbf{(2 Marks)}$$

$$C_1 \to C_1 - C_3,\ C_2 \to C_2 - C_3$$

$$\Delta = (a-b)(c-a)(b-c)\begin{vmatrix} 0 & 0 & -1 \\ -a-b-c & a+b+c & -a \\ (a+b)^2-ab & c^2-ab & ab \end{vmatrix}$$

$$\Delta = (a-b)(b-c)(c-a)\{[(a+b+c)$$
$$(c^2-ab)]+(a+b+c)[(a+b)^2-ab]\}$$
$$= (a-b)(b-c)(c-a)(a+b+c)[c^2-ab+$$
$$a^2+2ab+b^2-ab]$$
$$\Delta = (a-b)(b-c)(c-a)(a+b+c)(a^2+b^2+$$
$$c^2) = \text{R.H.S.}$$

Hence Proved. **(2 Marks)**

Note

Use properties of determinant to obtain maximum number of zeroes in a row or a column.

34. $A(2, -2),\ B(4, 5),\ C(6, 2)$

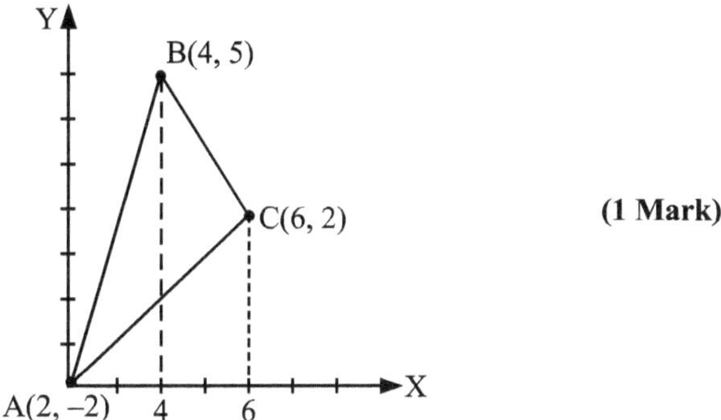

(1 Mark)

Equation of line

$$y - y_1 = \frac{y_2 - y_1}{x_2 - x_1}(x - x_1)$$ **(½ Mark)**

Equation of line AB:

$$y - 5 = \frac{-2 - 5}{2 - 4}(x - 4)$$

$$y - 5 = \frac{-7}{-2}(x - 4)$$

$$\Rightarrow y = \frac{7}{2}x - \frac{28}{2} + 5$$

$$\Rightarrow y = \frac{7}{2}x - 9$$ **(½ Mark)**

Equation of line BC:

$$y - 5 = \frac{2 - 5}{6 - 4}(x - 4)$$

$$\Rightarrow y = \frac{-3}{2}x + \frac{12}{2} + 5$$

$$\Rightarrow y = \frac{-3}{2}x + 6 + 5$$

$$\Rightarrow y = \frac{-3}{2}x + 11$$ **(½ Mark)**

Equation of line AC:

$$y - 2 = \frac{-2 - 2}{2 - 6}(x - 6)$$

$$\Rightarrow y - 2 = \frac{4}{4}(x - 6)$$

$$\Rightarrow y - 2 = x - 6$$
$$\Rightarrow y = x - 4$$ **(½ Mark)**

Area of ΔABC

$$= \int_2^4 AB\,dx + \int_4^6 (BC)\,dx - \int_2^6 (CA)\,dx$$ **(1 Mark)**

$$= \int_2^4 \left(\frac{7}{2}x - 9\right)dx + \int_4^6 \left(\frac{-3}{2}x + 11\right)dx - \int_2^6 (x - 4)\,dx$$

$$= \left[\frac{7x^2}{4} - 9x\right]_2^4 + \left[\frac{-3x^2}{4} + 11x\right]_4^6 - \left[\frac{x^2}{2} - 4x\right]_2^6$$

$$= [(28 - 36) - (7 - 18)] + [(-27 + 66) - (-12 + 44)]$$
$$- [(18 - 24) - (2 - 8)]$$

$$= [(-8) - (-11)] + [39 - (32)] - [(-6) - (-6)]$$

$$= 3 + 7 - 0 = 10 \text{ sq. units}$$

Area of $\Delta ABC = 10$ sq. units **(2 Marks)**

To check the answer find the area of triangles by $\frac{1}{2} \times b \times h$ *and trapezium by* $\frac{1}{2}$ *(sum of parallel side) × height.*

35.

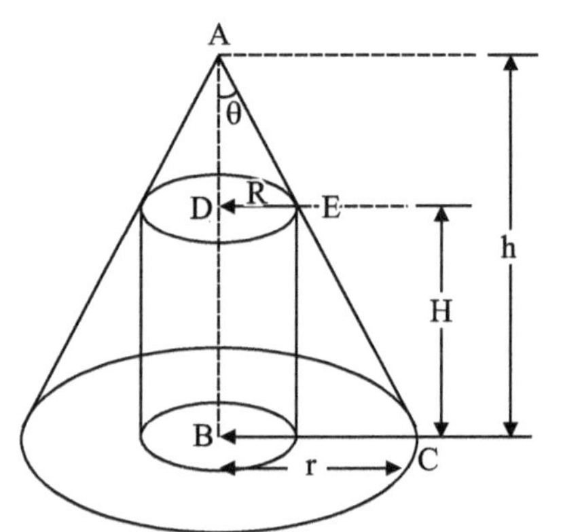

(1 Mark)

Given height of cone be h and radius of cone be r

Let height of cylinder be H and radius of cylinder be R

Volume of cylinder $V = \pi R^2 H$ ...(1)

In right ΔADE

$$\tan\theta = \frac{R}{h - H}$$ **(½ Mark)**

In right ΔABC

$$\tan\theta = \frac{r}{h}$$

$$\Rightarrow \quad \frac{r}{h} = \frac{R}{h - H}$$

$$\Rightarrow \quad rh - rH = hR$$

$$\Rightarrow \quad R = r - \frac{rH}{h}$$

$$\Rightarrow \quad R = r\left(1 - \frac{H}{h}\right)$$ ...(2) **(½ Mark)**

From (1)

$$V = \pi r^2 \left(1-\frac{H}{h}\right)^2 H \qquad \textbf{(1 Mark)}$$

Differentiate both sides w.r.t. H

$$\frac{dV}{dH} = \pi r^2 \left[\left(1-\frac{H}{h}\right)^2 + H2\left(1-\frac{H}{h}\right)\left(\frac{-1}{h}\right)\right]$$

$$= \pi r^2 \left(1-\frac{H}{h}\right)\left[1-\frac{H}{h}-\frac{2H}{h}\right]$$

$$= \pi r^2 \left(1-\frac{H}{h}\right)\left[1-\frac{3H}{h}\right] = 0$$

$$\because \quad 1-\frac{H}{h} \neq 0 \qquad \textbf{(1 Mark)}$$

$$\therefore \quad 1-\frac{3H}{h} = 0 \;\Rightarrow\; H = \frac{h}{3} \qquad \ldots(3)$$

$$\therefore \quad \frac{d^2V}{dH^2} = \pi r^2 \left[\frac{-1}{h}\left(1-\frac{3H}{h}\right)+\left(1-\frac{H}{h}\right)\left(\frac{-3}{h}\right)\right]$$

Put $H = \dfrac{h}{3}$

$$= \pi r^2 \left[0+\left(1-\frac{1}{3}\right)\left(\frac{-3}{h}\right)\right]$$

$$= \pi r^2 \left(\frac{-2}{h}\right) < 0$$

$\therefore$ Volume is maximum when $H = \dfrac{h}{3}$.

Volume of cylinder $= \pi r^2 \left(1-\dfrac{H}{h}\right)^2 H$

Putting $H = \dfrac{h}{3}$; $V = \pi r^2 \left(1-\dfrac{1}{3}\right)^2 \cdot \dfrac{h}{3}$

$$= \pi r^2 \frac{4}{9} h = \frac{4}{9}\pi r^2 h$$

$$= \frac{4}{9} \times \text{volume of cone.} \qquad \textbf{(2 Marks)}$$

Hence proved.

 **Note**

When right circular cylinder inscribed in a right circular cone then $\triangle ADE \sim \triangle ABC$ i.e. $\dfrac{AD}{AB} = \dfrac{DE}{BC} = \dfrac{AE}{AC}$.

36. Plane passing through $A(2, 1, -1)$ and perpendicular to line of intersection of 2 planes

$2x + y - z = 3$ and $x + 2y + z = 2$

Since plane is perpendicular to the line of intersection. Therefore, normal of the required plane is parallel to the line of intersection and perpendicular to a normal of both given plane.

$\vec{n}_1 \to$ Normal vector of first given plane.

$\vec{n}_2 \to$ Normal vector of second given plane.

$\vec{N} \to$ Normal vector of required plane.

$$\vec{N} \parallel \vec{n}_1 \times \vec{n}_2 \qquad (\because \vec{N} \perp n_1, \vec{N} \perp n_2)$$

Normal vector, $\vec{N} = \begin{vmatrix} \hat{i} & \hat{j} & \hat{k} \\ 2 & 1 & -1 \\ 1 & 2 & 1 \end{vmatrix} = 3\hat{i} - 3\hat{j} + 3\hat{k}$

$\therefore$ Direction ratios of normal are $3, -3, 3$ **(1 Mark)**

Equation of plane passing through (x_1, y_1, z_1) is given by

$A(x - x_1) + B(y - y_1) + c(z - z_1) = 0$

Where A, B, C are the direction ratios of normal to the plane.

$A(x - 2) + B(y - 1) + C(z + 1) = 0$

$\Rightarrow \quad 3(x - 2) - 3(y - 1) + 3(z + 1) = 0$

$\Rightarrow \quad (x - 2) - (y - 1) + (z + 1) = 0$

$\Rightarrow \quad x - 2 - y + 1 + z + 1 = 0$

$\Rightarrow \quad x - y + z = 0 \qquad \textbf{(2 Marks)}$

$$\cos\theta = \frac{|\vec{N} \cdot \vec{b}|}{|\vec{N}||\vec{b}|} \qquad \textbf{(1 Mark)}$$

Direction vector of y axis is $\vec{b} = 0\hat{i} + \hat{j} + 0\hat{k}$

$$\cos\theta = \frac{|(3\hat{i} - 3\hat{j} + 3\hat{k})(0\hat{i} + \hat{j} + 0\hat{k})|}{\sqrt{3^2 + 3^2 + 3^2}\sqrt{1^2}}$$

$$\Rightarrow \quad \cos\theta = \frac{|-1|}{\sqrt{3}} = \frac{1}{\sqrt{3}}$$

$$\Rightarrow \quad \theta = \cos^{-1}\left(\frac{1}{\sqrt{3}}\right) \qquad \textbf{(2 Marks)}$$

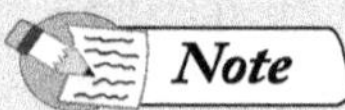

> **Note**
>
> *Equation of line of intersection of two plane $a_1x + b_1y + c_1z + d_1 = 0$ and $a_2x + b_2y + c_2z + d_2 = 0$ is $a_1x + b_1y + c_1z + d_1 = a_2x + b_2y + c_2z + d_2 = 0$.*

OR

$\vec{r} = (3\hat{i} - 2\hat{j} + 6\hat{k}) + \lambda(2\hat{i} - \hat{j} + 2\hat{k})$ line equation

$\vec{r}.(\hat{i} - \hat{j} + \hat{k}) = 6$ plane equation

From line equation

$$x = 3 + 2\lambda$$
$$y = -2 - \lambda$$
$$z = 6 + 2\lambda$$

Equation of plane can be written as

$$x - y + z = 6$$
$$\Rightarrow (3 + 2\lambda) - (-2 - \lambda) + (6 + 2\lambda) = 6$$
$$\Rightarrow 3 + 2\lambda + 2 + \lambda + 6 + 2\lambda = 6$$
$$\Rightarrow 5\lambda + 11 = 6$$

$$\Rightarrow \lambda = \frac{-5}{5} = -1$$

$$\Rightarrow \lambda = -1 \qquad \text{(1 Mark)}$$

Point of intersection

$$x = 3 + 2(-1) = 1$$
$$y = -2 + 1 = -1$$
$$z = 6 - 2 = 4$$

$Q(1, -1, 4)$

$P(-2, -4, 7)$ **(1 Mark)**

$$\text{Distance} = \sqrt{(x_2 - x_1)^2 + (y_2 - y_1)^2 + (z_2 - z_1)^2}$$
$$= \sqrt{(-2 - 1)^2 + (-4 + 1)^2 + (7 - 4)^2}$$
$$= \sqrt{3^2 + 3^2 + 3^2} = 3\sqrt{3} \qquad \text{(2 Marks)}$$

Vector equation of PQ

$$\vec{r} = (\hat{i} - \hat{j} + 4\hat{k}) + \lambda\left[(1 + 2)\hat{i} + (-1 + 4)\hat{j} + (4 - 7)\hat{k}\right]$$
$$\vec{r} = (\hat{i} - \hat{j} + 4\hat{k}) + \lambda(3i + 3\hat{j} - 3\hat{k})$$
$$= (\hat{i} - \hat{j} + 4\hat{k}) + \lambda(i + \hat{j} - \hat{k}) \qquad \text{(2 Marks)}$$

Delhi **2020**

CBSE Board Solved Paper

Time Allowed : 3 Hours   *Maximum Marks : 100*

General Instructions:

Read the following instructions very carefully and strictly follow them:

(i)   This question paper comprises **four** Sections A, B, C and D. This question paper carries **36** questions. **All** questions are compulsory.

(ii) **Section A:** Questions no. **1** to **20** comprises of **20** questions of **1** mark each.

(iii) **Section B:** Questions no. **21** to **26** comprises of **6** questions of **2** marks each.

(iv) **Section C:** Questions no. **27** to **32** comprises of **6** questions of **4** marks each.

(v)   **Section D:** Questions no. **33** to **36** comprises of **4** questions of **6** marks each.

(vi) There is no overall choice in the question paper. However, an internal choice has been provided in **3** questions of **one** mark, **2** questions of **two** marks, **2** questions of **four** marks and **2** questions of **six** marks. Only one of the choices in such questions have to be attempted.

(vii) In addition to this, separate instructions are given with each section and question, wherever necessary.

(viii) Use of calculators is not permitted.

SECTION - A

Question numbers 1 to 20 carry 1 mark each.

Question numbers 1 to 10 are multiple choice type questions. Select the correct option.

1. The area of a triangle formed by vertices O, A and B, where $\overrightarrow{OA} = \overrightarrow{OA} = \hat{i} + 2\hat{j} + 3\hat{k}$ and $\overrightarrow{OB} = -3\hat{i} - 2\hat{j} + \hat{k}$ is

(a) $3\sqrt{5}$ sq. units   (b) $5\sqrt{5}$ sq. units

(c) $6\sqrt{5}$ sq. units   (d) 4 sq. units

2. If $\cos\left(\sin^{-1}\dfrac{2}{\sqrt{5}} + \cos^{-1}x\right) = 0,$ then x is equal to

(a) $\dfrac{1}{\sqrt{5}}$ (b) $-\dfrac{2}{\sqrt{5}}$

(c) $\dfrac{2}{\sqrt{5}}$ (d) 1

3. The interval in which of function f given by $f(x) = x^2 e^{-x}$ is strictly increasing, is

(a) $(-\infty, \infty)$ (b) $(-\infty, 0)$

(c) $(2, \infty)$ (d) $(0, 2)$

4. The function $f(x) = \dfrac{x-1}{x(x^2-1)}$ is discontinuous at

(a) exactly one point   (b) exactly two points

(c) exactly three points (d) no point

5. The function $f : R \to [-1, 1]$ defined by $f(x) = \cos x$ is

(a) both one-one and onto

(b) not one-one, but onto

(c) one-one, but not onto

(d) neither one-one, nor onto

6. The coordinates of the foot of the perpendicular drawn from the point $(2, -3, 4)$ on the y-axis is

(a) $(2, 3, 4)$ (b) $(-2, -3, -4)$

(c) $(0, -3, 0)$ (d) $(2, 0, 4)$

7. The relation R in the set $\{1, 2, 3\}$ given by $R = \{(1, 2), (2, 1), (1, 1)\}$ is

(a) symmetric and transitive, but not reflexive

(b) reflexive and symmetric, but not transitive

(c) symmetric, but neither reflexive nor transitive

(d) an equivalence relation

8. The angle between the vectors $\hat{i} - \hat{j}$ and $\hat{j} - \hat{k}$ is

(a) $-\dfrac{\pi}{3}$ (b) 0

(c) $\dfrac{\pi}{3}$ (d) $\dfrac{2\pi}{3}$

9. If A is a non-singular square matrix of order 3 such that $A^2 = 3A$, then value of $|A|$ is

   (a) -3 (b) 3

   (c) 9 (d) 27

10. If $|\vec{a}| = 4$ and $-3 \le \lambda \le 2$, then $|\lambda \vec{a}|$ lies in

   (a) $[0, 12]$ (b) $[2, 3]$

   (c) $[8, 12]$ (d) $[-12, 8]$

Fill in the blanks in question numbers 11 to 15.

11. If the radius of the circle is increasing at the rate of 0.5 cm/s, then the rate of increase of its circumference is __________.

12. If $\begin{vmatrix} 2x & -9 \\ -2 & x \end{vmatrix} = \begin{vmatrix} -4 & 8 \\ 1 & -2 \end{vmatrix}$, then value of x is __________.

13. The corner points of the feasible region of an LPP are $(0, 0)$, $(0, 8)$, $(2, 7)$, $(5, 4)$ and $(6, 0)$. The maximum profit $P = 3x + 2y$ occurs at the point __________.

14. The range of the principal value branch of the function $y = \sec^{-1} x$ is __________.

OR

The principal value of $\cos^{-1}\left(-\dfrac{1}{2}\right)$ is __________.

15. The distance between parallel planes $2x + y - 2z - 6 = 0$ and $4x + 2y - 4z = 0$ is __________ units.

OR

If $P(1, 0, -3)$ is the foot of the perpendicular from the origin to the plane, then the cartesian equation of the plane is __________.

Question numbers 16 to 20 are very short answer type questions.

16. Evaluate: $\displaystyle\int_{-\pi/2}^{\pi/2} x\cos^2 x\, dx$

17. Find the coordinates of the point where the line $\dfrac{x-1}{3} = \dfrac{y+4}{7} = \dfrac{z+4}{2}$ cuts the xy-plane.

18. Find the value of k, so that the function
$$f(x) = \begin{cases} kx^2 + 5 & \text{if} \quad x \le 1 \\ 2 & \text{if} \quad x > 1 \end{cases}$$
is continuous at $x = 1$.

19. Find the integrating factor of the differential equation
$$x\frac{dy}{dx} = 2x^2 + y$$

20. Differentiate $\sec^2(x^2)$ with respect to x^2.

OR

If $y = f(x^2)$ and $f'(x) = e^{\sqrt{x}}$, then find $\dfrac{dy}{dx}$.

SECTION - B

Question numbers 21 to 26 carry 2 marks each.

21. Find a vector $\vec{r}$ equally inclined to the three axes and whose magnitude is $3\sqrt{3}$ units.

OR

Find the angle between unit vectors $\vec{a}$ and $\vec{b}$ so that $\sqrt{3}\vec{a} - \vec{b}$ is also a unit vector.

22. If $A = \begin{bmatrix} -3 & 2 \\ 1 & -1 \end{bmatrix}$ and $I = \begin{bmatrix} 1 & 0 \\ 0 & 1 \end{bmatrix}$, find scalar k so that $A^2 + I = kA$.

23. If $f(x) = \sqrt{\dfrac{\sec x - 1}{\sec x + 1}}$, find $f'\left(\dfrac{\pi}{3}\right)$.

OR

Find $f'(x)$ if $f(x) = (\tan x)^{\tan x}$

24. Find: $\displaystyle\int \dfrac{\tan^3 x}{\cos^3 x}\, dx$

25. Show that the plane $x - 5y - 2z = 1$ contains the line $\dfrac{x-5}{3} = y = 2 - z$.

26. A fair dice is thrown two times. Find the probability distribution of the number of sixes. Also determine the mean of the number of sixes.

SECTION - C

Question number 27 to 32 carry 4 marks each.

27. Solve the following differential equation:
$$(1 + e^{y/x})dy + e^{y/x}\left(1 - \frac{y}{x}\right)dx = 0 \, (x \ne 0)$$

28. A cottage industry manufactures pedestal lamps and wooden shades. Both the products require machine time as well as craftsman time in the making. The number of hour(s) required for producing 1 unit of each and the corresponding profit is given in the following table:

Item	Machine Time	Craftsman Time	Profit (in ₹)
Pedestal lamp	1.5 hours	3 hours	30
Wooden shades	3 hours	1 hour	20

In a day, the factory has availability of not more than 42 hours of machine time and 24 hours of craftsman time.

Assuming that all items manufactured are sold, how should the manufacturer schedule his daily production in order to maximise the profit? Formulate it as an LPP and solve it graphically.

———

29. Evaluate: $\int \sin 2x \tan\ (\sin x)\,dx$

30. Check whether the relation R in the set N of natural numbers given by

R = {(a, b) : a is divisor of b}

is reflexive, symmetric or transitive. Also determine whether R is an equivalence relation.

OR

Prove that $\tan^{-1}\dfrac{1}{4} + \tan^{-1}\dfrac{2}{9} = \dfrac{1}{2}\sin^{-1}\left(\dfrac{4}{5}\right)$.

31. Find the equation of the plane passing through the points $(1, 0, -2)$, $(3, -1, 0)$ and perpendicular to the plane $2x - y + z = 8$. Also find the distance of the plane thus obtained from the origin.

32. If $\tan^{-1}\left(\dfrac{y}{x}\right) = \log\sqrt{x^2 + y^2}$, prove that $\dfrac{dy}{dx} = \dfrac{x + y}{x - y}$.

OR

If $y = e^{a\cos^{-1}x}, -1 < x < 1$, then show that

$$(1 - x^2)\dfrac{d^2y}{dx^2} - x\dfrac{dy}{dx} - a^2 y = 0$$

Question numbers 33 to 36 carry 6 marks each.

33. Amongst all open (from the top) right circular cylindrical boxes of volume 125π cm^3, find the dimensions of the box which has the least surface area.

34. Using integration, find the area lying above x-axis and included between the circle $x^2 + y^2 = 8x$ and inside the parabola $y^2 = 4x$.

OR

Using the method of integration, find the area of the triangle ABC, coordinates of whose vertices are A(2, 0), B(4, 5) and C(6, 3).

35. If A = $\begin{bmatrix} 5 & -1 & 4 \\ 2 & 3 & 5 \\ 5 & -2 & 6 \end{bmatrix}$, find A^{-1} and use it to solve the following system of equations:

$5x - y + 4z = 5$

$2x + 3y + 5z = 2$

$5x - 2y + 6z = -1$

OR

If x, y, z are different and $\begin{vmatrix} x & x^2 & 1+x^3 \\ y & y^2 & 1+y^3 \\ z & z^2 & 1+z^3 \end{vmatrix} = 0$, then using properties of determinants show that $1 + xyz = 0$.

36. A card from a pack of 52 cards is lost. From the remaining cards of the pack, two cards are drawn randomly one-by-one without replacement and are found to be both kings. Find the probability of the lost card being a king.

Solutions

SECTION - A

1. (a) $\overrightarrow{OA} = \hat{i} + 2\hat{j} + 3\hat{k}$, $\overrightarrow{OB} = -3\hat{i} - 2\hat{j} + \hat{k}$

$$\overrightarrow{OA} \times \overrightarrow{OB} = \begin{vmatrix} \hat{i} & \hat{j} & \hat{k} \\ 1 & 2 & 3 \\ -3 & -2 & 1 \end{vmatrix}$$

$$= \hat{i}(2-(-6)) - \hat{j}(1-(-9)) + \hat{k}(-2-(-6))$$

$$= 8\hat{i} - 10\hat{j} + 4\hat{k}$$

$$\left| \overrightarrow{OA} \times \overrightarrow{OB} \right| = \sqrt{a^2 + b^2 + c^2}$$

$$= \sqrt{8^2 + (-10)^2 + (4)^2}$$

$$= \sqrt{64 + 100 + 16}$$

$$= \sqrt{180} = 6\sqrt{5}$$

$\therefore$ Area of $\triangle OAB = \dfrac{1}{2}\left| \overrightarrow{OA} \times \overrightarrow{OB} \right|$

Area of $\triangle ABC = \dfrac{1}{2} \times 6\sqrt{5} = 3\sqrt{5}$ sq. units. **(1 Mark)**

2. (c) $\cos\left(\sin^{-1} \dfrac{2}{\sqrt{5}} + \cos^{-1} x \right) = 0$

$$\Rightarrow \quad \sin^{-1} \dfrac{2}{\sqrt{5}} + \cos^{-1} x = \cos^{-1} 0$$

$$\Rightarrow \quad \sin^{-1} \dfrac{2}{\sqrt{5}} + \cos^{-1} x = \dfrac{\pi}{2} \qquad \left[\because \cos^{-1} 0 = \dfrac{\pi}{2} \right]$$

$$\Rightarrow \quad \cos^{-1} x = \dfrac{\pi}{2} - \sin^{-1} \dfrac{2}{\sqrt{5}}$$

Taking cos on both sides

$$\cos(\cos^{-1} x) = \cos\left(\dfrac{\pi}{2} - \sin^{-1} \dfrac{2}{\sqrt{5}} \right)$$

$$\Rightarrow x = \sin\left(\sin^{-1} \dfrac{2}{\sqrt{5}} \right) \qquad \left[\because \cos\left(\dfrac{\pi}{2} - \theta \right) = \sin\theta \right]$$

$$\Rightarrow x = \dfrac{2}{\sqrt{5}} \qquad\qquad\qquad\qquad \textbf{(1 Mark)}$$

3. (d) $f(x) = x^2 e^{-x}$

$$f'(x) = x^2 \dfrac{d}{dx}(e^{-x}) + e^{-x} \dfrac{d}{dx} x^2$$

$$\left[\because \dfrac{d}{dx} uv = u\dfrac{d}{dx}v + v\dfrac{du}{dx} \right]$$

$$f'(x) = -x^2 e^{-x} + e^{-x}(2x) \left[\dfrac{d}{dx} x^n = nx^{n-1} \right]$$

$$= xe^{-x}(-x+2) = xe^{-x}(2-x)$$

Putting $f'(x) = 0$

$$\Rightarrow \quad xe^{-x}(2-x) = 0$$

e^{-x} is always positive for all $x \in R$

$\therefore x = 0$ and $x = 2$

Case I: for $-\infty < x < 0$

$$f'(x) = (-)\,(+)\,(+)$$

$$= -ve$$

$\therefore$ Function is strictly decreasing.

Case II: for $0 < x < 2$

$$f'(x) = (+)\,(+)\,(+) = +ve$$

Function is strictly increasing.

Case III: for $2 < x < \infty$

$$f'(x) = (+)\,(+)\,(-)$$

$$= -ve$$

Function is strictly decreasing.

Hence, $f(x)$ is strictly increasing in $(0, 2)$ **(1 Mark)**

> **Note**
>
> *A function f(x) is strictly increasing in interval I, if f'(x) > 0 $\forall x \in I$.*

4. (c) $f(x) = \dfrac{x-1}{x(x^2 - 1^2)}$

$$\Rightarrow \quad f(x) = \dfrac{x-1}{x(x-1)(x+1)}$$

$$[\because (a^2 - b^2) = (a-b)(a+b)]$$

Graph will be discontinuous at three points i.e. $x = 0, -1, 1$.

(1 Mark)

> **Note**
>
> *Every single function is continuous at its domain.*

5.   (b) $f(x) = \cos x$

$f : R \to [-1, 1]$

if $x_1 = \dfrac{\pi}{2}$

$f(x_1) = f\left(\dfrac{\pi}{2}\right) = \cos\dfrac{\pi}{2} = 0$

if $x_2 = -\dfrac{\pi}{2}$

$f(x_2) = f\left(\dfrac{-\pi}{2}\right) = \cos\left(\dfrac{-\pi}{2}\right) = \cos\dfrac{\pi}{2} = 0$

$$[\because \cos(-\theta) = \cos\theta]$$

$f(x_1) = f(x_2)$

But $x_1 \neq x_2$

So, $f(x)$ is not one-one

Also range of $\cos x$ is $[-1, 1]$

$\therefore$ Range = Co-domain

So, it is onto.   **(1 Mark)**

6.   (c)   As foot of
perpendicular

lies on y-axis.

So, $x = 0$ and $z = 0$

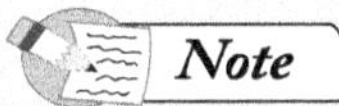

Therefore, the foot of perpendicular is $(0, -3, 0)$ **(1 Mark)**

7.   (a) Let set $A = \{1, 2, 3\}$

$\qquad R = \{(1, 2)\ (2, 1)\ (1, 1)\}$

(i)   Relation R is reflexive if

$\qquad a \in A$

$\quad (a, a) \in R$

But here $(2, 2)$ and $(3, 3)$ is missing.

So, R is not reflexive.

(ii) A relation R is symmetric if $(a, b) \in R$

then $(b, a) \in R$

Here R has $(1, 2)$ and $(2, 1)$

Therefore, R is symmetric.

(iii) A relation R is said to be transitive if

$(a, b) \in R$ and $(b, c) \in R$ then $(a, c) \in R$

$(1, 2) \in R,\ (2, 1) \in R$

Also $(1, 1) \in R$

Therefore, relation R is transitive.   **(1 Mark)**

8.   (d)   Let $\vec{a} = \hat{i} - \hat{j},\ \vec{b} = \hat{j} - \hat{k}$

$$\cos\theta = \dfrac{\vec{a}.\vec{b}}{|\vec{a}||\vec{b}|}$$

$\Rightarrow \quad \cos\theta = \dfrac{(\hat{i} - \hat{j}).(\hat{j} - \hat{k})}{\sqrt{1^2 + 1^2}\ \sqrt{1^2 + 1^2}}$

$\Rightarrow \quad \cos\theta = \dfrac{1(0) - 1(1) + 0(-1)}{\sqrt{2}\ \sqrt{2}}$

$\Rightarrow \quad \cos\theta = \dfrac{-1}{2} \Rightarrow \theta = \cos^{-1}\left(\dfrac{-1}{2}\right) \Rightarrow \theta = \cos^{-1}\left(\cos\dfrac{2\pi}{3}\right)$

$$\theta = \dfrac{2\pi}{3} \qquad\qquad\qquad \textbf{(1 Mark)}$$

9.   (d) $A^2 = 3A$

$\qquad |A^2| = |3A|$

$\Rightarrow \quad |A|^2 = 3^n |A| \qquad\qquad$ (Order = 3 and $|A^n| = |A|^n$)

$\Rightarrow \quad |A|^2 = 3^3 |A|$

$\Rightarrow \quad |A| = 27 \qquad\qquad\qquad\qquad\qquad$ **(1 Mark)**

> **Note**
>
> *A matrix is non-singular if and only if $|A| \neq 0$.*

10.   (a)   Given $|\vec{a}| = 4$ and $-3 \leq \lambda \leq 2$, then $|\lambda\vec{a}| = ?$

Let $\qquad \vec{a} = x_1\hat{i} + x_2\hat{j} + x_3\hat{k}$

So, $\qquad |\vec{a}| = \sqrt{x_1^2 + x_2^2 + x_3^2} = 4 \qquad\qquad$ ...(1)

$\qquad |\lambda\vec{a}| = |\lambda|\sqrt{x_1^2 + x_2^2 + x_3^2}$

$\Rightarrow \quad |\lambda\vec{a}| = |\lambda|.4 \qquad\qquad\qquad$ [from (1)]

Now $-3 \leq \lambda \leq 2$

then $0 \leq |\lambda| \leq 3$

Hence, $4.0 \leq 4|\lambda| \leq 4.3 \qquad$ (Multiplying with 4)

$\qquad 0 \leq |\lambda\vec{a}| \leq 12$

So, $|\lambda\vec{a}|$ lies between 0 and 12.   **(1 Mark)**

11.   [3.14 cm/s] $\dfrac{dr}{dt} = 0.5$ cm/s

Circumference, $C = 2\pi r$

$\qquad \dfrac{dC}{dt} = 2\pi\dfrac{dr}{dt} = 2\pi(0.5)$

$\qquad\qquad = \pi = 3.14$ cm/s   **(1 Mark)**

12.   [-3, 3] $\begin{vmatrix} 2x & -9 \\ -2 & x \end{vmatrix} = \begin{vmatrix} -4 & 8 \\ 1 & -2 \end{vmatrix}$

$\qquad 2x^2 - 18 = 8 - 8 \ \Rightarrow\ 2x^2 - 18 = 0$

$\Rightarrow \quad 2x^2 = 18 \quad \Rightarrow x^2 = 9$

$\Rightarrow \quad x = \pm 3$

Value of x is $-3, 3$.   **(1 Mark)**

13. **[(5, 4)]** $P = 3x + 2y$

At $(0, 0)$, $P = 3(0) + 2(0) = 0$

At $(0, 8)$, $P = 3(0) + 2(8) = 16$

At $(2, 7)$, $P = 3(2) + 2(7) = 6 + 14 = 20$

At $(5, 4)$, $P = 3(5) + 2(4) = 15 + 8 = 23$ (Max)

At $(6, 0)$, $P = 3(6) + 2(0) = 18 + 0 = 18$

Max. profit occurs at $(5, 4)$.   **(1 Mark)**

14. $[0, \pi] - \left[\dfrac{\pi}{2}\right]$

OR

$\left[\dfrac{2\pi}{3}\right]$

$\cos^{-1}\left(\dfrac{-1}{2}\right) = \pi - \cos^{-1}\left(\dfrac{1}{2}\right)$

$\left[\cos^{-1}(-\theta) = \pi - \cos^{-1}(\theta)\right]$

$= \pi - \dfrac{\pi}{3} = \dfrac{2\pi}{3}$ **(1 Mark)**

Note

The principal value of $\cos^{-1}\left(-\dfrac{1}{2}\right)$ can also determined as, $-\dfrac{1}{2}$ is the value of $\cos\left(\pi - \dfrac{\pi}{3}\right)$, then $\cos^{-1}\left[\cos\left(\pi - \dfrac{\pi}{3}\right)\right] = \dfrac{2\pi}{3}$.

15. **[2]** $d = \dfrac{|d_1 - d_2|}{\sqrt{a^2 + b^2 + c^2}}$

$2x + y - 2z - 6 = 0$

$\qquad d_1 = -6$

$4x + 2y - 4z = 0 \quad \Rightarrow 2(2x + y - 2z) = 0$

$\Rightarrow 2x + y - 2z = 0$

$\qquad d_2 = 0$

$d = \dfrac{|-6 - 0|}{\sqrt{(2)^2 + (1)^2 + (-2)^2}}$

$d = \dfrac{6}{\sqrt{4 + 1 + 4}} = \dfrac{6}{\sqrt{9}} = \dfrac{6}{3} = 2$

$d = 2$ **(1 Mark)**

OR

$[x - 3z = 10]$

$P(1, 0, -3)$

Since, $P(1, 0, -3)$ is the foot of perpendicular from origin to a plane.

Normal vector of plane is

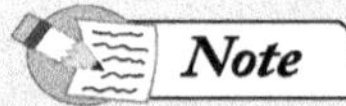

$\overrightarrow{OP} = \vec{n} = \hat{i} - 3\hat{k}$

Distance of the plane from origin

$\qquad d = |\,OP\,|$

$\qquad = \sqrt{(1)^2 + (-3)^2}$

$\qquad = \sqrt{1 + 9} \; = \; \sqrt{10}$

Unit normal vector

$\qquad \hat{n} = \dfrac{\vec{n}}{|\vec{n}|} = \dfrac{\hat{i} - 3\hat{k}}{\sqrt{10}}$

Vector equation of plane

$\qquad \vec{r} . \hat{n} = d$

$\qquad \vec{r} . \left(\dfrac{\hat{i} - 3\hat{k}}{\sqrt{10}}\right) = \sqrt{10}$

$\qquad \vec{r} . (\hat{i} - 3\hat{k}) = 10$

Cartesian equation : $x - 3z = 10$ **(1 Mark)**

Note

Foot of perpendicular from origin to the plane $lx + my + nz = d$ is (ld, md, nd).

16. $I = \displaystyle\int_{-\frac{\pi}{2}}^{\frac{\pi}{2}} x \cos^2 x \, dx$

$f(x) = x \cos^2 x$

$\Rightarrow \quad f(-x) = -x \cos^2(-x)$

$\Rightarrow \quad f(-x) = -x \cos^2 x$ $[\because \cos(-\theta) = \cos\theta]$

$\therefore f(x)$ is an odd function.   **(½ Mark)**

We know that for odd function

$\displaystyle\int_{-a}^{a} f(x)\, dx = 0$

$\therefore \quad I = 0$ **(½ Mark)**

17.   Let $\dfrac{x-1}{3} = \dfrac{y+4}{7} = \dfrac{z+4}{2} = \lambda$

$\Rightarrow x = 3\lambda + 1, \quad y = 7\lambda - 4, \quad z = 2\lambda - 4$ ...(1)

For xy plane

$\qquad z = 0$ **(½ Mark)**

$\Rightarrow \qquad 2\lambda - 4 = 0 \quad \Rightarrow 2\lambda = 4 \quad \Rightarrow \lambda = 2$

From (1)

$$x = 3(2) + 1 = 7$$
$$y = 7(2) - 4 = 10$$
$$z = 2(2) - 4 = 0$$

So, line will cut plane at (7, 10, 0)   (½ Mark)

18. $f(x) = \begin{cases} kx^2 + 5 & \text{if } x \leq 1 \\ 2 & \text{if } x > 1 \end{cases}$

L.H.L. $= \lim\limits_{x \to 1^-} k(x^2 + 5)$

$x = 1 - h$

$\quad = \lim\limits_{h \to 0} k(1-h)^2 + 5 = k(1-0)^2 + 5$

$\quad = k + 5$ (½ Mark)

R.H.L. $= \lim\limits_{x \to 1^+} 2 = 2$

As function is continuous at $x = 1$

L.H.L $=$ R.H.L $\Rightarrow k + 5 = 2$

$k = 2 - 5 = -3$ (½ Mark)

Note

A function $f(x)$ is continuous at $x = a$, if

$$\lim\limits_{x \to a^+} f(x) = \lim\limits_{x \to a^-} f(x) = f(a)$$

19. $x\dfrac{dy}{dx} = 2x^2 + y \Rightarrow \dfrac{dy}{dx} = 2x + \dfrac{y}{x}$

$\quad \dfrac{dy}{dx} - \dfrac{y}{x} = 2x$ (½ Mark)

Here $P = -\dfrac{1}{x}, Q = 2x$

$\text{I.F.} = e^{\int P(x)dx} = e^{\int -\frac{1}{x}dx} = e^{-\log x}$

$$[\because \log m^n = n \log m]$$

$= x^{-1} = \dfrac{1}{x}$

$\therefore \text{I.F.} = \dfrac{1}{x}$ (½ Mark)

20. Let $f(x) = \sec^2(x^2)$

Differentiate w.r.t. x^2; we get

$\dfrac{d}{dx^2} f(x) = 2 \sec x^2 \dfrac{d}{dx^2}(\sec x^2)$

$\quad = 2 \sec x^2 (\sec x^2 \tan x^2) \dfrac{d}{dx^2}(x^2)$

$$\left[\because \dfrac{d}{dx} \sec x = \sec x \tan x \right]$$

$= 2 \sec^2(x^2) \tan(x^2)$ **(1 Mark)**

OR

$f'(x) = e^{\sqrt{x}}$

$\Rightarrow \quad f'(x^2) = e^{\sqrt{x^2}} = e^x$ (½ Mark)

$y = f(x^2)$

$\dfrac{dy}{dx} = f'(x^2) \cdot \dfrac{dx^2}{dx}$

$\Rightarrow \quad \dfrac{dy}{dx} = e^x \cdot 2x = 2xe^x$ (½ Mark)

SECTION - B

21. $\vec{r}$ is equally inclined to three axes.

Therefore, direction cosines will be equal

$$\cos \alpha = \cos \beta = \cos \gamma$$
$$l = m = n \qquad \qquad ...(1)$$

We know that

$l^2 + m^2 + n^2 = 1 \Rightarrow l^2 + l^2 + l^2 = 1$ [from (1)]

$\Rightarrow \quad 3l^2 = 1 \Rightarrow l^2 = \dfrac{1}{3}$

$\quad l = \pm\dfrac{1}{\sqrt{3}}$ **(1 Mark)**

$|\vec{r}| = 3\sqrt{3}$ units   (given)

$\vec{r} = |\vec{r}|(l\hat{i} + m\hat{j} + n\hat{k})$

$\quad = 3\sqrt{3}\left(\pm\dfrac{1}{\sqrt{3}}\hat{i} \pm \dfrac{1}{\sqrt{3}}\hat{j} \pm \dfrac{1}{\sqrt{3}}\hat{k} \right)$

$\quad = \dfrac{3\sqrt{3}}{\sqrt{3}}\left(\pm\hat{i} \pm \hat{j} \pm \hat{k} \right) = 3\left(\pm\hat{i} \pm \hat{j} \pm \hat{k} \right)$ **(1 Mark)**

Note

Coefficient of $\hat{i}, \hat{j}$ and $\hat{k}$ of unit vector are called direction cosines but coefficient of $\hat{i}, \hat{j}$ and $\hat{k}$ of any vector are called direction ratio.

OR

$|\vec{a}| = 1, |\vec{b}| = 1$ $(\because \vec{a}$ and $\vec{b}$ are unit vectors)

Since, $(\sqrt{3}\vec{a} - \vec{b})$ is unit vector

$\quad |\sqrt{3}\vec{a} - \vec{b}| = 1$

$\Rightarrow (\sqrt{3}\vec{a} - \vec{b})(\sqrt{3}\vec{a} - \vec{b}) = 1$ $[\because |\vec{a}|^2 = \vec{a} \cdot \vec{a}]$

$\Rightarrow 3\vec{a}.\vec{a} + \vec{b}.\vec{b} - \sqrt{3}\vec{a}.\vec{b} - \sqrt{3}\vec{a}.\vec{b} = 1$

$\Rightarrow 3|\vec{a}|^2 + |\vec{b}|^2 - 2\sqrt{3}\vec{a}.\vec{b} = 1$

$$\Rightarrow 3(1) + 1 - 2\sqrt{3}\,\vec{a}.\vec{b} = 1 = 1 \qquad [\because |\vec{a}| = |\vec{b}| = 1]$$

$$4 - 2\sqrt{3}\,\vec{a}.\vec{b} = 1 \quad \Rightarrow \quad 2\sqrt{3}\,\vec{a}.\vec{b} = 3$$

$$\Rightarrow \vec{a}.\vec{b} = \frac{3}{2\sqrt{3}} \quad \Rightarrow \quad \vec{a}.\vec{b} = \frac{\sqrt{3}}{2} \qquad ...(1) \qquad \textbf{(1 Mark)}$$

$$\vec{a}.\vec{b} = |\vec{a}|\,|\vec{b}|\cos\theta$$

$$= 1.1\cos\theta$$

$$= \cos\theta \qquad ...(2)$$

From (1) and (2)

$$\cos\theta = \frac{\sqrt{3}}{2} \quad \Rightarrow \quad \cos\theta = \cos\frac{\pi}{6}$$

$$\theta = \frac{\pi}{6} \text{ or } 30° \qquad \textbf{(1 Mark)}$$

22.
$$A = \begin{bmatrix} -3 & 2 \\ 1 & -1 \end{bmatrix}, I = \begin{bmatrix} 1 & 0 \\ 0 & 1 \end{bmatrix}$$

$$A^2 = AA = \begin{bmatrix} -3 & 2 \\ 1 & -1 \end{bmatrix}\begin{bmatrix} -3 & 2 \\ 1 & -1 \end{bmatrix}$$

$$\Rightarrow \quad A^2 = \begin{bmatrix} 9+2 & -6-2 \\ -3-1 & 2+1 \end{bmatrix}$$

$$\Rightarrow \quad A^2 = \begin{bmatrix} 11 & -8 \\ -4 & 3 \end{bmatrix} \qquad \textbf{(1 Mark)}$$

$$A^2 + I = kA$$

$$\Rightarrow \quad \begin{bmatrix} 11 & -8 \\ -4 & 3 \end{bmatrix} + \begin{bmatrix} 1 & 0 \\ 0 & 1 \end{bmatrix} = k\begin{bmatrix} -3 & 2 \\ 1 & -1 \end{bmatrix}$$

$$\Rightarrow \quad \begin{bmatrix} 11+1 & -8+0 \\ -4+0 & 3+1 \end{bmatrix} = \begin{bmatrix} -3k & 2k \\ k & -k \end{bmatrix}$$

$$\Rightarrow \quad \begin{bmatrix} 12 & -8 \\ -4 & 4 \end{bmatrix} = \begin{bmatrix} -3k & 2k \\ k & -k \end{bmatrix}$$

Equating the element

$$-3k = 12 \quad \Rightarrow \quad k = -4 \qquad \textbf{(1 Mark)}$$

23.
$$f(x) = \sqrt{\frac{\sec x - 1}{\sec x + 1}}$$

$$f(x) = \sqrt{\frac{\dfrac{1}{\cos x} - 1}{\dfrac{1}{\cos x} + 1}} = \sqrt{\frac{1 - \cos x}{1 + \cos x}}$$

$$= \sqrt{\frac{2\sin^2 x/2}{2\cos^2\dfrac{x}{2}}} = \sqrt{\tan^2\frac{x}{2}}$$

$$= \tan\frac{x}{2} \qquad \textbf{(1 Mark)}$$

$$f'(x) = \sec^2\left(\frac{x}{2}\right)\cdot\frac{1}{2} \quad \Rightarrow \quad f'\left(\frac{\pi}{3}\right) = \frac{1}{2}\sec^2\frac{\pi}{6}$$

$$= \frac{1}{2}\left(\frac{2}{\sqrt{3}}\right)^2$$

$$= \frac{2}{3} \qquad \textbf{(1 Mark)}$$

OR

$$f(x) = (\tan x)^{\tan x}$$

Let
$$y = f(x) = (\tan x)^{\tan x}$$

$$y = (\tan x)^{\tan x}$$

Taking log on both sides

$$\log y = \log (\tan x)^{\tan x}$$

$$\Rightarrow \quad \log y = \tan x \log (\tan x) \quad [\because \log m^n = n\log m]$$

Differentiating on both sides w.r.t. x

$$\frac{d}{dx}\log y = \frac{d}{dx}[\tan x \log(\tan x)]$$

$$\Rightarrow \quad \frac{1}{y}\frac{dy}{dx} = \tan x \frac{d}{dx}\log(\tan x) + \log(\tan x)\frac{d}{dx}\tan x$$

$$\left[\because \frac{d}{dx}\log x = \frac{1}{x}, \frac{d}{dx}uv = u\frac{dv}{dx} + v\frac{du}{dx}\right]\textbf{(1 Mark)}$$

$$\Rightarrow \quad \frac{1}{y}\frac{dy}{dx} = \tan x\frac{1}{\tan x}\frac{d}{dx}\tan x + \log(\tan x)(\sec^2 x)$$

$$\left[\because \frac{d}{dx}\tan x = \sec^2 x\right]$$

$$\Rightarrow \quad \frac{1}{y}\frac{dy}{dx} = \sec^2 x + \sec^2 x \log(\tan x)$$

$$\Rightarrow \quad \frac{dy}{dx} = y(\sec^2 x + \sec^2 x \log(\tan x))$$

$$f'(x) = \frac{dy}{dx} = (\tan x)^{\tan x}\sec^2 x(1 + \log(\tan x)) \quad \textbf{(1 Mark)}$$

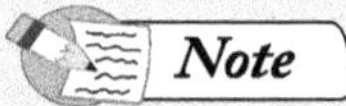

If function is in the form of variable to the power of variable then use log before differentiate.

24. Let $I = \int \dfrac{\tan^3 x}{\cos^3 x} dx$

$= \int \tan^3 x \cdot \sec^3 x \, dx = \int \tan^2 x \cdot \sec^2 x \cdot \tan x \cdot \sec x \, dx$

$= \int (\sec^2 x - 1) \sec^2 x \cdot \tan x \cdot \sec x \, dx$ **(1 Mark)**

Let $\sec x = t$, then $\tan x \cdot \sec x \, dx = dt$

$= \int (t^2 - 1) t^2 dt = \int (t^4 - t^2) dt$

$= \dfrac{t^5}{5} - \dfrac{t^3}{3} + C = \dfrac{1}{5} \sec^5 x - \dfrac{1}{3} \sec^3 x + C$ **(1 Mark)**

25. Equation of plane is $x - 5y - 2z = 1$ ...(1)

$a_1 = 1,\ b_1 = -5,\ c_1 = -2$

Equation of line is $\dfrac{x-5}{3} = y = -(z-2)$

$\dfrac{x-5}{3} = \dfrac{y-0}{1} = \dfrac{z-2}{-1}$

$x_1 = 5,\ y_1 = 0,\ z_1 = 2$

$a_2 = 3,\ b_2 = 1,\ c_3 = -1$

Substitute the point $(5, 0, 2)$ in equation of plane

$5 - 5\,(0) - 2(2) = 5 - 4 = 1$

Satisfy the equation (1)

So, point $(5, 0, 2)$ lies on plane **(1 Mark)**

Now,

$a_1 a_2 + b_1 b_2 + c_1 c_2$

$= 3.1 + (-5)\,(1) + (-2)\,(-1)) = 3 - 5 + 2 = 0$

So, line is perpendicular to normal of plane.

Hence, line lies on plane. **(1 Mark)**

26. Number of trial $= 2$

Number of sample space $= 36$

X (Number of sixes) $= 0, 1, 2$

X	P(X)	XP(X)
0	$\dfrac{25}{36}$	0
1	$\dfrac{10}{36}$	$\dfrac{10}{36}$
2	$\dfrac{1}{36}$	$\dfrac{2}{36}$

(1 Mark)

Mean $= \sum XP(X)$

$= 0 + \dfrac{10}{36} + \dfrac{2}{36}$

$= \dfrac{12}{36} = \dfrac{1}{3}$ **(1 Mark)**

SECTION - C

27. $(1 + e^{y/x}) dy + e^{y/x} \left(1 - \dfrac{y}{x}\right) dx = 0$

$\Rightarrow (1 + e^{y/x}) dy = -e^{y/x} \left(1 - \dfrac{y}{x}\right) dx$

$\Rightarrow \dfrac{dy}{dx} = \dfrac{-e^{y/x}\left(1 - \dfrac{y}{x}\right)}{(1 + e^{y/x})}$ ...(1)

$\therefore$ Equation is homogenous differential equation.

Now putting $y = vx$

$\dfrac{dy}{dx} = \dfrac{d}{dx}(vx)$

$\Rightarrow \dfrac{dy}{dx} = v + x \dfrac{dv}{dx}$ **(1 Mark)**

Putting value of $\dfrac{dy}{dx}$ and $y = vx$ in (1)

$v + x\dfrac{dv}{dx} = \dfrac{-e^v(1 - v)}{1 + e^v}$

$\Rightarrow x\dfrac{dv}{dx} = \dfrac{-e^v(1 - v)}{1 + e^v} - v$

$\Rightarrow x\dfrac{dv}{dx} = \dfrac{-e^v + ve^v - v - ve^v}{1 + e^v}$

$\Rightarrow x\dfrac{dv}{dx} = \dfrac{-e^v - v}{1 + e^v} = \dfrac{-(e + v)}{}$

$\Rightarrow \dfrac{1 + e^v}{e^v + v} dv = -\dfrac{dx}{x}$ **(1 Mark)**

Integrating on both sides

$\int \dfrac{1 + e^v}{e^v + v} dv = -\log|x| + \log C$

Let $e^v + v = t \Rightarrow e^v + 1 = \dfrac{dt}{dv}$

$\Rightarrow dt = (e^v + 1) dv$

$\Rightarrow \qquad \displaystyle\int \frac{dt}{t} = -\log |x| + \log C$

$\Rightarrow \qquad \log |t| = -\log |x| + \log C$

$\Rightarrow \log |v + e^v| = -\log |x| + \log C \qquad [\because t = v + e^v]$

$\Rightarrow \log |v + e^v| + \log |x| = \log C$

$\Rightarrow \log (|v + e^v| \times |x|) = \log C$

$\Rightarrow \log ((v + e^v) \times x) = \log C$

Putting, $\qquad v = \dfrac{y}{x}$

$\log\left(\dfrac{y}{x} \times x + e^{y/x} x \right) = \log C$

$\log (y + e^{y/x} x) = \log C$

$y + xe^{y/x} = C \qquad\qquad$ **(2 Marks)**

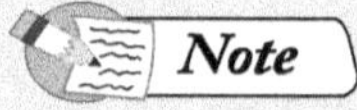

Note

Equation in the form $\dfrac{dy}{dx} = f\left(\dfrac{y}{x}\right)$ *or* $\dfrac{dy}{dx} = f\left(\dfrac{x}{y}\right)$ *is homogeneous differential equation.*

28. Let number of pedestal lamp be x and number of wooden shades be y

$\qquad 1.5x + 3y \le 42$

$\Rightarrow \quad 0.5x + y \le 14 \qquad\qquad\qquad ...(1)$

$\qquad 3x + 1y \le 24 \qquad\qquad\qquad ...(2)$

$\qquad\qquad x \ge 0, y \ge 0$

Maximize profit $Z = 30x + 20y$ **(2 Marks)**

Intersection point of (1) and (2) will be given as

$$\begin{array}{rcccr} 3x & + & 1y & = & 24 \\ 0.5x & + & y & = & 14 \\ - & & - & & - \\ \hline 2.5x & & & = & 10 \end{array}$$

$\qquad\qquad x = 4$

$\qquad 3(4) + 1y = 24 \Rightarrow y = 12$

Two lines intersect at (4, 12)

$\qquad 0.5x + y = 14$

x	0	28
y	14	0

$3x + 1y = 24$

x	0	8
y	24	0

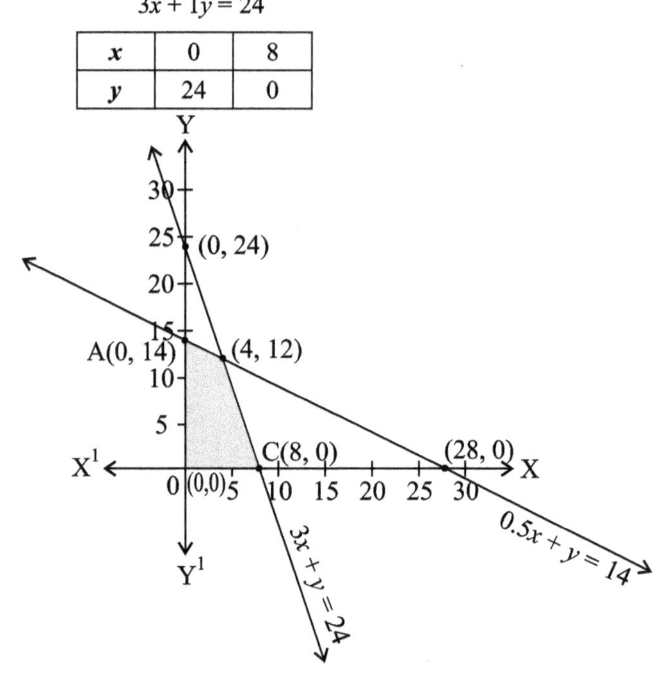

$\qquad\qquad$ **(1 Mark)**

OABC is desired region.

Corner points are O, A, B, C

Corner point	$z = 30x + 20y$
O(0, 0)	$z = 0$
A(0, 14)	$z = 0 + 20(14) = 280$
B(4, 12)	$z = 30(4) + 20(12) = 120 + 240 = 360$ (Max.)
C(8, 0)	$z = 30(8) + 0 = 240$

Profit will be maximum if

Number of lamps = 4

Number of wooden shades = 12

Maximum profit = ₹ 360 **(1 Mark)**

29. Let $\qquad I = \displaystyle\int_0^{\frac{\pi}{2}} \sin 2x \tan^{-1}(\sin x)\,dx$

$\Rightarrow \qquad I = \displaystyle\int_0^{\frac{\pi}{2}} (2\sin x \cos x) \tan^{-1}(\sin x)\,dx$

$[\because \sin 2\theta = 2\sin\theta.\cos\theta]$

Let $\sin x = t \Rightarrow \cos x\, dx = dt$

Limit $x = 0$, $t = \sin x = \sin 0 = 0$

$$x = \frac{\pi}{2}, t = \sin\left(\frac{\pi}{2}\right) = 1$$

$$I = 2\int_0^1 \underset{I}{t}\ \underset{II}{\tan^{-1}t}\ dt \qquad \textbf{(1 Mark)}$$

We know that

$$\int uv\,dx = u\int u\,dx - \int\left(\frac{d}{dx}u\int v\,dx\right)dx$$

$$\Rightarrow \quad I = 2\left[\tan^{-1}t\int t\,dt - \int\left(\frac{d}{dt}(\tan^{-1}t)\int t\,dt\right)dt\right]_0^1$$

$$= 2\left[\tan^{-1}t\left(\frac{t^2}{2}\right) - \int\frac{1}{1+t^2}\left(\frac{t^2}{2}\right)dt\right]_0^1$$

$$\left[\because \frac{d}{dx}\tan^{-1}x = \frac{1}{1+x^2}\right]$$

$$= 2\left(\frac{t^2}{2}\tan^{-1}t - \frac{1}{2}\int\frac{t^2}{1+t^2}dt\right)_0^1 \qquad \textbf{(1 Mark)}$$

Let $\quad I_1 = \int\dfrac{t^2}{1+t^2}$

$$I_1 = \int\left(\frac{t^2+1-1}{t^2+1}\right)dt = \int\left(1-\frac{1}{t^2+1}\right)dt$$

$$\Rightarrow \quad I_1 = \int dt - \int\frac{dt}{t^2+1}$$

$$\Rightarrow \quad I_1 = t - \tan^{-1}t \quad \left(\because \int\frac{1}{x^2+1} = \tan^{-1}x\right) \textbf{(1 Mark)}$$

$$\Rightarrow \quad I = 2\left(\frac{t^2}{2}\tan^{-1}t - \frac{1}{2}(t-\tan^{-1}t)\right)_0^1$$

$$= \left(t^2\tan^{-1}t - t + \tan^{-1}t\right)_0^1$$

$$= (1^2\times\tan^{-1}1 - 1 + \tan^{-1}1) - (0 - 0 + \tan^{-1}0)$$

$$= \left(\frac{\pi}{4} - 1 + \frac{\pi}{4}\right) - 0$$

$$= \frac{\pi}{2} - 1 \qquad \textbf{(1 Mark)}$$

30. $R = \{(a, b) : a \text{ is divisor of } b\}$

(i) Reflexive:

Since every natural number divisor of itself

$\therefore \forall\ a \in R \Rightarrow (a, a) \in R$

$\therefore$ R is reflexive. $\qquad$ **(1 Mark)**

(ii) Symmetric

Let $(2, 4) \in R \qquad$ (2 is divisor of 4)

but $(4, 2) \notin R \qquad$ (4 is not divisor of 2)

$\therefore$ R is not symmetric. $\qquad$ **(1 Mark)**

(iii) Transitive

Let $(a, b) \in R$, $(b, c) \in R\ \forall\ a, b, c \in N$

$\Rightarrow$ Let $b = ma \quad c = bn = n(ma)$

$= mna$

$\Rightarrow a$ is divisor of c

$\Rightarrow (a, c) \in R$

$\therefore$ R is transitive.

R is reflexive, transitive but not symmetric.

Therefore, R is not equivalence. $\qquad$ **(2 Marks)**

OR

$$\tan^{-1}\left(\frac{1}{4}\right) + \tan^{-1}\frac{2}{9} = \frac{1}{2}\sin^{-1}\left(\frac{4}{5}\right)$$

$$\text{L.H.S.} = \tan^{-1}\left(\frac{1}{4}\right) + \tan^{-1}\left(\frac{2}{9}\right)$$

$$= \tan^{-1}\left(\frac{\frac{1}{4}+\frac{2}{9}}{1-\frac{1}{4}\times\frac{2}{9}}\right)$$

$$\left[\because \tan^{-1}x + \tan^{-1}y = \tan^{-1}\frac{x+y}{1-xy}\right]$$

$$= \tan^{-1}\left(\frac{9+8}{36-2}\right) \qquad \textbf{(2 Marks)}$$

$$= \tan^{-1}\left(\frac{17}{34}\right) = \tan^{-1}\left(\frac{1}{2}\right) = \frac{1}{2}\times 2\tan^{-1}\left(\frac{1}{2}\right)$$

$$= \frac{1}{2}\sin^{-1}\left(\frac{2\times\frac{1}{2}}{1+\left(\frac{1}{2}\right)^2}\right)$$

$$\left[\because 2\tan^{-1}x = \sin^{-1}\frac{2x}{1+x^2}\right]$$

$$= \frac{1}{2}\sin^{-1}\left(\frac{1}{1+\frac{1}{4}}\right) = \frac{1}{2}\sin^{-1}\left(\frac{4}{5}\right)$$

L.H.S. = R.H.S.   **(2 Marks)**

Hence proved.

31. Let plane passes through P(1, 0, –2), Q(3, –1, 0)

Position vectors are

$$\vec{a} = \hat{i} - 2\hat{k}\,;\ \vec{b} = 3\hat{i} - \hat{j}$$

$$\overrightarrow{PQ} = \vec{b} - \vec{a} = (3-1)\hat{i} - \hat{j} + (0+2)\hat{k}$$

$$= 2\hat{i} - \hat{j} + 2\hat{k} \qquad \textbf{(1 Mark)}$$

Plane is perpendicular to given plane i.e.

$$2x - y + z = 8$$

Normal vector, $\vec{n}_1 = 2\hat{i} - \hat{j} + \hat{k}$

Normal vector of plane will be

$$\vec{n} = \vec{n}_1 \times \overrightarrow{PQ} = \begin{vmatrix} \hat{i} & \hat{j} & \hat{k} \\ 2 & -1 & 1 \\ 2 & -1 & 2 \end{vmatrix}$$

$$= \hat{i}(-2+1) - \hat{j}(4-2) + \hat{k}(-2+2)$$

$$= -\hat{i} - 2\hat{j} \qquad \textbf{(1 Mark)}$$

Equation of required plane

$$(\vec{r} - \vec{a}).\vec{n} = 0, \text{ where } \vec{r} = x\hat{i} + y\hat{j} + z\hat{k}$$

$$\Rightarrow\ (x\hat{i} + y\hat{j} + z\hat{k} - \hat{i} + 2\hat{k}).(-\hat{i} - 2\hat{j}) = 0$$

$$\Rightarrow\ [(x-1)\hat{i} + y\hat{j} + \hat{k}(z+2)](-\hat{i} - 2\hat{j}) = 0$$

$$\Rightarrow\ -(x-1) - 2y + (z+2)(0) = 0 \Rightarrow -x + 1 - 2y = 0$$

$$\Rightarrow\ -x - 2y = -1 \Rightarrow x + 2y = 1$$

Distance from origin

$$= \left|\frac{0 + 2(0) - 1}{\sqrt{1^2 + 2^2}}\right| = \frac{1}{\sqrt{5}}$$

(2 Marks)

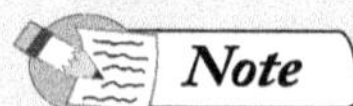

Note

The distance of the plane Ax + By + Cz = D from the origin is

calculated by $\left|\dfrac{D}{\sqrt{A^2 + B^2 + C^2}}\right|$

32. $\quad \tan^{-1}\left(\dfrac{y}{x}\right) = \log\sqrt{x^2 + y^2}$

$$\Rightarrow \tan^{-1}\left(\frac{y}{x}\right) = \log(x^2 + y^2)^{1/2}$$

$$\Rightarrow \tan^{-1}\left(\frac{y}{x}\right) = \frac{1}{2}\log(x^2 + y^2) \qquad [\because\ \log m^n = n\log m]$$

Differentiating on both sides w.r.t. x

$$\frac{1}{1+\left(\frac{y}{x}\right)^2}\frac{d}{dx}\left(\frac{y}{x}\right) = \frac{1}{2}\left(\frac{1}{x^2+y^2}\frac{d}{dx}(x^2+y^2)\right) \quad \textbf{(1 Mark)}$$

$$\left[\because \frac{d}{dx}\log x = \frac{1}{x}\right]\left[\because \frac{d}{dx}\tan^{-1}x = \frac{1}{1+x^2}\right]$$

$$\Rightarrow \frac{x^2}{x^2+y^2}\frac{d}{dx}\left(\frac{y}{x}\right) = \frac{1}{2(x^2+y^2)}\left[2x + 2y\frac{dy}{dx}\right]$$

$$\Rightarrow \frac{x^2}{x^2+y^2}\left(\frac{x\frac{dy}{dx} - y(1)}{x^2}\right) = \frac{1}{x^2+y^2}\left(x + y\frac{dy}{dx}\right) \textbf{(1 Mark)}$$

$$\left[\because \frac{d}{dx}\left(\frac{u}{v}\right) = \frac{v\frac{du}{dx} - u\frac{dv}{dx}}{v^2}\right]$$

$$\Rightarrow x\frac{dy}{dx} - y = x + y\frac{dy}{dx}$$

$$\Rightarrow x\frac{dy}{dx} - y\frac{dy}{dx} = x + y \Rightarrow \frac{dy}{dx}(x-y) = x + y$$

$$\frac{dy}{dx} = \frac{x+y}{x-y} \qquad \textbf{(2 Marks)}$$

Hence, proved.

OR

$$y = e^{a\cos^{-1}x}$$

$$\Rightarrow \quad \frac{dy}{dx} = e^{a\cos^{-1}x} \times a\frac{d}{dx}\cos^{-1}x$$

$$\Rightarrow \quad \frac{dy}{dx} = ae^{a\cos^{-1}x}\left(\frac{-1}{\sqrt{1-x^2}}\right)$$

$$\left[\because \frac{d}{dx}\cos^{-1}x = \frac{-1}{\sqrt{1-x^2}}\right]$$

$$\frac{dy}{dx} = \frac{-ay}{\sqrt{1-x^2}} \qquad \textbf{(1 Mark)}$$

Squaring on both sides

$$\left(\frac{dy}{dx}\right)^2 = \frac{a^2y^2}{1-x^2}$$

$$\Rightarrow \quad (1-x^2)\left(\frac{dy}{dx}\right)^2 = a^2y^2 \qquad \textbf{(1 Mark)}$$

Differentiating w.r.t. x

$$\left(\frac{dy}{dx}\right)^2 \frac{d}{dx}(1-x^2) + (1-x^2)\frac{d}{dx}\left(\frac{dy}{dx}\right)^2 = a^2\frac{d}{dx}(y^2)$$

$$\Rightarrow \left(\frac{dy}{dx}\right)(-2x) + (1-x^2)2\frac{dy}{dx}\frac{d\,y}{dx} = a^2(2y)\frac{dy}{dx}$$

$$\Rightarrow -x\left(\frac{dy}{dx}\right) + (1-x^2)\frac{d^2y}{dx^2} = a^2y$$

$$\Rightarrow (1-x^2)\frac{d^2y}{dx^2} - x\frac{dy}{dx} - a^2y = 0 \qquad \textbf{(2 Marks)}$$

SECTION - D

33. Volume of cylinder $= \pi r^2 h$

where r in radius and h is height of cylinder

$$\Rightarrow \qquad V = \pi r^2 h$$

$$\Rightarrow \qquad V = 125\,\pi \text{ cm}^3 \text{ (given)}$$

$$\Rightarrow \qquad \pi r^2 h = 125\,\pi \;\Rightarrow\; h = \frac{125\pi}{\pi r^2}$$

$$h = \frac{125}{r^2} \qquad ...(1) \qquad \textbf{(1 Mark)}$$

Surface area $= 2\pi rh + \pi r^2$

$$\Rightarrow \qquad S = 2\pi rh + \pi r^2 = 2\pi r\left(\frac{125}{r^2}\right) + \pi r^2 \text{ [from (1)]}$$

$$\Rightarrow \qquad S = \frac{250\pi}{r} + \pi r^2 \qquad \textbf{(1 Mark)}$$

Differentiating both sides w.r.t. r

$$\frac{dS}{dr} = 250\pi\left(\frac{-1}{r^2}\right) + 2\pi r \quad \left[\because \frac{d}{dx}x^n = nx^{n-1}\right]$$

$$\Rightarrow \qquad \frac{dS}{dr} = \frac{-250\pi}{r^2} + 2\pi r \qquad \textbf{(1 Mark)}$$

To get least surface

$$\frac{dS}{dr} = 0 \;\Rightarrow\; \frac{-250\pi}{r^2} + 2\pi r = 0 \;\Rightarrow\; 2\pi r = \frac{250\pi}{r^2}$$

$$\Rightarrow \qquad r^3 = 125,\, r = 5 \text{ cm} \qquad \textbf{(1 Mark)}$$

$$\frac{d^2S}{dr^2} = +\frac{500\pi}{r^3} + 2\pi > 0 \text{ [for } r = 5\text{]}$$

So, $\dfrac{d^2S}{dr^2} > 0$ $\qquad\qquad\qquad$ **(1 Mark)**

$\therefore$ Surface area is maximum at $r = 5$ cm

From (1)

$$h = \frac{125}{r^2} \;\Rightarrow\; h = \frac{125}{(5)^2} = \frac{125}{25} = 5$$

Radius $= 5$ cm, Height of cylinder $= 5$ cm $\qquad$ **(1 Mark)**

34. Equation of circle

$$x^2 + y^2 - 8x = 0 \;\Rightarrow\; x^2 - 8x + y^2 = 0$$

Using perfect square method

$$x^2 - 8x + y^2 + (4)^2 - (4)^2 = 0$$

$$\Rightarrow (x-4)^2 + y^2 = 4^2 \qquad ...(1) \qquad \textbf{(1 Mark)}$$

$$[\because (a-b)^2 = a^2 + b^2 - 2ab]$$

Parabola: $y^2 = 4x$ $\qquad\qquad ...(2)$

to find point of intersection

$$x^2 + y^2 - 8x = 0 \text{ and } y^2 = 4x$$

$$\Rightarrow x^2 + 4x - 8x = 0 \;\Rightarrow\; x^2 - 4x = 0 \;\Rightarrow\; x(x-4) = 0$$

$$x = 0,\, x = 4$$

$$y^2 = 4x$$

when $x = 0,\, y = 0$

when $x = 4$

$$y^2 = 4(4)$$

$$\Rightarrow \qquad y = 4 \qquad\qquad\qquad \textbf{(1 Mark)}$$

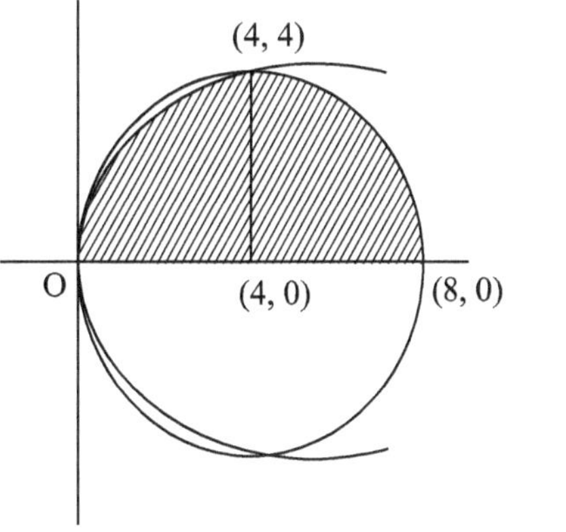

$\qquad\qquad\qquad\qquad\qquad\qquad\qquad$ **(1 Mark)**

$$\text{Required area} = \int_0^4 y_{\text{p}}\, dx + \int_4^8 y_{\text{circle}}\, dx$$

$$y^2 = 4x$$

$$\Rightarrow \qquad y = \sqrt{4x} = 2\sqrt{x}$$

$$(x-4)^2 + y^2 = 4^2 \;\Rightarrow\; y = \sqrt{4^2 - (x-4)^2}$$

Required area $= \int\limits_{0}^{4} 2\sqrt{x}\, dx + \int\limits_{4}^{8} \sqrt{4^2 - (x-4)^2}\, dx$ **(1 Mark)**

$= 2 \times \dfrac{2}{3}\Big[x^{3/2}\Big]_0^4 + \Big[\dfrac{x-4}{2}\sqrt{4^2-(x-4)^2} + \dfrac{16}{2}\sin^{-1}\dfrac{x-4}{4}\Big]_4^8$

$$\Big[\because \int \sqrt{a^2-x^2}\, dx = \dfrac{x}{2}\sqrt{a^2-x^2} + \dfrac{a^2}{2}\sin^{-1}\dfrac{x}{a}\Big]$$

$= \dfrac{4}{3}[4^{3/2} - 0] + [0 + 8\sin^{-1}(1) - (0+0)]$

$= \dfrac{4}{3}(2^2)^{3/2} + 8\sin^{-1}(1) = \dfrac{32}{3} + 8\Big(\dfrac{\pi}{2}\Big)$

$= \Big(\dfrac{32}{3} + 4\pi\Big)$ sq. units   **(2 Marks)**

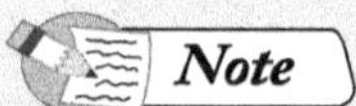

Note

If highest power of x and y are 2 and coefficient of x^2 and y^2 are equal then equation represent the equation of circle.

OR

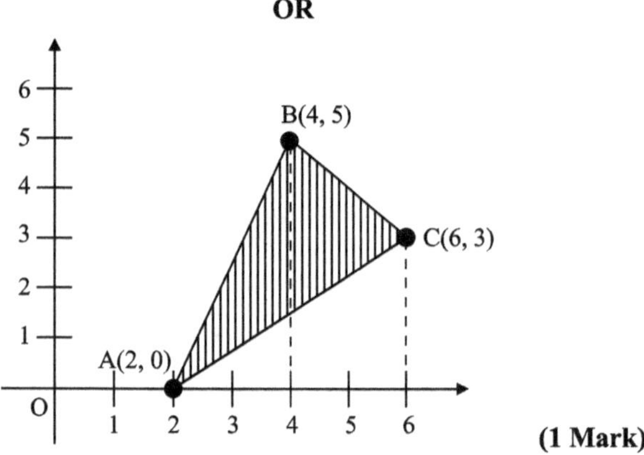

(1 Mark)

Equation of a line

$$y - y_1 = \dfrac{y_2 - y_1}{x_2 - x_1}(x - x_1)$$

Equation of AB

$$y - 0 = \dfrac{5-0}{4-2}(x-2)$$

$\Rightarrow \qquad y = \dfrac{5}{2}(x-2) = \dfrac{5x-10}{2}$ **(1 Mark)**

Equation of AC

$$y - 0 = \dfrac{3-0}{6-2}(x-2)$$

$\Rightarrow \qquad y = \dfrac{3}{4}(x-2) = \dfrac{3x-6}{4}$ **(1 Mark)**

Equation of BC

$$y - 3 = \dfrac{5-3}{4-6}(x-6)$$

$\Rightarrow \qquad y - 3 = \dfrac{2}{-2}(x-6)$

$\Rightarrow \qquad y = -x + 6 + 3 = -x + 9$ **(1 Mark)**

Area of $\triangle ABC = \int\limits_{2}^{4} y_{AB}\, dx + \int\limits_{4}^{6} y_{BC}\, dx - \int\limits_{2}^{6} y_{AC}\, dx$

Area of $\triangle ABC = \int\limits_{2}^{4}\Big(\dfrac{5x-10}{2}\Big) dx + \int\limits_{4}^{6}(9-x)\, dx - \int\limits_{2}^{6}\dfrac{3x-6}{4}\, dx$

$= \dfrac{1}{2}\Big(\dfrac{5x^2}{2} - 10x\Big)_2^4 + \Big(9x - \dfrac{x^2}{2}\Big)_4^6 - \dfrac{1}{4}\Big(\dfrac{3x^2}{2} - 6x\Big)_2^6$ **(1 Mark)**

$= \dfrac{1}{2}\Big[\Big(\dfrac{5\times16}{2} - 40\Big) - \Big(\dfrac{5\times4}{2} - 20\Big)\Big]$

$+ \Big[\Big(9\times6 - \dfrac{36}{2}\Big) - \Big(9\times4 - \dfrac{16}{2}\Big)\Big]$

$- \dfrac{1}{4}\Big[\Big(\dfrac{3\times36}{2} - 36\Big) - \Big(\dfrac{3\times4}{2} - 6\times2\Big)\Big]$

$= \dfrac{1}{2}[0+10] + [36-28] - \dfrac{1}{4}[18+6]$

$= 5 + 8 - 6 = 7$ sq. units   **(1 Mark)**

35. $\qquad A = \begin{bmatrix} 5 & -1 & 4 \\ 2 & 3 & 5 \\ 5 & -2 & 6 \end{bmatrix}$

$|A| = 5(18 - (-10)) + 1(12 - 25) + 4(-4 - 15)$

$= 140 - 13 - 76 = 140 - 89 = 51$ **(1 Mark)**

$$A_{11} = (-1)^2 \begin{vmatrix} 3 & 5 \\ -2 & 6 \end{vmatrix} = 18 + 10 = 28$$

$$A_{12} = (-1)^3 \begin{vmatrix} 2 & 5 \\ 5 & 6 \end{vmatrix} = (-1)(12 - 25) = 13$$

$$A_{13} = (-1)^4 \begin{vmatrix} 2 & 3 \\ 5 & -2 \end{vmatrix} = -4 - 15 = -19$$

$$A_{21} = (-1)^3 \begin{vmatrix} -1 & 4 \\ -2 & 6 \end{vmatrix} = (-1)(-6 + 8) = -2$$

$$A_{22} = (-1)^4 \begin{vmatrix} 5 & 4 \\ 5 & 6 \end{vmatrix} = 30 - 20 = 10$$

$$A_{23} = (-1)^5 \begin{vmatrix} 5 & -1 \\ 5 & -2 \end{vmatrix} = (-1)(-10 + 5) = 5$$

$$A_{31} = (-1)^4 \begin{vmatrix} -1 & 4 \\ 3 & 5 \end{vmatrix} = -5 - 12 = -17$$

$$A_{32} = (-1)^5 \begin{vmatrix} 5 & 4 \\ 2 & 5 \end{vmatrix} = (-1)(25 - 8) = -17$$

$$A_{33} = (-1)^6 \begin{vmatrix} 5 & -1 \\ 2 & 3 \end{vmatrix} = (15 + 2) = 17 \text{ (1 Mark)}$$

$$\text{adj } A = \begin{bmatrix} 28 & 13 & -19 \\ -2 & 10 & 5 \\ -17 & -17 & 17 \end{bmatrix}^T = \begin{bmatrix} 28 & -2 & -17 \\ 13 & 10 & -17 \\ -19 & 5 & 17 \end{bmatrix}$$

$$A^{-1} = \frac{\text{adj } A}{|A|} = \frac{1}{51} \begin{bmatrix} 28 & -2 & -17 \\ 13 & 10 & -17 \\ -19 & 5 & 17 \end{bmatrix} \quad \text{(1 Mark)}$$

$$5x - y + 4z = 5$$
$$2x + 3y + 5z = 2$$
$$5x - 2y + 6z = -1$$

$$A = \begin{bmatrix} 5 & -1 & 4 \\ 2 & 3 & 5 \\ 5 & -2 & 6 \end{bmatrix}, \; B = \begin{bmatrix} 5 \\ 2 \\ -1 \end{bmatrix}, \; X = \begin{bmatrix} x \\ y \\ z \end{bmatrix}$$

$$AX = B$$

$$X = A^{-1}B \quad \text{(1 Mark)}$$

$$\begin{bmatrix} x \\ y \\ z \end{bmatrix} = \frac{1}{51} \begin{bmatrix} 28 & -2 & -17 \\ 13 & 10 & -17 \\ -19 & 5 & 17 \end{bmatrix} \begin{bmatrix} 5 \\ 2 \\ -1 \end{bmatrix}$$

$$\Rightarrow \begin{bmatrix} x \\ y \\ z \end{bmatrix} = \frac{1}{51} \begin{bmatrix} 140 - 4 + 17 \\ 65 + 20 + 17 \\ -95 + 10 - 17 \end{bmatrix}$$

$$= \frac{1}{51} \begin{bmatrix} 153 \\ 102 \\ -102 \end{bmatrix} = \begin{bmatrix} \dfrac{153}{51} \\ \dfrac{102}{51} \\ \dfrac{-102}{51} \end{bmatrix} = \begin{bmatrix} 3 \\ 2 \\ -2 \end{bmatrix}$$

$$x = 3, \, y = 2, \, z = -2 \quad \text{(2 Marks)}$$

OR

$$\Delta = \begin{vmatrix} x & x^2 & 1+x^3 \\ y & y^2 & 1+y^3 \\ z & z^2 & 1+z^3 \end{vmatrix} = \begin{vmatrix} x & x^2 & 1 \\ y & y^2 & 1 \\ z & z^2 & 1 \end{vmatrix} + \begin{vmatrix} x & x^2 & x^3 \\ y & y^2 & y^3 \\ z & z^2 & z^3 \end{vmatrix}$$

(1 Mark)

Swapping $C_2 \leftrightarrow C_3$, then $C_2 \leftrightarrow C_1$ in 1st determinante

$$= (-1)^2 \begin{vmatrix} 1 & x & x^2 \\ 1 & y & y^2 \\ 1 & z & z^2 \end{vmatrix} + xyz \begin{vmatrix} 1 & x & x^2 \\ 1 & y & y^2 \\ 1 & z & z^2 \end{vmatrix}$$

$$= (1 + xyz) \begin{vmatrix} 1 & x & x^2 \\ 1 & y & y^2 \\ 1 & z & z^2 \end{vmatrix} \quad \text{(1 Mark)}$$

$R_1 \to R_1 - R_2$

$$\Delta = (1 + xyz) \begin{vmatrix} 0 & x-y & x^2-y^2 \\ 1 & y & y^2 \\ 1 & z & z^2 \end{vmatrix} \quad \text{(1 Mark)}$$

$R_2 \to R_2 - R_3$

$$\Delta = (1 + xyz) \begin{vmatrix} 0 & x-y & x^2-y^2 \\ 1 & y-z & y^2-z^2 \\ 1 & z & z^2 \end{vmatrix} \quad \text{(1 Mark)}$$

$$= (1 + xyz) \begin{vmatrix} 0 & x-y & (x-y)(x+y) \\ 1 & y-z & (y-z)(y+z) \\ 1 & z & z^2 \end{vmatrix}$$

$$= (1 + xyz)(x-y)(y-z) \begin{vmatrix} 0 & 1 & x+y \\ 0 & 1 & y+z \\ 1 & z & z^2 \end{vmatrix}$$

$$= (1 + xyz)(x-y)(y-z)(z-x) \quad \text{(1 Mark)}$$

if $\Delta = 0$

$(1 + xyz)(x - y)(y - z)(z - x) = 0$

x, y, z are different

$x - y \neq 0, y - z \neq 0, z - x \neq 0$

So $1 + xyz = 0$

Hence proved. **(1 Mark)**

36. Let, E_1 be event that lost card is king

E_2 be event that lost card is not a king

A be event that two cards drawn are king

$$P(E_1) = \frac{4}{52} = \frac{1}{13}, \quad P(E_2) = 1 - P(E_1) = 1 - \frac{1}{13} = \frac{12}{13}$$

(1 Mark)

$P\left(\dfrac{A}{E_1}\right)$ = Probability of getting 2 king cards if lost card is king (left king = 4 − 1 = 3)

$$= \frac{{}^3C_2}{{}^{51}C_2} = \frac{\dfrac{3!}{1!2!}}{\dfrac{51!}{49!2!}} \quad \left[\because {}^nC_n = \frac{n!}{r!(n-r)!}\right]$$

$$= \frac{3}{\dfrac{51 \times 50}{2}} = \frac{6}{51 \times 50} \qquad \textbf{(1 Mark)}$$

$P\left(\dfrac{A}{E_2}\right)$ = Probability of getting 2 king cards if lost card is not a king (king card = 4)

$$= \frac{{}^4C_2}{{}^{51}C_2}$$

$$= \frac{\dfrac{4!}{2!\,2!}}{\dfrac{51!}{2!\,49!}} = \frac{\dfrac{4 \times 3}{2}}{\dfrac{51 \times 50}{2}} = \frac{12}{51 \times 50} \qquad \textbf{(1 Mark)}$$

By Baye's theorem

$$P\left(\frac{E_1}{A}\right) = \frac{P(E_1).P\left(\dfrac{A}{E_1}\right)}{P(E_1).P\left(\dfrac{A}{E_1}\right) + P(E_2)P\left(\dfrac{A}{E_2}\right)} \qquad \textbf{(1 Mark)}$$

$$= \frac{\dfrac{1}{13} \times \dfrac{6}{51 \times 50}}{\dfrac{1}{13} \times \dfrac{6}{51 \times 50} + \dfrac{12}{13} \times \dfrac{12}{51 \times 50}}$$

$$= \frac{6}{6 + 144} = \frac{6}{150} = \frac{2}{50} = \frac{1}{25}$$

$$\therefore \quad P\left(\frac{E_1}{A}\right) = \frac{1}{25} \qquad \textbf{(2 Marks)}$$

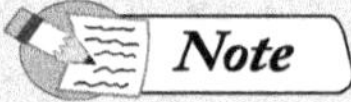

Note

If we have to find final event i.e. P(two cards drawn are king)

$$= P(E_1) \cdot P\left(\frac{A}{E_1}\right) + P(E_2) \cdot P\left(\frac{A}{E_2}\right).$$

It is called total probability.

All India *2019*

CBSE Board Solved Paper

Time Allowed : 3 Hours   *Maximum Marks : 100*

General Instructions:
(i) **All** questions are compulsory.
(ii) The question paper consists of **29** questions divided into four sections **A, B, C** and **D**. Section **A** comprises of **4** questions of **one mark** each, Section **B** comprises of **8** questions of **two marks** each, Section **C** comprises of **11** questions of **four marks** each and Section **D** comprises of **6** questions of **six marks** each.
(iii) All questions in Section **A** are to be answered in one word, one sentence or as per the exact requirement of the question.
(iv) There is no overall choice. However, internal choice has been provided in **1** question of Section A, **3** questions of Section B, **3** questions of Section C and **3** questions of Section D. You have to attempt only one of the alternatives in all such questions.
(v) Use of calculators is not permitted. You may ask for logarithmic tables, if required.

SECTION - A

1. Form the differential equation representing the family of curves $y = \dfrac{A}{x} + 5$, by eliminating the arbitrary constant A.

2. If A is a square matrix of order 3, with $|A| = 9$, then write the value of $|2.\text{adj}A|$.

3. Find the acute angle between the planes $\vec{r}.(\hat{i} - 2\hat{j} - 2\hat{k}) = 1$ and $\vec{r}.(3\hat{i} - 6\hat{j} + 2\hat{k}) = 0$.

OR

Find the length of the intercept, cut off by the plane $2x + y - z = 5$ on the x-axis.

4. If $y = \log (\cos e^x)$, then find $\dfrac{dy}{dx}$.

SECTION - B

5. Find: $\displaystyle\int_{-\frac{\pi}{4}}^{0} \frac{1 + \tan x}{1 - \tan x} dx$

6. Let * be an operation defined as $* : R \times R \to R$ such that $a * b = 2a + b$, $a, b \in R$. Check if * is a binary operation. If yes, find if it is associative too.

7. X and Y are two points with position vectors $3\vec{a} + \vec{b}$ and $\vec{a} - 3\vec{b}$ respectively. Write the position vector of a point Z which divides the line segment XY in the ratio 2 : 1 externally.

OR

Let $\vec{a} = \hat{i} + 2\hat{j} - 3\hat{k}$ and $\vec{b} = 3\hat{i} - \hat{j} + 2\hat{k}$ be two vectors. Show that the vectors $(\vec{a} + \vec{b})$ and $(\vec{a} - \vec{b})$ are perpendicular to each other.

8. If A and B are symmetric matrices, such that AB and BA are both defined, then prove that AB – BA is a skew symmetric matrix.

9. 12 cards numbered 1 to 12 (one number on one card), are placed in a box and mixed up thoroughly. Then a card is drawn at random from the box. If it is known that the number on the drawn card is greater than 5, find the probability that the card bears an odd number.

10. Out of 8 outstanding students of a school, in which there are 3 boys and 5 girls, a team of 4 students is to be selected for a quiz competition. Find the probability that 2 boys and 2 girls are selected.

OR

In a multiple choice examination with three possible answers for each of the five questions, what is the probability that a candidate would get four or more correct answers just by guessing?

11. Solve the following differential equation:

$$\frac{dy}{dx} + y = \cos x - \sin x$$

12. Find: $\int x.\tan^{-1} x\, dx$

OR

Find: $\int \dfrac{dx}{\sqrt{5 - 4x - 2x^2}}$

SECTION - C

13. Using properties of determinants, find the value of x for which

$$\begin{vmatrix} 4-x & 4+x & 4+x \\ 4+x & 4-x & 4+x \\ 4+x & 4+x & 4-x \end{vmatrix} = 0$$

14. Solve the differential equation $\dfrac{dy}{dx} = 1 + x^2 + y^2 + x^2 y^2$, given that $y = 1$ when $x = 0$.

OR

Find the particular solution of the differential equation $\dfrac{dy}{dx} = \dfrac{xy}{x^2 + y^2}$, given that $y = 1$ when $x = 0$.

15. Let $A = R - \{2\}$ and $B = R - \{1\}$. If $f : A \to B$ is a function defined by $f(x) = \dfrac{x-1}{x-2}$, show that f is one-one and onto. Hence, find f^{-1}.

OR

Show that the relation S on the set $A = \{x \in Z : 0 \le x \le 12\}$ given by $S = \{(a, b) : a, b \in Z, |a - b|$ is divisible by $3\}$ is an equivalence relation.

16. Integrate the function $\dfrac{\cos(x+a)}{\sin(x+b)}$ w.r.t.x.

17. If $x = \sin t$, $y = \sin pt$, prove that $(1 - x^2)\dfrac{d^2y}{dx^2} - x\dfrac{dy}{dx} + p^2 y = 0$.

OR

Differentiate $\tan^{-1}\left[\dfrac{\sqrt{1+x^2} - \sqrt{1-x^2}}{\sqrt{1+x^2} + \sqrt{1-x^2}}\right]$ with respect to $\cos^{-1}x^2$.

18. Prove that: $\cos^{-1}\left(\dfrac{12}{13}\right) + \sin^{-1}\left(\dfrac{3}{5}\right) = \sin^{-1}\left(\dfrac{56}{65}\right)$

19. If $y = (x)^{\cos x} + (\cos x)^{\sin x}$, find $\dfrac{dy}{dx}$.

20. Prove that $\displaystyle\int_0^a f(x)dx = \int_0^a f(a-x)dx$, and hence evaluate

$$\int_0^1 x^2 (1-x)^n \, dx.$$

21. Find the value of x, for which the four points $A(x, -1, -1)$, $B(4, 5, 1)$, $C(3, 9, 4)$ and $D(-4, 4, 4)$ are coplanar.

22. A ladder 13 m long is leaning against a vertical wall. The bottom of the ladder is dragged away from the wall along the ground at the rate of 2 cm/sec. How fast is the height on the wall decreasing when the foot of the ladder is 5 m away from the wall ?

23. Find the vector equation of the plane determined by the points $A(3, -1, 2)$, $B(5, 2, 4)$ and $C(-1, -1, 6)$. Hence, find the distance of the plane, thus obtained, from the origin.

SECTION - D

24. Using integration, find the area of the greatest rectangle that can be inscribed in an ellipse $\dfrac{x^2}{a^2} + \dfrac{y^2}{b^2} = 1$.

25. An insurance company insured 3000 cyclists, 6000 scooter drivers and 9000 car drivers. The probability of an accident involving a cyclist, a scooter driver and a car driver are 0.3, 0.05 and 0.02 respectively. One of the insured persons meets with an accident. What is the probability that he is a cyclist?

26. Using elementary row transformations, find the inverse of the matrix $\begin{bmatrix} 2 & -3 & 5 \\ 3 & 2 & -4 \\ 1 & 1 & -2 \end{bmatrix}$.

OR

Using matrices, solve the following system of linear equations:
$$x + 2y - 3z = -4$$
$$2x + 3y + 2z = 2$$
$$3x - 3y - 4z = 11$$

27. Using integration, find the area of the region bounded by the parabola $y^2 = 4x$ and the circle $4x^2 + 4y^2 = 9$.

OR

Using the method of integration, find the area of the region bounded by the lines $3x - 2y + 1 = 0$, $2x + 3y - 21 = 0$ and $x - 5y + 9 = 0$.

28. A dietician wishes to mix two types of food in such a way that the vitamin contents of the mixture contains at least 8 units of vitamin A and 10 units of vitamin C. Food I contains 2 units/kg of vitamin A and 1 unit/kg of vitamin C. It costs ₹ 50 per kg to produce food I. Food II contains 1 unit/kg of vitamin A and 2 units/kg of vitamin C and it costs ₹ 70 per kg to produce food II. Formulate this problem as a LPP to minimise the cost of a mixture that will produce the required diet. Also find the minimum cost.

29. Find the vector equation of a line passing through the point $(2, 3, 2)$ and parallel to the line $\vec{r} = (-2\hat{i} + 3\hat{j}) + \lambda(2\hat{i} - 3\hat{j} + 6\hat{k})$. Also, find the distance between these two lines.

OR

Find the coordinates of the foot of the perpendicular Q drawn from $P(3, 2, 1)$ to the plane $2x - y + z + 1 = 0$. Also, find the distance PQ and the image of the point P treating this plane as a mirror.

Solutions

SECTION - A

1. Here, $y = \dfrac{A}{x} + 5$ ...(1)

Differentiate the above equation w.r.t 'x', we get,

$\dfrac{dy}{dx} = -\dfrac{A}{x^2} \Rightarrow A = -x^2 \dfrac{dy}{dx}$ **(½ Mark)**

Put the value of A in equation (1), we get

$y = \dfrac{-x^2 \dfrac{dy}{dx}}{x} + 5 \Rightarrow x\dfrac{dy}{dx} + y = 5$ **(½ Mark)**

which is required differential equation

2. Here $|A| = 9$

We know that; $|\text{adj}(A)| = |A|^{n-1}$ **(½ Mark)**

where n = 3 (order)

$\therefore |2.\text{adj}(A)| = 2^n |\text{adj}(A)| = 2^3 |A|^{3-1} = 8 \times 9^2 = 648.$ **(½ Mark)**

3. Equation of two planes are:

$\vec{r}.\left(\hat{i} - 2\hat{j} - 2\hat{k}\right) = 1$ and $\vec{r}.\left(3\hat{i} - 6\hat{j} + 2\hat{k}\right) = 0$

$\therefore$ angle between them is given as:

$\cos\theta = \dfrac{\left|\left(\hat{i} - 2\hat{j} - 2\hat{k}\right).\left(3\hat{i} - 6\hat{j} + 2\hat{k}\right)\right|}{\sqrt{(1)^2 + (-2)^2 + (-2)^2}\sqrt{(3)^2 + (-6)^2 + (2)^2}}$ **(½ Mark)**

$\Rightarrow \cos\theta = \dfrac{|3 + 12 - 4|}{\sqrt{9} \times \sqrt{49}} = \dfrac{11}{21} \Rightarrow \theta = \cos^{-1}\left(\dfrac{11}{21}\right).$ **(½ Mark)**

OR

Equation of plane is : $2x + y - z = 5$ ...(1)

$\because$ We know that on x-axis $y = z = 0$ **(½ Mark)**

$\therefore$ Equation (1) becomes: $2x = 5$

$\Rightarrow \quad x = \dfrac{5}{2}$ (length of intercept).   **(½ Mark)**

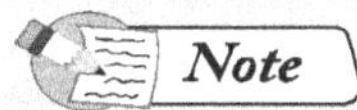

For length of intercept on the x-axis put y = z = 0, for on the y-axis put x = z = 0 and for on the z-axis put x = y = 0.

4. $y = \log(\cos e^x)$

$\Rightarrow \dfrac{dy}{dx} = \dfrac{1}{\cos e^x} \dfrac{d(\cos e^x)}{dx}$ **(½ Mark)**

$= \dfrac{1}{\cos e^x}.(-\sin e^x).\dfrac{de^x}{dx} = -\tan e^x . e^x = -e^x \tan e^x.$ **(½ Mark)**

SECTION - B

5. Since we know that; $\tan\left(\dfrac{\pi}{4} + A\right) = \dfrac{1 + \tan A}{1 - \tan A}$.

$\therefore \displaystyle\int_{-\frac{\pi}{4}}^{0} \dfrac{1 + \tan x}{1 - \tan x}dx = \int_{-\frac{\pi}{4}}^{0} \tan\left(\dfrac{\pi}{4} + x\right).dx$ **(1 Mark)**

$= \left[\log\left|\sec\left(\dfrac{\pi}{4} + x\right)\right|\right]_{-\frac{\pi}{4}}^{0}$ $\left(\because \int \tan x\, dx = \log|\sec x|\right)$

$= \left(\log\sec\left(\dfrac{\pi}{4}\right)\right) - (\log\sec(0)) = \log\sqrt{2} - \log 1 = \dfrac{1}{2}\log 2$

$(\because \log 1 = 0)$ **(1 Mark)**

6. Given operation: $a * b = 2a + b$, $a, b \in R$

If any operation is binary operation, it must follow closure property.

Let $a \in R$ and $b \in R$

Then $2a \in R$

Also $2a + b \in R$

So, $a * b \in R$

So * satisfies the closure property.

Since * is defined for all $a, b \in R$.

$\therefore$ * is a binary operation.   **(1 Mark)**

Now, $(a * b) * c = (2a + b) * c = 2(2a + b) + c = 4a + 2b + c$

$a * (b * c) = a * (2b + c) = 2a + (2b + c) = 2a + 2b + c$

$\therefore \quad (a * b) * c \neq a * (b * c)$

Hence, binary operation * is not associative.   **(1 Mark)**

7. Position vector of X $= 3\vec{a} + \vec{b}$.

Position vector of Y $= \vec{a} - 3\vec{b}$.

$\because$ Z divides XY externally in the ratio 2 : 1.

$\therefore$ position vector of Z $= \dfrac{2\left(\vec{a} - 3\vec{b}\right) - 1\left(3\vec{a} + \vec{b}\right)}{2 - 1}$

$= \dfrac{2\vec{a} - 6\vec{b} - 3\vec{a} - \vec{b}}{1} = -\vec{a} - 7\vec{b}.$ **(2 Marks)**

OR

$\vec{a} = \hat{i} + 2\hat{j} - 3\hat{k}$; $\vec{b} = 3\hat{i} - \hat{j} + 2\hat{k}$

$\therefore \vec{a} + \vec{b} = 4\hat{i} + \hat{j} - \hat{k}$ and $\vec{a} - \vec{b} = -2\hat{i} + 3\hat{j} - 5\hat{k}$ **(1 Mark)**

$\therefore \left(\vec{a} + \vec{b}\right).\left(\vec{a} - \vec{b}\right) = \left(4\hat{i} + \hat{j} - \hat{k}\right).\left(-2\hat{i} + 3\hat{j} - 5\hat{k}\right)$

$\qquad\qquad\qquad = -8 + 3 + 5 = 0$

Hence the two vectors $\left(\vec{a} + \vec{b}\right)$ and $\left(\vec{a} - \vec{b}\right)$ are perpendicular to each other.   **(1 Mark)**

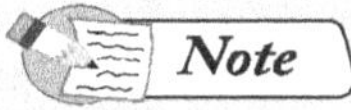

For two vectors to be perpendicular, their dot product should be zero.

8. A and B are symmetric matrices i.e. $A' = A$ and $B' = B$ Also $(AB)' = B'A'$.   **(1 Mark)**

Now, $(AB - BA)' = (AB)' - (BA)' = B'A' - A'B' = BA - AB$

$= -(AB - BA)$

Hence $AB - BA$ is skew symmetric matrix.   **(1 Mark)**

9. Let A be an event "the number on the card drawn is odd" and B be an event "the number on the drawn card is greater than 5". Then,

$S = \{1, 2, 3, 4, 5, 6, 7, 8, 9, 10, 11, 12\}$; $A = \{1, 3, 5, 7, 9, 11\}$;
$B = \{6, 7, 8, 9, 10, 11, 12\}$
$A \cap B = \{7, 9, 11\}$

$\therefore\ P(A) = \dfrac{6}{12} = \dfrac{1}{2}$; $P(B) = \dfrac{7}{12}$ and $P(A \cap B) = \left(\dfrac{3}{12}\right) = \dfrac{1}{4}$.

(1 Mark)

$\therefore$ Required probability

$= P\left(\dfrac{A}{B}\right) = \dfrac{P(A \cap B)}{P(B)} = \dfrac{\frac{1}{4}}{\frac{7}{12}} = \dfrac{1}{4} \times \dfrac{12}{7} = \dfrac{3}{7}.$ **(1 Mark)**

10. Let A be the event of selecting 2 boys & 2 girls and C be the event of selecting 4 students.
Then, $A = \{(2B, 2G)\}$ and $C = \{(1B, 3G), (2B, 2G), (3B, 1G), (0B, 4G)\}$ **(1 Mark)**
where B is used for boy and G is used for girl.

So, required probability $= P(A) = \dfrac{{}^3C_2 \cdot {}^5C_2}{{}^8C_4} = \dfrac{3}{7}$ **(1 Mark)**

As, ${}^mC_n = \dfrac{m!}{n!(m-n)!}$

OR

Let p be the probability of answer to be correct and q be answer to get wrong.

$p = \dfrac{1}{3}, q = 1 - p = 1 - \dfrac{1}{3} = \dfrac{2}{3}$; $n = 5, r = 4, 5$

and $P(X = r) = {}^nC_r \, p^r q^{(n-r)}$ **(1 Mark)**

P (Four or more successes) $= P(X = 4) + P(X = 5)$

$= {}^5C_4 \left(\dfrac{1}{3}\right)^4 \left(\dfrac{2}{3}\right)^1 + {}^5C_5 \left(\dfrac{1}{3}\right)^5 = \dfrac{11}{243}$ **(1 Mark)**

Note

In case of finding probability of at least two successes use $P(X \geq 2) = 1 - \{P(X = 0) + P(X = 1)\}$ in place of $P(X \geq 2) = P(X = 2) + P(X = 3) + P(X = 4) + P(X = 5)$.

11. Given, differential equation is $\dfrac{dy}{dx} + y = \cos x - \sin x$

which is of the form $\dfrac{dy}{dx} + Py = Q$

Here, $P = 1, Q = \cos x - \sin x$

$\Rightarrow$ I.F $= e^{\int P dx} = e^{\int 1 dx} = e^x$ **(1 Mark)**

Now, solution of diff eqn. is given by

$y \times \text{I.F} = \int (\text{I.F}) \times Q \, dx + c$

where c is constant of integration

$\Rightarrow\ y.e^x = \int e^x (\cos x - \sin x) \, dx + c$
$= e^x \cdot \cos x + c$

$\left[\because \int e^x [f(x) + f'(x)] dx = e^x \cdot f(x)\right]$

$\Rightarrow\ y = \cos x + ce^{-x}$

Hence, solution is $y = \cos x + ce^{-x}$ **(1 Mark)**

12. Let $I = \int x \tan^{-1} x \, dx$

$= \tan^{-1} x \left(\dfrac{x^2}{2}\right) - \int \dfrac{1}{1+x^2} \cdot \dfrac{x^2}{2} dx + c$ **(½ Mark)**

where c is constant of integration

$= \dfrac{x^2}{2} \tan^{-1} x - \dfrac{1}{2} \int \dfrac{x^2}{x^2 + 1} dx + c$

$= \dfrac{x^2}{2} \tan^{-1} x - \dfrac{1}{2} \int \dfrac{x^2 + 1 - 1}{1 + x^2} dx + c$ **(½ Mark)**

$= \dfrac{x^2}{2} \tan^{-1} x - \dfrac{1}{2} \int \left(1 - \dfrac{1}{1+x^2}\right) dx + c$

$= \dfrac{x^2}{2} \tan^{-1} x - \dfrac{1}{2} (x - \tan^{-1} x) + c$

$= \dfrac{x^2}{2} \tan^{-1} x - \dfrac{1}{2} x + \dfrac{1}{2} \tan^{-1} x + c$ **(1 Mark)**

OR

$\int \dfrac{dx}{\sqrt{5 - 4x - 2x^2}} = \int \dfrac{dx}{\sqrt{5 - \left(2x^2 + 4x\right)}}$

$= \int \dfrac{dx}{\sqrt{5 - 2\left(x^2 + 2x + 1\right) + 2}}$

$= \int \dfrac{dx}{\sqrt{7 - 2\left(x+1\right)^2}} = \dfrac{1}{\sqrt{2}} \int \dfrac{dx}{\sqrt{\left(\sqrt{\frac{7}{2}}\right)^2 - \left(x+1\right)^2}}$ **(1 Mark)**

$= \dfrac{1}{\sqrt{2}} \sin^{-1} \left[\dfrac{x+1}{\frac{\sqrt{7}}{\sqrt{2}}}\right] + c$ where c is constant of integration

$= \dfrac{1}{\sqrt{2}} \sin^{-1} \left(\dfrac{\sqrt{2}\left(x+1\right)}{\sqrt{7}}\right) + c$ **(1 Mark)**

13. Here, $\begin{vmatrix} 4-x & 4+x & 4+x \\ 4+x & 4-x & 4+x \\ 4+x & 4+x & 4-x \end{vmatrix} = 0$

$$\Rightarrow \begin{vmatrix} 12+x & 4+x & 4+x \\ 12+x & 4-x & 4+x \\ 12+x & 4+x & 4-x \end{vmatrix} = 0$$

(Operate : $C_1 \to C_1 + C_2 + C_3$) (1 Mark)

$$\Rightarrow (12+x)\begin{vmatrix} 1 & 4+x & 4+x \\ 1 & 4-x & 4+x \\ 1 & 4+x & 4-x \end{vmatrix} = 0$$

(Taking (12 +x) common from C_1). (1 Mark)

$$(12+x)\begin{vmatrix} 0 & 0 & 2x \\ 1 & 4-x & 4+x \\ 1 & 4+x & 4-x \end{vmatrix} = 0$$

(Operate : $R_1 \to R_1 - R_3$) (1 Mark)

Expanding along R_1, we get :

$(12+x)(2x)(4+x-4+x) = 0 \quad \Rightarrow (12+x)(2x)(2x) = 0$

$\Rightarrow x^2(x+12) = 0 \quad \Rightarrow x = 0$ or $x = -12$.   **(1 Mark)**

Note

If a matrix have like terms in column or row, then try to make single row or column to have same elements and then take common. This will simplify the matrix.

14. Given differential equation can be written as

$$\frac{dy}{dx} = (1+x^2) + y^2(1+x^2) = (1+x^2)(1+y^2)$$

$$\therefore \quad \frac{1}{1+y^2}dy = \left(1+x^2\right)dx \qquad \textbf{(1½ Marks)}$$

Integrating both sides

$$\Rightarrow \int \frac{1}{1+y^2}dy = \int \left(1+x^2\right)dx$$

$$\Rightarrow \tan^{-1}y = x + \frac{x^3}{3} + C \qquad \textbf{(1½ Marks)}$$

where C is constant of integration

Put y = 1 and x = 0 in the above equation, we get

$$\tan^{-1}1 = 0+0+C \Rightarrow \frac{\pi}{4} = C$$

Hence, $\tan^{-1}y = x + \dfrac{x^3}{3} + \dfrac{\pi}{4}$, is the required solution.

(1 Mark)

OR

$$\frac{dy}{dx} = \frac{xy}{x^2+y^2} \qquad \qquad ....(1)$$

This is a homogenous differential equation.

Substitute $y = vx$ ....(2)

$$\Rightarrow \frac{dy}{dx} = v + \frac{xdv}{dx} \qquad ....(3) \quad \textbf{(1 Mark)}$$

From (1), (2) and (3), we have

$$\frac{xdv}{dx} + v = \frac{x(vx)}{x^2+(vx)^2} = \frac{vx^2}{x^2(1+v^2)} \quad \Rightarrow \frac{xdv}{dx} + v = \frac{v}{1+v^2}$$

$$\Rightarrow \frac{xdv}{dx} = \frac{v}{1+v^2} - v = \frac{v-v-v^3}{1+v^2} \quad \Rightarrow \frac{xdv}{dx} = -\frac{v^3}{1+v^2}$$

$$\Rightarrow \frac{\left(1+v^2\right)}{v^3}dv = -\frac{dx}{x} \Rightarrow \left(\frac{1}{v^3} + \frac{1}{v}\right)dv = -\frac{dx}{x} \quad \textbf{(1 Mark)}$$

Integrating both sides, we have

$\dfrac{v^{-3+1}}{-3+1} + \ln|v| = -\ln|x| + C$, where C is constant of integration

$$\Rightarrow -\frac{1}{2v^2} + \ln|v| = -\ln|x| + C$$

$$\Rightarrow -\frac{1}{2v^2} + \ln|vx| = C \Rightarrow -\frac{x^2}{2y^2} + \ln|y| = C \quad \textbf{(1 Mark)}$$

Given $y = 1$ when $x = 0 \Rightarrow C = 0$

Thus, the particular solution of the given differential

equation is given by $\ln|y| = \dfrac{x^2}{2y^2}$ **(1 Mark)**

Note

Always put y = vx in the homogenous differential equation of

the form $\dfrac{dy}{dx} = \dfrac{\phi(y/x)}{\psi(y/x)}$ *and x = vy in the homogenous*

differential equation of the form $\dfrac{dx}{dy} = \dfrac{\psi(x/y)}{\phi(x/y)}$.

15. Let x_1, x_2 be any two elements of set A, such that $f(x_1) = f(x_2)$

$$\Rightarrow \frac{x_1-1}{x_1-2} = \frac{x_2-1}{x_2-2} \Rightarrow x_1x_2 - 2x_1 - x_2 + 2$$

$$= x_1x_2 - x_1 - 2x_2 + 2$$

$$\Rightarrow -2x_1 + x_1 = -2x_2 + x_2 \quad \Rightarrow x_1 = x_2$$

Thus, f is one-one, for all $x_1, x_2 \in A$.   **(1 Mark)**

Let y be an arbitrary element of B, then $f(x) = y$

$$\Rightarrow \frac{x-1}{x-2} = y, x \neq 2 \quad \Rightarrow x = \frac{1-2y}{1-y}$$

Clearly, $x = \dfrac{1-2y}{1-y}$ is a real number for all $y \neq 1$.

$\Rightarrow$ Corresponding to each $y \in B$, there exists

$\dfrac{1-2y}{1-y} \in A$, such that $f\left(\dfrac{1-2y}{1-y}\right) = y$ **(2 Marks)**

Thus, f is onto $\Rightarrow$ f is invertible.

$$x = \frac{1-2y}{1-y} \quad \Rightarrow \quad f^{-1}(y) = \frac{1-2y}{1-y}$$

Hence, $f^{-1}(x) = \dfrac{1-2x}{1-x}$ for all $x \in R - \{1\}$ **(1 Mark)**

OR

Given set $A = \{0, 1, 2, 3, 4, 5, 6, 7, 8, 9, 10, 11, 12\}$.
and $S = \{(a, b) : a, b \in Z, |a-b| \text{ is divisible by 3}\}$.
(i) For all $a \in A$, $(a, a) \in S$ ($\because a - a = 0$ is divisible by 3).
$\therefore$ S is reflexive on A. **(1 Mark)**
(ii) For all $a, b \in A$,
If $(a, b) \in S$, i.e, $|a-b|$ is divisible by 3.
$\Rightarrow |b-a|$ is also divisible by 3.
$\therefore$ S is symmetric on A. **(1 Mark)**
(iii) For all $a, b, c \in A$.
Let $(a, b) \in S$ and $(b, c) \in S$.
i.e; $|a-b|$ is divisible by 3 and $|b-c|$ is divisible by 3.
and let $(a-b) = \pm 3q$, $(b-c) = \pm 3p$.
Adding we get :
$$a - c = \pm 3(p+q) = \pm 3m \qquad \text{(say)}$$
$$\Rightarrow |a-c| = 3m \qquad \text{(divisible by 3)}.$$
$\therefore$ S is transitive in A.
Hence, S is an equivalence relation on A.
A relation is equivalence when it is reflexive, symmetric and transitive. **(2 Marks)**

16. Let $I = \displaystyle\int \frac{\cos(x+a)}{\sin(x+b)}\,dx = \int \frac{\cos[(x+b)+(a-b)]}{\sin(x+b)}\,dx$ **(1 Mark)**

$$= \int \frac{\cos(x+b)\cos(a-b) - \sin(x+b)\sin(a-b)}{\sin(x+b)}\,dx$$
(1 Mark)

$$= \cos(a-b)\int \frac{\cos(x+b)}{\sin(x+b)}\,dx - \sin(a-b)\int dx \text{ **(1 Mark)**}$$

$$= \cos(a-b)\int \cot(x+b)\,dx - \sin(a-b)\int dx$$

$= \cos(a-b).\ln|\sin(x+b)| - x\sin(a-b) + c$, where c is constant of integration **(1 Mark)**

17. $x = \sin t$ & $y = \sin pt$.

$\therefore \quad \dfrac{dx}{dt} = \cos t$ & $\dfrac{dy}{dt} = p\cos pt$

$$\Rightarrow \quad \frac{dy}{dx} = p\,\frac{\cos pt}{\cos t} \qquad \text{**(1 Mark)**}$$

$\Rightarrow \quad y'\cos t = p\cos pt \quad \left(\dfrac{dy}{dx} = y'\right)$

Squaring both sides we get:
$$y'^2 \cos^2 t = p^2 \cos^2 pt \qquad \text{**(1 Mark)**}$$
$$\Rightarrow \quad y'^2(1 - \sin^2 t) = p^2(1 - \sin^2 pt)$$
$$\Rightarrow \quad y'^2(1 - x^2) = p^2(1 - y^2)$$
Differentiate w.r.t. 'x' we get
$$2y'y''(1 - x^2) + (-2x)y'^2 = p^2(-2yy')$$
$$\Rightarrow y''(1 - x^2) - xy' = -p^2 y$$

$$\Rightarrow \quad (1 - x^2)\frac{d^2y}{dx^2} - x\frac{dy}{dx} + p^2 y = 0$$

(Hence proved). **(2 Marks)**

OR

$$y = \tan^{-1}\left(\frac{\sqrt{1+x^2} - \sqrt{1-x^2}}{\sqrt{1+x^2} + \sqrt{1-x^2}}\right)$$

Putting $x^2 = \cos 2\theta$, we have

$$y = \tan^{-1}\left(\frac{\sqrt{1+\cos 2\theta} - \sqrt{1-\cos 2\theta}}{\sqrt{1+\cos 2\theta} + \sqrt{1-\cos 2\theta}}\right)$$

$$\Rightarrow \quad y = \tan^{-1}\left(\frac{\sqrt{2\cos^2\theta} - \sqrt{2\sin^2\theta}}{\sqrt{2\cos^2\theta} + \sqrt{2\sin^2\theta}}\right)$$

$$\Rightarrow \quad y = \tan^{-1}\left(\frac{\cos\theta - \sin\theta}{\cos\theta + \sin\theta}\right)$$

$$\Rightarrow \quad y = \tan^{-1}\left(\frac{1 - \tan\theta}{1 + \tan\theta}\right) \qquad \text{**(1 Mark)**}$$

(Dividing the numerator and denominator by $\cos\theta$)

$$\Rightarrow \quad y = \tan^{-1}\left(\frac{\tan\dfrac{\pi}{4} - \tan\theta}{1 + \tan\dfrac{\pi}{4}\tan\theta}\right)$$

$$\Rightarrow \quad y = \tan^{-1}\left[\tan\left(\frac{\pi}{4} - \theta\right)\right] \quad \Rightarrow \quad y = \frac{\pi}{4} - \theta$$

$$\therefore \quad y = \frac{\pi}{4} - \frac{1}{2}\cos^{-1} x^2 \qquad (x^2 = \cos 2\theta) \quad \text{**(1 Mark)**}$$

Differentiating both sides with respect to x, we get

$$\frac{dy}{dx} = 0 - \frac{1}{2} \times \left(\frac{-1}{\sqrt{1 - (x^2)^2}}\right) \times 2x$$

$$\Rightarrow \quad \frac{dy}{dx} = \frac{x}{\sqrt{1 - x^4}} \qquad \text{**(1 Mark)**}$$

Now let, $z = \cos^{-1} x^2 \quad \Rightarrow \quad \dfrac{dz}{dx} = \dfrac{-1}{\sqrt{1-x^4}} \times 2x = \dfrac{-2x}{\sqrt{1-x^4}}$

$$\Rightarrow \quad \frac{dy}{dz} = \frac{\dfrac{dy}{dx}}{\dfrac{dz}{dx}} = \frac{x}{\sqrt{1-x^4}} \times \frac{\sqrt{1-x^4}}{-2x} = -2 \qquad \text{**(1 Mark)**}$$

Note

To simplify the inverse trigonometric function contain
$\left(\sqrt{1-x}, \sqrt{1+x}\right)$ or $\left(\sqrt{1-x^2}, \sqrt{1+x^2}\right)$ *put x or $x^2 = \cos\theta$ or*
$\cos 2\theta$ to remove square root.

18. Let $\cos^{-1}\dfrac{12}{13} = \alpha$, $\quad \therefore \cos\alpha = \dfrac{12}{13}$, $\sin\alpha = \dfrac{5}{13}$,

$\sin^{-1}\dfrac{3}{5} = \beta \quad \therefore \sin\beta = \dfrac{3}{5}$, $\cos\beta = \dfrac{4}{5}$ **(2 Marks)**

$\sin(\alpha+\beta)=\sin\alpha\cos\beta+\cos\alpha\sin\beta$

$=\dfrac{5}{13}\times\dfrac{4}{5}+\dfrac{12}{13}\times\dfrac{3}{5}=\dfrac{20+36}{65}=\dfrac{56}{65}$

$\therefore\quad \alpha+\beta=\sin^{-1}\dfrac{56}{65}$

$\Rightarrow\quad \cos^{-1}\dfrac{12}{13}+\sin^{-1}\dfrac{3}{5}=\sin^{-1}\dfrac{56}{65}.$ **(2 Marks)**

19. $y=(x)^{\cos x}+(\cos x)^{\sin x}$

Let $u=x^{\cos x}$

Taking log on both sides we get;

$\log u=\cos x\,\log x$

Differentiate both sides w.r.t. x we get;

$\dfrac{1}{u}\dfrac{du}{dx}=\cos x\left(\dfrac{1}{x}\right)+\log x(-\sin x)=\dfrac{\cos x}{x}-\sin x\log x$

$\Rightarrow\quad \dfrac{du}{dx}=x^{\cos x}\left[\dfrac{\cos x}{x}-\sin x\log x\right]$ **(1½ Marks)**

Now, let $v=(\cos x)^{\sin x}$

$\Rightarrow\quad \log v=\sin x\,\log(\cos x)$

$\Rightarrow\quad \dfrac{1}{v}\cdot\dfrac{dv}{dx}=\sin x\cdot\left(\dfrac{1}{\cos x}\right)\cdot(-\sin x)+\log(\cos x)\cdot(\cos x).$

$\Rightarrow\quad \dfrac{1}{v}\cdot\dfrac{dv}{dx}=\cos x\cdot\log(\cos x)-\sin x\cdot\tan x$

$\Rightarrow\quad \dfrac{dv}{dx}=(\cos x)^{\sin x}\left[\cos x\cdot\log(\cos x)-\sin x\tan x\right]$

(1½ Marks)

$\therefore\quad \dfrac{dy}{dx}=\dfrac{du}{dx}+\dfrac{dv}{dx}$

$=x^{\cos x}\left[\dfrac{\cos x}{x}-\sin x\cdot\log x\right]$

$\quad +(\cos x)^{\sin x}\left[\cos x\cdot\log(\cos x)-\sin x\cdot\tan x\right]$ **(1 Mark)**

20. Put $a-x=t\Rightarrow dx=-dt$

when $x=a,\,t=0$ and when $x=0,\,t=a$

$\therefore\quad \displaystyle\int_0^a f(a-x)\,dx=\int_a^0 f(t)(-dt)=-\int_a^0 f(t).dt$

$\displaystyle =\int_0^a f(t).dt=\int_0^a f(x).dx=\text{L.H.S}$

Hence proved. **(2 Marks)**

$\displaystyle\int_0^1 x^2(1-x)^n.\,dx=\int_0^1(1-x)^2\left(1-(1-x)\right)^n\cdot dx$

$\displaystyle =\int_0^1(1-x)^2 x^n.dx=\int_0^1(1+x^2-2x)x^n\cdot dx$

$\displaystyle =\int_0^1(x^n+x^{n+2}-2x^{n+1})dx=\left[\dfrac{x^{n+1}}{n+1}+\dfrac{x^{n+3}}{n+3}-2\dfrac{x^{n+2}}{n+2}\right]_0^1$

$\displaystyle =\left[\dfrac{1}{n+1}+\dfrac{1}{n+3}-\dfrac{2}{n+2}\right]=\dfrac{2}{(n+1)(n+2)(n+3)}$ **(2 Marks)**

21. Since the points $A(x,-1,-1),B(4,5,1),C(3,9,4)$ and $D(-4,4,4)$ are coplanar.

$\therefore\quad \begin{vmatrix} x-4 & -1-5 & -1-1 \\ 3-4 & 9-5 & 4-1 \\ -4-4 & 4-5 & 4-1 \end{vmatrix}=0$

$\Rightarrow\quad \begin{vmatrix} x-4 & -6 & -2 \\ -1 & 4 & 3 \\ -8 & -1 & 3 \end{vmatrix}=0$ **(2 Marks)**

$\Rightarrow\quad (x-4)(12+3)+6(-3+24)-2(1+32)=0$

$\Rightarrow\quad (x-4)15+6(21)-2(33)=0\Rightarrow 15(x-4)=66-126$

$\Rightarrow\quad x-4=-4\Rightarrow x=0.$ **(2 Marks)**

If four points are coplanar, then cartesian form will be equal to zero.

22. Let AB be the ladder and OB be the wall. At an instant, let

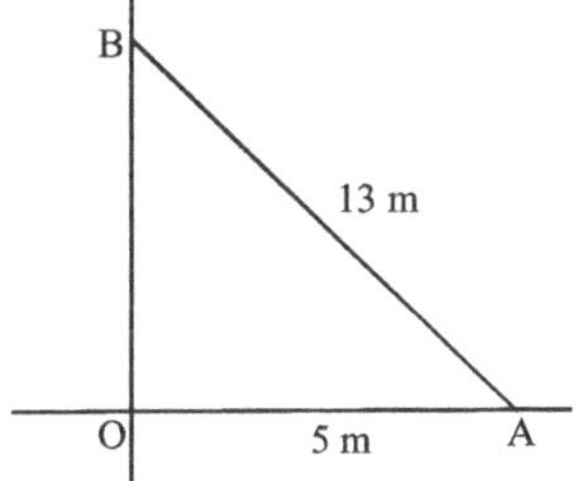

$OA=x,\,OB=y,\,x^2+y^2=169$ ...(i)

On differentiating, $2x\dfrac{dx}{dt}+2y\dfrac{dy}{dt}=0$

$\Rightarrow\quad x\dfrac{dx}{dt}+y\dfrac{dy}{dt}=0$ ...(ii) **(1 Mark)**

When $x=5$, then from (i),

we have $25+y^2=169$

$\Rightarrow\quad y^2=144\Rightarrow y=12$ **(1 Mark)**

As the bottom of ladder is dragged away at the rate of 2 cm/sec.

Now, $\dfrac{dx}{dt}=0.02$ m/sec. **(1 Mark)**

Put these values in (ii), $5\times0.02+12\times\dfrac{dy}{dt}=0$

$\Rightarrow\quad \dfrac{dy}{dt}=\dfrac{-0.1}{12}=\dfrac{-1}{120}$

Hence, the height of the ladder on the wall is decreasing at the rate of $\dfrac{1}{120}$ m/sec. $=\dfrac{5}{6}$ cm/sec. **(1 Mark)**

23. Given points are $A(3,-1,2)$ and $B(5,2,4)$ and $C(-1,-1,6)$

$\therefore\quad \overrightarrow{AB}=5\hat{i}+2\hat{j}+4\hat{k}-\left(3\hat{i}-\hat{j}+2\hat{k}\right)=2\hat{i}+3\hat{j}+2\hat{k}$ **(½ Mark)**

$\overrightarrow{AC}=-\hat{i}-\hat{j}+6\hat{k}-\left(3\hat{i}-\hat{j}+2\hat{k}\right)=-4\hat{i}+0\hat{j}+4\hat{k}$ **(½ Mark)**

Now, $\vec{n} = \overrightarrow{AB} \times \overrightarrow{AC} = \begin{vmatrix} \hat{i} & \hat{j} & \hat{k} \\ 2 & 3 & 2 \\ -4 & 0 & 4 \end{vmatrix} = 12\hat{i} - 16\hat{j} + 12\hat{k}$ **(1 Mark)**

The required plane passes through A $(3, -1, 2)$ and normal is along the vector $\vec{n}$

∴ The vector equation of the required plane is

$\vec{r}.\vec{n} = \vec{a}.\vec{n}$

$\Rightarrow \vec{r}.\left(12\hat{i} - 16\hat{j} + 12\hat{k}\right) = \left(3\hat{i} - \hat{j} + 2\hat{k}\right).\left(12\hat{i} - 16\hat{j} + 12\hat{k}\right)$

$= 36 + 16 + 24 = 76$

$\Rightarrow \vec{r}.4\left(3\hat{i} - 4\hat{j} + 3\hat{k}\right) = 4(19) \Rightarrow \vec{r}.\left(3\hat{i} - 4\hat{j} + 3\hat{k}\right) - 19 = 0$

(1 Mark)

The distance of the origin from this plane

$= \dfrac{\left|3 \times 0 - 4 \times 0 + 3 \times 0 - 19\right|}{\sqrt{3^2 + (-4)^2 + 3^2}} = \dfrac{|-19|}{\sqrt{9 + 16 + 9}} = \dfrac{19}{\sqrt{34}}$ units.

(1 Mark)

SECTION - D

24. Let the coordinates of the vertices of rectangle ABCD be
A $(a\cos\theta, b\sin\theta)$, B $(-a\cos\theta, b\sin\theta)$,
C $(-a\cos\theta, -b\sin\theta)$ and D $(a\cos\theta, -b\sin\theta)$
Length of rectangle, AB $= 2a\cos\theta$
Breadth of rectangle, AD $= 2b\sin\theta$
Area of rectangle ABCD $=$ AB $\times$ AD $= 2a\cos\theta \times 2b\sin\theta$

(1 Mark)

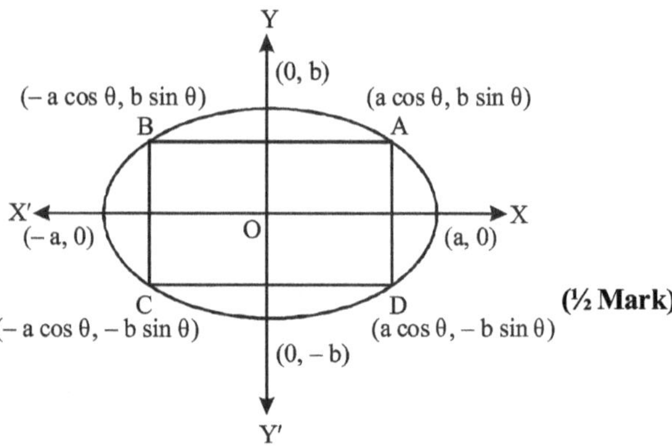

(½ Mark)

Area of rectangle (A) $= 2ab\sin 2\theta$

Differentiate w.r.t. 'θ'; $\dfrac{dA}{d\theta} = 2ab\cos 2\theta.(2)$ **(1 Mark)**

For, maximum or minimum,

put, $\dfrac{dA}{d\theta} = 0 \quad \Rightarrow 4ab\cos 2\theta = 0 \Rightarrow \cos 2\theta = 0$

$\Rightarrow \quad 2\theta = \dfrac{\pi}{2} \quad \Rightarrow \theta = \dfrac{\pi}{4}$ **(1 Mark)**

Also, $\dfrac{d^2A}{d\theta^2} = -8ab\sin 2\theta < 0$

∴   Area is maximum at $\theta = \dfrac{\pi}{4}$ **(1 Mark)**

∴   Co-ordinates of A are $\left(\dfrac{a}{\sqrt{2}}, \dfrac{b}{\sqrt{2}}\right)$ and coordinates of B are $\left(\dfrac{-a}{\sqrt{2}}, \dfrac{b}{\sqrt{2}}\right)$

∴   Equation of AB is: $y = \dfrac{b}{\sqrt{2}}$ **(½ Mark)**

∴   Required area

$= 4\displaystyle\int_0^{\frac{a}{\sqrt{2}}} \dfrac{b}{\sqrt{2}} \cdot dx = \dfrac{4b}{\sqrt{2}}[x]_0^{\frac{a}{\sqrt{2}}} = \dfrac{4b}{\sqrt{2}}\left[\dfrac{a}{\sqrt{2}}\right]$

$= \dfrac{4ab}{(\sqrt{2})^2} = 2ab$ sq. units   **(1 Mark)**

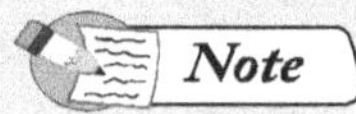 **Note**

Polar form of any point on ellipse $\dfrac{x^2}{a^2} + \dfrac{y^2}{b^2} = 1$ *in first quadrat is* $(a\cos\theta, b\sin\theta)$

25. An Insurance Company insured:
3000 cyclists ; 6000 scooter drivers and 9000 car drivers.
∴   total number of drivers $= 18,000$.

Probability of selecting a cyclist $= P(E_1) = \dfrac{3000}{18000} = \dfrac{1}{6}$.

Probability of selecting a scooter driver $= P(E_2) = \dfrac{6000}{18000} = \dfrac{1}{3}$.

Probability of selecting a car driver $= P(E_3) = \dfrac{9000}{18000} = \dfrac{1}{2}$.

(1½ Marks)

Let A be an event that insured person meets with an accident.

Probability of accident involving a cyclist $= P\left(\dfrac{A}{E_1}\right) = 0.3$

Probability of accident involving a scooter driver $= P\left(\dfrac{A}{E_2}\right) = 0.05$

Probability of accident involving a car driver $= P\left(\dfrac{A}{E_3}\right) = 0.02$

(1½ Marks)

∴   Probability of being a cyclist, given that he meets with an accident is given as :

$P\left(\dfrac{E_1}{A}\right) = \dfrac{P\left(\dfrac{A}{E_1}\right) \cdot P(E_1)}{P\left(\dfrac{A}{E_1}\right) \cdot P(E_1) + P\left(\dfrac{A}{E_2}\right) \cdot P(E_2) + P\left(\dfrac{A}{E_3}\right) \cdot P(E_3)}$

(1 Mark)

$$= \frac{0.3 \times \frac{1}{6}}{\left[0.3 \times \frac{1}{6}\right] + \left[0.05 \times \frac{1}{3}\right] + \left[0.02 \times \frac{1}{2}\right]}$$

$$= \frac{\frac{1}{20}}{\frac{1}{20} + \frac{1}{60} + \frac{1}{100}} = \frac{\frac{1}{2}}{\frac{1}{2} + \frac{1}{6} + \frac{1}{10}}$$

$$= \frac{\frac{1}{2}}{\frac{15+5+3}{30}} = \frac{1}{2} \times \frac{30}{23} = \frac{15}{23}$$ **(2 Marks)**

26. $\therefore$ Let $A = \begin{bmatrix} 2 & -3 & 5 \\ 3 & 2 & -4 \\ 1 & 1 & -2 \end{bmatrix}$

We know that; $A = IA$

$$\Rightarrow \begin{bmatrix} 2 & -3 & 5 \\ 3 & 2 & -4 \\ 1 & 1 & -2 \end{bmatrix} = \begin{bmatrix} 1 & 0 & 0 \\ 0 & 1 & 0 \\ 0 & 0 & 1 \end{bmatrix} A$$ **(½ Mark)**

Operate; $R_1 \to R_1 + 3R_3$ & $R_2 \to R_2 - 3R_3$, we get

$$\begin{bmatrix} 5 & 0 & -1 \\ 0 & -1 & 2 \\ 1 & 1 & -2 \end{bmatrix} = \begin{bmatrix} 1 & 0 & 3 \\ 0 & 1 & -3 \\ 0 & 0 & 1 \end{bmatrix} A$$ **(1 Mark)**

Operate $R_1 \to R_1 - 4R_3$, we get:

$$\begin{bmatrix} 1 & -4 & 7 \\ 0 & -1 & 2 \\ 1 & 1 & -2 \end{bmatrix} = \begin{bmatrix} 1 & 0 & -1 \\ 0 & 1 & -3 \\ 0 & 0 & 1 \end{bmatrix} A$$ **(½ Mark)**

Operate $R_3 \to 4R_3 + R_1$, we get:

$$\begin{bmatrix} 1 & -4 & 7 \\ 0 & -1 & 2 \\ 5 & 0 & -1 \end{bmatrix} = \begin{bmatrix} 1 & 0 & -1 \\ 0 & 1 & -3 \\ 1 & 0 & 3 \end{bmatrix} A$$ **(½ Mark)**

Operate $R_1 \to R_1 - 4R_2$, we get:

$$\begin{bmatrix} 1 & 0 & -1 \\ 0 & -1 & 2 \\ 5 & 0 & -1 \end{bmatrix} = \begin{bmatrix} 1 & -4 & 11 \\ 0 & 1 & -3 \\ 1 & 0 & 3 \end{bmatrix} A$$ **(1 Mark)**

Operate $R_3 \to R_3 - 5R_1$, we get:

$$\begin{bmatrix} 1 & 0 & -1 \\ 0 & -1 & 2 \\ 0 & 0 & 4 \end{bmatrix} = \begin{bmatrix} 1 & -4 & 11 \\ 0 & 1 & -3 \\ -4 & 20 & -52 \end{bmatrix} A$$ **(½ Mark)**

Operate $R_1 \to R_1 + \dfrac{R_3}{4}$, we get:

$$\begin{bmatrix} 1 & 0 & 0 \\ 0 & -1 & 2 \\ 0 & 0 & 4 \end{bmatrix} = \begin{bmatrix} 0 & 1 & -2 \\ 0 & 1 & -3 \\ -4 & 20 & -52 \end{bmatrix} A$$ **(½ Mark)**

Operate $R_2 \to R_2 - \dfrac{R_3}{2}$, we get:

$$\begin{bmatrix} 1 & 0 & 0 \\ 0 & -1 & 0 \\ 0 & 0 & 4 \end{bmatrix} = \begin{bmatrix} 0 & 1 & -2 \\ 2 & -9 & 23 \\ -4 & 20 & -52 \end{bmatrix} A$$ **(½ Mark)**

Operate $R_2 \to -R_2$ and $R_3 \to \dfrac{R_3}{4}$, we get:

$$\begin{bmatrix} 1 & 0 & 0 \\ 0 & 1 & 0 \\ 0 & 0 & 1 \end{bmatrix} = \begin{bmatrix} 0 & 1 & -2 \\ -2 & 9 & -23 \\ -1 & 5 & -13 \end{bmatrix} A$$

$$\Rightarrow A^{-1} = \begin{bmatrix} 0 & 1 & -2 \\ -2 & 9 & -23 \\ -1 & 5 & -13 \end{bmatrix}$$ **(1 Mark)**

OR

$$x + 2y - 3z = -4$$
$$2x + 3y + 2z = 2$$
$$3x - 3y - 4z = 11$$

Above system of equations can be written as: $AX = B$

where, $A = \begin{bmatrix} 1 & 2 & -3 \\ 2 & 3 & 2 \\ 3 & -3 & -4 \end{bmatrix}$; $X = \begin{bmatrix} x \\ y \\ z \end{bmatrix}$ & $B = \begin{bmatrix} -4 \\ 2 \\ 11 \end{bmatrix}$ **(1 Mark)**

$|A| = 1(-12 + 6) - 2(-8 - 6) - 3(-6 - 9) = -6 + 28 + 45 = 67 \neq 0$

$\Rightarrow A^{-1}$ exists. **(1 Mark)**

$\therefore$ The given system of equations will have a unique solution.

Cofactors of A :

$A_{11} = (-1)^2(-12 + 6) = -6$; $\quad A_{12} = (-1)^3(-8 - 6) = 14$;

$A_{13} = (-1)^4(-6 - 9) = -15$; $\quad A_{21} = (-1)^3(-8 - 9) = 17$;

$A_{22} = (-1)^4(-4 + 9) = 5$; $\quad A_{23} = (-1)^5(-3 - 6) = 9$;

$A_{31} = (-1)^4(4 + 9) = 13$; $\quad A_{32} = (-1)^5(2 + 6) = -8$ and

$A_{33} = (-1)^6(3 - 4) = -1.$ **(2 Marks)**

$$\therefore \ (\text{adj } A) = \begin{bmatrix} -6 & 14 & -15 \\ 17 & 5 & 9 \\ 13 & -8 & -1 \end{bmatrix}^T = \begin{bmatrix} -6 & 17 & 13 \\ 14 & 5 & -8 \\ -15 & 9 & -1 \end{bmatrix}$$

$$\therefore \ A^{-1} = \frac{1}{|A|}(\text{adj } A) = \frac{1}{67}\begin{bmatrix} -6 & 17 & 13 \\ 14 & 5 & -8 \\ -15 & 9 & -1 \end{bmatrix}$$ **(1 Mark)**

$$\text{Now; } A^{-1}\, B = \frac{1}{67}\begin{bmatrix} -6 & 17 & 13 \\ 14 & 5 & -8 \\ -15 & 9 & -1 \end{bmatrix}\begin{bmatrix} -4 \\ 2 \\ 11 \end{bmatrix}$$

$$= \frac{1}{67}\begin{bmatrix} 24 + 34 + 143 \\ -56 + 10 - 88 \\ 60 + 18 - 11 \end{bmatrix} = \frac{1}{67}\begin{bmatrix} 201 \\ -134 \\ 67 \end{bmatrix}$$

$$\because X = A^{-1}B \Rightarrow \begin{bmatrix} x \\ y \\ z \end{bmatrix} = \frac{1}{67}\begin{bmatrix} 201 \\ -134 \\ 67 \end{bmatrix}$$

$$\Rightarrow \quad x=3, y=-2, z=1. \qquad \textbf{(1 Mark)}$$

Note

If $|A| = 0$ and $(adjA)B = 0$ then equations have infinite many solutions and if $|A| = 0$ and $(adjA)B \neq 0$ then equations have no solutions.

27. Given equation of circle is $4x^2 + 4y^2 = 9$

$$\Rightarrow x^2 + y^2 = \frac{9}{4} \Rightarrow (x-0)^2 + (y-0)^2 = \left(\frac{3}{2}\right)^2$$

$\therefore$ Centre of the circle is $(0, 0)$ and radius $= \dfrac{3}{2}$

Now, equation of parabola is given by $y^2 = 4x$

Which is symmetric about x-axis

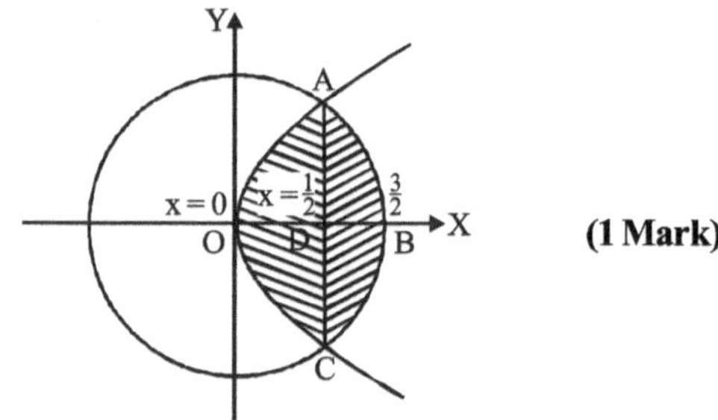

$\qquad\qquad\qquad$ **(1 Mark)**

$\therefore$ vertex at $(0, 0)$

Now, $x^2 + y^2 = \dfrac{9}{4} \Rightarrow y = \sqrt{\left(\dfrac{3}{2}\right)^2 - x^2}$

Also, $\qquad 4x^2 + 4y^2 = 9$
$\Rightarrow \quad 4x^2 + 4 \times 4x = 9 \qquad\qquad (\because y^2 = 4x)$
$\Rightarrow \quad 4x^2 + 16x - 9 = 0$

$$\Rightarrow (2x+9)(2x-1) = 0 \Rightarrow x = \frac{-9}{2}, \ x = \frac{1}{2}$$

Now, when $x = \dfrac{1}{2}, y = \sqrt{2}$ $\qquad\qquad$ **(1 Mark)**

$\therefore$ Area of shaded region

$$= 2\left[\int_0^{1/2} (y \text{ of parabola})\, dx + \int_{1/2}^{3/2} (y \text{ of circle})\, dx\right]$$

$$= 2\left[\int_0^{1/2} 2\sqrt{x}\, dx + \int_{1/2}^{3/2} \sqrt{\left(\frac{3}{2}\right)^2 - x^2}\, dx\right]. \qquad \textbf{(1 Mark)}$$

$$= 2 \times \frac{4}{3}\left[x^{3/2}\right]_0^{1/2} + 2\left[\frac{x}{2}\sqrt{\frac{9}{4} - x^2} + \frac{9}{8}\sin^{-1}\frac{x}{\frac{3}{2}}\right]_{1/2}^{3/2} \qquad \textbf{(1 Mark)}$$

$$\left[\because \int \sqrt{a^2 - x^2}\, dx = \frac{1}{2}x\sqrt{a^2 - x^2} + \frac{1}{2}a^2 \sin^{-1}\left(\frac{x}{a}\right) + c\right]$$

$$= \frac{8}{3}\left\{\left(\frac{1}{2}\right)^{3/2} - 0\right\} + 2\left[\frac{9}{8}\sin^{-1}1 - \frac{1}{4}\sqrt{2} - \frac{9}{8}\sin^{-1}\frac{1}{3}\right]$$

$$= \frac{8}{3}\left\{\left(\frac{1}{\sqrt{2}}\right)^3\right\} + 2\left[\frac{9}{8}\times\frac{\pi}{2} - \frac{1}{2\sqrt{2}} - \frac{9}{8}\sin^{-1}\frac{1}{3}\right]$$

$$\left(\because \sin\frac{\pi}{2} = 1\right)$$

$$= \frac{8}{3}\times\frac{1}{2\sqrt{2}} + \frac{9\pi}{8} - \frac{1}{\sqrt{2}} - \frac{9}{4}\sin^{-1}\frac{1}{3}$$

$$= \frac{4}{3\sqrt{2}} - \frac{1}{\sqrt{2}} + \frac{9\pi}{8} - \frac{9}{4}\sin^{-1}\frac{1}{3}$$

$$= \frac{1}{3\sqrt{2}} + \frac{9}{4}\left(\frac{\pi}{2} - \sin^{-1}\frac{1}{3}\right)$$

$$= \frac{\sqrt{2}}{6} + \frac{9}{4}\cos^{-1}\left(\frac{1}{3}\right) \text{ sq. units} \qquad \textbf{(2 Marks)}$$

OR

Given equation of lines are
$$3x - 2y = -1 \qquad\qquad \text{....... (i)}$$
$$2x + 3y = 21 \qquad\qquad \text{...... (ii)}$$
$$x - 5y = -9 \qquad\qquad \text{..... (iii)}$$

Solving eqs. (i) and (ii) as follows
$$2(3x - 2y = -1)$$
$$3(2x + 3y = 21)$$
$$\Rightarrow \quad 6x - 4y = -2$$
$$\underline{\quad 6x + 9y = \ 63 \quad}$$
$$-13y = -65$$

$$\Rightarrow \quad y = \frac{65}{13} = 5$$

Putting $y = 5$ in eq. (i)

$$3x - 2y = -1 \ \Rightarrow 3x - 10 = -1 \ \Rightarrow x = \frac{9}{3} = 3$$

Lines (i) and (ii) intersect each other at point $(3, 5)$. **(½ Mark)**

Now, solving eqs. (ii) and (iii), we get

$$y = \frac{39}{13} = 3$$

Putting $y = 3$ in eq. (iii), we get
$$x - 5y = -9 \Rightarrow x - 5(3) = -9 \Rightarrow x = 6$$
$$\therefore \quad x = 6, y = 3$$

So lines (ii) and (iii) intersect each other at point $(6, 3)$. Now solving eqs. (i) and (iii), we get **(½ Mark)**

$$y = \frac{26}{13} = 2$$

Put $y = 2$ in eq. (iii), we get
$$x - 5(2) = -9 \ \Rightarrow x - 10 = -9 \ \Rightarrow x = 1$$
$$\therefore \quad x = 1, y = 2$$

So, lines (i) and (ii) intersect each other at point $(1, 2)$ **(½ Mark)**

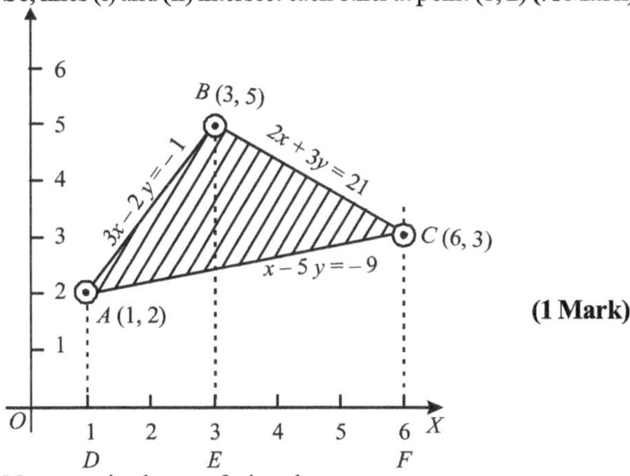

(1 Mark)

Now required area of triangle

= Area of (ABED) + Area of (BEFC) − Area of (ADFC)

$$= \int_1^3 \frac{3x+1}{2}\,dx + \int_3^6 \frac{21-2x}{3}\,dx - \int_1^6 \frac{x+9}{5}\,dx \qquad \textbf{(1 Mark)}$$

$$= \frac{1}{2}\left[\frac{3x^2}{2}+x\right]_1^3 + \frac{1}{3}\left[21x-\frac{2x^2}{2}\right]_3^6 - \frac{1}{5}\left[\frac{x^2}{2}+9x\right]_1^6 \qquad \textbf{(1 Mark)}$$

$$= \frac{1}{2}\left[\left(\frac{27}{2}+3\right)-\left(\frac{3}{2}+1\right)\right] + \frac{1}{3}\left[(126-36)-(63-9)\right]$$

$$-\frac{1}{5}\left[(18+54)-\left(\frac{1}{2}+9\right)\right]$$

$$= \frac{1}{2}\left[\frac{33}{2}-\frac{5}{2}\right] + \frac{1}{3}[90-54] - \frac{1}{5}\left[72-\frac{19}{2}\right]$$

$$= \frac{1}{2}\left[\frac{28}{2}\right] + \frac{1}{3}(36) - \frac{1}{5}\left(\frac{125}{2}\right)$$

$$= 7+12-\frac{25}{2} = \frac{14+24-25}{2} = \frac{13}{2} \text{ sq. units.} \qquad \textbf{(1½ Marks)}$$

28. The given data can be put in the tabular form as follows.

Food	Vitamin A	Vitamin C	Cost/Unit
I	2	1	₹ 50
II	1	2	₹ 70
Min. requirement	8	10	

Suppose the diet contains x units of food I and y units of food II.

Then, the required LPP is

Minimize $\quad Z = 50x + 70y$

Subject to the constraints,

$$2x+y \geq 8$$
$$x+2y \geq 10$$
$$x \geq 0, y \geq 0 \qquad \textbf{(2 Marks)}$$

Let us draw the lines,

$$2x+y=8 \qquad \text{...(i)}$$
$$x+2y=10 \qquad \text{...(ii)}$$

$2x+y=8$ passes through points $(0, 8)$ and $(4, 0)$.

∴ $\quad$ For $2x+y=8$

x	0	4
y	8	0

and the line $x+2y=10$ passes through points $(10, 0)$ and $(0, 5)$.

∴ $\quad$ For $x+2y=10$

x	10	0
y	0	5

(1 Mark)

Graph of above LPP is given as follows:

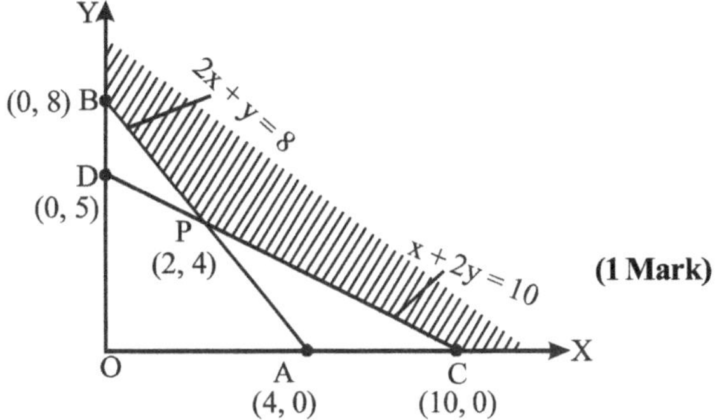

(1 Mark)

Multiplying eq. (i) by 2 and subtracting eq. (ii) from eq. (i), we get

$$\begin{aligned} 4x + 2y &= 16 \\ x + 2y &= 10 \\ \hline 3x &= 6 \end{aligned}$$

$$\Rightarrow \qquad x = 2$$

Putting $x = 2$ in eq (i), we get

$$2(2)+y=8 \quad \Rightarrow \quad y=8-4=4$$

These lines intersect at $P(2, 4)$. **(1 Mark)**

The solution set is shaded region.

∴ We have, the table with corner points and values of Z.

Corner point	Value of objective function $Z = 50x + 70y$	
C(10, 0)	$50(10) + 70(0) = 500$	
P(2, 4)	$50(2) + 70(4) = 100 + 280$ $= 380$ (minimum)	**(1 Mark)**
B(0, 8)	$50(0) + 70(8) = 0 + 560$ $= 560$	

Hence, the minimum cost is ₹ 380 when $x = 2$ and $y = 4$.

29. Given line is: $\quad \vec{r} = (-2\hat{i}+3\hat{j}) + \lambda(2\hat{i}-3\hat{j}+6\hat{k})$

it is parallel to $2\hat{i}-3\hat{j}+6\hat{k}$.

Also required line is parallel to the given line.

$\Rightarrow \quad$ Required line is parallel to $2\hat{i}-3\hat{j}+6\hat{k}$

Again required line passes through the point (2, 3, 2) or $(2\hat{i}+3\hat{j}+2\hat{k})$

$\therefore$ Equation of a line parallel to $2\hat{i}-3\hat{j}+6\hat{k}$ & passes through the point having position vector $2\hat{i}+3\hat{j}+2\hat{k}$ is given as:

$\vec{r}=\vec{a}+r\vec{b}$

$\vec{r}=(2\hat{i}+3\hat{j}+2\hat{k})+\mu(2\hat{i}-3\hat{j}+6\hat{k}).$ **(2 Marks)**

We know that distance between the parallel lines

$\vec{r}=\vec{a}_1+\lambda\vec{b}$ and $\vec{r}=\vec{a}_2+\mu\vec{b}$ is given as:

$$d=\left|\frac{(\vec{a}_2-\vec{a}_1)\times\vec{b}}{|\vec{b}|}\right|.$$ **(1 Mark)**

Here;

$\vec{a}_1=-2\hat{i}+3\hat{j};\quad \vec{a}_2=2\hat{i}+3\hat{j}+2\hat{k}\quad \& \vec{b}=2\hat{i}-3\hat{j}+6\hat{k}$

$\Rightarrow |\vec{b}|=\sqrt{2^2+3^2+6^2}=\sqrt{49}=7$ and $(\vec{a}_2-\vec{a}_1)=4\hat{i}+2\hat{k}$ **(1 Mark)**

$$(\vec{a}_2-\vec{a}_1)\times\vec{b}=\begin{vmatrix}\hat{i}&\hat{j}&\hat{k}\\4&0&2\\2&-3&6\end{vmatrix}=\hat{i}(+6)-\hat{j}(24-4)+\hat{k}(-12)$$

$$=6\hat{i}-20\hat{j}-12\hat{k}$$ **(1 Mark)**

$\left|(\vec{a}_2-\vec{a}_1)\times\vec{b}\right|=\sqrt{6^2+20^2+12^2}=2\sqrt{145}$

$\therefore\ d=\dfrac{2\sqrt{145}}{7}$ units. **(1 Mark)**

OR

Let Q be the foot of perpendicular and R (x_1, y_1, z_1) be the image of point P (3, 2, 1) on the plane whose equation is

$2x-y+z+1=0$ ...(i)

Here, the line PQ is normal to the given plane.
So, DR's of line PQ are proportional to DR's of normal of plane.

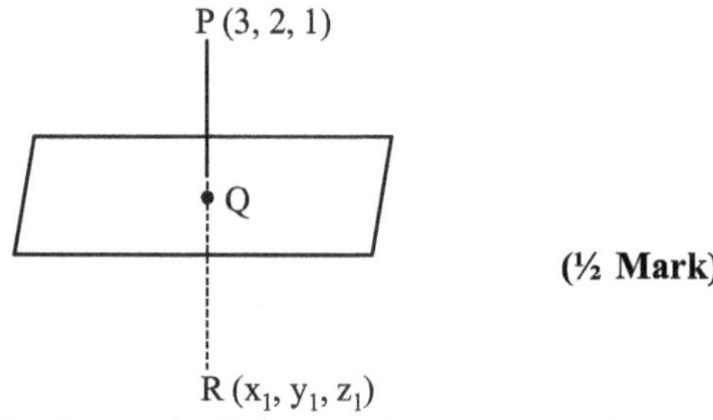

(½ Mark)

Now, DR's of normal of plane are 2, –1, 1. **(½ Mark)**

$\therefore$ Equation of line PQ where point P (3, 2, 1) is given by

$$\frac{x-3}{2}=\frac{y-2}{-1}=\frac{z-1}{1}$$ **(1 Mark)**

let $\dfrac{x-3}{2}=\dfrac{y-2}{-1}=\dfrac{z-1}{1}=\lambda$ (say)

$\Rightarrow x-3=2\lambda, y-2=-\lambda, z-1=\lambda$

$\Rightarrow x=2\lambda+3, y=2-\lambda, z=\lambda+1$

$\therefore$ Coordinates of Q are $(2\lambda+3, 2-\lambda, \lambda+1)$ ...(ii) **(1 Mark)**

As point Q lies on the plane, so its coordinates must satisfy equation of plane.

$\therefore$ Putting $x=2\lambda+3, y=2-\lambda, z=\lambda+1$ in Eq. (i), we get

$2(2\lambda+3)-(2-\lambda)+(\lambda+1)+1=0$

$\Rightarrow 4\lambda+6-2+\lambda+\lambda+1+1=0$

$\Rightarrow 6\lambda+6=0 \Rightarrow 6\lambda=-6 \Rightarrow \lambda=-1$ **(1 Mark)**

Putting $\lambda=-1$ in Eq. (ii), we get coordinates of foot of perpendicular on Q as: $Q(2\lambda+3, 2-\lambda, \lambda+1)=$ Q (1, 3, 0)

(½ Mark)

Also, perpendicular distance PQ is given by using distance formula as

$$PQ=\sqrt{(1-3)^2+(3-2)^2+(0-1)^2}$$

$=\sqrt{4+1+1}=\sqrt{6}$ units **(½ Mark)**

We find image of point P (3, 2, 1), Since Q is the mid-point of line PR.

$\therefore$ Using mid-point formula, we have

$$\left(\frac{x_1+3}{2},\frac{y_1+2}{2},\frac{z_1+1}{2}\right)=(1,3,0)$$

$\Rightarrow \dfrac{x_1+3}{2}=1, \dfrac{y_1+2}{2}=3, \dfrac{z_1+1}{2}=0$

$\Rightarrow x_1=2-3, y_1=6-2, z_1=0-1$

$\therefore\ R(x_1, y_1, z_1)=(-1, 4, -1)$

Hence the image of point P (3, 2, 1) is (–1, 4, –1).**(1 Mark)**

> **Note**
>
> *If a point (x_1, y_1, z_1) is given, which is perpendicular to a plane $ax+by+cz=d$, then foot (u, v, w) of perpendicular is given by*
>
> $$\frac{u-x_1}{a}=\frac{v-y_1}{b}=\frac{w-z_1}{c}$$

Delhi *2019*

CBSE Board Solved Paper

Time Allowed : 3 Hours   *Maximum Marks : 100*

General Instructions:

(i) **All** questions are compulsory.

(ii) This question paper contains **29** questions divided into four sections **A, B, C** and **D**. Section **A** comprises of **4** questions of **one** mark each, Section **B** comprises of **8** questions of **two** marks each, Section **C** comprises of **11** questions of **four** marks each and Section **D** comprises of **6** questions of **six** marks each.

(iii) All questions in Section **A** are to be answered is **one** word, **one** sentence or as per the exact requirement of the question.

(iv) There is no overall choice. However, internal choice has been provided in **1** question of Section **A**, **3** questions of Section **B**, **3** questions of Section **C** and **3** questions of Section **D**. You have to attempt only one of the alternatives in all such questions.

(v) Use of calculators is not permitted. You may ask logarithmic tables, if required.

SECTION - A

Question numbers 1 to 4 carry 1 mark each.

1. If $3A - B = \begin{bmatrix} 5 & 0 \\ 1 & 1 \end{bmatrix}$ and $B = \begin{bmatrix} 4 & 3 \\ 2 & 5 \end{bmatrix}$, then find the matrix A.

2. Write the order and the degree of the following differential equation: $x^3 \left(\dfrac{d^2 y}{dx^2} \right)^2 + x \left(\dfrac{dy}{dx} \right)^4 = 0$

3. If $f(x) = x + 1$, find $\dfrac{d}{dx}$ $(fof)(x)$.

4. If a line makes angles 90°, 135°, 45° with the x, y and z axes respectively, find its direction cosines.

OR

Find the vector equation of the line which passes through the point $(3, 4, 5)$ and is parallel to the vector $2\hat{i} + 2\hat{j} - 3\hat{k}$.

SECTION - B

Question numbers 5 to 12 carry 2 marks each.

5. Find : $\int \sin x . \log \cos x \, dx$.

6. Evaluate : $\displaystyle\int_{-\pi}^{\pi} (1 - x^2) \sin x \cos^2 x \, dx$

OR

Evaluate : $\displaystyle\int_{-1}^{2} \dfrac{|x|}{x} dx$

7. Examine whether the operation * defined on R by $a * b = ab + 1$ is (i) a binary or not. (ii) if a binary operation, is it associative or not?

8. Find a matrix A such that $2A - 3B + 5C = 0$, where $B = \begin{bmatrix} -2 & 2 & 0 \\ 3 & 1 & 4 \end{bmatrix}$ and $C = \begin{bmatrix} 2 & 0 & -2 \\ 7 & 1 & 6 \end{bmatrix}$.

9. A die marked 1, 2, 3 in red and 4, 5, 6 in green is tossed. Let A be the event "number is even" and B be the event "number is marked red". Find whether the events A and B are independent or not.

10. Form the differential equation representing the family of curves $y = e^{2x} (a + bx)$, where 'a' and 'b' are arbitrary constants.

11. A die is thrown 6 times. If "getting an odd number" is a "success", what is the probability of

(i) 5 successes?

(ii) atmost 5 successes?

OR

The random variable X has a probability distribution P(X) of the following form, where 'k' is some number.

$$P(X = x) = \begin{cases} k & , & \text{if } x = 0 \\ 2k & , & \text{if } x = 1 \\ 3k & , & \text{if } x = 2 \\ 0 & , & \text{otherwise} \end{cases}$$

Determine the value of 'k'.

12. If the sum of two unit vectors is a unit vector, prove that the magnitude of their difference is $\sqrt{3}$.

OR

If $\vec{a} = 2\hat{i} + 3\hat{j} + \hat{k}, \vec{b} = \hat{i} - 2\hat{j} + \hat{k}$ and $\vec{c} = -3\hat{i} + \hat{j} + 2\hat{k}$, find $[\vec{a} \ \vec{b} \ \vec{c}]$.

SECTION - C

Question numbers 13 to 23 carry 4 marks each.

13. Using properties of determinants, prove the following:

$$\begin{vmatrix} a & b & c \\ a-b & b-c & c-a \\ b+c & c+a & a+b \end{vmatrix} = a^3 + b^3 + c^3 - 3abc.$$

14. Solve : $\tan^{-1} 4x + \tan^{-1} 6x = \dfrac{\pi}{4}$.

15. Show that the relation R on $\mathbb{R}$ defined as R = $\{(a, b) : a \le b\}$, is reflexive, and transitive but not symmetric.

OR

Prove that the function $f : N \to N$, defined by $f(x) = x^2 + x + 1$ is one-one but not onto. Find inverse of $f : N \to S$, where S is range of f.

16. Find the equation of tangent to the curve $y = \sqrt{3x-2}$ which is parallel to the line $4x - 2y + 5 = 0$. Also, write the equation of normal to the curve at the point of contact.

17. If $\log (x^2 + y^2) = 2 \tan^{-1}\left(\dfrac{y}{x}\right)$, show that $\dfrac{dy}{dx} = \dfrac{x+y}{x-y}$.

OR

If $x^y - y^x = a^b$, find $\dfrac{dy}{dx}$.

18. If $y = (\sin^{-1}x)^2$, prove that $(1 - x^2)\dfrac{d^2y}{dx^2} - x\dfrac{dy}{dx} - 2 = 0$.

19. Prove that $\displaystyle\int_0^a f(x)dx = \int_0^a f(a-x)dx$, hence evaluate $\displaystyle\int_0^{\pi} \dfrac{x\sin x}{1+\cos^2 x}dx$.

20. Find : $\displaystyle\int \dfrac{\cos x}{(1+\sin x)(2+\sin x)}dx$

21. Solve the differential equation : $\dfrac{dy}{dx} - \dfrac{2x}{1+x^2}y = x^2 + 2$

OR

Solve the differential equation : $(x + 1)\dfrac{dy}{dx} = 2e^{-y} - 1$; $y(0) = 0$.

22. If $\hat{i} + \hat{j} + \hat{k}$, $2\hat{i} + 5\hat{j}$, $3\hat{i} + 2\hat{j} - 3\hat{k}$ and $\hat{i} - 6\hat{j} - \hat{k}$ respectively are the position vectors of points A, B, C and D, then find the angle between the straight lines AB and CD. Find whether $\overrightarrow{AB}$ and $\overrightarrow{CD}$ are collinear or not.

23. Find the value of λ, so that the lines $\dfrac{1-x}{3} = \dfrac{7y-14}{\lambda} = \dfrac{z-3}{2}$ and $\dfrac{7-7x}{3\lambda} = \dfrac{y-5}{1} = \dfrac{6-z}{5}$ are at right angles. Also, find whether the lines are intersecting or not.

SECTION - D

Question numbers 24 to 29 carry 6 marks each.

24. A tank with rectangular base and rectangular sides, open at the top is to be constructed so that its depth is 2 m and volume is 8 m³. If building of tank costs ₹ 70 per square metre for the base and ₹ 45 per square metre for the sides, what is the cost of least expensive tank?

25. If A = $\begin{bmatrix} 1 & 1 & 1 \\ 1 & 0 & 2 \\ 3 & 1 & 1 \end{bmatrix}$, find A⁻¹.

Hence, solve the system of equations $x + y + z = 6$, $x + 2z = 7$, $3x + y + z = 12$.

OR

Find the inverse of the following matrix using elementary operations.

$$A = \begin{bmatrix} 1 & 2 & -2 \\ -1 & 3 & 0 \\ 0 & -2 & 1 \end{bmatrix}$$

26. Prove that the curves $y^2 = 4x$ and $x^2 = 4y$ divide the area of the square bounded by sides $x = 0$, $x = 4$, $y = 4$ and $y = 0$ into three equal parts.

OR

Using integration, find the area of the triangle whose vertices are (2, 3), (3, 5) and (4, 4).

27. A manufacturer has employed 5 skilled men and 10 semi-skilled men and makes two models A and B of an article. The making of one item of model A requires 2 hours work by a skilled man and 2 hours work by a semi-skilled man. One item of model B requires 1 hour by a skilled man and 3 hours by a semi-skilled man. No man is expected to work more than 8 hours per day. The manufacturer's profit on an item of model A is ₹ 15 and on an item of model B is ₹ 10. How many of items of each model should be made per day in order to maximize daily profit? Formulate the above LPP and solve it graphically and find the maximum profit.

28. Find the vector and Cartesian equations of the plane passing through the points (2, 2, – 1), (3, 4, 2) and (7, 0, 6). Also find the vector equation of a plane passing through (4, 3, 1) and parallel to the plane obtained above.

OR

Find the vector equation of the plane that contains the lines $\vec{r} = (\hat{i} + \hat{j}) + \lambda(\hat{i} + 2\hat{j} - \hat{k})$ and the point (–1, 3, –4). Also, find the length of the perpendicular drawn from the point (2, 1, 4) to the plane thus obtained.

29. Two cards are drawn simultaneously (or successively without replacement) from a well shuffled pack of 52 cards. Find the mean and variance of the number of kings.

Solutions

SECTION - A

1. $3A - \begin{bmatrix} 4 & 3 \\ 2 & 5 \end{bmatrix} = \begin{bmatrix} 5 & 0 \\ 1 & 1 \end{bmatrix}$

Taking B to Right hand side

$3A = \begin{bmatrix} 5 & 0 \\ 1 & 1 \end{bmatrix} + \begin{bmatrix} 4 & 3 \\ 2 & 5 \end{bmatrix} \Rightarrow 3A = \begin{bmatrix} 9 & 3 \\ 3 & 6 \end{bmatrix}$

$A = \begin{bmatrix} 3 & 1 \\ 1 & 2 \end{bmatrix}$ **(1 Mark)**

2.   Highest order derivative is $\dfrac{d^2y}{dx^2}$.

So, order of the differential equation is 2.   **(½ Mark)**

Power of $\dfrac{d^2y}{dx^2}$ is 2 in the given equation.

So, degree of the differential equation is 2.

∴   Order is 2 and degree is 2.   **(½ Mark)**

 **Note**

Order is the highest order derivative present in the differential equation and degree is the power of highest order derivative.

3.   Given: $f(x) = x + 1$

$(fof)(x) = f(f(x)) = f(x + 1) = (x + 1) + 1 = x + 2$

                                                      (½ Mark)

Differentiating on both sides

$\dfrac{d}{dx}(fof)(x) = \dfrac{d}{dx}(x + 2)$

$= \dfrac{d(x)}{dx} + \dfrac{d(2)}{dx} = 1$ **(½ Mark)**

4.   Direction cosines of the line are cos 90°, cos 135°, cos 45°

cos 90° = 0

$\cos 135° = \cos(90 + 45°) = -\sin 45° = -\dfrac{1}{\sqrt{2}}$

$\cos 45° = \dfrac{1}{\sqrt{2}}$

Direction cosines of the line are $0, \dfrac{-1}{\sqrt{2}}, \dfrac{1}{\sqrt{2}}$ **(1 Mark)**

OR

The vector equation of a line passing through a point having position vector $\vec{a}$ and parallel to vector $\vec{b}$ is

$\vec{r} = \vec{a} + \lambda\vec{b}$, where λ is a parameter   **(½ Mark)**

$\vec{b} = 2\hat{i} + 2\hat{j} - 3\hat{k}$ (given)

Point (3, 4, 5) (given)

∴ $\vec{a} = 3\hat{i} + 4\hat{j} + 5\hat{k}$

Hence $\vec{r} = 3\hat{i} + 4\hat{j} + 5\hat{k} + \lambda(2\hat{i} + 2\hat{j} - 3\hat{k})$ **(½ Mark)**

SECTION - B

5. $\int \sin x \log \cos x\, dx$

Let $\cos x = t \Rightarrow -\sin x\, dx = dt$

$\int -\log t\, dt = \int (-\log t)\, dt = -\int 1.\log t\, dt$ **(1 Mark)**

$\left[\because \int u.v\, dx = u\int v\, dx - \left[\int \dfrac{du}{dx}\left(\int v\, dx \right) dx \right] \right]$

$-\int (\log t)(1)\, dt = -\left[\log t \int dt - \left[\dfrac{d(\log t)}{dt} \int dt . dt \right] \right]$

$= -\left[t\log t - \int 1.dt \right] \Rightarrow -\int \log t\, dt = -t \log t + t + C$

$\int \sin x(\log x)\, dx = -\cos x \log \cos x + \cos x + C$

                                          [Putting value of t]

                                                      (1 Mark)

6.   As we know that

$\int_{-a}^{a} f(x)\, dx = \begin{cases} 2\int_{0}^{a} f(x)\, dx & , \ \ \text{if } f(x) \text{ is an even function} \\ 0 & , \ \ \text{if } f(x) \text{ is an odd function} \end{cases}$

$\int_{-\pi}^{\pi} (1 - x^2) \sin x \cos^2 x\, dx$

Let $f(x) = (1 - x^2) \sin x \cos^2 x$

$f(-x) = (1 - (-x)^2) \sin (-x) \cos^2 (-x)$

$f(-x) = (1 - x^2)[(-\sin x) \cos^2 x]$

                [$\because \sin(-\theta) = -\sin\theta \ \cos (-\theta) = \cos\theta$]

$f(-x) = -(1 - x^2) \sin x \cos^2 x$

$f(-x) = -f(x)$

Hence f is an odd function   **(1 Mark)**

∴ $\int_{-\pi}^{\pi} (1 - x^2) \sin x \cos^2 x\, dx = 0$ **(1 Mark)**

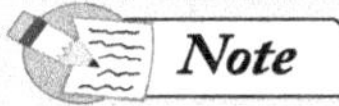 **Note**

If f(–x) = f(x) then f is an even function and if f(–x) = –f(x) then f is an odd function

OR

$|x| = x$ when $x \geq 0$

$\quad\quad = -x$ when $x < 0$

$\therefore \dfrac{|x|}{x} = 1$ when $x \geq 0$

$\quad\quad = -1$ when $x < 0$ **(1 Mark)**

$\displaystyle \int_{-1}^{2} \dfrac{|x|}{x}\, dx = \int_{-1}^{0}(-1)\, dx + \int_{0}^{2}(1)\, dx$

As $= -\left(x\right)_{-1}^{0} + \left(x\right)_{0}^{2} = -[0 - (-1)] + [2 - 0]$

$= -1 + 2 = 1$ **(1 Mark)**

7. (i)   Let $a \in R$ and $b \in R$

       then $ab \in R$

       Also $ab + 1 \in R$

       So $a * b \in R$

       So $*$ satisfies the closure property.

       Since $*$ is defined for all $a, b \in R$.

       $\therefore$ $*$ is a binary operation.   **(1 Mark)**

(ii)   For $*$ to be associative

$(a * b) * c = (ab + 1) * c = (ab + 1)c + 1$

$\quad\quad\quad\quad = abc + c + 1$ ...(1)

$a * (b * c) = a * (bc + 1) = a(bc + 1) + 1$

$\quad\quad\quad\quad = abc + a + 1$ ...(2)

       From equation (1) & (2)

       $(a * b) * c \neq a * (b * c)$

       $\therefore$ $*$ is not associative   **(1 Mark)**

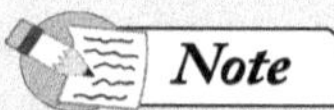

Note

If any operation is a binary operation, it must follow closure property i.e. result is also belongs to given set.

8. Given: $2A - 3B + 5C = 0$

Both B and C are of order 2×3. Therefore A should be of order 2×3.

$2A - 3\begin{bmatrix} -2 & 2 & 0 \\ 3 & 1 & 4 \end{bmatrix} + 5\begin{bmatrix} 2 & 0 & -2 \\ 7 & 1 & 6 \end{bmatrix} = 0$

$2A - \begin{bmatrix} -6 & 6 & 0 \\ 9 & 3 & 12 \end{bmatrix} + \begin{bmatrix} 10 & 0 & -10 \\ 35 & 5 & 30 \end{bmatrix} = 0$

$2A + \begin{bmatrix} 16 & -6 & -10 \\ 26 & 2 & 18 \end{bmatrix} = 0$ **(1 Mark)**

$2A = -\begin{bmatrix} 16 & -6 & -10 \\ 26 & 2 & 18 \end{bmatrix}$

$A = \begin{bmatrix} \dfrac{16}{2} & \dfrac{6}{2} & \dfrac{10}{2} \\ -\dfrac{26}{2} & -\dfrac{2}{2} & -\dfrac{18}{2} \end{bmatrix}$

$A = \begin{bmatrix} -8 & 3 & 5 \\ -13 & -1 & -9 \end{bmatrix}$ **(1 Mark)**

Note

Two matrices can be added or subtracted if both have same order

9. When a die is thrown, the sample space (S) is

$S = [1, 2, 3, 4, 5, 6]$

Let A: the number is even $[2, 4, 6]$

$P(A) = \dfrac{\text{Number of favorable outcomes}}{\text{Total number of possible outcomes}} = \dfrac{3}{6} = \dfrac{1}{2}$

B: the number is marked red

$B = [1, 2, 3]$

$P(B) = \dfrac{3}{6} = \dfrac{1}{2}$ **(1 Mark)**

$P(A) \cdot P(B) = \dfrac{1}{2} \times \dfrac{1}{2} = \dfrac{1}{4}$

$P(A \cap B) = \dfrac{1}{6}$

     $[\because$ Only 2 is a number which is even and red$]$

As we can see that

$P(A \cap B) \neq P(A) \cdot P(B)$

$\therefore$ A and B are not independent events.   **(1 Mark)**

Note

$P(A \cap B)$ is the probability of having an event of A and B both.

10. Given: $y = e^{2x}(a + bx)$ ...(1)

Differentiating on both side with respect to x

$\dfrac{dy}{dx} = \dfrac{d}{dx}[e^{2x}(a + bx)]$

$\dfrac{dy}{dx} = \dfrac{d}{dx}(ae^{2x}) + \dfrac{d}{dx}(bxe^{2x})$

$\dfrac{dy}{dx} = 2a\, e^{2x} + b\left[e^{2x}\dfrac{dx}{dx} + x\dfrac{d}{dx}e^{2x}\right]$

$= 2a\, e^{2x} + b[e^{2x} + 2x\, e^{2x}]$

$= be^{2x} + 2(a + bx)e^{2x}$

$\dfrac{dy}{dx} = be^{2x} + 2y$ ...(2) $[\because y = e^{2x}(a + bx)]$

                              (1 Mark)

Differentiating the above equation

$\Rightarrow \dfrac{d^2y}{dx^2} = 2b\, e^{2x} + 2\dfrac{dy}{dx}$ ...(3)

Substituting the value of be^{2x} from (2) in equation (3)

$$\frac{d^2 y}{dx^2} = 2\left(\frac{dy}{dx} - 2\right) + 2\frac{dy}{dx}$$

$$\frac{d^2 y}{dx^2} - 4\frac{dy}{dx} + 4y = 0 \qquad \textbf{(1 Mark)}$$

11. Number of trial $= 6$

Random variable $(X) = 0, 1, 2, 3, 4, 5, 6$

p (Probability of odd numbers) $= \dfrac{3}{6} = \dfrac{1}{2}$

q (Probability of not odd) $= \dfrac{3}{6} = \dfrac{1}{2}$

$$[\because P(X = x) = {}^n C_x \, p^x \, q^{n-x}]$$

(i) $\quad P(X = 5) = {}^6 C_5 \left(\dfrac{1}{2}\right)^5 \left(\dfrac{1}{2}\right)^{6-5} = \dfrac{3}{32}$

$$\left[\because {}^n C_p = \frac{n!}{p!(n-p)!}\right] \quad \textbf{(1 Mark)}$$

(ii) Probability of getting atmost 5 successes

$\quad P(X \le 5) = 1 - P(p = 6)$

$$= 1 - {}^6 C_6 \left(\frac{1}{2}\right)^6 \left(\frac{1}{2}\right)^0 = 1 - \frac{1}{64} = \frac{63}{64} \quad \textbf{(1 Mark)}$$

OR

We know that sum of probabilities of a probability distribution of random variable is 1.

$\therefore \; k + 2k + 3k + 0 = 1 \qquad \textbf{(1 Mark)}$

$6k = 1$

$k = \dfrac{1}{6} \qquad \textbf{(1 Mark)}$

12. Given: $|\vec{x}| = 1$, $|\vec{y}| = 1$ and $|\vec{x} + \vec{y}| = 1$

Squaring on both side

$|\vec{x} + \vec{y}|^2 = 1^2$

$|\vec{x}|^2 + |\vec{y}|^2 + 2|\vec{x}||\vec{y}|\cos\theta = 1$

$$\left[\because |\vec{a} + \vec{b}|^2 = |\vec{a}|^2 + |\vec{b}|^2 + 2|\vec{a}||\vec{b}|\cos\theta\right]$$

$1 + 1 + 2\,(1)(1)\cos\theta = 1$

$2\cos\theta = -1 \quad ...(1) \qquad \textbf{(1 Mark)}$

$|\vec{x} - \vec{y}|^2 = |\vec{x}|^2 + |\vec{y}|^2 - 2|\vec{x}||\vec{y}|\cos\theta$

$$\left[\because |\vec{a} - \vec{b}|^2 = |\vec{a}|^2 + |\vec{b}|^2 - 2|\vec{a}||\vec{b}|\cos\theta\right]$$

$|\vec{x} - \vec{y}|^2 = 1 + 1 - 2(1)(1)\cos\theta = 2 - 2\cos\theta$

$= 2 - (-1) = 3 \;\; [\text{from (1)}]$

$|\vec{x} - \vec{y}| = \sqrt{3} \qquad \textbf{(1 Mark)}$

Hence proved.

OR

$$\begin{bmatrix} \vec{a} & \vec{b} & \vec{c} \end{bmatrix} = \begin{vmatrix} 2 & 3 & 1 \\ 1 & -2 & 1 \\ -3 & 1 & 2 \end{vmatrix}$$

$$= 2(-4 - 1) - 3(2 + 3) + 1(1 - 6)$$

$$= -30 \qquad \textbf{(2 Marks)}$$

Note

If $\quad \vec{x} = x_1 \hat{i} + x_2 \hat{j} + x_3 \hat{k}$

$\quad\quad \vec{y} = y_1 \hat{i} + y_2 \hat{j} + y_3 \hat{k}$

$\quad\quad \vec{z} = z_1 \hat{i} + z_2 \hat{j} + z_3 \hat{k}$, then

$$\begin{bmatrix} \vec{x} & \vec{y} & \vec{z} \end{bmatrix} = \begin{bmatrix} x_1 & x_2 & x_3 \\ y_1 & y_2 & y_3 \\ z_1 & z_2 & z_3 \end{bmatrix}$$

SECTION - C

13. $\Delta = \begin{vmatrix} a & b & c \\ a-b & b-c & c-a \\ b+c & c+a & a+b \end{vmatrix}$

Applying $R_2 \to R_2 - R_1$

$$\Delta = \begin{vmatrix} a & b & c \\ -b & -c & -a \\ b+c & c+a & a+b \end{vmatrix} \qquad \textbf{(½ Mark)}$$

Applying $R_3 \to R_3 + R_1$

$$\Delta = \begin{vmatrix} a & b & c \\ -b & -c & -a \\ a+b+c & a+b+c & a+b+c \end{vmatrix} \qquad \textbf{(½ Mark)}$$

Taking $(a + b + c)$ common

$$\Delta = (a + b + c) \begin{vmatrix} a & b & c \\ -b & -c & -a \\ 1 & 1 & 1 \end{vmatrix}$$

$$\textbf{(½ Mark)}$$

Applying $C_2 \to C_2 - C_3$

$$\Delta = (a + b + c) \begin{vmatrix} a & b-c & c \\ -b & -c+a & -a \\ 1 & 0 & 1 \end{vmatrix} \qquad \textbf{(½ Mark)}$$

Applying $C_1 \to C_1 - C_3$

$$\Delta = (a+b+c)\begin{vmatrix} a-c & b-c & c \\ -b+a & -c+a & -a \\ 0 & 0 & 1 \end{vmatrix}$$ **(1 Mark)**

$$\Delta = (a+b+c)[(a-c)(a-c)-(b-c)(a-b)]$$
$$= (a+b+c)\,[a^2+c^2-2ac-(ba-b^2-ca+cb)]$$
$$= (a+b+c)[a^2+b^2+c^2-ab-bc-ca]$$
$$\Delta = a^3+b^3+c^3-3abc$$

[By formula $x^3+y^3+z^3-3xyz = (x+y+z)(x^2+y^2+z^2-xy-yz-za)$]

Hence proved. **(1 Mark)**

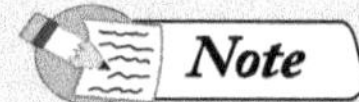

Note

If the quantities of corresponding elements of other column (or rows) are added to every element of any column (or row), then the value of determinants remain same.

14. We know that

$$\tan^{-1} x + \tan^{-1} y = \tan^{-1}\left(\frac{x+y}{1-xy}\right)$$

$$\tan^{-1} 4x + \tan^{-1} 6x = \frac{\pi}{4}$$

$$\tan^{-1}\left(\frac{4x+6x}{1-(4x)(6x)}\right) = \frac{\pi}{4}$$ **(1 Mark)**

Taking tan on both sides

$$\tan\left(\tan^{-1}\frac{10x}{1-24x^2}\right) = \tan\frac{\pi}{4}$$

$$\Rightarrow \frac{10x}{1-24x^2} = 1 \qquad \left[\because \tan\frac{\pi}{4}=1\right]$$ **(1 Mark)**

$$\Rightarrow 24x^2 + 10x - 1 = 0$$
$$\Rightarrow 24x^2 + 12x - 2x - 1 = 0 \qquad \text{[Middle Term Splitting]}$$
$$\Rightarrow 12x(2x+1) - 1(2x+1) = 0$$
$$\Rightarrow (2x+1)(12x-1) = 0$$ **(1 Mark)**

If $2x+1=0$ or $12x-1=0$

$$x = \frac{-1}{2} \qquad\qquad x = \frac{1}{12}$$

For $x = \dfrac{-1}{2}$, LHS will become negative. So, it does not satisfies equation.

$$\therefore x = \frac{1}{12}$$ **(1 Mark)**

15. Given: $R = [(a, b) : a \le b]$ and a, b $\in \mathbb{R}$

We know that

$a = a$

$\therefore a \le a \Rightarrow (a, a) \in R$

$\therefore R$ is reflexive **(1 Mark)**

To check R is symmetric or not

Let $a = 3, b = 7$

$(3, 7) \in R$ (as $3 < 7$)

But $(7, 3) \notin R$ because 7 is greater than 3

$\therefore R$ is not symmetric. **(1 Mark)**

If $a \le b$ & $b \le c$, then $a \le c$

$\therefore$ We can say that if $(a, b) \in R$ & $(b, c) \in R$,

then $(a, c) \in R$

Hence R is transitive. **(2 Marks)**

OR

Given function if

$f(x) = x^2 + x + 1, \quad f : N \to N$

Let $f(x_1) = f(x_2)$ when $x_1, x_2 \in$ N.

$$x_1^2 + x_1 + 1 = x_2^2 + x_2 + 1$$
$$x_1^2 - x_2^2 = x_2 - x_1 \quad [\because (a^2-b^2)=(a-b)(a+b)]$$
$$(x_1 - x_2)(x_1 + x_2) + (x_1 - x_2) = 0$$
$$(x_1 - x_2)(x_1 + x_2 + 1) = 0$$
$$x_1 - x_2 = 0 \Rightarrow x_1 = x_2$$

$\because x_1 + x_2 \ne -1$ (Sum of natural number is not negative)

So, $f(x_2) = f(x_1)$ only for $x_1 = x_2$

$\therefore f(x)$ is one-one function **(1 Mark)**

$$f(x) = x^2 + x + 1$$

$$f(x) = x^2 + x + 1 + \left(\frac{1}{2}\right)^2 - \left(\frac{1}{2}\right)^2 = \left(x+\frac{1}{2}\right)^2 + 1 - \frac{1}{4}$$

$$= \left(x+\frac{1}{2}\right)^2 + \frac{3}{4}$$

$\left(x+\dfrac{1}{2}\right)^2$ is always positive

$\therefore f(x)$ is increasing function

If $x = 1, f(1) = 3$

$x = 2, f(2) = 7$

Range of $f(x)$ [3, 7, ...]

But $f(x)$ does not have 1, 2

$\therefore f(x)$ is an into function, not onto function. **(1 Mark)**

Let f^{-1} denote inverse of f

$fof^{-1}(x) = x$ for all $x \in$ Range (f)

$f(f^{-1}(x)) = x$ for all $x \in$ Range (f)

$\Rightarrow [f^{-1}(x)]^2 + f^{-1}(x) + 1 = x$ for all $x \in$ Range (f)

$\Rightarrow [f^{-1}(x)]^2 + f^{-1}(x) + (1 - x) = 0$

$f^{-1}(x) = \dfrac{-1 \pm \sqrt{1 - 4(1)(1 - x)}}{2}$ $\qquad \begin{bmatrix} \because \text{ for } ax^2 + bx + c = 0 \\ x = \dfrac{-b \pm \sqrt{b^2 - 4ac}}{2a} \end{bmatrix}$

$f^{-1}(x) = \dfrac{-1 \pm \sqrt{4x - 3}}{2}$ **(2 Marks)**

16. Slope of line $4x - 2y + 5 = 0$

$m = \dfrac{-a}{b} = \dfrac{-4}{-2} = 2$

$\therefore$ Slope of given line is 2

$y = \sqrt{3x - 2}$

Differentiate on both side

$\dfrac{dy}{dx} = \dfrac{3}{2\sqrt{3x - 2}}$ $\qquad \left[\because \dfrac{d}{dx}\sqrt{x} = \dfrac{1}{2\sqrt{x}} \right]$ **(1 Mark)**

Tangent is parallel to the line $4x - 2y + 5 = 0$

$\therefore$ Slope of tangent = Slope of $4x - 2y + 5 = 0$

$\dfrac{3}{2\sqrt{3x - 2}} = 2 \ \Rightarrow \ 3 = 4\sqrt{3x - 2}$

Squaring on both sides

$9 = 16(3x - 2) \ \Rightarrow \ 3x - 2 = \dfrac{9}{16} \ \Rightarrow \ x = \dfrac{41}{48}$

$y = \sqrt{3 \times \left(\dfrac{41}{48}\right) - 2}$

$= \sqrt{\dfrac{9}{16}} = \dfrac{3}{4}$ **(1 Mark)**

Equation of tangents

$y - y_1 = m(x - x_1)$

$y - \dfrac{3}{4} = 2\left(x - \dfrac{41}{48}\right)$

$\Rightarrow \dfrac{4y - 3}{4} = 2\left(\dfrac{48x - 41}{48}\right) \ \Rightarrow \ \dfrac{4y - 3}{4} = \dfrac{48x - 41}{24}$

$\Rightarrow 6(4y - 3) = 48x - 41 \ \Rightarrow \ 48x - 24y - 23 = 0$

Required equation of tangent is

$48x - 2y = 23$ **(½ Mark)**

To find equation of normal to the curve at the point of contact.

$y - y_1 = m_1(x - x_1)$

Slope of normal $= \dfrac{-1}{\text{Slope of the tangent}}$

$m_1 = -\dfrac{1}{2}$ $[\because$ Slope of tangent = 2$]$ **(½ Mark)**

Equation of Normal

$y - y_1 = m_1(x - x_1) \ \Rightarrow y - \dfrac{3}{4} = \dfrac{-1}{2}\left(x - \dfrac{41}{48}\right)$

$\Rightarrow 4y - 3 = -\dfrac{(48x - 41)}{24}$

$\Rightarrow 24(4y - 3) = -48x + 41 \ \Rightarrow \ 48x + 96y = 113$

Equation of normal is $48x + 96y = 113$ **(1 Mark)**

17. Given: $\log (x^2 + y^2) = 2 \tan^{-1}\left(\dfrac{y}{x}\right)$

Differentiating with respect to x

$\dfrac{d}{dx}[\log (x^2 + y^2)] = \dfrac{d}{dx}\left[2 \tan^{-1}(y/x)\right]$ ...(1)

$\Rightarrow \dfrac{1}{x^2 + y^2}\dfrac{d}{dx}(x^2 + y^2) = 2 \times \dfrac{1}{1 + \left(\dfrac{y}{x}\right)^2}\dfrac{d}{dx}\left(\dfrac{y}{x}\right)$ **(2 Marks)**

$\Rightarrow \dfrac{1}{x^2 + y^2}\left[2x + 2y\dfrac{dy}{dx}\right] = \dfrac{2}{\dfrac{x^2 + y^2}{x^2}}\left[\dfrac{x\dfrac{dy}{dx} - y(1)}{x^2}\right]$

$\Rightarrow \dfrac{1}{x^2 + y^2}\left[2x + 2y\dfrac{dy}{dx}\right] = \dfrac{2}{x^2 + y^2}\left[x\dfrac{dy}{dx} - y\right]$

$\Rightarrow 2x + 2y\dfrac{dy}{dx} = 2\left[x\dfrac{dy}{dx} - y\right]$

$\Rightarrow 2x + 2y\dfrac{dy}{dx} = 2x\dfrac{dy}{dx} - 2y \ \Rightarrow 2x + 2y = 2x\dfrac{dy}{dx} - 2y\dfrac{dy}{dx}$

$\Rightarrow 2(x + y) = 2\dfrac{dy}{dx}(x - y) \ \Rightarrow x + y = \dfrac{dy}{dx}(x - y)$

$\Rightarrow \dfrac{dy}{dx} = \dfrac{x + y}{x - y}$ **(2 Marks)**

Hence proved.

OR

Let $x^y = u$, $y^x = v$

$x^y - y^x = a^b$

$u - v = a^b$

Differentiating with respect to x

$\dfrac{d}{dx}u - \dfrac{d}{dx}v = \dfrac{d}{dx}a^b$

$\dfrac{du}{dx} - \dfrac{dv}{dx} = 0$ ...(1) $[\because$ Differentiation of constant term is 0$]$ **(1 Mark)**

Now $u = x^y$

Taking log on both sides

$\log u = \log(x^y)$

$\log u = y \log x$ $[\because \log m^n = n \log m]$

Differentiating on both sides

$$\frac{d}{dx}[\log u] = \frac{d}{dx}[y \log x]$$

$$\frac{1}{u}\frac{d}{dx}u = y\frac{d}{dx}\log x + \log x\frac{dy}{dx}$$

$$\left[\because \frac{d}{dx}[f(x).g(x)] = f(x)\frac{d}{dx}g(x) + g(x)\frac{d}{dx}f(x)\right]$$

$$\Rightarrow \frac{1}{u}\frac{du}{dx} = \frac{y}{x} + \log x\frac{dy}{dx}$$

$$\Rightarrow \frac{du}{dx} = u\left[\frac{y}{x} + \log x\frac{dy}{dx}\right]$$

$$\Rightarrow \frac{du}{dx} = x^y\left[\frac{y}{x} + \log x\frac{dy}{dx}\right] \qquad [\because u = x^y]$$

$$\Rightarrow \frac{du}{dx} = y x^{y-1} + x^y \log x\frac{dy}{dx} \qquad ...(2) \quad \textbf{(1 Mark)}$$

Also $v = y^x$

Taking log on both sides

$\log v = \log(y^x)$

$\log v = x \log y$

Differentiating on both sides

$$\frac{d}{dx}(\log v) = \frac{d}{dx}(x \log y)$$

$$\Rightarrow \frac{1}{v}\frac{dv}{dx} = x\frac{d}{dx}(\log y) + \log y\frac{d}{dx}x$$

$$\Rightarrow \frac{1}{v}\frac{dv}{dx} = \frac{x}{y}\frac{dy}{dx} + \log y$$

$$\Rightarrow \frac{dv}{dx} = v\left[\frac{x}{y}\frac{dy}{dx} + \log y\right]$$

$$\Rightarrow \frac{dv}{dx} = y^x\left[\frac{x}{y}\frac{dy}{dx} + \log y\right] \qquad [\because v = y^x]$$

$$\frac{dv}{dx} = y^{x-1}x\frac{dy}{dx} + y^x \log y \qquad ...(3) \quad \textbf{(1 Mark)}$$

From (1)

$$\frac{du}{dx} - \frac{dv}{dx} = 0$$

Putting the values of $\dfrac{du}{dx}$ and $\dfrac{dv}{dx}$ from (2) and (3) in (1).

$$\left(y.x^{y-1} + x^y \log x\frac{dy}{dx}\right) - \left(x\, y^{x-1}\frac{dy}{dx} + y^x \log y\right) = 0$$

$$y\, x^{y-1} + x^y \log x\,\frac{dy}{dx} - xy^{x-1}\frac{dy}{dx} - y^x \log y = 0$$

$$\frac{dy}{dx}(x^y \log x - x\, y^{x-1}) = y^x \log y - y\, x^{y-1}$$

$$\frac{dy}{dx} = \frac{y^x \log y - y\, x^{y-1}}{x^y \log x - x\, y^{x-1}} \qquad \textbf{(1 Mark)}$$

18. $y = (\sin^{-1} x)^2$ (1)

Differentiating both sides with respect to x

$$\Rightarrow \frac{dy}{dx} = 2 \sin^{-1} x\, \frac{d}{dx}(\sin^{-1} x) \qquad \text{(Using chain rule)}$$

$$\Rightarrow \frac{dy}{dx} = \frac{2\sin^{-1} x}{\sqrt{1-x^2}} \qquad \textbf{(1 Mark)}$$

$$\sqrt{1-x^2}\,\frac{dy}{dx} = 2\sin^{-1} x$$

Squaring both sides

$$\left(1-x^2\right)\left(\frac{dy}{dx}\right)^2 = 4\left(\sin^{-1} x\right)^2$$

$$\left(1-x^2\right)\left(\frac{dy}{dx}\right)^2 = 4y \qquad \text{(From 1)} \qquad \textbf{(1 Mark)}$$

Differentiating both sides, we get

$$(-2x)\left(\frac{dy}{dx}\right)^2 + \left(1-x^2\right)\frac{2dy}{dx}\frac{d^2 y}{dx^2} = 4\frac{dy}{dx} \qquad \textbf{(1 Mark)}$$

$$(1 - x^2)\frac{d^2 y}{dx^2} - x\frac{dy}{dx} - 2 = 0 \qquad \textbf{(1 Mark)}$$

Hence proved.

19. Let $a - x = t$

Differentiate w.r. to x

$$-1 = \frac{dt}{dx} \Rightarrow dx = -dt \qquad \begin{bmatrix} \text{As,} & x = 0, & t = a \\ & x = a, & t = 0 \end{bmatrix}$$

$$\therefore \int_0^a f(x)\, dx = -\int_a^0 f(a-t)\, dt \qquad [\because a-x=t \quad x=a-t]$$

$$= \int_0^a f(a-t)\, dt \qquad \left[\because \int_a^b f(x)\, dx = -\int_b^a f(x)\, dx\right]$$

$$= \int_0^a f(a-x)\, dx$$

$[\because$ Integeration is independent of the change of variable$]$

$$\int_0^a f(x)\, dx = \int_0^a f(a-x)\, dx$$

Hence proved. **(2 Marks)**

Let $I = \displaystyle\int_0^\pi \frac{x \sin x}{1 + \cos^2 x}\, dx$

$$I = \int_0^\pi \frac{(\pi - x)\sin(\pi - x)}{1 + \cos^2(\pi - x)}\, dx \left[\int_0^a f(x)\, dx = \int_0^a f(a-x)\, dx\right]$$

$$\Rightarrow I = \int_0^\pi \frac{(\pi - x)\sin x}{1 + \cos^2 x} dx \qquad \begin{bmatrix} \because & \sin(\pi - \theta) = \sin\theta \\ & \cos(\pi - \theta) = -\cos\theta \\ & \cos^2(\pi - \theta) = \cos\theta \end{bmatrix}$$

$$\Rightarrow I = \int_0^\pi \frac{\pi\sin x}{1 + \cos^2 x} dx - \int_0^\pi \frac{x\sin x}{1 + \cos^2 x} dx$$

$$\Rightarrow I = \int_0^\pi \frac{\pi\sin x}{1 + \cos^2 x} dx - I$$

$$2I = \int_0^\pi \frac{\pi\sin x}{1 + \cos^2 x} dx \qquad \textbf{(1 Mark)}$$

Let $\cos x = t \Rightarrow -\sin x\, dx = dt$

As, $x = 0$, $t = 1$ and $x = \pi$, $t = -1$

$$2I = -\pi \int_1^{-1} \frac{dt}{1 + t^2}$$

$$\Rightarrow I = -\frac{\pi}{2}\Big[\tan^{-1} t\Big]_1^{-1} \qquad \left[\because \int \frac{1}{1 + x^2} = \tan^{-1} x\right]$$

$$\Rightarrow I = -\frac{\pi}{2}\,[\tan^{-1}(-1) - \tan^{-1}(1)]$$

$$\Rightarrow I = -\frac{\pi}{2}\left[\left(-\frac{\pi}{4}\right) - \left(\frac{\pi}{4}\right)\right] \qquad \left[\because \tan^{-1}(1) = \frac{\pi}{4}\right]$$

$$= -\frac{\pi}{2}\left(-\frac{2\pi}{4}\right) \Rightarrow I = \frac{\pi^2}{4}$$

$$\int_0^\pi \frac{x\sin x}{1 + \cos^2 x} dx = \frac{\pi^2}{4} \qquad \textbf{(1 Mark)}$$

20. Let $1 + \sin x = u$

$\cos x\, dx = du$

$$\int \frac{\cos x}{(1 + \sin x)} \frac{dx}{(2 + \sin x)} = \int \frac{du}{u(1 + u)}$$

$$\begin{bmatrix} \because 2 + \sin x = 1 + 1 + \sin x \\ = 1 + u \end{bmatrix}$$

$$= \int \left(\frac{1}{u} - \frac{1}{1 + u}\right) dx \qquad \textbf{(2 Marks)}$$

$$= \int \frac{1}{u} du - \int \frac{1}{1 + u} du$$

$$= \log u - \log(1 + u) + C \qquad \left[\because \int \frac{1}{x} dx = \log x\right]$$

$$= \log(1 + \sin x) - \log(2 + \sin x) + C$$

$$= \log\left(\frac{1 + \sin x}{2 + \sin x}\right) + C \qquad \left[\because \log m - \log n = \log \frac{m}{n}\right]$$

$$\therefore \int \frac{\cos x\, dx}{(1 + \sin x)(2 + \sin x)} = \log\left(\frac{1 + \sin x}{2 + \sin x}\right) + C$$

$$\textbf{(2 Marks)}$$

21. Given differential equation is

$$\frac{dy}{dx} - \frac{2x}{1 + x^2} y = x^2 + 2$$

This is a linear differential equation of the form

$$\frac{dy}{dx} + py = Q, \text{ where}$$

$$P = \frac{-2x}{1 + x^2} \text{ and } Q = x^2 + 2$$

$$\therefore \text{ I.F.} = e^{\int P\, dx} = e^{\int \frac{-2x}{1 + x^2} dx} = e^{-\log(1 + x^2)} = e^{\log[(1 + x^2)^{-1}]}$$

$$\text{I.F.} = e^{\log\left(\frac{1}{1 + x^2}\right)} = \frac{1}{1 + x^2} \qquad \textbf{(2 Marks)}$$

General solution of the given differential equation is

$$y \cdot (\text{I.F.}) = \int Q(\text{I.F.})\, dx + C$$

$$y\left(\frac{1}{1 + x^2}\right) = \int \frac{x^2 + 2}{1 + x^2} dx + C$$

$$= \int \left(1 + \frac{1}{1 + x^2}\right) dx + C$$

$$= \int 1.dx + \int \frac{1}{1 + x^2} dx + C$$

$$= x + \tan^{-1} x + C \qquad \left[\because \int \frac{1}{1 + x^2} dx = \tan^{-1} x\right]$$

$$y\left(\frac{1}{1 + x^2}\right) = x + \tan^{-1} x + C$$

$$y = (1 + x^2)(x + \tan^{-1}x + C) \qquad \textbf{(2 Marks)}$$

OR

$$(x + 1)\frac{dy}{dx} = 2e^{-y} - 1 \Rightarrow (x + 1)dy = (2e^{-y} - 1)dx$$

$$\Rightarrow \frac{1}{2e^{-y} - 1} dy = \frac{1}{x + 1} dx$$

Integerating on both sides

$$\int \frac{1}{2e^{-y} - 1} dy = \int \frac{1}{x + 1} dx \qquad \textbf{(½ Mark)}$$

$$\Rightarrow \int \frac{1}{2e^{-y} - 1} dy = \log|x + 1| + \log C \qquad \left[\because \int \frac{1}{x} dx = \log|x|\right]$$

$$\Rightarrow -\int \frac{e^y}{e^y - 2} dy = \log|x + 1| + \log C \;\;...(1) \quad \textbf{(½ Mark)}$$

Let $e^y - 2 = t \Rightarrow e^y\, dy = dt$

Substituting these values in equation (1)

$$-\int \frac{dt}{t} = \log|x + 1| + \log C$$

$$\Rightarrow -\log|t| = \log|x + 1| + \log C \qquad \textbf{(1 Mark)}$$

$$\Rightarrow -\log|e^y - 2| = \log|x + 1| + \log C$$

$$\Rightarrow \log\left|\frac{1}{e^y - 2}\right| = \log|x + 1| + \log C$$

$$\Rightarrow \log \left| \frac{1}{e^y - 2} \right| = \log |C(x + 1)|$$

$$\Rightarrow \left| \frac{1}{e^y - 2} \right| = |C(x + 1)| \qquad ...(2) \qquad \textbf{(1 Mark)}$$

Given that $x = 0$, $y = 0$

$$\left| \frac{1}{e^0 - 2} \right| = C(0 + 1) \Rightarrow \left| \frac{1}{1 - 2} \right| = C \Rightarrow C = 1$$

Putting the value of C in (1)

$$\left| \frac{1}{e^y - 2} \right| = |x + 1| \Rightarrow |(x + 1)(e^y - 2)| = 1$$

$$\Rightarrow (x + 1)(e^y - 2) = 1 \Rightarrow (x + 1)(e^y - 2) = 1$$

$$\Rightarrow e^y - 2 = \frac{1}{x+1} \Rightarrow e^y = 2 + \frac{1}{x+1}$$

$$y = \log\left(2 + \frac{1}{x+1}\right) \qquad \textbf{(1 Mark)}$$

Note

If after integration all functions are log function then take constant c as a log function i.e. (log c).

22. $\overrightarrow{AB} = (x_2 - x_1)\hat{i} + (y_2 - y_1)\hat{j} + (z_2 - z_1)\hat{k}$

$\qquad = (2-1)\hat{i} + (5-1)\hat{j} + (0-1)\hat{k} = 1\hat{i} + 4\hat{j} - \hat{k}$

$AB = |\overrightarrow{AB}| = \sqrt{(x_2 - x_1)^2 + (y_2 - y_1)^2 + (z_2 - z_1)^2}$

$\qquad = \sqrt{1^2 + 4^2 + (-1)^2} = \sqrt{18} \quad 3\sqrt{2} \qquad \textbf{(1 Mark)}$

$\overrightarrow{CD} = (x_2 - x_1)\hat{i} + (y_2 - y_1)\hat{j} + (z_2 - z_1)\hat{k}$

$\overrightarrow{CD} = (1-3)\hat{i} + (-6-2)\hat{j} + (-1+3)\hat{k}$

$\qquad = -2\hat{i} - 8\hat{j} + 2\hat{k}$

$CD = |\overrightarrow{CD}| = \sqrt{(-2)^2 + (-8)^2 + 2^2}$

$\qquad = \sqrt{4 + 64 + 4} = \sqrt{72} = 6\sqrt{2} \qquad \textbf{(1 Mark)}$

$\cos\theta = \dfrac{\overrightarrow{AB}.\overrightarrow{CD}}{|\overrightarrow{AB}||\overrightarrow{CD}|} = \dfrac{(\hat{i} + 4\hat{j} - \hat{k})(-2\hat{i} - 8\hat{j} + 2\hat{k})}{3\sqrt{2} \times 6\sqrt{2}}$

$= \dfrac{1(-2) + 4(-8) + (-1)(2)}{36} = \dfrac{-2 - 32 - 2}{36} = \dfrac{-36}{36} = -1$

$\cos\theta = -1 \Rightarrow \theta = 180°$

As the angle between $\overrightarrow{AB}$ and $\overrightarrow{CD}$ is $180°$

$\therefore$ $\overrightarrow{AB}$ and $\overrightarrow{CD}$ are collinear $\qquad \textbf{(2 Marks)}$

23. $\dfrac{1-x}{3} = \dfrac{7y - 14}{\lambda} = \dfrac{z-3}{2}$

$\Rightarrow \dfrac{x-1}{-3} = \dfrac{7(y-2)}{\lambda} = \dfrac{z-3}{2}$

$\Rightarrow \dfrac{x-1}{-3} = \dfrac{y-2}{\lambda/7} = \dfrac{z-3}{2}$

Here $a_1 = -3$, $b_1 = \dfrac{\lambda}{7}$, $c_1 = 2$ $\qquad \textbf{(½ Mark)}$

$\dfrac{7 - 7x}{3\lambda} = \dfrac{y - 5}{1} = \dfrac{6 - z}{5}$

$\Rightarrow \dfrac{-7(x-1)}{3\lambda} = \dfrac{y-5}{1} = \dfrac{-(z-6)}{5}$

$\Rightarrow \dfrac{x-1}{\dfrac{-3\lambda}{7}} = \dfrac{y-5}{1} = \dfrac{z-6}{-5}$

$a_2 = \dfrac{-3\lambda}{7}$, $b_2 = 1$, $c_2 = -5$ $\qquad \textbf{(½ Mark)}$

If two lines are perpendicular, then

$a_1 a_2 + b_1 b_2 + c_1 c_2 = 0$

$(-3)\left(-\dfrac{3\lambda}{7}\right) + \left(\dfrac{\lambda}{7}\right)(1) + (2)(-5) = 0$

$\Rightarrow \dfrac{9\lambda}{7} + \dfrac{\lambda}{7} - 10 = 0 \Rightarrow \dfrac{9\lambda + \lambda - 70}{7} = 0$

$\Rightarrow 10\lambda - 70 = 0 \Rightarrow 10\lambda = 70 \Rightarrow \lambda = 7 \qquad \textbf{(1 Mark)}$

Substituting the value of λ in both the equation

$\dfrac{x-1}{-3} = \dfrac{y-2}{1} = \dfrac{z-3}{2} = A \qquad ...(1)$

$x - 1 = -3A \Rightarrow x = -3A + 1$

$y - 2 = A \Rightarrow y = A + 2$

$z - 3 = 2A \Rightarrow z = 2A + 3$

Coordinates of a general points on first line are

$(-3A + 1, A + 2, 2A + 3)$

second equation:

$\dfrac{x-1}{-3} = \dfrac{y-5}{1} = \dfrac{z-6}{-5} = B \qquad ...(2)$

$x - 1 = -3B \Rightarrow x = -3B + 1$

$y - 5 = B \Rightarrow y = B + 5$

$z - 6 = -5B \Rightarrow z = -5B + 6 \qquad \textbf{(1 Mark)}$

Coordinates of a general points on second line are
$(-3B + 1, B + 5, -5B + 6)$

If the lines are intersecting, then they have common point. So, for some value of A and B, we must have

$x = -3A + 1 = -3B + 1$

$A = B \qquad ...(3)$

$y = A + 2 = B + 5$

A = B + 3

B = B + 3   [from (3)]

1 = 3

It is not possible

So, both of these lines are not intersecting.   **(1 Mark)**

SECTION - D

24.   Depth of tank, $h = 2m$

Volume of tank = $8m^3$

Let length of tank be l, breadth be b

Volume of tank = $L \times B \times H$

$l \times b \times h = 8 \Rightarrow l\, b\, (2) = 8$

$l = \dfrac{4}{b}$ ...(i)   **(1 Mark)**

Area of base = $L \times B = lb$

$\therefore$ Cost of base = 70 (lb)[$\because$ cost of base ₹70 per sq mtr]

Area of 4 sides = $(H \times L) + (H \times B) + (H \times L) + (H \times B)$

$= 2(H \times L + H \times B) = 2(hl + hb) = 4(l + b)$ $[\because h = 2]$

Cost of making sides = Cost of making sides ₹ 45 per sq. mtr $\times$ Area of 4 sides

$= 45[4(l + b)] = 180\,(l + b)$

Let total cost of tank be C(l).

Total cost = cost of base + cost of making sides

$C(l) = 70(lb) + 180(l + b)$

$= 70(4) + 180\left(l + \dfrac{4}{l}\right)$ $\left[\because b = \dfrac{4}{l}\right]$

$= 280 + 180\left(l + \dfrac{4}{l}\right)$ **(2 Marks)**

Differentiating the equation with respect to l

$\dfrac{d}{dl}C(l) = 0 + 180\left(1 - \dfrac{4}{l^2}\right)\left[\because \dfrac{d}{dx}x^n = nx^{n-1}\right]$

$\Rightarrow \dfrac{d}{dl}C(l) = 180\left(1 - \dfrac{4}{l^2}\right)$

Putting $\dfrac{d}{dl}C(l) = 0$

$0 = 180\left(1 - \dfrac{4}{l^2}\right) \Rightarrow \left(1 - \dfrac{4}{l^2}\right) = 0$

$l^2 = 4 \Rightarrow l = 2$ **(1 Mark)**

Length cannot be negative

So, length of tank is 2 metre

Again differentiating $\dfrac{d}{dl}C(l)$

$\dfrac{d^2C(l)}{dl^2} = 180\left[0 - \dfrac{4(-2)}{l^3}\right] = \dfrac{1440}{l^3}$ $\left[\because \dfrac{d}{dx}x^n = nx^{n-1}\right]$

Put $l = 2$

$\dfrac{d^2}{dl}C(l) = \dfrac{1440}{2^3} > 0$

So, $l = 2$ is a point of minima   **(1 Mark)**

$C(l)$ is least at $l = 2$

Least cost of construction

$C(l) = 280 + 180\left(2 + \dfrac{4}{2}\right) = 280 + 180(4) = 1000$

Hence, least cost of construction is ₹1000.   **(1 Mark)**

25. $A = \begin{bmatrix} 1 & 1 & 1 \\ 1 & 0 & 2 \\ 3 & 1 & 1 \end{bmatrix}$

$|A| = 1(0 - 2) - 1(1 - 6) + 1(1 - 0) = -2 + 5 + 1 = 4$

$\because |A| = 4 \neq 0$ $\therefore A^{-1}$ exists   **(1 Mark)**

To find Adj A, we have to find cofactors

$c_{11} = \begin{vmatrix} 0 & 2 \\ 1 & 1 \end{vmatrix} = 0 - 2 = -2$

$c_{12} = -\begin{vmatrix} 1 & 2 \\ 3 & 1 \end{vmatrix} = -1(1 - 6) = 5$

$c_{13} = \begin{vmatrix} 1 & 0 \\ 3 & 1 \end{vmatrix} = 1 - 0 = 1$

$c_{21} = -\begin{vmatrix} 1 & 1 \\ 1 & 1 \end{vmatrix} = -(1 - 1) = 0$

$c_{22} = -\begin{vmatrix} 1 & 1 \\ 3 & 1 \end{vmatrix} = 1 - 3 = -2$

$c_{23} = -\begin{vmatrix} 1 & 1 \\ 3 & 1 \end{vmatrix} = -(1 - 3) = 2$

$c_{31} = \begin{vmatrix} 1 & 1 \\ 0 & 2 \end{vmatrix} = (2 - 0) = 2$

$c_{32} = -\begin{vmatrix} 1 & 1 \\ 1 & 2 \end{vmatrix} = -(2 - 1) = -1$

$c_{33} = \begin{vmatrix} 1 & 1 \\ 1 & 0 \end{vmatrix} = 0 - 1 = -1$ **(2 Marks)**

$$\text{Adj } A = \begin{bmatrix} -2 & 5 & 1 \\ 0 & -2 & 2 \\ 2 & -1 & -1 \end{bmatrix}^T = \begin{bmatrix} -2 & 0 & 2 \\ 5 & -2 & -1 \\ 1 & 2 & -1 \end{bmatrix}$$

$$\therefore A^{-1} = \frac{\text{Adj}A}{|A|} = \frac{1}{4}\begin{bmatrix} -2 & 0 & 2 \\ 5 & -2 & -1 \\ 1 & 2 & -1 \end{bmatrix} \qquad \textbf{(1 Mark)}$$

Equations are

$x + y + z = 6$

$x + 2z = 7$

$3x + y + z = 12$

It can be written as

$AX = B$

where $A = \begin{bmatrix} 1 & 1 & 1 \\ 1 & 0 & 2 \\ 3 & 1 & 1 \end{bmatrix}, B = \begin{bmatrix} 6 \\ 7 \\ 12 \end{bmatrix}, X = \begin{bmatrix} x \\ y \\ z \end{bmatrix}$

$AX = B$

$X = A^{-1}B$ [Multiplying A^{-1} on both sides] $\qquad \textbf{(1 Mark)}$

$$X = \begin{bmatrix} 1 & 1 & 1 \\ 1 & 0 & 2 \\ 3 & 1 & 1 \end{bmatrix}^{-1}\begin{bmatrix} 6 \\ 7 \\ 12 \end{bmatrix}$$

$$= \frac{1}{4}\begin{bmatrix} -2 & 0 & 2 \\ 5 & -2 & -1 \\ 1 & 2 & -1 \end{bmatrix}\begin{bmatrix} 6 \\ 7 \\ 12 \end{bmatrix}$$

$$= \frac{1}{4}\begin{bmatrix} -12+24 \\ 30-14-12 \\ 6+14-12 \end{bmatrix}$$

$$= \frac{1}{4}\begin{bmatrix} 12 \\ 4 \\ 8 \end{bmatrix} = \begin{bmatrix} \frac{12}{4} \\ \frac{4}{4} \\ \frac{8}{4} \end{bmatrix} = \begin{bmatrix} 3 \\ 1 \\ 2 \end{bmatrix}$$

$\therefore$ Solutions of equations is $x = 3, y = 1, z = 2$

$\qquad\qquad\qquad\qquad\qquad\qquad\qquad \textbf{(1 Mark)}$

OR

We know that

$A = IA$

$$\begin{bmatrix} 1 & 2 & -2 \\ -1 & 3 & 0 \\ 0 & -2 & 1 \end{bmatrix} = \begin{bmatrix} 1 & 0 & 0 \\ 0 & 1 & 0 \\ 0 & 0 & 1 \end{bmatrix}A \qquad \textbf{(½ Mark)}$$

$R_2 \rightarrow R_2 + R_1$

$$\begin{bmatrix} 1 & 2 & -2 \\ 0 & 5 & -2 \\ 0 & -2 & 1 \end{bmatrix} = \begin{bmatrix} 1 & 0 & 0 \\ 1 & 1 & 0 \\ 0 & 0 & 1 \end{bmatrix}A \qquad \textbf{(1 Mark)}$$

$R_2 \rightarrow R_2 + 2R_3$

$$\begin{bmatrix} 1 & 0 & -2 \\ 0 & 1 & 0 \\ 0 & -2 & 1 \end{bmatrix} = \begin{bmatrix} 1 & 0 & 0 \\ 1 & 1 & 2 \\ 0 & 0 & 1 \end{bmatrix}A \qquad \textbf{(1 Mark)}$$

$R_1 \rightarrow R_1 - 2R_2$

$$\begin{bmatrix} 1 & 0 & -2 \\ 0 & 1 & 0 \\ 0 & -2 & 1 \end{bmatrix} = \begin{bmatrix} -1 & -2 & -4 \\ 1 & 1 & 2 \\ 0 & 0 & 1 \end{bmatrix}A \qquad \textbf{(1 Mark)}$$

$R_3 \rightarrow R_3 + 2R_2$

$$\begin{bmatrix} 1 & 0 & -2 \\ 0 & 1 & 0 \\ 0 & 0 & 1 \end{bmatrix} = \begin{bmatrix} -1 & -2 & -4 \\ 1 & 1 & 2 \\ 2 & 2 & 5 \end{bmatrix}A \qquad \textbf{(1 Mark)}$$

$R_1 \rightarrow R_1 + 2R_3$

$$\begin{bmatrix} 1 & 0 & 0 \\ 0 & 1 & 0 \\ 0 & 0 & 1 \end{bmatrix} = \begin{bmatrix} 3 & 2 & 6 \\ 1 & 1 & 2 \\ 2 & 2 & 5 \end{bmatrix}A \qquad \textbf{(1 Mark)}$$

Hence $A^{-1} = \begin{bmatrix} 3 & 2 & 6 \\ 1 & 1 & 2 \\ 2 & 2 & 5 \end{bmatrix}$ $\qquad \textbf{(½ Mark)}$

26.

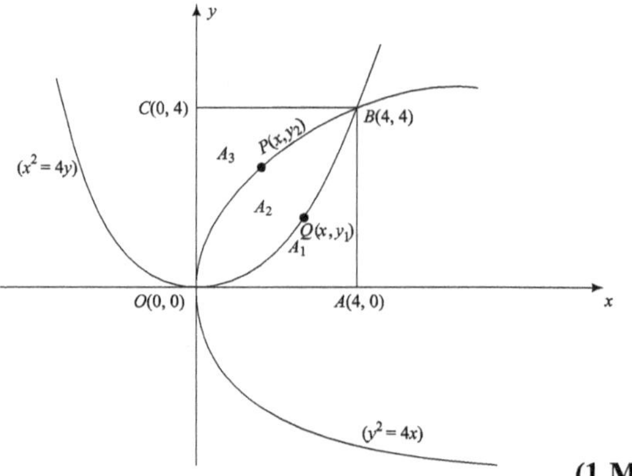

$\qquad\qquad\qquad\qquad\qquad\qquad\qquad \textbf{(1 Mark)}$

Let A_1, A_2, A_3 be the areas of region $OABQO$, $OQBPO$, $OPBCO$

$$A_1 = \int_0^4 |y_1| \, dx = \int_0^4 y_1 dx \qquad [\because y_1 > 0 \ \therefore |y_1| = y_1]$$

(x, y_1) lies on $x^2 = 4y$

$$y_1 = \frac{x^2}{4}$$

$$A_1 = \int_0^4 \frac{x^2}{4} \, dx = \frac{1}{4}\left[\frac{x^3}{3}\right]_0^4 = \frac{1}{4 \times 3}\left[(4)^3 - (0)^3\right]$$

$= \dfrac{1}{4} \times \dfrac{64}{3} = \dfrac{16}{3}$ sq. units   ...(1)   **(1 Mark)**

For A_2,

$A_2 = \int\limits_0^4 (y_2 - y_1)dx \quad [\because |y_2 - y_1| = y_2 - y_1 \text{ as } y_2 - y_1 > 0]$

(x, y_2) lie on $y^2 = 4x$

$y_2 = 2\sqrt{x}$

$A_2 = \int\limits_0^4 \left[2\sqrt{x} - \dfrac{x^2}{4} \right] dx$

$= \left[\dfrac{4}{3}x^{3/2} - \dfrac{x^3}{12} \right]_0^4 \quad \left[\because \int x^n dx = \dfrac{x^{n+1}}{n+1} \right]$

$= \dfrac{4}{3} \times (4)^{3/2} - \dfrac{(4)^3}{12}$

$A_2 = \dfrac{64}{12} = \dfrac{16}{3}$

$A_2 = \dfrac{16}{3}$ sq. units   ...(2)   **(2 Marks)**

For A_3,

$\because (x_1, y)$ lies on $y^2 = 4x \Rightarrow y^2 = 4x_1 \Rightarrow x_1 = \dfrac{y^2}{4}$

$A_3 = \int\limits_0^4 |x_1| dy = \int\limits_0^4 \dfrac{y^2}{4} dy = \dfrac{1}{4}\left[\dfrac{y^3}{3} \right]_0^4$

$= \dfrac{1}{4} \times \dfrac{64}{3} = \dfrac{16}{3}$ ...(3)   **(1½ Marks)**

From (1), (2) & (3)

$A_1 = A_2 = A_3 = \dfrac{16}{3}$ sq. units.

Hence proved.   **(½ Mark)**

OR

Let $A(2, 3)$, $B(3, 5)$ & $C(4, 4)$ be the vertices of $\triangle ABC$.

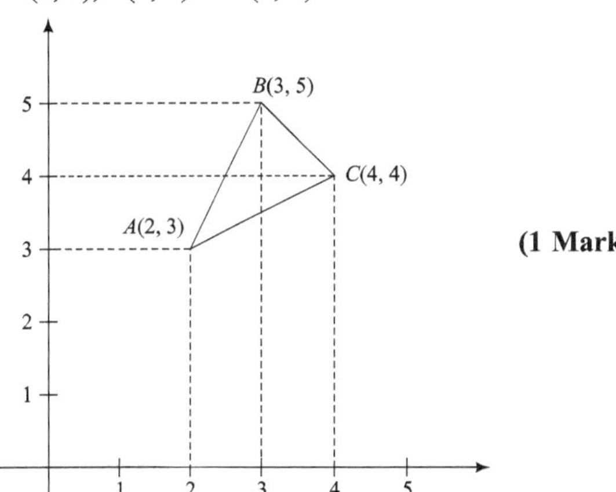

    (1 Mark)

Equation of line AB is

$\dfrac{y - y_1}{y_2 - y_1} = \dfrac{x - x_1}{x_2 - x_1} \Rightarrow \dfrac{y - 3}{5 - 3} = \dfrac{x - 2}{3 - 2}$

$\Rightarrow \dfrac{y - 3}{2} = \dfrac{x - 2}{1}$

$\Rightarrow y - 3 = 2(x - 2) \Rightarrow y = 2x - 1$ ...(1)   **Mark**

Equation of line BC is

$\dfrac{y - 5}{4 - 5} = \dfrac{x - 3}{4 - 3} \Rightarrow \dfrac{y - 5}{-1} = \dfrac{x - 3}{1}$

$\Rightarrow y - 5 = -x + 3$

$\Rightarrow y = -x + 8$ ...(2)   **(1 Mark)**

Equation of line CA is

$\dfrac{y - 4}{3 - 4} = \dfrac{x - 4}{2 - 4} \Rightarrow \dfrac{y - 4}{-1} = \dfrac{x - 4}{-2}$

$\Rightarrow 2y - 8 = x - 4 \Rightarrow 2y = x + 4$

$\Rightarrow y = \dfrac{x + 4}{2}$ ...(3)   **(1 Mark)**

Let area of triangle ABC be A

$A = \int\limits_2^3 |y_1| dx + \int\limits_3^4 |y_2| dx - \int\limits_2^4 |y_3| dx$

$= \int\limits_2^3 (2x - 1)dx + \int\limits_3^4 (-x + 8)dx - \int\limits_2^4 \left(\dfrac{x + 4}{2} \right) dx$

      [From (1), (2) & (3)]

$= \left[\dfrac{2x^2}{2} - x \right]_2^3 + \left[\dfrac{-x^2}{2} + 8x \right]_3^4 - \dfrac{1}{2}\left[\dfrac{x^2}{2} + 4x \right]_2^4$

$= \left[(3)^2 - 3 - (2)^2 + 2 \right] + \left[-\dfrac{(4)^2}{2} + 32 + \dfrac{9}{2} - 24 \right]$

$\qquad\qquad - \dfrac{1}{2}\left[\dfrac{16}{2} + 16 - \dfrac{4}{2} - 8 \right]$

$= 9 - 3 - 4 + 2 - \dfrac{16}{2} + 32 + \dfrac{9}{2} - 24 - \dfrac{1}{2} \times 14$

$= \dfrac{3}{2}$ sq. units   **(2 Marks)**

Area of required triangle $= \dfrac{3}{2}$ sq. units

27. Let number of articles of model A be x and number of articles of model B be y

Mathematical formulation of the given linear programming problem is

$$\text{Max } Z = 15x + 10y$$

Subjected to

$$2x + y \le 40, \quad 2x + 3y \le 80$$
$$x \ge 0, y \ge 0 \qquad \textbf{(2 Marks)}$$

Let $\qquad 2x + y = 40$

x	0	20
y	40	0

$2x + 3y = 80$

x	0	40
y	80/3	0

(1 Mark)

Intersection point of $2x + y = 40$ and $2x + 3y = 80$ is B(10, 20).

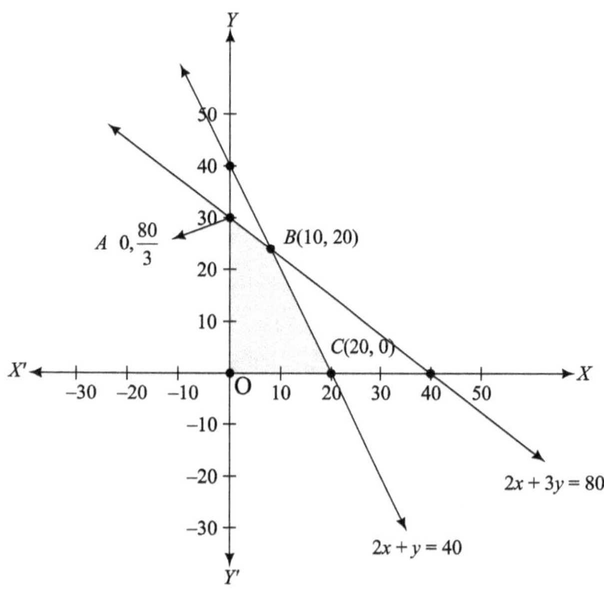

(1 Mark)

Corner points are $A\left(0, \dfrac{80}{3}\right)$, B(10, 20), O(0, 0) and C(20, 0)

Corner point	Value of Z = 15x + 10y
$A\left(0, \dfrac{80}{3}\right)$	$Z = \dfrac{800}{3}$
B (10, 20)	$Z = 350$
O (0, 0)	$Z = 0$
C (20, 0)	$Z = 300$

Maximum value of Z is ₹ 350 which is attained at B(10, 20)

∴ Maximum profit is ₹ 350 obtained when 10 articles of model A and 20 articles of model B are produced.

(2 Marks)

28. The given points are $A(2, 2, -1)$, $B(3, 4, 2)$ and $C(7, 0, 6)$

Let $\vec{a} = 2\hat{i} + 2\hat{j} - \hat{k}$, $\vec{b} = 3\hat{i} + 4\hat{j} + 2\hat{k}$ and $\vec{c} = 7\hat{i} + 6\hat{k}$

Hence the vector equation of the plane

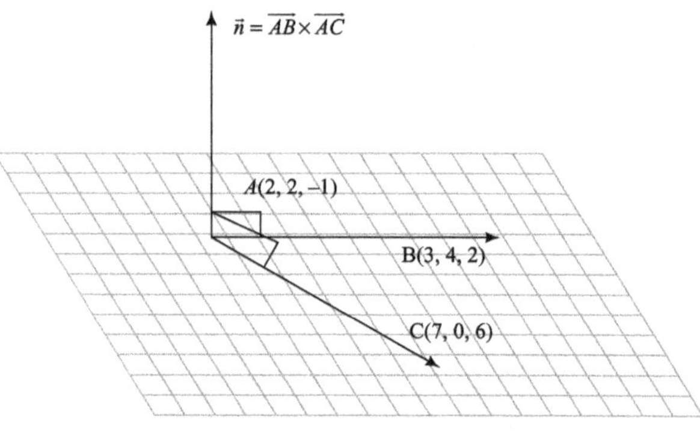

Normal to the vector $\vec{n}$ given by $\vec{n} = \overline{AB} \times \overline{AC}$

Clearly $\overline{AB} = (3\hat{i} + 4\hat{j} + 2\hat{k}) - (2\hat{i} + 2\hat{j} - \hat{k}) = \hat{i} + 2\hat{j} + 3\hat{k}$

$\overline{AC} = (7\hat{i} + 0\hat{j} + 6\hat{k}) - (2\hat{i} + 2\hat{j} - \hat{k}) = 5\hat{i} - 2\hat{j} + 7\hat{k}$

$$\therefore \vec{n} = \overline{AB} \times \overline{AC} \begin{vmatrix} \hat{i} & \hat{j} & \hat{k} \\ 1 & 2 & 3 \\ 5 & -2 & 7 \end{vmatrix} \qquad \textbf{(2 Marks)}$$

$= (14 + 6)\hat{i} - (7 - 15)\hat{j} + (-2 - 10)\hat{k}$

$= 20\hat{i} + 8\hat{j} - 12\hat{k}$

The vector equation of the required plane is

$\vec{r}.\vec{n} = \vec{a}.\vec{n}$

$\vec{r} \cdot (20\hat{i} + 8\hat{j} - 12\hat{k}) = (2\hat{i} + 2\hat{j} - \hat{k}).(20\hat{i} + 8\hat{j} - 12\hat{k})$

$\Rightarrow \vec{r}(20\hat{i} + 8\hat{j} - 12\hat{k}) = 68$

$\Rightarrow \vec{r}(5\hat{i} + 2\hat{j} - 3\hat{k}) = 17 \qquad \textbf{(1 Mark)}$

The Cartesian equation of the plane is given by

$\Rightarrow 5x + 2y - 3z = 17 \qquad \textbf{(1 Mark)}$

As we can see that the above plane is perpendicular to $5\hat{i} + 2\hat{j} - 3\hat{k}$

Also required plane is parallel to the above plane

∴ Required plane is $5x + 2y - 3z + \lambda = 0$

It passes through (4, 3, 1)

$5 \times 4 + 2 \times 3 - 3 \times 1 + \lambda = 0$

$\Rightarrow 20 + 6 - 3 + \lambda = 0 \quad \Rightarrow \lambda = -23$

∴ Equation of plane: $5x + 2y - 3z - 23 = 0$

$$5x + 2y - 3z = 23$$

Vector form of equation of plane is $r \cdot (5\hat{i} + 2\hat{j} - 3\hat{k}) = 23$

(2 Marks)

OR

Let the vector equation of required plane is $(\vec{r} - \vec{a}).\vec{n} = 0$

Plane contains the line $\vec{r} = (\hat{i} + \hat{j}) + \lambda(\hat{i} + 2\hat{j} - \hat{k})$

$\therefore$ A(1, 1, 0) and $\vec{b} = \hat{i} + 2\hat{j} - \hat{k}$

Plane passes through $A(1, 1, 0)$ & $B(-1, 3, -4)$

So $\vec{n}$ will be parallel to the vector $\overrightarrow{AB} \times \vec{b}$

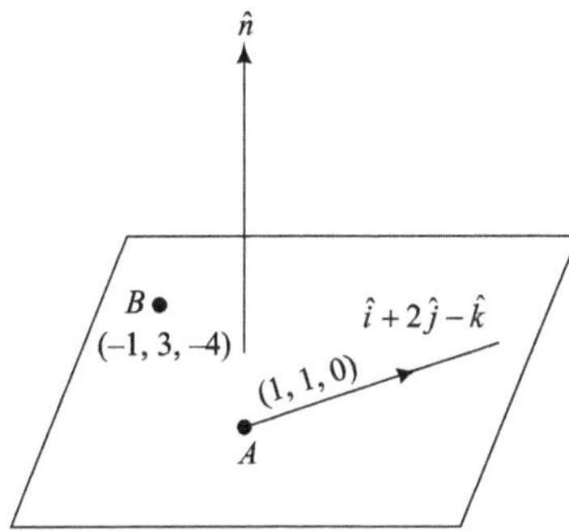

$\overrightarrow{AB} = (1 + 1)\hat{i} + (1 - 3)\hat{j} + (0 + 4)\hat{k}$

$\Rightarrow \overrightarrow{AB} = 2\hat{i} + (-2)\hat{j} + 4\hat{k}$

$\vec{n} = \overrightarrow{AB} \times \vec{b}$ $[\because \vec{n}$ is perpendicular to both $\overrightarrow{AB}$ & $\vec{b}\,]$

$$\vec{n} = \begin{vmatrix} \hat{i} & \hat{j} & \hat{k} \\ 2 & -2 & 4 \\ 1 & 2 & -1 \end{vmatrix}$$ **(2 Marks)**

$\vec{n} = \hat{i}(2 - 8) - \hat{j}(-2 - 4) + \hat{k}(4 + 2)$

$\Rightarrow \vec{n} = -6\hat{i} + 6\hat{j} + 6\hat{k}$

Equation of plane is given as

$(\vec{r} - \vec{a}) \cdot \vec{n} = 0$ or

$\vec{r}.\vec{n} = \vec{a} \cdot \vec{n}$ ...(1)

Where $\vec{a} = -\hat{i} + 3\hat{j} - 4\hat{k}$ $[\because \vec{a}$ is position vector of $B]$

From (1)

$\vec{r} \cdot (-6\hat{i} + 6\hat{j} + 6\hat{k}) = (-\hat{i} + 3\hat{j} - 4\hat{k}) \cdot (-6\hat{i} + 6\hat{j} + 6\hat{k})$

$= 6 + 18 - 24 = 0$

$\vec{r}(-6\hat{i} + 6\hat{j} + 6\hat{k}) = 0$

Equation of plane is $\vec{r}(-6\hat{i} + 6\hat{j} + 6\hat{k}) = 0$

$\vec{r}(\hat{i} - \hat{j} - \hat{k}) = 0$ **(1 Mark)**

Cartesian form of equation is

$x - y - z = 0$ **(1 Mark)**

Length of perpendicular from $p(2, 1, 4)$ to the plane $x - y - z = 0$

$$d = \left| \frac{ax_1 + by_1 + cz_1 + d}{a^2 + b^2 + c^2} \right|$$

$$\Rightarrow d = \frac{|2(1) + 1(-1) + 4(-1) + 0|}{\sqrt{(1)^2 + (-1)^2 + (-1)^2}} = \frac{|2 - 1 - 4|}{\sqrt{3}} = \frac{3}{\sqrt{3}} = \sqrt{3}$$

$\Rightarrow d = \sqrt{3}$ unit.   **(2 Marks)**

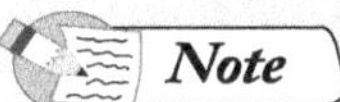 **Note**

For finding the normal of plane, use cross multiplication of any two vector lies on plane.

29. No. of trial = 2

X (No. of king cards) = 0, 1, 2

No. of king cards = 4 and no. of other cards = 48

P (X = O) = P (Two cards other than king)

$$= \frac{48_{C_2}}{52_{C_2}} = \frac{1128}{1326}$$

$P(X = 1) = $ P (One king and one other card)

$$= \frac{4_{C_1} \times 48_{C_1}}{52_{C_1}}$$

$$= \frac{192}{1326}$$ **(½ Mark)**

P (X = 2) = P (Two king cards)

$$= \frac{4c_2}{52c_2} = \frac{6}{1326}$$ **(½ Mark)**

X	0	1	2	Total
P(X)	$\dfrac{1128}{1326}$	$\dfrac{192}{1326}$	$\dfrac{6}{1326}$	1
XP(X)	0	$\dfrac{192}{1326}$	$\dfrac{12}{1326}$	$\dfrac{204}{1326}$
X²P(X)	0	$\dfrac{192}{1326}$	$\dfrac{24}{1326}$	$\dfrac{216}{1326} = \dfrac{36}{221}$

(2 Marks)

Mean $= \Sigma XP(X) = \dfrac{204}{1326} = \dfrac{2}{13}$ **(1 Mark)**

Variance $= \Sigma X^2 P(X) - (\Sigma XP(X))^2$

$$= \frac{36}{221} - \left(\frac{34}{221}\right)^2 = \frac{1}{221}\left[36 - \frac{34^2}{221}\right]$$

$$= \frac{1}{221}\left[\frac{36 \times 221 - 1156}{221}\right]$$

$$= \frac{6800}{(221)^2} \qquad \textbf{(2 Marks)}$$

$$\therefore \ \text{Variance} = \frac{6800}{(221)^2} = 0.139$$

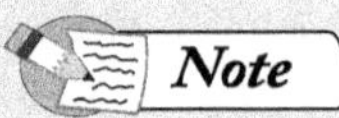

In without replacement quantity will be reduced in every drawn but in with replacement quantity will be same in every drawn.

All India *2018*

CBSE Board Solved Paper

Time Allowed : 3 Hours   *Maximum Marks : 100*

General Instructions:

(i)   **All** questions are compulsory.

(ii)   The question paper consists of **29** questions divided into four sections **A, B, C** and **D**. Section **A** comprises of **4** questions of **one mark** each, Section **B** comprises of **8** questions of **two marks** each, Section **C** comprises of **11** questions of **four marks** each and Section **D** comprises of **6** questions of **six marks** each.

(iii)   All questions in Section **A** are to be answered in one word, one sentence or as per the exact requirement of the question.

(iv)   There is no overall choice. However, internal choice has been provided in **3** questions of four marks each and **3** questions of six marks each. You have to attempt only one of the alternatives in all such questions.

(v)   Use of calculators is not permitted. You may ask for logarithmic tables, if required.

SECTION - A

1. If $a * b$ denotes the larger of 'a' and 'b' and if $a \circ b = (a * b) + 3$, then write the value of $(5) \circ (10)$, where $*$ and $\circ$ are binary operations.

2. Find the magnitude of each of the two vectors $\vec{a}$ and $\vec{b}$, having the same magnitude such that the angle between them is 60° and their scalar product is $\dfrac{9}{2}$.

3. If the matrix $A = \begin{bmatrix} 0 & a & -3 \\ 2 & 0 & -1 \\ b & 1 & 0 \end{bmatrix}$ is skew symmetric, find the values of 'a' and 'b'.

4. Find the value of $\tan^{-1} \sqrt{3} - \cot^{-1} (-\sqrt{3})$.

SECTION - B

5. The total cost $C(x)$ associated with the production of x units of an item is given by $C(x) = 0.005x^3 - 0.02x^2 + 30x + 5000$. Find the marginal cost when 3 units are produced, where by marginal cost we mean the instantaneous rate of change of total cost at any level of output.

6. Differentiate $\tan^{-1}\left(\dfrac{1+\cos x}{\sin x}\right)$ with respect to x.

7. Given $A = \begin{bmatrix} 2 & -3 \\ -4 & 7 \end{bmatrix}$, compute A^{-1} and show that $2A^{-1} = 9I - A$.

8. Prove that:
$$3\sin^{-1} x = \sin^{-1} (3x - 4x^3), x \in \left[-\dfrac{1}{2}, \dfrac{1}{2}\right]$$

9. A black and a red die are rolled together. Find the conditional probability of obtaining the sum 8, given that the red die resulted in a number less than 4.

10. If θ is the angle between two vectors $\hat{i} - 2\hat{j} + 3\hat{k}$ and $3\hat{i} - 2\hat{j} + \hat{k}$, find $\sin \theta$.

11. Find the differential equation representing the family of curves $y = a\, e^{bx + 5}$ where a and b are arbitrary constants.

12. Evaluate:
$$\int \dfrac{\cos 2x + 2\sin^2 x}{\cos^2 x} dx$$

SECTION - C

13. If $y = \sin(\sin x)$, prove that

$$\frac{d^2 y}{dx^2} + \tan x \; \frac{dy}{dx} + y \cos^2 x = 0.$$

14. Find the particular solution of the differential equation

$$e^x \tan y \, dx + (2 - e^x) \sec^2 y \, dy = 0, \text{ given that } y = \frac{\pi}{4} \text{ when}$$

$x = 0.$

OR

Find the particular solution of the differential equation

$$\frac{dy}{dx} + 2y \tan x = \sin x, \text{ given that } y = 0 \text{ when } x = \frac{\pi}{3}.$$

15. Find the shortest distance between the lines

$$\vec{r} = (4\hat{i} - \hat{j}) + \lambda(\hat{i} + 2\hat{j} - 3\hat{k}) \text{ and}$$

$$\vec{r} = (\hat{i} - \hat{j} + 2\hat{k}) + \mu(2\hat{i} + 4\hat{j} - 5\hat{k}).$$

16. Two numbers are selected at random (without replacement) from the first five positive integers. Let X denote the larger of the two numbers obtained. Find the mean and variance of X.

17. Using properties of determinants, prove that

$$\begin{vmatrix} 1 & 1 & 1+3x \\ 1+3y & 1 & 1 \\ 1 & 1+3z & 1 \end{vmatrix} = 9 \, (3xyz + xy + yz + zx)$$

18. Find the equations of the tangent and the normal, to the curve $16x^2 + 9y^2 = 145$ at the point (x_1, y_1), where $x_1 = 2$ and $y_1 > 0$.

OR

Find the intervals in which the function

$$f(x) = \frac{x^4}{4} - x^3 - 5x^2 + 24x + 12 \text{ is}$$

(a) strictly increasing, (b) strictly decreasing.

19. Find:

$$\int \frac{2 \cos x}{(1 - \sin x)(1 + \sin^2 x)} dx$$

20. Suppose a girl throws a die. If she gets 1 or 2, she tosses a coin three times and notes the number of tails. If she gets 3, 4, 5 or 6, she tosses a coin once and notes whether a 'head' or 'tail' is obtained. If she obtained exactly one 'tail', what is the probability that she threw 3, 4, 5 or 6 with the die?

21. Let $\vec{a} = 4\hat{i} + 5\hat{j} - \hat{k}, \vec{b} = \hat{i} - 4\hat{j} + 5\hat{k}$ and $\vec{c} = 3\hat{i} + \hat{j} - \hat{k}$. Find a vector $\vec{d}$ which is perpendicular to both $\vec{c}$ and $\vec{b}$ and $\vec{d} \cdot \vec{a} = 21.$

22. An open tank with a square base and vertical sides is to be constructed from a metal sheet so as to hold a given quantity of water. Show that the cost of material will be least when depth of the tank is half of its width. If the cost is to be borne by nearby settled lower income families, for whom water will be provided, what kind of value is hidden in this question?

23. If $(x^2 + y^2)^2 = xy$, find $\dfrac{dy}{dx}$.

OR

If $x = a \, (2\theta - \sin 2\theta)$ and $y = a \, (1 - \cos 2\theta)$, find $\dfrac{dy}{dx}$ when θ

$$= \frac{\pi}{3}.$$

SECTION - D

24. Evaluate :

$$\int_0^{\pi/4} \frac{\sin x + \cos x}{16 + 9 \sin 2x} dx$$

OR

Evaluate :

$$\int_1^3 (x^2 + 3x + e^x) dx$$

as the limit of the sum.

25. A factory manufactures two types of screws A and B, each type requiring the use of two machines, an automatic and a hand-operated. It takes 4 minutes on the automatic and 6 minutes on the hand-operated machines to manufacture a packet of screws 'A' while it takes 6 minutes on the automatic and 3 minutes on the hand-operated machine to manufacture a packet of screws 'B'. Each machine is available for at most 4 hours on any day. The manufacture can sell a packet of screws 'A' at a profit of 70 paise and screws 'B' at a profit of ₹ 1. Assuming that he can sell all the screws he manufactures, how many packets of each type should the factory owner produce in a day in order to maximize his profit? Formulate the above LPP and solve it graphically and find the maximum profit?

26. Let $A = \{x \in Z : 0 \le x \le 12\}$. Show that $R = \{(a, b) : a, b \in A, |a - b| \text{ is divisible by } 4\}$ is an equivalence relation. Find the set of all elements related to 1. Also write the equivalence class [2].

OR

Show that the function $f : \mathbf{R} \to \mathbf{R}$ defined by $f(x) = \dfrac{x}{x^2 + 1}, \ \forall \, x \in \mathbf{R}$ is neither one-one nor onto. Also, if $g : \mathbf{R} \to \mathbf{R}$ is defined as $g(x) = 2x - 1$, find $fog(x)$.

27. Using integration, find the area of the region in the first quadrant enclosed by the x-axis, the line $y = x$ and the circle $x^2 + y^2 = 32$.

28. If $A = \begin{bmatrix} 2 & -3 & 5 \\ 3 & 2 & -4 \\ 1 & 1 & -2 \end{bmatrix}$, find A^{-1}.

Use it to solve the system of equations

$$2x - 3y + 5z = 11$$
$$3x + 2y - 4z = -5$$
$$x + y - 2z = -3.$$

OR

Using elementary row transformations, find the inverse of

the matrix $A = \begin{bmatrix} 1 & 2 & 3 \\ 2 & 5 & 7 \\ -2 & -4 & -5 \end{bmatrix}$.

29. Find the distance of the point $(-1, -5, -10)$ from the point of intersection of the line $\vec{r} = 2\hat{i} - \hat{j} + 2\hat{k} + \lambda(3\hat{i} + 4\hat{j} + 2\hat{k})$ and the plane $\vec{r} \cdot (\hat{i} - \hat{j} + \hat{k}) = 5$.

Solutions

SECTION - A

1. $(5) \circ (10) = (5 * 10) + 3$
$= 10 + 3 = 13 \quad (\because 10 > 5)$ **(1 Mark)**

2. As $\vec{a} \cdot \vec{b} = |\vec{a}||\vec{b}| \cos\theta$, where θ is the angle between $\vec{a}$ and $\vec{b}$. **(½ Mark)**

$\therefore \quad \dfrac{9}{2} = |\vec{a}|^2 \cos 60° \qquad (\because |\vec{a}| = |\vec{b}| \text{ given})$

$\Rightarrow \quad \dfrac{9}{2} = |\vec{a}|^2 \cdot \dfrac{1}{2} \Rightarrow 9 = |\vec{a}|^2$

$\therefore |\vec{a}| = 3$ **(½ Mark)**

Hence magnitude of each of the vectors $\vec{a}$ and $\vec{b}$ is 3.

3. $A = \begin{bmatrix} 0 & a & -3 \\ 2 & 0 & -1 \\ b & 1 & 0 \end{bmatrix}$ is skew symmetric.

$\begin{bmatrix} 0 & 2 & b \\ a & 0 & 1 \\ -3 & -1 & 0 \end{bmatrix} = \begin{bmatrix} 0 & -a & 3 \\ -2 & 0 & 1 \\ -b & -1 & 0 \end{bmatrix} \qquad (\because A^T = -A)$

$\therefore \quad a = -2, b = 3$ **(1 Mark)**

Note

Diagonal elements of skew symmetric matrix are zero and $A + A' = O$

4. $\tan^{-1}\sqrt{3} - \cot^{-1}(-\sqrt{3})$

$= \tan^{-1}\sqrt{3} - [\pi - \cot^{-1}(\sqrt{3})] \quad [\because \cot^{-1}(-x) = \pi - \cot^{-1}x]$

$= (\tan^{-1}\sqrt{3} + \cot^{-1}\sqrt{3}) - \pi$

$= \left(\dfrac{\pi}{3} + \dfrac{\pi}{6}\right) - \pi = \pi/2 - \pi = -\pi/2$ **(1 Mark)**

SECTION - B

5. As $C(x) = 0.005x^3 - 0.02x^2 + 30x + 5000$
$\therefore \quad$ Marginal cost $= C'(x)$
$= 3(0.005x^2) - 0.02(2x) + 30$
$= 0.015x^2 - 0.04x + 30$ **(1 Mark)**
Marginal cost when 3 units are produced
$= C'(3) = 0.015(3)^2 - 0.04(3) + 30$
$= 0.135 - 0.12 + 30$

$= 30.135 - 0.120 = 30.015$ **(1 Mark)**

6. Let $f(x) = \tan^{-1}\left(\dfrac{1 + \cos x}{\sin x}\right)$

$= \tan^{-1}\left(\dfrac{2\cos^2\dfrac{x}{2}}{2\sin\dfrac{x}{2} \cdot \cos\dfrac{x}{2}}\right) = \tan^{-1}\left(\dfrac{\cos\dfrac{x}{2}}{\sin\dfrac{x}{2}}\right)$

$= \tan^{-1}\left(\cot\dfrac{x}{2}\right) = \tan^{-1}\left[\tan\left(\dfrac{\pi}{2} - \dfrac{x}{2}\right)\right]$

$f(x) = \dfrac{\pi}{2} - \dfrac{x}{2}$ **(1 Mark)**

$f'(x) = -\dfrac{1}{2}$ **(1 Mark)**

7. $A = \begin{bmatrix} 2 & -3 \\ -4 & 7 \end{bmatrix}$

$C_{11} = (-1)^{1+1}(7) = 7,$
$C_{12} = (-1)^{1+2}(-4) = 4,$
$C_{21} = (-1)^{2+1}(-3) = 3,$
$C_{22} = (-1)^{2+2}\, 2 = 2$

$\text{Adj } A = \begin{bmatrix} 7 & 4 \\ 3 & 2 \end{bmatrix}' = \begin{bmatrix} 7 & 3 \\ 4 & 2 \end{bmatrix}$

$|A| = 2 \times 7 - (-3) \times (-4) = 14 - 12 = 2 \neq 0$

$\therefore \quad A^{-1} = \dfrac{1}{|A|}\text{ adj } A = \dfrac{1}{2}\begin{bmatrix} 7 & 3 \\ 4 & 2 \end{bmatrix} = \begin{bmatrix} 7/2 & 3/2 \\ 2 & 1 \end{bmatrix}$
(1 Mark)

$\text{L.H.S.} = 2A^{-1} = 2\begin{bmatrix} 7/2 & 3/2 \\ 2 & 1 \end{bmatrix} = \begin{bmatrix} 7 & 3 \\ 4 & 2 \end{bmatrix}$

$\text{R.H.S.} = 9I - A = 9\begin{bmatrix} 1 & 0 \\ 0 & 1 \end{bmatrix} - \begin{bmatrix} 2 & -3 \\ -4 & 7 \end{bmatrix}$

$= \begin{bmatrix} 9 & 0 \\ 0 & 9 \end{bmatrix} - \begin{bmatrix} 2 & -3 \\ -4 & 7 \end{bmatrix}$

$= \begin{bmatrix} 9-2 & 3 \\ 4 & 9-7 \end{bmatrix} = \begin{bmatrix} 7 & 3 \\ 4 & 2 \end{bmatrix}$

$\therefore \quad$ L.H.S. = R.H.S.
Hence verified that $2A^{-1} = 9I - A$. **(1 Mark)**

8. $3\sin^{-1} x = \sin^{-1}(3x - 4x^3),\ x \in \left[-\dfrac{1}{2}, \dfrac{1}{2}\right]$

Let $\sin^{-1} x = \theta \Rightarrow x = \sin\theta$

L.H.S. $= 3\theta$ **(1 Mark)**

R.H.S. $= \sin^{-1}(3\sin\theta - 4\sin^3\theta) = \sin^{-1}(\sin 3\theta) = 3\theta$

$\therefore$ LHS $=$ RHS   **(1 Mark)**

Hence, $3\sin^{-1} x = \sin^{-1}(3x - 4x^3)$

9. Let A be the event of obtaining sum as 8 and B be the event that red die resulted in a number less than 4. Let black die be represented by first number in the ordered pair.

$\therefore$ B has the following outcomes

$(1,1),(2,1),(3,1),(4,1),(5,1),(6,1),(1,2),(2,2),(3,2),$
$(4,2),(5,2),(6,2),(1,3),(2,3),(3,3),(4,3),(5,3),(6,3).$

So, B has 18 outcomes.

A has $(2,6),(3,5),(4,4),(5,3),(6,2)$

So, A has 5 outcomes.   **(1 Mark)**

$A \cap B$ has 2 outcomes $(5,3)$ and $(6,2)$.

$\therefore$ $P(A/B) = \dfrac{P(A \cap B)}{P(B)} = \dfrac{2}{18} = \dfrac{1}{9}$ **(1 Mark)**

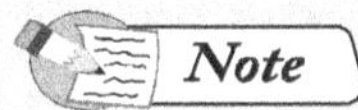

Conditional probability P(A/B) applied when probability of occurence of event A is under the condition that B has already occured and P(B) $\neq$ 0.

10. $\because$ $\vec{a} \times \vec{b} = \begin{vmatrix} \hat{i} & \hat{j} & \hat{k} \\ 1 & -2 & 3 \\ 3 & -2 & 1 \end{vmatrix}$

$= \hat{i}(-2+6) - \hat{j}(1-9) + \hat{k}(-2+6)$

$= 4\hat{i} + 8\hat{j} + 4\hat{k}$

$\therefore |\vec{a} \times \vec{b}| = \sqrt{4^2 + 8^2 + 4^2}$

$= \sqrt{16 + 64 + 16} = \sqrt{96} = 4\sqrt{6}$

$|\vec{a}| = \sqrt{1^2 + (-2)^2 + 3^2} = \sqrt{14}$

$|\vec{b}| = \sqrt{3^2 + (-2)^2 + 1^2} = \sqrt{14}$ **(1 Mark)**

$\because$ $|\vec{a} \times \vec{b}| = |\vec{a}||\vec{b}|\sin\theta$

where θ is the angle between $\vec{a}$ and $\vec{b}$.

$\Rightarrow$ $\sin\theta = \dfrac{4\sqrt{6}}{\sqrt{14}\sqrt{14}} = \dfrac{4\sqrt{6}}{14} = \dfrac{2}{7}\sqrt{6}$

$\Rightarrow$ $\sin\theta = \dfrac{2}{7}\sqrt{6}$ **(1 Mark)**

11. $y = ae^{bx+5}$ ... (i)

$\Rightarrow$ $y' = ba\,e^{bx+5} = by$ ... (ii)

$\Rightarrow$ $y'' = b^2 a\,e^{bx+5}$ **(1 Mark)**

$\Rightarrow$ $y'' = b^2 y$ [By using (i)]

$\Rightarrow$ $y'' = \left(\dfrac{y'}{y}\right)^2 y$ [By using (ii)]

$\Rightarrow$ $yy'' - (y')^2 = 0$ **(1 Mark)**

This represent the differential equation representing the family of curves $y = ae^{bx+5}$, where a and b are arbitrary constrants.

12. $\displaystyle\int \dfrac{\cos 2x + 2\sin^2 x}{\cos^2 x}\,dx$

$= \displaystyle\int \dfrac{2\cos^2 x - 1 + 2(1 - \cos^2 x)}{\cos^2 x}\,dx$ $\begin{bmatrix} \text{Put}\cos 2x = 2\cos^2 x - 1 \\ \&\ \sin^2 x = 1 - \cos^2 x \end{bmatrix}$

     (1 Mark)

$= \displaystyle\int \dfrac{1}{\cos^2 x}\,dx = \int \sec^2 x\,dx = \tan x + c$ **(1 Mark)**

SECTION - C

13. As $y = \sin(\sin x)$

$\Rightarrow$ $\dfrac{dy}{dx} = \cos(\sin x)\cos x$ ... (i)   **(1 Mark)**

and $\dfrac{d^2 y}{dx^2} = \cos(\sin x)(-\sin x) - \cos^2 x(\sin(\sin x))$

     (1 Mark)

Now $\dfrac{d^2 y}{dx^2} + \tan x\,\dfrac{dy}{dx} + y\cos^2 x$

$= -\sin x\cos(\sin x) - \cos^2 x\sin(\sin x)$

$\qquad + \dfrac{\sin x}{\cos x} \times \cos x\cos(\sin x) + \sin(\sin x)\cos^2 x$

$= -\sin x\cos(\sin x) - \cos^2 x\sin(\sin x) + \sin x\cos(\sin x)$
$\qquad\qquad\qquad\qquad\qquad\qquad + \cos^2 x\sin(\sin x)$

$= 0 = $ R.H.S.   **(2 Marks)**

Hence proved

14. $e^x \tan y\,dx + (2 - e^x)\sec^2 y\,dy = 0$

$\Rightarrow$ $e^x \tan y\,dx = (e^x - 2)\sec^2 y\,dy$

or $\displaystyle\int \frac{\sec^2 y}{\tan y} dy = \int \frac{e^x}{e^x - 2} dx$ ...(i)

Let $\tan y = t$

$\qquad \sec^2 y\, dy = dt$

$$\int \frac{\sec^2 y}{\tan y} dy = \int \frac{dt}{t} = \log|t| + c = \log|\tan y| + c_1$$

(1 Mark)

Let $e^x - 2 = t$

$\qquad e^x dx = dt$

$$\int \frac{e^x}{e^x - 2} dx = \int \frac{1}{t} dt = \log|t| + c_2 = \log|e^x - 2| + c_2$$

Put in (i), we get

$\Rightarrow \quad \log|\tan y| = \log|e^x - 2| + c$ **(1 Mark)**

$\Rightarrow \quad \log|\tan y| = \log|e^x - 2| + \log k$ where $\log k = c$

$\Rightarrow \quad \log|\tan y| = \log|k(e^x - 2)|$

$\Rightarrow \quad \tan y = k(e^x - 2)$ is general solution **(1 Mark)**

Now for particular solution

$$y = \frac{\pi}{4} \text{ where } x = 0$$

$\Rightarrow \quad \tan \dfrac{\pi}{4} = k(e^0 - 2)$

$\Rightarrow \quad 1 = k(1 - 2)$

$\qquad -1 = k$

$\therefore \quad \tan y = -(e^x - 2) = 2 - e^x$ is the particular solution.

(1 Mark)

OR

$$\frac{dy}{dx} + 2y \tan x = \sin x$$

It is linear differential equation of first order, $\dfrac{dy}{dx} + Py = Q$

where $P = 2 \tan x$

$\qquad Q = \sin x$

Integrating factor $= e^{\int 2 \tan x\, dx}$

$\qquad = e^{2 \log(\sec x)} = e^{\log \sec^2 x} = \sec^2 x$ $[e^{\log x} = x]$ **(1 Mark)**

$y.\text{I.F.} = \int \text{I.F.Q. } dx$

$\therefore \quad y \cdot \sec^2 x = \int \sin x \times \sec^2 x\, dx$

$\qquad = \int \dfrac{\sin x}{\cos^2 x} dx = \int \tan x \cdot \sec x\, dx$

$y \sec^2 x = \sec x + c$ **(2 Marks)**

For particular solution:

$$y = 0 \text{ where } x = \frac{\pi}{3}$$

$\Rightarrow \quad y \sec^2 \dfrac{\pi}{3} = \sec \dfrac{\pi}{3} + c$

$0 = 2 + c \Rightarrow -2 = c$

$\therefore \quad y \sec^2 x = \sec x - 2$ is the particular solution.

(1 Mark)

15. As $\vec{r} = (4\hat{i} - \hat{j}) + \lambda(\hat{i} + 2\hat{j} - 3\hat{k})$ and

$\vec{r} = (\hat{i} - \hat{j} + 2\hat{k}) + \mu(2\hat{i} + 4\hat{j} - 5\hat{k})$ are the two lines.

$\vec{a_1} = 4\hat{i} - \hat{j}, \vec{b_1} = \hat{i} + 2\hat{j} - 3\hat{k}$

$\vec{a_2} = \hat{i} - \hat{j} + 2\hat{k}, \vec{b_2} = 2\hat{i} + 4\hat{j} - 5\hat{k}$ **(1 Mark)**

Shortest distance, $d = \left| \dfrac{(\vec{b_1} \times \vec{b_2}) \cdot (\vec{a_2} - \vec{a_1})}{|\vec{b_1} \times \vec{b_2}|} \right|$ **(1 Mark)**

$$\vec{b_1} \times \vec{b_2} = \begin{vmatrix} \hat{i} & \hat{j} & \hat{k} \\ 1 & 2 & -3 \\ 2 & 4 & -5 \end{vmatrix}$$

$= \hat{i}(2) - \hat{j}(1) + \hat{k}(0) = 2\hat{i} - \hat{j}$

$|\vec{b_1} \times \vec{b_2}| = \sqrt{4 + 1} = \sqrt{5}$ **(1 Mark)**

$\vec{a_2} - \vec{a_1} = -3\hat{i} + 0\hat{j} + 2\hat{k}$

$(\vec{a_2} - \vec{a_1}) \cdot (\vec{b_1} \times \vec{b_2}) = -6 + 0 + 0 = -6$

$\therefore \quad d = \left| \dfrac{-6}{\sqrt{5}} \right| = \dfrac{6}{\sqrt{5}}$ **(1 Mark)**

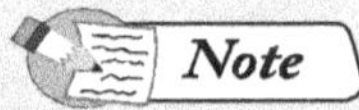

Note

If $\vec{b_1} \times \vec{b_2} = 0$ then $\vec{b_1}$ is parallel to $\vec{b_2}$.

16. First five positive integers are 1, 2, 3, 4, 5.

Two numbers are selected at random without replacement and X denotes the larger of the two numbers.

X can have values 2, 3, 4, 5.

Two number being selected from 1, 2, 3, 4, 5 in $5 \times 4 = 20$ ways

$\therefore P(2) = \dfrac{2}{20}$ (cases (1, 2) and (2, 1))

$\therefore P(3) = \dfrac{4}{20}$ (cases (1, 3), (3, 1), (3, 2) and (2, 3))

$\therefore P(4) = \dfrac{6}{20} \left(\begin{array}{l} \text{cases 1, 4), (4, 1), (4, 2), (2, 4), (3, 4)} \\ \text{and (4, 3)} \end{array} \right)$

$\therefore P(5) = \dfrac{8}{20} \left(\begin{array}{l} \text{cases (1, 5), (5, 1), (5, 2), (2, 5), (3, 5),} \\ \text{(5, 3), (5, 4) and (4, 5)} \end{array} \right)$

[1 Mark]

x	2	3	4	5
P(X)	2/20	4/20	6/20	8/20

Now, mean $= E(X) = \sum P_i X_i$ **[1 Mark]**

$\Rightarrow \displaystyle\sum_{i=2}^{5} X \times P(X) = 2 \times \frac{2}{20} + 3 \times \frac{4}{20} + 4 \times \frac{6}{20} + 5 \times \frac{8}{20}$

$$\Rightarrow \frac{4+12+24+40}{20} = \frac{80}{20} = 4 \qquad \textbf{[1 Mark]}$$

$$\text{Variance} = \sum_{i=2}^{5} X^2 \times P(X) - \left(\sum_{i=2}^{5} X \times P(X)\right)^2$$

$$\Rightarrow 17 - 16 = 1 \qquad \textbf{[1 Mark]}$$

17.
$$\begin{vmatrix} 1 & 1 & 1+3x \\ 1+3y & 1 & 1 \\ 1 & 1+3z & 1 \end{vmatrix}$$

L.H.S. $= R_1 \to R_1 + R_2 + R_3$

$$\begin{vmatrix} 3+3y & 3+3z & 3+3x \\ 1+3y & 1 & 1 \\ 1 & 1+3z & 1 \end{vmatrix} \qquad \textbf{(½ Mark)}$$

Taking 3 common from R_1

$$= 3\begin{vmatrix} 1+y & 1+z & 1+x \\ 1+3y & 1 & 1 \\ 1 & 1+3z & 1 \end{vmatrix} \qquad \textbf{(½ Mark)}$$

$R_2 \to R_2 - R_1$

$$= 3\begin{vmatrix} 1+y & 1+z & 1+x \\ 2y & -z & -x \\ 1 & 1+3z & 1 \end{vmatrix} \qquad \textbf{(½ Mark)}$$

$R_1 \to R_1 - \dfrac{1}{2} R_2$

$$= 3\begin{vmatrix} 1 & 1+\frac{3}{2}z & 1+\frac{3}{2}x \\ 2y & -z & -x \\ 1 & 1+3z & 1 \end{vmatrix} \qquad \textbf{(½ Mark)}$$

$R_3 \to R_3 - R_1$

$$= 3\begin{vmatrix} 1 & 1+\frac{3}{2}z & 1+\frac{3}{2}x \\ 2y & -z & -x \\ 0 & \frac{3}{2}z & -\frac{3}{2}x \end{vmatrix} \qquad \textbf{(½ Mark)}$$

$R_2 \to R_2 - 2y R_1$

$$= 3\begin{vmatrix} 1 & 1+\frac{3}{2}z & 1+\frac{3}{2}x \\ 0 & -z-2y-3yz & -x-2y-3yx \\ 0 & \frac{3}{2}z & -\frac{3}{2}x \end{vmatrix} \qquad \textbf{(½ Mark)}$$

Expanding along C_1

$$= 3 \times 1 \times \left[(-z-2y-3yz)\left(\frac{-3}{2}x\right) \right.$$

$$\left. -\left(\frac{3}{2}z\right)(-x-2y-3yx) \right]$$

$$= 3 \times \left(\frac{-3}{2}\right)(-xz-2yx-3xyz-xz-2yz-3xyz)$$

$$= 3 \times \left(\frac{-3}{2}\right)(-6xyz-2xy-2yz-2xz)$$

$$= 9\,(3xyz+xy+yz+zx)$$

$$= \text{R.H.S.} \qquad \textbf{(1 Mark)}$$

18. $16x^2 + 9y^2 = 145$ is the curve and point is (x_1, y_1) where $x_1 = 2$ and $y_1 > 0$

$$\Rightarrow 16(2)^2 + 9\,y_1^2 = 145$$

$$\Rightarrow 9\,y_1^2 = 145 - 64 = 81$$

$$\Rightarrow y_1^2 = 9$$

$$y_1 = \pm 3$$

Since $y_1 > 0$

$$\therefore \quad y_1 = 3$$

So, required point is $(2, 3)$. $\qquad \textbf{(1 Mark)}$

Now $16x^2 + 9y^2 = 145$, on differentiating w.r.t. x gives

$$16(2x) + 18y\frac{dy}{dx} = 0$$

$$\frac{dy}{dx} = -\frac{32x}{18y} = -\frac{16x}{9y} \qquad \textbf{(1 Mark)}$$

Slope of tangent at $(2, 3) = \dfrac{dy}{dx}\bigg]_{(2,3)}$

$$= -\frac{16 \times 2}{9 \times 3} = \frac{-32}{27}$$

So, equation of tangent is
$$y - y_1 = m\,(x - x_1)$$

$$y - 3 = \frac{-32}{27}\,(x-2)$$

$$27y - 81 = -32x + 64$$

$$\Rightarrow 32x + 27y = 145 \text{ is the equation of tangent} \qquad \textbf{(1 Mark)}$$

Slope of normal is $\dfrac{-1}{m} = \dfrac{-1}{\frac{-32}{27}} = \dfrac{27}{32}$

Equation of normal is

$$y - 3 = \frac{27}{32}\,(x-2)$$

$$\Rightarrow 32y - 96 = 27x - 54$$

$$\Rightarrow 27x - 32y = 54 - 96 = -42$$

$$\Rightarrow 27x - 32y + 42 = 0 \qquad \textbf{(1 Mark)}$$

OR

As $f(x) = \dfrac{x^4}{4} - x^3 - 5x^2 + 24x + 12$

$$\Rightarrow f'(x) = \frac{4x^3}{4} - 3x^2 - 10x + 24 \qquad \textbf{(1 Mark)}$$

$$= x^3 - 3x^2 - 10x + 24$$

Let $f'(x) = 0 \Rightarrow x^3 - 3x^2 - 10x + 24 = 0$

$x - 2$ is factor of $f'(x)$

$$x-2\overline{)\,x^3-3x^2-10x+24\,}\bigg(x^2-x-12$$

$$\underline{x^3-2x^2}$$
$$\underline{-\quad +\qquad\qquad\qquad}$$
$$-x^2-10x+24$$
$$-x^2+2x$$
$$\underline{+\quad -\qquad\qquad}$$
$$-12x+24$$
$$-12x+24$$
$$\underline{+\quad -\qquad\qquad}$$
$$0$$

$$\Rightarrow\quad (x-2)(x^2-x-12)=0$$
$$\Rightarrow\quad (x-2)(x+3)(x-4)=0$$
$$x=2,-3,4 \hspace{2cm} \textbf{(2 Marks)}$$

$$\Rightarrow\quad f'(x)=(x-2)(x+3)(x-4)$$

Interval	Sign of $f'(x)$	Nature of $f(x)$
$(-\infty,-3)$	$(-)(-)(-)<0$	$f(x)$ is strictly decreasing
$(-3,2)$	$(-)(+)(-)>0$	$f(x)$ is strictly increasing
$(2,4)$	$(+)(+)(-)<0$	$f(x)$ is strictly decreasing
$(4,\infty)$	$(+)(+)(+)>0$	$f(x)$ is strictly increasing

(1 Mark)

> **Note**
>
> *To get strictly increasing and strictly decreasing interval, draw a number line and plot all the values of variable in it. It is necessary to check all intervals by putting the any value within interval in f'(x).*

19. Let $I=\displaystyle\int\frac{2\cos x}{(1-\sin x)(1+\sin^2 x)}dx$

$$=\int\frac{2}{(1-t)(1+t^2)}dt \quad \text{where } t=\sin x \Rightarrow dt=\cos x\,dx$$

(1 Mark)

$$\frac{2}{(1-t)(1+t^2)}=\frac{A}{1-t}+\frac{Bt+C}{1+t^2}$$
$$2=A(1+t^2)+(Bt+C)(1-t)$$
$$2=A+At^2+Bt-Bt^2+C-Ct$$

Comparing coefficients of t^2, t and constant terms on both sides, we get
$$0=A-B,\ 0=B-C \text{ and } 2=A+C$$
We get, $A=1,B=1,C=1$ **(1 Mark)**

$$\therefore\quad I=\int\frac{1}{1-t}dt+\int\frac{t+1}{t^2+1}dt$$

$$=-\log|1-t|+\frac{1}{2}\int\frac{2t}{t^2+1}dt+\int\frac{1}{t^2+1}dt$$

$$=-\log|1-t|+\frac{1}{2}\log|t^2+1|+\tan^{-1}t+C$$

$$I=-\log|1-\sin x|+\frac{1}{2}\log|\sin^2 x+1|+\tan^{-1}(\sin x)+C$$

(2 Marks)

20. E_1 = Getting 1 and 2 when throwing a die.
E_2 = Getting 3, 4, 5 and 6 when throwing a die.
F = Event getting exactly one tail

$$\therefore P(E_1)=\frac{2}{6}=\frac{1}{3};\ P(E_2)=\frac{4}{6}=\frac{2}{3}.$$

$P(F/E_1)$ = P(Getting one tail in 3 times tosses a coin when die comes us 1 and 2.) = {THH, HTH, HHT}

$$=\frac{3}{8}$$

$P(F/E_2)$ = P(Getting one tail in one time tosses a coin when die comes up 3, 4, 5 and 6)

$$=\frac{1}{2} \hspace{3cm} \textbf{(1½ Marks)}$$

$$\therefore P(E_2/F)=\frac{P(F/E_2)\times P(E_2)}{P(E_1)\times P(F/E_2)+P(E_2)\times P(F/E_2)}$$

(1 Mark)

$$=\frac{\dfrac{1}{2}\times\dfrac{2}{3}}{\dfrac{1}{3}\times\dfrac{3}{8}+\dfrac{1}{2}\times\dfrac{2}{3}}=\frac{\dfrac{1}{3}}{\dfrac{1}{8}+\dfrac{1}{3}}$$

$$=\frac{1}{3}\times\frac{24}{11}=\frac{8}{11}. \hspace{2cm} \textbf{(1½ Marks)}$$

21. $\vec{a}=4\hat{i}+5\hat{j}-\hat{k}, \vec{b}=\hat{i}-4\hat{j}+5\hat{k}$, $\vec{c}=3\hat{i}+\hat{j}-\hat{k}$
$\vec{d}\perp\vec{c}, \vec{d}\perp\vec{b}, \vec{d}\cdot\vec{a}=21$
Let $\vec{d}=x\hat{i}+y\hat{j}+z\hat{k}$
As $\vec{d}\perp\vec{c}\Rightarrow 3x+y-z=0$ ...(i)
As $\vec{d}\perp\vec{b}\Rightarrow x-4y+5z=0$ ...(ii)
As $\vec{d}\cdot\vec{a}=21\Rightarrow 4x+5y-z=21$ ...(iii)   **(1½ Marks)**
By (iii) – (i), we get
    $x+4y=21$ ...(iv)
By (ii) + 5(i), we get
    $16x+y=0$ ...(v)   **(1½ Marks)**
By solving (iv) & (v)

$$\therefore\quad x=\frac{-1}{3},y=\frac{16}{3},z=\frac{13}{3}$$

$$\therefore\quad \vec{d}=-\frac{\hat{i}}{3}+\frac{16}{3}\hat{j}+\frac{13}{3}\hat{k} \hspace{1.5cm} \textbf{(1 Mark)}$$

> 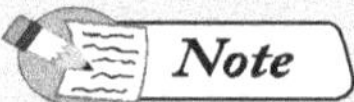 **Note**
>
> *If two vectors are perpendicular then their dot product will always be zero.*

22. An open square box with base length x and breadth x and height y is considered.

Let volume of water it holds be V (constant).

Volume $= l \cdot b \cdot h$

$V = x \cdot x \cdot y = x^2 y$

Now cost of making box is minimum if area of sheet used in making open box is minimum.

$\therefore \quad A(x) = x^2 + 4xy$

$$= x^2 + 4x \cdot \frac{V}{x^2} \qquad (\because V = x^2 y)$$

$$A(x) = x^2 + \frac{4V}{x} \qquad \textbf{(1 Mark)}$$

$$\therefore \quad A'(x) = 2x - \frac{4V}{x^2} \qquad \textbf{(½ Mark)}$$

Let $A'(x) = 0 \Rightarrow 2x - \dfrac{4V}{x^2} = 0 \Rightarrow 4V = 2x^3$

$\Rightarrow \quad 2V = x^3$ or $2x^2 y = x^3 \Rightarrow 2y = x$

$$y = \frac{x}{2} \text{ or height} = \frac{\text{width}}{2} \qquad \textbf{(1 Mark)}$$

Now $A''(x) = 2 + \dfrac{4V(2)}{x^3} = 2 + \dfrac{8V}{x^3} > 0 \, \forall \, x$

$$\therefore \; A(x) \text{ is minimum at } y = \frac{x}{2}. \qquad \textbf{(½ Mark)}$$

The value hidden in the question is that people can solve their problems locally by contributing for a common cause.

$$\textbf{(1 Mark)}$$

> **Note**
>
> *If double differentiation of a function is greater than zero, then it will always give minimum value, vice-versa.*

23. $(x^2 + y^2)^2 = xy$

Differentiating both sides w.r.t. x

$$2(x^2 + y^2)\left(2x + 2y\frac{dy}{dx}\right) = \frac{xdy}{dx} + y.1 \qquad \textbf{(2 Marks)}$$

$$\Rightarrow \quad 2(x^2 + y^2)2x + 2(x^2 + y^2).2y\frac{dy}{dx} = x\frac{dy}{dx} + y$$

$$\Rightarrow \quad (4x^2 y + 4y^3 - x)\frac{dy}{dx} = y - 4x(x^2 + y^2)$$

$$\therefore \quad \frac{dy}{dx} = \frac{y - 4x(x^2 + y^2)}{4x^2 y + 4y^3 - x} \qquad \textbf{(2 Marks)}$$

OR

$x = a(2\theta - \sin 2\theta)$ and $y = a(1 - \cos 2\theta)$

$$\frac{dx}{d\theta} = a(2 - 2\cos 2\theta) \text{ and } \frac{dy}{d\theta} = a(2\sin 2\theta) \qquad \textbf{(2 Marks)}$$

$$\therefore \quad \frac{dy}{dx} = \frac{dy/d\theta}{dx/d\theta} = \frac{2a\sin 2\theta}{a.2(1 - \cos 2\theta)} = \frac{\sin 2\theta}{2\sin^2 \theta} \qquad \textbf{(1 Mark)}$$

$$\frac{dy}{dx} = \frac{2\sin\theta\cos\theta}{2\sin^2\theta} = \cot\theta$$

$$\left.\frac{dy}{dx}\right]_{\theta = \pi/3} = \cot \pi/3 = \frac{1}{\sqrt{3}} \qquad \textbf{(1 Mark)}$$

SECTION - D

24. Let $I = \displaystyle\int_0^{\pi/4} \frac{\sin x + \cos x}{16 + 9\sin 2x}dx$

As $(\sin x - \cos x)^2 = \sin^2 x + \cos^2 x - 2\sin x \cos x$

$\therefore \quad \sin 2x = 1 - (\sin x - \cos x)^2$

$\Rightarrow \quad 16 + 9\sin 2x = 16 + 9 - 9(\sin x - \cos x)^2$

$\qquad = 25 - 9(\sin x - \cos x)^2$

$$\therefore \quad I = \int_0^{\pi/4} \frac{\sin x + \cos x}{25 - 9(\sin x - \cos x)^2}dx \qquad \textbf{(2 Marks)}$$

Let $\sin x - \cos x = t$

$\therefore \quad (\cos x + \sin x)\,dx = dt$

$\therefore \quad$ When $x = 0,\ \sin 0 - \cos 0 = t \Rightarrow t = -1$

when $x = \pi/4,\ \sin \pi/4 - \cos \pi/4 = t \Rightarrow t = 0$

$$\therefore \quad I = \int_{-1}^{0} \frac{dt}{25 - 9t^2} = \frac{1}{9}\int_{-1}^{0} \frac{dt}{\frac{25}{9} - t^2} = \frac{1}{9}\int_{-1}^{0} \frac{dt}{\left(\frac{5}{3}\right)^2 - t^2}$$

$$\textbf{(2 Marks)}$$

As $\displaystyle\int \frac{dt}{a^2 - t^2} = \frac{1}{2a}\log\frac{|a + x|}{|a - x|} + c$

$$= \frac{1}{9} \cdot \frac{1}{2\left(\frac{5}{3}\right)} \cdot \left[\log\left|\frac{5/3 + t}{5/3 - t}\right|\right]_{-1}^{0}$$

$$= \frac{1}{9} \cdot \frac{3}{2 \times 5}\left[\log 1 - \log\frac{2}{8}\right]$$

$$= \frac{1}{30}\log 4 = \frac{1}{15}\log 2 \qquad \textbf{(2 Marks)}$$

OR

Let $I = \displaystyle\int_1^3 (x^2 + 3x + e^x)dx$

We have $\displaystyle\int_a^b f(x)dx = \lim_{\substack{h \to 0 \\ n \to \infty}} h\,[f(a) + f(a+h) + f(a+2h) + \dots$

$$+ f(a + (n-1)h)]$$

Where $h = \dfrac{b - a}{n}$

$$h = \frac{3 - 1}{n} = \frac{2}{n} \qquad \textbf{(1 Mark)}$$

$$\therefore I = \lim_{\substack{h\to 0 \\ n\to\infty}} h[(1+3+e)+((1+h)^2+3(1+h)+e^{1+h})$$
$$+((1+2h)^2+3(1+2h)+e^{1+2h})+....+(1+(n-1)h)^2$$
$$+3(1+(n-1)h)+e^{1+(n-1)}h]$$

$$= \lim_{\substack{h\to 0 \\ n\to\infty}} h[(1+3+e)+(1+h^2+2h+3+3h+e^{1+h})$$

$$+(1+4h^2+4h+3+6h+e^{1+2h})+....+(1+(n-1)^2h^2$$
$$+2(n-1)h+3+3(n-1)h+e^{1+(n-1)h})]$$

$$= \lim_{\substack{h\to 0 \\ n\to\infty}} h[(4+4+4+....n\,\text{times})+e(1+e^h+e^{2h}+....e^{(n-1)h})$$

$$+(5h+10h+....+5(n-1)h)+h^2(1+4+....+(n-1)^2)]$$
(2 Marks)

$$= \lim_{\substack{h\to 0 \\ x\to\infty}} h\left[4n+\frac{(n-1)n(2n-1)h^2}{6}+5h\frac{(n-1)n}{2}+\frac{e(e^{nh}-1)}{e^h-1} \right]$$

$$= \lim_{\substack{h\to 0 \\ x\to\infty}} \frac{2}{n}\left[4n+\frac{n(n-1)(2n-1)4}{6n^2}+5.2.\frac{(n-1)}{2}+\frac{e(e^2-1)}{e^h-1} \right]$$
(2 Marks)

$$= \lim_{\substack{h\to 0 \\ x\to\infty}} \left[8+\frac{1.(1-1/n)(2-1/n).4}{3}+10\left(1-\frac{1}{n}\right)+\frac{\dfrac{e(e^2-1)}{e^h-1}}{h} \right]$$

$$= 8+\frac{8}{3}+10+\frac{e(e^2-1)}{1} \qquad \left[\because \lim_{h\to 0}\frac{e^h-1}{h}=1 \right]$$

$$= \frac{54+8}{3}+e(e^2-1)$$

$$= \frac{62}{3}+e(e^2-1) \qquad\qquad\qquad\qquad \textbf{(1 Mark)}$$

25. Let packets of type of screws A be x and packets of types of screws B be y

Machines screws	Automatic Time(min)	handoperated Time(min).	Profit
$A\ (x)$	4	6	70 Paise
$B\ (y)$	6	3	1 Rs.
Maximum time	4hours = 240 min	4hours = 240 min	

$\therefore 4x+6y\le 240$ and $6x+3y\le 240$

or $\quad 2x+3y\le 120$ and $2x+y\le 80$

where $x\ge 0$ and $y\ge 0$

Profit on type of screw A is $70P = ₹\dfrac{70}{100} = ₹\,0.70$

Profit on type of screw B is $₹\,1$

$\therefore \quad$ Profit function $= P(x) = 0.7x+y$ **[1 Mark]**

Now LPP is

Maximize $P(x) = 0.7x+y$

subjected to

$2x+3y\le 120$

$2x+y\le 80$

$x\ge 0$ and $y\ge 0$ **(1 Mark)**

Now we'll draw the graphs for the constraints

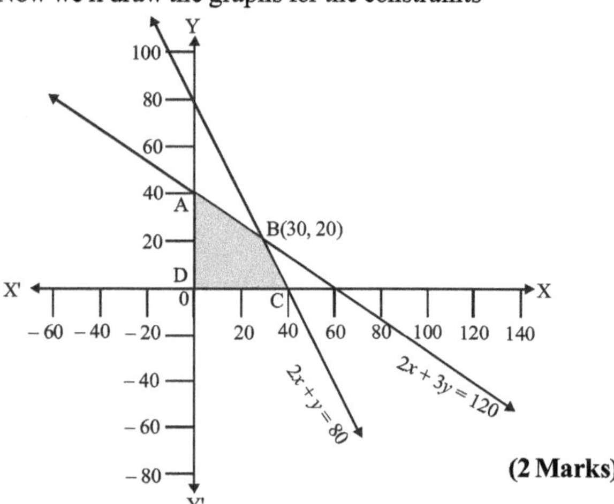

(2 Marks)

The feasible region ABCD has corner points as A(0, 40), B(30, 20), C(40, 0) and D(0, 0). The value of $p(x)$ at different corner points:

At A(0, 40), $P(x) = 40$

At B(30, 20), $P(x) = 0.7\times 30+20 = 21+20 = 41$

At C(40, 0), $P(x) = 0.7\times 40 = 28$

At D(0, 0), $P(x) = 0$

$\therefore\quad$ Maximum value of profit function is $₹\ 41$ at $x = 30$, $y = 20$

$\therefore\quad$ 30 packets of screw A and 20 packets of screws B should be produced. **(2 Marks)**

26. Let $A = \{x\in z : 0\le x\le 12\}$

$\therefore\quad A = \{0, 1, 2, 3, 4, 5, 6, 7, 8, 9, 10, 11, 12\}$

Now $R = \{(a, b): a, b\in A, |a-b|\ \text{is divisible by 4}\}$

$\therefore\ R = \{(0, 4), (0, 8), (0, 12), (1, 5), (1, 9), (2, 6), (2, 10), (3, 7),$ $(3, 11), (4, 8), (4, 12), (9, 1), (9, 5), (10, 2), (10, 6), (11, 7), (11, 3),$ $(12, 4)\ (12, 8), (0, 0), (1, 1), (2, 2), (3, 3), (4, 4), (5, 5), (6, 6),$ $(7, 7), (8, 8), (9, 9), (10, 10), (11, 11), (12, 12), (4, 0), (8, 0), (12, 0),$ $(5, 1), (6, 2), (6, 10), (7, 3), (7, 11), (8, 4), (8, 12)\}$ **(1 Mark)**

Now we see is that

(i) $(a, a)\in R$ as $|a-a| = 0$ which is divisible by 4

$\qquad \therefore R$ is reflexive **(1 Mark)**

(ii) If $(a, b)\in R$, then $(b, a)\in R$ as if $|a-b|$ is divisible by 4, then $|b-a|$ is also divisible by 4.

$\qquad \therefore R$ is symmetric **(1 Mark)**

(iii) If $(a, b)\in R$ and $(b, c)\in R$, then $(a, c)\in R$

$\qquad$ If $|a-b|$ is divisible by 4

$\qquad \Rightarrow\quad a-b = \pm 4k_1$ ...(i)

$\qquad$ and $|\,b-c\,|$ is divisible by 4

$\qquad \Rightarrow\quad b-c = \pm 4k_2$ ...(ii)

$\qquad$ Adding (i) and (ii)

$a - b + b - c = a - c = \pm 4(k_1 + k_2)$
$\Rightarrow \quad |a - c|$ is divisible by 4.
$\therefore \quad R$ is transitive   **(1 Mark)**
Hence R is Reflexive Symmetric and Transitive
$\Rightarrow \quad R$ is equivalence relation   **(1 Mark)**
All elements related to 1
$\{(1, 1), (1, 5), (5, 1), (1, 9), (9, 1)\}$
$\therefore \quad \{1, 5, 9\}$ is set of elements related to 1.
Equivalence class [2]
$= \{(2, 6), (2, 10), (10, 2), (6, 2), (2, 2)\}$ **(1 Mark)**

To check relation is equivalence or not, first verify whether it is reflexive, transitive, symmetric or not.

OR

$f(x) = \dfrac{x}{x^2 + 1}, \forall\, x \in \mathbf{R}$

Let $f(x_1) = f(x_2)$

$\Rightarrow \quad \dfrac{x_1}{x_1^2 + 1} = \dfrac{x_2}{x_2^2 + 1}$

$x_1\left(x_2^2 + x_1\right) = x_2\left(x_1^2 + x_2\right)$

$x_1 x_2^2 - x_2 x_1^2 + x_1 - x_2 = 0$

$(x_1 x_2)(x_2 - x_1) + (x_1 - x_2) = 0$

$(x_2 - x_1)(x_1 x_2 - 1) = 0$

Eiher $x_1 = x_2$ or $x_1 x_2 - 1 = 0 \;\chi\; x_1 x_2 = 1$
As $x_1 x_2 = 1$, it is not necessary $x_1 = x_2$
$\therefore \quad f(x)$ is not one-one   **(2 Marks)**
Now let $f(x) = 1$

$\therefore \quad 1 = \dfrac{x}{x^2 + 1} \Rightarrow x^2 - x + 1 = 0 \Rightarrow x$ is not real

Now $x \in \mathbf{R}$
So there does not exist any $x \in R$ such that

$f(x) = 1 = \dfrac{x}{x^2 + 1}$

$\therefore \quad f(x)$ is not onto   **(2 Marks)**
Now $g(x) = 2x - 1$
$\therefore \quad \text{fog}(x) = f(g(x))$

$\qquad = \dfrac{2x - 1}{(2x - 1)^2 + 1} = \dfrac{2x - 1}{4x^2 + 1 - 4x + 1}$

$\qquad = \dfrac{2x - 1}{4x^2 - 4x + 2}$ **(2 Marks)**

If function is not one-one and onto, then it will never be invertible.

27. $y = x$ and $x^2 + y^2 = 32$
$x^2 + y^2 = \left(4\sqrt{2}\right)^2$

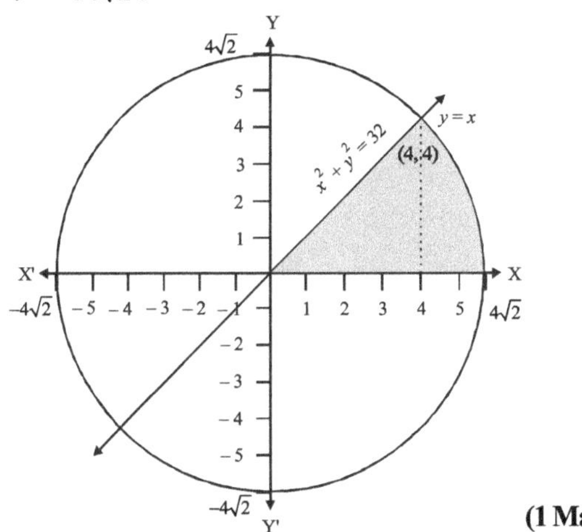

(1 Mark)

Solving $y = x$ and $x^2 + y^2 = 32$
$\Rightarrow \quad x^2 + x^2 = 32$
$\Rightarrow \quad x^2 = 16$
$x = \pm 4$
$\therefore \quad 4^2 + y^2 = 32$
$y^2 = 16$
$y = \pm 4$ **(1 Mark)**
To find area between x axis, $y = x$ and $x^2 + y^2 = 32$

$A = \displaystyle\int_0^4 x\,dx + \int_4^{4\sqrt{2}} \sqrt{(32 - x^2)}\; dx$ **(1 Mark)**

$= \left[\dfrac{x^2}{2}\right]_0^4 + \left[\dfrac{x}{2}\sqrt{32 - x^2} + \dfrac{32}{2}\sin^{-1}\left(\dfrac{x}{4\sqrt{2}}\right)\right]_4^{4\sqrt{2}}$ **(1 Mark)**

$\left[\because \displaystyle\int \sqrt{a^2 - x^2}\,dx = \dfrac{1}{2}x\sqrt{a^2 - x^2} + \dfrac{1}{2}a^2\sin^{-1}\left(\dfrac{x}{a}\right) + \mathrm{C}\right]$

$= \left(\dfrac{16}{2}\right) + \left(0 + 16 \times \dfrac{\pi}{2} - \dfrac{4}{2} \times 4 - 16\dfrac{\pi}{4}\right)$
$= 8 + 8\pi - 8 - 4\pi$
$= 4\pi$ sq units   **(2 Marks)**

28. $A = \begin{bmatrix} 2 & -3 & 5 \\ 3 & 2 & -4 \\ 1 & 1 & -2 \end{bmatrix}$

$|A| = 2(-4 + 4) + 3(-6 + 4) + 5(3 - 2)$
$\qquad = -6 + 5 = -1 \neq 0$
$\therefore \quad A^{-1}$ exists   **(1 Mark)**

$A_{11} = (-1)^2 \begin{vmatrix} 2 & -4 \\ 1 & -2 \end{vmatrix} = -4 - (-4) = 0$

$A_{12} = (-1)^3 \begin{vmatrix} 3 & -4 \\ 1 & -2 \end{vmatrix} = -(-6 + 4) = 2$

$A_{13} = (-1)^4 \begin{vmatrix} 3 & 2 \\ 1 & 1 \end{vmatrix} = 3 - 2 = 1$

$A_{21} = (-1)^3 \begin{vmatrix} -3 & 5 \\ 1 & -2 \end{vmatrix} = -1$

$$A_{22} = (-1)^4 \begin{vmatrix} 2 & 5 \\ 1 & -2 \end{vmatrix} = -9; \quad A_{23} = (-1)^5 \begin{vmatrix} 2 & -3 \\ 1 & 1 \end{vmatrix} = -5$$

$$A_{31} = (-1)^4 \begin{vmatrix} -3 & 5 \\ 2 & -4 \end{vmatrix} = 2$$

$$A_{32} = (-1)^5 \begin{vmatrix} 2 & 5 \\ 3 & -4 \end{vmatrix} = 23$$

$$A_{33} = (-1)^6 \begin{vmatrix} 2 & -3 \\ 3 & 2 \end{vmatrix} = 13$$ **(1 Mark)**

$$\text{Adj } A = \begin{bmatrix} 0 & 2 & 1 \\ -1 & -9 & -5 \\ 2 & 23 & 13 \end{bmatrix}' = \begin{bmatrix} 0 & -1 & 2 \\ 2 & -9 & 23 \\ 1 & -5 & 13 \end{bmatrix}$$

$$A^{-1} = \frac{\text{Adj } A}{|A|} = \begin{bmatrix} 0 & 1 & -2 \\ -2 & 9 & -23 \\ -1 & 5 & -13 \end{bmatrix}$$ **(2 Marks)**

$$2x - 3y + 5z = 11; \quad 3x + 2y - 4z = -5$$
$$x + y - 2z = -3$$

Matrix form :
$$\begin{vmatrix} 2 & -3 & 5 \\ 3 & 2 & -4 \\ 1 & 1 & -2 \end{vmatrix} \begin{bmatrix} x \\ y \\ z \end{bmatrix} = \begin{bmatrix} 11 \\ -5 \\ -3 \end{bmatrix}$$

$$AX = B$$

$$\therefore \quad X = A^{-1}B = \begin{bmatrix} 0 & 1 & -2 \\ -2 & 9 & -23 \\ -1 & 5 & -13 \end{bmatrix} \begin{bmatrix} 11 \\ -5 \\ -3 \end{bmatrix}$$ **(1 Mark)**

$$\begin{bmatrix} x \\ y \\ z \end{bmatrix} = \begin{bmatrix} 0-5+6 \\ -22-45+69 \\ -11-25+39 \end{bmatrix} = \begin{bmatrix} 1 \\ 2 \\ 3 \end{bmatrix}$$

$$\therefore \quad x = 1, y = 2, z = 3$$ **(1 Mark)**

> **Note**
>
> *If coefficient matrix of system of equations in transpose matrix of given matrix then use $(A^T)^{-1} = (A^{-1})^T$. i.e. Transpose the inverse matrix when multiply with matrix B.*

OR

Let $A = \begin{bmatrix} 1 & 2 & 3 \\ 2 & 5 & 7 \\ -2 & -4 & -5 \end{bmatrix}$

$\therefore \quad A = IA$

$$\begin{bmatrix} 1 & 2 & 3 \\ 2 & 5 & 7 \\ -2 & -4 & -5 \end{bmatrix} = \begin{bmatrix} 1 & 0 & 0 \\ 0 & 1 & 0 \\ 0 & 0 & 1 \end{bmatrix} A$$ **(½ Mark)**

$$R_2 \to R_2 + R_3$$

$$\begin{bmatrix} 1 & 2 & 3 \\ 0 & 1 & 2 \\ -2 & -4 & -5 \end{bmatrix} = \begin{bmatrix} 1 & 0 & 0 \\ 0 & 1 & 1 \\ 0 & 0 & 1 \end{bmatrix} A$$ **(½ Mark)**

$$R_1 \to R_1 - 2R_2$$

$$\begin{bmatrix} 1 & 0 & -1 \\ 0 & 1 & 2 \\ -2 & -4 & -5 \end{bmatrix} = \begin{bmatrix} 1 & -2 & -2 \\ 0 & 1 & 1 \\ 0 & 0 & 1 \end{bmatrix} A$$ **(1 Mark)**

$$R_3 \to R_3 + 2R_1$$

$$\begin{bmatrix} 1 & 0 & -1 \\ 0 & 1 & 2 \\ 0 & -4 & -7 \end{bmatrix} = \begin{bmatrix} 1 & -2 & -2 \\ 0 & 1 & 1 \\ 2 & -4 & -3 \end{bmatrix} A$$ **(1 Mark)**

$$R_3 \to R_3 + 4R_2$$

$$\begin{bmatrix} 1 & 0 & -1 \\ 0 & 1 & 2 \\ 0 & 0 & 1 \end{bmatrix} = \begin{bmatrix} 1 & -2 & -2 \\ 0 & 1 & 1 \\ 2 & 0 & 1 \end{bmatrix} A$$ **(1 Mark)**

$$R_2 \to R_2 - 2R_3$$

$$\begin{bmatrix} 1 & 0 & -1 \\ 0 & 1 & 0 \\ 0 & 0 & 1 \end{bmatrix} = \begin{bmatrix} 1 & -2 & -2 \\ -4 & 1 & -1 \\ 2 & 0 & 1 \end{bmatrix} A$$ **(1 Mark)**

$$R_1 \to R_1 + R_3$$

$$\begin{bmatrix} 1 & 0 & 0 \\ 0 & 1 & 0 \\ 0 & 0 & 1 \end{bmatrix} = \begin{bmatrix} 3 & -2 & -1 \\ -4 & 1 & -1 \\ 2 & 0 & 1 \end{bmatrix} A$$ **(½ Mark)**

$$\therefore \quad A^{-1} = \begin{bmatrix} 3 & -2 & -1 \\ -4 & 1 & -1 \\ 2 & 0 & 1 \end{bmatrix}$$ **(½ Mark)**

29. Given point is $(-1, -5, -10)$

Line is $\vec{r} = 2\hat{i} - \hat{j} + 2\hat{k} + \lambda(3\hat{i} + 4\hat{j} + 2\hat{k})$

or $\dfrac{x-2}{3} = \dfrac{y+1}{4} = \dfrac{z-2}{2} = r$ (let)

$\therefore \quad x = 3r + 2, y = 4r - 1, z = 2r + 2$ **(2 Marks)**

And plane is $\vec{r} \cdot (\hat{i} - \hat{j} + \hat{k}) = 5$

or $\quad x - y + z = 5$ ... (i)

Put the point in (i)

$3r + 2 - 4r + 1 + 2r + 2 = 5$

$r + 5 = 5$

$r = 0$

$\therefore$ Required point of intersection of line and plane is $(2, -1, 2)$ **(2 Marks)**

Required distance of $(-1, -5, -10)$ from $(2, -1, 2)$ is

$$D = \sqrt{(x_2 - x_1)^2 + (y_2 - y_1)^2 + (z_2 - z_1)^2}$$

$$= \sqrt{(2+1)^2 + (-1+5)^2 + (2+10)^2}$$

$$= \sqrt{(3)^2 + 4^2 + (12)^2}$$

$$= \sqrt{9 + 16 + 144} = \sqrt{169} = 13 \text{ units}$$ **(2 Marks)**

> **Note**
>
> *Alternate method to find intersection point by substitute $\vec{r}$ from equation of line in equation plane, we get value of λ. Putting the value of λ in equation of line we get intersection point.*

All India *2017*

CBSE Board Solved Paper

Time Allowed : 3 Hours   *Maximum Marks : 100*

General Instructions:
(i) All questions are compulsory.
(ii) This question paper contains **29** questions.
(iii) Question 1-4 in **Section A** are very short-answer type questions carrying **1** mark each.
(iv) Questions 5-12 in **Section B** are short-answer type questions carrying **2** marks each.
(v) Question 13-23 in **Section C** are long-answer-**I** type questions carrying **4** marks each.
(vi) Question 24-29 in **Section D** are long answer-**II** Type Questions carrying **6** marks each.
(vii) Please write down the serial number of the Question before attempting it.

SECTION - A

1. If for any 2×2 square matrix A, $A\,(\text{adj } A) = \begin{bmatrix} 8 & 0 \\ 0 & 8 \end{bmatrix}$, then write the value of $|A|$.

2. Determine the value of 'k' for which the following function is continuous at $x = 3$:

$$f(x) = \begin{cases} \dfrac{(x+3)^2 - 36}{x-3}, & x \neq 3 \\ k, & x = 3 \end{cases}$$

3. Find : $\displaystyle \int \frac{\sin^2 x - \cos^2 x}{\sin x \cos x}\, dx$

4. Find the distance between the planes $2x - y + 2z = 5$ and $5x - 2.5y + 5z = 20$.

SECTION - B

5. If A is a skew-symmetric matrix of order 3, then prove that $\det A = 0$.

6. Find the value of c in Rolle's theorem for the function $f(x) = x^3 - 3x$ in $\left[-\sqrt{3}, 0 \right]$.

7. The volume of a cube is increasing at the rate of $9\,\text{cm}^3/\text{s}$. How fast is its surface area increasing when the length of an edge is 10 cm?

8. Show that the function $f(x) = x^3 - 3x^2 + 6x - 100$ is increasing on R.

9. The x–coordinate of a point on the line joining the points $P\,(2, 2, 1)$ and $Q\,(5, 1, -2)$ is 4. Find its z-coordinate.

10. A die, whose faces are marked 1, 2, 3 in red and 4, 5, 6 in green, is tossed. Let A be the event "number obtained is even" and B be the event "number obtained is red." Find if A and B are independent events.

11. Two tailors, A and B earn ₹ 300 and ₹ 400 per day respectively. A can stitch 6 shirts and 4 pairs of trousers while B can stitch 10 shirts and 4 pairs of trousers per day. To find how many days should each of them work and if it is desired to produce at least 60 shirts and 32 pairs of trousers at a minimum labour cost, formulate this as an LPP.

12. Find : $\displaystyle \int \frac{dx}{5 - 8x - x^2}$

SECTION - C

13. If $\tan^{-1}\dfrac{x-3}{x-4} + \tan^{-1}\dfrac{x+3}{x+4} = \dfrac{\pi}{4}$, then find the value of x.

14. Using properties of determinants, prove that

$$\begin{vmatrix} a^2 + 2a & 2a+1 & 1 \\ 2a+1 & a+2 & 1 \\ 3 & 3 & 1 \end{vmatrix} = (a-1)^3$$

OR

Find matrix A such that

$$\begin{pmatrix} 2 & -1 \\ 1 & 0 \\ -3 & 4 \end{pmatrix} A = \begin{pmatrix} -1 & -8 \\ 1 & -2 \\ 9 & 22 \end{pmatrix}$$

15. If $x^y + y^x = a^b$, then find $\dfrac{dy}{dx}$.

OR

If $e^y(x+1) = 1$, then show that $\dfrac{d^2 y}{dx^2} = \left(\dfrac{dy}{dx}\right)^2$.

16. Find: $\displaystyle\int \dfrac{\cos\theta}{(4+\sin^2\theta)(5-4\cos^2\theta)}\, d\theta$

17. Evaluate: $\displaystyle\int_0^\pi \dfrac{x\tan x}{\sec x + \tan x}\, dx$

OR

Evaluate: $\displaystyle\int_1^4 \left\{|x-1|+|x-2|+|x-4|\right\}dx$

18. Solve the differential equation $(\tan^{-1} x - y)\, dx = (1+x^2)\, dy$.

19. Show that the points A, B, C with position vectors $2\hat{i} - \hat{j} + \hat{k}, \hat{i} - 3\hat{j} - 5\hat{k}$ and $3\hat{i} - 4\hat{j} - 4\hat{k}$ respectively, are the vertices of a right-angled triangle. Hence find the area of the triangle.

20. Find the value of λ, if four points with position vectors $3\hat{i} + 6\hat{j} + 9\hat{k}, \hat{i} + 2\hat{j} + 3\hat{k}, 2\hat{i} + 3\hat{j} + \hat{k}$ and $4\hat{i} + 6\hat{j} + \lambda\hat{k}$ are coplanar.

21. There are 4 cards numbered 1, 3, 5 and 7, one number on one card. Two cards are drawn at random without replacement. Let X denote the sum of the numbers on the two drawn cards. Find the mean and variance of X.

22. Of the students in a school, it is known that 30% have 100% attendance and 70% students are irregular. Previous year results report that 70% of all students who have 100% attendance attain A grade and 10% irregular students attain A grade in their annual examination. At the end of the year, one students is chosen at random from the school and he was found to have an A grade. What is the probability that the student has 100% attendance? Is regularity required only in school? Justify your answer.

23. Maximise $Z = x + 2y$
subject to the constraints
$x + 2y \geq 100$
$2x - y \leq 0$
$2x + y \leq 200$
$x, y \geq 0$
Solve the above LPP graphically.

SECTION - D

24. Determine the product $\begin{bmatrix} -4 & 4 & 4 \\ -7 & 1 & 3 \\ 5 & -3 & -1 \end{bmatrix}\begin{bmatrix} 1 & -1 & 1 \\ 1 & -2 & -2 \\ 2 & 1 & 3 \end{bmatrix}$ and use it to solve the system of equations $x - y + z = 4$, $x - 2y - 2z = 9, 2x + y + 3z = 1$.

25. Consider $f: R - \left\{-\dfrac{4}{3}\right\} \to R - \left\{\dfrac{4}{3}\right\}$ given by

$f(x) = \dfrac{4x+3}{3x+4}$. Show that f is bijective. Find the inverse of f and hence find $f^{-1}(0)$ and x such that $f^{-1}(x) = 2$.

OR

Let $A = Q \times Q$ and let $*$ be a binary operation on A defined by $(a, b) * (c, d) = (ac, b + ad)$ for $(a, b), (c, d) \in A$. Determine, whether $*$ is commutative and associative. Then, with respect to $*$ on A
(i) find the identity element in A
(ii) find the invertible elements of A

26. Show that the surface area of a closed cuboid with square base and given volume is minimum, when it is a cube.

27. Using the method of integration, find the area of the triangle ABC, coordinates of whose vertices are A(4, 1), B(6, 6) and C(8, 4).

OR

Find the area enclosed between the parabola $4y = 3x^2$ and the straight line $3x - 2y + 12 = 0$.

28. Find the particular solution of the differential equation

$(x - y)\dfrac{dy}{dx} = (x + 2y)$, given that $y = 0$ when $x = 1$.

29. Find the coordinates of the point where the line through the points $(3, -4, -5)$ and $(2, -3, 1)$ crosses the plane determined by the points $(1, 2, 3), (4, 2, -3)$ and $(0, 4, 3)$.

OR

A variable plane which remains at a constant distance 3p from the origin cuts the coordinate axes at A, B, C. Show that the locus of the centroid of triangle ABC is

$$\dfrac{1}{x^2} + \dfrac{1}{y^2} + \dfrac{1}{z^2} = \dfrac{1}{p^2}.$$

Solutions

SECTION - A

1. Since $A(\text{adj } A) = \begin{bmatrix} 8 & 0 \\ 0 & 8 \end{bmatrix} = 8\begin{bmatrix} 1 & 0 \\ 0 & 1 \end{bmatrix}$

$\Rightarrow A(\text{adj } A) = 8\, I_2$ ...(i) **(½ Mark)**

We know that.

$A(\text{adj } A) = |A|\, I_2$ ...(ii)

From (i) and (ii)

$|A| = 8$ **(½ Mark)**

2. Since $f(x)$ is continuous at $x = 3$

$\therefore \lim\limits_{x \to 3^-} f(x) = \lim\limits_{x \to 3^+} f(x) = f(3)$ **(½ Mark)**

$\Rightarrow f(3) = \lim\limits_{x \to 3} f(x)$

$\Rightarrow k = \lim\limits_{x \to 3} \dfrac{(x+3)^2 - 36}{x-3} = \lim\limits_{x \to 3} \dfrac{(x+3)^2 - (6)^2}{x-3}$

$\Rightarrow k = \lim\limits_{x \to 3} \dfrac{(x+3-6)(x+3+6)}{(x-3)}$

$\Rightarrow k = \lim\limits_{x \to 3} \dfrac{(x-3)(x+9)}{x-3}$

$\Rightarrow k = \lim\limits_{x \to 3} (x+9) = 3 + 9$

$\Rightarrow k = 12$ **(½ Mark)**

3. $\displaystyle\int \dfrac{\sin^2 x - \cos^2 x}{\sin x - \cos x}\, dx$

$= \displaystyle\int \dfrac{\sin^2 x}{\sin x \cos x}\, dx - \int \dfrac{\cos^2 x}{\sin x \cos x}\, dx$ **(½ Mark)**

$= \displaystyle\int \tan x\, dx - \int \cot x\, dx$

$= \log|\sec x| - \log|\sin x| + C$ **(½ Mark)**

4. Since equation of planes are: $2x - y + 2z = 5$

and $5x - 2.5y + 5z = 20$

or $\quad 2x - y + 2z = 5 \,\&\, 2x - y + 2z = 8$

It is clear that these two planes are parallel planes.

The distance between the two parallel planes $ax + by + cz + d_1 = 0$ and $ax + by + cz + d_2 = 0$ is given by:

$d = \left| \dfrac{(d_2 - d_1)}{\sqrt{a^2 + b^2 + c^2}} \right|$ **(½ Mark)**

Therefore distance between two given planes is :

$d = \left| \dfrac{(5-8)}{\sqrt{2^2 + (-1)^2 + 2^2}} \right|$

$= \left| \dfrac{-3}{\sqrt{4+1+4}} \right| = \left| \dfrac{-3}{3} \right|$

$\Rightarrow \quad d = 1\,\text{unit}$ **(½ Mark)**

SECTION - B

5. Since A is a skew-symmetric matrix of order 3.

$\therefore \quad A^T = -A$

$\therefore \quad |A^T| = |-A| = |A|$

$\Rightarrow \quad |A| = |(-1)\,A|$

$\Rightarrow |A| = (-1)^3\, |A|$ **(1 Mark)**

$|kA| = k^n|A|$, where n is the order of the matrix

$\Rightarrow |A| = -|A|$

$\Rightarrow 2|A| = 0$

$\Rightarrow |A| = 0$ **(1 Mark)**

6. Since $f(x) = x^3 - 3x$

We know that polynomial function is continuous and differentiable everywhere , therefore $f(x)$ is continuous on $\left[-\sqrt{3}, 0\right]$ and differentiable on $\left(-\sqrt{3}, 0\right)$

Also, $f\left(-\sqrt{3}\right) = \left(-\sqrt{3}\right)^3 - 3\left(-\sqrt{3}\right) = -3\sqrt{3} + 3\sqrt{3} = 0$

$f(0) = (0)^3 - 3 \times 0 = 0$

As all the three conditions of Rolle's theorem are satisfied, therefore there exists a point $c \in \left(-\sqrt{3}, 0\right)$ such that $f(c) = 0$.

$f(x) = x^3 - 3x$ **(1 Mark)**

$f'(x) = 3x^2 - 3$

$\therefore f'(c) = 0$

$\Rightarrow 3c^2 - 3 = 0 \Rightarrow c^2 - 1 = 0$

$\Rightarrow (c+1)(c-1) = 0$

$\Rightarrow c = -1 \text{ or } c = 1$

Now, $c \neq 1 \left[\because 1 \notin \left(-\sqrt{3}, 0\right)\right]$

$\therefore c = -1$, where $c \in \left(-\sqrt{3}, 0\right)$

Thus -1 is the required value of c **(1 Mark)**

Note

Rolle's theorem is applicable only when function is continuous in [a, b], differentiable in (a, b) and f(a) = f(b).

7. Let x = length of one side.

$\therefore$ Volume $= V = x^3$ (say)

Surface area $= S = 6x^2$.

Also $\dfrac{dV}{dt} = 9 \text{ cm}^3/\text{sec}$ (given)

$$\Rightarrow 9 = \frac{dV}{dt} = \frac{d(x^3)}{dt} = 3x^2 \cdot \frac{dx}{dt}$$

$$\Rightarrow \frac{dx}{dt} = \frac{3}{x^2} \qquad ...(i)$$ **(1 Mark)**

Also, $\dfrac{dS}{dt} = \dfrac{d(6x^2)}{dt} = 12x \cdot \dfrac{dx}{dt}$

$$= 12x \cdot \frac{3}{x^2} \qquad \text{From (i)}$$

$$= \frac{36}{x}$$

$$\Rightarrow \frac{dS}{dt} = 3.6 \, \text{cm}^2/\text{sec} \qquad (\because x = 10\,\text{cm}).$$ **(1 Mark)**

8. Since $f(x) = x^3 - 3x^2 + 6x - 100$

$\therefore f'(x) = 3x^2 - 6x + 6$ **(1 Mark)**

$\qquad = 3(x^2 - 2x + 2)$

$\qquad = 3(x^2 - 2x + 1) + 3$

$\qquad = 3(x-1)^2 + 3 \geq 0 \quad \forall x \in R$

$\therefore f'(x) > 0 \quad \forall x \in R$

Hence, the given function is increasing on R. **(1 Mark)**

9. Let R be the point dividing PQ in the ratio $\lambda : 1$.

Then, the coordinates of R will be

$$\left(\frac{5\lambda + 2}{\lambda + 1}, \frac{\lambda + 2}{\lambda + 1}, \frac{-2\lambda + 1}{\lambda + 1} \right)$$ **(1 Mark)**

$$\overset{\lambda \qquad R \qquad 1}{\underline{\hspace{8cm}}}$$
P(2, 2, 1) $\qquad\qquad\qquad$ Q(5, 1, –2)

Since x-coordinate of R is 4.

$$\therefore \frac{5\lambda + 2}{\lambda + 1} = 4$$

$$\Rightarrow 5\lambda + 2 = 4\lambda + 4$$

$$\Rightarrow 5\lambda - 4\lambda = 4 - 2$$

$$\Rightarrow \lambda = 2$$

$$\therefore z\text{–coordinate of R} = \frac{-2\lambda + 1}{\lambda + 1} = \frac{-2 \times 2 + 1}{2 + 1} = \frac{-3}{3} = -1$$

Hence, the z–coordinate of the point is –1. **(1 Mark)**

10. Total number of outcomes = 6

The outcomes in favour of the event A are 2, 4, 6.

$\therefore$ Number of outcomes in favour of event A = 3

$$\therefore P(A) = \frac{3}{6} = \frac{1}{2}$$ **(½ Mark)**

The outcomes in favour of the event B are 1, 2, 3.

$\therefore$ Number of outcomes in favour of event B = 3

$$\therefore P(B) = \frac{3}{6} = \frac{1}{2}$$ **(½ Mark)**

$$\therefore P(A)P(B) = \frac{1}{2} \times \frac{1}{2} = \frac{1}{4}$$ **(½ Mark)**

Now,

$A \cap B$ is the event "number obtained is even and red".

The outcomes in favour of the event $A \cap B$ is 2.

$\therefore$ Number of outcomes in favour of event $A \cap B = 1$

$$\therefore P(A \cap B) = \frac{1}{6} \neq P(A)\,P(B)$$ **(½ Mark)**

Therefore, the events A and B are not independent events.

11. Let tailor A & B work for x and y days respectively.

In one day, A can stitch 6 shirts and 4 pairs of trousers Whereas B can stitch 10 shirts and 4 pairs of trousers.

Thus, in x days A can stitch 6x shirts and 4x pairs of trousers, and in y days B can stitch 10y shirts and 4y pairs of trousers. Since the minimum requirement of the shirts and pairs of trousers are 60 and 32 respectively.

$\therefore 6x + 10y \geq 60$

$4x + 4y \geq 32$

Also A and B earns ₹ 300 and ₹ 400 per day respectively.

Let Z denotes the total cost

$\therefore Z = \text{Rs}\,(300\,x + 400\,y)$

Number of days cannot be negative.

$\therefore x, y \geq 0$

Hence, the required LPP is given as :

Minimize $Z = 300x + 400y$ **(½ Mark)**

Subject to

$6x + 10y \geq 60$ **(½ Mark)**

$4x + 4y \geq 32$ **(½ Mark)**

$x \geq 0, y \geq 0$ **(½ Mark)**

12. $\displaystyle \int \frac{dx}{5 - 8x - x^2}$

$$= \int \frac{dx}{5 - (8x + x^2)}$$

$$= \int \frac{dx}{5 - (x^2 + 8x + 16 - 16)}$$

$$= \int \frac{dx}{21 - (x + 4)^2}$$ **(1 Mark)**

$$= \int \frac{dx}{\left(\sqrt{21}\right)^2 - (x + 4)^2}$$

$$= \frac{1}{2\sqrt{21}} \log \left| \frac{\sqrt{21} + (x + 4)}{\sqrt{21} - (x + 4)} \right| + C$$

$$= \frac{1}{2\sqrt{21}} \log\left|\frac{\sqrt{21}+x+4}{\sqrt{21}-x-4}\right| + C \qquad \textbf{(1 Mark)}$$

Note

If there is quadratic equation in denominator, then to solve integeration, make perfect square of that equation.

SECTION - C

13. Since; $\tan^{-1}\dfrac{x-3}{x-4} + \tan^{-1}\dfrac{x+3}{x+4} = \dfrac{\pi}{4}$

$\Rightarrow \tan^{-1}\dfrac{x-3}{x-4} = \dfrac{\pi}{4} - \tan^{-1}\dfrac{x+3}{x+4}$

$\Rightarrow \tan^{-1}\dfrac{x-3}{x-4} = \tan^{-1}1 - \tan^{-1}\dfrac{x+3}{x+4} \qquad \textbf{(1 Mark)}$

$\Rightarrow \tan^{-1}\dfrac{x-3}{x-4} = \tan^{-1}\left(\dfrac{1-\dfrac{x+3}{x+4}}{1+\dfrac{x+3}{x+4}}\right) \qquad \textbf{(1 Mark)}$

$$\left[\because \tan^{-1}A - \tan^{-1}B = \tan^{-1}\left(\dfrac{A-B}{1+AB}\right)\right]$$

$\Rightarrow \tan^{-1}\dfrac{x-3}{x-4} = \tan^{-1}\left(\dfrac{\dfrac{x+4-x-3}{x+4}}{\dfrac{x+4+x+3}{x+4}}\right)$

$\Rightarrow \tan^{-1}\dfrac{x-3}{x-4} = \tan^{-1}\left(\dfrac{1}{2x+7}\right)$

$\Rightarrow \dfrac{x-3}{x-4} = \dfrac{1}{2x+7} \qquad \textbf{(1 Mark)}$

$\Rightarrow (x-3)(2x+7) = x-4$

$\Rightarrow 2x^2 + x - 21 = x - 4$

$\Rightarrow 2x^2 = 17$

$\Rightarrow x = \pm\sqrt{\dfrac{17}{2}} \qquad \textbf{(1 Mark)}$

14. Let $\Delta = \begin{vmatrix} a^2+2a & 2a+1 & 1 \\ 2a+1 & a+2 & 1 \\ 3 & 3 & 1 \end{vmatrix}$

Applying $R_1 \to R_1 - R_3$ and $R_2 \to R_2 - R_3$

$$\Delta = \begin{vmatrix} a^2+2a-3 & 2a-2 & 0 \\ 2a-2 & a-1 & 0 \\ 3 & 3 & 1 \end{vmatrix} \qquad \textbf{(1 Mark)}$$

$$\Rightarrow \quad \Delta = \begin{vmatrix} (a+3)(a-1) & 2(a-1) & 0 \\ 2(a-1) & a-1 & 0 \\ 3 & 3 & 1 \end{vmatrix}$$

$$\Rightarrow \quad \Delta = (a-1)^2 \begin{vmatrix} (a+3) & 2 & 0 \\ 2 & 1 & 0 \\ 3 & 3 & 1 \end{vmatrix} \qquad \textbf{(2 Marks)}$$

Expanding along C_3

$\therefore \quad \Delta = (a-1)^2 [0-0+1\times(a+3-4)]$

$\Rightarrow \quad \Delta = (a-1)^3 \qquad \textbf{(1 Mark)}$

OR

$$\begin{bmatrix} 2 & -1 \\ 1 & 0 \\ -3 & 4 \end{bmatrix} A = \begin{bmatrix} -1 & -8 \\ 1 & -2 \\ 9 & 22 \end{bmatrix}$$

Here 3×2 matrix is multiplied with A and the result is 3×2 matrix so, A is a 2×2 matrix

& let $A = \begin{bmatrix} x & y \\ a & b \end{bmatrix} \qquad \textbf{(1 Mark)}$

$$\therefore \begin{bmatrix} 2 & -1 \\ 1 & 0 \\ -3 & 4 \end{bmatrix}\begin{bmatrix} x & y \\ a & b \end{bmatrix} = \begin{bmatrix} -1 & -8 \\ 1 & -2 \\ 9 & 22 \end{bmatrix}$$

$$\begin{bmatrix} 2x-a & 2y-b \\ x & y \\ -3x+4a & -3y+4b \end{bmatrix} = \begin{bmatrix} -1 & -8 \\ 1 & -2 \\ 9 & 22 \end{bmatrix} \qquad \textbf{(1 Mark)}$$

On equating the corresponding elements of the two matrices, we get:

$2x - a = -1$

$2y - b = -8$

$x = 1$

$y = -2$

On solving the above equations , we get a = 3 and b = 4

$$\therefore A = \begin{bmatrix} 1 & -2 \\ 3 & 4 \end{bmatrix} \qquad \textbf{(2 Marks)}$$

15. Let $u = x^y$ and $v = y^x$

Then $u + v = a^b$

On differentiating both the sides w.r.t.x, we get

$$\frac{du}{dx} + \frac{dv}{dx} = 0 \qquad \qquad .....(i)$$

Now, $u = x^y$

Taking logarithm on both the sides

$\Rightarrow \log u = y \log x$

On differentiating w.r.t.x, we have

$$\Rightarrow \frac{1}{u}\frac{du}{dx} = y \times \frac{1}{x} + \log x \frac{dy}{dx}$$

$$\Rightarrow \frac{du}{dx} = u\left(\frac{y}{x} + \log x \frac{dy}{dx}\right) \Rightarrow \frac{du}{dx} = x^y\left(\frac{y + x\log x \dfrac{dy}{dx}}{x}\right)$$

$$\Rightarrow \frac{du}{dx} = x^{y-1}\left(y + x\log x \frac{dy}{dx}\right) \qquad ...(ii) \qquad \textbf{(1½ Marks)}$$

Now, $v = y^x$

Taking logarithm on both the sides

$\Rightarrow \log v = x \log y$

On differentiating w.r.t. x, we have

$$\Rightarrow \frac{1}{v}\frac{dv}{dx} = x \times \frac{1}{y} \times \frac{dy}{dx} + \log y$$

$$\Rightarrow \frac{dv}{dx} = v\left(\frac{x}{y} \times \frac{dy}{dx} + \log y\right) \Rightarrow \frac{dv}{dx} = y^x\left(\frac{x \times \dfrac{dy}{dx} + y\log y}{y}\right)$$

$$\Rightarrow \frac{dv}{dx} = y^{x-1}\left(x\frac{dy}{dx} + y\log y\right) \qquad ....(iii) \qquad \textbf{(1½ Marks)}$$

From equations (i), (ii) and (iii), we have

$$x^{y-1}\left(y + x\log x \frac{dy}{dx}\right) + y^{x-1}\left(x\frac{dy}{dx} + y\log y\right) = 0$$

$$\Rightarrow x^{y-1}y + x^y\log x\frac{dy}{dx} + xy^{x-1}\frac{dy}{dx} + y^x\log y = 0$$

$$\Rightarrow (x^y\log x + xy^{x-1})\frac{dy}{dx} = -(y^x\log y + x^{y-1}y)$$

$$\Rightarrow \frac{dy}{dx} = \frac{-(y^x\log y + x^{y-1}y)}{x^y\log x + xy^{x-1}} \qquad \textbf{(1 Mark)}$$

OR

Since $e^y(x+1) = 1$

$$\Rightarrow x+1 = \frac{1}{e^y}$$

$$\Rightarrow x+1 = e^{-y} \qquad ....(i) \qquad \textbf{(1 Mark)}$$

Differentiate equation (i) with respect to x, we get

$$\frac{dx}{dx} + \frac{d(1)}{dx} = \frac{d(e^{-y})}{dx}$$

$$\Rightarrow \quad 1 + 0 = -e^{-y} \times \frac{dy}{dx}$$

$$\Rightarrow \quad 1 = -\frac{1}{e^y} \times \frac{dy}{dx}$$

$$\Rightarrow \quad \frac{dy}{dx} = -e^y \qquad ...(ii) \qquad \textbf{(1 Mark)}$$

Again differentiating (ii) with respect to x, we get

$$\frac{d^2y}{dx^2} = -e^y\frac{dy}{dx}$$

$$\Rightarrow \frac{d^2y}{dx^2} = \frac{dy}{dx} \times \frac{dy}{dx} \qquad \qquad ...\text{From (ii)}$$

$$\Rightarrow \frac{d^2y}{dx^2} = \left(\frac{dy}{dx}\right)^2$$

Hence proved $\qquad \qquad \textbf{(2 Marks)}$

16. Let $I = \displaystyle\int \frac{\cos\theta}{(4 + \sin^2\theta)(5 - 4\cos^2\theta)}d\theta$

$$= \int \frac{\cos\theta}{(4 + \sin^2\theta)(5 - 4(1 - \sin^2\theta))}d\theta$$

$$= \int \frac{\cos\theta}{(4 + \sin^2\theta)(1 + 4\sin^2\theta)}d\theta \qquad ....(i) \qquad \textbf{(½ Mark)}$$

Let $\sin\theta = t \Rightarrow \cos\theta d\theta = dt$

So, equation (i) becomes $I = \displaystyle\int \frac{dt}{(4 + t^2)(1 + 4t^2)} \quad ...(ii) \; \textbf{(½ Mark)}$

Let, $t^2 = y$

$$\frac{1}{(4+y)(1+4y)} = \frac{A}{(4+y)} + \frac{B}{(1+4y)} \text{ (by partial fraction)}$$

$$\Rightarrow 1 = A(1 + 4y) + B(4 + y)$$

$$\Rightarrow A = \frac{-1}{15}, B = \frac{4}{15} \qquad \textbf{(½ Mark)}$$

Putting the values of A & B in (ii), we get

$$I = \int \left[\dfrac{\dfrac{-1}{15}}{4+t^2} + \dfrac{\dfrac{4}{15}}{1+4t^2} \right] dt$$

$$\Rightarrow I = \dfrac{-1}{15} \int \dfrac{dt}{4+t^2} + \dfrac{4}{15} \int \dfrac{dt}{1+4t^2} \qquad \textbf{(½ Mark)}$$

$$\Rightarrow I = \dfrac{-1}{15} \int \dfrac{dt}{4+t^2} + \dfrac{4}{15} \int \dfrac{dt}{4\left(\dfrac{1}{4}+t^2\right)}$$

$$\Rightarrow I = \dfrac{-1}{15} \int \dfrac{dt}{4+t^2} + \dfrac{1}{15} \int \dfrac{dt}{\left(\dfrac{1}{4}+t^2\right)}$$

$$\Rightarrow I = \dfrac{-1}{15} \left[\dfrac{1}{2} \tan^{-1} \dfrac{t}{2} \right] + \dfrac{1}{15}\left[2 \tan^{-1} 2t \right] + C$$

$$\left[\because \int \dfrac{dx}{a^2+x^2} = \dfrac{1}{a} \tan^{-1} \dfrac{x}{a} + C \right]$$

$$\Rightarrow I = \dfrac{-1}{30} \tan^{-1}\left(\dfrac{\sin\theta}{2} \right) + \dfrac{2}{15} \tan^{-1}(2\sin\theta) + C$$

$$(\because t = \sin\theta) \qquad \textbf{(2 Marks)}$$

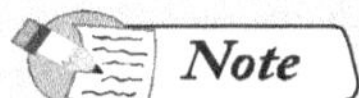 **Note**

For integral of function in the form $\dfrac{1}{(x^2+a)(x^2+b)}$ *be take*
$x^2 = y$ *and split using partical fraction then put* $y = x^2$ *before integration.*

17. Let $I = \displaystyle\int_0^\pi \dfrac{x\tan x}{\sec x + \tan x} dx \qquad \text{...(i)}$

$$I = \int_0^\pi \left\{ \dfrac{(\pi-x)\tan(\pi-x)}{\sec(\pi-x)+\tan(\pi-x)} \right\} dx \qquad \textbf{(½ Mark)}$$

$$\left(\because \int_0^\pi f(x)dx = \int_0^\pi f(a-x)dx \right)$$

$$\Rightarrow I = \int_0^\pi \left\{ \dfrac{-(\pi-x)\tan x}{-(\sec x + \tan x)} \right\} dx$$

$$\Rightarrow I = \int_0^\pi \dfrac{(\pi-x)\tan x}{\sec x + \tan x} dx \qquad \text{...(ii)}$$

Adding (i) and (ii), we get,

$$2I = \int_0^\pi \dfrac{\pi\tan x}{\sec x + \tan x} dx \qquad \textbf{(1 Mark)}$$

$$\Rightarrow 2I = \pi\int_0^\pi \dfrac{\dfrac{\sin x}{\cos x}}{\dfrac{1}{\cos x} + \dfrac{\sin x}{\cos x}} dx$$

$$\Rightarrow 2I = \pi\int_0^\pi \dfrac{\sin x + 1 - 1}{1 + \sin x} dx$$

$$\Rightarrow 2I = \pi\int_0^\pi 1.dx - \pi\int_0^x \dfrac{1}{1+\sin x} dx \qquad \textbf{(½ Mark)}$$

$$\Rightarrow 2I = \pi[x]_0^\pi - \pi\int_0^\pi \dfrac{1-\sin x}{\cos^2 x} dx$$

$$2I = \pi^2 - \pi\int_0^\pi \left(\dfrac{1}{\cos^2 x} - \dfrac{\sin x}{\cos x}\cdot\dfrac{1}{\cos x} \right) dx$$

$$\Rightarrow 2I = \pi^2 - \pi\int_0^\pi (\sec^2 x - \tan x \sec x)\,dx$$

$$\Rightarrow 2I = \pi^2 - \pi[\tan x - \sec x]_0^\pi$$

$$\Rightarrow 2I = \pi^2 - \pi[\tan\pi - \sec\pi - \tan 0 + \sec 0]$$

$$\Rightarrow 2I = \pi^2 - \pi[0-(-1)-0+1]$$

$$\Rightarrow 2I = \pi^2 - 2\pi$$

$$\Rightarrow 2I = \pi(\pi-2)$$

$$\Rightarrow I = \dfrac{\pi}{2}(\pi-2) \qquad \textbf{(2 Marks)}$$

OR

Suppose $I = \displaystyle\int_1^4 \left(|x-1| + |x-2| + |x-4| \right) dx$

$$\Rightarrow I = \int_1^4 |x-1|\,dx + \int_1^4 |x-2|\,dx + \int_1^4 |x-4|\,dx$$

Now,

$$|x-1| = \begin{cases} -(x-1), & x \le 1 \\ x-1, & 1 < x \le 4 \end{cases}$$

$$|x-2| = \begin{cases} -(x-2), & 1 \le x \le 2 \\ x-2, & 2 < x \le 4 \end{cases}$$

$$|x-4| = \begin{cases} -(x-4), & 1 \le x \le 4 \\ x-4, & x > 4 \end{cases} \qquad \textbf{(1 Mark)}$$

$$\therefore I = \int_1^4 (x-1)dx - \int_1^2 (x-2)dx + \int_2^4 (x-2)dx - \int_1^4 (x-4)dx$$

$$\textbf{(1 Mark)}$$

$$\Rightarrow I = \left[\frac{x^2}{2} - x\right]_1^4 - \left[\frac{x^2}{2} - 2x\right]_1^2 + \left[\frac{x^2}{2} - 2x\right]_2^4 - \left[\frac{x^2}{2} - 4x\right]_1^4$$

(1 Mark)

$$\Rightarrow I = \left[(8-4) - \left(\frac{1}{2} - 1\right)\right] - \left[(2-4) - \left(\frac{1}{2} - 2\right)\right] +$$

$$\left[(8-8) - (2-4)\right] - \left[(8-16) - \left(\frac{1}{2} - 4\right)\right]$$

$$\Rightarrow I = \frac{9}{2} + \frac{1}{2} + 2 + \frac{9}{2}$$

$$\Rightarrow I = \frac{23}{2}$$

(1 Mark)

Note

Always there are two possible ways of function in between mod. Function can be positive or negative. So while solving integration take all possible ways of it.

18. Since $(\tan^{-1}x - y)\,dx = (1+x^2)\,dy$

$$\Rightarrow \quad (1+x^2)\frac{dy}{dx} + y = \tan^{-1} x$$

$$\Rightarrow \quad \frac{dy}{dx} + \frac{y}{1+x^2} = \frac{\tan^{-1} x}{1+x^2} \qquad ....(i)$$

Thus, it is clear that equation (i) is a linear differential equation of the form

$$\frac{dy}{dx} + Py = Q$$

where, $P = \dfrac{1}{1+x^2} \,\&\, Q = \dfrac{\tan^{-1} x}{1+x^2}$ **(1 Mark)**

$$\therefore \text{I.F.} = e^{\int P dx} = e^{\int \frac{1}{1+x^2}dx}$$

$$\Rightarrow \text{I.F.} = e^{\tan^{-1}x}$$

(1 Mark)

I.F. $y = \int Q \cdot \text{I.F.}\, dx + C$

$$e^{\tan^{-1}x} y = \int \frac{\tan^{-1} x \times e^{\tan^{-1} x}}{1+x^2} dx + C \qquad ...(ii)$$

Let, $I = \displaystyle\int \frac{\tan^{-1} x \times e^{\tan^{-1} x}}{1+x^2} dx$

Put $\tan^{-1} x = t$

$$\Rightarrow \frac{1}{1+x^2} dx = dt$$

$$\therefore I = \int t e^t dt$$

$$= t\int e^t dt - \int\left[\frac{d}{dt}(t)\int e^t dt\right]dt$$

$$= te^t - e^t = (t-1)e^t$$

$$= (\tan^{-1} x - 1)e^{\tan^{-1} x}$$

On substituting the value of I in (ii), we get

$$e^{\tan^{-1}x} y = (\tan^{-1}x - 1)e^{\tan^{-1x}} + C$$

$$\Rightarrow y = \tan^{-1} x - 1 + Ce^{-\tan^{-1}x} \qquad .....(iii) \quad \textbf{(2 Marks)}$$

Hence, equation (iii) is the required solution.

19. Since

$$\overrightarrow{OA} = 2\hat{i} - \hat{j} + \hat{k},\ \overrightarrow{OB} = \hat{i} - 3\hat{j} - 5\hat{k} \text{ and } \overrightarrow{OC} = 3\hat{i} - 4\hat{j} - 4\hat{k}$$

And $\overrightarrow{AB}, \overrightarrow{BC}, \overrightarrow{CA}$ represent the sides of $\triangle ABC$

$$\therefore \overrightarrow{AB} = (1-2)\hat{i} + (-3+1)\hat{j} + (-5-1)\hat{k} = -\hat{i} - 2\hat{j} - 6\hat{k}$$

(1 Mark)

$$\Rightarrow |\overrightarrow{AB}| = \sqrt{(-1)^2 + (-2)^2 + (-6^2)} = \sqrt{1+4+36} = \sqrt{41}$$

$$\overrightarrow{BC} = (3-1)\hat{i} + (-4+3)\hat{j} + (-4+5)\hat{k} = 2\hat{i} - \hat{j} + \hat{k}$$

$$\Rightarrow |\overrightarrow{BC}| = \sqrt{(2)^2 + (-1)^2 + (1)^2} = \sqrt{4+1+1} = \sqrt{6} \ \textbf{(1 Mark)}$$

$$\overrightarrow{CA} = (2-3)\hat{i} + (-1+4)\hat{j} + (1+4)\hat{k} = -\hat{i} + 3\hat{j} + 5\hat{k}$$

$$\Rightarrow |\overrightarrow{CA}| = \sqrt{(-1)^2 + (3)^2 + (5)^2} = \sqrt{1+9+25} = \sqrt{35}$$

$$\therefore |\overrightarrow{BC}|^2 + |\overrightarrow{CA}|^2 = 6 + 35 = 41 = |\overrightarrow{AB}|^2 \qquad \textbf{(1 Mark)}$$

Hence, $\triangle ABC$ is a right-angled triangle.

Area of $\triangle ABC$

$$= \frac{1}{2} \times \text{Base} \times \text{Altitude}$$

$$= \frac{1}{2} \times |\overrightarrow{BC}| \times |\overrightarrow{CA}|$$

$$= \frac{1}{2} \times \sqrt{6} \times \sqrt{35} = \sqrt{\frac{105}{2}} \text{ sq. units.} \qquad \textbf{(1 Mark)}$$

20. Let $\overrightarrow{OA} = 3\hat{i} + 6\hat{j} + 9\hat{k}$

$$\overrightarrow{OB} = \hat{i} + 2\hat{j} + 3\hat{k}$$

$$\overrightarrow{OC} = 2\hat{i} + 3\hat{j} + \hat{k} \ \& \ \overrightarrow{OD} = 4\hat{i} + 6\hat{j} + \lambda\hat{k}$$

$$\therefore \overrightarrow{AB} = (\hat{i} + 2\hat{j} + 3\hat{k}) - (3\hat{i} + 6\hat{j} + 9\hat{k}) = -2\hat{i} - 4\hat{j} - 6\hat{k}$$

$$\overrightarrow{AC} = (2\hat{i} + 3\hat{j} + \hat{k}) - (3\hat{i} + 6\hat{j} + 9\hat{k}) = -\hat{i} - 3\hat{j} - 8\hat{k}$$

$$\overrightarrow{AD} = (4\hat{i} + 6\hat{j} + \lambda\hat{k}) - (3\hat{i} + 6\hat{j} + 9\hat{k}) = \hat{i} + (\lambda - 9)\hat{k}$$

Since the given four points are coplanar.   **(1 Mark)**

Therefore $\overrightarrow{AB}, \overrightarrow{AC}$ & $\overrightarrow{AD}$ are also coplanar .

$$\therefore \left[\overrightarrow{AB}\,\overrightarrow{AC}\,\overrightarrow{AD} \right] = 0 \qquad\qquad \textbf{(1 Mark)}$$

$$\Rightarrow \begin{vmatrix} -2 & -4 & -6 \\ -1 & -3 & -8 \\ 1 & 0 & \lambda - 9 \end{vmatrix} = 0$$

$$\Rightarrow -2(-3\lambda + 27) + 4(-\lambda + 9 + 8) - 6(3) = 0$$

$$\Rightarrow 6\lambda - 54 - 4\lambda + 68 - 18 = 0$$

$$\Rightarrow 2\lambda - 4 = 0$$

$$\Rightarrow \lambda = 2 \qquad\qquad \textbf{(2 Marks)}$$

21. Here X can take the values 4, 6, 8, 10 and 12

Now, P $(X = 4)$ = Probability of getting 4 as sum

= P [(Getting 1 in the first draw and 3 in the second draw)
or (Getting 3 in the first draw and 1 in the second draw)]

$$= \frac{1}{4} \times \frac{1}{3} + \frac{1}{4} \times \frac{1}{3} = \frac{2}{12} = \frac{1}{6}$$

Similarly,

$$P(X = 6) = \frac{1}{4} \times \frac{1}{3} + \frac{1}{4} \times \frac{1}{3} = \frac{2}{12} = \frac{1}{6} \qquad \{\because (1,5)(5,1)\}$$

$$P(X = 8) = \frac{1}{4} \times \frac{1}{3} + \frac{1}{4} \times \frac{1}{3} + \frac{1}{4} \times \frac{1}{3} + \frac{1}{4} \times \frac{1}{3} = \frac{4}{12} = \frac{2}{6}$$

$$\{\because (1,7)(3,5)(5,3)(7,1)\}$$

$$P(X = 10) = \frac{1}{4} \times \frac{1}{3} + \frac{1}{4} \times \frac{1}{3} = \frac{2}{12} = \frac{1}{6} \qquad \{\because (3,7)(7,3)\}$$

$$P(X = 12) = \frac{1}{4} \times \frac{1}{3} + \frac{1}{4} \times \frac{1}{3} = \frac{2}{12} = \frac{1}{6} \qquad \{\because (7,5)(5,7)\}$$

(2 Marks)

Thus, the probability distribution of X is given below.

X	4	6	8	10	12
$P(X)$	$\frac{1}{6}$	$\frac{1}{6}$	$\frac{2}{6}$	$\frac{1}{6}$	$\frac{1}{6}$

$$\sum p_i = \frac{1}{6} + \frac{1}{6} + \frac{2}{6} + \frac{1}{6} + \frac{1}{6} = \frac{6}{6} = 1$$

Now, $\displaystyle\sum p_i x_i = \frac{1}{6} \times 4 + \frac{1}{6} \times 6 + \frac{2}{6} \times 8 + \frac{1}{6} \times 10 + \frac{1}{6} \times 12$

$$= \frac{1}{6} \times (4 + 6 + 16 + 10 + 12)$$

$$= \frac{1}{6} \times 48 = 8$$

$$\therefore \quad \text{Mean } [E(X)] = \frac{\sum p_i x_i}{\sum p_i} = \frac{8}{1} = 8 \qquad \textbf{(1 Mark)}$$

$$\sum p_i x_i^2 = \frac{1}{6} \times 16 + \frac{1}{6} \times 36 + \frac{2}{6} \times 64 + \frac{1}{6} \times 100 + \frac{1}{6} \times 144$$

$$= \frac{1}{6} \times (16 + 36 + 128 + 100 + 144)$$

$$= \frac{1}{6} \times 424 = \frac{212}{3}$$

$$\text{Variance} = \sum p_i x_i^2 - \left(\sum p_i x_i \right)^2 \Rightarrow \sum P_i x_1^2 - (\text{Mean})^2$$

$$\Rightarrow \frac{212}{3} - 64 = \frac{212 - 192}{3} = \frac{20}{3}$$

(1 Mark)

 **Note**

A distribution is a probability distribution of a random variable
X, (i) $\Sigma P(X) = 1$ (ii) $O < P(X) < 1$.

22. Let E_1 : the event that the student has 100% attendance

E_2 the event that the student does not has 100% attendance

A : the event that student gets grade A

So,

$$P(E_1) = \frac{30}{100}$$

$$P\left(\frac{A}{E_1}\right) = \frac{70}{100}$$

$$P(E_2) = \frac{70}{100}$$

$$P\left(\frac{A}{E_2}\right) = \frac{10}{100} \qquad \textbf{(1 Mark)}$$

Using Baye's theorem, we have
Required probability

= Probability that the student has 100% attendance given that he was found to have an A grade

$$= P\left(\frac{E_1}{A}\right) = \frac{P(E_1)\,P\left(\dfrac{A}{E_1}\right)}{P(E_1)\,P\left(\dfrac{A}{E_1}\right) + P(E_2)\,P\left(\dfrac{A}{E_2}\right)}$$ **(1 Mark)**

$$= \frac{\dfrac{30}{100} \times \dfrac{70}{100}}{\dfrac{30}{100} \times \dfrac{70}{100} + \dfrac{70}{100} \times \dfrac{10}{100}} = \frac{21}{28} = \frac{3}{4}$$ **(1 Mark)**

No, regularity is not required only in school but also in colleges, offices and even in day to day life. Suppose a person jobs everyday and if he misses a day, he will feel layness all day long. Thus regularity is needs everywhere and in everything. **(1 Mark)**

23. Since $x + 2y \geq 100, 2x + y \leq 200, 2x - y \leq 0, x \geq 0, y \geq 0$.

Converting the given inequations into equation, we have

$x + 2y = 100, 2x + y = 200, 2x - y = 0, x = 0, y = 0$

The line x + 2y = 100 meets the x- axis at $A_1(100, 0)$ and y-axis $B_1\ (0, 50)$. Join these points to obtain the line. $x + 2y = 100$. It is clear that $(0,0)$ does not satisfy the inequation $x + 2y \geq 100$. Thus, the region not containing the origin represents the solution set of the inequation $x - 2y \geq 100$.

The line $2x + y = 200$ meets the X-axis at $A_1(100, 0)$ and Y-axis $B_2\ (0, 200)$. Join these points to obtain the line $2x + y = 200$. It is clear that $(0, 0)$ satisfies the inequation $2x + y \leq 200$. Thus, the region containing the origin represents the solution set of the inequation $2x + y \leq 200$.

The line $2x - y = 0$ is the line that passes through the origin.

Point of intersection of line 2x − y = 0 with line $2x + y = 200$ is R $(50,100)$

Point of intersection of line 2x − y = 0 with line x + 2y = 100 is Q $(20, 40)$

For $x \geq 0$ and $y \geq 0$, the first quadrant is the region represented by the inequations $x \geq 0$ and $y \geq 0$.

The feasible region determined by the system of constraints is shown below. **(2 Marks)**

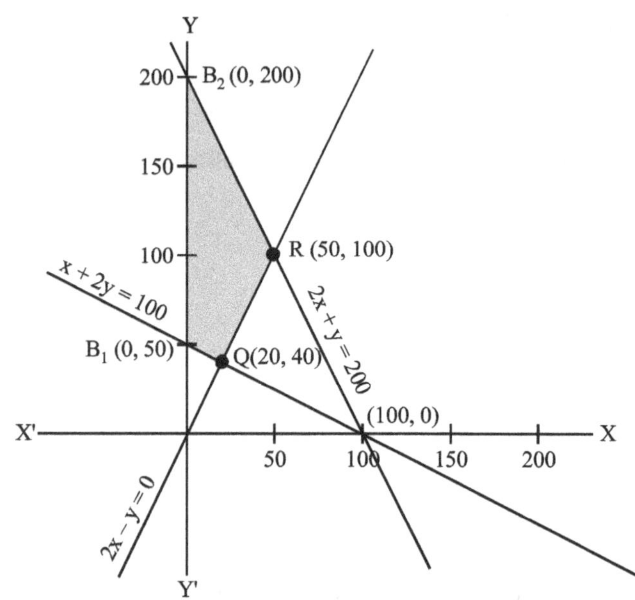

(1 Mark)

The corner points of the feasible region are $B_1(0,50), B_2(0,200), R(50,100)$ and $Q(20,40)$.

The values of Z at these corner points are as follows.

Corner points	Value of the objective function
	$Z = x + 2y$
$B_1(0,50)$	$Z = 0 + 2 \times 50 = 100$
$B_2(0.200)$	$Z = 0 + 2 \times 200 = 400 \text{(maximum)}$
$R(50, 100)$	$Z = 50 + 2 \times 100 = 250$
$Q(20.40)$	$Z = 20 + 2 \times 40 = 100$

Thus the maximum value of the objective function Z is 400 which is obtained at $x = 0$ and $y = 200$. **(1 Mark)**

 **Note**

If in equality has sign of greater than or equal to (≥) than shade the upward portion of the line in graph. If sign is of less than equal to (≤) then shade the downward portion of the line.

SECTION - D

24. Let $A = \begin{bmatrix} 1 & -1 & 1 \\ 1 & -2 & -2 \\ 2 & 1 & -3 \end{bmatrix}$ and $B = \begin{bmatrix} -4 & 4 & 4 \\ -7 & 1 & 3 \\ 5 & -3 & -1 \end{bmatrix}$

$\therefore\ BA = \begin{bmatrix} -4 & 4 & 4 \\ -7 & 1 & 3 \\ 5 & -3 & -1 \end{bmatrix}\begin{bmatrix} 1 & -1 & 1 \\ 1 & -2 & -2 \\ 2 & 1 & 3 \end{bmatrix}$

$$\Rightarrow BA = \begin{bmatrix} -4+4+8 & 4-8+4 & -4-8+12 \\ -7+1+6 & 7-2+3 & -7-2+9 \\ 5-3-2 & -5+6-1 & 5+6-3 \end{bmatrix}$$

$$\Rightarrow BA = \begin{bmatrix} 8 & 0 & 0 \\ 0 & 8 & 0 \\ 0 & 0 & 8 \end{bmatrix} \Rightarrow BA = 8\begin{bmatrix} 1 & 0 & 0 \\ 0 & 1 & 0 \\ 0 & 0 & 1 \end{bmatrix}$$

$$\Rightarrow BA = 8I_3 \qquad \textbf{(2 Marks)}$$

$$\Rightarrow \frac{1}{8}BA = I_3$$

$$\Rightarrow \left(\frac{1}{8}B\right)A = I_3$$

$$\Rightarrow A^{-1} = \frac{1}{8}B$$

$$\Rightarrow A^{-1} = \frac{1}{8}\begin{bmatrix} -4 & 4 & 4 \\ -7 & 1 & 3 \\ 5 & -3 & -1 \end{bmatrix} \qquad \textbf{(1 Mark)}$$

The given system of equations can be written in matrix form as

$$\begin{bmatrix} 1 & -1 & 1 \\ 1 & -2 & -2 \\ 2 & 1 & 3 \end{bmatrix}\begin{bmatrix} x \\ y \\ z \end{bmatrix} = \begin{bmatrix} 4 \\ 9 \\ 1 \end{bmatrix}$$

or $AX = D$, where $A = \begin{bmatrix} 1 & -1 & 1 \\ 1 & -2 & -2 \\ 2 & 1 & 3 \end{bmatrix}, X = \begin{bmatrix} x \\ y \\ z \end{bmatrix}$ and $D = \begin{bmatrix} 4 \\ 9 \\ 1 \end{bmatrix}$

$$\Rightarrow X = A^{-1}D \qquad \textbf{(1 Mark)}$$

$$\Rightarrow X = \frac{1}{8}\begin{bmatrix} -4 & 4 & 4 \\ -7 & 1 & 3 \\ 5 & -3 & -1 \end{bmatrix}\begin{bmatrix} 4 \\ 9 \\ 1 \end{bmatrix}$$

$$\Rightarrow \begin{bmatrix} x \\ y \\ z \end{bmatrix} = \frac{1}{8}\begin{bmatrix} -16+36+4 \\ -28+9+3 \\ 20-27-1 \end{bmatrix}$$

$$\Rightarrow \begin{bmatrix} x \\ y \\ z \end{bmatrix} = \frac{1}{8}\begin{bmatrix} 24 \\ -16 \\ -8 \end{bmatrix}$$

$$\Rightarrow \begin{bmatrix} x \\ y \\ z \end{bmatrix} = \begin{bmatrix} 3 \\ -2 \\ -1 \end{bmatrix}$$

$$\therefore x = 3, y = -2 \text{ and } z = -1 \qquad \textbf{(2 Marks)}$$

25. The function $f : R - \left\{-\dfrac{4}{3}\right\} \to R - \left\{\dfrac{4}{3}\right\}$ is given by

$$f(x) = \frac{4x+3}{3x+4}$$

Injectivity: Let $x, y \in R - \left\{-\dfrac{4}{3}\right\}$ be such that

$$f(x) = f(y)$$

$$\Rightarrow \frac{4x+3}{3x+4} = \frac{4y+3}{3y+4}$$

$$\Rightarrow (4x+3)(3y+4) = (4y+3)(3x+4)$$

$$\Rightarrow 12xy+9y+16x+12 = 12xy+9x+16y+12$$

$$\Rightarrow 7x = 7y$$

$$\Rightarrow x = y$$

Hence, f is one-one function $\qquad$ **(1 Mark)**

Surjectivity. Let y be an arbitrary element of $R - \left\{\dfrac{4}{3}\right\}$ then,

$$f(x) = y$$

$$\Rightarrow \frac{4x+3}{3x+4} = y$$

$$\Rightarrow 4x+3 = 3xy+4y$$

$$\Rightarrow 4x-3xy = 4y-3 \Rightarrow x = \frac{4y-3}{4-3y}$$

As, $y \in R - \left\{\dfrac{4}{3}\right\}, \dfrac{4y-3}{4-3y} \in R$ $\qquad$ **(1 Mark)**

Also $\dfrac{4y-3}{4-3y} \neq -\dfrac{4}{3}$ because $\dfrac{4y-3}{4-3y} = -\dfrac{4}{3}$

$$\Rightarrow 12y-9 = -16+12y$$

$$\Rightarrow 9 = 16 \text{ which is impossible}$$

Thus $x = \dfrac{4y-3}{4-3y} \in R - \left\{-\dfrac{4}{3}\right\}$ such that

$$f(x) = f\left(\frac{4y-3}{4-3y}\right) = \frac{4\left(\frac{4y-3}{4-3y}\right)+3}{3\left(\frac{4y-3}{4-3y}\right)+4}$$

$$= \frac{16y-12+12-9y}{12y-9+16-12y} = \frac{7y}{7} = y.$$ So every elements in

$R-\left\{\frac{4}{3}\right\}$ has pre-image in $R-\left\{-\frac{4}{3}\right\}$

Hence, f is onto.   **(1 Mark)**
Thus f is bijective.

Now, $x = \dfrac{4y-3}{4-3y}$

Replacing x by $f^{-1}(x)$ and y by x, we have

$$f^{-1}(x) = \frac{4x-3}{4-3x}$$ **(1 Mark)**

$$\therefore f^{-1}(0) = \frac{4\times 0-3}{4-3\times 0} = -\frac{3}{4}$$ **(1 Mark)**

Now,

$$f^{-1}(x) = 2$$

$$\Rightarrow \frac{4x-3}{4-3x} = 2$$

$$\Rightarrow 4x-3 = 8-6x$$

$$\Rightarrow 10x = 11$$

$$\Rightarrow x = \frac{11}{10}$$ **(1 Mark)**

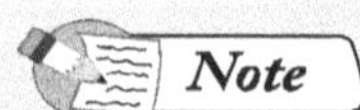

Injective (one-one)function can be proved in two ways.

(i) $f(x_1) = f(x_2) \Rightarrow x_1 = x_2$ or (ii) $x_1 \neq x_2 \Rightarrow f(x_1) \neq f(x_2)$

OR

Since $A = Q \times Q$ and * be a binary operation on A defined

by $(a,b)*(c,d) = (ac, b+ad)$ for $(a,b),(c,d) \in A$.

Commutativity:

Let, $X = (a,b)$ and $Y = (c,d) \in A, \forall a, c \in Q$ and $b, d \in Q$.
Then,
$X*Y = (ac, b+ad)$
$Y*X = (ca, d+cb)$
Therefore,

$$X*Y \neq Y*X \;\; \forall X, Y \in A$$

Thus * is not commutative on A   **(1 Mark)**
Associativity:

Let $X = (a,b), Y = (c,d)$ and $Z = (e,f), \forall a, c, e \in Q$ and

$b, d, f \in Q$

$X*(Y*Z) = (a,b)*(ce, d+cf)$
$\qquad\qquad = (ace, b + ad +acf)$
$(X*Y)*Z = (ac, b+ad)*(e,f)$
$\qquad\qquad = (ace, b + ad+acf)$
$\therefore X*(Y*Z) = (X*Y)*Z, \forall X, Y, Z \in A$
Thus, * is associative on A.   **(1 Mark)**
(i) Let $E = (x, y)$ be the identity element in A with respect to
$*, \forall x \in Q$ and $Y \in Q$ such that

$$X*E = X = E*X, \forall X \in A$$

$$\Rightarrow X*E = X \text{ and } E*X = X$$

$$\Rightarrow (ax, b+ay) = (a,b) \text{ and } (xa, y+xb) = (a,b)$$

Considering $(ax, b+ay) = (a,b)$
$\Rightarrow ax = a \Rightarrow x = 1$
And $b + ay = b$
$\Rightarrow y = 0$
Considering $(xa, y + xb) = (a, b)$
$\Rightarrow xa = a$
$\Rightarrow x = 1$
and $y + xb = b$
$\Rightarrow y = 0$ $[\because x = 1]$
$\therefore (1, 0)$ is the identity element in A with respect to *.

                                    (2 Marks)

(ii) Let $F = (m, n)$ be the inverse in $A \forall m \in Q$ and $n \in Q$.
$X * F = E$ and $F * X = E$
$\Rightarrow (am, b +an) = (1, 0)$ and $(ma, n + mb) = (1, 0)$
Considering $(am, b +an) = (1, 0)$
$\Rightarrow am = 1$

$$\Rightarrow m = \frac{1}{a} \text{ and } b + an = 0$$

$$\Rightarrow n = -\frac{b}{a}$$

Considering $(ma, n+ mb) = (1, 0)$

$$\Rightarrow ma = 1 \Rightarrow m = \frac{1}{a}$$

and $n + mb = 0$

$$\Rightarrow n = \frac{-b}{a} \left[\because m = \frac{a}{b}\right]$$

$\therefore$ The inverse of $(a, b) \in A$ with respect to * is $\left(\dfrac{1}{a}, \dfrac{-b}{a}\right)$

(2 Marks)

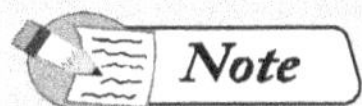

Invertable element of binary operation will be exist if identity element will be exit.

26. Let, length = breadth = x,

height = y

Surface area = S & Fixed volume = V of a closed cuboid

$V = x^2 y$ ...(i)

and $S = 2(x^2 + xy + xy) = 2x^2 + 4xy$ ...(ii)

Now $S = 2x^2 + 4xy$

$\Rightarrow S = 2x^2 + 4x\dfrac{V}{x^2}$

$\Rightarrow S = 2x^2 + 4\dfrac{V}{x}$ **(2 Marks)**

$\Rightarrow \dfrac{dS}{dx} = 4x - 4\dfrac{V}{x^2}$ ...(iii)   **(1 Mark)**

For maximum or minimum value, we have

$\Rightarrow \dfrac{dS}{dx} = 0$

$\Rightarrow 4x - 4\dfrac{V}{x^2} = 0$

$\Rightarrow V = x^3$

$\Rightarrow x^2 y = x^3$

$\Rightarrow x = y$ **(1 Mark)**

Differentiating equation (iii) with respect to x.

$\dfrac{d^2 S}{dx^2} = 4 + \dfrac{8V}{x^3} = 4 + \dfrac{8x^2 y}{x^3} = 4 + \dfrac{8y}{x}$

$\Rightarrow \left[\dfrac{d^2 S}{dx^2}\right]_{y=x} = 12 > 0$

Hence, S is minimum where length = x, bredth = x and height = x, i.e., when it is a cube.   **(2 Marks)**

To check whether the value is minimum or maximum, always find double differentation of function. If double differentation is negative, the value of function will be maximum, vice-versa.

27. The vertices of the triangle ABC are A(4,1) B (6, 6) and C (8, 4)

The equation of AB is $y - 1 = \left(\dfrac{6-1}{6-4}\right)(x-4)$

$\Rightarrow 2y - 2 = 5x - 20$

$\Rightarrow 2y = 5x - 18$

$\Rightarrow y = \dfrac{5x - 18}{2} = \dfrac{5x}{2} - 9$ ...(i)   **(1 Mark)**

The equation of BC is $y - 6 = \left(\dfrac{4-6}{8-6}\right)(x-6)$

$\Rightarrow y - 6 = -(x-6)$

$\Rightarrow y = 12 - x$ ....(ii)   **(1 Mark)**

The equation of CA is

$y - 4 = \left(\dfrac{1-4}{4-8}\right)(x-8)$

$\Rightarrow 4y - 16 = 3x - 24$

$\Rightarrow 4y = 3x - 8$

$\Rightarrow y = \dfrac{3x - 8}{4} = \dfrac{3x}{4} - 2$ ...(iii)   **(1 Mark)**

The region bounded by these line is shown below

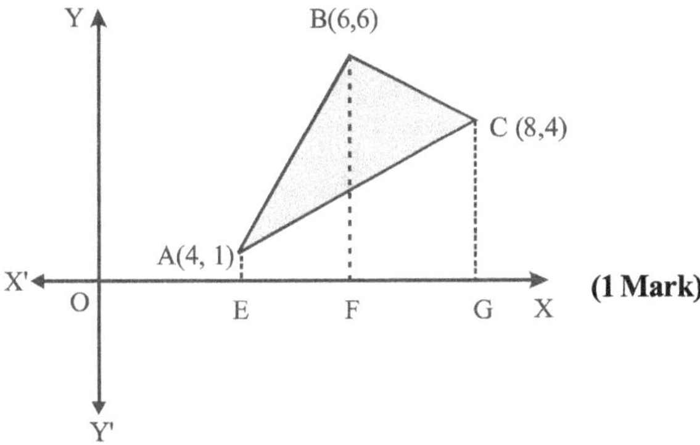

(1 Mark)

$\therefore$ Area of $\triangle ABC$

= Area of ABFE + Area of BCGF − Area of ACGF

$= \int_4^6 \left(\dfrac{5x}{2} - 9\right) dx + \int_6^8 (12 - x) dx - \int_4^8 \left(\dfrac{3x}{4} - 2\right) dx$ **(1 Mark)**

$= \left[\dfrac{5x^2}{4} - 9x\right]_4^6 + \left[12x - \dfrac{x^2}{2}\right]_6^8 - \left[\dfrac{3x^2}{8} - 2x\right]_4^8$

$= \left[(45 - 54) - (20 - 36)\right] + \left[(96 - 32) - (72 - 18)\right]$

$\quad - \left[(24 - 16) - (6 - 8)\right]$

$= (-9 + 16) + (64 - 54) - (8 + 2)$

$= 7 + 10 - 10 = 7 \text{ square units}$ **(1 Mark)**

OR

The equations of the curve are

$$4y = 3x^2 \qquad ....(i)$$

$$3x - 2y + 12 = 0 \qquad ...(ii)$$

The curve (i) represents a parabola having vertex at the origin, axis along the positive direction of Y-axis and opens upwards. The curve (ii) represents a straight line.

This straight lines meets the x-axis at (–4, 0) and y-axis at (0, 6). Solving (i) and (ii), we get

$$3x - 2\left(\frac{3x^2}{4}\right) + 12 = 0$$

$$\Rightarrow 6x - 3x^2 + 24 = 0$$

$$\Rightarrow x^2 - 2x - 8 = 0$$

$$\Rightarrow (x + 2)(x - 4) = 0$$

$$\Rightarrow x = -2, 4$$

When $x = -2, y = 3$ & $x = 4, y = 12$

Therefore the point of intersection of the given curves is $(-2, 3)$ and $(4, 12)$ **(1 Mark)**

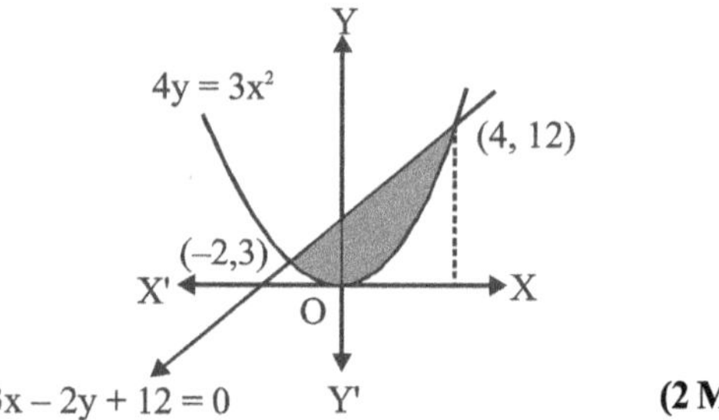

(2 Marks)

$\therefore$ Required area
= Area of the shaded region

$$= \int_{-2}^{4} \left(\frac{3x + 12}{2} - \frac{3}{4}x^2\right) dx \qquad \textbf{(1 Mark)}$$

$$= \left[\frac{3}{4}x^2 + 6x - \frac{x^3}{4}\right]_{-2}^{4}$$

$$= \left(\frac{3}{4} \times 16 + 6 \times 4 - \frac{64}{4}\right) - \left(\frac{3}{4} \times 4 + 6 \times (-2) + \frac{8}{4}\right)$$

$$= 20 - (-7)$$

$$= 27 \text{ square units} \qquad \textbf{(2 Marks)}$$

28. Since, $(x - y)\dfrac{dy}{dx} = x + 2y$

$$\Rightarrow \frac{dy}{dx} = \frac{x + 2y}{x - y}$$

This is a homogeneous differential equation.

Putting $y = vx$ and $\dfrac{dy}{dx} = v + x\dfrac{dv}{dx}$, we get

$$v + x\frac{dv}{dx} = \frac{x + 2vx}{x - vx} \quad \Rightarrow v + x\frac{dv}{dx} = \frac{1 + 2v}{1 - v}$$

$$\Rightarrow x\frac{dv}{dx} = \frac{1 + 2v}{1 - v} - v \quad \Rightarrow x\frac{dv}{dx} = \frac{1 + 2v - v + v^2}{1 - v}$$

$$\Rightarrow x\frac{dv}{dx} = \frac{1 + v + v^2}{1 - v} \quad \Rightarrow \frac{1 - v}{1 + v + v^2} dv = \frac{1}{x} dx$$

(1 Mark)

Integrating both sides, we get

$$\int \frac{1 - v}{1 + v + v^2} dv = \int \frac{1}{x} dx$$

$$\Rightarrow \frac{1}{2}\int \frac{2v - 2}{v^2 + v + 1} dv = \int \frac{-dx}{x}$$

$$\Rightarrow \int \frac{(2v + 1) - 3}{v^2 + v + 1} dv = -\int \frac{2dx}{x}$$

$$\Rightarrow \int \frac{(2v + 1)}{v^2 + v + 1} dv - \int \frac{3}{v^2 + v + 1} dv = -\int \frac{2dx}{x} \quad ...(i) \ \textbf{(1 Mark)}$$

Let $I_1 = \int \dfrac{(2v + 1)}{v^2 + v + 1} dv$ and $I_2 = \int \dfrac{3}{v^2 + v + 1} dv$

$$I_1 = \int \frac{2v + 1}{v^2 + v + 1} dv$$

Let $v^2 + v + 1 = t \Rightarrow (2v + 1) dv = dt$

$$\therefore I_1 = \int \frac{dt}{t} = \log|t| = \log|v^2 + v + 1| \qquad \textbf{(1 Mark)}$$

Also,

$$I_2 = \int \frac{3}{v^2 + v + 1} dv$$

$$= \int \frac{3dv}{v^2 + 2 \times v \times \frac{1}{2} + \left(\frac{1}{2}\right)^2 - \left(\frac{1}{2}\right)^2 + 1}$$

$$= 3\int \frac{1}{\left(v + \frac{1}{2}\right)^2 + \left(\frac{\sqrt{3}}{2}\right)^2} dv = 3\left(\frac{2}{\sqrt{3}}\right)\tan^{-1}\left(\frac{v + \frac{1}{2}}{\frac{\sqrt{3}}{2}}\right)$$

$$= 2\sqrt{3}\,\tan^{-1}\left(\dfrac{v+\dfrac{1}{2}}{\dfrac{\sqrt{3}}{2}}\right) \qquad \textbf{(1 Mark)}$$

Therefore from eq (i), we have

$$\log|v^2+v+1| - 2\sqrt{3}\,\tan^{-1}\left(\dfrac{v+\dfrac{1}{2}}{\dfrac{\sqrt{3}}{2}}\right) = -2\log|x| + C$$

Putting the value of $v = \dfrac{y}{x}$ in the above equation, we get

$$\log|x^2+y^2+xy| = 2\sqrt{3}\,\tan^{-1}\left(\dfrac{x+2y}{x\sqrt{3}}\right)+C \quad ...\text{(ii)} \ \textbf{(1 Mark)}$$

At : $y=0$ & $x=1$. eqn . (ii) becomes

$$\log|1| = 2\sqrt{3}\,\tan^{-1}\left(\dfrac{1}{\sqrt{3}}\right)+C \ \Rightarrow\ 0 = 2\sqrt{3}\times\dfrac{\pi}{6}+C$$

$$\Rightarrow C = -\dfrac{\pi}{\sqrt{3}}$$

Putting $C = -\dfrac{\pi}{\sqrt{3}}$ in eqn (ii), we have

$$\log|x^2+y^2+xy| = 2\sqrt{3}\,\tan^{-1}\left(\dfrac{x+2y}{x\sqrt{3}}\right) - \dfrac{\pi}{\sqrt{3}} \ ....\text{(iii)}$$

Hence eqn. (iii) is the required solution.   **(1 Mark)**

29. The cartesian equation of a line passing through two points (x_1, y_1, z_1) and (x_2, y_2, z_2) is given as.

$$\dfrac{x-x_1}{x_2-x_1} = \dfrac{y-y_1}{y_2-y_1} = \dfrac{z-z_1}{z_2-z_1}$$

Therefore the equation of a line passing through

$(3, -4, -5)$ and $(2, -3, 1)$ is $\dfrac{x-3}{2-3} = \dfrac{y-(-4)}{-3-(-4)} = \dfrac{z-(-5)}{1-(-5)}$

$$\Rightarrow \dfrac{x-3}{-1} = \dfrac{y+4}{1} = \dfrac{z+5}{6} \qquad \textbf{(2 Marks)}$$

Now the coordinates of any point on this line are given by

$$\dfrac{x-3}{-1} = \dfrac{y+4}{1} = \dfrac{z+5}{6} = k$$

$\Rightarrow x = 3-k,\ y = k-4,\ z = 6k-5$, where k is a constant.

Let $(3-k, k-4, 6k-5)$ be the required point of intersection.   **(1 Mark)**

Now, Let the equation of a plane passing through $(1, 2, 3)$ be

$a(x-1) + b(y-2) + c(z-3) = 0 \qquad\qquad ....\text{(i)}$

where a, b, c are the direction ratios of the normal to the plane.

Since the plane (i) passes through $(4, 2, -3)$ & $(0, 4, 3)$

$\therefore\ a(4-1) + b(2-2) + c(-3-3) = 0$

$\Rightarrow 3a - 6c = 0 \qquad\qquad\qquad\qquad\qquad ...\text{(ii)}$

& $a(0-1) + b(4-2) + c(3-3) = 0$

$\Rightarrow -a + 2b = 0 \qquad\qquad\qquad\qquad\qquad ...\text{(iii)}$

We can solve (ii) and (iii) using the method of cross multiplication, as given below

$$\dfrac{a}{0+12} = \dfrac{b}{6-0} = \dfrac{c}{6+0}$$

$$\Rightarrow \dfrac{a}{12} = \dfrac{b}{6} = \dfrac{c}{6}$$

$$\Rightarrow \dfrac{a}{2} = b = c = \lambda \ \text{(Say)}$$

$\Rightarrow a = 2\lambda,\ b = \lambda,\ c = \lambda$

From (i), we get

$2\lambda(x-1) + \lambda(y-2) + \lambda(z-3) = 0$

$\Rightarrow 2x + y + z - 7 = 0 \qquad\qquad ......\text{(iv)}\ \textbf{(2 Marks)}$

Putting $x = 3-k,\ y = k-4,\ z = 6k-5$ in (iv), we get

$\Rightarrow 2(3-k) + (k-4) + (6k-5) - 7 = 0$

$\Rightarrow 5k - 10 = 0$

$\Rightarrow k = 2$

$\therefore$ required point of intersection is

$(3-k, k-4, 6k-5)$ or $(3-2, 2-4, 6\times2-5)$ or $(1, -2, 7)$

    (1 Mark)

OR

Suppose this plane meets the X, Y and Z axis at A $(a, 0, 0)$, B $(0, b, 0)$ and C $(0, 0, c)$.

Equation of plnae is :

$$\dfrac{x}{a} + \dfrac{y}{b} + \dfrac{z}{c} = 1 \qquad\qquad ...\text{(i)}\ \ \textbf{(2 Marks)}$$

Let the coordinates of the centroid of triangle ABC be (α, β, λ)

$$\therefore\ \alpha = \dfrac{a+0+0}{3} = \dfrac{a}{3},\ \beta = \dfrac{0+b+0}{3} = \dfrac{b}{3},\ \gamma = \dfrac{0+0+c}{3} = \dfrac{c}{3}$$

$\Rightarrow a = 3\alpha,\ b = 3\beta,\ c = 3\gamma \qquad\qquad \textbf{(1 Mark)}$

Since required plane is at a distance of 3p from the origin.

$\therefore\ 3p = $ Length of perpendicular from $(0, 0, 0)$ to the plane (i)

$$\Rightarrow 3p = \dfrac{\left|\dfrac{0}{a} + \dfrac{0}{b} + \dfrac{0}{c} - 1\right|}{\sqrt{\left(\dfrac{1}{a}\right)^2 + \left(\dfrac{1}{b}\right)^2 + \left(\dfrac{1}{c}\right)^2}} \qquad \textbf{(1 Mark)}$$

$$\Rightarrow 3p = \dfrac{1}{\sqrt{\dfrac{1}{a^2} + \dfrac{1}{b^2} + \dfrac{1}{c^2}}}$$

$$\Rightarrow \sqrt{\dfrac{1}{a^2} + \dfrac{1}{b^2} + \dfrac{1}{c^2}} = \dfrac{1}{3p}$$

Squaring both sides, we get

$$\frac{1}{a^2}+\frac{1}{b^2}+\frac{1}{c^2}=\frac{1}{9p^2} \qquad ...(ii)$$

Substituting the values of a, b and c in (ii), we get

$$\frac{1}{9\alpha^2}+\frac{1}{9\beta^2}+\frac{1}{9\gamma^2}=\frac{1}{9p^2}$$

$$\Rightarrow \frac{1}{\alpha^2}+\frac{1}{\beta^2}+\frac{1}{\gamma^2}=\frac{1}{p^2}$$

or $\dfrac{1}{x^2}+\dfrac{1}{y^2}+\dfrac{1}{z^2}=\dfrac{1}{p^2}$ **(2 Marks)**

Which is the required locus of the centroid of the triangle ABC.

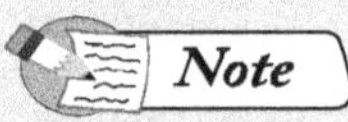

Note

When a plane intersect the axes at a, b and c then equation of

plane is $\dfrac{x}{a}+\dfrac{y}{b}+\dfrac{z}{c}=1$

Delhi *2017*
CBSE Board Solved Paper

Time Allowed : 3 Hours   *Maximum Marks : 100*

General Instructions:

(i) All questions are compulsory.

(ii) This question paper contains **29** questions.

(iii) Question **1-4** in **Section A** are very short-answer type questions carrying **1** mark each.

(iv) Question **5-12** in **Section B** are short-answer type questions carrying **2** marks each.

(v) Question **13-23** in **Section C** are long-answer I type questions carrying **4** marks each.

(vi) Question **24-29** in **Section D** are long-answer **II** type questions carrying **6** marks each.

SECTION - A

Question numbers 1 to 4 carry 1 mark each.

1. If A is a 3×3 invertible matrix, then what will be the value of k if $\det(A^{-1}) = (\det A)^k$.

2. Determine the value of the constant 'k' so that the function
$$f(x) = \begin{cases} \dfrac{kx}{|x|} & , \ \text{if } x < 0 \\ 3 & , \ \text{if } x \geq 0 \end{cases}$$
is continuous at $x = 0$.

3. Evaluate : $\displaystyle\int_{2}^{3} 3^x \, dx$.

4. If a line makes angles $90°$ and $60°$ respectively with the positive directions of x and y axes, find the angle which it makes with the positive direction of z-axis.

SECTION - B

Question numbers 5 to 12 carry 2 marks each.

5. Show that all the diagonal elements of a skew symmetric matrix are zero.

6. Find $\dfrac{dy}{dx}$ at $x = 1$, $y = \dfrac{\pi}{4}$ if $\sin^2 y + \cos xy = \text{K}$.

7. The volume of a sphere is increasing at the rate of 3 cubic centimeter per second. Find the rate of increase of its surface area, when the radius is 2 cm.

8. Show that the function $f(x) = 4x^3 - 18x^2 + 27x - 7$ is always increasing on R.

9. Find the vector equation of the line passing through the point A(1, 2, −1) and parallel to the line
$$5x - 25 = 14 - 7y = 35z.$$

10. Prove that if E and F are independent events, then the events E and F' are also independent.

11. A small firm manufactures necklaces and bracelets. The total number of necklaces and bracelets that it can handle per day is at most 24. It takes one hour to make a bracelet and half an hour to make a necklace. The maximum number of hours available per day is 16. If the profit on a necklace is ₹ 100 and that on a bracelet is ₹ 300. Formulate on L.P.P. for finding how many of each should be produced daily to maximize the profit? It is being given that at least one of each must be produced.

12. Find : $\displaystyle\int \dfrac{dx}{x^2 + 4x + 8}$

SECTION - C

Question numbers 13 to 23 carry 4 marks each.

13. Prove that $\tan\left\{\dfrac{\pi}{4} + \dfrac{1}{2}\cos^{-1}\dfrac{a}{b}\right\} + \tan\left\{\dfrac{\pi}{4} - \dfrac{1}{2}\cos^{-1}\dfrac{a}{b}\right\} = \dfrac{2b}{a}$

14. Using properties of determinants, prove that
$$\begin{vmatrix} x & x+y & x+2y \\ x+2y & x & x+y \\ x+y & x+2y & x \end{vmatrix} = 9y^2(x+y).$$

OR

Let $A = \begin{pmatrix} 2 & -1 \\ 3 & 4 \end{pmatrix}$, $B = \begin{pmatrix} 5 & 2 \\ 7 & 4 \end{pmatrix}$, $C = \begin{pmatrix} 2 & 5 \\ 3 & 8 \end{pmatrix}$, find a matrix D such that $CD - AB = O$.

15. Differentiate the function $(\sin x)^x + \sin^{-1}\sqrt{x}$ with respect to x.

OR

If $x^m y^n = (x + y)^{m+n}$, prove that $\dfrac{d^2 y}{dx^2} = 0$.

16. Find : $\displaystyle\int \dfrac{2x}{(x^2 + 1)(x^2 + 2)^2}\, dx$

17. Evaluate : $\displaystyle\int_0^{\pi} \dfrac{x \sin x}{1 + \cos^2 x}\, dx$

OR

Evaluate : $\displaystyle\int_0^{3/2} |\, x \sin \pi x\,|\, dx$

18. Prove that $x^2 - y^2 = C(x^2 + y^2)^2$ is the general solution of the differential equation
$(x^3 - 3xy^2)dx = (y^3 - 3x^2y)dy$, where C is a parameter.

19. Let $\vec{a} = \hat{i} + \hat{j} + \hat{k}$, $\vec{b} = \hat{i}$ and $\vec{c} = c_1\hat{i} + c_2\hat{j} + c_3\hat{k}$, then

(a) Let $c_1 = 1$ and $c_2 = 2$, find c_3 which makes $\vec{a}, \vec{b}$ and $\vec{c}$ coplanar.

(b) If $c_2 = -1$ and $c_3 = 1$, show that no value of c_1 can make $\vec{a}, \vec{b}$ and $\vec{c}$ coplanar.

20. If $\vec{a}, \vec{b}, \vec{c}$ are mutually perpendicular vectors of equal magnitudes, show that the vector $\vec{a} + \vec{b} + \vec{c}$ is equally inclined to $\vec{a}, \vec{b}$ and $\vec{c}$. Also, find the angle which $\vec{a} + \vec{b} + \vec{c}$ makes with $\vec{a}$ or $\vec{b}$ or $\vec{c}$.

21. The random variable X can take only the values 0, 1, 2, 3. Given that $P(X = 0) = P(X = 1) = p$ and $P(X = 2) = P(X = 3)$ such that $\Sigma p_i x_i^2 = 2\Sigma p_i x_i$, find the value of p.

22. Often it is taken that a truthful person commands, more respect in the society. A man is known to speak the truth 4 out of 5 times. He throws a die and reports that it is a six. Find the probability that it is actually a six.

Do you also agree that the value of truthfulness leads to more respect in the society?

23. Solve the following L.P.P. graphically:

Minimise $Z = 5x + 10y$

Subject to Constraints

$$x + 2y \le 120$$
$$x + y \ge 60$$
$$x - 2y \ge 0$$

and $\qquad x, y \ge 0$

$$x + 3z = 9,$$
$$-x + 2y - 2z = 4,$$
$$2x - 3y + 4z = -3.$$

25. Consider $f : R^+ \to [-5, \infty)$ given by $f(x) = 9x^2 + 6x - 5$. Show that f is invertible with

$$f^{-1}(y) = \left(\dfrac{\sqrt{y + 6} - 1}{3} \right).$$

Hence find:

(i) $f^{-1}(10)$

(ii) y if $f^{-1}(y) = \dfrac{4}{3}$,

where R^+ is the set of all non-negative real numbers.

OR

Discuss the commutativity and associativity of binary operation '*' defined on $A = Q - \{1\}$ by the rule $a * b = a - b + ab$ for all $a, b \in A$. Also find the identity element of * in A and hence find the invertible elements of A.

26. If the sum of lengths of the hypotenuse and a side of a right angled triangle is given show that the area of the triangle is maximum, when the angle between them is $\dfrac{\pi}{3}$.

27. Using integration, find the area of region bounded by the triangle whose vertices are $(-2, 1)$, $(0, 4)$ and $(2, 3)$.

OR

Find the area bounded by the circle $x^2 + y^2 = 16$ and the line $\sqrt{3}\,y = x$ in the first quadrant, using integration.

28. Solve the differential equation $x\dfrac{dy}{dx} + y = x \cos x + \sin x$, given that $y = 1$ when $x = \dfrac{\pi}{2}$

29. Find the equation of the plane through the line of intersection of $\vec{r}.(2\hat{i} - 3\hat{j} + 4\hat{k}) = 1$ and $\vec{r}.(\hat{i} - \hat{j}) + 4 = 0$ and perpendicular to the plane $\vec{r}.(2\hat{i} - \hat{j} + \hat{k}) + 8 = 0$. Hence find whether the plane thus obtained contains the line $x - 1 = 2y - 4 = 3z - 12$.

OR

Find the vector and Cartesian equations of a line passing through $(1, 2, -4)$ and perpendicular to the two lines

$$\dfrac{x-8}{3} = \dfrac{y+19}{-16} = \dfrac{z-10}{7} \text{ and } \dfrac{x-15}{3} = \dfrac{y-29}{8} = \dfrac{z-5}{-5}$$

SECTION - D

Question numbers 24 to 29 carry 6 marks each.

24. Use product $\begin{bmatrix} 1 & -1 & 2 \\ 0 & 2 & -3 \\ 3 & -2 & 4 \end{bmatrix}\begin{bmatrix} -2 & 0 & 1 \\ 9 & 2 & -3 \\ 6 & 1 & -2 \end{bmatrix}$ to solve the system of equations

Solutions

SECTION - A

1. $|A^{-1}| = \dfrac{1}{|A|}$ **(½ Mark)**

$|A^{-1}| = |A|^K$

$\therefore \quad K = -1$ **(½ Mark)**

 **Note**

An square matrix is invertible if and only if det (A) ≠ 0

2. $\displaystyle\lim_{x \to 0^-} f(x) = \lim_{x \to 0^-} \dfrac{kx}{|x|} = \lim_{x \to 0^-} \dfrac{kx}{(-x)} = -k$ **(½ Mark)**

As function is continuous at $x = 0$

$\displaystyle\lim_{x \to 0^+} f(x) = \lim_{x \to 0^-} f(x)$

$3 = -k$

$k = -3$ **(½ Mark)**

Note

A function f(x) is continuous at x = a

if $\displaystyle\lim_{x \to a^-} f(x) = f(a) = \lim_{x \to a^+} f(x)$

3. Let $I = \displaystyle\int_2^3 3^x \, dx = \left[\dfrac{3^x}{\log 3}\right]_2^3$ $\left[\because \displaystyle\int a^x dx = \dfrac{a^x}{\log a}\right]$

$= \dfrac{1}{\log 3}[3^3 - 3^2] = \dfrac{18}{\log 3}$ **(1 Mark)**

4. Given: $\alpha = 90°$, $\beta = 60°$

$\cos^2\alpha + \cos^2\beta + \cos^2\gamma = 1$ **(½ Mark)**

$\cos^2 90° + \cos^2 60° + \cos^2\gamma = 1$

$0 + \left(\dfrac{1}{2}\right)^2 + \cos^2\gamma = 1$

$\cos^2\gamma = \dfrac{3}{4}$

$\cos\gamma = \pm\dfrac{\sqrt{3}}{2}$

$\therefore \quad \gamma = \dfrac{\pi}{6} \text{ or } \dfrac{5\pi}{6}$ **(½ Mark)**

Note

If a line passes through origin and makes direction angles α, β, and γ with x, y and z-axes respectively, then the relation between direction cosines is cos²α + cos²β + cos²γ = 1

SECTION - B

5. Let $A = [a_{ij}]_{n \times n}$ be skew symmetric matrix

A is skew symmetric

$\therefore \quad A = -A'$ **(1 Mark)**

$\Rightarrow \quad a_{ij} = -a_{ij} \; \forall \, i, j$

For diagonal element $i = j$.

$a_{ii} = -a_{ii}$

$2\,a_{ii} = 0$

$a_{ii} = 0$

Therefore diagonal elements are zero.   **(1 Mark)**

6. $\sin^2 y + \cos xy = K$

Differentiating on both sides w.r.t. x

$2\sin y \cos y \dfrac{dy}{dx} - \sin xy\left[x\dfrac{dy}{dx} + y\right] = 0$ **(1 Mark)**

$\sin 2y \dfrac{dy}{dx} - x \sin xy \dfrac{dy}{dx} - y \sin xy = 0$

$\dfrac{dy}{dx}(\sin 2y - x \sin xy) - y \sin xy = 0$

$\dfrac{dy}{dx} = \dfrac{y \sin xy}{\sin 2y - x \sin xy}$

$\therefore \quad \dfrac{dy}{dx}\bigg|_{x=1, y=\frac{\pi}{4}} = \dfrac{\pi}{4(\sqrt{2}-1)}$ **(1 Mark)**

7. Volume of sphere, $V = \dfrac{4}{3}\pi r^3$

Differentiating w.r.t. t

$\dfrac{dV}{dt} = \dfrac{4}{3}\pi(3r^2)\dfrac{dr}{dt} = 4\pi r^2 \dfrac{dr}{dt}$ ...(1)

$\dfrac{dV}{dt} = 3$ (given)   ...(2)

$\therefore \quad \dfrac{dr}{dt} = \dfrac{3}{4\pi r^2}$ [From (1) and (2)]   **(1 Mark)**

Surface area of sphere, $S = 4\pi r^2$

$\dfrac{dS}{dt} = 8\pi r \dfrac{dr}{dt} = 8\pi r\left(\dfrac{3}{4\pi r^2}\right) = \dfrac{6}{r}$

$\dfrac{dS}{dt}\bigg|_{r=2} = 3 \text{ cm}^2/\text{s}$ **(1 Mark)**

8. $f(x) = 4x^3 - 18x^2 + 27x - 7$

Differentiating w.r.t. x

$f'(x) = 12x^2 - 36x + 27 = 3(4x^2 - 12x + 9)$ **(1 Mark)**

$= 3(2x-3)^2 \geq 0 \; \forall \; x \in R$

$\therefore \; f(x)$ is increasing on R. **(1 Mark)**

9. Given line: $5x - 25 = 14 - 7y = 35z$

$$\frac{x-5}{1/5} = \frac{y-2}{-1/7} = \frac{z}{1/35}$$

Direction ratios $\left(\frac{1}{5}, \frac{-1}{7}, \frac{1}{35}\right)$ **(1 Mark)**

Required line passes through $(1, 2, -1)$

$$\vec{r} = (\hat{i} + 2\hat{j} - \hat{k}) + \lambda\left(\frac{1}{5}\hat{i} - \frac{1}{7}\hat{j} + \frac{1}{35}\hat{k}\right)$$

$$\vec{r} = (\hat{i} + 2\hat{j} - \hat{k}) + \lambda(7\hat{i} - 5\hat{j} + \hat{k})$$ **(1 Mark)**

10. $P(E \cap F') = P(E) - P(E \cap F)$ **(1 Mark)**

$= P(E) - P(E) \cdot P(F) = P(E)[1 - P(F)] = P(E) \cdot P(F')$

Therefore E and F' are independent events. **(1 Mark)**

 **Note**

Two events E and F are independent if $P(E \cap F) = P(E) \cdot P(F)$.

11. Let number of necklaces manufactured be x and number of braceletes be y

$\therefore \;\;\; LPP$ is

Maximum profit, $P = 100x + 300y$

$x, y \geq 1$

$x + y \leq 24$

$\dfrac{1}{2}x + y \leq 16 \quad$ or $\quad x + 2y \leq 32$ **(2 Mark)**

12. Let $I = \displaystyle\int \frac{dx}{x^2 + 4x + 8} = \int \frac{dx}{x^2 + 4x + 8 + (2)^2 - (2)^2}$ **(1 Mark)**

$$= \int \frac{dx}{(x+2)^2 + (2)^2} = \frac{1}{2}\tan^{-1}\left(\frac{x+2}{2}\right) + C$$

$$\left[\because \int \frac{dx}{x^2 + a^2} = \frac{1}{a}\tan^{-1}\frac{x}{a} + C\right]$$ **(1 Mark)**

 **Note**

Convert the denominator which is a quadratic polynomial of the integral in the form $(x \pm \alpha)^2 \pm \beta^2$, where α and β are constants.

SECTION - C

13. L.H.S.

$$\tan\left(\frac{\pi}{4} + \frac{1}{2}\cos^{-1}\frac{a}{b}\right) + \tan\left(\frac{\pi}{4} - \frac{1}{2}\cos^{-1}\frac{a}{b}\right)$$

Let $\dfrac{1}{2}\cos^{-1}\dfrac{a}{b} = x$ **(1 Mark)**

$$\tan\left(\frac{\pi}{4} + x\right) + \tan\left(\frac{\pi}{4} - x\right)$$

$$\frac{\tan\frac{\pi}{4} + \tan x}{1 - \tan\frac{\pi}{4} \cdot \tan x} + \frac{\tan\frac{\pi}{4} - \tan x}{1 + \tan\frac{\pi}{4} \cdot \tan x}$$

$$\left[\because \tan(A+B) = \frac{\tan A + \tan B}{1 - \tan A \cdot \tan B}\right]$$

$$= \frac{1 + \tan x}{1 - \tan x} + \frac{1 - \tan x}{1 + \tan x}$$ **(1 Mark)**

$$= \frac{1 + \tan^2 x + 2\tan x + 1 + \tan^2 x - 2\tan x}{(1 - \tan x)(1 + \tan x)}$$

$$= \frac{2(1 + \tan^2 x)}{1 - \tan^2 x} \qquad [\because (a+b)(a-b) = a^2 - b^2]$$

$$= \frac{2(\cos^2 x + \sin^2 x)}{(\cos^2 x - \sin^2 x)} \qquad \left[\because \tan x = \frac{\sin x}{\cos x}\right]$$

$$= \frac{2}{\cos 2x} \quad [\because \cos 2\theta = \cos^2\theta - \sin^2\theta, \; \cos^2\theta + \sin^2\theta = 1]$$ **(1 Mark)**

$$= \frac{2}{\cos 2\left(\frac{1}{2}\cos^{-1}\frac{a}{b}\right)} = \frac{2b}{a} = \text{R.H.S.}$$ **(1 Mark)**

14. L.H.S. $\begin{vmatrix} x & x+y & x+2y \\ x+2y & x & x+y \\ x+y & x+2y & x \end{vmatrix}$

Applying $R_1 \to R_1 + R_2 + R_3$

$$= \begin{vmatrix} 3(x+y) & 3(x+y) & 3(x+y) \\ x+2y & x & x+y \\ x+y & x+2y & x \end{vmatrix}$$ **(1 Mark)**

$$= 3(x+y)\begin{vmatrix} 1 & 1 & 1 \\ x+2y & x & x+y \\ x+y & x+2y & x \end{vmatrix}$$ **(1 Mark)**

Applying $C_2 \to C_2 - C_1, \; C_3 \to C_3 - C_1$

$$= 3(x+y)\begin{vmatrix} 1 & 0 & 0 \\ x+2y & -2y & -y \\ x+y & y & -y \end{vmatrix}$$ **(1 Mark)**

$= 3(x+y)[1(2y^2 + y^2)]$

$= 9y^2(x+y) = \text{R.H.S.}$

L.H.S. = R.H.S. **(1 Mark)**

Hence proved.

OR

Let $D = \begin{bmatrix} x & y \\ z & w \end{bmatrix}$

$CD - AB = O$

$CD = O + AB$

$CD = AB$　　　　　　　　　　　　　　**(1 Mark)**

$\begin{bmatrix} 2 & 5 \\ 3 & 8 \end{bmatrix}\begin{bmatrix} x & y \\ z & w \end{bmatrix} = \begin{bmatrix} 2 & -1 \\ 3 & 4 \end{bmatrix}\begin{bmatrix} 5 & 2 \\ 7 & 4 \end{bmatrix}$

$\begin{bmatrix} 2x+5z & 2y+5w \\ 3x+8z & 3y+8w \end{bmatrix} = \begin{bmatrix} 10-7 & 4-4 \\ 15+28 & 6+16 \end{bmatrix}$

$\begin{bmatrix} 2x+5z & 2y+5w \\ 3x+8z & 3y+8w \end{bmatrix} = \begin{bmatrix} 3 & 0 \\ 43 & 22 \end{bmatrix}$　　　**(1 Mark)**

On equating

$2x + 5z = 3$

$3x + 8z = 43$

$2y + 5w = 0$

$3y + 8w = 22$

On solving equations

$x = -191,\ y = -110,\ z = 77,\ w = 44$

$\therefore D = \begin{bmatrix} -191 & -110 \\ 77 & 44 \end{bmatrix}$　　　**(2 Marks)**

15.　Let $y = (\sin x)^x + \sin^{-1}\sqrt{x}$

$y = u + v$

$\dfrac{dy}{dx} = \dfrac{du}{dx} + \dfrac{dv}{dx}$　　　...(1)　　**(1 Mark)**

$u = (\sin x)^x$

Taking log on both sides

$\log u = x \log \sin x$

Differentiating on both sides w.r.t. x

$\dfrac{1}{u}\dfrac{du}{dx} = x\dfrac{\cos x}{\sin x} + \log \sin x$

$\dfrac{du}{dx} = u[x \cot x + \log \sin x]$

$\dfrac{du}{dx} = (\sin x)^x [x \cot x + \log \sin x]$　...(2)　**(1½ Marks)**

Now $v = \sin^{-1}\sqrt{x}$

$\dfrac{dv}{dx} = \dfrac{1}{2\sqrt{x}\sqrt{1-(\sqrt{x})^2}}$　　$\left[\because \dfrac{d}{dx}\sin^{-1} x = \dfrac{1}{\sqrt{1-x^2}}\right]$

$\dfrac{dv}{dx} = \dfrac{1}{2\sqrt{x-x^2}}$　　　...(2)　　**(1 Mark)**

Putting values of $\dfrac{du}{dx}$ and $\dfrac{dv}{dx}$ in (1)

$\dfrac{dy}{dx} = (\sin x)^x [x \cot x + \log \sin x] + \dfrac{1}{2\sqrt{x-x^2}}$

　　　　　　　　　　　　　　　　(½ Mark)

OR

$x^m\, y^n = (x + y)^{m+n}$

Taking log on both sides

$\log(x^m\, y^n) = \log (x + y)^{m+n}$

$\log x^m + \log y^n = \log(x + y)^{m+n}$

　　　　　　　　　　$[\because \log uv = \log u + \log v]$

$m \log x + n \log y = (m + n)\log (x + y)$

　　　　　　$[\because \log m^n = n \log m]$　　**(1 Mark)**

Differentiating on both sides w.r.t. x

$\dfrac{m}{x} + \dfrac{n}{y}\dfrac{dy}{dx} = \dfrac{m+n}{x+y}\left[1+\dfrac{dy}{dx}\right]\left[\because \dfrac{d}{dx}\log x = \dfrac{1}{x}\right]$　**(1 Mark)**

$\dfrac{dy}{dx}\left[\dfrac{n}{y} - \dfrac{m+n}{x+y}\right] = \dfrac{m+n}{x+y} - \dfrac{m}{x}$

$\dfrac{dy}{dx}\left[\dfrac{nx+ny-my-ny}{y(x+y)}\right] = \dfrac{mx+nx-mx-my}{x(x+y)}$

$\dfrac{dy}{dx} = \dfrac{y}{x}$　　　　　　...(1)　　**(1 Mark)**

Again differentiating w.r.t. x

$\dfrac{d^2y}{dx^2} = \dfrac{x\dfrac{dy}{dx} - y}{x^2}$　　$\left[\because \dfrac{d}{dx}\left(\dfrac{u}{v}\right) = \dfrac{v\dfrac{du}{dx} - u\dfrac{dv}{dx}}{v^2}\right]$

$= \dfrac{x\dfrac{y}{x} - y}{x^2} = 0$　　　　[By using (1)]　**(1 Mark)**

L.H.S. = R.H.S.

Hence proved.

16.　Let $I = \displaystyle\int \dfrac{2x\ dx}{(x^2+1)(x^2+2)^2}$

Let $x^2 = y$

$2x\, dx = dy$

$I = \displaystyle\int \dfrac{dy}{(y+1)(y+2)^2}$　　　**(1 Mark)**

Using partial fraction

$\dfrac{1}{(y+1)(y+2)^2} = \dfrac{A}{y+1} + \dfrac{B}{(y+2)^2} + \dfrac{C}{(y+2)}$

$1 = A(y + 2)^2 + B(y + 1) + C(y + 1)(y + 2)$

When $y = -2$

$\qquad B = -1$

When $y = -1$

$\qquad A = 1$

Put $y = 0$

$\qquad 1 = 4 - 1 + 2C$

$\qquad C = -1$

$\therefore \quad \dfrac{1}{(y+1)(y+2)^2} = \dfrac{1}{y+1} - \dfrac{1}{y+2} - \dfrac{1}{(y+2)^2}$ **(2 Marks)**

$I = \displaystyle\int \dfrac{dy}{y+1} - \int \dfrac{dy}{y+2} - \int \dfrac{dy}{(y+2)^2}$

$= \log(y + 1) - \log(y + 2) + \dfrac{1}{y+2} + C \left[\because \displaystyle\int \dfrac{1}{x} dx = \log x \right]$

$\therefore \quad I = \log(x^2 + 1) - \log(x^2 + 2) + \dfrac{1}{x^2+2} + C$ **(1 Mark)**

17. Let $I = \displaystyle\int_0^\pi \dfrac{x \sin x}{1+\cos^2 x} dx$

$I = \displaystyle\int_0^\pi \dfrac{(\pi - x)\sin(\pi - x)}{1+\cos^2(\pi - x)} dx \quad \left[\displaystyle\int_0^a f(x)dx = \int_0^a f(a-x)dx \right]$

$I = \displaystyle\int_0^\pi \dfrac{\pi \sin x}{1+\cos^2 x} dx - I$

$2I = \displaystyle\int_0^\pi \dfrac{\pi \sin x}{1+\cos^2 x} dx$ **(1 Mark)**

Let $\cos x = t$ then $-\sin x\, dx = dt$

When $x = 0$, then $t = 1$

When $x = \pi$, then $t = -1$

$2I = -\pi \displaystyle\int_1^{-1} \dfrac{dt}{1+t^2}$ **(1 Mark)**

$2I = \pi \displaystyle\int_{-1}^1 \dfrac{dt}{1+t^2} \quad \left[\because \displaystyle\int_{-a}^a f(x)dx = -\int_a^{-a} f(x)dx \right]$

$2I = \pi \left[\tan^{-1} t \right]_{-1}^1$

$2I = \pi \left[\dfrac{\pi}{4} + \dfrac{\pi}{4} \right]$

$2I = \dfrac{\pi^2}{2}$

$I = \dfrac{\pi^2}{4}$ **(2 Marks)**

OR

Let $I = \displaystyle\int_0^{3/2} |x \sin \pi x|\, dx$

$|x \sin \pi x| = \begin{cases} -x\sin \pi x & 1 < x < \dfrac{3}{2} \\[2mm] x \sin \pi x & 0 < x < 1 \end{cases}$ **(1 Mark)**

$I = \displaystyle\int_0^1 x \sin \pi x\, dx - \int_1^{3/2} x \sin \pi x\, dx$

As $\displaystyle\int uv\, dx = u\int v\, dx - \int \left(\dfrac{d}{dx} u \right)\left(\int v\, dx \right) dx$ **(1 Mark)**

$I = \left[\dfrac{-x\cos \pi x}{\pi} + \int \dfrac{\cos \pi x}{\pi} dx \right]_0^1 - \left[\dfrac{-x\cos \pi x}{\pi} + \int \dfrac{\cos \pi x}{\pi^2} \right]_1^{3/2}$

$= \left[\dfrac{-x\cos \pi x}{\pi} + \dfrac{\sin \pi x}{\pi^2} \right]_0^1 - \left[\dfrac{-x\cos \pi x}{\pi} + \dfrac{\sin \pi x}{\pi^2} \right]_1^{3/2}$

$\qquad\qquad\qquad\qquad = \dfrac{2}{\pi} + \dfrac{1}{\pi^2}$ **(2 Marks)**

18. $x^2 - y^2 = C(x^2 + y^2)^2 \qquad\qquad …(1)$

Differentiating on both sides

$2x - 2y \dfrac{dy}{dx} = 2C(x^2 + y^2)\left(2x + 2y\dfrac{dy}{dx} \right)$ **(1 Mark)**

$x - y\dfrac{dy}{dx} = C(x^2 + y^2)\left(2x + 2y\dfrac{dy}{dx} \right) \quad …(2)$

From (1)

$C = \dfrac{x^2 - y^2}{(x^2 + y^2)^2}$

Putting value of C in (2)

$x - y\dfrac{dy}{dx} = \dfrac{x^2 - y^2}{x^2 + y^2}\left(2x + 2y\dfrac{dy}{dx} \right)$ **(1 Mark)**

$(x^2 + y^2)\left(x - y\dfrac{dy}{dx} \right) = (x^2 - y^2)\left(2x + 2y\dfrac{dy}{dx} \right)$

$\dfrac{dy}{dx}[-2y(x^2 - y^2) - y(x^2 + y^2)] = 2x(x^2 - y^2) - x(y^2 + x^2)$

$\dfrac{dy}{dx}[-2yx^2 + 2y^3 - yx^2 - y^3] = 2x^3 - 2xy^2 - xy^2 - x^3$

$\dfrac{dy}{dx}(y^3 - 3x^2 y) = (x^3 - 3xy^2)$

$(y^3 - 3x^2 y)dy = (x^3 - 3xy^2)dx$ **(2 Marks)**

Hence $x^2 - y^2 = C(x^2 + y^2)^2$ is the solution of given differential equation.

19. $\vec{a} = \hat{i} + \hat{j} + \hat{k}$

$\vec{b} = \hat{i}$

$\vec{c} = c_1 \hat{i} + c_2 \hat{j} + c_3 \hat{k}$

$\vec{a}, \vec{b}, \vec{c}$ will be copalanar if

$$\begin{bmatrix} \vec{a} & \vec{b} & \vec{c} \end{bmatrix} = 0 \qquad \textbf{(1 Mark)}$$

$$\begin{bmatrix} \vec{a} & \vec{b} & \vec{c} \end{bmatrix} = \begin{vmatrix} 1 & 1 & 1 \\ 1 & 0 & 0 \\ c_1 & c_2 & c_3 \end{vmatrix} = c_2 - c_3 \qquad \textbf{(1 Mark)}$$

(a) $c_1 = 1,\ c_2 = 2$

$$\begin{bmatrix} \vec{a} & \vec{b} & \vec{c} \end{bmatrix} = 2 - c_3$$

As $\vec{a}, \vec{b}, \vec{c}$ are coplanar

$$2 - c_3 = 0$$

$$c_3 = 2 \qquad \textbf{(1 Mark)}$$

(b) $c_2 = -1,\ c_3 = 1$

$$\begin{bmatrix} \vec{a} & \vec{b} & \vec{c} \end{bmatrix} = c_2 - c_3$$
$$= -1 - 1 = -2 \neq 0$$

Therefore, no value of c_1 can make $\vec{a}, \vec{b}, \vec{c}$ coplanar.
(1 Mark)

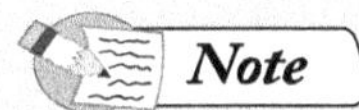
Note

Three or more non-zero vectors are coplanar if they lie in the same plane.

20. Given: $|\vec{a}| = |\vec{b}| = |\vec{c}|$ ...(1)

As vectors are perpendiculars

$$\therefore \quad \vec{a}.\vec{b} = \vec{b}.\vec{c} = \vec{c}.\vec{a} = 0 \qquad ...(2) \quad \textbf{(1 Mark)}$$

Let α, β, γ be the angles made by $(\vec{a}+\vec{b}+\vec{c})$ with $\vec{a},\vec{b},\vec{c}$ respectively

$$|\vec{a}+\vec{b}+\vec{c}|^2 = |\vec{a}|^2 + |\vec{b}|^2 + |\vec{c}|^2 + 2(\vec{a}.\vec{b}+\vec{b}.\vec{c}+\vec{c}.\vec{a})$$

$$|\vec{a}+\vec{b}+\vec{c}|^2 = 3|\vec{a}|^2 + 2(0) \qquad \text{[From (1) \& (2)]}$$

$$|\vec{a}+\vec{b}+\vec{c}|^2 = 3|\vec{a}|^2 \qquad ...(3) \quad \textbf{(1 Mark)}$$

We know that

$$(\vec{a}+\vec{b}+\vec{c}).\vec{a} = |\vec{a}+\vec{b}+\vec{c}||\vec{a}|\cos\alpha$$

$$\alpha = \cos^{-1}\left(\frac{|\vec{a}|}{|\vec{a}+\vec{b}+\vec{c}|}\right)$$

$$\alpha = \cos^{-1}\left(\frac{1}{\sqrt{3}}\right) \qquad \text{[From (3)]}$$

$$\therefore \quad \alpha = \cos^{-1}\left(\frac{1}{\sqrt{3}}\right) \qquad \textbf{(1 Mark)}$$

Similarly, $\beta = \cos^{-1}\left(\dfrac{|\vec{b}|}{|\vec{a}+\vec{b}+\vec{c}|}\right)$

$$\beta = \cos^{-1}\left(\frac{1}{\sqrt{3}}\right)$$

$$\& \quad \gamma = \cos^{-1}\left[\frac{|\vec{c}|}{|\vec{a}+\vec{b}+\vec{c}|}\right]$$

$$\gamma = \cos^{-1}\left(\frac{1}{\sqrt{3}}\right) \qquad \textbf{(1 Mark)}$$

21. Let $P(X = 2) = P(X = 3) = K$

(X)	$P(X)$
0	p
1	p
2	k
3	k

$$\sum P(X) = 2p + 2k \qquad \textbf{(½ Mark)}$$

Also $\sum P(X) = 1$ ($\because$ Sum of probability of all event is 1)

$$\therefore \quad 2p + 2k = 1$$

$$2k = 1 - 2p$$

$$k = \frac{1}{2} - p \qquad \textbf{(½ Mark)}$$

X_i	P_i	P_iX_i	$P_iX_i^2$
0	p	0	0
1	p	p	p
2	$\dfrac{1}{2} - p$	$1 - 2p$	$2 - 4p$
3	$\dfrac{1}{2} - p$	$\dfrac{3}{2} - 3p$	$\dfrac{9}{2} - 9p$
		$\sum P_iX_i = \dfrac{5}{4} - 4p$	$\sum P_iX_i^2 = \dfrac{13}{2} - 12p$

(2 Marks)

$$\sum P_iX_i^2 = 2\sum P_iX_i^2 \qquad \text{(given)}$$

$$\frac{13}{2} - 12p = 2\left(\frac{5}{2} - 4p\right)$$

$$\frac{13}{2} - \frac{10}{2} = 12p - 8p$$

$$\frac{3}{2} = 4p$$

$$p = \frac{3}{8} \qquad \textbf{(1 Mark)}$$

22. Let H_1 be the event that 6 appears on throwing a die

H_2 be the event that 6 does not appear on throwing a die

E be the event that he reports it is six. **(½ Mark)**

$$P(H_1) = \frac{1}{6}$$

$$P(H_2) = 1 - \frac{1}{6} = \frac{5}{6}$$

$$P(E/H_1) = \frac{4}{5}$$

$$P(E/H_2) = \frac{1}{5}$$ **(1 Mark)**

Using Bayes theorem

$$P(H_1/E) = \frac{P(H_1).P(E/H_1)}{P(H_1)P(E/H_1) + P(H_2)P(E/H_2)}$$ **(1 Mark)**

$$P(H_1/E) = \frac{\frac{1}{6} \times \frac{4}{5}}{\frac{1}{6} \times \frac{4}{5} + \frac{5}{6} \times \frac{1}{5}}$$

$$P(H_1/E) = \frac{4}{9}$$ **(1 Mark)**

Yes, Truthfulness leads to more respect in society.

(½ Mark)

23. Minimise $z = 5x + 10y$

$x + 2y = 120$

x	0	120	60
y	60	0	30

$x + y = 60$

x	0	60	40
y	60	0	20

$x - 2y = 0$

x	0	60	40
y	0	30	20

$, x \geq 0, y \geq 0$

(1 Mark)

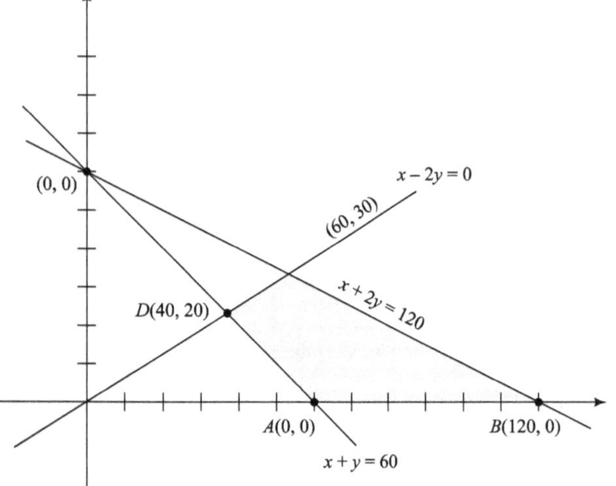

(2 Marks)

Corner Points	$Z = 5x + 10y$
(60, 0)	300
(120, 0)	600
(40, 20)	400
(60, 30)	600

Minimum value of $Z = 300$ at (60, 0). **(1 Mark)**

SECTION - D

24. Let $A = \begin{bmatrix} 1 & -1 & 2 \\ 0 & 2 & -3 \\ 3 & -2 & 4 \end{bmatrix}$

$$B = \begin{bmatrix} -2 & 0 & 1 \\ 9 & 2 & -3 \\ 6 & 1 & -2 \end{bmatrix}$$

$$AB = \begin{bmatrix} 1 & -1 & 2 \\ 0 & 2 & -3 \\ 3 & -2 & 4 \end{bmatrix}\begin{bmatrix} -2 & 0 & 1 \\ 9 & 2 & -3 \\ 6 & 1 & -2 \end{bmatrix}$$

$$= \begin{bmatrix} -2-9+12 & 0-2+2 & 1+3-4 \\ 0+18-18 & 0+4-3 & 0-6+6 \\ -6-18+24 & 0-4+4 & 3+6-8 \end{bmatrix}$$

$$= \begin{bmatrix} 1 & 0 & 0 \\ 0 & 1 & 0 \\ 0 & 0 & 1 \end{bmatrix} = I$$ **(2 Marks)**

$AB = I$

$B = A^{-1} I$

$B = A^{-1}$

$$A^{-1} = \begin{bmatrix} -2 & 0 & 1 \\ 9 & 2 & -3 \\ 6 & 1 & -2 \end{bmatrix}$$ **(1 Mark)**

Given equations: $x + 3z = 9$

$-x + 2y - 2z = 4$

$2x - 3y + 4z = -3$

Matrix form

$$\begin{bmatrix} 1 & 0 & 3 \\ -1 & 2 & -2 \\ 2 & -3 & 4 \end{bmatrix}\begin{bmatrix} x \\ y \\ z \end{bmatrix} = \begin{bmatrix} 9 \\ 4 \\ -3 \end{bmatrix}$$ **(1 Mark)**

$A^T X = C$

$X = (A^T)^{-1} C$

$X = (A^{-1})^T C$ **(1 Mark)**

$$\begin{bmatrix} x \\ y \\ z \end{bmatrix} = \begin{bmatrix} -2 & 9 & 6 \\ 0 & 2 & 1 \\ 1 & -3 & -2 \end{bmatrix} \begin{bmatrix} 9 \\ 4 \\ -3 \end{bmatrix}$$

$$\begin{bmatrix} x \\ y \\ z \end{bmatrix} = \begin{bmatrix} -18+36-18 \\ 0+8-3 \\ 9-12+6 \end{bmatrix}$$

$$\begin{bmatrix} x \\ y \\ z \end{bmatrix} = \begin{bmatrix} 0 \\ 5 \\ 3 \end{bmatrix}$$

$$\therefore \quad x = 0, \, y = 5, \, z = 3 \qquad \textbf{(1 Mark)}$$

25. Clearly $f^{-1}(y) = g(y) : [-5, \infty) \to R_+$

$$f(x) = 9x^2 + 6x - 5$$

$$fog(y) = f\left(\frac{\sqrt{y+6}-1}{3}\right)$$

$$= 9\left[\frac{\sqrt{y+6}-1}{3}\right]^2 + 6\left[\frac{\sqrt{y+6}-1}{3}\right] - 5 = y \qquad \textbf{(1 Mark)}$$

and $gof(x) = g(9x^2 + 6x - 5)$

$$= \frac{\sqrt{9x^2+6x+1}-1}{3} = x \qquad \textbf{(1 Mark)}$$

$$\therefore \quad g = f^{-1}$$

$\therefore f$ is invertible $\qquad \textbf{(1 Mark)}$

(i) $f^{-1}(10) = \dfrac{\sqrt{10+6}-1}{3} = \dfrac{\sqrt{16}-1}{3} = \dfrac{3}{3} = 1$ **(1 Mark)**

(ii) $f^{-1}(y) = \dfrac{4}{3}$

$$\frac{\sqrt{y+6}-1}{3} = \frac{4}{3}$$

$$\sqrt{y+6} = 5$$

Squaring on both sides

$$y + 6 = 25$$

$$y = 19 \qquad \textbf{(2 Marks)}$$

OR

$a * b = a - b + ab \; \forall \, a, b \in A = Q - [1]$

$b * a = b - a + ba$

$a * b \neq b * a$

$\therefore *$ is not commutative $\qquad \textbf{(1 Mark)}$

$$(a * b) * c = (a - b + ab) * c$$
$$= a - b - c + ab + ac - bc + abc$$
$$a * (b * c) = a * (b - c + bc)$$
$$= a - b + c + ab - bc + abc$$

$$(a * b) * c \neq a * (b * c)$$

$\therefore *$ is not associative $\qquad \textbf{(2 Marks)}$

Existence of identity

$$a * e = a - e + ae = a$$
$$\Rightarrow \quad e(a - 1) = 0$$
$$e = 0$$
$$e * a = e - a + ea = a$$
$$e(1 + a) = 2a$$
$$e = \frac{2a}{1+a}$$

$\therefore e$ is not unique $\qquad \textbf{(2 Marks)}$

$\therefore$ No identity element exists.

$$a * b = e = b * e$$

$\therefore$ No identity element exists.

Inverse element does not exist. $\qquad \textbf{(1 Mark)}$

26. Let base and hypotenous of right angle triangle be x and y respectively.

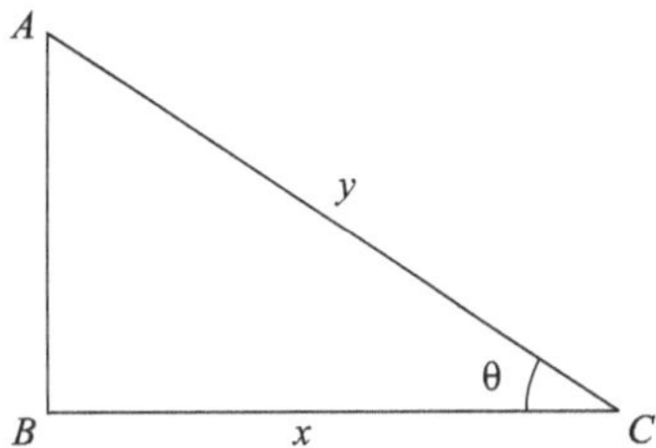

Also θ be angle between them.

Given: Sum of length of side and hypotenous

$$\therefore \quad x + y = k$$

Area of triangle $= \dfrac{1}{2} \times$ Base $\times$ height $\qquad$ ...(1)

$AB^2 = AC^2 - BC^2 \quad$ (By pythagoras theorem)

$AB = \sqrt{y^2 - x^2} \qquad\qquad$ ...(2) $\quad$ **(½ Mark)**

$$\therefore \quad \text{Area of } \Delta = \frac{1}{2}x\sqrt{y^2 - x^2}$$

$$A = \frac{1}{2}x\sqrt{(k-x)^2 - x^2} \qquad [\because x + y = k]$$

$$A = \frac{1}{2}x\sqrt{k^2 + x^2 - 2kx - x^2}$$

$$A = \frac{1}{2}x\sqrt{k^2 - 2kx} \qquad \textbf{(½ Mark)}$$

Squaring on both sides

$$A^2 = \frac{1}{4}x^2(k^2 - 2kx)$$

Let $A^2 = Z = \dfrac{1}{4}(k^2 x^2 - 2kx^3)$

$$\frac{dZ}{dx} = \frac{1}{4}[2k^2x - 6kx^2] \qquad \textbf{(1 Mark)}$$

$$\frac{dZ}{dx} = 0$$

$$2k^2x - 6k\,x^2 = 0$$

$$2k^2x = 6k\,x^2$$

$$x = \frac{k}{3} \qquad \ldots(3) \quad \textbf{(1 Mark)}$$

$$x = \frac{x+y}{3} \qquad [\because\ k = x + y]$$

$$3x - x = y$$

$$2x = y \qquad \ldots(4) \quad \textbf{(1 Mark)}$$

$$\frac{d^2z}{dx^2} = \frac{1}{4}[2k^2 - 12kx]$$

$$\left.\frac{d^2z}{dx^2}\right|_{x=\frac{k}{3}} = \frac{1}{4}[2k^2 - 4k^2] = -\frac{k^2}{2} < 0 \qquad \textbf{(1 Mark)}$$

$\therefore$ Area will be maximum for $2x = y$

$$\cos\theta = \frac{x}{y}$$

$$\cos\theta = \frac{x}{2x} = \frac{1}{2}$$

$$\cos\theta = \cos\frac{\pi}{3}$$

$$\theta = \frac{\pi}{3} \qquad \textbf{(1 Mark)}$$

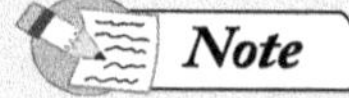

> **Note**
>
> *For maximum or minimum point* $\dfrac{dy}{dx} = 0$

27. Vertices of triangle $(-2, 1)$, $(0, 4)$ and $(2, 3)$

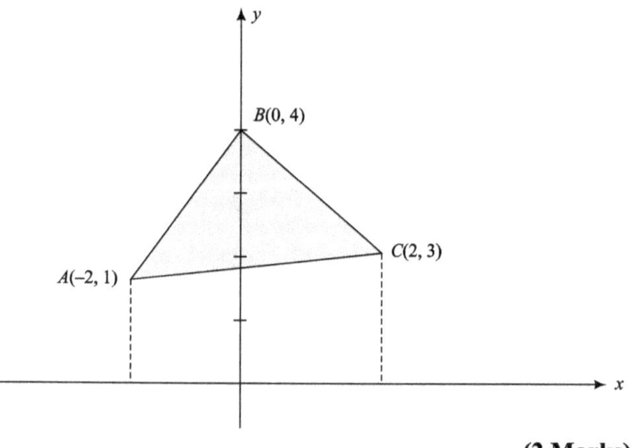

(2 Marks)

Equation of AB:

$$y - y_1 = \frac{y_2 - y_1}{x_2 - x_1}(x - x_1)$$

$$y - 1 = \frac{4-1}{2}(x + 2)$$

$$y - 1 = \frac{3}{2}x + 3$$

$$y = \frac{3}{2}x + 4 \qquad \textbf{(1 Mark)}$$

Similarly, equation of BC:

$$y = 4 - \frac{x}{2}$$

Equation of AC

$$y = \frac{1}{2}x + 2 \qquad \textbf{(1 Mark)}$$

Required area $= \int_{-2}^{0}(AB)\,dx + \int_{0}^{2}(BC)\,dx - \int_{-2}^{2}(AC)\,dx$

$$= \int_{-2}^{0}\left(\frac{3}{2}x + 4\right)dx + \int_{0}^{2}\left(4 - \frac{x}{2}\right)dx - \int_{-2}^{2}\left(\frac{1}{2}x + 2\right)dx$$

(1 Mark)

$$= \left(\frac{3}{4}x^2 + 4x\right)_{-2}^{0} + \left(4x - \frac{x^2}{4}\right)_{0}^{2} - \left(\frac{x^2}{4} + 2x\right)_{-2}^{2}$$

$$= 5 + 7 - 8 = 4 \text{ sq. units.} \qquad \textbf{(1 Mark)}$$

OR

$$x^2 + y^2 = 16 \qquad\qquad x = \sqrt{3}y$$

$$\Rightarrow x^2 = 3y^2$$

$$x^2 + y^2 = 16$$

$$3y^2 + y^2 = 16$$

$$y^2 = 4$$

$$y = \pm 2$$

$$x^2 = 12$$

$$x = \pm 2\sqrt{3}$$

Point of intersection $(2\sqrt{3}, 2)$ & $(-2\sqrt{3}, -2)$ **(1 Mark)**

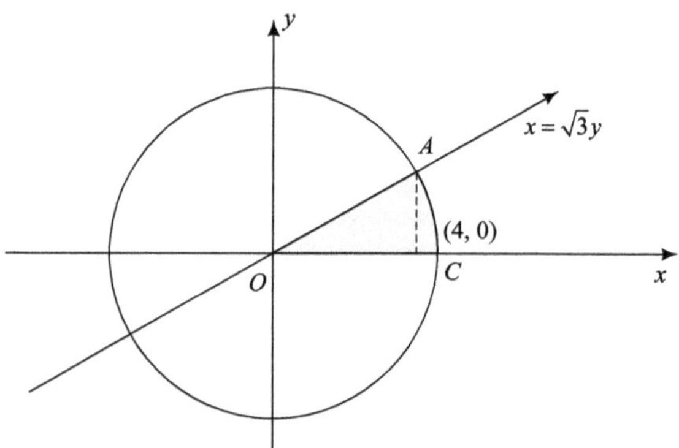

(1 Mark)

There are 2 possible region.

Req. area $= \int_0^{2\sqrt{3}} OA\, dx + \int_{2\sqrt{3}}^{4} \text{Curve } AC\, dx$

$= \int_0^{2\sqrt{3}} \dfrac{x}{\sqrt{3}}\, dx + \int_{2\sqrt{3}}^{4} \sqrt{4^2 - x^2}\, dx$ **(1 Mark)**

$= \dfrac{1}{2\sqrt{3}}\left(x^2\right)_0^{2\sqrt{3}} + \left[\dfrac{x\sqrt{16-x^2}}{2} + 8\sin^{-1}\dfrac{x}{4}\right]_{2\sqrt{3}}^{4}$

$$\left[\because \int \sqrt{a^2 - x^2}\, dx = \dfrac{x}{2}\sqrt{a^2 - x^2} + \dfrac{a^2}{2}\sin^{-1}\dfrac{x}{a}\right]$$

$= 2\sqrt{3} + 8\left(\dfrac{\pi}{2} - \dfrac{\pi}{3}\right) - 2\sqrt{3}$

$= \dfrac{4\pi}{3}$ sq. units   **(1 Mark)**

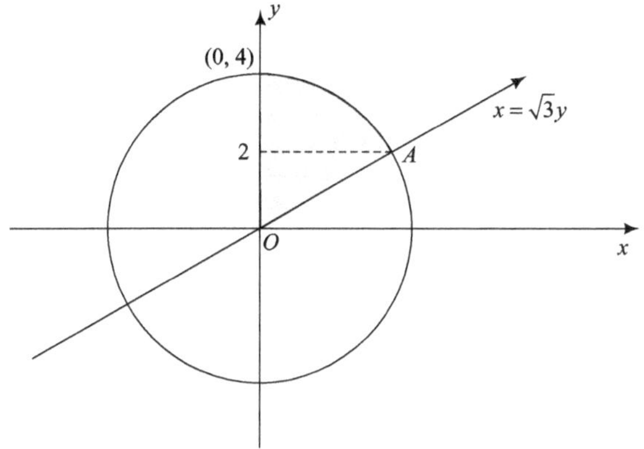

(1 Mark)

Required area $= \sqrt{3}\int_0^{2} y\, dx + \int_2^{4} \sqrt{4^2 - y^2}\, dy$

$= \sqrt{3}\left[\dfrac{y^2}{2}\right]_0^{2} + \left[\dfrac{y}{2}\sqrt{16 - y^2} + 8\sin^{-1}\dfrac{y}{4}\right]_2^{4}$

$= 2\sqrt{3} + 4\pi - 2\sqrt{3} - \dfrac{4\pi}{3} = \dfrac{8\pi}{3}$ sq. units   **(1 Mark)**

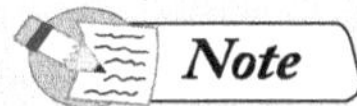 **Note**

Area of bounded region is obtain only by use of integration not by area formula.

28. $x\dfrac{dy}{dx} + y = x\cos x + \sin x$

$\dfrac{dy}{dx} + \dfrac{y}{x} = \cos x + \dfrac{\sin x}{x}$ **(1 Mark)**

This is linear differential equation of the form

$\dfrac{dy}{dx} + Py = Q$

where $P = \dfrac{1}{x}$, $Q = \cos x + \dfrac{\sin x}{x}$

$\therefore$ Integerating factor

I.F. $= e^{\int P\,dx} = e^{\int \frac{1}{x}\,dx} = e^{\log_x} = x$ **(2 Marks)**

$\therefore$ Solution is

$y \cdot x = \int \left(\dfrac{x\cos x + \sin x}{x}\right) x\, dx + C$

$y \cdot x = \int x\cos x\, dx + \int \sin x\, dx + C$

$xy = x\sin x - \int \sin x\, dx + \int \sin x\, dx + C$

$$\left[\because \int uv\, dx = u\int v\, dx - \int \dfrac{du}{dx}\left(\int v\, dx\right) dx\right]$$

$xy = x\sin x + C$ **(2 Marks)**

$y = \sin x + \dfrac{C}{x}$

when $x = \dfrac{\pi}{2}$, $y = 1$

$1 = \sin \dfrac{\pi}{2} + \dfrac{C}{x}$

$C = 0$

$\therefore$ Particular solution of the given differential equation is $y = \sin x$.   **(1 Mark)**

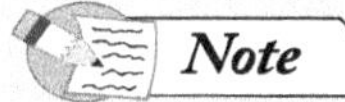 **Note**

Particular solution contains no arbitrary constants.

29. The equation of the plane passing through the intersection of planes

$\vec{r}\cdot\left[\left(2\hat{i} - \hat{j} + \hat{k}\right) + \lambda\left(\hat{i} - \hat{j}\right)\right] + 4\lambda - 1 = 0$

$\vec{r}\cdot\left[\left(2+\lambda\right)\hat{i} - \left(3+\lambda\right)\hat{j} + 4\hat{k}\right] + \left(4\lambda - 1\right) = 0$ ...(1) **(1 Mark)**

and it is perpendicular to the plane

$\vec{r}\cdot\left(2\hat{i} - \hat{j} + \hat{k}\right) + 8 = 0$

$\therefore \quad 2(2 + \lambda) - 1(-3 - \lambda) + 4 \times 1 = 0$

$4 + 2\lambda + 3 + \lambda + 4 = 0$

$3\lambda = -11$

$\lambda = -\dfrac{11}{3}$ **(1 Mark)**

Putting the value of λ in (1)

$\vec{r}\cdot\left[\left(2 - \dfrac{11}{3}\right)\hat{i} - \left(3 - \dfrac{11}{3}\right)\hat{j} + 4\hat{k}\right] + \left[4\times\left(\dfrac{-11}{3}\right) - 1\right] = 0$

$$\vec{r}.\left[\frac{-5}{3}\hat{i}+\frac{2}{3}\hat{j}+4\hat{k}\right]+\left[\frac{-47}{3}\right]=0$$

$$\vec{r}.\left(-5\hat{i}+2\hat{j}+12\hat{k}\right)=47 \qquad\qquad \textbf{(1 Mark)}$$

Cartesian equation

$$-5x + 2y + 12z - 47 = 0 \qquad\qquad \textbf{(½ Mark)}$$

It is required equation of plane

Line $\dfrac{x-1}{1}=\dfrac{y-2}{\frac{1}{2}}=\dfrac{z-4}{\frac{1}{3}}$ lies on the plane.

This line passes through the point (1, 2, 4)   **(½ Mark)**

Now putting this point in the equation of plane,

we have

$$\text{L.H.S.} = \left(\hat{i}+2\hat{j}+4\hat{k}\right).\left(-5\hat{i}+2\hat{j}+12\hat{k}\right)$$

$$= 1(-5) + 2 \times 2 + 4 \times 12$$

$$= -5 + 4 + 48 = 47 = \text{R.H.S.} \qquad\qquad \textbf{(1 Mark)}$$

So (1, 2, 4) lies on the given plane.

Also, $1 \times (-5) + 2 \times \dfrac{1}{2} + 12 \times \dfrac{1}{3} = -5 + 1 + 4 = 0$

So the vector normal to the plane and vector parallel to the line are perpendicular to each other. Hence, the plane thus contains the given line.   **(1 Mark)**

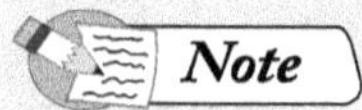
Note

Line of intersection of two planes is perpendicular to normals of both planes.

OR

Given lines:

$$\frac{x-8}{3}=\frac{y+19}{-16}=\frac{z-10}{7} \qquad ...(1)$$

and $\dfrac{x-15}{3}=\dfrac{y-29}{8}=\dfrac{z-5}{-5}$ ...(2)

Let a, b, c be the direction ratios of the required line. Since the required line is perpendicular to (1) and (2), we have

$$3a - 16b + 7c = 0 \qquad ...(3)$$

and $3a + 8b - 5c = 0$ ...(4)   **(2 Marks)**

Solving (3) and (4) by the method of cross multiplication, we have

$$\frac{a}{80-50}=\frac{b}{21+15}=\frac{c}{24+48}$$

$$\frac{a}{24}=\frac{b}{36}=\frac{c}{72}$$

$$\frac{a}{2}=\frac{b}{3}=\frac{c}{6}$$

Thus, the required line has the direction ratios 2, 3, 6.

(2 Marks)

Thus, the cartesian equation of the required line passing through (1, 2, –4) is:

$$\frac{x-1}{2}=\frac{y-2}{3}=\frac{z+4}{6} \qquad\qquad \textbf{(1 Mark)}$$

Also its vector equation is

$$\vec{r} = \left(\hat{i}+2\hat{j}-4\hat{k}\right)+\lambda\left(2\hat{i}+3\hat{j}+6\hat{k}\right) \qquad \textbf{(1 Mark)}$$

CBSE Board Solved Paper

Time Allowed : 3 Hours   *Maximum Marks : 100*

General Instructions:
  (i)   All questions are compulsory.
  (ii)   Please check that this Question Paper contains 26 questions.
  (iii) Marks for each question are indicated against it.
  (iv) Question **1** to **6** in **Section-A** are Very Short Answer Type Questions carrying **one** mark each.
  (v)   Question **7** to **19** in **Section-B** are Long Answer **I** Type Questions carrying **4** marks each.
  (vi) Question **20** to **26** in **Section-C** are Long Answer **II** Type Questions carrying **6** marks each.
  (vii) Please write down the serial number of the Question before attempting it.

SECTION - A

1. The two vectors $\hat{j}+\hat{k}$ and $3\hat{i}-\hat{j}+4\hat{k}$ represent the two sides AB and AC, respectively of a $\triangle$ABC. Find the length of the median through A.

2. Find the vector equation of a plane which is at a distance of 5 units from the origin and its normal vector is $2\hat{i}-3\hat{j}+6\hat{k}$.

3. Find the maximum value of $\begin{vmatrix} 1 & 1 & 1 \\ 1 & 1+\sin\theta & 1 \\ 1 & 1 & 1+\cos\theta \end{vmatrix}$

4. If A is a square matrix such that $A^2 = I$, then find the simplified value of $(A-I)^3 + (A+I)^3 - 7A$.

5. Matrix $A = \begin{bmatrix} 0 & 2b & -2 \\ 3 & 1 & 3 \\ 3a & 3 & -1 \end{bmatrix}$ is given to be symmetric, find values of a and b.

6. Find the position vector of a point which divides the join of points with position vectors $\vec{a}-2\vec{b}$ and $2\vec{a}+\vec{b}$ externally in the ratio $2:1$.

SECTION - B

7. Find the general solution of the following differential equation :
$$\left(1+y^2\right)+\left(x-e^{\tan^{-1}y}\right)\frac{dy}{dx} = 0$$

8. Show that the vectors $\vec{a}, \vec{b}$ and $\vec{c}$ are coplanar if $\vec{a}+\vec{b}, \vec{b}+\vec{c}$ and $\vec{c}+\vec{a}$ are coplanar.

9. Find the vector and Cartesian equations of the line through the point $(1, 2, -4)$ and perpendicular to the two lines.
$$\vec{r} = \left(8\hat{i}-19\hat{j}+10\hat{k}\right)+\lambda\left(3\hat{i}-16\hat{j}+7\hat{k}\right) \text{ and}$$
$$\vec{r} = \left(15\hat{i}+29\hat{j}+5\hat{k}\right)+\mu\left(3\hat{i}+8\hat{j}-5\hat{k}\right)$$

10. Three persons A, B and C apply for a job of Manager in a Private Company. Chances of their selection (A, B and C) are in the ratio $1:2:4$. The probabilities that A, B and C can introduce changes to improve profits of the company are 0.8, 0.5 and 0.3 respectively. If the change does not take place, find the probability that it is due to the appointment of C.

OR

A and B throw a pair of dice alternately. A wins the game if he gets a total of 7 and B wins the game if he gets a total of 10. If A starts the game, then find the probability that B wins.

11. Prove that:
$$\tan^{-1}\frac{1}{5}+\tan^{-1}\frac{1}{7}+\tan^{-1}\frac{1}{3}+\tan^{-1}\frac{1}{8} = \frac{\pi}{4}$$

OR

Solve for x :
$$2\tan^{-1}(\cos x) = \tan^{-1}(2\,\mathrm{cosec}\,x)$$

12. The monthly incomes of Aryan and Babban are in the ratio $3:4$ and their monthly expenditures are in the ratio $5:7$. If each saves ₹15,000 per month, find their monthly incomes using matrix method. This problem reflects which value?

13. If $x = a \sin 2t\,(1 + \cos 2t)$ and $y = b \cos 2t\,(1 - \cos 2t)$, find the values of $\dfrac{dy}{dx}$ at $t = \dfrac{\pi}{4}$ and $t = \dfrac{\pi}{3}$.

OR

If $y = x^x$, prove that $\dfrac{d^2 y}{dx^2} - \dfrac{1}{y}\left(\dfrac{dy}{dx}\right)^2 - \dfrac{y}{x} = 0.$

14. Find the values of p and q for which

$$f(x) = \begin{cases} \dfrac{1 - \sin^3 x}{3 \cos^2 x} & , \text{ if } x < \dfrac{\pi}{2} \\[2mm] p & , \text{ if } x = \pi/2 \\[2mm] \dfrac{q(1 - \sin x)}{(\pi - 2x)^2} & , \text{ if } x > \pi/2 \end{cases}$$

is continuous at $x = \pi/2$.

15. Show that the equation of normal at any point t on the curve $x = 3 \cos t - \cos^3 t$ and $y = 3 \sin t - \sin^3 t$ is

$4\,(y \cos^3 t - x \sin^3 t) = 3 \sin 4t.$

16. Find $\displaystyle\int \dfrac{(3 \sin\theta - 2)\cos\theta}{5 - \cos^2\theta - 4\sin\theta}\,d\theta$

OR

Evaluate $\displaystyle\int_0^\pi e^{2x} \cdot \sin\left(\dfrac{\pi}{4} + x\right) dx$

17. Find $\displaystyle\int \dfrac{\sqrt{x}}{\sqrt{a^3 - x^3}}\,dx.$

18. Evaluate $\displaystyle\int_{-1}^{2} \left|x^3 - x\right|\,dx.$

19. Find the particular solution of the differential equation $(1 - y^2)(1 + \log x)\,dx + 2xy\,dy = 0$, given that $y = 0$ when $x = 1$.

SECTION - C

20. Find the coordinate of the point P where the line through A$(3, -4, -5)$ and B$(2, -3, 1)$ crosses the plane passing through three points L$(2, 2, 1)$, M$(3, 0, 1)$ and N$(4, -1, 0)$. Also, find the ratio in which P divides the line segment AB.

21. An urn contains 3 white and 6 red balls. Four balls are drawn one by one with replacement from the urn. Find the probability distribution of the number of red balls drawn. Also find mean and variance of the distribution.

22. A manufacturer produces two products A and B. Both the products are processed on two different machines. The available capacity of first machine is 12 hours and that of second machine is 9 hours per day. Each unit of product A requires 3 hours on both machines and each unit of product B requires 2 hours on first machine and 1 hour on second machine. Each unit of product A is sold at ₹7 profit and B at a profit of ₹4. Find the production level per day for maximum profit graphically.

23. Let $f : N \to N$ be a function defined as $f(x) = 9x^2 + 6x - 5$. Show that $f : N \to S$, where S is the range of f, is invertible. Find the inverse of f and hence find $f^{-1}(43)$ and $f^{-1}(163)$.

24. Prove that $\begin{vmatrix} yz - x^2 & zx - y^2 & xy - z^2 \\ zx - y^2 & xy - z^2 & yz - x^2 \\ xy - z^2 & yz - x^2 & zx - y^2 \end{vmatrix}$ is divisible by $(x + y + z)$ and hence find the quotient.

OR

Using elementary transformations, find the inverse of the matrix $A = \begin{pmatrix} 8 & 4 & 3 \\ 2 & 1 & 1 \\ 1 & 2 & 2 \end{pmatrix}$ and use it to solve the following system of linear equations :

$8x + 4y + 3z = 19$

$2x + y + z = 5$

$x + 2y + 2z = 7$

25. Show that the altitude of the right circular cone of maximum volume that can be inscribed in a sphere of radius r is $\dfrac{4r}{3}$. Also find maximum volume in terms of volume of the sphere.

OR

Find the intervals in which $f(x) = \sin 3x - \cos 3x$, $0 < x < \pi$, is strictly increasing or strictly decreasing.

26. Using integration find the area of the region $\left\{(x, y) : x^2 + y^2 \le 2ax,\ y^2 \ge ax,\ x, y \ge 0\right\}.$

Solutions

SECTION - A

1.

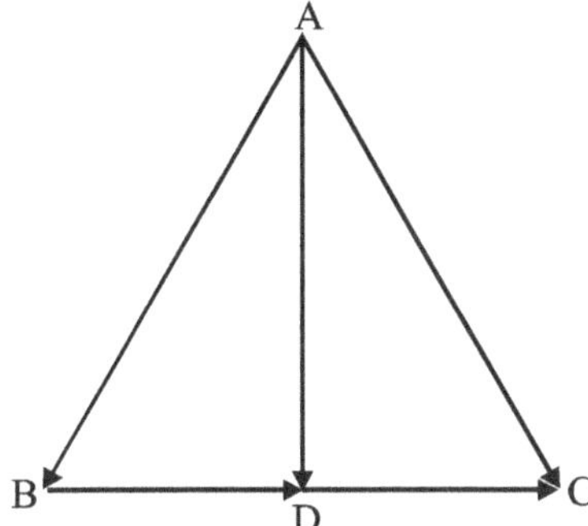

In the given ΔABC, we have

$\overrightarrow{BC} = \overrightarrow{AC} - \overrightarrow{AB}$ (Triangle Law of Vector Addition)

$= \left(3\hat{i} - \hat{j} + 4\hat{k}\right) - \left(\hat{j} + \hat{k}\right) = 3\hat{i} - 2\hat{j} + 3\hat{k}$ **(½ Mark)**

Here, AD is the median.

$\therefore \overrightarrow{BD} = \dfrac{1}{2}\overrightarrow{BC} = \dfrac{3}{2}\hat{i} - \hat{j} + \dfrac{3}{2}\hat{k}$

In ΔABD, using the triangle law of vector addition, we have $\overrightarrow{AD} = \overrightarrow{AB} + \overrightarrow{BD}$

So, $\overrightarrow{AD} = \left(\hat{j} + \hat{k}\right) + \left(\dfrac{3}{2}\hat{i} - \hat{j} + \dfrac{3}{2}\hat{k}\right) = \dfrac{3}{2}\hat{i} + 0\hat{j} + \dfrac{5}{2}\hat{k}$

$\therefore AD = \sqrt{\left(\dfrac{3}{2}\right)^2 + 0^2 + \left(\dfrac{5}{2}\right)^2} = \dfrac{1}{2}\sqrt{34}$ **(½ Mark)**

Hence, the length of the median through A is $\dfrac{1}{2}\sqrt{34}$ units.

2.   Normal vector, $\vec{n} = 2\hat{i} - 3\hat{j} + 6\hat{k}$

Then, $\hat{n} = \dfrac{\vec{n}}{|\vec{n}|} = \dfrac{2\hat{i} - 3\hat{j} + 6\hat{k}}{\sqrt{2^2 + 3^2 + 6^2}} = \dfrac{2\hat{i} - 3\hat{j} + 6\hat{k}}{\sqrt{49}} = \dfrac{2\hat{i} - 3\hat{j} + 6\hat{k}}{7}$

   (½ Mark)

Here, $d = 5$

Vector equation of the plane is given by

$\vec{r} \cdot \hat{n} = d$

Hence, the required equation of the plane is

$\vec{r} \cdot \left(\dfrac{2}{7}\hat{i} - \dfrac{3}{7}\hat{j} + \dfrac{6}{7}\hat{k}\right) = 5$ **(½ Mark)**

3. $\begin{vmatrix} 1 & 1 & 1 \\ 1 & 1+\sin\theta & 1 \\ 1 & 1 & 1+\cos\theta \end{vmatrix}$

Applying $R_2 \to R_2 - R_1$ and $R_3 \to R_3 - R_1$

$\Rightarrow \begin{vmatrix} 1 & 1 & 1 \\ 0 & \sin\theta & 0 \\ 0 & 0 & \cos\theta \end{vmatrix}$ **(½ Mark)**

$= \sin\theta \cos\theta = \dfrac{\sin 2\theta}{2}$

We know that, $-1 \le \sin 2\theta \le 1$

Therefore, required maximum value $= \dfrac{1}{2} \times 1 = \dfrac{1}{2}$ **(½ Mark)**

 **Note**

To find the value of determinant make two zero in any one row or column by using properties of determinate then expand through that row or column.

4. $(A-I)^3 + (A+I)^3 - 7A$

$= A^3 - I^3 - 3A^2 I + 3AI^2 + A^3 + I^3 + 3A^2 I + 3AI^2 - 7A$

   (½ Mark)

$= 2A^3 + 6AI^2 - 7A$

$= 2A \cdot A^2 + 6AI^2 - 7A$ (Given : $A^2 = I$)

$= 8A - 7A$

$= A$ **(½ Mark)**

5.   Given : $A = \begin{bmatrix} 0 & 2b & -2 \\ 3 & 1 & 3 \\ 3a & 3 & -1 \end{bmatrix}$

$\Rightarrow A^T = \begin{bmatrix} 0 & 3 & 3a \\ 2b & 1 & 3 \\ -2 & 3 & -1 \end{bmatrix}$ **(½ Mark)**

A matrix is symmetric if $A = A^T$.

Thus, $\begin{bmatrix} 0 & 2b & -2 \\ 3 & 1 & 3 \\ 3a & 3 & -1 \end{bmatrix} = \begin{bmatrix} 0 & 3 & 3a \\ 2b & 1 & 3 \\ -2 & 3 & -1 \end{bmatrix}$

Comparing both sides, we get

$$2b = 3 \Rightarrow b = \frac{3}{2}$$

And, $3a = -2 \Rightarrow a = \frac{-2}{3}$

Therefore, $a = \frac{-2}{3}$ and $b = \frac{3}{2}$ **(½ Mark)**

6. Let A and B be the points with position vectors $\vec{a} - 2\vec{b}$ and $2\vec{a} + \vec{b}$ respectively.

Also, assume that R divides AB externally in the ratio 2 : 1.

Therefore, position vector of $R = \dfrac{2 \times (2\vec{a} + \vec{b}) - 1 \times (\vec{a} - 2\vec{b})}{2 - 1}$

$$= 3\vec{a} + 4\vec{b}$$ **(1 Mark)**

SECTION - B

7. Given : $\left(1 + y^2\right) + \left(x - e^{\tan^{-1} y}\right) \dfrac{dy}{dx} = 0$

Let $\tan^{-1} y = t$

$\Rightarrow \quad y = \tan t$

$\Rightarrow \quad \dfrac{dy}{dx} = \sec^2 t \dfrac{dt}{dx}$ **(½ Mark)**

Therefore, the equation becomes

$$\left(1 + \tan^2 t\right) + \left(x - e^t\right) \sec^2 t \frac{dt}{dx} = 0$$

$$\Rightarrow \quad \sec^2 t + \left(x - e^t\right)\left(\sec^2 t\right)\frac{dt}{dx} = 0$$

$$\Rightarrow \quad \sec^2 t \left[1 + \left(x - e^t\right)\frac{dt}{dx}\right] = 0$$

$$\Rightarrow \quad 1 + \left(x - e^t\right)\frac{dt}{dx} = 0 \quad \Rightarrow \quad \left(x - e^t\right)\frac{dt}{dx} = -1$$

$$\Rightarrow \quad x - e^t = -\frac{dx}{dt} \quad \Rightarrow \quad \frac{dx}{dt} + 1.x = e^t$$ **(1½ Marks)**

The above equation is a linear first order differential equation

of the form $\dfrac{dx}{dt} + Px = Q$

Integrating factor, $\text{I.F.} = e^{\int 1.dt} = e^t$ **(½ Mark)**

Solution of the differential equation is given by

$$x \times \text{I.F.} = \int Q \times \text{I.F.} \ dt + C$$

$$x \times e^t = \int \left(e^t \times e^t\right) dt + C = \int e^{2t} dt + C$$

$$x e^t = \frac{1}{2} e^{2t} + C$$ ...(1)   **(1 Mark)**

Substituting the value of t in (1), we get

$$x e^{\tan^{-1} y} = \frac{1}{2} e^{2 \tan^{-1} y} + C_1$$

$$\Rightarrow \quad e^{2 \tan^{-1} y} = 2x e^{\tan^{-1} y} + C$$

It is the required general solution.   **(½ Mark)**

8. It is given that $\vec{a} + \vec{b}$, $\vec{b} + \vec{c}$ and $\vec{c} + \vec{a}$ are coplanar.

Therefore,

Scalar triple product = Volume of the parallelopiped = 0

$$\left(\vec{a} + \vec{b}\right).\left[\left(\vec{b} + \vec{c}\right) \times \left(\vec{c} + \vec{a}\right)\right] = 0$$ **(1 Mark)**

$$\Rightarrow \quad \left(\vec{a} + \vec{b}\right).\left[\left(\vec{b} \times \vec{c}\right) + \left(\vec{b} \times \vec{a}\right) + 0 + \left(\vec{c} \times \vec{a}\right)\right] = 0$$ **(1 Mark)**

$$\Rightarrow \quad \vec{a}.\left(\vec{b} \times \vec{c}\right) + \vec{a}.\left(\vec{b} \times \vec{a}\right) + \vec{a}.\left(\vec{c} \times \vec{a}\right)$$
$$+ \ \vec{b}.\left(\vec{b} \times \vec{c}\right) + \vec{b}.\left(\vec{b} \times \vec{a}\right) + \vec{b}.\left(\vec{c} \times \vec{a}\right) = 0$$ **(1 Mark)**

$$\Rightarrow \quad [\vec{a}\ \vec{b}\ \vec{c}] + 0 + 0 + 0 + 0 + [\vec{b}\ \vec{c}\ \vec{a}] = 0$$

$$\left(\because [\vec{a}\ \vec{b}\ \vec{c}] = [\vec{b}\ \vec{c}\ \vec{a}]\right)$$

$$\Rightarrow \quad 2[\vec{a}\ \vec{b}\ \vec{c}] = 0 \quad \Rightarrow [\vec{a}\ \vec{b}\ \vec{c}] = 0$$ **(1 Mark)**

Therefore, the vectors $\vec{a}$, $\vec{b}$ and $\vec{c}$ are coplanar.

9. The equations of the given lines are

$$\vec{r} = \left(8\hat{i} - 19\hat{j} + 10\hat{k}\right) + \lambda\left(3\hat{i} - 16\hat{j} + 7\hat{k}\right)$$ ...(1)

$$\vec{r} = \left(15\hat{i} + 29\hat{j} + 5\hat{k}\right) + \mu\left(3\hat{i} + 8\hat{j} - 5\hat{k}\right)$$ ...(2)

Vector parallel to (1) is $\vec{b_1} = 3\hat{i} - 16\hat{j} + 7\hat{k}$

Vector parallel to (2) is $\vec{b_2} = 3\hat{i} + 8\hat{j} - 5\hat{k}$ **(1 Mark)**

The required line is perpendicular to the given lines. So, the vector $\overrightarrow{b}$ parallel to the required line is perpendicular to $\overrightarrow{b_1}$ and $\overrightarrow{b_2}$.

$$\therefore \ \overrightarrow{b} = \overrightarrow{b_1} \times \overrightarrow{b_2} = \begin{vmatrix} \hat{i} & \hat{j} & \hat{k} \\ 3 & -16 & 7 \\ 3 & 8 & -5 \end{vmatrix} = 24\hat{i} + 36\hat{j} + 72\hat{k} \quad \textbf{(1 Mark)}$$

As, line passes through $(1, 2, -4)$

$$\overrightarrow{a} = \hat{i} + 2\hat{j} - 4\hat{k} \qquad \textbf{(½ Mark)}$$

Thus, the vector equation of the required line is $\overrightarrow{r} = \overrightarrow{a} + k\,\overrightarrow{b}$

$$\Rightarrow \quad \overrightarrow{r} = \left(\hat{i} + 2\hat{j} - 4\hat{k}\right) + k\left(24\hat{i} + 36\hat{j} + 72\hat{k}\right) \qquad \textbf{(1 Mark)}$$

Also, the Cartesian equation of required line is

$$\frac{x-1}{24} = \frac{y-2}{36} = \frac{z+4}{72} \qquad \textbf{(½ Mark)}$$

 **Note**

If a line is perpendicular to the given two lines, then normal vector of required line and given lines will be parallel to each other.

10. Let x, 2x and 4x be the events denoting the selection of A, B and C as managers, respectively.

$$\therefore \ \text{Probability of selection of } \ A = \frac{x}{x + 2x + 4x} = \frac{1}{7}$$

$$\text{Probability of selection of } B = \frac{2x}{x + 2x + 4x} = \frac{2}{7}$$

$$\text{Probability of selection of } C = \frac{4x}{x + 2x + 4x} = \frac{4}{7} \quad \textbf{(1 Mark)}$$

Let A be the event denoting the change not taking place.

$$\therefore \ P\left(\frac{A}{E_1}\right) = \text{Probability that A does not introduce change} = 0.2$$

$$P\left(\frac{A}{E_2}\right) = \text{Probability that B does not introduce change} = 0.5$$

$$P\left(\frac{A}{E_3}\right) = \text{Probability that C does not introduce change} = 0.7$$

$$\textbf{(1 Mark)}$$

$$\therefore \ \text{Required probability} = P\left(\frac{E_3}{A}\right)$$

Using Bayes' theorem, we have

$$P\left(\frac{E_3}{A}\right) = \frac{P(E_3)P\left(\dfrac{A}{E_3}\right)}{P(E_1)P\left(\dfrac{A}{E_1}\right) + P(E_2)P\left(\dfrac{A}{E_2}\right) + P(E_3)P\left(\dfrac{A}{E_3}\right)}$$

$$\textbf{(1 Mark)}$$

$$= \frac{\dfrac{4}{7} \times 0.7}{\dfrac{1}{7} \times 0.2 + \dfrac{2}{7} \times 0.5 + \dfrac{4}{7} \times 0.7} = \frac{2.8}{0.2 + 1 + 2.8} = \frac{2.8}{4} = 0.7$$

$$\textbf{(1 Mark)}$$

OR

Total of 7 on the dice can be obtained in the following ways:
$(1, 6), (6, 1), (2, 5), (5, 2), (3, 4), (4, 3)$

$$\text{Probability of getting a total of } 7 = \frac{6}{36} = \frac{1}{6}$$

$$\text{Probability of not getting a total of } 7 = 1 - \frac{1}{6} = \frac{5}{6}$$

Total of 10 on the dice can be obtained in the following ways: $(4, 6), (6, 4), (5, 5)$

$$\text{Probability of getting a total of } 10 = \frac{3}{36} = \frac{1}{12}$$

$$\text{Probability of not getting a total of } 10 = 1 - \frac{1}{12} = \frac{11}{12}$$

$$\textbf{(1 Mark)}$$

Let E and F be the two events, defined as follows:

E = Getting a total of 7 in a single throw of a dice

F = Getting a total of 10 in a single throw of a dice

$$P(E) = \frac{1}{6}, \ P(F) = \frac{1}{12} \Rightarrow P\left(\overline{E}\right) = \frac{5}{6}, \ P\left(\overline{F}\right) = \frac{11}{12} \quad \textbf{(½ Mark)}$$

A wins if he gets a total of 7 in 1st, 3rd or 5th .... throws & so on.

$$\text{Probability of A getting a total of 7 in the 1st throw} = \frac{1}{6}$$

A will get the 3rd throw if he fails in the 1st throw and B fails in the 2nd throw.

Probability of A getting a total of 7 in the 3rd throw

$$= P\left(\overline{E}\right)P\left(\overline{F}\right)P(E) = \frac{5}{6} \times \frac{11}{12} \times \frac{1}{6}$$

Similarly, probability of getting a total of 7 in the 5th throw is

$$P(\overline{E})P(\overline{F})P(\overline{E})P(\overline{F})P(E) = \frac{5}{6} \times \frac{11}{12} \times \frac{5}{6} \times \frac{11}{12} \times \frac{1}{6}$$ **(1 Mark)**

Probability of winning of A

$$= \frac{1}{6} + \left(\frac{5}{6} \times \frac{11}{12} \times \frac{1}{6}\right) + \left(\frac{5}{6} \times \frac{11}{12} \times \frac{5}{6} \times \frac{11}{12} \times \frac{1}{6}\right) + ...$$

$$= \frac{\dfrac{1}{6}}{1 - \dfrac{5}{6} \times \dfrac{11}{12}} = \frac{\dfrac{1}{6}}{\dfrac{72 - 55}{72}} = \frac{12}{17}$$ **(1 Mark)**

Probability of winning of B = 1 – Probability of winning of A

$$= 1 - \frac{12}{17} = \frac{5}{17}$$ **(½ Mark)**

11. $\left(\tan^{-1}\dfrac{1}{5} + \tan^{-1}\dfrac{1}{7}\right) + \left(\tan^{-1}\dfrac{1}{3} + \tan^{-1}\dfrac{1}{8}\right)$

$$= \tan^{-1}\left(\frac{\dfrac{1}{5} + \dfrac{1}{7}}{1 - \dfrac{1}{5} \times \dfrac{1}{7}}\right) + \tan^{-1}\left(\frac{\dfrac{1}{3} + \dfrac{1}{8}}{1 - \dfrac{1}{3} \times \dfrac{1}{8}}\right)$$ **(1½ Marks)**

$$\left[\because \tan^{-1}X + \tan^{-1}Y = \tan^{-1}\left(\frac{X+Y}{1-XY}\right)\right]$$

$$= \tan^{-1}\frac{6}{17} + \tan^{-1}\frac{11}{23} = \tan^{-1}\left(\frac{\dfrac{6}{17} + \dfrac{11}{23}}{1 - \dfrac{6}{17} \times \dfrac{11}{23}}\right)$$ **(1½ Marks)**

$$= \tan^{-1}\left(\frac{325}{325}\right) = \tan^{-1}1 = \frac{\pi}{4}$$ **(1 Mark)**

Hence, proved.

OR

$2\tan^{-1}(\cos x) = \tan^{-1}(2\operatorname{cosec} x)$ **(1 Mark)**

$$\Rightarrow \tan^{-1}\left(\frac{2\cos x}{1 - \cos^2 x}\right) = \tan^{-1}(2\operatorname{cosec} x)$$ **(1 Mark)**

$$\left[\because 2\tan^{-1}x = \tan^{-1}\left(\frac{2x}{1-x^2}\right)\right]$$

$$\Rightarrow \frac{2\cos x}{\sin^2 x} = 2\operatorname{cosec} x$$

$\Rightarrow \cos x = \sin x \Rightarrow \tan x = 1$

$$\therefore \ x = \frac{\pi}{4}$$ **(2 Marks)**

12. Let the monthly incomes of Aryan and Babban be $3x$ and $4x$, respectively. Suppose their monthly expenditures are $5y$ and $7y$, respectively. Since each saves ₹ 15,000 per month,

Monthly savings of Aryan : $3x - 5y = 15000$

Monthly savings of Babban : $4x - 7y = 15000$

The above system of equations can be written in the matrix form as follows:

$$\begin{bmatrix} 3 & -5 \\ 4 & -7 \end{bmatrix}\begin{bmatrix} x \\ y \end{bmatrix} = \begin{bmatrix} 15000 \\ 15000 \end{bmatrix}$$ **(1 Mark)**

or $AX = B$, where

$$A = \begin{bmatrix} 3 & -5 \\ 4 & -7 \end{bmatrix}, \ X = \begin{bmatrix} x \\ y \end{bmatrix} \text{ and } B = \begin{bmatrix} 15000 \\ 15000 \end{bmatrix}$$

Now, $|A| = \begin{vmatrix} 3 & -5 \\ 4 & -7 \end{vmatrix} = -21 - (-20) = -1$ **(1 Mark)**

$$\text{Adj } A = \begin{bmatrix} -7 & -4 \\ 5 & 3 \end{bmatrix}^T = \begin{bmatrix} -7 & 5 \\ -4 & 3 \end{bmatrix}$$

So, $A^{-1} = \dfrac{1}{|A|}\text{Adj } A = -1\begin{bmatrix} -7 & 5 \\ -4 & 3 \end{bmatrix} = \begin{bmatrix} 7 & -5 \\ 4 & -3 \end{bmatrix}$ **(1 Mark)**

$\therefore \ X = A^{-1}B$

$$\Rightarrow \begin{bmatrix} x \\ y \end{bmatrix} = \begin{bmatrix} 7 & -5 \\ 4 & -3 \end{bmatrix}\begin{bmatrix} 15000 \\ 15000 \end{bmatrix}$$

$$\Rightarrow \begin{bmatrix} x \\ y \end{bmatrix} = \begin{bmatrix} 105000 - 75000 \\ 60000 - 45000 \end{bmatrix}$$

$$\Rightarrow \begin{bmatrix} x \\ y \end{bmatrix} = \begin{bmatrix} 30000 \\ 15000 \end{bmatrix}$$

$\Rightarrow x = 30,000 \text{ and } y = 15,000$

Therefore,

Monthly income of Aryan = $3 \times$ ₹ 30,000 = ₹ 90,000

Monthly income of Babban = $4 \times$ ₹ 30,000 = ₹ 1,20,000

Here, we are encouraged to understand the importance of savings. We should save certain part of our monthly income for the future. **(1 Mark)**

Note

Any given number of equations can be converted into matrix form to get the solution.

13. Given that :

$x = a\sin 2t(1 + \cos 2t)$

$y = b\cos 2t(1 - \cos 2t)$

Differentiating the above equations w.r.t. t, we get

$$\frac{dx}{dt} = 2a\cos 2t\,(1+\cos 2t) - 2a\sin^2 2t$$

$$= 2a\cos 2t + 2a(\cos^2 2t - \sin^2 2t)$$

$$\frac{dx}{dt} = a\left[2\cos 2t + 2\cos 4t\right] \qquad \textbf{(1 Mark)}$$

$$\frac{dy}{dt} = -2b\sin 2t(1-\cos 2t) + b\cos 2t\,(2\sin 2t)$$

$$= -2b\sin 2t + 4b\sin 2t\cos 2t$$

$$= -2b\sin 2t + 2b\sin 4t$$

and $\dfrac{dy}{dt} = b\left[-2\sin 2t + 2\sin 4t\right] \qquad \textbf{(1 Mark)}$

Now, $\dfrac{dy}{dx} = \dfrac{\dfrac{dy}{dt}}{\dfrac{dx}{dt}} = \dfrac{b\left[-2\sin 2t + 2\sin 4t\right]}{a\left[2\cos 2t + 2\cos 4t\right]}$

$$\Rightarrow \frac{dy}{dx} = \frac{b}{a}\left[\frac{-2\sin 2t + 2\sin 4t}{2\cos 2t + 2\cos 4t}\right] \qquad \textbf{(1 Mark)}$$

$$\therefore \left.\frac{dy}{dx}\right|_{t=\frac{\pi}{4}} = \frac{b}{a}\left[\frac{-2+0}{0-2}\right] = \frac{b}{a}$$

and $\left.\dfrac{dy}{dx}\right|_{t=\frac{\pi}{3}} = \dfrac{b}{a}\left[\dfrac{-2\sqrt{3}}{-2}\right] = \dfrac{\sqrt{3}b}{a} \qquad \textbf{(1 Mark)}$

OR

$y = x^x$

Taking logarithm on both sides, we have

$\log y = x\log x$

$$\frac{1}{y}\frac{dy}{dx} = \log x + x\times\frac{1}{x} = 1 + \log x$$

$$\frac{dy}{dx} = x^x[1+\log x] \qquad \textbf{(1 Mark)}$$

$$\frac{d^2 y}{dx^2} = \frac{d(x^x)}{dx}(1+\log x) + x^x\left[\frac{d}{dx}(1+\log x)\right]$$

$$= x^x(1+\log x)(1+\log x) + x^x\left[\frac{1}{x}\right]$$

$$= x^x(1+\log x)^2 + x^{x-1} \qquad \textbf{(1 Mark)}$$

Putting the values of $\dfrac{d^2 y}{dx^2}$, $\dfrac{dy}{dx}$ and y in the expression

$\dfrac{d^2 y}{dx^2} - \dfrac{1}{y}\left(\dfrac{dy}{dx}\right)^2 - \dfrac{y}{x}$, we have

$$x^x(1+\log x)^2 + x^{x-1} - \frac{1}{x^x}\left(x^x(1+\log x)\right)^2 - \frac{x^x}{x}$$

$$x^x(1+\log x)^2 + x^{x-1} - \frac{1}{x^x}\times x^{2x}(1+\log x)^2 - x^{x-1}$$

$$x^x(1+\log x)^2 - x^x(1+\log x)^2 = 0$$

Hence, proved. $\qquad \textbf{(2 Marks)}$

14. $f(x) = \begin{cases} \dfrac{1-\sin^3 x}{3\cos^2 x} & , \text{ if } x < \dfrac{\pi}{2} \\[2mm] p & , \text{ if } x = \dfrac{\pi}{2} \\[2mm] \dfrac{q(1-\sin x)}{(\pi-2x)^2} & , \text{ if } x > \dfrac{\pi}{2} \end{cases}$

For f(x) to be continuous at $x = \dfrac{\pi}{2}$,

$$\lim_{x\to\frac{\pi^-}{2}} f(x) = \lim_{x\to\frac{\pi^+}{2}} f(x) = f\left(\frac{\pi}{2}\right) \qquad \textbf{(1 Mark)}$$

L.H.L: $\displaystyle\lim_{x\to\frac{\pi^-}{2}} f(x) = \lim_{x\to\frac{\pi^-}{2}}\left(\frac{1-\sin^3 x}{3\cos^2 x}\right)$

$$= \lim_{x\to\frac{\pi^-}{2}} \frac{(1-\sin x)(1+\sin^2 x + \sin x)}{3\left[1-\sin^2 x\right]}$$

$$= \lim_{x\to\frac{\pi^-}{2}} \frac{1+\sin^2 x + \sin x}{3(1+\sin x)} = \frac{1+1+1}{3(2)} = \frac{1}{2} \qquad \textbf{(1 Mark)}$$

R.H.L: $\displaystyle\lim_{x\to\frac{\pi^+}{2}} f(x) = \lim_{x\to\frac{\pi^+}{2}} \frac{q(1-\sin x)}{(\pi-2x)^2}$

$$\lim_{x\to\frac{\pi^+}{2}} \frac{q(1-\sin x)}{(\pi-2x)^2} = \lim_{h\to 0} \frac{q\left[1-\sin\left(\frac{\pi}{2}+h\right)\right]}{\left[\pi-2\left(\frac{\pi}{2}+h\right)\right]^2}$$

$$= \lim_{h\to 0} \frac{q(1-\cos h)}{4h^2}$$

$$= \lim_{h\to 0} \frac{q\cdot 2\sin^2\frac{h}{2}}{2\frac{h^2}{4}\times 4} \qquad \left[\because \lim_{\theta\to 0}\frac{\sin\theta}{\theta} = 1\right]$$

$$= \frac{q}{8} \qquad \textbf{(1 Mark)}$$

Now, $\lim\limits_{x\to\frac{\pi}{2}^-} f(x) = \lim\limits_{x\to\frac{\pi}{2}^+} f(x) = f\left(\frac{\pi}{2}\right)$

$\Rightarrow \dfrac{1}{2} = \dfrac{q}{8} = p$

Therefore, $p = \dfrac{1}{2}$ and $q = \dfrac{8}{2} = 4$ **(1 Mark)**

15. Given:

$$x = 3\cos t - \cos^3 t$$

$$y = 3\sin t - \sin^3 t$$

Slope of the tangent,

$$\dfrac{dy}{dx} = \dfrac{\dfrac{dy}{dt}}{\dfrac{dx}{dt}} = \dfrac{3\cos t - 3\sin^2 t\,\cos t}{-3\sin t + 3\cos^2 t\,\sin t}$$

$$= \dfrac{3\cos t\left[\cos^2 t\right]}{-3\sin t\left[\sin^2 t\right]} = \dfrac{-\cos^3 t}{\sin^3 t} \qquad \textbf{(1½ Marks)}$$

$\therefore$ Slope of the normal $= \dfrac{-1}{\dfrac{dy}{dx}} = \dfrac{\sin^3 t}{\cos^3 t}$ **(½ Mark)**

The equation of the normal is given by

$$\dfrac{y-(3\sin t - \sin^3 t)}{x-(3\cos t - \cos^3 t)} = \dfrac{\sin^3 t}{\cos^3 t}$$

$\Rightarrow y\cos^3 t - 3\sin t\cos^3 t + \sin^3 t\cos^3 t$
$$= x\sin^3 t - 3\cos t\sin^3 t + \sin^3 t\cos^3 t$$

$\Rightarrow y\cos^3 t - x\sin^3 t = 3(\sin t\cos^3 t - \cos t\sin^3 t)$

$\Rightarrow y\cos^3 t - x\sin^3 t = 3\sin t\cos t\,(\cos^2 t - \sin^2 t)$

$\Rightarrow y\cos^3 t - x\sin^3 t = \dfrac{3}{2}\sin 2t\cos 2t$

$\Rightarrow y\cos^3 t - x\sin^3 t = \dfrac{3}{4} \times 2\sin 2t\cos 2t$

$\Rightarrow 4(y\cos^3 t - x\sin^3 t) = 3\sin 4t$

Hence, proved. **(2 Marks)**

16. Let $I = \displaystyle\int \dfrac{(3\sin\theta - 2)\cos\theta}{5 - \cos^2\theta - 4\sin\theta}\,d\theta$

$\Rightarrow I = \displaystyle\int \dfrac{(3\sin\theta - 2)\cos\theta}{5 - (1-\sin^2\theta) - 4\sin\theta}\,d\theta \quad \left(\because \cos^2\theta = 1 - \sin^2\theta\right)$

$\Rightarrow I = \displaystyle\int \dfrac{(3\sin\theta - 2)\cos\theta}{\sin^2\theta - 4\sin\theta + 4}\,d\theta$

Now, substitute $\sin\theta = t.$ $\Rightarrow \cos\theta\,d\theta = dt$

$\therefore \quad I = \displaystyle\int \dfrac{(3t - 2)\,dt}{t^2 - 4t + 4}$

$\Rightarrow 3t - 2 = A\dfrac{d}{dx}(t^2 - 4t + 4) + B$ **(½ Mark)**

$\Rightarrow 3t - 2 = A(2t - 4) + B$

$\Rightarrow 3t - 2 = (2A)t + B - 4A$

Comparing the coefficients of the like powers of t, we get

$$2A = 3 \Rightarrow A = \dfrac{3}{2}$$

and $B - 4A = -2 \;\Rightarrow\; B - 4\times\dfrac{3}{2} = -2 \;\Rightarrow\; B = -2 + 6 = 4$

Substituting the values of A and B, we get

$\therefore \quad I = \displaystyle\int \dfrac{(3t-2)\,dt}{t^2-4t+4} = \int \left(\dfrac{\dfrac{3}{2}(2t-4) + 4}{t^2 - 4t + 4}\right) dt$

$$= \dfrac{3}{2}\int\left(\dfrac{2t-4}{t^2-4t+4}\right)dt + 4\int\dfrac{dt}{t^2-4t+4}$$

$$= \dfrac{3}{2}I_1 + 4I_2 \qquad \text{...(1)} \qquad \textbf{(½ Mark)}$$

Here,

$$I_1 = \int\dfrac{(2t-4)\,dt}{t^2-4t+4} \quad\text{and}\quad I_2 = \int\dfrac{dt}{t^2-4t+4}$$

Now,

$$I_1 = \int\dfrac{(2t-4)\,dt}{t^2-4t+4}$$

Let $t^2 - 4t + 4 = p$

$\Rightarrow (2t - 4)dt = dp$

$$I_1 = \int\dfrac{(2t-4)\,dt}{t^2-4t+4} = \int\dfrac{dp}{p}$$

$$= \log|p| + C_1 = \log|t^2 - 4t + 4| + C_1 \quad\text{...(2)}\quad \textbf{(1 Mark)}$$

and $I_2 = \displaystyle\int\dfrac{dt}{t^2-4t+4} = \int\dfrac{dt}{(t-2)^2}$

$$= \int (t-2)^{-2}\,dt = \dfrac{(t-2)^{-2+1}}{-2+1} + C_2$$

$$= \dfrac{-1}{t-2} + C_2 \qquad\text{...(3)}\qquad \textbf{(1 Mark)}$$

From equations (1), (2) and (3), we get

$$I = \frac{3}{2}\log\left|t^2 - 4t + 4\right| + 4 \times \frac{-1}{t-2} + C_1 + C_2$$

$$= \frac{3}{2}\log\left|\sin^2\theta - 4\sin\theta + 4\right| + \frac{4}{2-t} + C \quad (\text{where } C = C_1 + C_2)$$

$$= \frac{3}{2}\log\left|(\sin\theta - 2)^2\right| + \frac{4}{2-\sin\theta} + C$$

$$= \frac{3}{2} \times 2\log\left|\sin\theta - 2\right| + \frac{4}{2-\sin\theta} + C$$

$$= 3\log\left|2 - \sin\theta\right| + \frac{4}{2-\sin\theta} + C$$

$$= 3\log(2-\sin\theta) + \frac{4}{2-\sin\theta} + C \ (\text{Since, } 2 - \sin\theta \text{ is always positive})$$

(1 Mark)

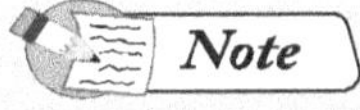

In the case of integral of function in the form of $\dfrac{px + q}{ax^2 + bx + c}$,

then use $px + q = \dfrac{A\,d\left(ax^2 + bx + c\right)}{dx} + B$

OR

Let $I = \displaystyle\int_0^\pi e^{2x}\sin\left(\frac{\pi}{4} + x\right)dx$

Integrating by parts, we get

$$I = \frac{1}{2}\left[e^{2x}\sin\left(\frac{\pi}{4} + x\right)\right]_0^\pi - \frac{1}{2}\int_0^\pi e^{2x}\cos\left(\frac{\pi}{4} + x\right)dx$$

$$\left[\because \int uv\,dx = u\int v\,dx - \int\left(u'\int v\,dx\right)dx\right] \quad \textbf{(1 Mark)}$$

Now, integrating the second term by parts, we get

$$\Rightarrow I = \frac{1}{2}\left[e^{2x}\sin\left(\frac{\pi}{4} + x\right)\right]_0^\pi - \frac{1}{2}\left\{\begin{array}{l}\left[\frac{1}{2}e^{2x}\cos\left(\frac{\pi}{4} + x\right)\right]_0^\pi \\[2mm] + \frac{1}{2}\int_0^\pi e^{2x}\sin\left(\frac{\pi}{4} + x\right)dx\end{array}\right\}$$

(1 Mark)

$$\Rightarrow I = \frac{1}{2}\left[e^{2x}\sin\left(\frac{\pi}{4} + x\right)\right]_0^\pi - \frac{1}{4}\left[e^{2x}\cos\left(\frac{\pi}{4} + x\right)\right]_0^\pi - \frac{1}{4}I$$

$$\Rightarrow I + \frac{1}{4}I = \frac{1}{2}\left[e^{2\pi}\sin\left(\pi + \frac{\pi}{4}\right) - \sin\left(\frac{\pi}{4}\right)\right]$$

$$- \frac{1}{4}\left[e^{2\pi}\cos\left(\pi + \frac{\pi}{4}\right) - \cos\left(\frac{\pi}{4}\right)\right]$$

(1 Mark)

$$\Rightarrow \frac{5}{4}I = \frac{1}{2}\left[-e^{2\pi} \times \frac{1}{\sqrt{2}} - \frac{1}{\sqrt{2}}\right] - \frac{1}{4}\left[-e^{2\pi} \times \frac{1}{\sqrt{2}} - \frac{1}{\sqrt{2}}\right]$$

$$\Rightarrow \frac{5}{4}I = -\frac{1}{2\sqrt{2}}e^{2\pi} - \frac{1}{2\sqrt{2}} + \frac{1}{4\sqrt{2}}e^{2\pi} + \frac{1}{4\sqrt{2}}$$

$$\Rightarrow I = -\frac{1}{5\sqrt{2}}\left(e^{2\pi} + 1\right) \quad \textbf{(1 Mark)}$$

17. $I = \displaystyle\int \frac{\sqrt{x}}{\sqrt{a^3 - x^3}}dx$

Substitute $x^{\frac{3}{2}} = t \quad \Rightarrow \frac{3}{2}x^{\frac{1}{2}}dx = dt \quad \left[\because \frac{d}{dx}x^n = nx^{n-1}\right]$

$$\Rightarrow x^{\frac{1}{2}}dx = \frac{2}{3}dt$$

and $x^{\frac{3}{2}} = t \quad \Rightarrow \left(x^3\right)^{\frac{1}{2}} = t \Rightarrow x^3 = t^2$ **(1 Mark)**

Putting the values in I, we get

$$I = \int \frac{\sqrt{x}}{\sqrt{a^3 - x^3}}dx = \frac{2}{3}\int \frac{1}{\sqrt{a^3 - t^2}}dt$$

Using the following formula of integration, we get

$$\int \frac{dx}{\sqrt{a^2 - x^2}} = \sin^{-1}\left(\frac{x}{a}\right)$$

$$\therefore \quad \frac{2}{3}\int \frac{1}{\sqrt{\left(a^{3/2}\right)^2 - t^2}}dt = \frac{2}{3}\sin^{-1}\left(\frac{t}{a^{\frac{3}{2}}}\right) + C \quad \textbf{(1 Mark)}$$

Again, putting the value of t, we get

$$\frac{2}{3}\int\frac{1}{\sqrt{a^3-t^2}}\,dt = \frac{2}{3}\sin^{-1}\left(\frac{t}{3^{\frac{1}{2}}}\right)+C = \frac{2}{3}\sin^{-1}\left(\frac{x^{\frac{3}{2}}}{a^{\frac{3}{2}}}\right)+C$$

Here, C is a constant of integration.   **(2 Marks)**

18. Let $I = \int_{-1}^{2}\left|x^3-x\right|dx$

$f(x)=x^3-x$

$\Rightarrow f(x) = x(x-1)(x+1)$

The signs of $f(x)$ for the different values are as follows:

$f(x)>0$ for all $x \in (-1,0)\cup(1,2)$

$f(x)<0$ for all $x \in (0,1)$

Therefore,

$$\left|x^3-x\right| = \begin{cases} x^3-x, & x \in (-1,0)\cup(1,2) \\ -\left(x^3-x\right), & x \in (0,1) \end{cases}$$ **(1 Mark)**

$$\therefore I = \int_{-1}^{2}\left|x^3-x\right|dx$$

$$= \int_{-1}^{0}\left|x^3-x\right|dx + \int_{0}^{1}\left|x^3-x\right|dx + \int_{1}^{2}\left|x^3-x\right|dx$$

$$= \int_{-1}^{0}\left(x^3-x\right)dx - \int_{0}^{1}\left(x^3-x\right)dx + \int_{1}^{2}\left(x^3-x\right)dx$$ **(1 Mark)**

$$= \left[\frac{x^4}{4}-\frac{x^2}{2}\right]_{-1}^{0} - \left[\frac{x^4}{4}-\frac{x^2}{2}\right]_{0}^{1} + \left[\frac{x^4}{4}-\frac{x^2}{2}\right]_{1}^{2}$$

$$= -\left(\frac{1}{4}-\frac{1}{2}\right) - \left(\frac{1}{4}-\frac{1}{2}\right) + \left(\frac{16}{4}-\frac{4}{2}\right) - \left(\frac{1}{4}-\frac{1}{2}\right)$$

$$= \frac{3}{4}+(4-2) = \frac{11}{4}$$ **(2 Marks)**

Note

Find the internal of $|x^3-x|$ by equate $x^3-x=0$ and solve, we get $x = 0, 1$ and 2 we number line

19. The given differential equation is

$(1-y^2)(1+\log x)dx + 2xy\,dy = 0$

Separate the variables

$\Rightarrow (1-y^2)(1+\log x)dx = -2xy\,dy$

$\Rightarrow \left(\frac{1+\log x}{2x}\right)dx = -\left(\frac{y}{1-y^2}\right)dy$ ...(1)   **(1 Mark)**

Integrating both sides

$$\int\frac{1+\log x}{2x}\,dx = -\int\frac{y}{1-y^2}\,dy$$

Substitute

$1+\log x = t$ and $(1-y^2)=p$

$\Rightarrow \dfrac{1}{x}dx = dt$ and $-2y\,dy = dp$

Therefore, (1) becomes

$$\int\frac{t}{2}\,dt = \int\frac{1}{2p}\,dp$$ **(1 Mark)**

$$\Rightarrow \frac{t^2}{4} = \frac{\log p}{2}+C$$ ...(2)

Substituting the values of t and p in (2), we get

$$\frac{(1+\log x)^2}{4} = \frac{\log\left(1-y^2\right)}{2}+C$$ ...(3)   **(1 Mark)**

At $x=1$ and $y=0$, equation (3) becomes

$$C = \frac{1}{4}$$

Substituting the value of C in equation (3), we get

$$\frac{(1+\log x)^2}{4} = \frac{\log\left(1-y^2\right)}{2}+\frac{1}{4}$$

$\Rightarrow (1+\log x)^2 = 2\log(1-y^2)+1$

$\Rightarrow 1+(\log x)^2+2\log x = 2\log(1-y^2)+1$

$\Rightarrow (\log x)^2 + \log x^2 = \log(1-y^2)^2$

This is the required particular solution.   **(1 Mark)**

SECTION - C

20. The equation of the plane passing through three given points can be given by

$$\begin{vmatrix} x-2 & y-2 & z-1 \\ 3-2 & 0-2 & 1-1 \\ 4-2 & -1-2 & 0-1 \end{vmatrix} = 0$$

$$\Rightarrow \quad \begin{vmatrix} x-2 & y-2 & z-1 \\ 1 & -2 & 0 \\ 2 & -3 & -1 \end{vmatrix} = 0$$

Solving the above determinant, we get

$\Rightarrow \quad (x-2)(2-0)-(y-2)(-1-0)+(z-1)(-3+4)=0$

$\Rightarrow \quad (2x-4)+(y-2)+(z-1)=0$

$\Rightarrow \quad 2x+y+z-7=0$ **(2 Marks)**

Therefore, the equation of the plane is $2x+y+z-7=0$

Now, the equation of the line passing through two given points is

$$\frac{x-3}{2-3}=\frac{y+4}{-3+4}=\frac{z+5}{1+5}=\lambda$$

$$\Rightarrow \quad \frac{x-3}{-1}=\frac{y+4}{1}=\frac{z+5}{6}=\lambda$$

$\Rightarrow \quad x=(-\lambda+3), y=(\lambda-4), z=(6\lambda-5)$ **(1 Mark)**

At the point of intersection, these points satisfy the equation of the plane $2x+y+z-7=0$

Putting the values of x, y and z in the equation of the plane, we get the value of λ

$2(-\lambda+3)+(\lambda-4)+(6\lambda-5)-7=0$

$\Rightarrow \quad -2\lambda+6+\lambda-4+6\lambda-5-7=0$

$\Rightarrow \quad 5\lambda=10$

$\Rightarrow \quad \lambda=2$

Thus, the point of intersection is $P(1,-2,7)$ **(1 Mark)**

Now, let P divide the line AB in the ratio m:n

By the section formula, we have

$$P=\left(\frac{2m+3n}{m+n},\frac{-3m-4n}{m+n},\frac{1m-5n}{m+n}\right)$$

$$(1,-2,7)=\left(\frac{2m+3n}{m+n},\frac{-3m-4n}{m+n},\frac{1m-5n}{m+n}\right)$$

Equating x-coordinate from both the sides.

$$1=\frac{2m+3n}{m+n}$$

$$\Rightarrow m+2n=0 \Rightarrow m=-2n \Rightarrow \frac{m}{n}=\frac{-2}{1}$$

Hence, P divides the line segment AB externally in the ratio $2:1$. **(2 Marks)**

21. Let X denote the total number of red balls when four balls are drawn one by one with replacement, P (getting a red ball in one draw) $=\dfrac{6}{9}=\dfrac{2}{3}=p$

P (getting a white ball in one draw) $=1-\dfrac{2}{3}=\dfrac{1}{3}=q$

We know that,

$P(X=x)={}^{n}C_x p^x q^{n-x}$ **(1 Mark)**

where, p = probability of success q = Probability of failure

X	0	1	2	3	4
P(X)	$\left(\dfrac{1}{3}\right)^4$	$\dfrac{2}{3}\left(\dfrac{1}{3}\right)^3 \cdot {}^4C_1$	$\left(\dfrac{2}{3}\right)^2\left(\dfrac{1}{3}\right)^2 \cdot {}^4C_2$	$\left(\dfrac{2}{3}\right)^3\left(\dfrac{1}{3}\right) \cdot {}^4C_3$	$\left(\dfrac{2}{3}\right)^4$
	$\dfrac{1}{81}$	$\dfrac{8}{81}$	$\dfrac{24}{81}$	$\dfrac{32}{81}$	$\dfrac{16}{81}$

Using the formula, for mean, we have **(2 Marks)**

$$\overline{X}=\sum P_i X_i$$

$$\text{Mean}\,(\overline{X})=\left(0\times\frac{1}{81}\right)+1\left(\frac{8}{81}\right)+2\left(\frac{24}{81}\right)+3\left(\frac{32}{81}\right)+4\left(\frac{16}{81}\right)$$

$$=\frac{1}{81}(8+48+96+64)=\frac{216}{81}=\frac{8}{3}$$ **(1 Mark)**

Using the formula for variance, we have

$$\text{Var}\,(X)=\sum P_i X_i^2 -\left(\sum P_i X_i\right)^2$$

$$\text{Var}\,(X)=\left\{\left(0\times\frac{1}{81}\right)+1\left(\frac{8}{81}\right)+4\left(\frac{24}{81}\right)+9\left(\frac{32}{81}\right)+16\left(\frac{16}{81}\right)\right.$$

$$\left.-\left(\frac{8}{3}\right)^2\right\}$$

$$=\frac{648}{81}-\frac{64}{9}=\frac{8}{9}$$ **(2 Marks)**

Hence, the mean of the distribution is $\dfrac{8}{3}$ and the variance of the distribution is $\dfrac{8}{9}$.

22. Let the number of units of products A and B to be produced be x and y, respectively.

Product	Machine	
	I(h)	II(h)
A	3	3
B	2	1

Total profit: Objective function, $Z=7x+4y$

We have to maximise $Z = 7x + 4y$, which is subject to constraints.

$3x + 2y \le 12$ (Constraint on machine I)

$3x + y \le 9$ (Constraint on machine II)

$\Rightarrow \quad x \ge 0$ and $y \ge 0$ **(2 Marks)**

The given information can be graphically expressed as follows:

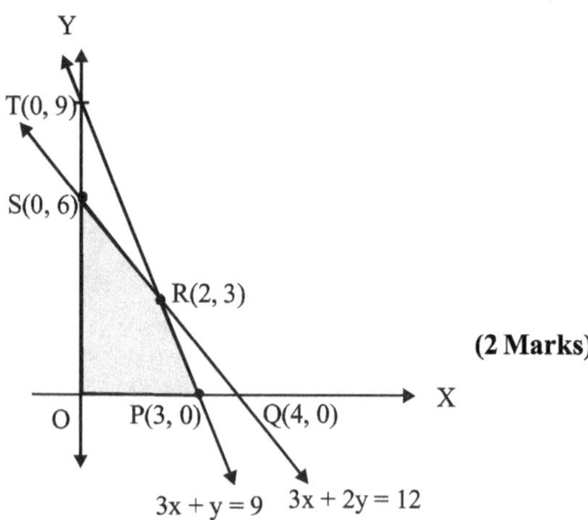

(2 Marks)

Values of the objective function $Z = 7x + 4y$ at the corner points are as follows:

Corner Point	$Z = 7x + 4y$
$(0,6)$	24
$(2,3)$	26
$(3,0)$	21

Therefore, the manufacturer has to produce 2 units of product A and 3 units of product B for getting the maximum profit of ₹ 26.   **(2 Marks)**

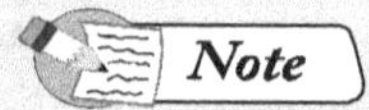
Note

To solve linear inequality, it is required to graph and get corner points from that. These points will help to get maximum or minimum desired value for the bounded region.

23. Let $y = 9x^2 + 6x - 5$

Complete the square by adding & subtracting 1,

$y = (9x^2 + 6x + 1) - 1 - 5$

$\Rightarrow \quad y = (3x + 1)^2 - 1 - 5 = (3x + 1)^2 - 6$

f is invertible $\Leftrightarrow$ f is one-one and onto

To show that f is one-one, let $f(x) = f(y)$, $x, y \in D_f$

$(3x + 1)^2 - 6 = (3y + 1)^2 - 6$

$\Rightarrow \quad (3x + 1)^2 = (3y + 1)^2$

$\Rightarrow \quad 3x + 1 = 3y + 1 \quad \Rightarrow 3x = 3y \quad \Rightarrow \quad x = y$

Therefore, f is one-one.   **(2 Marks)**

Let $y \in S$ (Range of f)

To show that f is onto, we need to find $x \in N$ such that $f(x) = y$

$\Rightarrow \quad (3x + 1)^2 - 6 = y \quad \Rightarrow (3x + 1)^2 = y + 6$

$\Rightarrow \quad 3x + 1 = \sqrt{y + 6}$

$\therefore$ there exists $x = \dfrac{\sqrt{y + 6} - 1}{3}$

such that $f(x) = y$

Therefore, f is onto   **(2 Marks)**

$\sqrt{y + 6} - 1 > 0$

$\Rightarrow \quad y + 6 > 1 \quad \Rightarrow y > -5$ and $y \in N$

So, the function is invertible if the range of the function f(x) is $\{1, 2, 3, ...\}$

Therefore, the inverse of the function f(x) is $f^{-1}(y)$, i.e.

$$f^{-1}(y) = \frac{\sqrt{y + 6} - 1}{3}$$ **(1 Mark)**

$$f^{-1}(43) = \frac{\sqrt{43 + 6} - 1}{3} = 2$$

$$f^{-1}(163) = \frac{\sqrt{163 + 6} - 1}{3} = 4$$ **(1 Mark)**

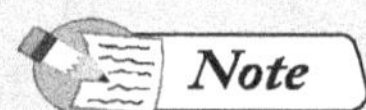
Note

A function is invertible only if it is both one-one and onto.

24. Let $\Delta = \begin{vmatrix} yz - x^2 & zx - y^2 & xy - z^2 \\ zx - y^2 & xy - z^2 & yz - x^2 \\ xy - z^2 & yz - x^2 & zx - y^2 \end{vmatrix}$

Applying $C_1 \rightarrow C_1 + C_2 + C_3$, we get

$$\Delta = \begin{vmatrix} xy + yz + zx - x^2 - y^2 - z^2 & zx - y^2 & xy - z^2 \\ xy + yz + zx - x^2 - y^2 - z^2 & xy - z^2 & yz - x^2 \\ xy + yz + zx - x^2 - y^2 - z^2 & yz - x^2 & zx - y^2 \end{vmatrix}$$

(1 Mark)

$$\Rightarrow \Delta = (xy + yz + zx - x^2 - y^2 - z^2) \begin{vmatrix} 1 & zx - y^2 & xy - z^2 \\ 1 & xy - z^2 & yz - x^2 \\ 1 & yz - x^2 & zx - y^2 \end{vmatrix}$$

(1 Mark)

Applying $R_2 \to R_2 - R_1$ and $R_3 \to R_3 - R_1$, we get
$$\Delta = (xy + yz + zx - x^2 - y^2 - z^2)$$

$$\begin{vmatrix} 1 & zx - y^2 & xy - z^2 \\ 0 & (x+y+z)(y-z) & (x+y+z)(z-x) \\ 0 & (x+y+z)(y-x) & (x+y+z)(z-y) \end{vmatrix}$$ **(1 Mark)**

$$\Rightarrow \Delta = (x+y+z)^2 (xy + yz + zx - x^2 - y^2 - z^2)$$

$$\begin{vmatrix} 1 & zx - y^2 & xy - z^2 \\ 0 & (y-z) & (z-x) \\ 0 & (y-x) & (z-y) \end{vmatrix}$$ **(1 Mark)**

Expanding along 1st column
$$\Rightarrow \Delta = (x+y+z)^2 (xy + yz + zx - x^2 - y^2 - z^2)\,[(y-z)(z-y)$$
$$- (z-x)(y-x) - 0 + 0]$$
$$\Rightarrow \Delta = (x+y+z)^2 (xy + yz + zx - x^2 - y^2 - z^2)^2 \quad \textbf{(1 Mark)}$$
We can see $(x + y + z)$ is a factor of Δ.

So, Δ is divisible by $(x + y + z)$

The quotient when Δ is divisible by $(x + y + z)$ is
$$(x+y+z)(xy + yz + zx - x^2 - y^2 - z^2)^2 \quad \textbf{(1 Mark)}$$

OR

Using elementary row transformations to find the inverse of A.

$$A = \begin{bmatrix} 8 & 4 & 3 \\ 2 & 1 & 1 \\ 1 & 2 & 2 \end{bmatrix}$$

$$A = IA$$

$$\begin{bmatrix} 8 & 4 & 3 \\ 2 & 1 & 1 \\ 1 & 2 & 2 \end{bmatrix} = \begin{bmatrix} 1 & 0 & 0 \\ 0 & 1 & 0 \\ 0 & 0 & 1 \end{bmatrix} A$$ **(½ Mark)**

Applying $R_1 \leftrightarrow R_3$, we get

$$\begin{bmatrix} 1 & 2 & 2 \\ 2 & 1 & 1 \\ 8 & 4 & 3 \end{bmatrix} = \begin{bmatrix} 0 & 0 & 1 \\ 0 & 1 & 0 \\ 1 & 0 & 0 \end{bmatrix} A$$ **(½ Mark)**

Applying $R_2 \to R_2 - 2R_1$, we get

$$\begin{bmatrix} 1 & 2 & 2 \\ 0 & -3 & -3 \\ 8 & 4 & 3 \end{bmatrix} = \begin{bmatrix} 0 & 0 & 1 \\ 0 & 1 & -2 \\ 1 & 0 & 0 \end{bmatrix} A$$ **(½ Mark)**

Applying $R_3 \to R_3 - 8R_1$, we get

$$\begin{bmatrix} 1 & 2 & 2 \\ 0 & -3 & -3 \\ 0 & -12 & -13 \end{bmatrix} = \begin{bmatrix} 0 & 0 & 1 \\ 0 & 1 & -2 \\ 1 & 0 & -8 \end{bmatrix} A$$ **(½ Mark)**

Applying $R_2 \to \dfrac{R_2}{-3}$, we get

$$\begin{bmatrix} 1 & 2 & 2 \\ 0 & 1 & 1 \\ 0 & -12 & -13 \end{bmatrix} = \begin{bmatrix} 0 & 0 & 1 \\ 0 & -\dfrac{1}{3} & \dfrac{2}{3} \\ 1 & 0 & -8 \end{bmatrix} A$$ **(½ Mark)**

Applying $R_1 \to R_1 - 2R_2$, we get

$$\begin{bmatrix} 1 & 0 & 0 \\ 0 & 1 & 1 \\ 0 & -12 & -13 \end{bmatrix} = \begin{bmatrix} 0 & \dfrac{2}{3} & -\dfrac{1}{3} \\ 0 & -\dfrac{1}{3} & \dfrac{2}{3} \\ 1 & 0 & -8 \end{bmatrix} A$$ **(½ Mark)**

Applying $R_3 \to R_3 + 12\,R_2$, we get

$$\begin{bmatrix} 1 & 0 & 0 \\ 0 & 1 & 1 \\ 0 & 0 & -1 \end{bmatrix} = \begin{bmatrix} 0 & \dfrac{2}{3} & -\dfrac{1}{3} \\ 0 & -\dfrac{1}{3} & \dfrac{2}{3} \\ 1 & -4 & 0 \end{bmatrix} A$$ **(½ Mark)**

Applying $R_3 \to -R_3$ and $R_2 \to R_2 - R_3$, we get

$$\begin{bmatrix} 1 & 0 & 0 \\ 0 & 1 & 0 \\ 0 & 0 & 1 \end{bmatrix} = \begin{bmatrix} 0 & \dfrac{2}{3} & -\dfrac{1}{3} \\ 1 & -\dfrac{13}{3} & \dfrac{2}{3} \\ -1 & 4 & 0 \end{bmatrix} A$$ **(½ Mark)**

Thus, we have

$$A^{-1} = \begin{bmatrix} 0 & \dfrac{2}{3} & -\dfrac{1}{3} \\ 1 & -\dfrac{13}{3} & \dfrac{2}{3} \\ -1 & 4 & 0 \end{bmatrix}$$ **(½ Mark)**

The given system of equations is

$$8x + 4y + 3z = 19$$
$$2x + y + z = 5$$
$$x + 2y + 2z = 7$$

The given system of equations can be written as AX = B,

$$\text{where } A = \begin{bmatrix} 8 & 4 & 3 \\ 2 & 1 & 1 \\ 1 & 2 & 2 \end{bmatrix}, X = \begin{bmatrix} x \\ y \\ z \end{bmatrix} \text{ and } B = \begin{bmatrix} 19 \\ 5 \\ 7 \end{bmatrix}$$ (½ Mark)

$$\therefore \quad X = A^{-1}B$$

$$\Rightarrow \begin{bmatrix} x \\ y \\ z \end{bmatrix} = \begin{bmatrix} 0 & \dfrac{2}{3} & -\dfrac{1}{3} \\ 1 & -\dfrac{13}{3} & \dfrac{2}{3} \\ -1 & 4 & 0 \end{bmatrix} \begin{bmatrix} 19 \\ 5 \\ 7 \end{bmatrix}$$

$$\Rightarrow \begin{bmatrix} x \\ y \\ z \end{bmatrix} = \begin{bmatrix} 0 + \dfrac{10}{3} - \dfrac{7}{3} \\ 19 - \dfrac{65}{3} + \dfrac{14}{3} \\ -19 + 20 + 0 \end{bmatrix} = \begin{bmatrix} 1 \\ 2 \\ 1 \end{bmatrix}$$

$$\therefore \quad x = 1, y = 2 \text{ and } z = 1$$ (1 Mark)

25. A sphere of fixed radius (r) is given.

Let R and h be the radius and the height of the cone, respectively.

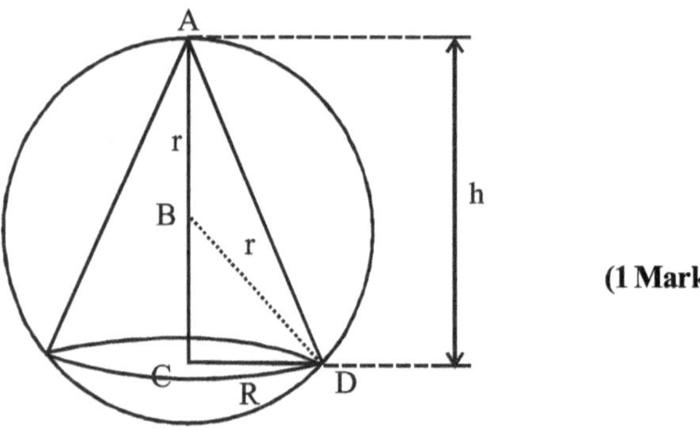

(1 Mark)

The volume (V) of the cone is given by,

$$V = \frac{1}{3}\pi R^2 h \qquad \text{...(i)}$$

Now, from the right triangle BCD, we have

$$BC = \sqrt{r^2 - R^2} \Rightarrow h - r = \sqrt{r^2 - R^2}$$

$$\therefore \quad h = r + \sqrt{r^2 - R^2}$$ (1 Mark)

Put the value of h in (i)

$$\therefore \quad V = \frac{1}{3}\pi R^2 \left(r + \sqrt{r^2 - R^2} \right) = \frac{1}{3}\pi R^2 r + \frac{1}{3}\pi R^2 \sqrt{r^2 - R^2}$$

Differentiating both sides w.r.t R

$$\therefore \quad \frac{dV}{dR} = \frac{2}{3}\pi Rr + \frac{2}{3}\pi R\sqrt{r^2 - R^2} + \frac{\pi R^2}{3} \cdot \frac{(-2R)}{2\sqrt{r^2 - R^2}}$$ (1 Mark)

$$= \frac{2}{3}\pi Rr + \frac{2}{3}\pi R\sqrt{r^2 - R^2} - \frac{\pi R^3}{3\sqrt{r^2 - R^2}}$$

$$= \frac{2}{3}\pi Rr + \frac{2\pi R\left(r^2 - R^2\right) - \pi R^3}{3\sqrt{r^2 - R^2}} = \frac{2}{3}\pi Rr + \frac{2\pi Rr^2 - 3\pi R^3}{3\sqrt{r^2 - R^2}}$$

Now, $\dfrac{dV}{dR} = 0$

$$\Rightarrow \quad \frac{2\pi rR}{3} = \frac{3\pi R^3 - 2\pi Rr^2}{3\sqrt{r^2 - R^2}}$$

$$\Rightarrow \quad 2r\sqrt{r^2 - R^2} = 3R^2 - 2r^2$$
$$\Rightarrow \quad 4r^2(r^2 - R^2) = (3R^2 - 2r^2)^2$$
$$\Rightarrow \quad 4r^4 - 4r^2R^2 = 9R^4 + 4r^4 - 12R^2r^2$$
$$\Rightarrow \quad 9R^4 - 8r^2R^2 = 0$$

$$\Rightarrow \quad 9R^2 = 8r^2 \quad \Rightarrow \quad R^2 = \frac{8r^2}{9}$$ (1 Mark)

Now,

$$\frac{d^2V}{dR^2} = \frac{2\pi r}{3} + \frac{\begin{bmatrix} 3\sqrt{r^2 - R^2}\left(2\pi r^2 - 9\pi R^2\right) \\ -\left(2\pi Rr^2 - 3\pi R^3\right)(-6R)\dfrac{1}{2\sqrt{r^2 - R^2}} \end{bmatrix}}{9\left(r^2 - R^2\right)}$$

$$= \frac{2\pi r}{3} + \frac{\begin{bmatrix} 3\sqrt{r^2 - R^2}\left(2\pi r^2 - 9\pi R^2\right) \\ +\left(2\pi Rr^2 - 3\pi R^3\right)(3R)\dfrac{1}{\sqrt{r^2 - R^2}} \end{bmatrix}}{9\left(r^2 - R^2\right)}$$

           115

Now, when $R^2 = \dfrac{8r^2}{9}$, it can be shown that $\dfrac{d^2V}{dR^2} < 0$.

$\therefore$ The volume is the maximum when $R^2 = \dfrac{8r^2}{9}$.

When $R^2 = \dfrac{8r^2}{9}$, height of the cone

$$= r + \sqrt{r^2 - \dfrac{8r^2}{9}} = r + \sqrt{\dfrac{r^2}{9}} = r + \dfrac{r}{3} = \dfrac{4r}{3}$$

Hence, the altitude of a right circular cone of maximum volume that can be inscribed in a sphere of radius r is $\dfrac{4r}{3}$. **(1 Mark)**

Let volume of the sphere be $V_s = \dfrac{4}{3}\pi r^3$.

$$r = \sqrt[3]{\dfrac{3V_s}{4\pi}}$$

$\therefore$ Volume of cone,

$$V = \dfrac{1}{3}\pi R^2 h \Rightarrow R = \dfrac{2\sqrt{2}}{3} r$$

$$V = \dfrac{1}{3}\pi \left(\dfrac{2\sqrt{2}}{3} r\right)^2 \times \dfrac{4r}{3} \Rightarrow V = \dfrac{1}{3}\pi \dfrac{8r^2}{9} \times \dfrac{4r}{3}$$

$$V = \dfrac{32\pi r^3}{81} = \dfrac{32}{81}\pi \left[\dfrac{3V_s}{4\pi}\right]$$

$\therefore$ Volume of cone in terms of sphere $= \dfrac{8V_s}{27}$ **(1 Mark)**

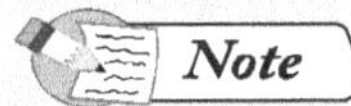

Note

Cone inscribed in sphere means cone exactly fitting inside the sphere and cone circumscribed the sphere means sphere exactly fitting inside the cone.

OR

Consider the function $f(x) = \sin 3x - \cos 3x,\ 0 < x < \pi$

$f'(x) = 3\cos 3x + 3\sin 3x)$

$\qquad = 3(\sin 3x + \cos 3x)$

$\qquad = 3\sqrt{2}\left(\sin 3x.\dfrac{1}{\sqrt{2}} + \cos 3x.\dfrac{1}{\sqrt{2}}\right)$

$\qquad = 3\sqrt{2}\left\{\sin 3x.\cos\left(\dfrac{\pi}{4}\right) + \cos 3x \sin\left(\dfrac{\pi}{4}\right)\right\}$

$\qquad = 3\sqrt{2}\left\{\sin\left(3x + \dfrac{\pi}{4}\right)\right\}$ **(1 Mark)**

$$[\because\ \sin A \cos B + \cos A \sin B = \sin(A+B)]$$

For the increasing interval $f'(x) > 0$

$$3\sqrt{2}\left\{\sin\left(3x + \dfrac{\pi}{4}\right)\right\} > 0$$

$$\sin\left(3x + \dfrac{\pi}{4}\right) > 0 \Rightarrow 0 < 3x + \dfrac{\pi}{4} < \pi$$

$$\Rightarrow\quad 0 < 3x < \dfrac{3\pi}{4} \Rightarrow 0 < x < \dfrac{\pi}{4}\quad (\text{Since } x \in (0, \pi))$$

(1 Mark)

Also, $\sin\left(3x + \dfrac{\pi}{4}\right) > 0$

when, $2\pi < 3x + \dfrac{\pi}{4} < 3\pi \Rightarrow \dfrac{7\pi}{4} < 3x < \dfrac{11\pi}{4}$

$$\Rightarrow\quad \dfrac{7\pi}{12} < x < \dfrac{11\pi}{12}$$

Therefore, intervals in which function is strictly increasing is $\left(0, \dfrac{\pi}{4}\right) \cup \left(\dfrac{7\pi}{12}, \dfrac{11\pi}{12}\right)$ **(1 Mark)**

Similarly, for the decreasing interval $f'(x) < 0$

$$3\sqrt{2}\left\{\sin\left(3x + \dfrac{\pi}{4}\right)\right\} < 0$$

$$\sin\left(3x + \dfrac{\pi}{4}\right) < 0 \Rightarrow \pi < 3x + \dfrac{\pi}{4} < 2\pi$$

$$\Rightarrow \dfrac{3\pi}{4} < 3x < \dfrac{7\pi}{4} \Rightarrow \dfrac{\pi}{4} < x < \dfrac{7\pi}{12}$$ **(1 Mark)**

Also, $\sin\left(3x + \dfrac{\pi}{4}\right) < 0$

When $3\pi < 3x + \dfrac{\pi}{4} < 4\pi,\ \Rightarrow \dfrac{11\pi}{4} < 3x < \dfrac{15\pi}{4}$

$$\Rightarrow \dfrac{11\pi}{12} < x < \dfrac{15\pi}{12}$$

The function is strictly decreasing in the interval

$$\left(\dfrac{\pi}{4}, \dfrac{7\pi}{12}\right) \cup \left(\dfrac{11\pi}{12}, \pi\right)$$ **(2 Marks)**

Alternate method,

$$\sin\left(3x+\frac{\pi}{4}\right)=0 \Rightarrow 3x+\frac{\pi}{4}=n\pi$$

$$\Rightarrow x=\frac{1}{3}\left(n\pi-\frac{\pi}{4}\right), n \in z$$

Find all values within $0 < x < \pi$ and make interval to check increasing and decreasing.

26. **Given :** $x^2+y^2 \leq 2ax, y^2 \geq ax, x, y \geq 0$

$\Rightarrow \quad x^2+y^2-2ax \leq 0, y^2 \geq ax, x, y \geq 0$

$\Rightarrow \quad x^2+y^2-2ax+a^2-a^2 \leq 0, y^2 \geq ax, x, y \geq 0$

$\Rightarrow \quad (x-a)^2+y^2 \leq a^2, y^2 \geq ax, x, y \geq 0$ **(1 Mark)**

To find the points of intersection of the circle $[(x-a)^2+y^2=a^2]$ and the parabola $[y^2=ax]$, we will substitute $y^2 = ax$ in $(x-a)^2+y^2=a^2$.

$(x-a)^2+ax=a^2$

$\Rightarrow \quad x^2+a^2-2ax+ax=a^2 \quad \Rightarrow x(x-a)=0 \quad \Rightarrow \quad x=0, a$

Therefore, the points of intersection are $(0, 0)$, (a, a) and $(a, -a)$. **(1 Mark)**

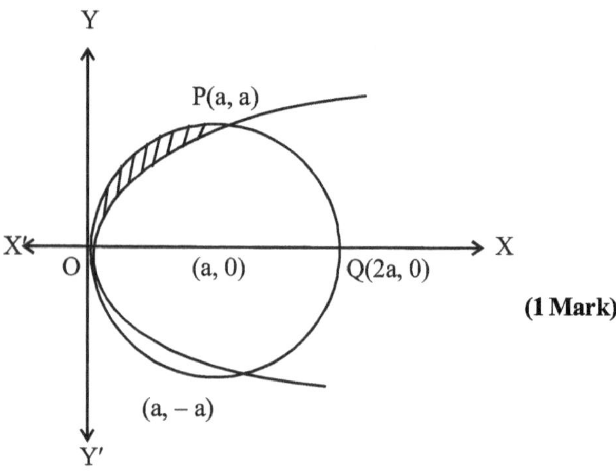

(1 Mark)

Now, find the area of shaded region.

Area of the shaded region from $x = 0$ to $x = a$

$$=\left[\int_0^a\left(\sqrt{a^2-(x-a)^2}\right)dx-\int_0^a\sqrt{ax}\,dx\right]$$ **(1 Mark)**

Let $x-a=t$ for the first part of the integral

$\Rightarrow \quad dx=dt$

$$\therefore \quad A_I=\int_{-a}^0\sqrt{a^2-t^2}\,dt-2\frac{\sqrt{a}}{3}x^{\frac{3}{2}}\Big|_0^a$$

$$=\left|\frac{t}{2}\sqrt{a^2-t^2}+\frac{1}{2}a^2\sin^{-1}\frac{t}{a}\right|_{-a}^0-\frac{2a^2}{3}$$

$$=0-\left(-\frac{\pi a^2}{4}\right)-\frac{2a^2}{3}$$

$$A_I=\left(\frac{\pi}{4}-\frac{2}{3}\right)a^2$$

$\therefore$ Area of the shaded region $=\left(\frac{\pi}{4}-\frac{2}{3}\right)a^2$ square units.

(2 Marks)

For shading the region, put the coordinate of testing point (0,0) or any point on x-axis or y-axis in given inequality if condition is true then shading towards testing point otherwise away from testing point.

CBSE Board Solved Paper

Time Allowed : 3 Hours   *Maximum Marks : 100*

General Instructions:

  (i)   **All** questions are compulsory.

  (ii)   Please check that this Question Paper contains **26** questions.

  (iii)   Marks for each question are indicated against it.

  (iv)   Questions **1** to **6** in Section A are Very Short Answer Type Questions carrying **one** mark each.

  (v)   Questions **7** to **19** in Section B are Long Answer **I** Type Questions carrying **4** marks each.

  (vi)   Questions **20** to **26** in Section C are Long Answer **II** Type Questions carrying **6** marks each.

  (vii)   Please write down the serial number of the question before attempting it.

SECTION - A

Question numbers 1 to 6 carry 1 mark each.

1. Matrix $A = \begin{bmatrix} 0 & 2b & -2 \\ 3 & 1 & 3 \\ 3a & 3 & -1 \end{bmatrix}$ is given to be symmetric, find values of a and b.

2. Find the position vector of a point which divides the join of points with position vectors $\vec{a} - 2\vec{b}$ and $2\vec{a} + \vec{b}$ externally in the ratio 2 : 1.

3. The two vectors $\hat{j} + \hat{k}$ and $3\hat{i} - \hat{j} + 4\hat{k}$ represent the two sides AB and AC, respectively of a $\triangle$ABC. Find the length of the median through A.

4. Find the vector equation of a plane which is at a distance of 5 units from the origin and its nomral vector is $2\hat{i} - 3\hat{j} + 6\hat{k}$.

5. Find the maximum value of $\begin{vmatrix} 1 & 1 & 1 \\ 1 & 1+\sin\theta & 1 \\ 1 & 1 & 1+\cos\theta \end{vmatrix}$

6. If A is a square matrix such that $A^2 = I$, then find the simplified value of $(A - I)^3 + (A + I)^3 - 7A$.

SECTION - B

Question numbers 7 to 19 carry 4 marks each.

7. Show that the equation of normal at any point t on the curve $x = 3 \cos t - \cos^3 t$ and $y = 3 \sin t - \sin^3 t$ is

$4(y \cos^3 t - x \sin^3 t) = 3 \sin 4t$.

8. Find : $\displaystyle\int \frac{(3\sin\theta - 2)\cos\theta}{5 - \cos^2\theta - 4\sin\theta} d\theta.$

OR

Evaluate : $\displaystyle\int_0^\pi e^{2x} \cdot \sin\left(\frac{\pi}{4} + x\right) dx$

9. Find : $\displaystyle\int \frac{\sqrt{x}}{\sqrt{a^3 - x^3}} dx.$

10. Evaluate : $\displaystyle\int_{-1}^{2} |x^3 - x| \, dx$

11. Find the particular solution of the differential equation $(1 - y^2)(1 + \log x)dx + 2xy \, dy = 0$, given that $y = 0$ when $x = 1$.

12. Find the general solution of the following differential equation:

$(1 + y^2) + (x - e^{\tan^{-1} y}) \dfrac{dy}{dx} = 0$

13. Show that the vectors $\vec{a}, \vec{b}$ and $\vec{c}$ are coplanar if $\vec{a} + \vec{b}, \vec{b} + \vec{c}$ and $\vec{c} + \vec{a}$ are coplanar.

14. Find the vector and Cartesian equations of the line through the point (1, 2, –4) and perpendicular to the two lines.

$\vec{r} = (8\hat{i} - 19\hat{j} + 10\hat{k}) + \lambda(3\hat{i} - 16\hat{j} + 7\hat{k})$ and

$\vec{r} = (15\hat{i} + 29\hat{j} + 5\hat{k}) + \mu(3\hat{i} + 8\hat{j} - 5\hat{k})$

15. Three persons A, B and C apply for a job of Manager in a Private Company. Chances of their selection (A, B and C) are in the ratio 1 : 2 : 4. The probabilities that A, B and C can introduce changes to improve profits of the company are 0.8, 0.5 and 0.3 respectively. If the change does not take place, find the probability that it is due to the appointment of C.

OR

A and B throw a pair of dice alternately. A wins the game if he gets a total of 7 and B wins the game if he gets a total of 10. If A starts the game, then find the probability that B wins.

16. Prove that : $\tan^{-1}\dfrac{1}{5} + \tan^{-1}\dfrac{1}{7} + \tan^{-1}\dfrac{1}{3} + \tan^{-1}\dfrac{1}{8} = \dfrac{\pi}{4}$

OR

Solve for x : $2\tan^{-1}(\cos x) = \tan^{-1}(2\operatorname{cosec} x)$

17. The monthly incomes of Aryan and Babban are in the ratio 3 : 4 and their monthly expenditures are in the ratio 5 : 7. If each saves ₹ 15,000 per month, find their monthly incomes using matrix method. This problem reflects which value?

18. If $x = a\sin 2t(1 + \cos 2t)$ and $y = b\cos 2t\,(1 - \cos 2t)$, find the values of $\dfrac{dy}{dx}$ at $t = \dfrac{\pi}{4}$ and $t = \dfrac{\pi}{3}$.

OR

If $y = x^x$, prove that $\dfrac{d^2y}{dx^2} - \dfrac{1}{y}\left(\dfrac{dy}{dx}\right)^2 - \dfrac{y}{x} = 0$.

19. Find the values of p and q, for which

$$f(x) = \begin{cases} \dfrac{1-\sin^3 x}{3\cos^2 x} & , \text{ if } x < \dfrac{\pi}{2} \\[2mm] p & , \text{ if } x = \dfrac{\pi}{2} \\[2mm] \dfrac{q(1-\sin x)}{(\pi - 2x)^2} & , \text{ if } x > \dfrac{\pi}{2} \end{cases}$$ is continuous at $x = \dfrac{\pi}{2}$.

SECTION - C

Question numbers 20 to 26 carry 6 marks each.

20. Show that the altitude of the right circular cone of maximum volume that can be inscribed in a sphere of radius r is $\dfrac{4r}{3}$.

Also find maximum volume in terms of volume of the sphere.

OR

Find the intervals in which $f(x) = \sin 3x - \cos 3x$, $0 < x < \pi$, is strictly increasing or strictly decreasing.

21. Using integration find the area of the region $\{(x, y) : x^2 + y^2 \le 2ax,\ y^2 \ge ax,\ x, y \ge 0\}$.

22. Find the coordinate of the point P where the line through A(3, −4, −5) and B(2, −3, 1) crosses the plane passing through three points L(2, 2, 1), M(3, 0, 1) and N(4, −1, 0). Also, find the ratio in which P divides the line segment AB.

23. An urn contains 3 white and 6 red balls. Four balls are drawn one by one with replacement from the urn. Find the probability distribution of the number of red balls drawn. Also find mean and variance of the distribution.

24. A manufacturer produces two products A and B. Both the products are processed on two different machines. The available capacity of first machine is 12 hours and that of second machine is 9 hours per day. Each unit of product A requires 3 hours on both machines and each unit of product B requires 2 hours on first machine and 1 hour on second machine. Each unit of product A is sold at ₹ 7 profit and that of B at a profit of ₹ 4. Find the production level per day for maximum profit graphically.

25. Let $f : \text{N} \to \text{N}$ be a function defined as $f(x) = 9x^2 + 6x - 5$. Show that $f : \text{N} \to \text{S}$, where S is the range of f, is invertible. Find the inverse of f and hence find $f^{-1}(43)$ and $f^{-1}(163)$.

26. Prove that $\begin{vmatrix} yz - x^2 & zx - y^2 & xy - z^2 \\ zx - y^2 & xy - z^2 & yz - x^2 \\ xy - z^2 & yz - x^2 & zx - y^2 \end{vmatrix}$ is divisible by $(x + y + z)$, and hence find the quotient.

OR

Using elementary transformations, find the inverse of the matrix $A = \begin{pmatrix} 8 & 4 & 3 \\ 2 & 1 & 1 \\ 1 & 2 & 2 \end{pmatrix}$ and use it to solve the following system of linear equations:

$8x + 4y + 3z = 19$

$2x + y + z = 5$

$x + 2y + 2z = 7$

Solutions

SECTION - A

1. $A = \begin{bmatrix} 0 & 2b & -2 \\ 3 & 1 & 3 \\ 3a & 3 & -1 \end{bmatrix}$

$A^T = \begin{bmatrix} 0 & 3 & 3a \\ 2b & 1 & 3 \\ -2 & 3 & -1 \end{bmatrix}$

As matrix A is symmetric   **(½ Mark)**

$\therefore A = A^T$

$\begin{bmatrix} 0 & 2b & -2 \\ 3 & 1 & 3 \\ 3a & 3 & -1 \end{bmatrix} = \begin{bmatrix} 0 & 3 & 3a \\ 2b & 1 & 3 \\ -2 & 3 & -1 \end{bmatrix}$

$2b = 3 \Rightarrow b = \dfrac{3}{2}$

$3a = -2 \Rightarrow a = \dfrac{-2}{3}$ **(½ Mark)**

2. Let $\vec{r}$ be the position vector of the point which divides $\vec{r_1} = \vec{a} - 2\vec{b}$ and $\vec{r_2} = 2\vec{a} + \vec{b}$ externally in the ratio 2 : 1

$\vec{r} = \dfrac{m_1 \vec{r_2} - m_2 \vec{r_1}}{m_1 - m_2}$ **(½ Mark)**

$\vec{r} = \dfrac{2(2\vec{a} + \vec{b}) - 1(\vec{a} - 2\vec{b})}{2 - 1}$

$= 4\vec{a} + 2\vec{b} - \vec{a} + 2\vec{b}$ **(½ Mark)**

$\vec{r} = 3\vec{a} + 4\vec{b}$

3. Given: $\overrightarrow{AB} = \hat{j} + \hat{k}$

$\overrightarrow{AC} = 3\hat{i} - \hat{j} + 4\hat{k}$

By triangle law of addition

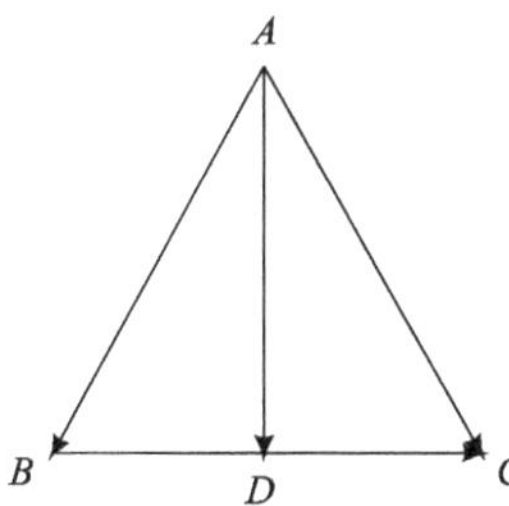

$\overrightarrow{AB} + \overrightarrow{BC} = \overrightarrow{AC}$

$\overrightarrow{BC} = \overrightarrow{AC} - \overrightarrow{AB}$

$= (3\hat{i} - \hat{j} + 4\hat{k}) - (\hat{j} + \hat{k})$

$= 3\hat{i} - 2\hat{j} + 3\hat{k}$ **(½ Mark)**

AD is median, so it will bisect BC

$\overrightarrow{BD} = \dfrac{1}{2}\overrightarrow{BC}$

$\overrightarrow{BD} = \dfrac{1}{2}(3\hat{i} - 2\hat{j} + 3\hat{k})$

$= \dfrac{3}{2}\hat{i} - \hat{j} + \dfrac{3}{2}\hat{k}$

$\overrightarrow{AB} + \overrightarrow{BD} = \overrightarrow{AD}$ [triangle law of addition]

$\overrightarrow{AD} = (\hat{j} + \hat{k}) + \left(\dfrac{3}{2}\hat{i} - \hat{j} + \dfrac{3}{2}\hat{k}\right)$

$= \dfrac{3}{2}\hat{i} + 0\hat{j} + \dfrac{5}{2}\hat{k}$

Length of median $\overrightarrow{AD} = |\overrightarrow{AD}|$

$|\overrightarrow{AD}| = \sqrt{\left(\dfrac{3}{2}\right)^2 + \left(\dfrac{5}{2}\right)^2}$

$|\overrightarrow{AD}| = \dfrac{1}{2}\sqrt{34}$ units   **(½ Mark)**

4. Given: $d = 5$

$\vec{n} = 2\hat{i} - 3\hat{j} + 6\hat{k}$

$\therefore \hat{n} = \dfrac{\vec{n}}{|\vec{n}|}$

$= \dfrac{2\hat{i} - 3\hat{j} + 6\hat{k}}{\sqrt{(2)^2 + (-3)^2 + (6)^2}} = \dfrac{2\hat{i} - 3\hat{j} + 6\hat{k}}{\sqrt{49}}$

$= \dfrac{2\hat{i} - 3\hat{j} + 6\hat{k}}{7}$ **(½ Mark)**

$\therefore$ Equation of plane is

$\vec{r} \cdot \hat{n} = d$

$\vec{r}\left(\dfrac{2\hat{i} - 3\hat{j} + 6\hat{k}}{7}\right) = 5$

$\vec{r}(2\hat{i} - 3\hat{j} + 6\hat{k}) = 35$ **(½ Mark)**

Note

Foot of perpendicular from origin to plane lx + my + nz = d (normal form) is (ld, md, nd).

5. Let $|A| = \begin{vmatrix} 1 & 1 & 1 \\ 1 & 1+\sin\theta & 1 \\ 1 & 1 & 1+\cos\theta \end{vmatrix}$

$R_3 \rightarrow R_3 - R_1$

$|A| = \begin{vmatrix} 1 & 1 & 1 \\ 1 & 1+\sin\theta & 1 \\ 0 & 0 & \cos\theta \end{vmatrix}$

$R_2 \rightarrow R_2 - R_1$

$|A| = \begin{vmatrix} 1 & 1 & 1 \\ 0 & \sin\theta & 0 \\ 0 & 0 & \cos\theta \end{vmatrix}$

$|A| = \sin\theta \cdot \cos\theta$

$= \dfrac{1}{2}(2\sin\theta \cdot \cos\theta)$

$= \dfrac{1}{2}\sin 2\theta \qquad [\because \sin 2\theta = 2\sin\theta \cdot \cos\theta]$ **(½ Mark)**

Maximum value of $\sin 2\theta$ is 1

$|A|_{\max} = \dfrac{1}{2}(1) = \dfrac{1}{2}$

Hence maximum value is $\dfrac{1}{2}$ **(½ Mark)**

6. $(A - I)^3 + (A + I)^3 - 7A = A^3 - I^3 - 3A^2I + 3I^2A + A^3 + I^3$
$$+ 3A^2I + 3I^2A - 7A$$

$[\because (x - y)^3 = x^3 - y^3 - 3x^2y + 3xy^2, (x + y)^3 = x^3 + y^3$
$$+ 3x^2y + 3xy^2]$$ **(½ Mark)**

$= 2A^3 + 6I^2A - 7A$

$= 2A \cdot A^2 + 6A - 7A \qquad\qquad [\because I^2 = I, IA = A]$

$= 2IA + 6A - 7A \qquad\qquad\qquad [\because A^2 = I]$

$= 2A + 6A - 7A$

$= A$ **(½ Mark)**

SECTION - B

7. $x = 3\cos t - \cos^3 t$

$y = 3\sin t - \sin^3 t$

$\dfrac{dx}{dt} = -3\sin t - 3\cos^2 t\,(-\sin t)$

$\qquad = -3\sin t\,(1 - \cos^2 t)$

$\qquad = -3\sin^3 t \qquad [\because 1 - \cos^2\theta = \sin^2\theta]$ **(1 Mark)**

$\dfrac{dy}{dt} = 3\cos t - 3\sin^2 t\,(\cos t)$

$\qquad = 3\cos t\,(1 - \sin^2 t)$

$\qquad = 3\cos^3 t \qquad [\because 1 - \sin^2\theta = \cos^2\theta]$ **(1 Mark)**

$\dfrac{dy}{dx} = \dfrac{\dfrac{dy}{dt}}{\dfrac{dx}{dt}} = \dfrac{3\cos^3 t}{-3\sin^3 t} = \dfrac{-\cos^3 t}{\sin^3 t}$

$\therefore$ Slope of tangent $= \dfrac{-\cos^3 t}{\sin^3 t}$

Slope of normal, $m_1 = \dfrac{-1}{\dfrac{dy}{dx}} = = \dfrac{\sin^3 t}{\cos^3 t}$ **(1 Mark)**

Equation of normal

$y - y_1 = m_1\,(x - x_1)$

$y - (3\sin t - \sin^3 t) = \dfrac{\sin^3 t}{\cos^3 t}\,[(x - (3\cos t - \cos^3 t)]$

$y\cos^3 t - 3\sin t\cos^3 t + \cos^3 t\sin^3 t = x\sin^3 t - 3\cos t\sin^3 t$
$$+ \cos^3 t\sin^3 t$$

$y\cos^3 t - x\sin^3 t = 3\sin t\cos t\,(\cos^2 t - \sin^2 t)$

$y\cos^3 t - x\sin^3 t = \dfrac{3}{2}(2\sin t\cos t)(\cos 2t)$

$$[\because \cos 2\theta = \cos^2\theta - \sin^2\theta]$$

$y\cos^3 t - x\sin^3 t = \dfrac{3}{2}\sin 2t\cos 2t$

$$[\because \sin 2\theta = 2\sin\theta \cdot \cos\theta]$$

$y\cos^3 t - x\sin^3 t = \dfrac{3}{4}\sin 4t$

$4(y\cos^3 t - x\sin t) = 3\sin 4t$

Hence proved. **(1 Mark)**

8. Let $I = \displaystyle\int \dfrac{(3\sin\theta - 2)\cos\theta}{5 - \cos^2\theta - 4\sin\theta}\,d\theta$

$I = \displaystyle\int \dfrac{(3\sin\theta - 2)\cos\theta}{5 - (1 - \sin^2\theta) - 4\sin\theta}\,d\theta$

$= \displaystyle\int \dfrac{(3\sin\theta - 2)\cos\theta}{4 + \sin^2\theta - 4\sin\theta}\,d\theta$

$= \displaystyle\int \dfrac{(3\sin\theta - 2)\cos\theta}{(2 - \sin\theta)^2}\,d\theta$ **(1 Mark)**

Let $2 - \sin\theta = t$

$-\cos\theta\,d\theta = dt$

$I = \displaystyle\int \dfrac{(3(2 - t) - 2)}{t^2}\,-dt$ **(1 Mark)**

$= -\displaystyle\int \dfrac{4 - 3t}{t^2}\,dt$

$= -4\displaystyle\int \dfrac{1}{t^2}\,dt + 3\displaystyle\int \dfrac{1}{t}\,dt$ **(1 Mark)**

$$= -4\left(\frac{-1}{t}\right) + 3 \log |t| + C \qquad \left[\because \int x^n dx = \frac{x^{n+1}}{n+1}\right]$$

$$= \frac{4}{2-\sin\theta} + 3 \log |2 - \sin\theta| + C \qquad \textbf{(1 Mark)}$$

OR

Let $I = \int\limits_0^\pi e^{2x} \sin\left(\frac{\pi}{4} + x\right) dx$

Using $\int uv\,dx = u\int v\,dx - \int\left[\frac{du}{dx}\int v\,dx\right]dx$.

Here, $u = \sin\left(\frac{\pi}{4} + x\right)$, $v = e^{2x}$

$$I = \left[\sin\left(\frac{\pi}{4} + x\right)\frac{e^{2x}}{2}\right]_0^\pi - \int\limits_0^\pi \cos\left(\frac{\pi}{4} + x\right)\frac{e^{2x}}{2}dx \quad \textbf{(1 Mark)}$$

$$= \frac{1}{2}\left[e^{2x}\sin\left(\frac{\pi}{4} + x\right)\right]_0^\pi - \frac{1}{2}\int\limits_0^\pi \cos\left(\frac{\pi}{4} + x\right)e^{2x}dx$$

$$= \frac{1}{2}\left[e^{2x}\sin\left(\frac{\pi}{4} + x\right)\right]_0^\pi - \frac{1}{2}\left[\left(\frac{1}{2}\cos\left(\frac{\pi}{4} + x\right)e^{2x}\right)\right]_0^\pi$$

$$- \frac{1}{2}\int\limits_0^\pi\left[\left(-\sin\left(\frac{\pi}{4} + x\right)e^{2x}dx\right)\right]$$

(1 Mark)

$$= \frac{1}{2}\left[e^{2x}\sin\left(\frac{\pi}{4} + x\right)\right]_0^\pi - \frac{1}{4}\left[\cos\left(\frac{\pi}{4} + x\right)e^{2x}\right]_0^\pi$$

$$- \frac{1}{4}\int\limits_0^\pi \sin\left(\frac{\pi}{4} + x\right)e^{2x}dx$$

$$I = \frac{1}{2}\left[e^{2x}\sin\left(\frac{\pi}{4} + x\right)\right]_0^\pi - \frac{1}{4}\left[\left(\cos\left(\frac{\pi}{4} + x\right)e^{2x}\right)\right]_0^\pi - \frac{1}{4}I$$

(1 Mark)

$$\frac{5I}{4} = \frac{1}{4}\left[\left(2\sin\left(\frac{\pi}{4} + x\right) - \cos\left(\frac{\pi}{4} + x\right)\right)e^{2x}\right]_0^\pi$$

$$\frac{5I}{4} = \frac{1}{4}\left[e^{2\pi}\left(2\sin\frac{5\pi}{4} - \cos\frac{5\pi}{4}\right)\right]$$

$$- \frac{1}{4}\left[\left(2\sin\frac{\pi}{4} - \cos\frac{\pi}{4}\right)e^{o}\right]$$

$$\frac{5I}{4} = \frac{1}{4}\left[e^{2\pi}\left(2\left(-\frac{1}{\sqrt{2}}\right) + \frac{1}{\sqrt{2}}\right)\right] - \frac{1}{4}\left[2\left(\frac{1}{\sqrt{2}}\right) - \frac{1}{\sqrt{2}}\right]$$

$$\frac{5I}{4} = \frac{1}{4}\left[-\frac{e^{2\pi}}{\sqrt{2}}\right] - \frac{1}{4}\left[\frac{1}{\sqrt{2}}\right]$$

$$I = \frac{1}{5\sqrt{2}}\left(e^{2\pi} + 1\right) \qquad \textbf{(1 Mark)}$$

Applying the by part in definite integral. First simple integrate by applying by part, after that put limit.

9. Let $I = \int \dfrac{\sqrt{x}}{\sqrt{a^3 - x^3}}dx$

$$I = \int \frac{\sqrt{x}}{\sqrt{\left(a^{\frac{3}{2}}\right)^2 - \left(x^{\frac{3}{2}}\right)^2}}dx \qquad \textbf{(1 Mark)}$$

Put $x^{3/2} = t$

$$\frac{3}{2}x^{\frac{1}{2}}dx = dt$$

$$\sqrt{x}\,dx = \frac{2}{3}dt$$

$$I = \int \frac{dt}{\sqrt{\left(a^{3/2}\right)\;t^2}} \qquad \textbf{(1 Mark)}$$

$$= \frac{2}{3}\sin^{-1}\frac{t}{a^{3/2}} + C \qquad \left[\because \int\frac{dx}{\sqrt{a^2 - x^2}} = \sin^{-1}\frac{x}{a} + C\right]$$

$$= \frac{2}{3}\sin^{-1}\frac{x^{3/2}}{a^{3/2}} + C = \frac{2}{3}\sin^{-1}\sqrt{\frac{x^3}{a^3}} + C \qquad \textbf{(2 Marks)}$$

10. Let $I = \int\limits_{-1}^2 \left|x^3 - x\right| dx$

Here $f(x) = x^3 - x$

$= x(x^2 - 1) = x(x - 1)(x + 1)$

Turning points of $f(x)$ are $0, 1, -1$

$$\begin{array}{c|c|c|c|c}
\hline
-1 & & 0 & & 1 \qquad\qquad 2 \\
\hline
\end{array}$$

$\therefore f(x) > 0$ for all $x \in (-1, 0)$

$f(x) < 0$ for all $x \in (0, 1)$

$f(x) > 0$ for all $x \in (1, 2)$ **(1 Mark)**

$$I = \int\limits_{-1}^0 |x^3 - x|\,dx + \int\limits_0^1 |x^3 - x|\,dx + \int\limits_1^2 |x^3 - x|\,dx$$

$$I = \int\limits_{-1}^0 (x^3 - x)dx - \int\limits_0^1 (x^3 - x)dx + \int\limits_1^2 (x^3 - x)dx \qquad \textbf{(1 Mark)}$$

$$I = \left[\frac{x^4}{4} - \frac{x^2}{2}\right]_{-1}^0 - \left[\frac{x^4}{4} - \frac{x^2}{2}\right]_0^1 + \left[\frac{x^4}{4} - \frac{x^2}{2}\right]_1^2$$

$$\left[\because \int x^n dx = \frac{x^{n+1}}{n+1} + c\right] \quad \textbf{(1 Mark)}$$

$$I = -\frac{1}{4} + \frac{1}{2} - \frac{1}{4} + \frac{1}{2} + 4 - 2 - \frac{1}{4} + \frac{1}{2}$$

$$I = \frac{-3}{4} + \frac{3}{2} + 2$$

$$I = \frac{11}{4} \qquad \textbf{(1 Mark)}$$

11. $(1 - y^2)(1 + \log x)dx + 2xy\, dy = 0$

$$(1 - y^2)(1 + \log x)dx = -2xy\, dy$$

$$\frac{(1+\log x)}{x} dx = -2\frac{y}{1-y^2} dy \qquad \textbf{(1 Mark)}$$

Integrating on both sides

$$\int \frac{(1+\log x)}{x} dx = -2\int \frac{y}{1-y^2} dy \qquad ...(1)$$

Let $I_1 = \int \frac{(1+\log x)}{x} dx$

Let $1 + \log x = t$

$$\frac{1}{x} dx = dt$$

$$I_1 = \int t\, dt$$

$$= \frac{t^2}{2} + C_1$$

$$= \frac{(1+\log x)^2}{2} + C_1 \qquad ...(2) \quad \textbf{(1 Mark)}$$

Let $I_2 = -2\int \frac{y}{1-y^2} dy$

Let $1 - y^2 = t$

$$-2y\, dy = dt$$

$$I_2 = \int \frac{dt}{t} = \log|t| + C_2 = \log|1-y^2| + C_2 \quad ..(3) \ \textbf{(1 Mark)}$$

Putting the value of I_1 and I_2 in eq. (1)

$$\frac{(1+\log x)^2}{2} = \log(1-y^2) + C \quad ...(3) \quad \{C_1 + C_2 = C\}$$

Given that $y = 0$ at $x = 1$

$$\frac{(1+0)^2}{2} = \log 1 + C \Rightarrow C = \frac{1}{2}$$

From (3)

$$\frac{(1+\log x)^2}{2} = \log (1-y^2) + \frac{1}{2}$$

$$(1 + \log x)^2 = 2\log(1-y^2) + 1 \qquad \textbf{(1 Mark)}$$

12. $(1 + y^2) + \left(x - e^{\tan^{-1} y}\right)\dfrac{dy}{dx} = 0$

$$\left(x - e^{\tan^{-1} y}\right)\frac{dy}{dx} = -(1 + y^2)$$

$$\frac{dy}{dx} = \frac{-(1+y^2)}{x - e^{\tan^{-1}y}}$$

$$\frac{dx}{dy} = -\frac{x - e^{\tan^{-1}y}}{1+y^2}$$

$$\frac{dx}{dy} + \frac{1}{1+y^2} x = \frac{e^{\tan^{-1}y}}{1+y^2} \qquad \textbf{(1 Mark)}$$

This is in the form of linear differential equation

$$\frac{dx}{dy} + px = Q$$

Here $P = \dfrac{1}{1+y^2}$, $Q = \dfrac{e^{\tan^{-1}y}}{1+y^2}$

$$\text{I.F} = e^{\int P dy}$$

$$= e^{\int \frac{1}{1+y^2} dy}$$

$$= e^{\tan^{-1}y} \qquad \textbf{(1 Mark)}$$

$\therefore$ Solution of differential equation is

$$x(IF) = \int Q.(IF)dy$$

$$xe^{\tan^{-1}y} = \int \frac{e^{\tan^{-1}y}}{1+y^2} e^{\tan^{-1}y} dy$$

$$xe^{\tan^{-1}y} = \int \frac{e^{2\tan^{-1}y}}{1+y^2} dy$$

Let $\tan^{-1} y = t$

$$\frac{1}{1+y^2} dy = dt$$

$$xe^{\tan^{-1}y} = \int e^{2t} dt$$

$$xe^{\tan^{-1}y} = \frac{e^{2t}}{2} + C$$

$$2xe^{\tan^{-1}y} = e^{2\tan^{-1}y} + C \qquad [C = 2c] \quad \textbf{(1 Mark)}$$

13. Given that $\vec{a}+\vec{b}, \vec{b}+\vec{c}$ and $\vec{c}+\vec{a}$ are coplanar

$$\therefore (\vec{a}+\vec{b}).[(\vec{b}+\vec{c})\times(\vec{c}+\vec{a})] = 0 \qquad \textbf{(1 Mark)}$$

$$(\vec{a}+\vec{b})[\vec{b}\times\vec{c} + \vec{b}\times\vec{a} + \vec{c}\times\vec{c} + \vec{c}\times\vec{a}] = 0$$

$$\vec{a}.[\vec{b}\times\vec{c} + \vec{b}\times\vec{a} + \vec{c}\times\vec{a}] + \vec{b}.[\vec{b}\times\vec{c} + \vec{b}\times\vec{a} + \vec{c}\times\vec{a}] = 0$$

$$[\because \vec{c}\times\vec{c} = 0] \quad \textbf{(1 Mark)}$$

$\vec{a}.(\vec{b}\times\vec{c})+\vec{a}.(\vec{b}\times\vec{a})+\vec{a}.(\vec{c}\times\vec{a})+$
$$\vec{b}.(\vec{b}\times\vec{c})+\vec{b}.(\vec{b}\times\vec{a})+\vec{b}.(\vec{c}\times\vec{a})=0 \quad ...(1)$$

As $\vec{a}.(\vec{b}\times\vec{a})=0$, $\vec{a}.(\vec{c}\times\vec{a})=0$

$\vec{b}.(\vec{b}\times\vec{c})=0$, $\vec{b}.(\vec{b}\times\vec{a})=0$ **(1 Mark)**

From eq. (1)

$\vec{a}.(\vec{b}\times\vec{c})+\vec{b}.(\vec{c}\times\vec{a})=0$

$\vec{a}.(\vec{b}\times\vec{c})+\vec{a}.(\vec{b}\times\vec{c})=0\,[\because \vec{a}.(\vec{b}\times\vec{c})=\vec{b}.(\vec{c}\times\vec{a})=\vec{c}.(\vec{b}\times\vec{a})]$

$2[\vec{a}.(\vec{b}\times\vec{c})]=0$

$[a\ b\ c]=0$

$\therefore$ Vector a, b, c are coplanar. **(1 Mark)**

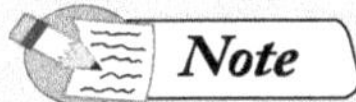 **Note**

When any two out of three vectors are same then its scalar triple product is zero.

14. $\vec{r}=(8\hat{i}-19\hat{j}+10\hat{k})+\lambda(3\hat{i}-16\hat{j}+7\hat{k})$

$\vec{r}=(15\hat{i}+29\hat{j}+5\hat{k})+\vec{r}(3\hat{i}+8\hat{j}-5\hat{k})$

Direction vectors of both the lines are

$\vec{b_1}=3\hat{i}-16\hat{j}+7\hat{k}$

$\vec{b_2}=3\hat{i}+8\hat{j}\_5\hat{k}$ **(1 Mark)**

Direction vector of required line will be

$\vec{b}=\vec{b_1}\times\vec{b_2}\,[\because \text{Line is perpendicular to both the lines}]$

$\vec{b}=\begin{vmatrix} \hat{i} & \hat{j} & \hat{k} \\ 3 & -16 & 7 \\ 3 & 8 & -5 \end{vmatrix}$

$=\hat{i}(80-56)-\hat{j}(-15-21)+\hat{k}(24+48)$

$=24\,\hat{i}+36\,\hat{j}+72\,\hat{k}$ **(1 Mark)**

As the required line passes through $(1, 2, -4)$

$\therefore \vec{a}=1\hat{i}+2\hat{j}-4\hat{k}$

$\vec{r}=\vec{a}+\gamma\vec{b}$

$\vec{r}=(1\hat{i}+2\hat{j}-4\hat{k})+\gamma(24\hat{i}+36\hat{j}+72\hat{k})$

$\vec{r}=(1\hat{i}+2\hat{j}-4\hat{k})+12\gamma(2\hat{i}+3\hat{j}+6\hat{k})$

$\vec{r}=(1\hat{i}+2\hat{j}-4\hat{k})+\gamma'(2\hat{i}+3\hat{j}+6\hat{k})$

Cartesian form

$$\frac{x-1}{2}=\frac{y-2}{3}=\frac{z+4}{6}$$ **(2 Marks)**

15. Let E_1, E_2, E_3 be the events of selecting A, B, C as managers respectively.

$\therefore P(E_1)=\dfrac{1}{7}$, $P(E_2)=\dfrac{2}{7}$, $P(E_3)=\dfrac{4}{7}$ **(1 Mark)**

Let A be the event denoting the change is not taking place

$P(A/E_1)$ = Probability of A does not introducing change

$\qquad = 1-0.8=0.2$

Similarly $P(A/E_2)=1-0.5=0.5$

$\qquad P(A/E_3)=1-0.3=0.7$ **(1 Mark)**

Probability of change does not take place due to appointment of $C=P(E_3/A)$

$P(E_3/A)$

$=\dfrac{P(A/E_3)\times P(E_3)}{P(A/E_1)\times P(E_1)+P(A/E_2)\times P(E_2)+P(A/E_3)\times P(E_3)}$

$P(E_3/A)=\dfrac{\dfrac{4}{7}\times 0.7}{\dfrac{1}{7}\times 0.2+\dfrac{2}{7}\times 0.5+\dfrac{4}{7}\times 0.7}$

$=\dfrac{2.8}{0.2+1+2.8}=\dfrac{2.8}{4}$

$P(E_3/A)=0.7$ **(2 Marks)**

OR

Total possible outcome for A to win $=[(1, 6), (2, 5), (3, 4), (4, 3), (5, 2), (6, 1)]=6$

Total sample space 36

Probability of A winning $=\dfrac{6}{36}=\dfrac{1}{6}$

Probability of A not winning $=1-\dfrac{1}{6}=\dfrac{5}{6}$ **(1 Mark)**

Total possible outcome for B to win

$=[(4, 6), (5, 5), (6, 4)]=3$

Probability of B winning $=\dfrac{3}{36}=\dfrac{1}{12}$

Probability of B not winning $=1-\dfrac{1}{12}=\dfrac{11}{12}$ **(1 Mark)**

A wins if he gets total of 7 in 1st, 3rd, 5th, ... throws

Probability of winning of A

$=\left(\dfrac{1}{6}\right)+\left(\dfrac{5}{6}\times\dfrac{11}{12}\times\dfrac{1}{6}\right)+\left(\dfrac{5}{6}\times\dfrac{11}{12}\times\dfrac{5}{6}\times\dfrac{11}{12}\times\dfrac{1}{6}\right)+.....$

This is in the form of $G.P$

$a=\dfrac{1}{6}, r=\dfrac{5}{6}\times\dfrac{11}{12}=\dfrac{55}{72}$

Probability of winning of A

$$= \frac{a}{1-r} = \frac{\frac{1}{6}}{1-\frac{55}{72}} = \frac{\frac{1}{6}}{\frac{17}{72}} = \frac{12}{17}$$ **(1 Mark)**

$\therefore$ Probability of winning of $B = 1 - $ (Probability of winning A)

$$= 1 - \frac{12}{17} = \frac{5}{17}$$ **(1 Mark)**

Note

Sum of infinite terms of G.P. when $0 < |r| < 1$ is $s = \dfrac{a}{1-r}$.

16. L.H.S $= \tan^{-1}\dfrac{1}{5} + \tan^{-1}\dfrac{1}{7} + \tan^{-1}\dfrac{1}{3} + \tan^{-1}\dfrac{1}{8}$

As we know that

$\tan^{-1} x + \tan^{-1} y = \tan^{-1}\left(\dfrac{x+y}{xy}\right)$, if $xy < 1$ **(1 Mark)**

$= \left(\tan^{-1}\dfrac{1}{5} + \tan^{-1}\dfrac{1}{7}\right) + \left(\tan^{-1}\dfrac{1}{3} + \tan^{-1}\dfrac{1}{8}\right)$

$$= \tan^{-1}\left(\frac{\frac{1}{5}+\frac{1}{7}}{1-\frac{1}{5}\times\frac{1}{7}}\right) + \tan^{-1}\left(\frac{\frac{1}{3}+\frac{1}{8}}{1-\frac{1}{3}\times\frac{1}{8}}\right)$$ **(1 Mark)**

$= \tan^{-1}\left(\dfrac{12}{34}\right) + \tan^{-1}\left(\dfrac{11}{23}\right)$

$= \tan^{-1}\left(\dfrac{6}{17}\right) + \tan^{-1}\left(\dfrac{11}{23}\right)$

$$= \tan^{-1}\left(\frac{\frac{6}{7}+\frac{11}{23}}{1-\frac{6}{7}\times\frac{11}{23}}\right)$$ **(1 Mark)**

$= \tan^{-1}\left(\dfrac{325}{325}\right) = \tan^{-1} 1 = \dfrac{\pi}{4} = $ R.H.S **(1 Mark)**

Hence proved.

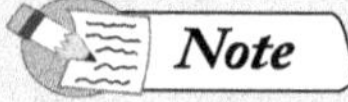
Note

If $xy > 1$, then $tan^{-1}x + tan^{-1}y = \pi + tan^{-1}\left(\dfrac{x+y}{1-xy}\right)$

OR

$2 \tan^{-1}(\cos x) = \tan^{-1}(2 \operatorname{cosec} x)$

$\Rightarrow \tan^{-1}\left(\dfrac{2\cos x}{1-\cos^2 x}\right) = \tan^{-1}(2 \operatorname{cosec} x)$

$\left[\because 2\tan^{-1}x = \tan^{-1}\dfrac{x}{1-x^2}\right]$ **(1 Mark)**

$\tan^{-1}\left(\dfrac{2\cos x}{\sin^2 x}\right) = \tan^{-1}\left(\dfrac{2}{\sin x}\right)$

$\left[\because \sin^2 x = 1 - \cos^2 x\right]$ **(1 Mark)**

$\dfrac{2\cos x}{\sin^2 x} = \dfrac{2}{\sin x}$

$\cot x = 1$

$x = \dfrac{\pi}{4}$ **(2 Marks)**

17. Let the monthly income of Aryan and Babban be $3x$ and $4x$ and their monthly expenditures be $5y$ and $7y$ respectively.

$\therefore$ Monthly saving of Aryan will be

$3x - 5y = 15000$ ...(1)

Monthly saving of Babban will be

$4x - 7y = 15000$ ...(2) **(1 Mark)**

Equation (1) and (2) can be written in matrix form as $AX = B$

where $A = \begin{bmatrix} 3 & -5 \\ 4 & -7 \end{bmatrix}$, $X = \begin{bmatrix} x \\ y \end{bmatrix}$, $B = \begin{bmatrix} 15000 \\ 15000 \end{bmatrix}$

$\begin{bmatrix} 3 & -5 \\ 4 & -7 \end{bmatrix}\begin{bmatrix} x \\ y \end{bmatrix} = \begin{bmatrix} 15000 \\ 15000 \end{bmatrix}$

$\begin{bmatrix} x \\ y \end{bmatrix} = \begin{bmatrix} 3 & -5 \\ 4 & -7 \end{bmatrix}^{-1}\begin{bmatrix} 15000 \\ 15000 \end{bmatrix}$ ...(1) **(1 Mark)**

$A = \begin{bmatrix} 3 & -5 \\ 4 & -7 \end{bmatrix}$

$|A| = -21 + 20 = -1 \neq 0$, A^{-1} exist

$\text{Adj }(A) = \begin{bmatrix} -7 & -4 \\ 5 & 3 \end{bmatrix}^T$

$= \begin{bmatrix} -7 & 5 \\ -4 & 3 \end{bmatrix}$

$A^{-1} = \dfrac{\text{Adj}(A)}{|A|}$

$A^{-1} = (-1)\begin{bmatrix} -7 & 5 \\ -4 & 3 \end{bmatrix} = \begin{bmatrix} 7 & -5 \\ 4 & -3 \end{bmatrix}$ **(1 Mark)**

From (1)

$\begin{bmatrix} x \\ y \end{bmatrix} = \begin{bmatrix} 7 & -5 \\ 4 & -3 \end{bmatrix}\begin{bmatrix} 15000 \\ 15000 \end{bmatrix}$

$$\begin{bmatrix} x \\ y \end{bmatrix} = \begin{bmatrix} 105000 - 75000 \\ 60000 - 45000 \end{bmatrix}$$

$$\begin{bmatrix} x \\ y \end{bmatrix} = \begin{bmatrix} 30000 \\ 15000 \end{bmatrix} \Rightarrow x = 30000$$

$$y = 15000$$

$\therefore$ Monthly income of Aryan $= 3x$

$$= ₹3 \times 30000 = ₹90,000$$

Monthly income of Babban $= 4x$

$$= ₹4 \times 30000 = ₹1,20,000$$

These value reflected that we should save some part of our money from monthly income.   **(1 Mark)**

18. $x = a \sin 2t \,(1 + \cos 2t)$ ...(1)

$y = b \cos 2t \,(1 - \cos 2t)$ ...(2)

Differentiating equation (1) & (2) w.r.t. t

$$\frac{dx}{dt} = 2a \cos 2t \,(1 + \cos 2t) + a \sin 2t \,(-2 \sin 2t)$$

$$\frac{dx}{dt} = 2a \cos 2t + 2a \cos^2 2t - 2a \sin^2 2t$$

$$\frac{dx}{dt} = 2a \cos 2t + 2a \,(\cos^2 2t - \sin^2 2t)$$

$$\frac{dx}{dt} = 2a \cos 2t + 2a \cos 4t$$

$$[\because \cos 2\theta = \cos^2\theta - \sin^2\theta] \quad \textbf{(1 Mark)}$$

Similarly, $\dfrac{dy}{dt} = -2b \sin 2t \,(1 - \cos 2t) + b \cos 2t \,(2 \sin 2t)$

$$\frac{dy}{dt} = -2b \sin 2t + 2b \sin 2t \cos 2t + b(2 \sin 2t \cos 2t)$$

$$\frac{dy}{dt} = -2b \sin 2t + b \sin 4t + b \sin 4t$$

$$[\because \sin 2\theta = 2 \sin\theta \,.\, \cos\theta]$$

$$\frac{dy}{dt} = -2b \sin 2t + 2b \sin 4t \qquad \textbf{(1 Mark)}$$

$$\therefore \frac{dy}{dx} = \frac{\dfrac{dy}{dt}}{\dfrac{dx}{dt}} = \frac{-2b \sin 2t + 2b \sin 4t}{2a \cos 2t + 2a \cos 4t}$$

$$\frac{dy}{dt} = \frac{-2b \sin 2t + 2b \sin 4t}{2a \cos 2t + 2a \cos 4t}$$

When $x = \dfrac{\pi}{4}$

$$\left.\frac{dy}{dt}\right|_{x=\frac{\pi}{4}} = \frac{-2b \sin 2\left(\dfrac{\pi}{4}\right) + 2b \sin 4\left(\dfrac{\pi}{4}\right)}{2a \cos 2\left(\dfrac{\pi}{4}\right) + 2a \cos 4\left(\dfrac{\pi}{4}\right)}$$

$$= \frac{-2b + 2b(0)}{2a(0) + 2a(-1)} = \frac{-2b}{-2a}$$

$$\left.\frac{dy}{dt}\right|_{x=\frac{\pi}{4}} = \frac{b}{a} \qquad \textbf{(1 Mark)}$$

When $x = \dfrac{\pi}{3}$

$$\left.\frac{dy}{dt}\right|_{x=\frac{\pi}{3}} = \frac{-2b \sin 2\left(\dfrac{\pi}{3}\right) + 2b \sin 4\left(\dfrac{\pi}{3}\right)}{2a \cos 2\left(\dfrac{\pi}{3}\right) + 2a \cos 4\left(\dfrac{\pi}{3}\right)}$$

$$= \frac{-2b\left(\dfrac{\sqrt{3}}{2}\right) + 2b\left(\dfrac{-\sqrt{3}}{2}\right)}{2a\left(\dfrac{-1}{2}\right) + 2a\left(\dfrac{-1}{2}\right)}$$

$$= \frac{-2b\sqrt{3}}{-2a}$$

$$\left.\frac{dy}{dt}\right|_{x=\frac{\pi}{3}} = \frac{b\sqrt{3}}{a} \qquad \textbf{(1 Mark)}$$

OR

$y = x^x$

Taking log on both sides

$\log y = x \log x$ $[\because \log m^n = n \log m]$

Differentiate w.r.t. x

$$\frac{1}{y}\frac{dy}{dx} = 1 \,.\, \log x + x \,.\, \frac{1}{x}$$

$$\frac{1}{y}\frac{dy}{dx} = \log x + 1$$

$$\frac{dy}{dx} = y(\log x + 1)$$

$$\frac{dy}{dx} = x^x(\log x + 1) \qquad ...(1) \quad \textbf{(1 Mark)}$$

Again differentiating w.r.t. x

$$\frac{d^2y}{dx^2} = x^x\left(\frac{1}{x}\right) + (\log x + 1)\frac{dx^x}{dx}$$

$$= x^x\left(\frac{1}{x}\right) + (\log x + 1)x^x(\log x + 1) \qquad \text{[From (1)]}$$

$$= x^x\left(\frac{1}{x}\right) + x^x(\log x + 1)^2 \qquad ...(2) \quad \textbf{(1 Mark)}$$

L.H.S.

$$\frac{d^2y}{dx^2} - \frac{1}{y}\left(\frac{dy}{dx}\right)^2 - \frac{y}{x}$$

$$= \frac{1}{x}\cdot x^x + x^x(\log x + 1)^2 - \frac{1}{x^x}[x^x(\log x + 1)]^2 - \frac{x^x}{x}$$

$$= 0 = \text{R.H.S.}$$

L.H.S. = R.H.S. $\qquad\qquad\qquad\qquad$ **(2 Marks)**

Hence proved.

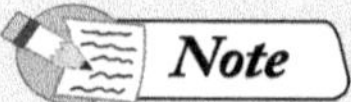

Note

When function in the form of variable to the power of variable then logrithum is used before differentiation.

19. $f(x) = \begin{cases} \dfrac{1-\sin^3 x}{3\cos^2 x}, & \text{if } x < \dfrac{\pi}{2} \\[2ex] p, & \text{if } x = \dfrac{\pi}{2} \\[2ex] \dfrac{q(1-\sin x)}{(\pi - 2x)^2}, & \text{if } x > \dfrac{\pi}{2} \end{cases}$

Given that $f(x)$ is continuous at $x = \dfrac{\pi}{2}$

$$\therefore \lim_{x\to\frac{\pi}{2}^-} f(x) = f\left(\frac{\pi}{2}\right) = \lim_{x\to\frac{\pi}{2}^+} f(x)$$

$$\text{L.H.L.} = \lim_{x\to\frac{\pi}{2}^-} f(x) = \lim_{x\to\frac{\pi}{2}^-} \frac{(1)^3 - \sin^3 x}{3\cos^2 x}$$

$$= \lim_{x\to\frac{\pi}{2}^-} \frac{(1-\sin x)(1+\sin^2 x + \sin x)}{3(1-\sin^2 x)}$$

$$\left[\because (a^3 - b^3) = (a-b)(a^2 + b^2 + ab), 1 - \sin^2 x = \cos^2 x\right]$$

$$= \lim_{x\to\frac{\pi}{2}^-} \frac{(1-\sin x)(1+\sin^2 x + \sin x)}{3(1-\sin x)(1+\sin x)}$$

$$= \lim_{x\to\frac{\pi}{2}^-} \frac{1+\sin^2 x + \sin x}{3(1+\sin x)}$$

$$= \lim_{h\to 0} \frac{\left[1+\sin^2\left(\frac{\pi}{2}-h\right) + \sin\left(\frac{\pi}{2}-h\right)\right]}{3\left[1+\sin\left(\frac{\pi}{2}-h\right)\right]}$$

$$= \lim_{h\to 0} \frac{\left[1+\cos^2 h + \cos h\right]}{3(1+\cos h)}$$

$$= \frac{1+1+1}{3(1+1)} = \frac{1}{2} \qquad\qquad \textbf{(1½ Marks)}$$

As $\lim_{x\to\frac{\pi}{2}^-} f(x) = f\left(\frac{\pi}{2}\right)$

$$\frac{1}{2} = P$$

$$\therefore P = \frac{1}{2} \qquad\qquad\qquad\qquad \textbf{(½ Mark)}$$

$$\text{R.H.L.} = \lim_{x\to\frac{\pi}{2}^+} f(x) = \lim_{x\to\frac{\pi}{2}^+} q\frac{(1-\sin x)}{(\pi - 2x)^2}$$

$$= \lim_{h\to 0} q\frac{\left[1-\sin\left(\frac{\pi}{2}+h\right)\right]}{\left[\pi - 2\left(\frac{\pi}{2}+h\right)\right]^2}$$

$$= \lim_{h\to 0} q\frac{(1-\cos h)}{(-2h)^2}$$

$$= \lim_{h\to 0} q\frac{2\sin^2\frac{h}{2}}{4h^2} \qquad\qquad [\because \cos 2\theta = 1 - 2\sin^2\theta]$$

$$= \lim_{h\to 0} q\frac{\sin^2\frac{h}{2}}{2\frac{h^2}{4}\times 4}$$

$$= \frac{q}{8} \qquad \left[\because \lim_{n\to 0}\frac{\sin x}{x} = 1\right] \quad \textbf{(1½ Marks)}$$

As $\lim_{x\to\frac{\pi}{2}^+} f(x) = \lim_{x\to\frac{\pi}{2}^-} f(x)$

$$\frac{q}{8} = \frac{1}{2}$$

$$q = 4 \qquad\qquad\qquad\qquad \textbf{(½ Mark)}$$

SECTION - C

20. Let r be the radius of sphere and R be the radius of cone.

Let AC be the axis of cone and B is the centre of the sphere such that $BC = x$.

Height of cone $= AC = AB + BC = r + x$

In right triangle BCD

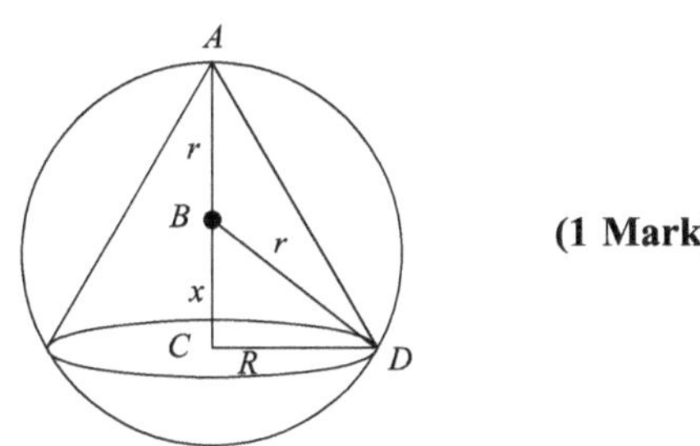

(1 Mark)

$BD^2 = BC^2 + DC^2$ [By pythagoras theorem]

$r^2 = x^2 + R^2$

$R^2 = r^2 - x^2$ ...(1)   **(1 Mark)**

Volume of the cone, $V = \dfrac{1}{3}\pi R^2(r + x)$

$$\left[\because \text{Volume of cone} = \frac{1}{3}\pi r^2 h\ \right]$$

$V = \dfrac{1}{3}\pi(r^2 - x^2)(r + x)$ ...(2)   [From (1)]

$\therefore \dfrac{dV}{dx} = \dfrac{1}{3}\pi[(r + x)(-2x) + r^2 - x^2]$

$= \dfrac{1}{3}\pi[-2xr - 2x^2 + r^2 - x^2]$

$= \dfrac{1}{3}\pi(r^2 - 3x^2 - 2xr)$ **(1 Mark)**

For critical points of maxima or minima

$\dfrac{dV}{dx} = 0$

$\dfrac{1}{3}\pi(r^2 - 3x^2 - 2xr) = 0$

$3x^2 + 2xr - r^2 = 0$

$3x^2 + 3xr - 1xr - r^2 = 0$

$3x(x + r) - r(x + r) = 0 \Rightarrow (x + r)(3x - r) = 0$

$x = -r$ or $x = \dfrac{r}{3}$ **(1 Mark)**

x cannot be negative $x \neq -r$. $\therefore x = \dfrac{r}{3}$

$\dfrac{dV}{dx} = \dfrac{1}{3}\pi(r^2 - 3x^2 - 2xr)$

$\dfrac{d^2V}{dx^2} = \dfrac{1}{3}\pi(-6x - 2r)$

$= -\dfrac{1}{3}\pi(6x + 2r)$

$= -\dfrac{1}{3}\pi\left[6\left(\dfrac{r}{3}\right) + 2r\right] = -\dfrac{4}{3}\pi r < 0$

$\therefore V$ will be maximum at $x = \dfrac{r}{3}$ **(1 Mark)**

Height of cone $= r + x$

$= r + \dfrac{r}{3} = \dfrac{4r}{3}$

$\therefore$ Volume of sphere, $V = \dfrac{1}{3}\pi\left(r^2 - \dfrac{r^2}{9}\right)\left(r + \dfrac{r}{3}\right)$

[From (2)]

$V = \dfrac{1}{3}\pi\left(\dfrac{8r^2}{9}\right)\left(\dfrac{4r}{3}\right)$

$= \dfrac{8}{27}\left(\dfrac{4}{3}\pi r^2\right)$

$\therefore$ Volume of the largest cone that can be inscribed in a sphere of radius r is $\dfrac{8}{27}$ of the volume of sphere.

(1 Mark)

OR

$f(x) = \sin 3x - \cos 3x,\ 0 < x < \pi.$

Differentiating $f(x)$ w.r.t. x

$f'(x) = 3(\cos 3x + \sin 3x)$

$= 3\sqrt{2}\left(\dfrac{1}{\sqrt{2}}\cos 3x + \dfrac{1}{\sqrt{2}}\sin 3x\right)$

$= 3\sqrt{2}\left(\sin\left(\dfrac{\pi}{4}\right)\cos 3x + \cos\left(\dfrac{\pi}{4}\right)\sin 3x\right)$

$= 3\sqrt{2}\sin\left(3x + \dfrac{\pi}{4}\right)$

$[\because \sin(A + B) = \sin A \cdot \cos B + \cos A \cdot \sin B]$ **(2 Marks)**

For increasing interval

$f'(x) > 0$

$$3\sqrt{2}\sin\left(3x+\frac{\pi}{4}\right) > 0$$

$$\sin\left(3x+\frac{\pi}{4}\right) > 0$$

$$\Rightarrow 0 < 3x + \frac{\pi}{4} < \pi$$

$$0 < 3x < \frac{3\pi}{4} \qquad [\because 0 < x < \pi] \quad \textbf{(1 Mark)}$$

$$0 < x < \frac{\pi}{4}$$

Also $\sin\left(3x+\frac{\pi}{4}\right) > 0$

when $2\pi < 3x + \dfrac{\pi}{4} < 3\pi$

$$\frac{7\pi}{4} < 3x < \frac{11\pi}{4}$$

$$\frac{7\pi}{12} < x < \frac{11\pi}{12}$$

$\therefore$ $f(x)$ is strictly increasing in

$$0 < x < \frac{\pi}{4} \text{ and } \frac{7\pi}{12} < x < \frac{11\pi}{12} \qquad \textbf{(1 Mark)}$$

For decreasing interval

$$f'(x) < 0$$

$$3\sqrt{2}\sin\left(3x+\frac{\pi}{4}\right) < 0$$

$$\sin\left(3x+\frac{\pi}{4}\right) < 0$$

$$\pi < 3x + \frac{\pi}{4} < 2\pi$$

$$\frac{3\pi}{4} < 3x < \frac{7\pi}{4}$$

$$\frac{\pi}{4} < x < \frac{7\pi}{12} \qquad \textbf{(1 Mark)}$$

Also $\sin\left(3x+\dfrac{\pi}{4}\right) < 0$

when $3\pi < 3x + \dfrac{\pi}{4} < 4\pi$

$$\frac{11\pi}{4} < 3x < \frac{15\pi}{4}$$

$$\frac{11\pi}{12} < x < \pi \qquad\qquad [\because 0 < x < \pi]$$

$\therefore$ $f(x)$ is strictly decreasing in $\left(\dfrac{\pi}{4},\dfrac{7\pi}{12}\right)$ and $\left(\dfrac{11\pi}{12},\pi\right)$

(1 Mark)

21.

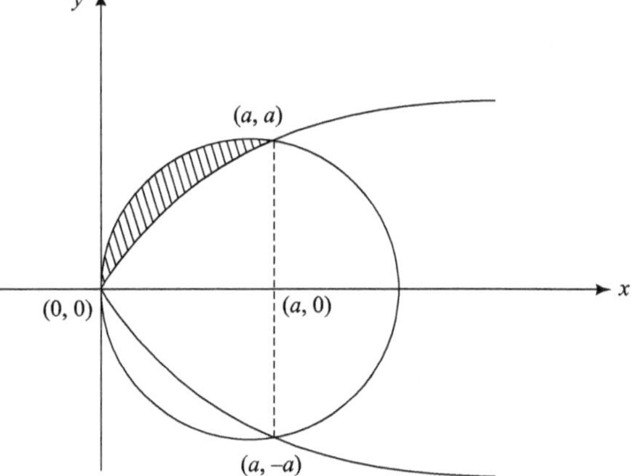

> **Note**
>
> *An equation which has highest power of x and y = 2 and coefficient of x^2 and y^2 will be same then it is equation of circle. By completing square method convert in the form $(x-h)^2 + (y-k)^2 = r^2$*

Given: $x^2 + y^2 \le 2ax$

$$x^2 - 2ax + y^2 \le 0$$

$$x^2 - 2ax + a^2 - a^2 + y^2 \le 0$$

$$(x-a)^2 + y^2 \le a^2 \qquad \textbf{(1 Mark)}$$

To find point of intersection of

$(x-a)^2 + y^2 = a^2$ and $y^2 = ax$

$$(x-a)^2 + ax = a^2$$

$$x^2 + a^2 - 2ax + ax = a^2$$

$$x^2 + a^2 - ax = a^2$$

$$x^2 - ax = 0$$

$$x(x-a) = 0$$

$$x = 0 \text{ or } x = a$$

$$y = 0 \text{ or } y^2 = a(a) = a^2$$

$$y = \pm a$$

$$y = 0, a, -a \qquad \textbf{(1 Mark)}$$

(1 Mark)

Area of shaded portion, $A = \displaystyle\int_0^a \left(\sqrt{a^2 - (x-a)^2} - \sqrt{ax}\right) dx$

(1 Mark)

$$A = \left[\frac{x-a}{2}\sqrt{a^2-(x-a)^2} + \frac{a^2}{2}\sin^{-1}\frac{(x-a)}{a} - \frac{2\sqrt{a}}{3}x^{3/2} \right]_0^a$$

(1 Mark)

$$\left[\because \int x^n dx = \frac{x^{n+1}}{n+1}+c, \int \sqrt{a^2-x^2}\,dx = \frac{x}{2}\sqrt{a^2-x^2}+\frac{a^2}{2}\sin^{-1}\frac{x}{a} \right]$$

$$A = \left[0+0-\frac{2\sqrt{a}}{3}a^{3/2} - \left(0+\frac{a^2}{2}\sin^{-1}(-1)-0 \right) \right]$$

$$A = -\frac{2}{3}a^2 + \frac{a^2}{2}\frac{\pi}{2}$$

$$A = a^2\left(\frac{\pi}{4}-\frac{2}{3} \right) \text{ square units} \qquad \textbf{(1 Mark)}$$

22. Equation of the plane passing through $L(2, 2, 1)$, $M(3, 0, 1)$ and $N(4, -1, 0)$ is

$$\begin{vmatrix} x-x_1 & y-y_1 & z-z_1 \\ x_2-x_1 & y_2-y_1 & z_2-z_1 \\ x_3-x_1 & y_3-y_1 & z_3-z_1 \end{vmatrix} = 0 \qquad \textbf{(1 Mark)}$$

$$\begin{vmatrix} x-2 & y-2 & z-1 \\ 3-2 & 0-2 & 1-1 \\ 4-2 & -1-2 & 0-1 \end{vmatrix} = 0$$

$$\begin{vmatrix} x-2 & y-2 & z-1 \\ 1 & -2 & 0 \\ 2 & -3 & -1 \end{vmatrix} = 0$$

$(x-2)(2-0) - (y-2)(-1-0) + (z-1)(-3+4) = 0$

$2x - 4 + y - 2 + z - 1 = 0$

$2x + y + z - 7 = 0$ **(1 Mark)**

Equation of line passing through $A(3, -4, -5)$ and $B(2, -3, 1)$

$$\frac{x-3}{2-3} = \frac{y+4}{-3+4} = \frac{z+5}{1+5} = \lambda$$

$$\frac{x-3}{-1} = \frac{y+4}{1} = \frac{z+5}{6} = \lambda$$

$x = -\lambda + 3,\ y = \lambda - 4,\ z = 6\lambda - 5$ **(1 Mark)**

To find point of intersection P

$2x + y + z - 7 = 0$

$2(-\lambda + 3) + (\lambda - 4) + (6\lambda - 5) - 7 = 0$

$5\lambda = 10$

$\lambda = 2$

$x = -2 + 3 = 1$

$y = 2 - 4 = -2$

$z = 6(2) - 5 = 7$

$P(1, -2, 7)$ **(1 Mark)**

Let P divides AB in the ratio $m : n$

$$P = \left(\frac{2m+3n}{m+n}, \frac{-3m-4n}{m+n}, \frac{1m-5n}{m+n} \right)$$

$$(1, -2, 7) = \left(\frac{2m+3n}{m+n}, \frac{-3m-4n}{m+n}, \frac{1m-5n}{m+n} \right)$$

$$\frac{2m+3n}{m+n} = 1$$

$2m + 3n = m + n$

$m = -2n$

$$\frac{m}{n} = \frac{-2}{1}$$

Hence P externally divides the line segment AB in the ratio $2 : 1$.   **(2 Marks)**

23. Let x denotes the total number of red balls when four balls are drawn one by one with replacement.

Probability of getting a red ball in one drawn,

$$P = \frac{6}{9} = \frac{2}{3}$$

Probability of not getting a red ball in one drawn,

$$q = 1 - \frac{2}{3} = \frac{1}{3}$$

As $P(x=r) = n_{C_r} p^r q^{n-r}$ **(1 Mark)**

Probability distribution:

$$P(x = 0) = 4_{C_0}\left(\frac{2}{3} \right)^0 \left(\frac{1}{3} \right)^4$$

$$= \frac{4!}{0!4!}\left(\frac{1}{3} \right)^4 \qquad \left[\because {}^m C_n = \frac{m!}{n!(m-n)!} \right]$$

$$= \frac{1}{81}$$

$$P(x = 1) = {}^4C_1\left(\frac{2}{3} \right)^1 \left(\frac{1}{3} \right)^3$$

$$= \frac{4!}{1!3!}\left(\frac{2}{3} \right)\left(\frac{1}{27} \right)$$

$$= \frac{8}{81}$$

$$P(x = 2) = {}^4C_2\left(\frac{2}{3} \right)^2 \left(\frac{1}{3} \right)^2 = \frac{24}{81}$$

$$P(x = 3) = {}^4C_3\left(\frac{2}{3} \right)^3 \left(\frac{1}{3} \right)^1 = \frac{32}{81}$$

$$P(x = 4) = {}^4C_4 \left(\frac{2}{3}\right)^4 \left(\frac{1}{3}\right)^0 = \frac{16}{81}$$ **(1½ Marks)**

To find mean and variance

x_i	$P(x_i)$	$x_i P(x)$	$x_i^2 P(x_i)$
0	$\frac{1}{81}$	0	0
1	$\frac{8}{81}$	$\frac{8}{81}$	$\frac{8}{81}$
2	$\frac{24}{81}$	$\frac{48}{81}$	$\frac{96}{81}$
3	$\frac{32}{81}$	$\frac{96}{81}$	$\frac{288}{81}$
4	$\frac{16}{81}$	$\frac{64}{81}$	$\frac{256}{81}$

(1½ Marks)

$$\therefore \text{Mean } \overline{X} = \sum P(x_i).x_i = \frac{8}{81} + \frac{48}{81} + \frac{96}{81} + \frac{64}{81}$$

$$= \frac{216}{81} = \frac{8}{3}$$ **(1 Mark)**

$$\text{Variance} = \sum P(x_i) x_i^2 - \left[\sum P(x_i).x_i\right]^2$$

$$= \frac{648}{81} - \frac{64}{9} = \frac{8}{9}$$ **(1 Mark)**

Note

For binomial distribution mean = np and variance = n pq.

24. Let the numbers of units of products A and B to be produced be x and y

Product	Machine 1	Machine 2
A	3	3
B	2	1

$$3x + 2y \leq 12$$
$$3x + 1y \leq 9$$
$$Z = 7x + 4y$$

We have to maximize $Z = 7x + 4y$

Also $x \geq 0, y \geq 0$ **(2 Marks)**

$3x + 2y = 12$

x	0	4	2
y	6	0	3

$3x + y = 9$

x	0	3	2
y	9	0	3

Point of intersection (2, 3)

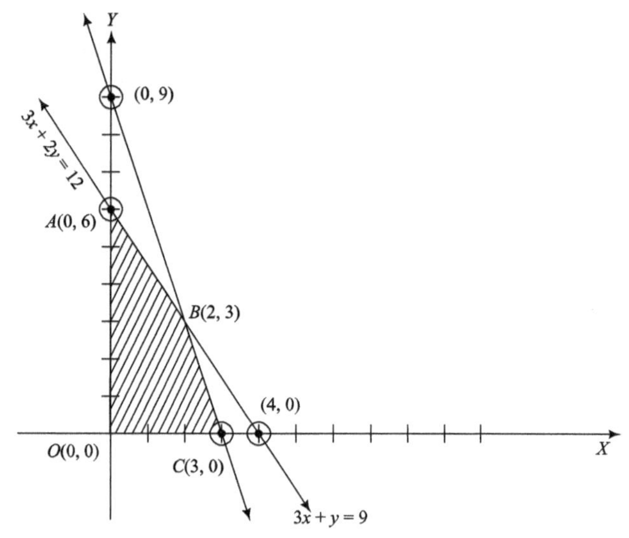

(2 Marks)

$OABC$ is the required region.

Corner Points	Z = 7x + 4y	
(0, 6)	24	
(2, 3)	14 + 12 = 26	$\Rightarrow$ Max
(3, 0)	21	

Z will be maximum at (2, 3).

$\therefore$ Manufactures has to produce 2 units of product A and 3 units of product B for maximum profit of Rs 26.

(2 Marks)

Note

The problem has multiple optimal solutions at the corner points A and B then every point on the line segment AB give the same maximum value.

25. $f : N \to S$ will be invertible if it is one–one and onto

$$f(x_1) = f(x_2)$$
$$9x_1^2 + 6x_1 - 5 = 9x_2^2 + 6x_2 - 5$$
$$9x_1^2 + 6x_1 = 9x_2^2 + 6x_2$$
$$9(x_1^2 - x_2^2) + 6(x_1 - x_2) = 0$$
$$9(x_1 - x_2)(x_1 + x_2) + 6(x_1 - x_2) = 0$$
$$(x_1 - x_2)(9x_1 + 9x_2 + 6) = 0$$
$$x_1 = x_2 \text{ or } 9x_1 + 9x_2 + 6 = 0$$

As $x_1 > 0, x_2 > 0$

$$9x_1 + 9x_2 + 6 = 0 \quad \text{(wrong)}$$

$\therefore x_1 = x_2$

$\therefore f$ is one-one.   **(1 Mark)**

$f : N \to S$

f is onto because S is range of f

$f(x) = y = 9x^2 + 6x - 5$

$9x^2 + 6x - 5 - y = 0$

$9x^2 + 6x - (5 + y) = 0$

$x = \dfrac{-6 \pm \sqrt{(6)^2 - 4(9)\left(-(5+y)\right)}}{18}$

$= \dfrac{-6 \pm \sqrt{36 + 36(5 + y)}}{18}$

$= \dfrac{-6 \pm 6\sqrt{1 + 5 + y}}{18}$

$= \dfrac{-1 \pm \sqrt{6 + y}}{3}$ **(2 Marks)**

x is cannot be negative

$g(y) = \dfrac{-1 + \sqrt{6 + y}}{3}$

$f[g(y)] = 9\left(\dfrac{-1 + \sqrt{6 + y}}{3}\right)^2 + 6\left(\dfrac{-1 + \sqrt{6 + y}}{3}\right) - 5 = y$

$\therefore f(x)$ is invertable.

$\Rightarrow f^{-1}(y) = \dfrac{-1 + \sqrt{6 + y}}{3}$ $[f^{-1} : y \to N]$

$f^{-1}(43) = \dfrac{-1 + \sqrt{6 + 43}}{3} = \dfrac{-1 + \sqrt{49}}{3} = \dfrac{-1 + 7}{3} = 2$

                                                         (2 Marks)

$f^{-1}(163) = \dfrac{-1 + \sqrt{6 + 163}}{3} = \dfrac{-1 + \sqrt{169}}{3} = \dfrac{-1 + 13}{3}$

$= \dfrac{12}{3} = 4$ **(1 Mark)**

26. $\begin{vmatrix} yz - x^2 & zx - y^2 & xy - z^2 \\ zx - y^2 & xy - z^2 & yz - x^2 \\ xy - z^2 & yz - x^2 & zx - y^2 \end{vmatrix}$

$R_1 \to R_1 + R_2 + R_3$

$= \begin{vmatrix} xy + yz + zx - (x^2 + y^2 + z^2) & xy + yz + zx - (x^2 + y^2 + z^2) & xy + yz + zx - (x^2 + y^2 + z^2) \\ zx - y^2 & xy - z^2 & yz - x^2 \\ xy - z^2 & yz - x^2 & zx - y^2 \end{vmatrix}$

                                                         (1 Mark)

$[xy + yz + zx - (x^2 + y^2 + z^2)]$

$\times \begin{vmatrix} 1 & 1 & 1 \\ zx - y^2 & xy - z^2 & yz - x^2 \\ xy - z^2 & yz - x^2 & zx - y^2 \end{vmatrix}$ **(1 Mark)**

$C_2 \to C_2 - C_1, C_3 \to C_3 - C_1$

$= [xy + yz + zx - (x^2 + y^2 + z^2)]$

$\times \begin{vmatrix} 1 & 0 & 0 \\ zx - y^2 & xy - zx - z^2 + y^2 & yz - zx - x^2 + y^2 \\ xy - z^2 & yz - xy - x^2 + z^2 & zx - xy - y^2 + z^2 \end{vmatrix}$ **(1 Mark)**

$= [xy + yz + zx - (x^2 + y^2 + z^2)]$

$\times \begin{vmatrix} 1 & 0 & 0 \\ zx - y^2 & x(y-z) + (y-z)(y+z) & z(y-x) + (y-x)(y+x) \\ xy - z^2 & y(z-x) + (z-x)(x+z) & x(z-y) + (z-y)(z+y) \end{vmatrix}$

$= [xy + yz + zx - (x^2 + y^2 + z^2)]$

$\times \begin{vmatrix} 1 & 0 & 0 \\ zx - y^2 & (x+y+z)(y-z) & (x+y+z)(y-x) \\ xy - z^2 & (x+y+z)(z-x) & (x+y+z)(z-y) \end{vmatrix}$ **(1 Mark)**

$= [xy + yz + zx - (x^2 + y^2 + z^2)] \, (x + y + z)^2$

$\times \begin{vmatrix} 1 & 0 & 0 \\ zx - y^2 & (y-z) & (y-x) \\ xy - z^2 & (z-x) & (z-y) \end{vmatrix}$

$= [xy + yz + zx - (x^2 + y^2 + z^2)] \, (x + y + z)^2 \, [-(z - y)^2 - (y - x)\,(z - x)]$

$= [xy + yz + zx - (x^2 + y^2 + z^2)]^2 \, (x + y + z)^2$

$\therefore$ It is divided by $(x + y + z)$ as one of its factor is $(x + y + z)$ **(1½ Marks)**

Quotient after division will be

$[xy + yz + zx - (x^2 + y^2 + z^2)]^2 \, (x + y + z)$ **(½ Marks)**

OR

$$A = \begin{bmatrix} 8 & 4 & 3 \\ 2 & 1 & 1 \\ 1 & 2 & 2 \end{bmatrix}$$

$A = IA$

$$\begin{bmatrix} 8 & 4 & 3 \\ 2 & 1 & 1 \\ 1 & 2 & 2 \end{bmatrix} = \begin{bmatrix} 1 & 0 & 0 \\ 0 & 1 & 0 \\ 0 & 0 & 1 \end{bmatrix} A$$

Applying $R_1 \Rightarrow R_3$

$$\begin{bmatrix} 1 & 2 & 2 \\ 2 & 1 & 1 \\ 8 & 4 & 3 \end{bmatrix} = \begin{bmatrix} 0 & 0 & 1 \\ 0 & 1 & 0 \\ 1 & 0 & 0 \end{bmatrix} A \qquad \textbf{(1 Mark)}$$

Applying $R_2 \to R_2 - 2R_1$ and $R_3 \to R_3 - 8R_1$

$$\begin{bmatrix} 1 & 2 & 2 \\ 0 & -3 & -3 \\ 0 & -12 & -13 \end{bmatrix} = \begin{bmatrix} 0 & 0 & 1 \\ 0 & 1 & -2 \\ 1 & 0 & -8 \end{bmatrix} A \qquad \textbf{(1 Mark)}$$

$R_2 \to \dfrac{R_2}{-3}$

$$\begin{bmatrix} 1 & 2 & 2 \\ 0 & 1 & 1 \\ 0 & -12 & -13 \end{bmatrix} = \begin{bmatrix} 0 & 0 & 1 \\ 0 & -\dfrac{1}{3} & \dfrac{2}{3} \\ 1 & 0 & -8 \end{bmatrix} A$$

$R_1 \to R_1 - 2R_2$ & $R_3 \to R_3 + 12R_2$

$$\begin{bmatrix} 1 & 0 & 0 \\ 0 & 1 & 1 \\ 0 & 0 & -1 \end{bmatrix} = \begin{bmatrix} 0 & \dfrac{2}{3} & -\dfrac{1}{3} \\ 0 & -\dfrac{1}{3} & \dfrac{2}{3} \\ 1 & -4 & 0 \end{bmatrix} A \qquad \textbf{(1 Mark)}$$

Applying $R_3 \to -R_3$ & $R_2 \to R_2 - R_3$

$$\begin{bmatrix} 1 & 0 & 0 \\ 0 & 1 & 0 \\ 0 & 0 & 1 \end{bmatrix} = \begin{bmatrix} 0 & \dfrac{2}{3} & -\dfrac{1}{3} \\ 1 & -\dfrac{13}{3} & \dfrac{2}{3} \\ -1 & 4 & 0 \end{bmatrix} A$$

As $I = A^{-1} A$

$$\therefore A^{-1} = \begin{bmatrix} 0 & \dfrac{2}{3} & -\dfrac{1}{3} \\ 1 & -\dfrac{13}{3} & \dfrac{2}{3} \\ -1 & 4 & 0 \end{bmatrix} \qquad \textbf{(1 Mark)}$$

The given system of equations is:

$8x + 4y + 2z = 19$

$2x + y + z = 5$

$x + 2y + 2z = 7$

It can be written as

$AX = B$

$\Rightarrow X = A^{-1} B$

$$\begin{bmatrix} x \\ y \\ z \end{bmatrix} = \begin{bmatrix} 0 & \dfrac{2}{3} & \dfrac{1}{3} \\ 1 & \dfrac{13}{3} & \dfrac{2}{3} \\ 1 & 4 & 0 \end{bmatrix} \begin{bmatrix} 19 \\ 5 \\ 7 \end{bmatrix}$$

$$\begin{bmatrix} x \\ y \\ z \end{bmatrix} = \begin{bmatrix} \dfrac{10}{3} - \dfrac{7}{3} \\ 19 - \dfrac{65}{3} + \dfrac{14}{3} \\ -19 + 20 \end{bmatrix}$$

$$\begin{bmatrix} x \\ y \\ z \end{bmatrix} = \begin{bmatrix} 1 \\ 2 \\ 1 \end{bmatrix}$$

$\therefore x = 1, y = 2, z = 1 \qquad \textbf{(2 Marks)}$

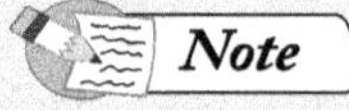

For elementary column transformation use property $A = AI$.

CBSE Board Solved Paper

Time Allowed : 3 Hours $\qquad$ *Maximum Marks : 100*

General Instructions:
(i)   **All** questions are compulsory.
(ii) Please check that this Question Paper contains **26** questions.
(iii) Marks for each question are indicated against it.
(iv) Question **1** to **6** in **Section-A** are Very Short Answer Type Questions carrying **one** mark each.
(v)   Question **7** to **19** in **Section-B** are Long Answer I Type Questions carrying **4** marks each.
(vi) Question **20** to **26** in **Section-C** are Long Answer II Type Questions carrying **6** marks each.
(vii) Please write down the serial number of the Question before attempting it.

SECTION - A

1. Write the value of $\vec{a} \cdot (\vec{b} \times \vec{a})$.

2. If $\vec{a} = \hat{i} + 2\hat{j} - \hat{k}, \vec{b} = 2\hat{i} + \hat{j} + \hat{k}$ and $\vec{c} = 5\hat{i} - 4\hat{j} + 3\hat{k}$, then find the value of $(\vec{a} + \vec{b}) \cdot \vec{c}$.

3. Write the direction ratios of the following line:
$$x = -3, \frac{y-4}{3} = \frac{2-z}{1}$$

4. If $A = \begin{bmatrix} 2 & 3 \\ 5 & -2 \end{bmatrix}$, then write A^{-1}.

5. Find the differential equation representing the curve $y = cx + c^2$.

6. Write the integrating factor of the following differential equation:
$$(1 + y^2)dx - (\tan^{-1} y - x)\, dy = 0$$

SECTION - B

7. Using the properties of determinants, prove the following:
$$\begin{vmatrix} 1 & x & x+1 \\ 2x & x(x-1) & x(x+1) \\ 3x(1-x) & x(x-1)(x-2) & x(x+1)(x-1) \end{vmatrix}$$
$$= 6x^2\left(1 - x^2\right)$$

8. If $x = \alpha \sin 2t\,(1 + \cot 2t)$ and $y = \beta \cos 2t\,(1 - \cos 2t)$. show that $\dfrac{dy}{dx} = \dfrac{\beta}{\alpha}\tan t$.

9. Find: $\dfrac{d}{dz} \cos^{-1}\left(\dfrac{z - z^{-1}}{z + z^{-1}}\right)$

10. Find the derivative of the following function
$$f(x) = \cos^{-1}\left[\sin\sqrt{\frac{1+z}{2}}\right] + x^x \quad \text{w.r.t. } x, \text{ at } x = 1$$

11. Evaluate:
$$\int_0^{\frac{\pi}{2}} \frac{2^{\sin x}}{2^{\sin x} + 2^{\cos x}}dx$$

OR

Evaluate : $\displaystyle\int_0^{\frac{3}{2}} |x \cdot \cos(\pi x)|\, dx$

12. To raise money for an orphanage, students of three schools A, B and C organised an exhibition in their locality, where they sold paper bags, scrap-books and pastel sheets made by them using recycled paper, at the rate of ₹ 20, ₹ 15 and ₹ 5 per unit respectively. School A sold 25 paper bags, 12 scrap-books and 34 pastel sheets. School B sold 22 paper bags, 15 scrap-books and 28 pastel sheets while school C sold 26 paper bags, 18 scrap-books and 36 pastel sheets. Using matrix, find the total amount raised by each school.
By such exhibition, which values are generated in the students?

13. Prove that:

$$2\tan^{-1}\left(\sqrt{\frac{a-b}{a+b}}\,\tan\frac{x}{2}\right) = \cos^{-1}\left(\frac{a\cos x+b}{a+b\cos x}\right)$$

OR

Solve the following for x :

$$\tan^{-1}\left(\frac{x-2}{x-3}\right) + \tan^{-1}\left(\frac{x+2}{x+3}\right) = \frac{\pi}{4}, |\,x\,|<1.$$

14. If $A = \begin{pmatrix} 2 & 0 & 1 \\ 2 & 1 & 3 \\ 1 & -1 & 0 \end{pmatrix}$, find $A^2 - 5A + 16I$.

15. Show that four points A, B, C and D whose position vectors are $4\hat{i}+5\hat{j}+\hat{k}, -\hat{j}-\hat{k}, 3\hat{i}+9\hat{j}+4\hat{k}$ and $4\left(-\hat{i}+\hat{j}+\hat{k}\right)$ respectively are coplanar.

16. Show that the following two lines are coplanar:

$$\frac{x-a+d}{a-d} = \frac{y-a}{a} = \frac{z-a-d}{a+d} \text{ and}$$

$$\frac{x-b+c}{\beta-\tau} = \frac{y-b}{\beta} = \frac{z-b-c}{\beta+\tau}$$

OR

Find the acute angle between the plane $5x - 4y + 7z - 13 = 0$ and the y-axis.

17. A and B throw a die alternatively till one of them gets a number greater than four and wins the game. If A starts the game, what is the probability of B winning?

OR

A die is thrown three times. Events A and B are defined as below:

A: 5 on the first and 6 on the second throw.

B: 3 or 4 on the third throw.

Find the probability of B, given that A has already occurred.

18. Evaluate: $\int\left(\sqrt{\cot x}+\sqrt{\tan x}\right) dx$

19. Find: $\int\dfrac{x^3-1}{x^3+x}dx$

SECTION - C

20. Using integration, find the area of the region bounded by the lines $y = 2 + x$, $y = 2 - x$, $x = 2$.

21. Find the differential equation for all the straight lines, which are at a unit distance from the origin.

OR

Show that the differential equation : $2xy\dfrac{dy}{dx} = x^2 + 3y^2$

is homogeneous and solve it.

22. Find the direction ratios of the normal to the plane, which passes through the points $(1,0,0)$ and $(0,1,0)$ and makes angle $\dfrac{\pi}{4}$ with the plane x + y = 3. Also find the equation of the plane.

23. If the function $f : R \to R$ be defined by $f(x) = 2x - 3$ and $g : R \to R$ by $g(x) = x^3 + 5$, then find the value of $(\text{fog})^{-1}(x)$.

OR

Let A = Q × Q, where Q is the set of all rational numbers, and x be a binary opertation defined on A by $(a, b)* (c,d) = (ac, b + ad)$, for all (a, b) $(c,d) \in$ A.
Find
(i)   the identity element in A
(ii)   the invertible element of A.

24. If the function $f(x) = 2x^3 - 9mx^2 + 12m^2x+ 1.$ where $m > 0$ attains its maximum and minimum at p and q respectively such that $p^2 = q$, then find the value of m.

25. The postmaster of a local post office wishes to hire extra helpers during the Deepawali season because of large increase in the volume of mail handling and delivery. Because of the limited office space and the budgetary conditions, the number of temporary helpers must not exceed 10. According to past experience, a man can handle 300 letters and 80 packages per day, on the average, and a woman can handle 400 letters and 50 packets per day. The postmaster believes that the daily volume of extra mail and packages will be no less than 3400 and 680 respectively. A man receives ₹ 225 a day and a woman receives ₹ 200 a day. How many men and women helpers should be hired to keep the pay-roll at a minimum? Formulate an LPP and solve it graphically.

26. 40% students of a college reside in hostel and the remaining reside outside. At the end of the year, 50% of the hostelers got A grade while from outside students, only 30% got A grade in the examination. At the end of the year, a student of the college was chosen at random and was found to have gotten A grade. What is the probability that the selected student was a hosteler?

Solutions

SECTION - A

1. Let: $\vec{a} = a_1\hat{i} + a_2\hat{j} + a_3\hat{k}$

$\vec{b} = b_1\hat{i} + b_2\hat{j} + b_3\hat{k}$

$\therefore \ \vec{a} \cdot (\vec{b} \times \vec{a})$

$= \left(a_1\hat{i} + a_2\hat{j} + a_3\hat{k}\right) \cdot \left[\left(b_1\hat{i} + b_2\hat{j} + b_3\hat{k}\right) \times \left(a_1\hat{i} + a_2\hat{j} + a_3\hat{k}\right)\right]$

(½ Mark)

$= \begin{vmatrix} a_1 & a_2 & a_3 \\ b_1 & b_2 & b_3 \\ a_1 & a_2 & a_3 \end{vmatrix}$

$= (b_2 a_3 - b_3 a_2)a_1 - (b_1 a_3 - b_3 a_1)a_2 + (b_1 a_2 - b_2 a_1)a_3$
$= a_1 a_3 b_2 - a_1 a_2 b_3 - a_2 a_3 b_1 + a_1 a_2 b_3 + a_2 a_3 b_1 - a_1 a_3 b_2$
$= 0$ (½ Mark)

Alternate Method:

$\vec{b} \times \vec{a}$ is a vector perpendicular to both $\vec{a}$ and $\vec{b}$.

$\therefore \ \vec{b} \times \vec{a} \perp \vec{a}$ and $\vec{b} \times \vec{a} \perp \vec{b}$

$\Rightarrow \vec{a} \cdot (\vec{b} \times \vec{a}) |\vec{a}| |\vec{b} \times \vec{a}| \cos 90° = 0$ (1 Mark)

2. $(\vec{a} + \vec{b}) \cdot \vec{c}$

$= \left(\hat{i} + 2\hat{j} - \hat{k} + 2\hat{i} + \hat{j} + \hat{k}\right) \cdot \left(5\hat{i} - 4\hat{j} + 3\hat{k}\right)$

$= \left(3\hat{i} + 3\hat{j}\right) \cdot \left(5\hat{i} - 4\hat{j} + 3\hat{k}\right)$

$= (3 \times 5) + (3 \times (-4)) + (0 \times 3)$
$= 15 - 12 = 3$ (1 Mark)

3. The equation of the given line can be rewritten as:

$\dfrac{x+3}{0} = \dfrac{y-4}{3} = \dfrac{z-2}{-1}$

Thus, the given line has direction ratios proportional to $0, 3, -1$.   (1 Mark)

4. $A = \begin{bmatrix} 2 & 3 \\ 5 & -2 \end{bmatrix}$

$\therefore |A| = \begin{vmatrix} 2 & 3 \\ 5 & -2 \end{vmatrix} = -4 - 15 = -19 \neq 0$

So, A is a non-singular matrix. Therefore, it is invertible. Now,

$\therefore \operatorname{adj} A = \begin{bmatrix} -2 & -5 \\ -3 & 2 \end{bmatrix}^T = \begin{bmatrix} -2 & -3 \\ -5 & 2 \end{bmatrix}$ (½ Mark)

We know

$A^{-1} = \dfrac{1}{|A|} \operatorname{adj} A$

$\therefore A^{-1} = \dfrac{1}{(-19)} \begin{bmatrix} -2 & -3 \\ -5 & 2 \end{bmatrix} = \begin{bmatrix} \dfrac{2}{19} & \dfrac{3}{19} \\ \dfrac{5}{19} & \dfrac{-2}{19} \end{bmatrix}$ (½ Mark)

> **Note**
>
> A^{-1} exist only when $|A| \neq 0$

5. We have
$y = cx + c^2$ ...(i)
Differentiating both side of equation (i) with respect to x, we get

$\dfrac{dy}{dx} = c$ (½ Mark)

Substituting $c = \dfrac{dy}{dx}$ in eqn. (i), we get

$y = x\dfrac{dy}{dx} + \left(\dfrac{dy}{dx}\right)^2$

$\Rightarrow \left(\dfrac{dy}{dx}\right)^2 + x\dfrac{dy}{dx} - y = 0$ (½ Mark)

This is the differential equation, which is representing the given curve.

> **Note**
>
> *To form the differential equation, elliminate the arbitrary constants from the given curve.*

6. $(1 + y^2)dx - (\tan^{-1} y - x)\,dy = 0$

$\Rightarrow \left(1 + y^2\right)\dfrac{dx}{dy} = \tan^{-1} y - x$

$\Rightarrow \left(1 + y^2\right)\dfrac{dx}{dy} + x = \tan^{-1} y$

$\Rightarrow \dfrac{dx}{dy} + \dfrac{1}{\left(1 + y^2\right)}x = \dfrac{\tan^{-1} y}{\left(1 + y^2\right)}$ (½ Mark)

$\therefore$ Integrating factor (IF) $= e^{\int \frac{1}{1+y^2}dy}$

$= e^{\tan^{-1} y}$ (½ Mark)

SECTION - B

7. $\begin{vmatrix} 1 & x & x+1 \\ 2x & x(x-1) & x(x+1) \\ 3x(1-x) & x(x-1)(x-2) & x(x+1)(x-1) \end{vmatrix}$

[Taking out common x from C_2 and $(x + 1)$ from C_3]

$$= x(1+x)\begin{vmatrix} 1 & 1 & 1 \\ 2x & (x-1) & x \\ 3x(1-x) & (x-1)(x-2) & x(x-1) \end{vmatrix}$$ **(1 Mark)**

[Taking out $(1 - x)$ common from R_3]

$$= x(1-x)(1+x)\begin{vmatrix} 1 & 1 & 1 \\ 2x & (x-1) & x \\ 3x & -(x-2) & -x \end{vmatrix}$$ **(1 Mark)**

[Applying $C_1 \to C_1 - C_2$ and $C_2 \to C_2 - C_3$]

$$= x(1-x^2)\begin{vmatrix} 0 & 0 & 1 \\ x+1 & -1 & x \\ 4x-2 & 2 & -x \end{vmatrix}$$ **(1 Mark)**

$$= x(1-x^2)[2(x+1)+4x-2] \text{ [Expanding along } R_1]$$

$$= 6x^2(1-x^2)$$ **(1 Mark)**

Hence, proved.

8. $x = \alpha \sin 2t (1 + \cos 2t)$

$$\Rightarrow x = \alpha \sin 2t + \frac{\alpha}{2} \times 2 \sin 2t \cos 2t$$

$$\Rightarrow x = \alpha \sin 2t + \frac{\alpha}{2} \sin 4t$$ **(1 Mark)**

Differentiating both sides w.r.t. t.we get,

$$\frac{dx}{dt} = \alpha \cos 2t \times 2 + \frac{\alpha}{2} \cos 4t \times 4$$

$$\Rightarrow \frac{dx}{dt} = 2\alpha(\cos 2t + \cos 4t)$$

$$\Rightarrow \frac{dx}{dt} = 2\alpha(\cos 2t + 2\cos^2 2t - 1)$$

$$\frac{dx}{dt} = 2\alpha(2\cos^2 2t + \cos 2t - 1)$$

$$= 2\alpha(2\cos^2 2t + 2\cos 2t - \cos 2t - 1)$$

$$\Rightarrow \frac{dx}{dt} = 2\alpha(\cos 2t + 1)(2\cos 2t - 1)$$ **(1 Mark)**

Now,

$$y = \beta \cos 2t (1 - \cos 2t)$$

$$\Rightarrow y = \beta \cos 2t - \beta \cos^2 2t$$

Differentiating both sides w.r.t. t, we get

$$\frac{dy}{dt} = -\beta \sin 2t \times 2 + \beta \times 2 \cos 2t \times \sin 2t \times 2$$

$$\Rightarrow \frac{dy}{dt} = -2\beta \sin 2t + 4\beta \cos 2t . \sin 2t$$

$$\Rightarrow \frac{dy}{dt} = 2\beta \sin 2t (2 \cos 2t - 1)$$ **(1 Mark)**

We know

$$\frac{dy}{dx} = \frac{\dfrac{dy}{dt}}{\dfrac{dx}{dt}} = \frac{2\beta \sin 2t (2\cos 2t - 1)}{2\alpha(\cos 2t + 1)(2\cos 2t - 1)}$$

$$= \frac{\beta \sin 2t}{\alpha(\cos 2t + 1)} = \frac{\beta \times 2 \sin t \cos t}{\alpha \times 2 \cos^2 t} = \frac{\beta}{\alpha} \tan t$$ **(1 Mark)**

> **Note**
>
> In case of to find $\dfrac{d^2 y}{dx^2}$ when $\dfrac{dy}{dx} = f(t)$,
>
> use $\dfrac{d^2 y}{dx^2} = f'(t) \cdot \dfrac{dt}{dx}$.

9. $y = \cos^{-1}\left(\dfrac{z - z^{-1}}{z + z^{-1}}\right) = \cos^{-1}\left(\dfrac{z^2 - 1}{z^2 + 1}\right)$

Let $z = \tan \theta$

$$\therefore y = \cos^{-1}\left(\frac{\tan^2 \theta - 1}{\tan^2 \theta + 1}\right) = \cos^{-1}\left(-\frac{1 - \tan^2 \theta}{1 + \tan^2 \theta}\right)$$

$$= \pi - \cos^{-1}(\cos 2\theta) \quad [\because \cos^{-1}(-x) = \pi - \cos^{-1} x]$$

$$= \pi - 2\theta = \pi - 2\tan^{-1} Z$$ **(2 Marks)**

Differentiating both sides w.r.t. z, we have

$$\frac{dy}{dz} = 0 - 2 \times \frac{1}{1 + z^2}$$

$$\therefore \frac{d}{dz} \cos^{-1}\left(\frac{z - z^{-1}}{z + z^{-1}}\right) = \frac{-2}{1 + z^2}$$ **(2 Marks)**

10. $f(x) = \cos^{-1}\left[\sin\sqrt{\dfrac{1+x}{2}}\right] + x^x$

Let $f_1(x) = \cos^{-1}\left[\sin\sqrt{\dfrac{1+x}{2}}\right]$ and $f_2(x) = x^x$

Now,

$$f_1(x) = \cos^{-1}\left[\sin\sqrt{\frac{1+x}{2}}\right]$$

$$= \cos^{-1}\left[\cos\left(\frac{\pi}{2} - \sqrt{\frac{1+x}{2}}\right)\right] \quad \left[\because \cos\left(\frac{\pi}{2} - x\right) = \sin x\right]$$ **(1 Mark)**

$$= \frac{\pi}{2} - \sqrt{\frac{1+x}{2}}$$

$$\Rightarrow f_1'(x) = -\frac{1}{2}\sqrt{\frac{2}{1+x}} = -\sqrt{\frac{1}{2(1+x)}}$$ **(1 Mark)**

and $f_2(x) = x^x$

Taking log on both sides, we get

$\log f_2(x) = x \log x$

$$\Rightarrow \frac{1}{f_2(x)} f_2'(x) = \log x + x \cdot \frac{1}{x}$$

$$\Rightarrow \frac{1}{f_2(x)} f_2'(x) = \log x + 1$$

$$\Rightarrow f_2'(x) = f_2(x)(\log x + 1)$$

$$\Rightarrow f_2' = x^x(\log x + 1)$$ **(1 Mark)**

$$\because f(x) = f_1(x) + f_2(x)$$

$$\therefore f'(x) = f_1'(x) + f_2'(x)$$

$$= -\sqrt{\frac{1}{2(1+x)}} + x^x(\log x + 1)$$

At $x = 1$

$$f'(1) = -\sqrt{\frac{1}{2(1+1)}} + 1^1(\log 1 + 1)$$

$$= -\frac{1}{2} + 1 = \frac{1}{2}$$ **(1 Mark)**

11. Let $I = \displaystyle\int_0^{\frac{\pi}{2}} \frac{2^{\sin x}}{2^{\sin x} + 2^{\cos x}} dx$ ....(1)

Then,

$$I = \int_0^{\frac{\pi}{2}} \frac{2^{\sin\left(\frac{\pi}{2}-x\right)}}{2^{\sin\left(\frac{\pi}{2}-x\right)} + 2^{\cos\left(\frac{\pi}{2}-x\right)}} dx \left[\because \int_0^a f(x)dx = \int_0^a f(a-x)dx\right]$$

   (1 Mark)

$$I = \int_0^{\frac{\pi}{2}} \frac{2^{\cos x}}{2^{\cos x} + 2^{\sin x}} dx \quad ...(2)$$ **(1 Mark)**

Adding equations (1) and (2), we get

$$2I = \int_0^{\frac{\pi}{2}} \frac{2^{\sin x}}{2^{\sin x} + 2^{\cos x}} dx + \int_0^{\frac{\pi}{2}} \frac{2^{\cos x}}{2^{\cos x} + 2^{\sin x}} dx$$ **(1 Mark)**

$$2I = \int_0^{\frac{\pi}{2}} dx$$

$$2I = [x]_0^{\frac{\pi}{2}}$$

$$2I = \frac{\pi}{2}$$

$$I = \frac{\pi}{4}$$

$$\therefore \int_0^{\frac{\pi}{2}} \frac{2^{\sin x}}{2^{\sin x} + 2^{\cos x}} dx = \frac{\pi}{4}$$ **(1 Mark)**

OR

$$f(x) = |x \cdot \cos(\pi x)| = \begin{cases} x \cdot \cos(\pi x), & \text{for} \quad 0 < x \le \frac{1}{2} \\ -x \cdot \cos(\pi x), & \text{for} \quad \frac{1}{2} < x \le \frac{3}{2} \end{cases}$$

$$\therefore \int_0^{\frac{3}{2}} |x \cdot \cos(\pi x)| \, dx = \int_0^{\frac{1}{2}} x \cdot \cos(\pi x) \, dx + \int_{\frac{1}{2}}^{\frac{3}{2}} -x \cdot \cos(\pi x) \, dx$$

   (2 Marks)

Integrating both integrals on right hand side, we get

$$\int_0^{\frac{3}{2}} |x \cdot \cos(\pi x)| \, dx$$

$$= \left[x\frac{\sin \pi x}{\pi} + \frac{\cos \pi x}{\pi^2}\right]_0^{\frac{1}{2}} - \left[x\frac{\sin \pi x}{\pi} + \frac{\cos x}{\pi^2}\right]_{\frac{1}{2}}^{\frac{3}{2}}$$ **(1 Mark)**

$$= \left[\left(\frac{\frac{1}{2}\times 1}{\pi} + 0\right) - \left(0 + \frac{1}{\pi^2}\right)\right] - \left[\left(\frac{\frac{3}{2}\times(-1)}{\pi} + 0\right) - \left(\frac{\frac{1}{2}\times 1}{\pi} + 0\right)\right]$$

$$= \frac{1}{2\pi} - \frac{1}{\pi^2} + \frac{3}{2\pi} + \frac{1}{2\pi}$$

$$= \frac{5}{2\pi} - \frac{1}{\pi^2}$$ **(1 Mark)**

Note

To evaluate the integral of the form $\displaystyle\int_\alpha^\beta |f(x)| dx$, *first find the intervals in which integrand is negative and positive and then use*

$$\int_\alpha^\phi -f(x)dx + \int_\phi^\beta f(x)dx, \; \alpha < \phi < \beta$$

12. School

Article	A	B	C
Paper Bags	25	22	26
Scrapbooks	12	15	18
Pastel Sheets	34	28	36

The number of articles sold by each school can be written in the matrix form as follows:

$$X = \begin{bmatrix} 25 & 22 & 26 \\ 12 & 15 & 18 \\ 34 & 28 & 36 \end{bmatrix}$$ **(1 Mark)**

The rate of each article can be written in the matrix form as follows:

$$Y = \begin{bmatrix} 20 & 15 & 5 \end{bmatrix}$$

The amount collected by each school is given by

$$YX = \begin{bmatrix} 20 & 15 & 5 \end{bmatrix} \begin{bmatrix} 25 & 22 & 26 \\ 12 & 15 & 18 \\ 34 & 28 & 36 \end{bmatrix}$$

$$YX = \begin{bmatrix} 850 & 805 & 970 \end{bmatrix}$$ **(2 Marks)**

Thus, the amount collected by schools A, B and C are
₹ 850, ₹ 805 and ₹ 970. respectively

$\therefore$ Total amount collected $= ₹ (850 + 805 + 970)$

$$= ₹\ 2{,}625$$ **(1 Mark)**

The situation highlights the helpful nature of the students.

13. $2\tan^{-1}\left(\sqrt{\dfrac{a-b}{a+b}}\ \tan\dfrac{x}{2}\right)$

$$= \cos^{-1}\left\{\frac{1-\left(\sqrt{\dfrac{a-b}{a+b}}\ \tan\dfrac{x}{2}\right)^2}{1+\left(\sqrt{\dfrac{a-b}{a+b}}\ \tan\dfrac{x}{2}\right)^2}\right\}$$

$$\left[\because 2\tan^{-1}(x) = \cos^{-1}\left(\frac{1-x^2}{1+x^2}\right)\right]$$ **(1 Mark)**

$$= \cos^{-1}\left\{\frac{1-\dfrac{a-b}{a+b}\tan^2\dfrac{x}{2}}{1+\dfrac{a-b}{a+b}\tan^2\dfrac{x}{2}}\right\}$$

$$= \cos^{-1}\left\{\frac{a+b-(a-b)\tan^2\dfrac{x}{2}}{a+b+(a-b)\tan^2\dfrac{x}{2}}\right\}$$

$$= \cos^{-1}\left\{\frac{a+b-a\tan^2\dfrac{x}{2}+b\tan^2\dfrac{x}{2}}{a+b+a\tan^2\dfrac{x}{2}-b\tan^2\dfrac{x}{2}}\right\}$$

$$= \cos^{-1}\left\{\frac{a\left(1-\tan^2\dfrac{x}{2}\right)+b\left(1+\tan^2\dfrac{x}{2}\right)}{a\left(1+\tan^2\dfrac{x}{2}\right)+b\left(1-\tan^2\dfrac{x}{2}\right)}\right\}$$ **(1 Mark)**

[Diving the numerator and the denominator by $1+\tan^2\dfrac{x}{2}$]

$$= \cos^{-1}\left\{\frac{a\left(\dfrac{1-\tan^2\dfrac{x}{2}}{1+\tan^2\dfrac{x}{2}}\right)+b\left(\dfrac{1+\tan^2\dfrac{x}{2}}{1+\tan^2\dfrac{x}{2}}\right)}{a\left(\dfrac{1+\tan^2\dfrac{x}{2}}{1+\tan^2\dfrac{x}{2}}\right)+b\left(\dfrac{1-\tan^2\dfrac{x}{2}}{1-\tan^2\dfrac{x}{2}}\right)}\right\}$$ **(1 Mark)**

$$= \cos^{-1}\left\{\frac{a\left(\dfrac{1-\tan^2\dfrac{x}{2}}{1+\tan^2\dfrac{x}{2}}\right)+b}{a+b\left(\dfrac{1-\tan^2\dfrac{x}{2}}{1+\tan^2\dfrac{x}{2}}\right)}\right\}$$

$$= \cos^{-1}\left\{\frac{a\cos x+b}{a+b\cos x}\right\}$$ **(1 Mark)**

OR

$$\tan^{-1}\frac{x-2}{x-3}+\tan^{-1}\frac{x+2}{x-3}=\frac{\pi}{4}$$

$$\Rightarrow \tan^{-1}\frac{x-2}{x-3}+\tan^{-1}\frac{x+2}{x+3}=\tan^{-1}1$$ **(1 Mark)**

$$\Rightarrow \tan^{-1}\left\{\frac{\dfrac{x-2}{x-3}+\dfrac{x+2}{x+3}}{1-\left(\dfrac{x-2}{x-3}\right)\left(\dfrac{x+2}{x+3}\right)}\right\}=\tan^{-1}1$$

$$\Rightarrow \tan^{-1}\left(\frac{x^2+x-6+x^2-x-6}{x^2-9-x^2+4}\right)=\tan^{-1}1$$ **(1 Mark)**

$$\Rightarrow \tan^{-1}\left(\frac{2x^2-12}{-5}\right)=\tan^{-1}1$$

$$\Rightarrow 2x^2-12=-5$$ **(1 Mark)**

$$\Rightarrow 2x^2=7$$

$$\Rightarrow x=\pm\sqrt{\frac{7}{2}}$$ **(1 Mark)**

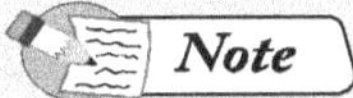

Use $\tan^{-1}\alpha \pm \tan^{-1}\beta = \tan^{-1}\left(\dfrac{\alpha \pm \beta}{1 \pm \alpha\beta}\right)$ to solve the

equation of the form $\tan^{-1}\alpha \pm \tan^{-1}\beta = k$ and then take tan on both sides of the equation.

14. $A = \begin{bmatrix} 2 & 0 & 1 \\ 2 & 1 & 3 \\ 1 & -1 & 0 \end{bmatrix}$

$$\therefore A^2 = A \cdot A = \begin{bmatrix} 2 & 0 & 1 \\ 2 & 1 & 3 \\ 1 & -1 & 0 \end{bmatrix}\begin{bmatrix} 2 & 0 & 1 \\ 2 & 1 & 3 \\ 1 & -1 & 0 \end{bmatrix}$$

$$\Rightarrow A^2 = \begin{bmatrix} 4+0+1 & 0+0-1 & 2+0+0 \\ 4+2+3 & 0+1-3 & 2+3+0 \\ 2-2+0 & 0-1+0 & 1-3+0 \end{bmatrix} = \begin{bmatrix} 5 & -1 & 2 \\ 9 & -2 & 5 \\ 0 & -1 & -2 \end{bmatrix}$$

(2 Marks)

Thus,

$$A^2 - 5A + 16I = \begin{bmatrix} 5 & -1 & 2 \\ 9 & -2 & 5 \\ 0 & -1 & -2 \end{bmatrix} - 5\begin{bmatrix} 2 & 0 & 1 \\ 2 & 1 & 3 \\ 1 & -1 & 0 \end{bmatrix} + 16\begin{bmatrix} 1 & 0 & 0 \\ 0 & 1 & 0 \\ 0 & 0 & 1 \end{bmatrix}$$

$$= \begin{bmatrix} 5 & -1 & 2 \\ 9 & -2 & 5 \\ 0 & -1 & -2 \end{bmatrix} - \begin{bmatrix} 10 & 0 & 5 \\ 10 & 5 & 15 \\ 5 & -5 & 0 \end{bmatrix} + \begin{bmatrix} 16 & 0 & 0 \\ 0 & 16 & 0 \\ 0 & 0 & 16 \end{bmatrix}$$

$$= \begin{bmatrix} 5-10+16 & -1-0+0 & 2-5+0 \\ 9-10+0 & -2-5+16 & 5-15+0 \\ 0-5+0 & -1+5+0 & -2-0+16 \end{bmatrix}$$

$$= \begin{bmatrix} 11 & -1 & -3 \\ -1 & 9 & -10 \\ -5 & 4 & 14 \end{bmatrix}$$

(2 Marks)

15. The position vectors of the points A, B, C and D are

$4\hat{i} + 5\hat{j} + \hat{k}, -\hat{j} - \hat{k}, 3\hat{i} + 9\hat{j} + 4\hat{k}$ and $4\left(-\hat{i} + \hat{j} + \hat{k}\right)$,

respectively, then

$$\overrightarrow{BA} = \left(4\hat{i} + 5\hat{j} + \hat{k}\right) - \left(0\hat{i} - \hat{j} - \hat{k}\right) = 4\hat{i} + 6\hat{j} + 2\hat{k}$$

$$\overrightarrow{BC} = \left(3\hat{i} + 9\hat{j} + 4\hat{k}\right) - \left(0\hat{i} - \hat{j} - \hat{k}\right) = 3\hat{i} + 10\hat{j} + 5\hat{k}$$

$$\overrightarrow{BD} = \left(-4\hat{i} + 4\hat{j} + 4\hat{k}\right) - \left(0\hat{i} - \hat{j} - \hat{k}\right) = -4\hat{i} + 5\hat{j} + 5\hat{k}$$

(2 Marks)

The given points are coplanar if vectors $\overrightarrow{BA}, \overrightarrow{BC}$ and $\overrightarrow{BD}$ are coplanar.

Now,

$$\overrightarrow{BA} \cdot \left(\overrightarrow{BC} \times \overrightarrow{BD}\right)$$

$$= \begin{vmatrix} 4 & 6 & 2 \\ 3 & 10 & 5 \\ -4 & 5 & 5 \end{vmatrix}$$

$$= 4(50 - 25) - 6(15 + 20) + 2(15 + 40)$$
$$= 100 - 210 + 110$$
$$= 0 \qquad\qquad \textbf{(2 Marks)}$$

Hence, the four points A, B, C and D are coplanar.

16. We know that the lines

$$\frac{x - x_1}{l_1} = \frac{y - y_1}{m_1} = \frac{z - z_1}{n_1} \text{ and } \frac{x - x_2}{l_2} = \frac{y - y_2}{m_2} = \frac{z - z_2}{n_2}$$

are coplanar, if $\begin{vmatrix} x_2 - x_1 & y_2 - y_1 & z_2 - z_1 \\ l_1 & m_1 & n_1 \\ l_2 & m_2 & n_2 \end{vmatrix} = 0$

(2 Marks)

Now, the equations of the given lines are

$$\frac{x - a + d}{a - d} = \frac{y - a}{a} = \frac{z - a - d}{a + d} \text{ and}$$

$$\frac{x - b + c}{\beta - \tau} = \frac{y - b}{\beta} = \frac{z - b - c}{\beta + \tau}$$

These can be rewritten as

$$\frac{x - (a - d)}{a - d} = \frac{y - a}{a} = \frac{z - (a + d)}{a + d} \text{ and}$$

$$\frac{x - (b - c)}{\beta - \tau} = \frac{y - b}{\beta} = \frac{z - (b + c)}{\beta + \tau}$$

$$\therefore \begin{vmatrix} (b - c) - (a - d) & b - a & (b + c) - (a + d) \\ a - d & a & a + d \\ \beta - \tau & \beta & \beta + \tau \end{vmatrix}$$

Applying $C_1 \to C_1 + C_3$

$$= \begin{vmatrix} 2(b - a) & b - a & (b + c) - (a + d) \\ 2a & a & a + d \\ 2\beta & \beta & \beta + \tau \end{vmatrix}$$

$$= 2\begin{vmatrix} (b - a) & b - a & (b + c) - (a + d) \\ a & a & a + d \\ \beta & \beta & \beta + \tau \end{vmatrix}$$

$$= 0 \quad [C_1 \text{ and } C_2 \text{ are identical}] \qquad \textbf{(2 Marks)}$$

Hence, the given lines are coplanar.

OR

The equation of the y-axis is

$$\frac{x - 0}{0} = \frac{y - 0}{1} = \frac{z - 0}{0}$$

The direction ratios of the y-axis are 0, 1, 0.

The equation of the given plane is $5x - 4y + 7z - 13 = 0$.

So, the direction ratios of the normal to the plane are $5, -4, 7$. **(1 Mark)**

Let θ be the acute angle between the given plane and the y-axis.

$$\therefore \sin\theta = \left| \frac{a_1 a_2 + b_1 b_2 + c_1 c_2}{\sqrt{a_1^2 + b_1^2 + c_1^2}\sqrt{a_2^2 + b_2^2 + c_2^2}} \right| \qquad \textbf{(1 Mark)}$$

$$\Rightarrow \sin\theta = \left| \frac{0\times 5 - 4\times 1 + 0\times 7}{\sqrt{0+1+0}\sqrt{25+16+49}} \right| = \left| \frac{-4}{3\sqrt{10}} \right|$$

$$\Rightarrow \theta = \sin^{-1}\left(\frac{4}{3\sqrt{10}} \right) = \sin^{-1}\left(\frac{2}{15}\sqrt{10} \right)$$

Hence, the acute angle between the given plane and the

y-axis is $\sin^{-1}\left(\frac{2}{15}\sqrt{10} \right)$ **(2 Marks)**

17. Let S denote the success, i.e. getting a number greater than four and F denote the failure.i.e. getting a number less than four.

$$\therefore P(S) = \frac{2}{6} = \frac{1}{3}, P(F) = 1 - \frac{1}{3} = \frac{2}{3} \qquad \textbf{(1 Mark)}$$

Now, B gets the second throw, if A fails in the first throw.

$\therefore$ P(B wins in the second throw) = P(FS) = P(F)P(S)

$$= \frac{2}{3} \times \frac{1}{3} \qquad \textbf{(1 Mark)}$$

Similarly, P(B wins in the fourth throw) = P(FFFS)

$$= P(F)P(F)P(F)P(S) = \left(\frac{2}{3}\right)^3 \times \frac{1}{3}$$

P(B wins in the sixth throw) = P(FFFFFS)

$$= P(F)P(F)P(F)P(F)P(F)P(S) = \left(\frac{2}{3}\right)^5 \times \frac{1}{3} \text{ and so on.}$$

(1 Mark)

Hence.

$$P(B \text{ wins}) = \frac{2}{3}\times\frac{1}{3} + \left(\frac{2}{3}\right)^3 \times\frac{1}{3} + \left(\frac{2}{3}\right)^5 \times\frac{1}{3} + ...$$

$$= \frac{2}{3}\times\frac{1}{3}\times\left[1 + \left(\frac{2}{3}\right)^2 + \left(\frac{2}{3}\right)^4 + ... \right]$$

$$= \frac{2}{3}\times\frac{1}{3}\times\left(\frac{1}{1-\frac{2}{3}} \right) = \frac{2}{3} \quad \left[\because a + ar + ar^2 + ... = \frac{a}{1-r} \right]$$

Thus, the probability that B wins is $\frac{2}{3}$. **(1 Mark)**

OR

A is an event getting 5 on the first throw and 6 on the second throw

Then

A = {(5,6,1) (5,6,2) (5,6,3) (5,6,4) (5,6,5), (5,6,6)} **(1 Mark)**

Also B is an event of getting 3 or 4 on the third throw.

$$\therefore A \cap B = \{(5,6,3),(5,6,4)\} \qquad \textbf{(1 Mark)}$$

Required probability, $P(B \mid A) = \dfrac{n(A\cap B)}{n(A)} = \dfrac{2}{6} = \dfrac{1}{3}$

Thus, the probability of B, given that A has already

occurred is $\dfrac{1}{3}$. **(2 Marks)**

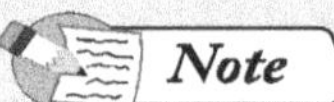 **Note**

Conditional probability P(B/A) applied when probability of occurence of event B is under the condition that A has already occured and $P(B) \neq 0$.

18. $I = \int\left(\sqrt{\cot x} + \sqrt{\tan x}\right)dx$

$$= \int\left[\sqrt{\tan x}\,(1 + \cot x) \right]dx \qquad \textbf{(1 Mark)}$$

Let $\tan x = t^2$

Differentiating both sides w.r.t x, we get

$\sec^2 x\, dx = 2t\,dt$

$(1 + \tan^2 x)\, dx = 2t\, dt$

$(1 + t^4)dx = 2t\, dt$

$$\Rightarrow dx = \frac{2t\,dt}{1+t^4} \qquad \textbf{(1 Mark)}$$

$$\therefore I = \int t\left(1 + \frac{1}{t^2}\right) \times \frac{2t}{1+t^4}\,dt$$

$$= 2\int\frac{t^2+1}{t^4+1}\,dt = 2\int\frac{1+\frac{1}{t^2}}{t^2+\frac{1}{t^2}}$$

$$= 2\int\frac{\left(1+\frac{1}{t^2}\right)dt}{\left(t-\frac{1}{t}\right)^2 + 2} \qquad \textbf{(1 Mark)}$$

Let $t - \dfrac{1}{t} = y$

$$\Rightarrow \left(1 + \frac{1}{t^2}\right)dt = dy$$

$$\therefore I = 2\int\frac{dy}{y^2 + \left(\sqrt{2}\right)^2}$$

$$= 2 \times \frac{1}{\sqrt{2}} \tan^{-1} \frac{y}{\sqrt{2}} + C \quad = \sqrt{2} \tan^{-1} \frac{\left(t - \frac{1}{t}\right)}{\sqrt{2}} + C$$

$$= \sqrt{2} \tan^{-1} \left(\frac{t^2 - 1}{\sqrt{2}\, t}\right) + C$$

$$= \sqrt{2} \tan^{-1} \left(\frac{\tan x - 1}{\sqrt{2 \tan x}}\right) + C \qquad \textbf{(1 Mark)}$$

19. Let

$$I = \int \frac{x^3 - 1}{x^3 + x}\,dx \;=\; \int \frac{x^3 + x - x - 1}{x^3 + x}\,dx$$

$$= \int \left[\frac{\left(x^3 + x\right)}{x^3 + x} - \frac{\left(x + 1\right)}{x^3 + x}\right] dx$$

$$= \int \left[1 - \frac{\left(x + 1\right)}{x^3 + x}\right] dx \qquad \textbf{(1 Mark)}$$

$$= \int 1\,dx - \int \frac{x + 1}{x^3 + x}\,dx$$

$$= x + C_1 - \int \frac{\left(x + 1\right)}{x^3 + x}\,dx$$

Let $I_1 = \int \frac{\left(x + 1\right)}{x^3 + x}\,dx$

Then
$$I = x + C_1 - I_1 \qquad ....(i)$$
Now,

$$I_1 = \int \frac{\left(x + 1\right)}{x^3 + x}\,dx$$

Let $\dfrac{\left(x + 1\right)}{x\left(x^2 + 1\right)} = \dfrac{A}{x} + \dfrac{Bx + C}{x^2 + 1}$

$$\Rightarrow \frac{\left(x + 1\right)}{x\left(x^2 + 1\right)} = \frac{\left(A + B\right)x^2 + Cx + A}{x\left(x^2 + 1\right)}$$

Comparing the coefficients of numerator, we get
A = 1, B = −1 and C = 1

So, $I_1 = \int \dfrac{\left(x + 1\right)}{x\left(x^2 + 1\right)}\,dx = \int \dfrac{1}{x}\,dx + \int \dfrac{-x + 1}{x^2 + 1}\,dx$ **(1 Mark)**

$$\Rightarrow I_1 = \log |x| + \int \frac{-x + 1}{x^2 + 1}\,dx$$

$$\Rightarrow I_1 = \log |x| - \frac{1}{2}\int \frac{2x}{x^2 + 1}\,dx + \int \frac{1}{x^2 + 1}\,dx$$

$$\Rightarrow I_1 = \log |x| - \frac{1}{2}\log |x^2 + 1| + \tan^{-1}\left(x^2 + 1\right) + C_2 \;...(ii)$$
(1 Mark)

From (i) and (ii), we get

$$I = x - \log|x| + \frac{1}{2}\log |x^2 + 1| - \tan^{-1}\left(x^2 + 1\right) + C \;\textbf{(1 Mark)}$$

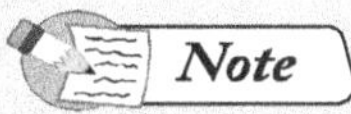

Note

In case of integral of rational polynomial $\dfrac{p(x)}{q(x)}$. If degree of $p(x) \geq$ degree of $q(x)$ then divide $p(x)$ by $q(x)$ and convert in the form of "Quotient $+ \dfrac{\text{Remainder}}{q(x)}$".

SECTION - C

20. The equations of the given lines are
$$y = 2 + x \qquad ... (1)$$
$$y = 2 - x \qquad ... (2)$$
$$x = 2 \qquad ... (3)$$
Solving (1), (2), and (3), we obtain the coordinates of the point of interesect A(0,2), B(2,4) and C(2,0). **(2 Marks)**
The graphs of these lines are drawn as shown in the figure below

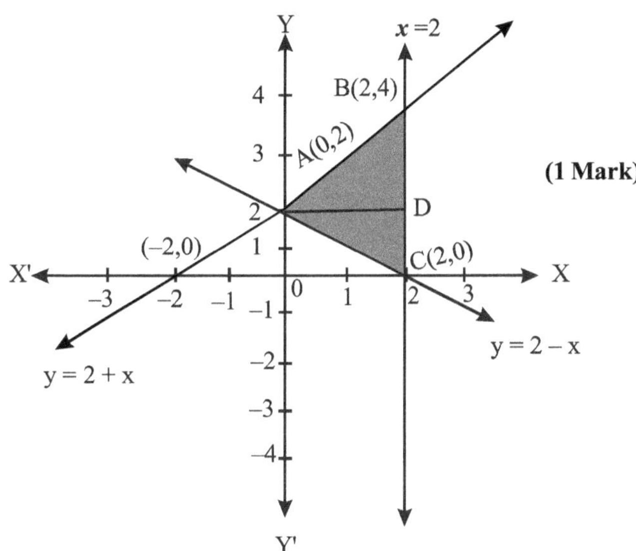

Here, the shaded region represents the area bounded by the given lines.
∴ Required area = Area of the region ABCA
= Area of region OABCO − Area of region OACO

$$\int_0^2 x_{AB}\,dx - \int_0^2 x_{AC}\,dx \qquad \textbf{(2 Marks)}$$

$$\int_0^2 (2 + x)\,dx - \int_0^2 (2 - x)\,dx$$

$$= \left(2x + \frac{x^2}{2}\right)\Bigg|_0^2 - \left(2x - \frac{x^2}{2}\right)\Bigg|_0^2$$

$$= [(4 + 2) - (0 - 0)] - (4 - 2)$$
$$= 6 - 2$$

= 4 square units

Thus, the area of the region bounded by the given lines is 4 square units. **(1 Mark)**

21. The general equation of a line that is at unit distance from the origin is given by

$$x \cos\alpha + y \sin\alpha = 1 \qquad \text{...(i)} \qquad \textbf{(1 Mark)}$$

Differentiating (i) w.r.t. x, we get

$$\cos\alpha + \frac{dy}{dx}\sin\alpha = 0$$

$$\Rightarrow \cot\alpha = -\frac{dy}{dx} \qquad \text{...(ii)} \qquad \textbf{(1 Mark)}$$

Dividing (i) by $\sin\alpha$, we get

$$x\frac{\cos\alpha}{\sin\alpha} + y\frac{\sin\alpha}{\sin\alpha} = \frac{1}{\sin\alpha}$$

$$\Rightarrow x\cot\alpha + y = \operatorname{cosec}\alpha$$

$$\Rightarrow x\cot\alpha + y = \sqrt{1+\cot^2\alpha} \qquad \text{... (iii)} \qquad \textbf{(1 Mark)}$$

Putting the value of (ii) in (iii), we get

$$x\left(-\frac{dy}{dx}\right) + y = \sqrt{1+\left(-\frac{dy}{dx}\right)^2} \qquad \text{...(iv)} \qquad \textbf{(1 Mark)}$$

Squaring (iv), we get

$$\left(-x\frac{dy}{dx}+y\right)^2 = \left(\sqrt{1+\left(\frac{dy}{dx}\right)^2}\right)^2$$

$$\Rightarrow \left(x^2-1\right)\left(\frac{dy}{dx}\right)^2 - 2xy\frac{dy}{dx} + y^2 - 1 = 0 \qquad \textbf{(2 Marks)}$$

OR

The given differential equation can be expressed as

$$\frac{dy}{dx} = \frac{x^2+3y^2}{2xy} \qquad \text{...(i)}$$

Let $F(x,y) = \dfrac{x^2+3y^2}{2xy}$

Now,

$$F(\lambda x, \lambda y) = \frac{(\lambda x)^2 + 3(\lambda y)^2}{2(\lambda x)(\lambda y)} = \frac{\lambda^2\left(x^2+3y^2\right)}{\lambda^2(2xy)}$$

$$= F(x,y) \qquad \textbf{(1 Mark)}$$

Therefore, $F(x, y)$ is a homogenous function of degree zero. So, the given differential equation is a homogenous differential equation.

Let $y = vx$ ...(ii)

Differentiating (ii) w.r.t. x, we get

$$\frac{dy}{dx} = v + x\frac{dv}{dx}$$

Substituting the value of y and $\dfrac{dy}{dx}$ in (i), we get

$$v + x\frac{dv}{dx} = \frac{1+3v^2}{2v} \qquad \textbf{(1 Mark)}$$

$$\Rightarrow x\frac{dv}{dx} = \frac{1+3v^2}{2v} - v \quad \Rightarrow x\frac{dv}{dx} = \frac{1+3v^2-2v^2}{2v}$$

$$\Rightarrow x\frac{dv}{dx} = \frac{1+v^2}{2v}$$

$$\Rightarrow \frac{2v}{1+v^2}dv = \frac{dx}{x} \qquad \text{... (iii)} \qquad \textbf{(1 Mark)}$$

Integrating both side of (iii), we get

$$\int\frac{2v}{1+v^2}\,dv = \int\frac{dx}{x}$$

$$\Rightarrow \log|1+v^2| = \log|x| + \log|C_1| \qquad \textbf{(1 Mark)}$$

$$\Rightarrow \log\left|\frac{1+v^2}{x}\right| = \log|C_1| \quad \Rightarrow \frac{1+v^2}{x} = \pm C_1$$

$$\Rightarrow \frac{1+\frac{y^2}{x^2}}{x} = \pm C_1 \quad \Rightarrow \frac{x^2+y^2}{x^3} = \pm C_1$$

or $x^2 + y^2 = Cx^3$ **(2 Marks)**

> **Note**
>
> *Differential equation in the form of* $\dfrac{dy}{dx} = \dfrac{f(x,y)}{g(x,y)}$. *If degree of each term of f(x, y) and g(x, y) will be same then it is called homogenous differential equation.*

22. Let the equation of the plane passing through (1,0,0) be

$a(x-1) + b(y-0) + c(z-0) = 0$ ...(1)

Here, a, b and c are the direction ratios of the normal to the plane.

If this plane passes through (0, 1, 0), then

$a(0-1) + b(1-0) + c(0-0) = 0$

$$\Rightarrow -a+b = 0$$

$$\Rightarrow a = b \quad \text{... (2)} \qquad \textbf{(1 Mark)}$$

It is given that plane (1) makes an angle of $\dfrac{\pi}{4}$ with the plane $x + y = 3$.

$$\therefore \cos\frac{\pi}{4} = \frac{(a\times1)+(b\times1)+(c\times0)}{\sqrt{a^2+b^2+c^2}\times\sqrt{1^2+1^2+0^2}} \qquad \textbf{(1 Mark)}$$

$$\Rightarrow \frac{1}{\sqrt{2}} = \frac{a+b}{\sqrt{a^2+b^2+c^2}\,\sqrt{2}}$$

$$\Rightarrow \sqrt{a^2+b^2+c^2} = a+b$$

Squaring on both sides, we get

$$a^2+b^2+c^2 = a^2+b^2+2ab$$

$$\Rightarrow c^2 = 2ab \qquad \text{...(3)}$$

From equations (2) and (3), we get

$c = \pm\sqrt{2}a$ **(1 Mark)**

So, the equation of the plane is

$a(x-1)+a(y-0)\pm\sqrt{2}a(z-0)=0$

$\Rightarrow x-1+y\pm\sqrt{2}z=0$

$\Rightarrow x+y\pm\sqrt{2}z=1$ **(2 Marks)**

Hence, the direction ratios of the normal to the plane

are proportional to $1, 1\pm\sqrt{2}$. **(1 Mark)**

 **Note**

Cartesian equation of a plane passing through (x, y, z) and having direction ratios proportional to a, b, c for its normal is $a(x - x_1) + b(y - y_1) + c(z - z_1) = 0$

23. Given:

$f(x) = 2x - 3$

$g(x) = x^3 + 5$

$(fog)(x) = f[g(x)] = f(x^3 + 5) = 2(x^3 + 5) - 3$

$= 2x^3 + 10 - 3 = 2x^3 + 7$ **(2 Marks)**

Let $(fog)(x) = y$

$\Rightarrow 2x^3 + 7 = y$

$\Rightarrow x = \left(\dfrac{y-7}{2}\right)^{\frac{1}{3}}$ **(1 Mark)**

$\Rightarrow (fog)^{-1}(y) = \left(\dfrac{y-7}{2}\right)^{\frac{1}{3}}$ **(1 Mark)**

Thus, $(fog)^{-1}(y)$: R $\to$ R be defined by

$(fog)^{-1}(x) = \left(\dfrac{x-7}{2}\right)^{\frac{1}{3}}$. **(2 Marks)**

OR

Then let $X = (a, b)$ and $Y = (c, d) \in A, \forall\, a, b, c$

and $d \in Q$ (i)

Let $E = (x, y)$ be the identity element in A with respect to *,

$\forall x, y \in Q$ such that

$X * E = X = E * X, \forall X \in A$

$\Rightarrow X * E = X$ and $E * X = X$

$\Rightarrow (ax, b + ay) = (a, b)$ and $(xa, y + xb) = (a, b)$

(1 Mark)

Considering $(ax, b + ay) = (a, b)$

$\Rightarrow ax = a$

$\Rightarrow x = 1$

and $b + ay = b$

$\Rightarrow y = 0$ $[\because x = 1]$

Also, considering $(xa, y + xb) = (a, b)$

$\Rightarrow xa = a$

$\Rightarrow x = 1$ **(1 Mark)**

and $y + xb = b$

$\Rightarrow y = 0$ $[\because x = 1]$ **(1 Mark)**

$\therefore (1, 0)$ is the identity element in A with respect to *.

(ii) Let $F = (m, n)$ be the inverse in $A, \forall m, n \in Q$

$X * F = E$ and $F * X = E$

$\Rightarrow (am, b + an) = (1, 0)$ and $(ma, n + mb) = (1, 0)$

Considering $(am, b + an) = (1, 0)$

$\Rightarrow am = 1$

$\Rightarrow m = \dfrac{1}{a}$ **(1 Mark)**

and $b + an = 0$

$\Rightarrow n = \dfrac{-b}{a}$

Also,

Considering $(ma, n + mb) = (1, 0)$

$\Rightarrow ma = 1$

$\Rightarrow m = \dfrac{1}{a}$

and $n + mb = 0 \Rightarrow n = \dfrac{-b}{a}$ $\left(\because m = \dfrac{1}{a}\right)$ **(1 Mark)**

$\therefore$ The inverse of $(a, b) \in A$ with respect to * is

$\left(\dfrac{1}{a}, \dfrac{-b}{a}\right) \in A^{-1}$. **(1 Mark)**

24. We have

$f(x) = 2x^3 - 9mx^2 + 12m^2x + 1$

$\Rightarrow f'(x) = 6x^2 - 18mx + 12m^2$

Also, $f''(x) = 12x - 18m$ **(1 Mark)**

Since, $f(x)$ attains its maximum and minimum values at $x = p$ and $x = q$, respectively, so $f'(p) = 0$ and $f'(q) = 0$

$f'(p) = 0$

$\Rightarrow 6p^2 - 18\,mp + 12m^2 = 0 \Rightarrow p^2 - 3mp + 2m^2 = 0$

$\Rightarrow (p - 2m)(p - m) = 0$

$\Rightarrow p - 2m = 0$ or $p - m = 0$

$\Rightarrow p = 2m$ or $p = m$ **(1 Mark)**

Similarly,

$f'(q) = 0$

$\Rightarrow q = 2m$ or $q = m$ **(1 Mark)**

Now, consider the following cases:

Case I:

If $p = 2m$ and $q = 2m$, then

$p^2 = q$

$\Rightarrow 4m^2 = 2m \Rightarrow 2m^2 - m = 0 \Rightarrow m(2m - 1) = 0$

$\therefore m = \dfrac{1}{2}$ $(\because\ m > 0)$

But, this gives $p = 1$ as the point of minima, which is not true. **(1 Mark)**

Case II:

If $p = 2\,m$ and $q = m$, then

$p^2 = q$

$\Rightarrow 4m^2 = m \Rightarrow 4m^2 - m = 0$

$\Rightarrow m(4m - 1) = 0$

$\therefore m = \dfrac{1}{4}$ $(\because\ m > 0)$

But, this gives $p = \dfrac{1}{2}$ as the point of minima, which is not true.

Case III:

If $p = m$ and $q = 2m$, then

$p^2 = q$

$\Rightarrow m^2 = 2m \Rightarrow m^2 - 2m = 0$

$\Rightarrow m(m - 2) = 0$

$\therefore m = 2 \quad (\because m > 0)$

For this case, $p = 2$ and $q = 4$ are the points of maxima and minima, respectively. **(1 Mark)**

Case IV:

If $p = m$ and $q = m$, then

$p^2 = q$

$\Rightarrow m^2 = m \Rightarrow m^2 - m = 0$

$\Rightarrow m(m - 1) = 0$

$\therefore m = 1 \,(\because m > 0)$

But, this gives $q = 1$ as the point of maxima, which is not true.

Hence, the value of m is 2. **(1 Mark)**

 **Note**

In order to find point of maxima and minima, put all values in equation seperately and then check for it.

25. Let the postmaster hire x men and y women.

Clearly, $x \geq 0, y \geq 0$

Also, it is given that the number of temporary helpers must not exceed 10.

$\therefore x + y \leq 10$

The given information can be represented in the tabular forms as

	Men (x)	Women (y)	Minimum Volume of Mails
Letters	300	400	3400
packages	80	50	680
Payroll (₹)	225	200	

Thus, the given LPP can be stated mathematically as follows:

Minimise $Z = 225x + 200y$

Subject to the constraints:

$x + y \leq 10 \qquad \dots (1)$

$300x + 400y \geq 3400$ (constraint on letters)

$\Rightarrow 3x + 4y \geq 34 \quad \dots (2)$

$80x + 50y \geq 680$ (constraint on packages)

$8x + 5y \geq 68 \qquad \dots (3)$

and $x, y \geq 0 \qquad \dots (4)$ **(2 Marks)**

Converting the inequations into equations, we obtain the lines $x + y = 10$, $3x + 4y = 34$, $8x + 5y = 68$, $x = 0$ and $y = 0$.

These lines are drawn and the feasible region of the LPP is shaded. It is observed that the feasible region is a point $(6, 4)$.

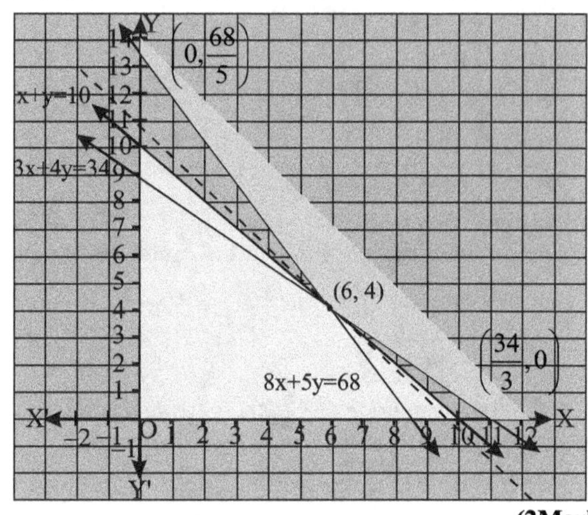

(2Marks)

The value of the objective function at this point is given as $Z = ₹\,2,150$.

But it is unbounded

$\therefore$ Let $225x + 200y < 2,150$

Draw this graph we observe

no any common point with feasible rigion.

So, the minimum value of Z is ₹ 2150 at the point $(6, 4)$.

Hence, the postmaster should hire 6 men and 4 women to keep pay-roll at a minimum of ₹ 2, 150. **(2 Marks)**

26. Let E_1 and E_2 be the events that the student is a hosteller and an outside student, respectively and A be the event that the chosen student gets A grade.

$\therefore P(E_1) = 40\% = 0.4$ **(1 Mark)**

$P(E_2) = (100 - 40)\% = 60\% = 0.6$ **(1 Mark)**

$P(A \mid E_1) = $ P (Student getting A grade is a hosteller)
$= 50\% = 0.5$ **(1 Mark)**

$P(A \mid E_2) = $ P (Student getting A grade is an outside student) $= 30\% = 0.3$ **(1 Mark)**

The probability that a randomly choosen student is a hosteller, given that he got A grade, is given by $P(E_1|A)$. Using Bayes' theorem, we get

$$P(E_1 / A) = \frac{P(E_1) \cdot P(A / E_1)}{P(E_1) \cdot P(A / E_1) + P(E_2) \cdot P(A / E_2)}$$

(1 Mark)

$$= \frac{0.4 \times 0.5}{0.4 \times 0.5 + 0.6 \times 0.3} = \frac{0.20}{0.35} = \frac{4}{7}$$ **(1 Mark)**

Delhi *2015*

CBSE Board Solved Paper

Time Allowed : 3 Hours   *Maximum Marks : 100*

General Instructions:

(i)   All questions are compulsory.

(ii)   Please check that this Question Paper contains **26** Questions.

(iii)   Marks for each question are indicated against it.

(iv)   Questions **1** to **6** in Section **A** are Very Short Answer Type Questions carrying **one** mark each.

(v)   Questions **7** to **19** in Section **B** are Long Answer I Type Questions carrying **4** marks each.

(vi)   Questions **20** to **26** in Section **C** are Long Answer II Type Questions carrying **6** marks each.

(vii)   Please write down the serial number of the Question before attempting it.

SECTION - A

Question numbers 1 to 6 carry 1 mark each.

1.   If $\vec{a} = 7\hat{i} + \hat{j} - 4\hat{k}$ and $\vec{b} = 2\hat{i} + 6\hat{j} + 3\hat{k}$, then find the projection of $\vec{a}$ on $\vec{b}$.

2.   Find λ, if the vector $\vec{a} = \hat{i} + 3\hat{j} + \hat{k}$, $\vec{b} = 2\hat{i} - \hat{j} - \hat{k}$ and $\vec{c} = \lambda\hat{j} + 3\hat{k}$ are coplanar.

3.   If a line makes angles 90°, 60° and θ with x, y and z-axis respectively, where θ is acute, then find θ.

4.   Write the element a_{23} of a 3×3 matrix A = (a_{ij}) whose elements a_{ij} are given by $a_{ij} = \dfrac{|i - j|}{2}$.

5.   Find the differential equation representing the family of curves $v = \dfrac{A}{r} + B$, where A and B are arbitrary constants.

6.   Find the integrating factor of the differential equation $\left(\dfrac{e^{-2\sqrt{x}}}{\sqrt{x}} - \dfrac{y}{\sqrt{x}} \right) \dfrac{dx}{dy} = 1$.

SECTION - B

Question numbers 7 to 19 carry 4 marks each.

7.   If A = $\begin{bmatrix} 2 & 0 & 1 \\ 2 & 1 & 3 \\ 1 & -1 & 0 \end{bmatrix}$ find $A^2 - 5A + 4I$ and hence find a matrix X such that $A^2 - 5A + 4I + X = O$

OR

If A = $\begin{bmatrix} 1 & -2 & 3 \\ 0 & -1 & 4 \\ -2 & 2 & 1 \end{bmatrix}$, find $(A')^{-1}$.

8.   If $f(x) = \begin{vmatrix} a & -1 & 0 \\ ax & a & -1 \\ ax^2 & ax & a \end{vmatrix}$, using properties of determinants find the value of $f(2x) - f(x)$.

9.   Find : $\displaystyle\int \dfrac{dx}{\sin x + \sin 2x}$

OR

Integrate the following w.r.t. x

$$\dfrac{x^2 - 3x + 1}{\sqrt{1 - x^2}}$$

10.   Evaluate : $\displaystyle\int_{-\pi}^{\pi} (\cos ax - \sin bx)^2 \, dx$

11.   A bag A contains 4 black and 6 red balls and bag B contains 7 black and 3 red balls. A die is thrown. If 1 or 2 appears on it, then bag A is chosen, otherwise bag B. If two balls are drawn at random (without replacement) from the selected bag, find the probability of one of them being red and another black.

OR

An unbiased coin is tossed 4 times. Find the mean and variance of the number of heads obtained.

12. If $\vec{r} = x\hat{i} + y\hat{j} + z\hat{k}$, find $(\vec{r} \times \hat{i}) \cdot (\vec{r} \times \hat{j}) + xy$

13. Find the distance between the point $(-1, -5, -10)$ and the point of intersection of the line

$$\frac{x-2}{3} = \frac{y+1}{4} = \frac{z-2}{12} \text{ and the plane } x - y + z = 5.$$

14. If $\sin[\cot^{-1}(x+1)] = \cos(\tan^{-1}x)$, then find x.

OR

If $(\tan^{-1}x)^2 + (\cot^{-1}x)^2 = \dfrac{5\pi^2}{8}$, then find x.

15. If $y = \tan^{-1}\left(\dfrac{\sqrt{1+x^2} + \sqrt{1-x^2}}{\sqrt{1+x^2} - \sqrt{1-x^2}}\right)$, $x^2 \le 1$, then find $\dfrac{dy}{dx}$.

16. If $x = a\cos\theta + b\sin\theta$, $y = a\sin\theta - b\cos\theta$, show that

$$\frac{d^2y}{dx^2} - x\frac{dy}{dx} + y = 0.$$

17. The side of an equilateral triangle is increasing at the rate of 2 cm/s. At what rate is its area increasing when the side of the triangle is 20 cm?

18. Find : $\int (x+3)\sqrt{3 - 4x - x^2}\, dx$.

19. Three schools A, B and C organized a mela for collecting funds for helping the rehabilitation of flood victims. They sold hand made fans, mats and plates from recycled material at a cost of ₹ 25, ₹ 100 and ₹ 50 each. The number of articles sold are given below:

Article/School	A	B	C
Hand-fans	40	25	35
Mats	50	40	50
Plates	20	30	40

Find the funds collected by each school separately by selling the above articles. Also find the total funds collected for the purpose.

Write one value generated by the above situation.

Question numbers 20 to 26 carry 6 marks each.

20. Let N denote the set of all natural numbers and R be the relation on N × N defined by (a, b) R (c, d) if $ad(b+c) = bc(a+d)$. Show that R is an equivalence relation.

21. Using integration find the area of the triangle formed by positive x-axis and tangent and normal to the circle $x^2 + y^2 = 4$ at $(1, \sqrt{3})$.

OR

Evaluate $\displaystyle\int_1^3 (e^{2-3x} + x^2 + 1)dx$ as a limit of a sum.

22. Solve the differential equation: $(\tan^{-1}y - x)dy = (1 + y^2)dx$.

OR

Find the particular solution of the differential equation

$$\frac{dy}{dx} = \frac{xy}{x^2 + y^2} \text{ given that } y = 1, \text{ when } x = 0.$$

23. If lines $\dfrac{x-1}{2} = \dfrac{y+1}{3} = \dfrac{z-1}{4}$ and $\dfrac{x-3}{1} = \dfrac{y-k}{2} = \dfrac{z}{1}$

intersect, then find the value of k and hence find the equation

of the plane containing these lines.

24. If A and B are two independent events such that $P(\overline{A} \cap B) = \dfrac{2}{15}$ and $P(A \cap \overline{B}) = \dfrac{1}{6}$, then find P(A) and P(B).

25. Find the local maxima and local minima, of the function $f(x) = \sin x - \cos x$, $0 < x < 2\pi$. Also find the local maximum and local minimum values.

26. Find graphically, the maximum value of $z = 2x + 5y$, subject to constraints given below:

$$2x + 4y \le 8;\ 3x + y \le 6;\ x + y \le 4;\ x \ge 0, y \ge 0$$

Solutions

SECTION - A

1. Given: $\vec{a} = 7\hat{i} + \hat{j} - 4\hat{k}$

$$\vec{b} = 2\hat{i} + b\hat{j} + 3\hat{k}$$

$\therefore$ Projection of $\vec{a}$ on $\vec{b} = \dfrac{\vec{a}.\vec{b}}{|\vec{b}|}$ (½ **Mark**)

$$= \frac{(7\hat{i} + \hat{j} - 4\hat{k}).(2\hat{i} + 6\hat{j} + 3\hat{k})}{\sqrt{(2)^2 + (6)^2 + (3)^2}} = \frac{(7 \times 2) + (1 \times 6) + (-4 \times 3)}{\sqrt{4 + 36 + 9}}$$

$$= \frac{8}{\sqrt{49}} = \frac{8}{7}$$ (½ **Mark**)

> **Note**
>
> *The vector projection of $\vec{a}$ on $\vec{b}$ means the resolved component of $\vec{a}$ in the direction of $\vec{b}$.*

2. Given: $\vec{a} = \hat{i} + 3\hat{j} + \hat{k}$

$$\vec{b} = 2\hat{i} - \hat{j} - \hat{k}$$

$$\vec{c} = \lambda\hat{j} + 3\hat{k}$$

Since given vectors are copalanar

$[\vec{a}\,\vec{b}\,\vec{c}] = 0$ (½ **Mark**)

$$[\vec{a}\,\vec{b}\,\vec{c}] = \begin{vmatrix} 1 & 3 & 1 \\ 2 & -1 & -1 \\ 0 & \lambda & 3 \end{vmatrix} = 0$$

$1(-3 + \lambda) - 3(6) + 1(2\lambda) = 0 \Rightarrow 3\lambda - 21 = 0$

$\Rightarrow \lambda = 7$ (½ **Mark**)

> **Note**
>
> *Three or more vectors are called coplanar if all vecters lies in one plane.*

3. Given angles are

$\alpha = 90°$

$\beta = 60°$

$\lambda = \theta$

Let l, m, n are direction cosines of the given line

$l = \cos\alpha$, $m = \cos\beta$, $n = \cos\lambda$

We know that

$l^2 + m^2 + n^2 = 1$ (½ **Mark**)

$\cos^2\alpha + \cos^2\beta + \cos^2\lambda = 1$

$\cos^2(90°) + \cos^2(60°) + \cos^2\theta = 1$

$$0 + \left(\frac{1}{2}\right)^2 + \cos^2\theta = 1$$

$$\cos\theta = \frac{\sqrt{3}}{2}$$

$\cos\theta = \cos(30°)$ ($\because \theta$ is acute)

$\theta = 30°$ (½ **Mark**)

4. $a_{ij} = \dfrac{|i - j|}{2}$

$a_{23} = \dfrac{|2 - 3|}{2}$ ($\because i = 2, j = 3$)   (½ **Mark**)

$a_{23} = \dfrac{|-1|}{2} = \dfrac{1}{2}$ (½ **Mark**)

5. $v = \dfrac{A}{r} + B$ ...(1)

Given equation has two arbitrary constants, so we will differentiate it two times.

Differentiating equation (1) w.r.t. r,

$$\frac{dv}{dr} = -\frac{A}{r^2}$$

$$r^2 \frac{dv}{dr} = -A \quad ...(2)$$ (½ **Mark**)

Again differentiating equation (2) w.r.t. r

$$r^2 \frac{d^2v}{dr^2} + 2r\frac{dv}{dr} = 0 \qquad \left[\because \frac{d}{dx}(uv) = u\frac{dv}{dx} + v\frac{du}{dx} \right]$$

$$r\frac{d^2v}{dr^2} + 2\frac{dv}{dr} = 0$$ (½ **Mark**)

> **Note**
>
> *To find the differential equation of any given family of curves, differentiate it as many numbers of times as the number of arbitrary constants presents in the equation of curve.*

6. $\left(\dfrac{e^{-2\sqrt{x}}}{\sqrt{x}} - \dfrac{y}{\sqrt{x}}\right)\dfrac{dx}{dy} = 1$

$$\frac{dy}{dx} = \frac{e^{-2\sqrt{x}}}{\sqrt{x}} - \frac{y}{\sqrt{x}}$$

$$\frac{dy}{dx} + \frac{y}{\sqrt{x}} = \frac{e^{-2\sqrt{x}}}{\sqrt{x}}$$ **(½ Mark)**

It is in the form of linear differential equation

$$\frac{dy}{dx} + py = Q$$

Where $P = \dfrac{1}{\sqrt{x}}$, $Q = \dfrac{e^{-2\sqrt{x}}}{\sqrt{x}}$

$\therefore$ I.F. $= e^{\int pdx}$

$$= e^{\int \frac{1}{\sqrt{x}}dx}$$

$$= e^{2\sqrt{x}} \qquad \left[\because \int x^n dx = x^{n+1}\right] \quad \textbf{(½ Mark)}$$

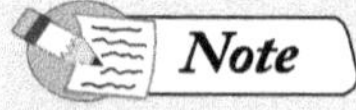

Note

Integrating factor is a function by which an ordinary differential equation can be multiplied to make the differential equation integrable.

SECTION - B

7. Given: $A = \begin{bmatrix} 2 & 0 & 1 \\ 2 & 1 & 3 \\ 1 & -1 & 0 \end{bmatrix}$

$$A^2 = A \cdot A = \begin{bmatrix} 2 & 0 & 1 \\ 2 & 1 & 3 \\ 1 & -1 & 0 \end{bmatrix}\begin{bmatrix} 2 & 0 & 1 \\ 2 & 1 & 3 \\ 1 & -1 & 0 \end{bmatrix}$$

$$= \begin{bmatrix} 4+1 & -1 & 2 \\ 4+2+3 & 1-3 & 2+3 \\ 2-2 & -1 & 1-3 \end{bmatrix} = \begin{bmatrix} 5 & -1 & 2 \\ 9 & -2 & 5 \\ 0 & -1 & -2 \end{bmatrix} \quad \textbf{(1 Mark)}$$

$$5A = 5\begin{bmatrix} 2 & 0 & 1 \\ 2 & 1 & 3 \\ 1 & -1 & 0 \end{bmatrix} = \begin{bmatrix} 10 & 0 & 5 \\ 10 & 5 & 15 \\ 5 & -5 & 0 \end{bmatrix} \quad \textbf{(½ Mark)}$$

$$4I_3 = 4\begin{bmatrix} 1 & 0 & 0 \\ 0 & 1 & 0 \\ 0 & 0 & 1 \end{bmatrix} \quad \textbf{(½ Mark)}$$

$$= \begin{bmatrix} 4 & 0 & 0 \\ 0 & 4 & 0 \\ 0 & 0 & 4 \end{bmatrix}$$

$$A^2 - 5A + 4I = \begin{bmatrix} 5 & -1 & 2 \\ 9 & -2 & 5 \\ 0 & -1 & -2 \end{bmatrix} - \begin{bmatrix} 10 & 0 & 5 \\ 10 & 5 & 15 \\ 5 & -5 & 0 \end{bmatrix} + \begin{bmatrix} 4 & 0 & 0 \\ 0 & 4 & 0 \\ 0 & 0 & 4 \end{bmatrix}$$

$$A^2 - 5A + 4I = \begin{bmatrix} 5-10+4 & -1-0+0 & 2-5+0 \\ 9-10+0 & -2-5+4 & 5-15+0 \\ 0-5+0 & -1+5+0 & -2-0+4 \end{bmatrix}$$

$$= \begin{bmatrix} -1 & -1 & -3 \\ -1 & -3 & -10 \\ -5 & 4 & 2 \end{bmatrix} \quad \textbf{(1 Mark)}$$

Now $A^2 - 5A + 4I + X = 0$

$X = -(A^2 - 5A + 4I)$

$$= (-1)\begin{bmatrix} -1 & -1 & -3 \\ -1 & -3 & -10 \\ -5 & 4 & 2 \end{bmatrix}$$

$$= \begin{bmatrix} 1 & 1 & 3 \\ 1 & 3 & 10 \\ 5 & -4 & -2 \end{bmatrix} \quad \textbf{(1 Mark)}$$

OR

$$A = \begin{bmatrix} 1 & -2 & 3 \\ 0 & -1 & 4 \\ -2 & 2 & 1 \end{bmatrix}$$

$$A' = \begin{bmatrix} 1 & 0 & -2 \\ -2 & -1 & 2 \\ 3 & 4 & 1 \end{bmatrix}$$

$|A'| = 1(-1-8) - 0(-2-6) - 2(-8+3)$ **(1 Mark)**

$= -9 + 10 = 1 \neq 0$

$\therefore |A'|^{-1}$ exists or A' is invertible

$A'_{11} = (-1)^{1+1}(-1-8) = -9$

$A'_{12} = (-1)^{1+2}(-2-6) = 8$

$A'_{13} = (-1)^{1+3}(-8+3) = -5$

$A'_{21} = (-1)^{2+1}(0+8) = -8$

$A'_{22} = (-1)^{2+2}(1+6) = 7$

$A'_{23} = (-1)^{2+3}(4-0) = -4$

$A'_{31} = (-1)^{3+1}(0-2) = -2$

$A'_{32} = (-1)^{3+2}(2-4) = 2$

$A'_{33} = (-1)^{3+3}(-1+0) = -1$ **(1 Mark)**

$$\text{Adj } A' = \begin{bmatrix} -9 & 8 & -5 \\ -8 & 7 & -4 \\ -2 & 2 & -1 \end{bmatrix}^T$$

$$= \begin{bmatrix} -9 & -8 & -2 \\ 8 & 7 & 2 \\ -5 & -4 & -1 \end{bmatrix} \quad \textbf{(1 Mark)}$$

$$(A')^{-1} = \frac{1}{|A'|} \text{ adj } A'$$

$$(A')^{-1} = \begin{bmatrix} -9 & -8 & -2 \\ 8 & 7 & 2 \\ -5 & -4 & -1 \end{bmatrix} \quad [\because |A'| = 1] \quad \textbf{(1 Mark)}$$

8. Given: $f(x) = \begin{vmatrix} a & -1 & 0 \\ ax & a & -1 \\ ax^2 & ax & a \end{vmatrix}$

Taking (a) common from C_1

$f(x) = a \begin{vmatrix} 1 & -1 & 0 \\ x & a & -1 \\ x^2 & ax & a \end{vmatrix}$

Applying $C_2 \to C_2 + C_1$

$f(x) = a \begin{vmatrix} 1 & 0 & 0 \\ x & a+x & -1 \\ x^2 & ax+x^2 & a \end{vmatrix}$ **(1 Mark)**

$f(x) = a(a(a + x) + (ax + x^2))$

$f(x) = a(a^2 + ax + ax + x^2)$

$f(x) = a(a^2 + 2ax + x^2)$ ...(1)

To find $f(2x)$

$f(2x) = \begin{vmatrix} a & -1 & 0 \\ a(2x) & a & -1 \\ a(2x)^2 & a(2x) & a \end{vmatrix}$

$= \begin{vmatrix} a & -1 & 0 \\ 2ax & a & -1 \\ 4ax^2 & 2ax & a \end{vmatrix}$ **(1 Mark)**

Taking (a) common from C_1

$f(x) = a \begin{vmatrix} 1 & -1 & 0 \\ 2x & a & -1 \\ 4x^2 & 2ax & a \end{vmatrix}$

Applying $C_2 \to C_2 + C_1$

$\Rightarrow f(2x) = a \begin{vmatrix} 1 & 0 & 0 \\ 2x & 2x+a & -1 \\ 4x^2 & 2ax+4x^2 & a \end{vmatrix}$ **(1 Mark)**

$\Rightarrow f(2x) = a[a(2x + a) + 2ax + 4x^2]$

$\Rightarrow f(2x) = a[2xa + a^2 + 2ax + 4x^2]$

$\Rightarrow f(2x) = a[a^2 + 4ax + 4x^2]$ ...(2)

$\therefore f(2x) - f(x) = a(a^2 + 4ax + 4x^2) - a(a^2 + 2ax + x^2)$

(from (1) & (2))

$= a(a^2 + 4ax + 4x^2 - a^2 - 2ax - x^2)$

$= a(3x^2 + 2ax)$ **(1 Mark)**

9. Let $I = \int \dfrac{dx}{\sin x + \sin 2x}$

$I = \int \dfrac{dx}{\sin x + 2\sin x . \cos x}$ $\quad [\because \sin 2\theta = 2\sin\theta . \cos\theta]$ **(½ Mark)**

$= \int \dfrac{dx}{\sin x(1 + 2\cos x)}$

$I = \int \dfrac{\sin x\, dx}{\sin^2 x(1 + 2\cos x)}$

(By multiplying Num & Den by $\sin x$)

$= \int \dfrac{\sin x\, dx}{(1 - \cos^2 x)(1 + 2\cos x)}$ $\quad (\because \sin^2\theta = 1 - \cos^2\theta)$ **(½ Mark)**

Let $\cos x = t$

$-\sin x\, dx = dt$

$I = \int \dfrac{dt}{(1 - t^2)(1 + 2t)}$

$= \int \dfrac{-dt}{(1 + t)(1 - t)(1 + 2t)}$

$= \int \dfrac{-1}{(1 + t)(1 - t)(1 + 2t)}\, dt$

Let $\dfrac{-1}{(1 + t)(1 - t)(1 + 2t)} = \dfrac{A}{1 + t} + \dfrac{B}{1 - t} + \dfrac{C}{1 + 2t}$

$-1 = A(1 - t)(1 + 2t) + B(1 + t)(1 + 2t) + C(1 + t)(1 - t)$

Putting $t = -1$

$-1 = -2A \Rightarrow A = \dfrac{1}{2}$

Putting $t = 1$

$-1 = 6B \Rightarrow B = -\dfrac{1}{6}$

Putting $t = -\dfrac{1}{2}, \quad C = -\dfrac{4}{3}$

$\dfrac{-1}{(1 + t)(1 - t)(1 + 2t)} = \dfrac{1}{2(1 + t)} - \dfrac{1}{6(1 - t)} - \dfrac{4}{3(1 + 2t)}$ **(2 Marks)**

$I = \int \dfrac{1}{2(1 + t)}\, dt - \int \dfrac{1}{6(1 - t)}\, dt - \int \dfrac{4}{3(1 + 2t)}\, dt$

$I = \dfrac{1}{2}\, \log|1 + t| + \dfrac{1}{6}\, \log|1 - t| - \dfrac{4}{3 \times 2}\, \log|1 + 2t| + C$

$\left[\because \int \dfrac{1}{x}\, dx = \log|x| + c \right]$

$I = \dfrac{1}{2}\, \log|1 + \cos x| + \dfrac{1}{6}\, \log|1 - \cos x| - \dfrac{2}{3}\, \log$

$|1 + 2\cos x| + C$ **(1 Mark)**

OR

Let $I = \int \dfrac{x^2 - 3x + 1}{\sqrt{1 - x^2}}\, dx$

$= \int \dfrac{x^2 - 3x + 1 + 1 - 1}{\sqrt{1 - x^2}}\, dx$

$= \int \dfrac{x^2 - 1 + 2 - 3x}{\sqrt{1 - x^2}}\, dx$

$= \int \dfrac{-(1 - x^2) + (2 - 3x)}{\sqrt{1 - x^2}}\, dx$

$= \int \left(-\sqrt{1 - x^2} + \dfrac{2}{\sqrt{1 - x^2}} - \dfrac{3x}{\sqrt{1 - x^2}} \right) dx$

$= -\int \sqrt{1 - x^2}\, dx + \int \dfrac{2}{\sqrt{1 - x^2}}\, dx - 3\int \dfrac{x}{\sqrt{1 - x^2}}\, dx$

$= -\int \sqrt{1 - x^2}\, dx + \int \dfrac{2}{\sqrt{1 - x^2}}\, dx - 3\int \dfrac{x}{\sqrt{1 - x^2}}\, dx$ **(1 Mark)**

Let $I_1 = -\int \sqrt{1 - x^2}\, dx$

$= -\left[\dfrac{1}{2} x\sqrt{1 - x^2} + \dfrac{1}{2}\sin^{-1} x + C_1 \right]$

$\left[\because \int \sqrt{a^2 - x^2}\, dx = \dfrac{1}{2} x\sqrt{a^2 - x^2} + \dfrac{1}{2} a^2 \sin^{-1}\left(\dfrac{x}{a} \right) + C \right]$

$= -\dfrac{1}{2} x\sqrt{1 - x^2} - \dfrac{1}{2}\sin^{-1} x + C_1$ **(1 Mark)**

$I_2 = \int \dfrac{2}{\sqrt{1 - x^2}}\, dx$

$= 2\int \dfrac{1}{\sqrt{(1)^2 - x^2}}\, dx$

$= 2\sin^{-1} x + C_2$

$\left[\because \int \dfrac{1}{\sqrt{a^2 - x^2}}\, dx = \sin^{-1}\left(\dfrac{x}{a} \right) + C \right]$ **(1 Mark)**

$I_3 = -3\int \dfrac{x}{\sqrt{1 - x^2}}\, dx$

Let $1 - x^2 = t$

$-2x\, dx = dt$

$= \dfrac{-3}{2} \int \dfrac{-dt}{\sqrt{t}}$

$= \dfrac{3}{2} \int \dfrac{1}{\sqrt{t}}\, dt$

$= \dfrac{3}{2} \times 2\sqrt{t} + C_3$ $\left[\because \int x^n\, dx = \dfrac{x^{n+1}}{n+1} + C \right]$

$= 3\sqrt{t} + C_3$

$= 3\sqrt{1 - x^2} + C_3$

Putting the values of I_1, I_2, I_3 in I

$I = -\dfrac{1}{2} x\sqrt{1 - x^2} - \dfrac{1}{2}\sin^{-1} x + 2\sin^{-1} x + 3\sqrt{1 - x^2} + C$

(1 Mark)

10.   Let $I = \displaystyle\int_{-\pi}^{\pi} (\cos ax - \sin bx)^2\, dx$

$I = \displaystyle\int_{-\pi}^{\pi} (\cos^2 ax + \sin^2 bx - 2\cos ax \cdot \sin bx)\, dx$

$[\because (a - b)^2 = a^2 + b^2 - 2ab]$

$I = \displaystyle\int_{-\pi}^{\pi} \cos^2 ax\, dx + \int_{-\pi}^{\pi} \sin^2 bx\, dx - 2\int_{-\pi}^{\pi} (\cos ax \cdot \sin bx)\, dx$

(1 Mark)

Here, $\cos^2 ax$ and $\sin^2 bx$ are even functions.

$\cos ax \cdot \sin bx$ is an odd function.

As we know that

$$\int_{-a}^{a} f(x)\, dx = \begin{cases} 2\displaystyle\int_{0}^{a} f(x)\, dx, & \text{if } f(x) \text{ is an even function} \\ 0 & \text{if } f(x) \text{ is an odd function} \end{cases}$$

(1 Mark)

$\therefore I = 2\displaystyle\int_{0}^{\pi} \cos^2 ax\, dx + 2\int_{0}^{\pi} \sin^2 bx\, dx - 0$

$I = 2\displaystyle\int_{0}^{\pi} \left(\dfrac{1 + \cos 2ax}{2} \right) dx + 2\int_{0}^{\pi} \left(\dfrac{1 - \cos 2bx}{2} \right) dx$

$\left(\begin{array}{l} \because \quad \cos 2\theta = 2\cos^2 \theta - 1 \\ \quad\ \cos 2\theta = 1 - 2\sin^2 \theta \end{array} \right)$ **(1 Mark)**

$I = \displaystyle\int_{0}^{\pi} (1 + \cos 2ax)\, dx + \int_{0}^{\pi} (1 - \cos 2bx)\, dx$

$= \displaystyle\int (1 + \cos 2ax + 1 - \cos 2bx)\, dx$

$I = \displaystyle\int_{0}^{\pi} (2 + \cos 2ax - \cos 2bx)\, dx$

$I = 2[x]_0^{\pi} + \left[\dfrac{\sin 2ax}{2a} \right]_0^{\pi} - \left[\dfrac{\sin 2bx}{2b} \right]_0^{\pi}$

$I = 2\pi + \dfrac{\sin 2a\pi}{2a} - \dfrac{\sin 2\pi b}{2b}$ **(1 Mark)**

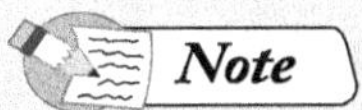

If $f(-x) = f(x)$ then $f(x)$ is called even function and if $f(-x) = -f(x)$ then $f(x)$ is called odd function.

11. Let E_1 be the probability of getting 1 or 2 on a die and E_2 be the probability of getting 3, 4, 5 or 6 on a die

$$P(E_1) = \frac{2}{6} = \frac{1}{3}$$

$$P(E_2) = \frac{4}{6} = \frac{2}{3} \qquad \textbf{(1 Mark)}$$

Also let E be the probability of getting one ball is red and another one is black

$\therefore \; P\left(\dfrac{E}{E_1}\right)$ = Probability of getting E when bag A is choosen.

$= P(BR) + P(RB)$

$$= \frac{4}{10} \times \frac{6}{9} + \frac{6}{10} \times \frac{4}{9} = \frac{8}{15} \qquad \textbf{(1 Mark)}$$

$P\left(\dfrac{E}{E_2}\right)$ = Probability of E when bag B is choosen

$$= \frac{3}{10} \times \frac{7}{9} + \frac{7}{10} \times \frac{3}{9}$$

$$= \frac{42}{90} = \frac{7}{15} \qquad \textbf{(1 Mark)}$$

$$P(E) = P(E_1)\, P\left(\frac{E}{E_1}\right) + P(E_2)\, P\left(\frac{E}{E_2}\right)$$

$$P(E) = \frac{1}{3} \times \frac{8}{15} + \frac{2}{3} \times \frac{7}{15}$$

$$P(E) = \frac{22}{45} \qquad \textbf{(1 Mark)}$$

OR

Let X denote the number of heads in the four tosses of the coin. X can be 0, 1, 2, 3, 4

$P(X = 0)$ Probability of getting no head (TTTT)

$$= \frac{\text{Number of favorable outcomes}}{\text{Total number of outcomes}}$$

Total number of outcomes $= 2^4 = 16$

$$(\because \text{coin is thrown 4 times})$$

$$P(X = 0) = \frac{1}{16}$$

$P(X = 1)$ = Probability of getting 1 head $\qquad$ **(1 Mark)**

[(HTTT), (THTT), (TTHT), (TTTH)]

$$= \frac{4}{16} = \frac{1}{4}$$

$P(X = 2)$ = Probability of getting 2 head

[(HHTT), (HTTH), (THTH), (TTHH), (HTHT), (THHT)]

$$= \frac{6}{16} = \frac{3}{8}$$

$P(X = 3)$ = Probability of getting 3 head

[(HHHT), (HHTH), (HTHH), (THHH)]

$$= \frac{4}{16} = \frac{1}{4}$$

$P(X = 4)$ = Probability of getting 4 head

(HHHH) $\qquad$ **(1 Mark)**

$$= \frac{1}{16}$$

Probability distribution of X is given below.

X_i	$P_i\ (X = X_i)$	$P_i\, X_i$	$P_i\, X_i^2$
0	$\dfrac{1}{16}$	0	0
1	$\dfrac{1}{4}$	$\dfrac{1}{4}$	$\dfrac{1}{4}$
2	$\dfrac{3}{8}$	$\dfrac{3}{4}$	$\dfrac{3}{2}$
3	$\dfrac{1}{4}$	$\dfrac{3}{4}$	$\dfrac{9}{4}$
4	$\dfrac{1}{16}$	$\dfrac{1}{4}$	1
	$\sum P_i = 1$	$\sum P_i X_i = 2$	$\sum P_i X_i^2 = 5$

(1 Mark)

$\therefore$ Mean $= \bar{X} = \sum P_i X_i = 2$

$$\text{Var}(x) = \sum P_i X_i^2 - \left(\sum P_i X_i\right)^2$$

$$= 5 - (2)^2$$

$$= 1$$

Hence, mean = 2 and variance = 1 $\qquad$ **(1 Mark)**

12. Given: $= x\hat{i} + y\hat{j} + z\hat{k}$

Now, $(\vec{r} \times \hat{i}).(\vec{r} \times \hat{j}) + xy$

$$= \left[(x\hat{i} + y\hat{j} + z\hat{k}) \times \hat{i}\right].\left[(x\hat{i} + y\hat{j} + z\hat{k}) \times \hat{j}\right] + xy$$

$$= (x\hat{i} \times \hat{i} + y\hat{j} \times \hat{i} + z\hat{k} \times \hat{i}).(x\hat{i} \times \hat{j} + y\hat{j} \times \hat{j} + z\hat{k} \times \hat{j}) + xy$$

(1 Mark)

As we know that

$\hat{i} \times \hat{j} = \hat{k}, \; \hat{j} \times \hat{i} = -\hat{k}$

$\hat{j} \times \hat{k} = \hat{i}, \; \hat{k} \times \hat{j} = -\hat{i}$

$\hat{k} \times \hat{i} = \hat{j}$, $\hat{i} \times \hat{k} = -\hat{j}$

$\hat{i} \times \hat{i} = 0$, $\hat{j} \times \hat{j} = 0$, $\hat{k} \times \hat{k} = 0$ **(2 Marks)**

$\therefore (\vec{r} \times \hat{i}).(\vec{r} \times \hat{j}) + xy = (0 - \hat{k}y + z\hat{j}).(x\hat{k} + 0 + z(-\hat{i})) + xy$

$$= -xy + xy$$

$$= 0 \qquad \textbf{(1 Mark)}$$

13. Given: $\dfrac{x-2}{3} = \dfrac{y+1}{4} = \dfrac{z-2}{12}$

Let $\dfrac{x-2}{3} = \dfrac{y+1}{4} = \dfrac{z-2}{12} = \lambda$

$x = 3\lambda + 2, \ y = 4\lambda - 1, \ z = 12\lambda + 2 \qquad ...(1)$

Coordinates of any point on the line are

$(3\lambda + 2, \ 4\lambda - 1, \ 12\lambda + 2)$ **(1½ Marks)**

To find point of intersection of line and plane, put these values of x, y, z in equation of plane.

$x - y + z = 5$

$(3\lambda + 2) - (4\lambda - 1) + (12\lambda + 2) = 5 \qquad$ (from (1))

$11\lambda + 5 = 5$

$\lambda = 0$

$x = 3\lambda + 2 = 2$

$y = 4\lambda - 1 = -1$

$z = 12\lambda + 2 = 2$ **(1½ Marks)**

$\therefore$ Point of intersection of line and plane is $(2, -1, 2)$

Given point is $(-1, -5, -10)$

Distance $= \sqrt{(x_2 - x_1)^2 + (y_2 - y_1)^2 + (z_2 - z_1)^2}$

Distance between $(2, -1, 2)$ and $(-1, -5, -10)$ is

Distance $= \sqrt{(-1 - 2)^2 + (-5 + 1)^2 + (-10 - 2)^2}$

$= \sqrt{(-3)^2 + (-4)^2 + (-12)^2}$

$= \sqrt{169} = 13$

Distance $= 13$ units

Hence distance between $(-1, -5, -10)$ and point of intersection of line and plane is 13 units. **(1 Mark)**

14. Given: $\sin[\cot^{-1}(x + 1)] = \cos(\tan^{-1} x)$

As, $\cot^{-1}(x + 1) = \sin^{-1} \dfrac{1}{\sqrt{1 + (x+1)^2}}$

$$\left[\because \cot^{-1} P = \sin^{-1} \dfrac{1}{\sqrt{1 + P^2}} \right]$$

and $\tan^{-1} x = \cos^{-1} \dfrac{1}{\sqrt{1 + x^2}}$

$$\left[\because \tan^{-1} P = \cos^{-1} \dfrac{1}{\sqrt{1 + P^2}} \right] \textbf{(1 Mark)}$$

$\therefore \sin\left(\sin^{-1} \dfrac{1}{\sqrt{1 + (x+1)^2}} \right) = \cos\left(\cos^{-1} \dfrac{1}{\sqrt{1 + x^2}} \right)$

$\dfrac{1}{\sqrt{1 + (x+1)^2}} = \dfrac{1}{\sqrt{1 + x^2}}$

$\sqrt{1 + x^2} = \sqrt{1 + (x+1)^2}$ **(1 Mark)**

Squaring on both sides, we get.

$1 + x^2 = 1 + (x^2 + 1 + 2x)$ **(1 Mark)**

$1 + x^2 = 2 + x^2 + 2x$

$2x + 2 + x^2 - x^2 - 1 = 0$

$2x = -1$

$x = -\dfrac{1}{2}$ **(1 Mark)**

OR

$(\tan^{-1} x)^2 + (\cot^{-1} x)^2 = \dfrac{5\pi^2}{8}$

$(\tan^{-1} x)^2 + (\cot^{-1} x)^2 + 2\tan^{-1} x \cot^{-1} x - 2\tan^{-1} x \cot^{-1} x$

$= \dfrac{5\pi^2}{8}$

$(\tan^{-1} x + \cot^{-1} x)^2 - 2\tan^{-1} x \cot^{-1} x = \dfrac{5\pi^2}{8} \qquad ...(\text{i})$

(1 Mark)

As we know that

$\tan^{-1} x + \cot^{-1} x = \dfrac{\pi}{2}$

From (i)

$\left(\dfrac{\pi}{2} \right)^2 - 2\tan^{-1} x \left(\dfrac{\pi}{2} - \tan^{-1} x \right) = \dfrac{5\pi^2}{8}$

$\dfrac{\pi^2}{4} - 2 \times \dfrac{\pi}{2} \tan^{-1} x + 2(\tan^{-1} x)^2 = \dfrac{5\pi^2}{8}$

$2(\tan^{-1} x)^2 - \pi \tan^{-1} x - \dfrac{3\pi^2}{8} = 0$ **(1 Mark)**

Let $\tan^{-1} x = t$

$2t^2 - \pi t - \dfrac{3\pi^2}{8} = 0$

Solving the quadratic equation

$t = \dfrac{\pi \pm \sqrt{\pi^2 - 4(2)\left(\dfrac{-3\pi^2}{8} \right)}}{4}$

$$\left[\because \text{For} \quad ax^2 + bx + c = 0 \right.$$
$$\left. x = \dfrac{-b \pm \sqrt{b^2 - 4ac}}{2a} \right]$$

$$t = \frac{\pi \pm \sqrt{4\pi^2}}{4} \Rightarrow t = \frac{\pi \pm 2\pi}{4}$$

$$t = \frac{3\pi}{4} \text{ or } -\frac{\pi}{4}$$ **(1 Mark)**

As, $-\dfrac{\pi}{2} \le \tan^{-1} x \le \dfrac{\pi}{2}$

$$\tan^{-1} x \ne \frac{3\pi}{4}, \ \tan^{-1} x = -\frac{\pi}{4}$$

$$x = \tan^{-1}\left(-\frac{\pi}{4}\right)$$

$$x = -1$$ **(1 Mark)**

15. $y = \tan^{-1}\left[\dfrac{\sqrt{1+x^2} + \sqrt{1-x^2}}{\sqrt{1+x^2} - \sqrt{1-x^2}}\right]$

Putting $x^2 = \cos 2\theta$

$$y = \tan^{-1}\left[\frac{\sqrt{1+\cos 2\theta} + \sqrt{1-\cos 2\theta}}{\sqrt{1+\cos 2\theta} - \sqrt{1-\cos 2\theta}}\right]$$ **(1 Mark)**

$$y = \tan^{-1}\left[\frac{\sqrt{2\cos^2\theta} + \sqrt{2\sin^2\theta}}{\sqrt{2\cos^2\theta} - \sqrt{2\sin^2\theta}}\right]$$

$$\left[\because\ \begin{array}{l} \cos 2\theta = 2\cos^2\theta - 1 \\ \cos 2\theta = 1 - 2\sin^2\theta \end{array}\right]$$

$$y = \tan^{-1}\left[\frac{\cos\theta + \sin\theta}{\cos\theta - \sin\theta}\right]$$ **(1 Mark)**

Dividing Num & Den by $\cos\theta$

$$y = \tan^{-1}\left[\frac{1+\tan\theta}{1-\tan\theta}\right]$$

$$= \tan^{-1}\left[\frac{\tan\dfrac{\pi}{4} + \tan\theta}{1 - \tan\dfrac{\pi}{4}.\tan\theta}\right] \qquad \left[\because \tan\frac{\pi}{4} = 1\right]$$

$$= \tan^{-1}\left[\tan\left(\frac{\pi}{4} + \theta\right)\right] \quad \left[\because \tan(A+B) = \frac{\tan A + \tan B}{1 - \tan A.\tan B}\right]$$

$$= \frac{\pi}{4} + \theta$$

$$= \frac{\pi}{4} + \frac{1}{2}\cos^{-1} x^2 \qquad (\because x^2 = \cos 2\theta)\ \textbf{(1 Mark)}$$

Differentiating w.r.t. x

$$\frac{dy}{dx} = 0 + \frac{1}{2}\left(\frac{-1}{\sqrt{1-(x^2)^2}}\right)\times 2x$$

$$\frac{dy}{dx} = \frac{-x}{\sqrt{1-x^4}} \qquad \left[\because \frac{d}{dx}\cos^{-1} x = -\frac{1}{\sqrt{1-x^2}}\right]$$

Hence $\dfrac{dy}{dx} = \dfrac{-x}{\sqrt{1-x^4}}$ **(1 Mark)**

16. $x = a\cos\theta + b\sin\theta$ ...(1)

$y = a\sin\theta - b\cos\theta$ ...(2)

On squaring and adding (1) & (2)

$x^2 + y^2 = (a\cos\theta + b\sin\theta)^2 + (a\sin\theta - b\cos\theta)^2$

$x^2 + y^2 = a^2\cos^2\theta + b^2\sin^2\theta + 2ab\cos\theta.\sin\theta$
$+ a^2\sin^2\theta + b^2\cos^2\theta - 2ab\cos\theta.\sin\theta$

$x^2 + y^2 = a^2(\cos^2\theta + \sin^2\theta) + b^2(\sin^2\theta + \cos^2\theta)$

$x^2 + y^2 = a^2 + b^2$ **(1 Mark)**

Differentiating w.r.t. x

$$2x + 2y\frac{dy}{dx} = 0 \Rightarrow 2y\frac{dy}{dx} = -2x$$

$$\frac{dy}{dx} = -\frac{x}{y} \qquad ...(3)\ \textbf{(1 Mark)}$$

Again differentiating w.r.t. x

$$\frac{d^2y}{dx^2} = -\left(\frac{y - x\dfrac{dy}{dx}}{y^2}\right) \left[\because \frac{d}{dx}\left(\frac{u}{v}\right) = \frac{v\dfrac{d}{dx}u - v\dfrac{dv}{dx}}{v^2}\right]$$

$$\frac{d^2y}{dx^2} = -\left(\frac{y - x\left(-\dfrac{x}{y}\right)}{y^2}\right) \qquad \text{[From (3)]}$$

$$\frac{d^2y}{dx^2} = -\left(\frac{y^2 + x^2}{y^3}\right) \qquad ...(4)\ \textbf{(1 Mark)}$$

L.H.S. $= y^2\dfrac{d^2y}{dx^2} - x\dfrac{dy}{dx} + y$

$$-y^2\left(\frac{y^2 + x^2}{y^3}\right) - x\left(-\frac{x}{y}\right) + y \qquad \text{[From (3) & (4)]}$$

$$= \frac{-y^2 - x^2}{y} + \frac{x^2}{y} + y$$

$$= \frac{-y^2 - x^2 + x^2 + y^2}{y}$$

$$= 0 = \text{R.H.S.}$$

L.H.S. = R.H.S.

Hence proved. **(1 Mark)**

17. Let a be the side of equilateral triangle

Area of equilateral triangle, $A = \dfrac{\sqrt{3}}{4}a^2$

Given that, $\dfrac{da}{dt} = 2$ cm/s   ...(1)

$A = \dfrac{\sqrt{3}}{4}a^2$ **(1 Mark)**

Differentiating w.r.t. t

$\dfrac{dA}{dt} = \dfrac{d}{dt}\left(\dfrac{\sqrt{3}}{4}a^2\right)$

$= \dfrac{\sqrt{3}}{4}(2a)\dfrac{da}{dt}$ **(1 Mark)**

$= \dfrac{\sqrt{3}}{2}a(2)$ [From (1)]

$= \sqrt{3}\, a$ cm^2/s

When, $a = 20$ cm

$\left(\dfrac{dA}{dt}\right)_{a=2} = \sqrt{3}(20)$ cm^2/s

$= 20\sqrt{3}$ cm^2/s

Hence, area is increasing at the rate of $20\sqrt{3}$ cm^2/s. When the side of triangle is 20 cm.   **(2 Marks)**

18. Let $I = \int(x+3)\sqrt{3-4x-x^2}\,dx$

Let $x + 3 = A\dfrac{d}{dx}(3 - 4x - x^2) + B$

$x + 3 = A(-4 - 2x) + B$

$x + 3 = -2Ax - 4A + B$

On comparing LHS & RHS

$1 = -2A \Rightarrow A = \dfrac{-1}{2}$

$-4A + B = 3 \Rightarrow -4\left(\dfrac{-1}{2}\right) + B = 3$

$B = 1$

$I = \int\left[\dfrac{1}{2}(4+2x)+1\right]\sqrt{3-4x-x^2}\,dx$ **(1 Mark)**

$I = \dfrac{1}{2}\int(4+2x)\sqrt{3-4x-x^2}\,dx + \int\sqrt{3-4x-x^2}\,dx$

$I = I_1 + I_2$

$I_1 = \dfrac{1}{2}\int(4+2x)\sqrt{3-4x-x^2}\,dx$

Let $3 - 4x - x^2 = t$

$(-4 - 2x)dx = dt$

$I_1 = -\dfrac{1}{2}\int\sqrt{t}\,dt$

$= \dfrac{-1}{2}\times\dfrac{2}{3}t^{3/2}+C_1$ $\left[\because \int x^n dx = \dfrac{x^{n+1}}{n+1}+C\right]$

$= \dfrac{-1}{3}(3-4x-x^2)^{3/2}+C$ $[\because t = 3 - 4x - x^2]$ **(1 Mark)**

$I_2 = \int\sqrt{3-4x-x^2}\,dx$

$= \int\sqrt{3-(4x+x^2)}\,dx$

$= \int\sqrt{3-(4x+x^2+2^2-2^2)}\,dx$

$= \int\sqrt{7-(x^2+4x+2^2)}\,dx$

$= \int\sqrt{(\sqrt{7})^2-(x+2)^2}\,dx$ **(1 Mark)**

As we know that

$\int\sqrt{a^2-x^2}\,dx = \dfrac{1}{2}x\sqrt{a^2-x^2}+\dfrac{1}{2}a^2\sin^{-1}\left(\dfrac{x}{a}\right)+C$

$\therefore I_2 = \dfrac{1}{2}(x+2)\sqrt{(\sqrt{7})^2-(x+2)^2}+\dfrac{1}{2}(\sqrt{7})^2\sin^{-1}\left(\dfrac{x+2}{\sqrt{7}}\right)+C_2$

$= \dfrac{1}{2}(x+2)\sqrt{3-4x-x^2}+\dfrac{7}{2}\sin^{-1}\left(\dfrac{x+2}{\sqrt{7}}\right)+C_2$

$I = I_1 + I_2$

$= \dfrac{-1}{3}(3-4x-x^2)^{3/2}+\dfrac{1}{2}(x+2)$

$\qquad \sqrt{3-4x-x^2}+\dfrac{7}{2}\sin^{-1}\left(\dfrac{x+2}{\sqrt{7}}\right)+C$ **(1 Mark)**

where $C = C_1 + C_2$

19. Number of articles sold can be represented as

$X = \begin{bmatrix} 40 & 25 & 35 \\ 50 & 40 & 50 \\ 20 & 30 & 40 \end{bmatrix}$ **(1 Mark)**

Cost of each article can be represented as

$Y = \begin{bmatrix} 25 & 100 & 50 \end{bmatrix}$ **(1 Mark)**

$\therefore$ Funds collected by each school separately is given by

$YX = \begin{bmatrix} 25 & 100 & 50 \end{bmatrix}\begin{bmatrix} 40 & 25 & 35 \\ 50 & 40 & 50 \\ 20 & 30 & 40 \end{bmatrix}$

$YX = \begin{bmatrix} 7000 & 6125 & 7875 \end{bmatrix}$ **(1 Mark)**

Funds collected by school A : ₹7000

Funds collected by school B : ₹6125

Funds collected by school C : ₹7875

Total funds collected = ₹(7000 + 6125 + 7875)

$\qquad\qquad\qquad\qquad = $ ₹21000

This shows helping nature of students.   **(1 Mark)**

SECTION - C

20. If relation R is reflexive, symmetric and transitive relation, then it will be equivalence relation.

(i) Let (a, b) be an arbitrary element of $N \times N$

Now $(a, b) \in N \times N$

$\quad a, b \in N$

$\Rightarrow \quad ab(a + b) = ba(a + b)$

$\Rightarrow \quad (a, b) R(a, b)$

$\therefore \quad (a, b) R(a, b) \ \forall \ (a, b) \in N \times N$

$\therefore \ R$ is reflexive on $N \times N$ **(1 Mark)**

(ii) Let $(a, b), (c, d)$ be an arbitrary element of $N \times N$

Such that $(a, b) R (c, d)$

Now $(a, b) R(c, d)$

$\Rightarrow \quad ad(b + c) = bc(a + d)$

$\Rightarrow \quad cb(d + a) = da(c + b)$

$\Rightarrow \quad (a, b) R(c, d) \Rightarrow (c, d) R(a, b) \ \forall \ (a, b),$
$\qquad\qquad\qquad\qquad\qquad\qquad (c, d) \in N \times N$

$\therefore \ R$ is symmetric on $N \times N$ **(1 Mark)**

(iii) Let $(a, b), (c, d), (e, f) \in N \times N$ such that

$(a, b) R(c, d)$ and $(c, d) R(e, f)$

$(a, b) R(c, d)$

$\Rightarrow ad(b + c) = bc(a + d)$

$\dfrac{b+c}{bc} = \dfrac{a+d}{ad}$

$\dfrac{1}{c}+\dfrac{1}{b} = \dfrac{1}{d}+\dfrac{1}{a} \qquad ...(1)$ **(1 Mark)**

Also $(c, d) R(e, f)$

$cf(d + e) = de(c + f)$

$\dfrac{d+e}{de} = \dfrac{c+f}{cf}$

$\dfrac{1}{d}+\dfrac{1}{e} = \dfrac{1}{c}+\dfrac{1}{f} \qquad ...(2)$ **(1 Mark)**

Adding (1) and (2)

$\dfrac{1}{b}+\dfrac{1}{c}+\dfrac{1}{d}+\dfrac{1}{e} = \dfrac{1}{a}+\dfrac{1}{d}+\dfrac{1}{c}+\dfrac{1}{f}$

$\dfrac{1}{b}+\dfrac{1}{e} = \dfrac{1}{a}+\dfrac{1}{f}$

$\dfrac{b+e}{be} = \dfrac{a+f}{af}$

$af(b + e) = be(a + f)$ **(1 Mark)**

$(a, b) R(e, f)$

Thus $(a, b) R(c, d)$ and $(c, d) R(e, b) \Rightarrow (a, b) R(e, f) \ \forall$
$\qquad\qquad\qquad\qquad (a, b) (c, d) (e, f) \in N \times N.$

$\therefore \ R$ is transitive on $N \times N$

Hence R being reflexive, symmetric and transitive is an equivalence relation on $N \times N$.   **(1 Mark)**

21. Given: $x^2 + y^2 = 4$

Normal at $(1, \sqrt{3})$ will also pass through $(0, 0)$. So, equation of normal:

$y - y_1 = \dfrac{y_2 - y_1}{x_2 - x_1}(x - x_1)$

$y - 0 = \dfrac{\sqrt{3} - 0}{1 - 0}(x - 0)$

$y = \sqrt{3}\, x \qquad\qquad ...(1)$ **(1 Mark)**

Slope of normal is $\sqrt{3}$

Slope of tangent $= \dfrac{-1}{\text{Slope of normal}} = \dfrac{-1}{\sqrt{3}}$

Equation of tangent at $(1, \sqrt{3})$ is

$y - \sqrt{3} = \dfrac{-1}{\sqrt{3}}(x - 1) \qquad [\because y - y_1 = m(x - x_1)]$

$\sqrt{3}\, y - 3 = -x + 1$

$y = \dfrac{-x + 4}{\sqrt{3}} \qquad\qquad ...(2)$ **(1 Mark)**

If $y = 0$, then x = 4

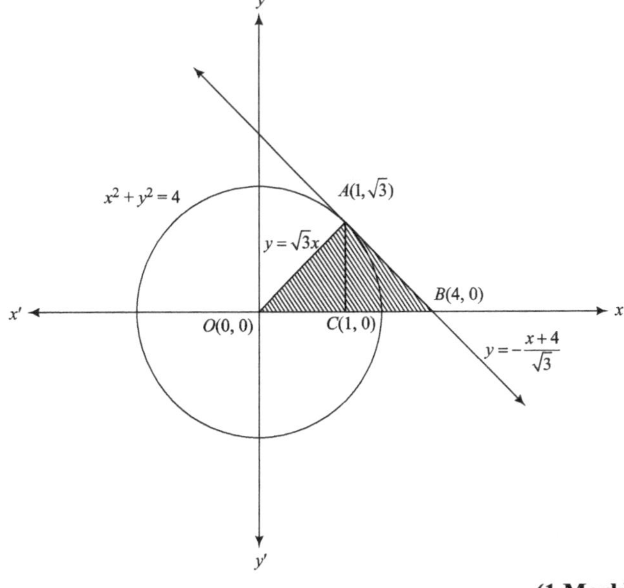

(1 Mark)

Thus, ΔAOB is formed by the tangent, normal and the positive x-axis

Area of ΔAOB = Area of ΔAOC + Area of ΔACB

$$= \int_0^1 y \, dx + \int_1^4 y \, dx$$

Area of $\Delta AOB = \int_0^1 \sqrt{3}x \, dx + \int_1^4 \left(\frac{-x+4}{\sqrt{3}}\right) dx \qquad \textbf{(1 Mark)}$

$$= \sqrt{3}\left(\frac{x^2}{2}\right)_0^1 + \frac{1}{\sqrt{3}}\left[\frac{-x^2}{2} + 4x\right]_1^4$$

$$= \frac{\sqrt{3}}{2}(1-0) + \frac{1}{\sqrt{3}}\left[\frac{-16}{2} + 16 - \left(\frac{-1}{2} + 4\right)\right]$$

$$= \frac{\sqrt{3}}{2} + \frac{1}{\sqrt{3}}\left[\frac{16}{2} - \frac{7}{2}\right] = \frac{\sqrt{3}}{2} + \frac{9}{2\sqrt{3}} \times \frac{\sqrt{3}}{\sqrt{3}}$$

$$= \frac{\sqrt{3}}{2} + \frac{9\sqrt{3}}{6} = 2\sqrt{3} \text{ sq. units}$$

Hence area of triangle is $2\sqrt{3}$ sq. units. $\qquad$ **(2 Marks)**

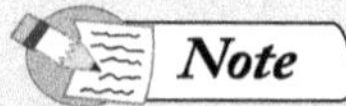
Note

Normal is perpendicular to the tangent at contact point. So, it is also passes through origin.

OR

$$\int_1^3 (e^{2-3x} + x^2 + 1) \, dx$$

$$\int f(x) \, dx = \lim_{\substack{h \to 0 \\ n \to \infty}} [f(a) + f(a+h) + f(a+2h) + \dots +$$

$$f(a + (n-1)h)] \quad \dots(1) \qquad \textbf{(1 Mark)}$$

where, $h = \dfrac{b-a}{n}$

Here, $b = 3$, $a = 1$

$$h = \frac{3-1}{n} = \frac{2}{n} \Rightarrow nh = 2$$

$f(x) = e^{2-3x} + x^2 + 1$

$f(a) = f(1) = e^{2-3(1)} + 1^2 + 1$

$f(a+h) = f(1+h) = e^{2-3(1+h)} + (1+h)^2 + 1$

$f(a+2h) = f(1+2h) = e^{2-3(1+2h)} + (1+2h)^2 + 1$

$f(a+(n-1)h) = f(1+(n-1)h) = e^{2-3[1+(n-1)h]} +$

$$[1 + (n-1)h]^2 = 1 \qquad \textbf{(1 Mark)}$$

$$\int_1^3 (e^{2-3x} + x^2 + 1)dx = \lim_{\substack{h \to 0 \\ n \to \infty}} [e^{2-3\times 1} + 1^2 + 1]$$

$$+ [e^{2-3(1+h)} + (1+h)^2 + 1]$$

$$+ [e^{2-3(1+2h)} + (1+2h)^2 + 1] + \dots +$$

$$[e^{2-3(1+(n-1)h)} + (1+(n-1)h)^2 + 1]$$

[By using (1)]

$$= \lim_{\substack{h \to 0 \\ n \to \infty}} [e^2(e^{-3} + e^{-3(1+h)} + e^{-3(1+2h)} + \dots$$

$$+ e^{-3(1+(n-1)h)}] + \lim_{h \to 0} [1^2 + (1+h)^2$$

$$+ (1+2h)^2 + \dots + (1+(n-1)h)^2]$$

$$+ \lim_{h \to 0} (1 + 1 + 1 \dots n \text{ times}] \qquad \textbf{(1 Mark)}$$

$$= \lim_{\substack{h \to 0 \\ n \to \infty}} h[e^2 \, e^{-3} (1 + e^{-3h} + e^{-3(2h)} + \dots + e^{-3(n-1)h}]$$

$$+ \lim_{h \to 0} [n + 2h\{1 + 2 + 3 +$$

$$\dots + (n-1)\} + h^2(1^2 + 2^2 + 3^2 + \dots + (n-1)^2)] + \lim_{h \to 0} nh$$

$$= \lim_{\substack{h \to 0 \\ n \to \infty}} h\left[e^{-1}\left(\frac{(e^{-3h})^n - 1}{e^{-3h} - 1}\right)\right]$$

$$+ \lim_{h \to 0} h\left[n + 2h\frac{n(n-1)}{2} + h^2\frac{n(n-1)(2n-1)}{6}\right] + \lim_{h \to 0} nh$$

$$\textbf{(1 Mark)}$$

$$\left[\because a + ar + ar^2 + \dots ar^{n-1} = a\left(\frac{r^n - 1}{r-1}\right), r \neq 1,\right.$$

$$1 + 2 + 3 + \dots + (n-1) = \frac{n(n-1)}{2}\right]$$

$$\left[1^2 + 2^2 + 3^2 + \dots + (n-1)^2 = \frac{n(n-1)(2n-1)}{6}\right]$$

$$= \lim_{\substack{h \to 0 \\ n \to \infty}} e^{-1}\left[\frac{e^{-3hn} - 1}{\left(\dfrac{e^{-3h} - 1}{h}\right)}\right] +$$

$$\lim_{\substack{h \to 0 \\ n \to \infty}}\left[nh + \frac{2hn(nh-h)}{2} + \frac{nh(nh-h)(2nh-h)}{6}\right] + \lim_{\substack{h \to 0 \\ n \to \infty}} nh$$

$$= \lim_{h \to 0} e^{-1}\left[\frac{e^{-6} - 1}{-3\left(\dfrac{e^{-3h} - 1}{-3h}\right)}\right] +$$

$$\lim_{h \to 0}\left[2 + 2(2-h) + \frac{2}{6}(2-h)(4-h)\right] + \lim_{h \to 0} 2$$

$$[\because nh = 2] \qquad \textbf{(1 Mark)}$$

$$= -\frac{e^{-1}}{3}(e^{-6} - 1) + 2 + 2(2-0) + \frac{2}{6}(2)(4) + 2$$

$$= -\frac{e^{-1}}{3}(e^{-6}-1)+8+\frac{8}{3}$$

$$= -\frac{1}{3}(e^{-7}-e^{-1})+\frac{32}{3}$$

$$\therefore \int_1^3 (e^{2-3x}+x^2+1)\,dx = \frac{-1}{3}(e^{-7}-e^{-1})+\frac{32}{3} \quad \textbf{(1 Mark)}$$

22. $(\tan^{-1} y - x)dy = (1 + y^2)dx$

$$\frac{dy}{dx} = \frac{1+y^2}{\tan^{-1} y - x}$$

$$\frac{dx}{dy} = \frac{\tan^{-1} y - x}{1+y^2}$$

$$\frac{dx}{dy} = \frac{\tan^{-1} y}{1+y^2} - \frac{x}{1+y^2}$$

$$\frac{dx}{dy} + \frac{1}{1+y^2}x = \frac{\tan^{-1} y}{1+y^2} \quad \textbf{(1 Mark)}$$

This is linear differential equation of the form

$$\frac{dx}{dy} + Px = Q.$$

$$P = \frac{1}{1+y^2}, Q = \frac{\tan^{-1} y}{1+y^2}$$

$$\text{I.F.} = e^{\int p\,dy}$$

$$= e^{\int \frac{1}{1+y^2}dy} = e^{\tan^{-1} y} \quad \textbf{(1 Mark)}$$

Required solution is given by

$$x(\text{I.F.}) = \int Q(\text{I.F.})dy + c$$

$$xe^{\tan^{-1} y} = \int\left(\frac{\tan^{-1} y}{1+y^2}e^{\tan^{-1} y}\right)dy + c \quad ...(1) \quad \textbf{(1 Mark)}$$

Let $I = \int \frac{\tan^{-1} y}{1+y^2}e^{\tan^{-1} y}\,dy$

Let $\tan^{-1} y = t$

$$\int \frac{1}{1+y^2}dy = dt$$

$$I = \int te^t\,dt$$

$$I = t \times \int e^t\,dt - \int\left[\frac{d}{dt}(t) \times \int e^t\,dt\right]dt$$

$$\left[\because \int uv\,dx = u\int v\,dx - \int\left(\frac{d}{dx}u\int v\,dx\right)dx\right] \quad \textbf{(1 Mark)}$$

$$= te^t - \int e^t\,dt$$

$$= t\,e^t - e^t$$

$$= \tan^{-1}y\ e^{\tan^{-1}y} - e^{\tan^{-1}y}$$

$$= e^{\tan^{-1}y}(\tan^{-1}y - 1)$$

Putting value of I in (1)

$$x\,e^{\tan^{-1}y} = e^{\tan^{-1}y}(\tan^{-1}y - 1) + C \quad \textbf{(2 Marks)}$$

OR

$$\frac{dy}{dx} = \frac{xy}{x^2+y^2} \quad ...(1)$$

This is a homogenous equation.

Putting $y = vx$

$$\frac{dy}{dx} = v + x\frac{dv}{dx}$$

Putting the value of y and $\dfrac{dy}{dx}$ in eq. (1) $\quad$ **(1 Mark)**

$$\frac{dy}{dx} = \frac{xy}{x^2+y^2}$$

$$v + x\frac{dv}{dx} = \frac{x(vx)}{x^2+(vx)^2}$$

$$v + x\frac{dv}{dx} = \frac{vx^2}{x^2+v^2x^2} \Rightarrow x\frac{dv}{dx} = \frac{v}{1+v^2} - v$$

$$x\frac{dv}{dx} = \frac{-v^3}{1+v^2} \Rightarrow \frac{1+v^2}{v^3}dv = -\frac{1}{x}dx$$

$$\left(\frac{1}{v^3}+\frac{1}{v}\right)dv = -\frac{1}{x}dx \quad \textbf{(1 Mark)}$$

Integerating both sides

$$\int\left(\frac{1}{v^3}+\frac{1}{v}\right)dv = -\int\frac{1}{x}dx$$

$$-\frac{v^{-2}}{2} + \log|v| = -\log|x| + C$$

$$\left[\begin{array}{l}\because \int x^n dx = \dfrac{x^{n+1}}{n+1}+C \\[2mm] \int \dfrac{1}{x}dx = \log|x|+ C\end{array}\right] \quad \textbf{(1 Mark)}$$

$$-\frac{1}{2v^2} + \log|v| + \log|x| = C$$

$$-\frac{1}{2v^2} + \log|vx| = C$$

$$\frac{-1}{2\left(\dfrac{y}{x}\right)^2}+\log\left|\frac{y}{x}x\right| = C \qquad \left[\because v = \frac{y}{x}\right]$$

$$\frac{-x^2}{2y^2} + \log|y| = C \quad ...(2) \quad \textbf{(1 Mark)}$$

$y = 1$ when $x = 0$ (given)

$C = 0$　(from (2))　　　　　　　　　**(1 Mark)**

$$\frac{-x^2}{2y^2} + \log|y| = 0 \Rightarrow \log|y| = \frac{x^2}{2y^2}$$

Hence $x^2 = 2y^2 \log|y|$ is the solution of given equation.

　　　　　　　　　　　　　　　　(1 Mark)

> **Note**
>
> *A solution of differential equation which does not contain any arbitrary constant is called the particular solution of differential equation.*

23. Let $\dfrac{x-1}{2} = \dfrac{y+1}{3} = \dfrac{z-1}{4} = \lambda$

$x = 2\lambda + 1,\ y = 3\lambda - 1,\ 2 = 4\lambda + 1$

Coordinates of any point on first line are

$(2\lambda + 1,\ 3\lambda - 1,\ 4\lambda + 1)$　　　**(½ Mark)**

Let $\dfrac{x-3}{1} = \dfrac{y-k}{2} = \dfrac{z}{1} = \mu$

$x = \mu + 3,\ y = 2\mu + k,\ z = \mu$

Coordinates of any point on second line are

$(\mu + 3,\ 2\mu + k,\ \mu)$　　　　　**(½ Mark)**

Comparing coordinates of both the lines

$2\lambda + 1 = \mu + 3 \Rightarrow 2\lambda - \mu = 2$　　...(1)

$3\lambda - 1 = 2\mu + k \Rightarrow 3\lambda - 2\mu = k + 1$　...(2)

$4\lambda + 1 = \mu \Rightarrow 4\lambda - \mu = -1$　　　...(3)

Solving (1) & (3)

$\lambda = \dfrac{-3}{2}\ \&\ \mu = -5$　　　　**(1 Mark)**

Putting values of λ & μ in (2)

$$3\left(\frac{-3}{2}\right) - 2(-5) = k + 1$$

$$\frac{-9}{2} + 10 = k + 1$$

$$k = \frac{9}{2}$$　　　　　　　　　　**(1 Mark)**

Point of intersection of both the lines

$P(2\lambda + 1,\ 3\lambda - 1,\ 4\lambda + 1)$

$$P\left(2\left(\frac{-3}{2}\right)+1, 3\left(\frac{-3}{2}\right)-1, 4\left(\frac{-3}{2}\right)+1\right)$$

$$P\left(-2, \frac{-11}{2}, -5\right)$$　　　　　**(1 Mark)**

Direction vector of both the lines are

$\vec{n}_1 = 2\hat{i} + 3\hat{j} + 4\hat{k}$

$\vec{n}_2 = \hat{i} + 2\hat{j} + \hat{k}$

Direction vector of normal of plane is given as

$$\vec{n} = \vec{n}_1 \times \vec{n}_2 = \begin{vmatrix} \hat{i} & \hat{j} & \hat{k} \\ 2 & 3 & 4 \\ 1 & 2 & 1 \end{vmatrix}$$

$= \hat{i}(3 - 8) - \hat{j}(2 - 4) + \hat{k}(4 - 3)$

$= -5\hat{i} + 2\hat{j} + \hat{k}$　　　　　**(1 Mark)**

Plane will also passes through $(1, -1, 1)$, then $\vec{a} = \hat{i} - \hat{j} + \hat{k}$

∴ Equation of plane is given as

$(\vec{r} - \vec{a}).\vec{n} = 0$

$\left[\vec{r} - (\hat{i} - \hat{j} + \hat{k})\right].(-5\hat{i} + 2\hat{j} + \hat{k}) = 0$

$\vec{r}.(-5\hat{i} + 2\hat{j} + \hat{k}) = (\hat{i} - \hat{j} + \hat{k})(-5\hat{i} + 2\hat{j} + \hat{k})$

$\vec{r}.(-5\hat{i} + 2\hat{j} + \hat{k}) = -5 - 2 + 1$

$\vec{r}.(-5\hat{i} + 2\hat{j} + \hat{k}) = -6$

Cartesian form

$5x - 2y - z - 6 = 0$　　　　　**(1 Mark)**

> **Note**
>
> *Cross multiplication of two given vectors gives third vector which is perpendicular to these two given vector.*

24. Let $P(A)$ be x & $P(B)$ be y

∴ $P(\bar{A}) = 1 - x$　　　$[\because P(\bar{A}) = 1 - P(A)]$

$P(\bar{B}) = 1 - y$　　　$[\because P(\bar{B}) = 1 - P(B)]$

$P(\bar{A} \cap B) = \dfrac{2}{15}$

$P(\bar{A}) \cdot P(B) = \dfrac{2}{15}$　　　$[\because A$ and B are independent]

$(1 - x)y = \dfrac{2}{15}$　　　　...(1)　　**(1 Mark)**

$P(A \cap \bar{B}) = \dfrac{1}{6}$

$P(A) \cdot P(\bar{B}) = \dfrac{1}{6}$

$x(1 - y) = \dfrac{1}{6}$

$x = \dfrac{1}{6 - 6y}$　　　　...(2)　　**(1 Mark)**

Putting the value of x in (1)

$$(1-x)y = \frac{2}{15}$$

$$\left(1-\frac{1}{6-6y}\right)y = \frac{2}{15}$$

$$\left(\frac{5-6y}{6-6y}\right)y = \frac{2}{15}$$

$$-90y^2 + 87y = 12$$

$$30y^2 - 29y + 4 = 0$$

$$y = \frac{-b \pm \sqrt{b^2 - 4ac}}{2a}$$

$$y = \frac{29 \pm \sqrt{(29)^2 - 4(30)(4)}}{60}$$

$$y = \frac{4}{5} \quad \text{or} \quad y = \frac{1}{6} \qquad \textbf{(2 Marks)}$$

From (2)

$$x = \frac{1}{6-6y}$$

if $y = \dfrac{4}{5}$

$$x = \frac{1}{6-6\left(\frac{4}{5}\right)} = \frac{5}{6}$$

if $y = \dfrac{1}{6}$

$$x = \frac{1}{6-6\left(\frac{1}{6}\right)} = \frac{1}{5}$$

$$\therefore\ P(A) = \frac{5}{6},\ P(B) = \frac{4}{5}$$

$$\text{or, } P(A) = \frac{1}{5},\ P(B) = \frac{1}{6} \qquad \textbf{(2 Marks)}$$

25. $f(x) = \sin x - \cos x,\ 0 < x < 2\pi$

On differentiating $f(x)$

$$\frac{d}{dx}f(x) = \cos x + \sin x \quad \dots(1) \qquad \textbf{(½ Mark)}$$

To find local maxima or local minima

$$\frac{d}{dx}f(x) = 0$$

$$\cos x = -\sin x$$

$$\tan x = -1$$

$$\Rightarrow x = \frac{3\pi}{4} \quad \text{or} \quad \frac{7\pi}{4} \qquad [\because\ 0 < x < 2\pi] \qquad \textbf{(1 Mark)}$$

Again differentiating (1)

$$\frac{d^2}{dx^2}f(x) = -\sin x + \cos x \qquad \textbf{(½ Mark)}$$

when, $x = \dfrac{3\pi}{4}$

$$\frac{d^2}{dx^2}f\left(\frac{3\pi}{4}\right) = -\sin\left(\frac{3\pi}{4}\right) + \cos\left(\frac{3\pi}{4}\right)$$

$$= -\frac{1}{\sqrt{2}} - \frac{1}{\sqrt{2}} = \frac{-2}{\sqrt{2}} = -\sqrt{2} < 0$$

$$\frac{d^2}{dx^2}f\left(\frac{3\pi}{4}\right) < 0$$

$\therefore\ x = \dfrac{3\pi}{4}$ is the point of local maximum   **(1 Mark)**

When $x = \dfrac{7\pi}{4}$

$$\frac{d^2}{dx^2}f\left(\frac{7\pi}{4}\right)$$

$$= -\sin\left(\frac{7\pi}{4}\right) - \cos\left(\frac{7\pi}{4}\right) = \frac{+1}{\sqrt{2}} + \frac{1}{\sqrt{2}} = +\sqrt{2} > 0$$

$$\frac{d^2 f}{dx^2}\left(\frac{7\pi}{4}\right) > 0$$

$\therefore\ x = \dfrac{7\pi}{4}$ is the point of local minimum   **(1 Mark)**

Local maximum value $= f\left(\dfrac{3\pi}{4}\right)$

$$= \sin\left(\frac{3\pi}{4}\right) - \cos\left(\frac{3\pi}{4}\right)$$

$$= \frac{1}{\sqrt{2}} + \frac{1}{\sqrt{2}} = \sqrt{2} \qquad \textbf{(1 Mark)}$$

Local minimum value $= f\left(\dfrac{7\pi}{4}\right)$

$$= \sin\left(\frac{7\pi}{4}\right) - \cos\left(\frac{7\pi}{4}\right)$$

$$= -\frac{1}{\sqrt{2}} - \frac{1}{\sqrt{2}} = -\sqrt{2} \qquad \textbf{(1 Mark)}$$

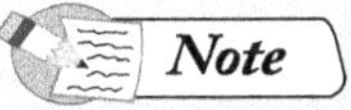

Note

General value if $\tan\theta = \tan\alpha$

$$\theta = n\pi + \alpha \qquad n \in Z$$

26. Given: $2x + 4y \leq 8$

$3x + y \leq 6$

$x + y \leq 4$

$x \geq 0, y \geq 0$

We first convert inequalities into equations to obtain lines

$$2x + 4y = 8$$
$$x + 2y = 4$$

x	0	4	2
y	2	0	1

$$x + y = 4$$

x	0	4	1
y	4	0	3

$$3x + y = 6$$

x	0	2	1
y	6	0	2

(1 Mark)

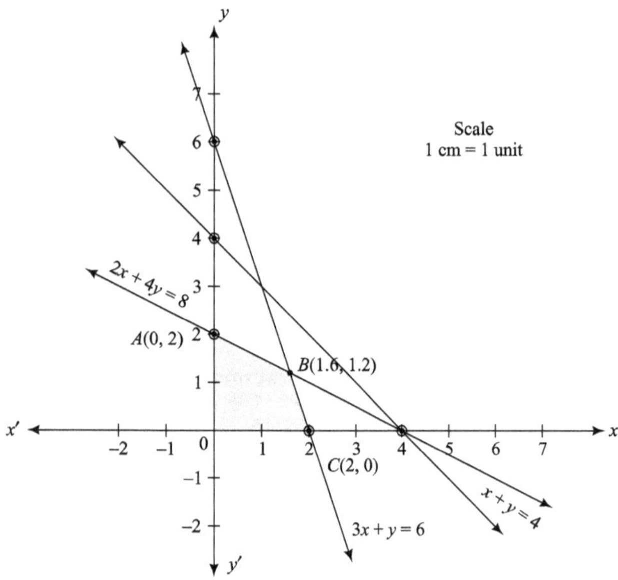

(2 Marks)

Point of intersection of $3x + y = 6$ & $2x + 4y = 8$ is (1.6, 1.2) **(1 Mark)**

Corner points are $O(0, 0)$, $A(0, 2)$, $B(1.6, 1.2)$, $C(2, 0)$

We have to maximize $Z = 2x + 5y$

Corner Points	**$Z = 2x + 5y$**
$O(0, 0)$	$Z = 0$
$A(0, 2)$	$Z = 10$ (maximum)
$B(1.6, 1.2)$	$Z = 1.6\,(2) + 5\,(1.2) = 9.2$
$C(2, 0)$	$Z = 4$

Z will be maximum at $A(0, 2)$

$\therefore$ Maximised value of Z is 10. **(2 Marks)**

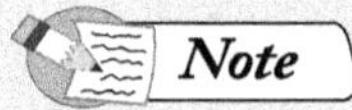 **Note**

The maximum value of an L.P.P. with bounded region is achieved at any corner point of the bounded region.

Time Allowed : 3 Hours   *Maximum Marks : 100*

General Instructions:

(i)   **All** questions are compulsory.

(ii)   The question paper consists of **29** questions divided into three sections A, B and C. Section A comprises of **10** questions of **one** mark each, section B comprises of **12** questions of **four** marks each and section C comprises of **07** questions of **six** marks each.

(iii)   All questions in Section A are to be answered in one word, one sentence or as per the exact requirement of the question.

(iv)   There is no overall choice. However, internal choice has been provided in **04** questions of **four** marks each and **02** questions of **six** marks each. You have to attempt only one of the alternatives in all such questions.

(v)   Use of calculator is not permitted. You may ask for logarithmic tables, if required.

SECTION - A

1. If R = {$(x, y) : x + 2y = 8$} is a relation on N, write the range of R.

2. If $\tan^{-1}x + \tan^{-1} y = \dfrac{\pi}{4}$, $xy < 1$, then write the value of $x + y + xy$.

3. If A is a square matrix such that $A^2 = A$, then write the value of $7A - (I + A)^3$, where I is an identity matrix.

4. If $\begin{bmatrix} x - y & z \\ 2x - y & w \end{bmatrix} = \begin{bmatrix} -1 & 4 \\ 0 & 5 \end{bmatrix}$, find the value of $x + y$.

5. If $\begin{vmatrix} 3x & 7 \\ -2 & 4 \end{vmatrix} = \begin{vmatrix} 8 & 7 \\ 6 & 4 \end{vmatrix}$, find the value of x.

6. If $f(x) = \displaystyle\int_0^x t \sin t \, dt$, then write the value of $f'(x)$

7. Evaluate: $\displaystyle\int_2^4 \dfrac{x}{x^2 + 1} dx$

8. Find the value of 'p' for which the vectors $3\hat{i} + 2\hat{j} + 9\hat{k}$ and $\hat{i} - 2p\hat{j} + 3\hat{k}$ are parallel.

9. Find $\vec{a}.(\vec{b} \times \vec{c})$, if $\vec{a} = 2\hat{i} + \hat{j} + 3\hat{k}$, $\vec{b} = -\hat{i} + 2\hat{j} + \hat{k}$ and $\vec{c} = 3\hat{i} + \hat{j} + 2\hat{k}$.

10. If the cartesian equations of a line are $\dfrac{3 - x}{5} = \dfrac{y + 4}{7} = \dfrac{2z - 6}{4}$, write the vector equation for the line.

SECTION - B

11. If the function $f : R \to R$ be given by $f(x) = x^2 + 2$ and $g : R \to R$ be given by $g(x) = \dfrac{x}{x - 1}$, $x \neq 1$, find fog and gof and hence find fog (2) and gof (–3).

12. Prove that
$$\tan^{-1}\left[\dfrac{\sqrt{1 + x} - \sqrt{1 - x}}{\sqrt{1 + x} + \sqrt{1 - x}}\right] = \dfrac{\pi}{4} - \dfrac{1}{2}\cos^{-1} x, \dfrac{-1}{\sqrt{2}} \leq x \leq 1$$

OR

If $\tan^{-1}\left(\dfrac{x - 2}{x - 4}\right) + \tan^{-1}\left(\dfrac{x + 2}{x + 4}\right) = \dfrac{\pi}{4}$, find the value of x.

13. Using properties of determinants, prove that
$$\begin{vmatrix} x + y & x & x \\ 5x + 4y & 4x & 2x \\ 10x + 8y & 8x & 3x \end{vmatrix} = x^3$$

14. Find the value of $\dfrac{dy}{dx}$ at $\theta = \dfrac{\pi}{4}$, if $x = ae^{\theta}(\sin\theta - \cos\theta)$ and $y = ae^{\theta}(\sin\theta + \cos\theta)$

15. If $y = Pe^{ax} + Qe^{bx}$, show that $\dfrac{d^2 y}{dx^2} - (a + b)\dfrac{dy}{dx} + aby = 0$.

16. Find the value(s) of x for which $y = [x(x - 2)]^2$ is an increasing function.

OR

Find the equations of the tangent and normal to the curve $\dfrac{x^2}{a^2} - \dfrac{y^2}{b^2} = 1$ at the point $(\sqrt{2}\,a, b)$.

17. Evaluate: $\displaystyle\int_0^{\pi}\frac{4x\sin x}{1+\cos^2 x}\,dx$

OR

Evaluate: $\displaystyle\int\frac{x+2}{\sqrt{x^2+5x+6}}\,dx$

18. Find the particular solution of the differential equation $\dfrac{dy}{dx}=1+x+y+xy$, given that $y=0$ when $x=1$.

19. Solve the differential equation

$$(1+x^2)\frac{dy}{dx}+y=e^{\tan^{-1}x}$$

20. Show that the four points A, B, C and D with position vectors $4\hat{i}+5\hat{j}+\hat{k},\ -\hat{j}-\hat{k},\ 3\hat{i}+9\hat{j}+4\hat{k}$ and $4(-\hat{i}+\hat{j}+\hat{k})$ respectively are coplanar.

OR

The scalar product of the vector $\vec{a}=\hat{i}+\hat{j}+\hat{k}$ with a unit vector along the sum of vectors $\vec{b}=2\hat{i}+4\hat{j}-5\hat{k}$ and $\vec{c}=\lambda\hat{i}+2\hat{j}+3\hat{k}$ is equal to one. Find the value of λ and hence find the unit vector along $\vec{b}+\vec{c}$.

21. A line passes through $(2,-1,3)$ and is perpendicular to the lines

$$\vec{r}=(\hat{i}+\hat{j}-\hat{k})+\lambda(2\hat{i}-2\hat{j}+\hat{k})\ \text{and}$$

$$\vec{r}=(2\hat{i}-\hat{j}-3\hat{k})+\mu(\hat{i}+2\hat{j}+2\hat{k}).$$

Obtain its equation in vector and cartesian form.

22. An experiment succeeds thrice as often as it fails. Find the probability that in the next five trials, there will be at least 3 successes.

SECTION - C

23. Two schools A and B want to award their selected students on the values of sincerity, truthfulness and helpfulness. The school A wants to award ₹ x each, ₹ y each and ₹ z each for the three respective values to 3, 2 and 1 students respectively with a total award money of ₹ 1,600. School B wants to spend ₹ 2,300 to award its 4, 1 and 3 students on the respective values (by giving the same award money to the three values as before). If the total amount of award for one prize on each value is ₹ 900, using matrices, find the award money for each value. Apart from these three values, suggest one more value which should be considered for award.

24. Show that the altitude of the right circular cone of maximum volume that can be inscribed in a sphere of radius r is $\dfrac{4r}{3}$.

Also show that the maximum volume of the cone is $\dfrac{8}{27}$ of the volume of the sphere.

25. Evaluate: $\displaystyle\int\frac{1}{\cos^4 x+\sin^4 x}\,dx$

26. Using integration, find the area of the region bounded by the triangle whose vertices are $(-1,2)$, $(1,5)$ and $(3,4)$.

27. Find the equation of the plane through the line of intersection of the planes $x+y+z=1$ and $2x+3y+4z=5$ which is perpendicular to the plane $x-y+z=0$. Also find the distance of the plane obtained above, from the origin.

OR

Find the distance of the point $(2,12,5)$ from the point of intersection of the line $\vec{r}=2\hat{i}-4\hat{j}+2\hat{k}+\lambda(3\hat{i}+4\hat{j}+2\hat{k})$ and the plane $\vec{r}.(\hat{i}-2\hat{j}+\hat{k})=0$

28. A manufacturing company makes two types of teaching aids A and B of Mathematics for class XII. Each type of A requires 9 labour hours for fabricating and 1 labour hour for finishing. Each type of B requires 12 labour hours for fabricating and 3 labour hours for finishing. For fabricating and finishing, the maximum labour hours available per week are 180 and 30 respectively. The company makes a profit of ₹ 80 on each piece of type A and ₹ 120 on each piece of type B. How many pieces of type A and type B should be manufactured per week to get a maximum profit? Make it as an LPP and solve graphically. What is the maximum profit per week?

29. There are three coins. One is a two-headed coin (having head on both faces), another is a biased coin that comes up heads 75% of the times and third is also a biased coin that comes up tails 40% of the times. One of the three coins is chosen at random and tossed, and it shows heads. What is the probability that it was the two-headed coin?

OR

Two numbers are selected at random (without replacement) from the first six positive integers. Let X denote the larger of the two numbers obtained. Find the probability distribution of the random variable X, and hence find the mean of the distribution.

Solutions

SECTION - A

1. $R = \{(x, y) : x + 2y = 8\}$

$x = 1$, $y = \dfrac{7}{2} \notin N$, $x = 5$, $y = \dfrac{3}{2} \notin N$

$x = 2$, $y = 3 \in N$, $x = 6$, $y = 1 \in N$

$x = 3$, $y = \dfrac{5}{2} \notin N$, $x = 7$, $y = \dfrac{1}{2} \notin N$

$x = 4, y = 2, \in N, x = 8, y = 0 \notin N$

$\therefore$ Range $(R) = \{1, 2, 3\}$ **(1 Mark)**

2. $\tan^{-1} x + \tan^{-1} y = \dfrac{\pi}{4}$, $xy < 1$

$\Rightarrow \quad \tan^{-1}\left(\dfrac{x+y}{1-xy}\right) = \dfrac{\pi}{4}$ **(½ Mark)**

$\Rightarrow \quad \dfrac{x+y}{1-xy} = \tan\dfrac{\pi}{4}$

$\Rightarrow \quad \dfrac{x+y}{1-xy} = 1$

$\Rightarrow \quad x + y = 1 - xy$

$\Rightarrow \quad x + y + xy = 1$ **(½ Mark)**

3. $A^2 = A$ (Given)

We have,

$7A - (I + A)^3$

$= 7A - (I^3 + A^3 + 3I^2 A + 3IA^2)$

$= 7A - (I + A^2 . A + 3IA + 3IA)$

$= 7A - (I + A^2 + 3A + 3A)$

$= 7A - (I + A + 6A)$

$= 7A - I - 7A$

$\therefore 7A - (I + A)^3 = -I$ **(1 Mark)**

4. We have

$\begin{bmatrix} x-y & z \\ 2x-y & w \end{bmatrix} = \begin{bmatrix} -1 & 4 \\ 0 & 5 \end{bmatrix}$

By the equality of matrices, we have

$x - y = -1$, $2x - y = 0$

On subtracting, we get

$$\begin{array}{r} 2x - y = 0 \\ x - y = -1 \\ \underline{- \quad + \quad +} \\ x = 1 \end{array}$$

$\Rightarrow \quad y = 2$

$\therefore \quad x + y = 3$ **(1 Mark)**

5. $\begin{vmatrix} 3x & 7 \\ -2 & 4 \end{vmatrix} = \begin{vmatrix} 8 & 7 \\ 6 & 4 \end{vmatrix}$

$\Rightarrow 12x + 14 = 32 - 42$

$\Rightarrow 12x = -10 - 14$

$\Rightarrow 12x = -24$

$\Rightarrow x = -2$ **(1 Mark)**

6. Let $f(x) = \int\limits_{0}^{x} t \sin t \, dt$

$f(x) = -t \cos t \Big|_{0}^{x} + \int\limits_{0}^{x} \cos t \, dt$

$f(x) = -x \cos x + \sin t \Big|_{0}^{x}$

$f(x) = -x \cos x + \sin x$

$f'(x) = -x(-\sin x) - \cos x + \cos x$

$\qquad = x \sin x$ **(1 Mark)**

 **Note**

Integration is also called antiderivative. So, if $f(x) = \int g(x)dx$ then $f'(x) = g(x)$.

7. $I = \int\limits_{2}^{4} \dfrac{x}{x^2 + 1} dx$

Put $x^2 + 1 = t$

$2x \cdot dx = dt$

$\therefore \quad x\,dx = \dfrac{dt}{2}$ **(1 Mark)**

When $x = 2$, $t = 5$

$x = 4$, $t = 17$

$I = \int_{5}^{17} \dfrac{1}{2t} dt = \dfrac{1}{2} \big[\log t\big]_{5}^{17}$

$I = \dfrac{1}{2}\left(\log \dfrac{17}{5}\right)$ **(1 Mark)**

8. Given $3\hat{i} + 2\hat{j} + 9\hat{k}$ and $\hat{i} - 2p\hat{j} + 3\hat{k}$ are parallel.

$\dfrac{3}{1} = \dfrac{2}{-2p} = \dfrac{9}{3}$

$\Rightarrow \dfrac{3}{1} = \dfrac{-1}{p} \Rightarrow p = \dfrac{-1}{3}$

 **Note**

If two lines are parallel and having direction ratios proportional to a_1, b_1, c_1 and $a_2, b_2, c_2,$ then $\dfrac{a_1}{a_2} = \dfrac{b_1}{b_2} = \dfrac{c_1}{c_2}$

9. $\vec{a} = 2\hat{i} + \hat{j} + 3\hat{k}$, $\vec{b} = -\hat{i} + 2\hat{j} + \hat{k}$ and $\vec{c} = 3\hat{i} + \hat{j} + 2\hat{k}$

We have,

$\vec{b} \times \vec{c} = \begin{vmatrix} \hat{i} & \hat{j} & \hat{k} \\ -1 & 2 & 1 \\ 3 & 1 & 2 \end{vmatrix}$

$$= (4-1)\,\hat{i} - (-2-3)\,\hat{j} + (-1-6)\,\hat{k}$$
$$= 3\hat{i} + 5\hat{j} - 7\hat{k} \qquad \text{(½ Mark)}$$

Now, $\vec{a}.(\vec{b} \times \vec{c}) = (2\hat{i} + \hat{j} + 3\hat{k}).(3\hat{i} + 5\hat{j} - 7\hat{k})$
$$= 6 + 5 - 21 = -10 \qquad \text{(½ Mark)}$$

10. Given equations of line.

$$\frac{x-3}{-5} = \frac{y+4}{7} = \frac{z-3}{2}$$

Comparing the given equation with the standard form:

$$\frac{x-x_1}{a} = \frac{y-y_1}{b} = \frac{z-z_1}{c}, \text{ we get}$$

$$x_1 = 3,\ y_1 = -4,\ z_1 = 3$$
$$a = -5,\ b = 7,\ c = 2$$

Let $\vec{r}$ be the position vector of any point on the line, then the vector equation of the line is given by

$$\vec{r} = 3\hat{i} - 4\hat{j} + 3\hat{k} + \lambda(-5\hat{i} + 7\hat{j} + 2\hat{k}) \qquad \text{(1 Mark)}$$

SECTION - B

11. Let $f(x) = x^2 + 2$ and $g(x) = \dfrac{x}{x-1},\ x \neq 1$

Consider

$$\text{fog}(x) = f[g(x)] = f\left[\frac{x}{x-1}\right] = \left[\frac{x}{x-1}\right]^2 + 2$$

$$= \frac{x^2 + 2x^2 + 2 - 4x}{(x^2 + 1 - 2x)} = \frac{3x^2 - 4x + 2}{x^2 - 2x + 1} \qquad \text{(1 Mark)}$$

$$\text{gof}(x) = g[f(x)] = g[x^2 + 2]$$

$$= \frac{x^2 + 2}{x^2 + 2 - 1} = \frac{x^2 + 2}{x^2 + 1} \qquad \text{(1 Mark)}$$

Now, $\text{gof}(-3) = \dfrac{(-3)^2 + 2}{(-3)^2 + 1} = \dfrac{9+2}{9+1} = \dfrac{11}{10} \qquad \text{(1 Mark)}$

and $\text{fog}(2) = \dfrac{3(2)^2 - 4(2) + 2}{(2)^2 - 2(2) + 1} = \dfrac{12 - 8 + 2}{4 - 4 + 1} = 6 \qquad \text{(1 Mark)}$

12. L.H.S.

$$\tan^{-1}\left[\frac{\sqrt{1+x} - \sqrt{1-x}}{\sqrt{1+x} + \sqrt{1-x}}\right]$$

Put $x = \cos 2\theta \Rightarrow \theta = \dfrac{1}{2}\cos^{-1} x$

$$= \tan^{-1}\left[\frac{\sqrt{1+\cos 2\theta} - \sqrt{1-\cos 2\theta}}{\sqrt{1+\cos 2\theta} + \sqrt{1-\cos 2\theta}}\right]$$

$$= \tan^{-1}\left[\frac{\sqrt{2\cos^2\theta} - \sqrt{2\sin^2\theta}}{\sqrt{2\cos^2\theta} + \sqrt{2\sin^2\theta}}\right] \qquad \text{(1 Mark)}$$

$$= \tan^{-1}\left[\frac{\cos\theta - \sin\theta}{\cos\theta + \sin\theta}\right] \qquad \text{(1 Mark)}$$

$$= \tan^{-1}\left[\frac{1 - \tan\theta}{1 + \tan\theta}\right] = \tan^{-1}\left[\tan\left(\frac{\pi}{4} - \theta\right)\right]$$

$$= \frac{\pi}{4} - \theta = \frac{\pi}{4} - \frac{1}{2}\cos^{-1}x,\ \frac{-1}{\sqrt{2}} \le x \le 1 \qquad \text{(2 Marks)}$$

= R.H.S.
Hence proved.

 **Note**

Another method to solve it by rationalise the denominator then put $x = \sin q$ and use formula $1 - \cos\theta = 2\sin^2\theta/2$, $\sin\theta = 2\sin\theta/2 \cos\theta/2$

OR

Let $\tan^{-1}\left[\dfrac{x-2}{x-4}\right] + \tan^{-1}\left[\dfrac{x+2}{x+4}\right] = \dfrac{\pi}{4}$

$$\Rightarrow \tan^{-1}\left(\frac{\dfrac{x-2}{x-4} + \dfrac{x+2}{x+4}}{1 - \dfrac{x-2}{x-4} \times \dfrac{x+2}{x+4}}\right) = \frac{\pi}{4} \qquad \text{(1 Mark)}$$

$$\Rightarrow \frac{(x-2)(x+4) + (x+2)(x-4)}{(x-4)(x+4) - (x-2)(x+2)} = \tan\frac{\pi}{4} \qquad \text{(1 Mark)}$$

$$\Rightarrow (x-2)(x+4) + (x+2)(x-4) = (x^2 - 16) - (x^2 - 4)$$
$$\Rightarrow x^2 + 2x - 8 + x^2 - 2x - 8 = -12$$
$$\Rightarrow 2x^2 - 16 + 12 = 0$$
$$\Rightarrow 2x^2 = 4 \Rightarrow x^2 = 2$$
$$\Rightarrow x = \pm\sqrt{2} \qquad \text{(2 Marks)}$$

13. Let $\Delta = \begin{vmatrix} x+y & x & x \\ 5x+4y & 4x & 2x \\ 10x+8y & 8x & 3x \end{vmatrix}$

Take x common from C_2 and C_3

$$\Delta = x^2 \begin{vmatrix} x+y & 1 & 1 \\ 5x+4y & 4 & 2 \\ 10x+8y & 8 & 3 \end{vmatrix} \qquad \text{(1 Mark)}$$

Apply $R_3 \to R_3 - R_2$

$$\Delta = x^2 \begin{vmatrix} x+y & 1 & 1 \\ 5x+4y & 4 & 2 \\ 5x+4y & 4 & 1 \end{vmatrix} \qquad \text{(1 Mark)}$$

Apply $R_2 \to R_2 - R_3$

$$\Delta = x^2 \begin{vmatrix} x+y & 1 & 1 \\ 0 & 0 & 1 \\ 5x+4y & 4 & 1 \end{vmatrix} \qquad \text{(1 Mark)}$$

$$= x^2\left[(x+y)(-4) - 1(-5x-4y) + 1(0)\right]$$

$= x^2[-4x - 4y + 5x + 4y] = x^2(x) = x^3$

Hence proved.   **(1 Mark)**

14. Let $x = ae^{\theta}(\sin\theta - \cos\theta)$

$$\frac{dx}{d\theta} = ae^{\theta}(\cos\theta + \sin\theta) + (\sin\theta - \cos\theta)a.e^{\theta}$$

$$= 2ae^{\theta}\sin\theta \qquad \textbf{(1 Mark)}$$

$y = ae^{\theta}(\sin\theta + \cos\theta)$

$$\frac{dy}{d\theta} = ae^{\theta}[\cos\theta - \sin\theta] + [\sin\theta + \cos\theta]a.e^{\theta}$$

$$= 2ae^{\theta}\cos\theta \qquad \textbf{(1 Mark)}$$

Now, $\dfrac{dy}{dx} = \dfrac{dy}{d\theta} \times \dfrac{d\theta}{dx} = \dfrac{2ae^{\theta}\cos\theta}{2ae^{\theta}\sin\theta} = \cot\theta$

Now, $\dfrac{dy}{dx}\bigg|_{\theta=\frac{\pi}{4}} = \cot\dfrac{\pi}{4} = 1$ **(2 Marks)**

15. Let $y = Pe^{ax} + Qe^{bx}$

$$\frac{dy}{dx} = Pae^{ax} + Qbe^{bx} \qquad .....(1)$$

$$\frac{d^2y}{dx^2} = Pa^2 e^{ax} + Qb^2 e^{bx} \qquad .....(2) \qquad \textbf{(1 Mark)}$$

$aby = ab[Pe^{ax} + Q\,e^{bx}]$

$aby = P\,a\,b\,e^{ax} + Q\,a\,b\,e^{bx}]\quad .....(3)$ **(1 Mark)**

Consider

$$\frac{d^2y}{dx^2} - (a+b)\frac{dy}{dx} + aby$$

$= (Pa^2 e^{ax} + Q.\,b^2\,e^{bx}) - (a+b)(Pae^{ax} + Q.be^{bx}) + Pabe^{ax}$
$\qquad\qquad\qquad\qquad + Q\,abe^{bx}\ \text{(from 1, 2 and 3)}$

$= Pa^2 e^{ax} + Q\,b^2\,e^{bx} - Pa^2 e^{ax} - Q.b^2\,e^{bx} - Pabe^{ax}$
$\qquad\qquad\qquad - Q\,a\,b\,e^{bx} + P\,a\,b\,e^{ax} + Q\,a\,b\,e^{bx} = 0$

Hence proved.   **(2 Marks)**

16. Let $f(x) = [x(x-2)]^2$

$f'(x) = 2[x(x-2)][x + x - 2]$

$= 2[x^2 - 2x][2x - 2]$

$= 4x(x-2)(x-1)$ **(1 Mark)**

For $f(x)$ to be increasing $f'(x) \geq 0$ **(1 Mark)**

$\Rightarrow\quad 4x(x-2)(x-1) \geq 0$

−   +   −   +
←—+—+—+—→
  0   1   2

$x \in [0, 1],\ \cup[2, \infty]$ **(2 Marks)**

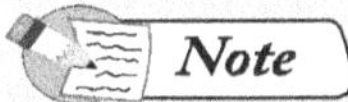

Real valued function f(x) of domain I is said to be

(i) Increasing on I if $x_1 < x_2$ then $f(x_1) \leq f(x_2)$, $\forall\ x_1, x_2 \in I$.

(ii) Decreasing on I if $x_1 < x_2$ then $f(x_1) \geq f(x_2)$, $\forall\ x_1, x_2 \in I$

OR

We have $\dfrac{x^2}{a^2} - \dfrac{y^2}{b^2} = 1$

Differentiating *w.r.t. x*, we get

$$\frac{2x}{a^2} - \frac{2y}{b^2}\frac{dy}{dx} = 0$$

$$\frac{dy}{dx} = \frac{b^2 x}{a^2 y} \qquad \textbf{(½ Mark)}$$

Now

$$\left(\frac{dy}{dx}\right)_{(\sqrt{2}\,a, b)} = \frac{b^2\sqrt{2}a}{a^2 b}$$

slope of the tangent $= \dfrac{\sqrt{2}b}{a}$ **(½ Mark)**

Since (x_0, y_0) lies on $\dfrac{x^2}{a^2} - \dfrac{y^2}{b^2} = 1$

$$\therefore\quad \frac{x_0^2}{a^2} - \frac{y_0^2}{b^2} = 1 \qquad .....(i)$$

Equation of the tangent is

$$y - y_0 = \frac{\sqrt{2}b}{a}(x - x_0) \Rightarrow y - b = \frac{\sqrt{2}b}{a}(x - \sqrt{2}a)$$

$$b\sqrt{2}x - ay - ab = 0 \qquad \textbf{(1 Mark)}$$

Now, slope of the normal is

$$\frac{-1}{\left(\dfrac{dy}{dx}\right)_{(\sqrt{2}a, b)}} = -\frac{a}{\sqrt{2}b} \qquad \textbf{(1 Mark)}$$

Equation of the normal is

$$y - y_0 = \frac{-a^2 y_0}{b^2 x_0}(x - x_0) \Rightarrow \frac{y - y_0}{a^2 y_0} + \frac{x - x_0}{b^2 x_0} = 0$$

$$\Rightarrow\quad \frac{y - b}{a^2 b} + \frac{x - \sqrt{2}a}{\sqrt{2}ab} = 0$$

$$\Rightarrow\quad (y - b)\sqrt{2}b + a(x - \sqrt{2}a) = 0$$

$$\Rightarrow\quad b\sqrt{2}y - \sqrt{2}b^2 + ax - \sqrt{2}a^2 = 0$$

$$\Rightarrow\quad ax + b\sqrt{2}y - \sqrt{2}(a^2 + b^2) = 0 \qquad \textbf{(1 Mark)}$$

17. Let $I = \displaystyle\int_0^{\pi} \frac{4x\sin x}{1 + \cos^2 x}\,dx \qquad .....(1)$

$$I = \int_0^\pi \frac{4(\pi - x)\sin(\pi - x)}{1 + \cos^2(\pi - x)}\,dx \qquad \textbf{(½ Mark)}$$

$$\left[\because \int_0^a f(x)\,dx = \int_0^a f(a - x)\,dx \right] \qquad \textbf{(½ Mark)}$$

$$I = \int_0^\pi \frac{(4\pi - 4x)\sin x}{1 + \cos^2 x}\,dx \qquad .....(2)$$

On adding (1) and (2), we get

$$2I = \int_0^\pi \frac{4\pi \sin x}{1 + \cos^2 x}\,dx \qquad \textbf{(1 Mark)}$$

$$= 4\pi \int_1^{-1} \frac{-dt}{1 + t^2} \qquad \left[\because \cos x = t,\ \sin x\, dx = -dt \right]$$

where $t = \cos x$
when $x = 0,\ t = 1$
$x = \pi,\ t = -1$

$$= -4\pi \int_{-1}^{1} \frac{dt}{1 + t^2} = 4\pi (\tan^{-1} t)_{-1}^{1} \qquad \textbf{(1 Mark)}$$

$$\left[\because \int_a^b f(x)\,dx = -\int_b^a f(x)\,dx \right]$$

$$= -4\pi \left[\tan^{-1}(1) - \tan^{-1}(-1) \right]$$

$$= -4\pi \left[\frac{\pi}{4} - \frac{3\pi}{4} \right] = -2\pi^2$$

$$\therefore \quad I = \pi^2 \qquad \textbf{(1 Mark)}$$

OR

Let $I = \int \dfrac{x + 2}{\sqrt{x^2 + 5x + 6}}\,dx$

$$= \frac{1}{2} \int \frac{2x + 4}{\sqrt{x^2 + 5x + 6}}\,dx$$

$$= \frac{1}{2} \int \frac{2x + 5 - 1}{\sqrt{x^2 + 5x + 6}}\,dx$$

$$= \frac{1}{2} \int \frac{(2x + 5)\,dx}{\sqrt{x^2 + 5x + 6}} - \frac{1}{2} \int \frac{dx}{\sqrt{x^2 + 5x + 6}} \qquad \textbf{(1 Mark)}$$

Consider

$$I_1 = \frac{1}{2} \int \frac{(2x + 5)\,dx}{\sqrt{x^2 + 5x + 6}}$$

Let $x^2 + 5x + 6 = t^2$

$$(2x + 5)\,dx = 2t\,dt$$

$$= \frac{1}{2} \int \frac{2t\,dt}{t} = \sqrt{x^2 + 5x + 6} \qquad \textbf{(1 Mark)}$$

$$I_2 = \int \frac{dx}{\sqrt{x^2 + 5x + 6}} = \int \frac{dx}{\sqrt{\left(x + \dfrac{5}{2}\right)^2 - \left(\dfrac{1}{2}\right)^2}}$$

$$= \log \left| \left(x + \frac{5}{2}\right) + \sqrt{\left(x + \frac{5}{2}\right)^2 - \left(\frac{1}{2}\right)^2} \right| + C \qquad \textbf{(1 Mark)}$$

$$= \log \left| \left(x + \frac{5}{2}\right) + \sqrt{x^2 + 5x + 6} \right| + C$$

$$= \log \left| \left(\frac{2x + 5}{2}\right) + \sqrt{x^2 + 5x + 6} \right| + C \qquad \textbf{(½ Mark)}$$

$$I = \sqrt{x^2 + 5x + 6} + \frac{1}{2}\left[\log \left| \frac{2x + 5}{2} + \sqrt{x^2 + 5x + 6} \right| \right] + C \qquad \textbf{(½ Mark)}$$

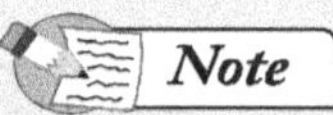

Note

Whenever there is a square root of quadratic equation in denominator, to simply the integeration, try to make perfect square of the equation.

18. Consider

$$\frac{dy}{dx} = 1 + x + y + xy$$

$$= 1 + x + y(1 + x)$$

$$= (1 + x)(1 + y) \qquad \textbf{(1 Mark)}$$

$$\Rightarrow \quad \frac{dy}{1 + y} = (1 + x)\,dx \quad \Rightarrow \quad \int \frac{dy}{1 + y} = \int (1 + x)\,dx$$

$$\Rightarrow \quad \log(1 + y) = x + \frac{x^2}{2} + C \qquad \textbf{(1 Mark)}$$

Putting $y = 0$ and $x = 1$, we get

$$\log 1 = 1 + \frac{1}{2} + C \Rightarrow C = \frac{-3}{2} \qquad \textbf{(1 Mark)}$$

$\therefore$ Particular solution is

$$\log(1 + y) = x + \frac{x^2}{2} - \frac{3}{2} \qquad \textbf{(1 Mark)}$$

19. Consider $(1 + x^2)\dfrac{dy}{dx} + y = e^{\tan^{-1} x}$

Dividing both the sides by $(1 + x^2)$, we get

$$\frac{dy}{dx} + \frac{y}{1+x^2} = \frac{e^{\tan^{-1}x}}{1+x^2}$$　　　(Linear form)　**(1 Mark)**

$$\text{I.F.} = e^{\int \frac{1}{1+x^2}dx} = e^{\tan^{-1}x}$$　　**(1 Mark)**

$$y(\text{I.F.}) = \int Q.\text{I.F.} + C$$

$$y.e^{\tan^{-1}x} = \int \frac{(e^{\tan^{-1}x})e^{\tan^{-1}x}}{1+x^2}dx + C$$

$$y.e^{\tan^{-1}x} = \int \frac{(e^{2\tan^{-1}x})}{1+x^2}dx + C$$　　**(1 Mark)**

Let $t = \tan^{-1}x$, $dt = \frac{1}{1+x^2}dx$

$$y.e^{\tan^{-1}x} = \int e^{2t}dt + C,$$

$$\Rightarrow y.e^{\tan^{-1}x} = \frac{e^{2\tan^{-1}x}}{2} + C$$　　**(1 Mark)**

20.　Let　$A = 4\hat{i} + 5\hat{j} + \hat{k}$

　　　　$B = -\hat{j} - \hat{k}$

　　　　$C = 3\hat{i} + 9\hat{j} + 4\hat{k}$

　　　　$D = 4(-\hat{i} + \hat{j} + \hat{k})$

Now, $\overrightarrow{AB} = -4\hat{i} - 6\hat{j} - 2\hat{k}$

　　　　$\overrightarrow{AC} = -\hat{i} + 4\hat{j} + 3\hat{k}$

　　　　$\overrightarrow{AD} = -8\hat{i} - \hat{j} + 3\hat{k}$　　**(1 Mark)**

These points are coplanar if the vectors $\overrightarrow{AB}$, $\overrightarrow{AC}$ and $\overrightarrow{AD}$ are coplanar.　　**(1 Mark)**

$$\left[\overrightarrow{AB}\ \overrightarrow{AC}\ \overrightarrow{AD}\right] = \begin{vmatrix} -4 & -6 & -2 \\ -1 & 4 & 3 \\ -8 & -1 & 3 \end{vmatrix}$$　　**(1 Mark)**

$= -4(12+3) + 6(-3+24) - 2(1+32)$
$= -60 + 126 - 66 = 0$
$\therefore$ Points A, B, C, D are coplanar.　　**(1 Mark)**

OR

Let $\vec{a} = \hat{i} + \hat{j} + \hat{k}$, $\vec{b} = 2\hat{i} + 4\hat{j} - 5\hat{k}$

$\vec{c} = \lambda\hat{i} + 2\hat{j} + 3\hat{k}$

$\vec{b} + \vec{c} = (2+\lambda)\hat{i} + 6\hat{j} - 2\hat{k}$

Let $\vec{r}$ be the unit vector along $\vec{b} + \vec{c}$

$$\therefore\quad \vec{r} = \frac{\vec{b}+\vec{c}}{|\vec{b}+\vec{c}|} = \frac{(2+\lambda)\hat{i} + 6\hat{j} - 2\hat{k}}{\sqrt{(2+\lambda)^2 + 40}}$$　　**(2 Marks)**

Now, $(\hat{i} + \hat{j} + \hat{k}).\hat{r} = 1$　　**(1 Mark)**

$\Rightarrow\ (\hat{i} + \hat{j} + \hat{k}) . \{(2+\lambda)\hat{i} + 6\hat{j} - 2\hat{k}\}$

$\qquad = \sqrt{(2+\lambda)^2 + 40}$
$\Rightarrow\ (\lambda+6)^2 = (2+\lambda)^2 + 40$
$\Rightarrow 8\lambda = 8 \Rightarrow \lambda = 1$　　**(1 Mark)**

21.　Let $\vec{r} = \vec{a} + \lambda\vec{b}$ be the vector form of the required equation. where $\vec{a}$ is the position vector and vector equation parallel to vector $\vec{b}$. Since, $a\hat{i} + b\hat{j} + c\hat{k}$ is perpendicular to the given lines

$\therefore\quad 2a - 2b + c = 0$　　　　　　.....(1)
$\qquad a + 2b + 2c = 0$　　　　　　.....(2)　**(1 Mark)**
On solving (1) and (2), we get
$\qquad a = 2b, c = -2b$
$\therefore\quad a : b : c = (2 : 1 : -2)$　　**(1 Mark)**
Also, required vector equation passes through $(2, -1, 3)$.

Hence, required vector equation is $\vec{r} = (2\hat{i} - \hat{j} + 3\hat{k})$

$+ \lambda(2\hat{i} + \hat{j} - 2\hat{k})$ and Cartesian form of equation is

$$\frac{x-2}{2} = \frac{y+1}{1} = \frac{z-3}{-2}$$　　**(2 Marks)**

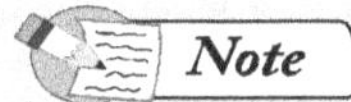

Note

Vector product of two vectors is vector which is perpendicular to these two vectors. So, another method to find direction cosine of required vector by $\vec{b_1} \times \vec{b_2}$.

22.　Let p denote the probability of succeeding in the experiment.

Given: $p = 3(1-p) \Rightarrow p = \frac{3}{4}$　　**(1 Mark)**

Let X = number of successes in 5 trials.
$\Rightarrow$　X follows binomial distribution with

$$n = 5,\ p = \frac{3}{4}, q = \frac{1}{4}\ \text{such that}$$　　**(½ Mark)**

$$P(X = r) = {}^5C_r\left(\frac{3}{4}\right)^r\left(\frac{1}{4}\right)^{5-r},\ r = 0, 1, 2, ..., 5$$　　**(½ Mark)**

Required probability = $P(X \geq 3)$
$= P(X=3) + P(X=4) + P(X=5)$

$$= {}^5C_3\left(\frac{3}{4}\right)^3\left(\frac{1}{4}\right)^2 + {}^5C_4\left(\frac{3}{4}\right)^4\left(\frac{1}{4}\right)^1 + {}^5C_5\left(\frac{3}{4}\right)^5$$

$$= 10\left(\frac{3}{4}\right)^3\left(\frac{1}{4}\right)^2 + 5\left(\frac{3}{4}\right)^4\left(\frac{1}{4}\right) + \left(\frac{3}{4}\right)^5$$

$$= \left(\frac{3}{4}\right)^3\left[\frac{10}{16} + 5\times\frac{3}{4}\times\frac{1}{4} + \frac{3\times3}{4\times4}\right]$$

$$= \frac{27}{64}\left[\frac{10}{16} + \frac{15}{16} + \frac{9}{16}\right]$$

$$= \frac{27}{64}\times\frac{34}{16} = \frac{27}{32}\times\frac{17}{16} = \frac{459}{512}$$ **(2 Marks)**

SECTION - C

23. The given information can be written as

$$3x + 2y + z = 1600 \qquad ....(1)$$
$$4x + y + 3z = 2300 \qquad ....(2)$$
$$x + y + z = 900 \qquad ....(3)$$

where,

$$A = \begin{bmatrix} 3 & 2 & 1 \\ 4 & 1 & 3 \\ 1 & 1 & 1 \end{bmatrix}, \quad B = \begin{bmatrix} 1600 \\ 2300 \\ 900 \end{bmatrix} \text{ and } X = \begin{bmatrix} x \\ y \\ z \end{bmatrix}$$

$$AX = B$$
$$\Rightarrow \quad X = A^{-1}B \qquad \textbf{(1 Mark)}$$

Now,

$$|A| = [3(1-3) - 2(4-3) + 1(4-1)]$$
$$= [3(-2) - 2\times1 + 3]$$
$$|A| = -5 \neq 0$$

So, A is invertible. **(1 Mark)**

Let C_{ij} be the cofactor of a_{ij} in $A = \begin{bmatrix} a_{ij} \end{bmatrix}$

We have

$$C_{11} = (-1)^2\begin{vmatrix} 1 & 3 \\ 1 & 1 \end{vmatrix} = -2$$

$$C_{12} = (-1)^3\begin{vmatrix} 4 & 3 \\ 1 & 1 \end{vmatrix} = -1$$

$$C_{13} = (-1)^4\begin{vmatrix} 4 & 1 \\ 1 & 1 \end{vmatrix} = 3$$

$$C_{21} = (-1)^3\begin{vmatrix} 2 & 1 \\ 1 & 1 \end{vmatrix} = -1$$

$$C_{22} = (-1)^4\begin{vmatrix} 3 & 1 \\ 1 & 1 \end{vmatrix} = 2$$

$$C_{23} = (-1)^5\begin{vmatrix} 3 & 2 \\ 1 & 1 \end{vmatrix} = -1$$

$$C_{31} = (-1)^4\begin{vmatrix} 2 & 1 \\ 1 & 3 \end{vmatrix} = 5$$

$$C_{32} = (-1)^5\begin{vmatrix} 3 & 1 \\ 4 & 3 \end{vmatrix} = -5$$

$$C_{33} = (-1)^6\begin{vmatrix} 3 & 2 \\ 4 & 1 \end{vmatrix} = -5$$

$$\therefore \quad adj\,A = \begin{bmatrix} -2 & -1 & 3 \\ -1 & 2 & -1 \\ 5 & -5 & -5 \end{bmatrix}^t \qquad \textbf{(1 Mark)}$$

$$= \begin{bmatrix} -2 & -1 & 5 \\ -1 & 2 & -5 \\ 3 & -1 & -5 \end{bmatrix}$$

$$A^{-1} = \frac{1}{|A|}adj\,A \Rightarrow \frac{1}{-5}\begin{bmatrix} -2 & -1 & 5 \\ -1 & 2 & -5 \\ 3 & -1 & -5 \end{bmatrix} \qquad \textbf{(1 Mark)}$$

Thus, the solution of the system of equations is given by $X = A^{-1}B$

$$X = \frac{1}{-5}\begin{bmatrix} -2 & -1 & 5 \\ -1 & 2 & -5 \\ 3 & -1 & -5 \end{bmatrix}\begin{bmatrix} 1600 \\ 2300 \\ 900 \end{bmatrix}$$

$$= \frac{1}{-5}\begin{bmatrix} -3200 - 2300 + 4500 \\ -1600 + 4600 - 4500 \\ 4800 - 2300 - 4500 \end{bmatrix}$$

$$X = -\frac{1}{5}\begin{bmatrix} -1000 \\ -1500 \\ -2000 \end{bmatrix}, X = \begin{bmatrix} 200 \\ 300 \\ 400 \end{bmatrix}$$

$$x = 200, y = 300, z = 400$$

Hence, the money awarded for sincerity, truthfulness and helpfulness are ₹ 200, ₹ 300 and ₹ 400 respectively.

$\therefore \quad x, y,$ and z will have unique solution:

$$x = ₹\,200, y = ₹\,300, \text{ and } z = ₹\,400. \qquad \textbf{(2 Marks)}$$

24. Let R and h be the radius and height of the cone and r be the radius of sphere.

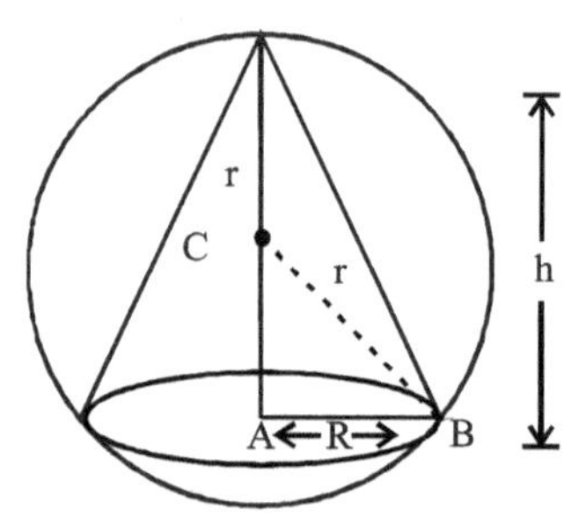

(½ Mark)

To show : $h = \dfrac{4r}{3}$ and

Maximum volume of sphere

$= \dfrac{8}{27}$ (Volume of Sphere)

Proof :

In $\triangle ABC$

$AC = h - r$

$r^2 = (h-r)^2 + R^2$ (By Pythagoras theorem)

$R^2 = r^2 - (h-r)^2$ **(½ Mark)**

Volume of cone $= \dfrac{1}{3}\pi R^2 h$

$V = \dfrac{1}{3}\pi\left[r^2 - \left(h-r\right)^2 \right]h$ ...... (1)

$= \dfrac{1}{3}\pi\left[2h^2 r - h^3 \right]$ **(1 Mark)**

For maxima or minima, $\dfrac{dV}{dh} = 0$

$\Rightarrow \quad \dfrac{1}{3}\pi\left[4hr - 3h^2 \right] = 0$

$h = \dfrac{4r}{3}$ **(1 Mark)**

$\dfrac{d^2 V}{dh^2} = \dfrac{1}{3}\pi\left[4r - 6h \right]$ **(½ Mark)**

Putting $h = \dfrac{4r}{3}$

$\dfrac{d^2 V}{dh^2} = \dfrac{1}{3}\pi\left[4r - \dfrac{24r}{3} \right] = \dfrac{-4}{3}\pi r < 0$

$\therefore$ Volume is maximum at $h = \dfrac{4r}{3}$ **(½ Mark)**

$V = \dfrac{1}{3}\pi\left[r^2 - \left(h-r\right)^2 \right]h$ [from (1)]

$= \dfrac{1}{3}\pi\left[r^2 - \left(\dfrac{4r}{3} - r\right)^2 \right]\dfrac{4r}{3} = \dfrac{1}{3}\pi\left[\dfrac{8r^2}{9} \right]\left[\dfrac{4r}{3} \right]$

$= \dfrac{8}{27}\left(\dfrac{4}{3}\pi r^3 \right) = \dfrac{8}{27}$ (Volume of sphere)

Hence, proved.   **(2 Marks)**

Note

Since perpendicular bisector of a chord passes through the centre of circle. So, centre of sphere lies on altitude of inscribed cone.

25. Let $I = \displaystyle\int \dfrac{1}{\cos^4 x + \sin^4 x}\, dx$

$= \displaystyle\int \dfrac{\sec^4 x\, dx}{1 + \tan^4 x}$

$= \displaystyle\int \dfrac{\sec^2 x \, \sec^2 x\, dx}{1 + \tan^4 x}$ **(1 Mark)**

Putting $\tan x = t \Rightarrow \sec^2 x\, dx = dt$

$= \displaystyle\int \dfrac{(1 + \tan^2 x)dt}{1 + t^4} = \int \dfrac{1 + t^2}{1 + t^4}\, dt$

$= \displaystyle\int \dfrac{1 + \dfrac{1}{t^2}}{t^2 + \dfrac{1}{t^2}}\, dt$

$= \displaystyle\int \dfrac{1 + \dfrac{1}{t^2}}{t^2 + \dfrac{1}{t^2} + 2 - 2}\, dt = \int \dfrac{1 + \dfrac{1}{t^2}}{\left(t - \dfrac{1}{t}\right)^2 + 2}$ **(2 Marks)**

Putting $t - \dfrac{1}{t} = z \Rightarrow 1 + \dfrac{1}{t^2}\, dt = dz$ **(1 Mark)**

$= \displaystyle\int \dfrac{dz}{\left(t - \dfrac{1}{t}\right)^2 + 2} = \int \dfrac{dz}{z^2 + 2} = \int \dfrac{dz}{z^2 + (\sqrt{2})^2}$

$= \dfrac{1}{\sqrt{2}} \tan^{-1} z + C$

$= \dfrac{1}{\sqrt{2}} \tan^{-1}\left(\tan x - \dfrac{1}{\tan x} \right) + c$

$= \dfrac{1}{\sqrt{2}} \tan^{-1}\left(\tan x - \cot x \right) + c$ **(2 Marks)**

26. The points A $(-1, 2)$, B$(1, 5)$ and C$(3, 4)$ are plotted and joined.

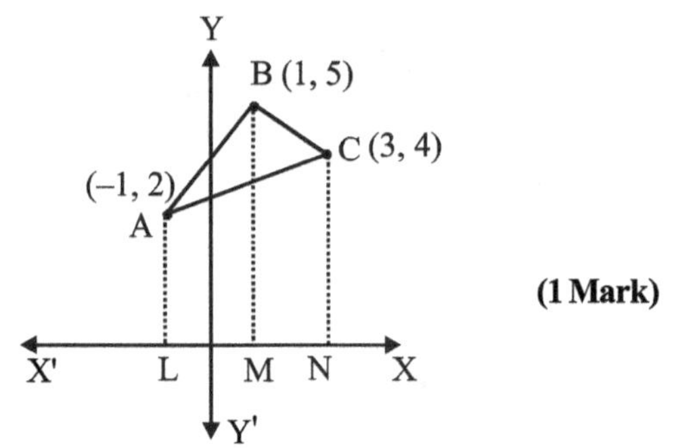

(1 Mark)

Equation of AB:

$$\frac{y-2}{x+1} = \frac{3}{2} \Rightarrow y = \frac{3x+7}{2}$$

Equation of BC :

$$\frac{y-5}{x-1} = \frac{-1}{2} \Rightarrow 2y - 10 = -x + 1$$

$$\Rightarrow \quad y = \frac{-x+11}{2}$$

Equation of CA:

$$\frac{y-4}{x-3} = \frac{1}{2} \Rightarrow 2y - 8 = x - 3$$

$$\Rightarrow \quad y = \frac{x+5}{2} \qquad \textbf{(1 Mark)}$$

Area of $\triangle$ABC = (Area of trapezium ABML + Area of trapezium BCNM) – (Area of trapezium ACNL)   **(1 Mark)**

$$= \int_{-1}^{1} \frac{3x+7}{2} dx + \int_{1}^{3} \frac{-x+11}{2} dx - \int_{-1}^{3} \frac{x+5}{2} dx \qquad \textbf{(1 Mark)}$$

$$\text{Required Area} = \frac{3}{2}\frac{x^2}{2} + \frac{7x}{2}\Big|_{-1}^{1}$$

$$+ \left[\frac{-x^2}{4} + \frac{11x}{2}\right]_{1}^{3} - \left[\frac{x^2}{4} + \frac{5x}{2}\right]_{-1}^{3}$$

$$= \left\{\left(\frac{3}{4} + \frac{7}{2}\right) - \left(\frac{3}{4} - \frac{7}{2}\right)\right\}$$

$$+ \left\{\left(\frac{-9}{4} + \frac{33}{2}\right) - \left(\frac{-1}{4} + \frac{11}{2}\right)\right\} - \left\{\left(\frac{9}{4} + \frac{15}{2}\right) - \left(\frac{1}{4} - \frac{5}{2}\right)\right\}$$

$$= \left(\frac{17}{4} + \frac{11}{4}\right) + \left(\frac{36}{4}\right) - \left(\frac{39}{4} + \frac{9}{4}\right) = \frac{28}{4} + \frac{36}{4} - \frac{48}{4}$$

$$= \frac{16}{4} = 4 \text{ sq. unit } \textbf{(2 Marks)}$$

 **Note**

To get required area, first find the total area then subtract unwanted area from it.

27. Given planes are

$$x + y + z - 1 = 0 \qquad \qquad \text{..........(i)}$$
$$2x + 3y + 4z - 5 = 0 \qquad \qquad \text{............(ii)}$$
$$x - y + z = 0 \qquad \qquad \text{............(iii)}$$

Any plane through the intersection of (i) and (ii) is
$$(1 + 2\lambda)x + (1 + 3\lambda)y + (1 + 4\lambda)z - 1 - 5\lambda = 0 \qquad \text{...... (iv)}$$
Direction ratio of the normal of (iii) are $1, -1, 1$
Also direction ratios of normal of (iv) are
$1 + 2\lambda, 1 + 3\lambda, 1 + 4\lambda$ **(1 Mark)**
Two planes are perpendicular if their normals are perpendicular.

$$\Rightarrow \quad 1 + 2\lambda - 1 - 3\lambda + 1 + 4\lambda = 0 \Rightarrow \lambda = \frac{-1}{3} \qquad \textbf{(1 Mark)}$$

Now equation of the required plane is
$$x - z + 2 = 0 \qquad \qquad \textbf{(1 Mark)}$$

$$\text{Distance} = d = \left|\frac{ax_1 + by_1 + cz_1 + d}{\sqrt{a^2 + b^2 + c^2}}\right| \qquad \textbf{(1 Mark)}$$

$$= \left|\frac{1(0) + 0(0) + (-1)(0) + 2}{\sqrt{(1)^2 + (0)^2 + (-1)^2}}\right|$$

$$= \left|\frac{2}{\sqrt{2}}\right| = \sqrt{2} \qquad \qquad \textbf{(2 Marks)}$$

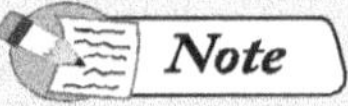 **Note**

The equation of the family of planes containing line $a_1 x + b_1 y + c_1 z + d_1 = 0 = a_2 x + b_2 y + c_2 z + d_2$ is $(a_1 x + b_1 y + c_1 z + d_1) + \lambda (a_2 x + b_2 y + c_2 z + d_2) = 0$, where λ is a parameter.

OR

The line and plane are

$$\vec{r} = (2\hat{i} - 4\hat{j} + 2\hat{k}) + \lambda(3\hat{i} + 4\hat{j} + 2\hat{k}) \qquad \text{.....(1)}$$

$$\vec{r}(\hat{i} - 2\hat{j} + \hat{k}) = 0 \qquad \text{..... (2)}$$

On solving (1) and (2)

$$\left[(2\hat{i} - 4\hat{j} + 2\hat{k}) + \lambda(3\hat{i} + 4\hat{j} + 2\hat{k})\right](\hat{i} - 2\hat{j} + \hat{k}) = 0$$

$$\text{or} \quad (2\hat{i} - 4\hat{j} + 2\hat{k})(\hat{i} - 2\hat{j} + \hat{k})$$

$$+ \lambda(3\hat{i} + 4\hat{j} + 2\hat{k})(\hat{i} - 2\hat{j} + \hat{k}) = 0$$

$$\text{or} \quad (2 + 8 + 2) + \lambda[3 - 8 + 2] = 0$$

$\Rightarrow \quad 12 + \lambda(-3) = 0$

$\Rightarrow \quad \lambda = 4$ **(1 Mark)**

$\therefore$ The point of intersection of line and the plane is

$14\hat{i} + 12\hat{j} + 10\hat{k}.$ **(2 Marks)**

The other point is $(2, 12, 5) = 2\hat{i} + 12\hat{j} + 5\hat{k}$ **(1 Mark)**

Distance between these points

$$= \sqrt{(14-2)^2 + (12-12)^2 + (10-5)^2}$$

$$= \sqrt{144 + 25} = \sqrt{169} = 13$$ **(2 Marks)**

28. Suppose x is the number of teaching aids A and y is the number of teaching aids B.

Then,

Total profit (in ₹) $= 80x + 120y$

$Z = 80x + 120y$ **(1 Mark)**

Let, we now have the following mathematical model for the given problem

Maximize $Z = 80x + 120y$ .....(1)

Subject to the constraints

$9x + 12y \le 180$ (fabricating constraint)

i.e. $3x + 4y \le 60$ .....(2)

$x + 3y \le 30$ (finishing constraint) .....(3)

$x \ge 0, y \ge 0$ (non-negative constraint) .....(4) **(2 Marks)**

The feasible region (shaded) OABC determined by the linear inequalities (2) to (4) is shown in the graph.

The feasible region is bounded.

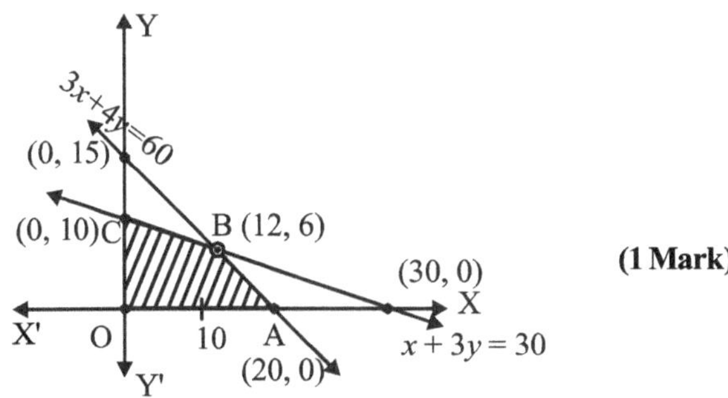

(1 Mark)

The objective function Z at each corner point is shown below:

Corner Point	$Z = 80x + 120y$
0 (0, 0)	0
A (20, 0)	1600
B (12, 6)	1680 (Maximum)
C (0, 10)	1200

The maximum value of Z is 1680 at point B(12, 6). Hence the company should produce 12 pieces of teaching aid A and 6 pieces of teaching aid B to realise maximum profit and maximum profit then will be ₹1680. **(2 Marks)**

29. Let E_1, E_2, E_3, and A denotes the following events:

E_1 = a two headed coin, E_2 = a biased coin that comes up head 75% of the times

E_3 = a biased coin that comes up tail 40% of the times

A = a head is shown **(1 Mark)**

Now,

$$P(A/E_1) = 1, \ P(A/E_2) = \frac{75}{100} = \frac{3}{4},$$

$$P(A/E_3) = \frac{60}{100} = \frac{3}{5}$$ **(2 Marks)**

By Baye's theorem,

$P(E_1/A)$

$$= \frac{P(E_1)P(A/E_1)}{P(E_1)P(A/E_1) + P(E_2)P(A/E_2) + P(E_3)P(A/E_3)}$$ **(1 Mark)**

$$P(E_1/A) = \frac{\dfrac{1}{3} \times 1}{\dfrac{1}{3} \times 1 + \dfrac{1}{3} \times \dfrac{3}{4} + \dfrac{1}{3} \times \dfrac{3}{5}}$$

$$= \frac{\dfrac{1}{3}}{\dfrac{1}{3}\left(1 + \dfrac{3}{4} + \dfrac{3}{5}\right)} = \frac{1}{\dfrac{20+15+12}{20}}$$

$$P(E_1/A) = \frac{20}{43} = \frac{20}{47}$$ **(2 Marks)**

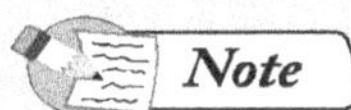

To apply Baye's theorem, E_1, E_2, E_3, ... En should be mutually exclusive and exhaustive events

OR

There are six numbers 1, 2, 3, 4, 5, 6 and one of them is selected in 6 ways.

When one of the numbers has been selected, 5 numbers are left. One number out of 5 may be selected in 5 ways.

$\therefore$ No. of ways of selecting two numbers without replacement out of 6 positive integers $= 6 \times 5 = 30$

(2 Marks)

Let X denotes larger of two number

When X = 2 then the two numbers are (1, 2), (1, 2)

$$\therefore \ P(X) = \frac{2}{30}$$

When X = 3 then the two numbers are (1, 3)(2, 3) (3, 1) (3, 2)

$$\therefore \ P(X) = \frac{4}{30}$$

When X = 4 then the two numbers are (2, 4) (3, 4) (4, 1) (4, 2) (4, 3) (1, 4)

$$\therefore \ P(X = 4) = \frac{6}{30}$$

When X = 5 then the two numbers are (1, 5) (2, 5) (3, 5) (4, 5) (5, 1) (5, 2) (5, 3) (5, 4)

$$P(x = 5) = \frac{8}{30}$$

When X = 6 then the two numbers are (1, 6) (2, 6) (3, 6) (4, 6) (5, 6) (6, 1) (6, 2) (6, 3) (6, 4) (6, 5)

$$P(X = 6) = \frac{10}{30}$$

The probability distribution is

X	2	3	4	5	6
$P(X)$	$\dfrac{2}{30}$	$\dfrac{4}{30}$	$\dfrac{6}{30}$	$\dfrac{8}{30}$	$\dfrac{10}{30}$

(2 Marks)

The mean of the distribution is

$$E(X) = \sum X \, P(X)$$

$$= 2 \times \frac{2}{30} + 3 \times \frac{4}{30} + 4 \times \frac{6}{30} + 5 \times \frac{8}{30} + 6 \times \frac{10}{30}$$

$$= \frac{1}{30}[4 + 12 + 24 + 40 + 60] = \frac{1}{30}(140)$$

$$E(X) = \frac{14}{3}$$

(2 Marks)

Delhi *2014*

CBSE Board Solved Paper

Time Allowed : 3 Hours   *Maximum Marks : 100*

General Instructions:

(i) All questions are compulsory.

(ii) The question paper consists of **29** questions divided into three Sections **A, B** and **C**. Section **A** comprises of **10** questions of **one** mark each, Section **B** comprises of **12** questions of **four** marks each and Section **C** comprises of **07** questions of **six** marks each.

(iii) All questions in Section **A** are to be answered is **one** word, **one** sentence or as per the exact requirement of the question.

(iv) There is no overall choice. However, internal choice has been provided in **04** questions of **four** marks each and **02** questions of **six** marks each. You have to attempt only one of the alternatives in all such questions.

(v) Use of calculators is **not** permitted. You may ask for logarithmic tables, if required.

SECTION - A

Question numbers 1 to 10 carry 1 mark each.

1. Let $*$ be a binary operation, on the set of all non-zero real numbers, given by $a * b = \dfrac{ab}{5}$ for all $a, b \in R - \{0\}$. Find the value of x, given that $2 * (x * 5) = 10$.

2. If $\sin\left(\sin^{-1}\dfrac{1}{5} + \cos^{-1} x\right) = 1$, then find the value of x.

3. If $2\begin{bmatrix} 3 & 4 \\ 5 & x \end{bmatrix} + \begin{bmatrix} 1 & y \\ 0 & 1 \end{bmatrix} = \begin{bmatrix} 7 & 0 \\ 10 & 5 \end{bmatrix}$, find $(x - y)$.

4. Solve the following matrix equation of x :

$$[x \ \ 1]\begin{bmatrix} 1 & 0 \\ -2 & 0 \end{bmatrix} = 0.$$

5. If $\begin{vmatrix} 2x & 5 \\ 8 & x \end{vmatrix} = \begin{vmatrix} 6 & -2 \\ 7 & 3 \end{vmatrix}$, write the value of x.

6. Write the anti derivative of $\left(3\sqrt{x} + \dfrac{1}{\sqrt{x}}\right)$.

7. Evaluate : $\displaystyle\int_{0}^{3} \dfrac{dx}{9 + x^2}$

8. Find the projection of the vector $\hat{i} + 3\hat{j} + 7\hat{k}$ on the vector $2\hat{i} - 3\hat{j} + 6\hat{k}$.

9. If $\vec{a}$ and $\vec{b}$ are two unit vectors such that $\vec{a} + \vec{b}$ is also a unit vector, then find the angle between $\vec{a}$ and $\vec{b}$.

10. Write the vector equation of the plane, passing through the point (a, b, c) and parallel to the plane $\vec{r}.(\hat{i} + \hat{j} + \hat{k}) = 2$.

SECTION - B

Question numbers 11 to 22 carry 4 marks each.

11. Let A $= \{1, 2, 3, \dots , 9\}$ and R be the relation in A $\times$ A defined by (a, b) R (c, d) if $a + d = b + c$ for $(a, b), (c, d)$ in A $\times$ A. Prove that R is an equivalence relation. Also obtain the equivalence class $[(2, 5)]$.

12. Prove that $\cot^{-1}\left(\dfrac{\sqrt{1+\sin x} + \sqrt{1-\sin x}}{\sqrt{1+\sin x} - \sqrt{1-\sin x}}\right) = \dfrac{x}{2}; x \in \left(0, \dfrac{\pi}{4}\right)$.

OR

Prove that $2\tan^{-1}\left(\dfrac{1}{5}\right) + \sec^{-1}\left(\dfrac{5\sqrt{2}}{7}\right) + 2\tan^{-1}\left(\dfrac{1}{8}\right) = \dfrac{\pi}{4}$.

13. Using properties of determinants, prove that

$$\begin{vmatrix} 2y & y-z-x & 2y \\ 2z & 2z & z-x-y \\ x-y-z & 2x & 2x \end{vmatrix} = (x+y+z)^3$$

14. Differentiate $\tan^{-1}\left(\dfrac{\sqrt{1-x^2}}{x}\right)$ with respect to $\cos^{-1}\left(2x\sqrt{1-x^2}\right)$, when $x \neq 0$.

15. If $y = x^x$, prove that $\dfrac{d^2y}{dx^2} - \dfrac{1}{y}\left(\dfrac{dy}{dx}\right)^2 - \dfrac{y}{x} = 0$.

16. Find the intervals in which the function $f(x) = 3x^4 - 4x^3 - 12x^2 + 5$ is

(a) strictly increasing

(b) strictly decreasing

OR

Find the equations of the tangent and normal to the curve

$x = a \sin^3\theta$ and $y = a \cos^3\theta$ at $\theta = \dfrac{\pi}{4}$.

17. Evaluate : $\displaystyle\int \dfrac{\sin^6 x + \cos^6 x}{\sin^2 x . \cos^2 x}\, dx$

OR

Evaluate : $\displaystyle\int (x-3)\sqrt{x^2 + 3x - 18}\, dx$

18. Find the particular solution of the differential equation

$e^x \sqrt{1-y^2}\, dx + \dfrac{y}{x}\, dy = 0$, given that $y = 1$ when $x = 0$.

19. Solve the following differential equation :

$(x^2 - 1)\dfrac{dy}{dx} + 2xy = \dfrac{2}{x^2 - 1}$.

20. Prove that, for any three vectors $\vec{a}, \vec{b}, \vec{c}$

$\left[\vec{a}+\vec{b},\ \vec{b}+\vec{c},\ \vec{c}+\vec{a}\right] = 2\left[\vec{a}, \vec{b}, \vec{c}\right]$

OR

Vectors $\vec{a}, \vec{b}$ and $\vec{c}$ are such that $\vec{a} + \vec{b} + \vec{c} = \vec{0}$ and $|\vec{a}| = 3, |\vec{b}| = 5$ and $|\vec{c}| = 7$. Find the angle between $\vec{a}$ and $\vec{b}$.

21. Show that the lines $\dfrac{x+1}{3} = \dfrac{y+3}{5} = \dfrac{z+5}{7}$ and $\dfrac{x-2}{1} = \dfrac{y-4}{3} = \dfrac{z-6}{5}$ intersect. Also find their point of intersection.

22. Assume that each born child is equally likely to be a boy or a girl. If a family has two children, what is the conditional probability that both are girls? Given that

   (a) the youngest is a girl.

   (b) atleast one is a girl.

SECTION - C

Question numbers 23 to 29 carry 6 marks each.

23. Two schools P and Q want to award their selected students on the values of Discipline, Politeness and Punctuality. The school P wants to award ₹ x each, ₹ y each and ₹ z each for the three respective values to its 3, 2 and 1 students with a total award money of ₹ 1,000. School Q wants to spend ₹ 1,500 to award its 4, 1 and 3 students on the respective values (by giving the same award money for the three values as before). If the total amount of awards for one prize on each value is ₹ 600, using matrices, find the award money for each value.

Apart from the above three values, suggest one more value for awards.

24. Show that the semi-vertical angle of the cone of the maximum volume and of given slant height is $\cos^{-1}\dfrac{1}{\sqrt{3}}$.

25. Evaluate : $\displaystyle\int_{\pi/6}^{\pi/3} \dfrac{dx}{1 + \sqrt{\cot x}}$

26. Find the area of the region in the first quadrant enclosed by the x-axis, the line $y = x$ and the circle $x^2 + y^2 = 32$.

27. Find the distance between the point (7, 2, 4) and the plane determined by the points A(2, 5, –3), B(–2, –3, 5) and C(5, 3, –3).

OR

Find the distance of the point (–1, –5, –10) from the point of intersection of the line $\vec{r} = 2\hat{i} - \hat{j} + 2\hat{k} + \lambda(3\hat{i} + 4\hat{j} + 2\hat{k})$ and the plane $\vec{r}.(\hat{i} - \hat{j} + \hat{k}) = 5$.

28. A dealer in rural area wishes to purchase a number of sewing machines. He has only ₹ 5,760 to invest and has space for at most 20 items for storage. An electronic sewing machine cost him ₹ 360 and a manually operated sewing machine ₹ 240. He can sell an electronic sewing machine at a profit of ₹ 22 and a manually operated sewing machine at a profit of ₹ 18. Assuming that he can sell all the items that he can buy, how should he invest his money in order to maximize his profit? Make it as a LPP and solve it graphically.

29. A card from a pack of 52 playing cards is lost. From the remaining cards of the pack three cards are drawn at random (without replacement) and are found to be all spades. Find the probability of the lost card being a spade.

OR

From a lot of 15 bulbs which include 5 defectives, a sample of 4 bulbs is drawn one by one with replacement. Find the probability distribution of number of defective bulbs. Hence find the mean of the distribution.

Solutions

SECTION - A

1. $a * b = \dfrac{ab}{5} \ \forall \ a, b \in R - \{0\}$

$2 * (x * 5) = 10 \ \Rightarrow \ 2 * \dfrac{5x}{5} = 10$ **(½ Mark)**

$\Rightarrow \ 2 * x = 10 \ \Rightarrow \ \dfrac{2x}{5} = 10$

$\Rightarrow \ x = 25$ **(½ Mark)**

2. $\sin\left(\sin^{-1}\dfrac{1}{5} + \cos^{-1}x\right) = 1$

$\Rightarrow \sin^{-1}\dfrac{1}{5} + \cos^{-1}x = \sin^{-1}1$

$\Rightarrow \sin^{-1}\dfrac{1}{5} + \cos^{-1}x = \dfrac{\pi}{2} \ \left(\because \sin^{-1}(1) = \dfrac{\pi}{2}\right)$ **(½ Mark)**

$\Rightarrow \sin^{-1}\dfrac{1}{5} = \dfrac{\pi}{2} - \cos^{-1}x$

$\Rightarrow \sin^{-1}\dfrac{1}{5} = \sin^{-1}x \ \left(\because \sin^{-1}x + \cos^{-1}x = \dfrac{\pi}{2}\right)$

$\Rightarrow \ x = \dfrac{1}{5}$ **(½ Mark)**

3. $2\begin{bmatrix} 3 & 4 \\ 5 & x \end{bmatrix} + \begin{bmatrix} 1 & y \\ 0 & 1 \end{bmatrix} = \begin{bmatrix} 7 & 0 \\ 10 & 5 \end{bmatrix}$

$\begin{bmatrix} 6 & 8 \\ 10 & 2x \end{bmatrix} + \begin{bmatrix} 1 & y \\ 0 & 1 \end{bmatrix} = \begin{bmatrix} 7 & 0 \\ 10 & 5 \end{bmatrix}$

$\Rightarrow \begin{bmatrix} 6+1 & 8+y \\ 10+0 & 2x+1 \end{bmatrix} = \begin{bmatrix} 7 & 0 \\ 10 & 5 \end{bmatrix}$

On comparing corresponding elements

$8 + y = 0 \Rightarrow y = -8$

$2x + 1 = 5$

$2x = 4$

$x = 2$ **(½ Mark)**

Now $x - y = 2 - (-8)$ **(½ Mark)**

> **Note**
>
> *Two equal matrices always have equal corresponding elements.*

4. $\begin{bmatrix} x & 1 \end{bmatrix} \begin{bmatrix} 1 & 0 \\ -2 & 0 \end{bmatrix} = 0$

$\begin{bmatrix} x-2 & 0+0 \end{bmatrix} = \begin{bmatrix} 0 & 0 \end{bmatrix}$ **(½ Mark)**

$x - 2 = 0$

$x = 2$ **(½ Mark)**

5. $\begin{vmatrix} 2x & 5 \\ 8 & x \end{vmatrix} = \begin{vmatrix} 6 & -2 \\ 7 & 3 \end{vmatrix}$

$2x^2 - 40 = 18 + 14$ **(½ Mark)**

$2x^2 = 32 + 40$

$2x^2 = 72$

$x^2 = 36$

$x = \pm 6$ **(½ Mark)**

6. Anti derivative = Integral

$\int\left(3\sqrt{x} + \dfrac{1}{\sqrt{x}}\right)dx = 3\dfrac{x^{3/2}}{3/2} + \dfrac{x^{\frac{1}{2}}}{\frac{1}{2}} + C$

$\left[\because \int x^n dx = \dfrac{x^{n+1}}{n+1} + c\right]$

$= 2x^{3/2} + 2x^{1/2} + C = 2x\sqrt{x} + 2\sqrt{x} + C$ **(½ Mark)**

$= 2\sqrt{x}\,(x + 1) + C$ **(½ Mark)**

7. $\displaystyle\int_0^3 \dfrac{dx}{9 + x^2} = \int_0^3 \dfrac{dx}{3^2 + x^2} = \dfrac{1}{3}\left[\tan^{-1}\dfrac{x}{3}\right]_0^3$

$\left[\because \int \dfrac{dx}{x^2 + a^2} = \dfrac{1}{a}\tan^{-1}\dfrac{x}{a}\right]$ **(½ Mark)**

$= \dfrac{1}{3}[\tan^{-1}1 - \tan^{-1}0] = \dfrac{1}{3}\left[\dfrac{\pi}{4} - 0\right] = \dfrac{\pi}{12}$ **(½ Mark)**

8. Let $\vec{a} = \hat{i} + 3\hat{j} + 7\hat{k}$

$\vec{b} = 2\hat{i} - 3\hat{j} + 6\hat{k}$

$\therefore$ Projection of $\vec{a}$ on $\vec{b} = \dfrac{\vec{a}.\vec{b}}{|\vec{b}|}$ **(½ Mark)**

$= \dfrac{(\hat{i} + 3\hat{j} + 7\hat{k})(2\hat{i} - 3\hat{j} + 6\hat{k})}{\sqrt{2^2 + (-3)^2 + (6)^2}}$

$= \dfrac{2 - 9 + 42}{\sqrt{49}} = \dfrac{35}{7} = 5$ **(½ Mark)**

9. Given: $|\vec{a}| = 1, \ |\vec{b}| = 1, \ |\vec{a} + \vec{b}| = 1$

Squaring on both sides

$|\vec{a} + \vec{b}|^2 = 1 \Rightarrow (\vec{a} + \vec{b}).(\vec{a} + \vec{b}) = 1$

$\Rightarrow \ \vec{a}.\vec{a} + \vec{a}.\vec{b} + \vec{b}.\vec{a} + \vec{b}.\vec{b} = 1$

$\Rightarrow \ |\vec{a}|^2 + |\vec{b}|^2 + 2\vec{a}.\vec{b} = 1$ **(½ Mark)**

$\Rightarrow \ 1 + 1 + 2\vec{a}.\vec{b} = 1$ $[\because |\vec{a}| = |\vec{b}| = 1]$

$\Rightarrow \ 2\vec{a}.\vec{b} = -1 \ \Rightarrow 2|\vec{a}||\vec{b}|\cos\theta = -1$

$\Rightarrow \ 2 . 1 . 1 \cos\theta = -1$

$$\Rightarrow \quad \cos \theta = \frac{-1}{2}$$

$$\Rightarrow \quad \cos \theta = \cos 120°$$
$$\Rightarrow \quad \theta = 120° \qquad \qquad \text{(½ Mark)}$$

10. Given: $\quad \vec{r}.(\hat{i}+\hat{j}+\hat{k}) = 2$

$$(x\hat{i}+y\hat{j}+z\hat{k}).(\hat{i}+\hat{j}+\hat{k}) = 2$$
$$x+y+z = 2$$

Equation of the plane parallel to given plane

$$x+y+z = k \qquad \qquad \text{(½ Mark)}$$

The plane is passing through (a, b, c)

$$k = a+b+c$$

∴ vector equation of required plane is

$$\vec{r}.(\hat{i}+\hat{j}+\hat{k}) = a+b+c \qquad \text{(½ Mark)}$$

Note

Direction ratios of two parallel planes are equal but constant term is different.

SECTION - B

11. Here $A = [1, 2, 3, ... 9]$ and R is a relation on $A \times A$ defined by

$$(a, b)\, R\, (c, d) \Leftrightarrow a+d = b+c \;\forall\, a, b, c, d \in A$$

(i) Let $(a, b) \in A \times A$

$$a+b = b+a$$
$$(a, b)\, R\, (a, b),\; \forall\, (a, b) \in A \times A$$
$$\Rightarrow R \text{ is reflexive on } A \qquad \text{(1 Mark)}$$

(ii) Let $(a, b)\, R\, (c, d)$

$$a+d = b+c$$
$$b+c = d+a$$
$$(c, d)\, R\, (a, b),\; \forall\, (a, b), (c, d) \in A \times A$$
$$\Rightarrow R \text{ is symmetric on } A \qquad \text{(1 Mark)}$$

(iii) Let $(a, b)\, R\, (c, d)$ and $(c, d)\, R\, (e, f),\; \forall\, (a, b), (c, d)$ and $(e, f) \in A \times A$

$$a+d = b+c \text{ and } c+f = d+e$$

On adding

$$(a+d)+(c+f) = (b+c)+(d+e)$$
$$\Rightarrow a+f = b+e$$
$$(a, b)\, R\, (e, f)$$
$$\Rightarrow R \text{ is transitive on } A.$$

Hence R is an equivalence relation on A **(1 Mark)**

Also equivalence class $[(2, 5)]$

$$= [(a, b) \in A \times A \mid (2, 5)\, R\, (a, b)]$$
$$= [(a, b) \in A \times A \mid 2+b = 5+a]$$
$$= [(a, b) \in A \times A \mid b = a+3]$$
$$= [(a, a+3) \mid a \in A \mid = \{(1, 4), (2, 5), (3, 6), (4, 7),$$
$$(5, 8), (6, 9)\} \quad \text{(1 Mark)}$$

12. L.H.S. $= \cot^{-1}\!\left(\dfrac{\sqrt{1+\sin x}+\sqrt{1-\sin x}}{\sqrt{1+\sin x}-\sqrt{1-\sin x}}\right)$

$$\Rightarrow \cot^{-1}\!\left(\frac{\sqrt{1+\sin x}+\sqrt{1-\sin x}}{\sqrt{1+\sin x}-\sqrt{1-\sin x}} \times \frac{\sqrt{1+\sin x}+\sqrt{1-\sin x}}{\sqrt{1+\sin x}+\sqrt{1-\sin x}}\right)$$

$$\text{(1 Mark)}$$

$$\Rightarrow \cot^{-1}\!\left(\frac{1+\sin x+1-\sin x+2\sqrt{(1+\sin x)(1-\sin x)}}{(1+\sin x)-(1-\sin x)}\right)$$

$$[\because (a+b)^2 = a^2+b^2+2ab]$$

$$\Rightarrow \cot^{-1}\!\left(\frac{2+2\sqrt{1-\sin^2 x}}{2\sin x}\right)$$

$$\Rightarrow \cot^{-1}\!\left(\frac{1+\cos x}{\sin x}\right) \quad [\because \cos^2 x = 1 - \sin^2 x] \quad \text{(1 Mark)}$$

$$\Rightarrow \cot^{-1}\!\left(\frac{2\cos^2 \dfrac{x}{2}}{2\sin \dfrac{x}{2}\cos \dfrac{x}{2}}\right)$$

$$\left[\because \sin 2\theta = 2\sin\theta.\cos\theta,\, 1+\cos\theta = 2\cos^2 \frac{\theta}{2}\right] \quad \text{(1 Mark)}$$

$$= \cot^{-1}\!\left(\frac{\cos \dfrac{x}{2}}{\sin \dfrac{x}{2}}\right) = \cot^{-1}\!\left(\cot \frac{x}{2}\right) = \frac{x}{2} = \text{R.H.S.}$$

Hence proved. **(1 Mark)**

Note

Alternate method to solve by convert

$$1+\sin x = \sin^2 \frac{x}{2}+\cos^2 \frac{x}{2}-2\sin \frac{x}{2}\cdot\cos \frac{x}{2}$$

$$= \left(\cos \frac{x}{2}+\sin \frac{x}{2}\right)^2$$

$$1-\sin x = \sin^2 \frac{x}{2}+\cos^2 \frac{x}{2}-2\sin \frac{x}{2}\cdot\cos \frac{x}{2}$$

$$= \left(\cos \frac{x}{2}-\sin \frac{x}{2}\right)^2$$

OR

L.H.S. $= 2\tan^{-1}\!\left(\dfrac{1}{5}\right) + \sec^{-1}\!\left(\dfrac{5\sqrt{2}}{7}\right) + 2\tan^{-1}\!\left(\dfrac{1}{8}\right)$

$$= 2\left(\tan^{-1}\frac{1}{5}+\tan^{-1}\frac{1}{8}\right) + \sec^{-1}\!\left(\frac{5\sqrt{2}}{7}\right)$$

$$= 2\tan^{-1}\!\left[\frac{\dfrac{1}{5}+\dfrac{1}{8}}{1-\dfrac{1}{5}\times\dfrac{1}{8}}\right] + \tan^{-1}\!\left[\sqrt{\left(\frac{5\sqrt{2}}{7}\right)^2 -1}\right] \quad \text{(1 Mark)}$$

$$\left[\because \tan^{-1}A+\tan^{-1}B = \tan^{-1}\!\left(\frac{A+B}{1-AB}\right),\, \sec^{-1}x = \tan^{-1}\sqrt{x^2-1}\right]$$

$$= 2\tan^{-1}\!\left(\frac{13/40}{39/40}\right) + \tan^{-1}\!\left(\sqrt{\frac{1}{49}}\right) = 2\tan^{-1}\frac{1}{3}+\tan^{-1}\frac{1}{7}$$

$$= \tan^{-1}\left(\frac{2 \times \frac{1}{3}}{1 - \left(\frac{1}{3}\right)^2}\right) + \tan^{-1}\frac{1}{7}$$

$$\left[\because 2\tan^{-1}x = \tan^{-1}\left(\frac{2x}{1-x^2}\right)\right] \quad \textbf{(1 Mark)}$$

$$= \tan^{-1}\left(\frac{\frac{2}{3}}{\frac{8}{9}}\right) + \tan^{-1}\frac{1}{7} = \tan^{-1}\left(\frac{3}{4}\right) + \tan^{-1}\left(\frac{1}{7}\right)$$

$$= \tan^{-1}\left(\frac{\frac{3}{4}+\frac{1}{7}}{1-\frac{3}{4}\cdot\frac{1}{7}}\right) = \tan^{-1}\left(\frac{\frac{25}{28}}{\frac{25}{28}}\right) = \tan^{-1}(1)$$

$$= \frac{\pi}{4} = \text{R.H.S.} \qquad\qquad \textbf{(2 Marks)}$$

Hence proved.

13. L.H.S. Let $\Delta = \begin{vmatrix} 2y & y-z-x & 2y \\ 2z & 2z & z-x-y \\ x-y-z & 2x & 2x \end{vmatrix}$

Applying $R_1 \to R_1 + R_2 + R_3$

$$\Delta = \begin{vmatrix} x+y+z & x+y+z & x+y+z \\ 2z & 2z & z-x-y \\ x-y-z & 2x & 2x \end{vmatrix} \qquad \textbf{(1 Mark)}$$

$$= (x+y+z)\begin{vmatrix} 1 & 1 & 1 \\ 2z & 2z & z-x-y \\ x-y-z & 2x & 2x \end{vmatrix} \qquad \textbf{(1 Mark)}$$

Applying $C_2 \to C_2 - C_1$ and $C_3 \to C_3 - C_1$

$$\Delta = (x+y+z)\begin{vmatrix} 1 & 0 & 0 \\ 2z & 0 & -(x+y+z) \\ x-y-z & x+y+z & (x+y+z) \end{vmatrix}$$

$$\textbf{(1 Mark)}$$

Expanding along R_1
$$\Delta = (x+y+z) \cdot 1\,(x+y+z)^2$$
$$= (x+y+z)^3 = \text{R.H.S.}$$
Hence proved. $\qquad\qquad\qquad\qquad$ **(1 Mark)**

14. Let $y = \tan^{-1}\left[\dfrac{\sqrt{1-x^2}}{x}\right]$ and $t = \cos^{-1}\left(2x\sqrt{1-x^2}\right)$

$$y = \tan^{-1}\left[\frac{\sqrt{1-x^2}}{x}\right]$$

Let $x = \cos\theta$

$$y = \tan^{-1}\left[\frac{\sqrt{1-\cos^2\theta}}{\cos\theta}\right]$$

$$\tan^{-1}\left[\frac{\sin\theta}{\cos\theta}\right] \qquad\qquad [\because \sin^2\theta = 1 - \cos^2\theta]$$

$$= \tan^{-1}\tan\theta = \theta \qquad\qquad \textbf{(1 Mark)}$$

Differentiating w.r.t. θ

$$\frac{dy}{d\theta} = 1 \qquad\qquad\qquad ...(1) \quad \textbf{(½ Mark)}$$

$$t = \cos^{-1}(2x\sqrt{1-x^2})\ (x \neq 0)$$

Putting $x = \cos\theta$

$$t = \cos^{-1}(2\cos\theta\sqrt{1-\cos^2\theta})$$
$$t = \cos^{-1}(2\cos\theta\sin\theta)$$
$$t = \cos^{-1}\sin 2\theta$$
$$t = \cos^{-1}\cos\left(\frac{\pi}{2} - 2\theta\right) \qquad \left[\because \cos\left(\frac{\pi}{2}-\theta\right) = \sin\theta\right]$$

$$t = \frac{\pi}{2} - 2\theta \qquad\qquad\qquad \textbf{(1 Mark)}$$

Differentiating w.r.t. θ,

$$\frac{dt}{d\theta} = 0 - 2 = -2 \qquad\qquad ...(2) \quad \textbf{(½ Mark)}$$

Dividing (1), (2)

$$\frac{dy}{dt} = \frac{\dfrac{dy}{d\theta}}{\dfrac{dt}{d\theta}} = -\frac{1}{2}$$

$$\frac{dy}{dt} = -\frac{1}{2} \qquad\qquad\qquad \textbf{(1 Mark)}$$

15. Given: $y = x^x$

Taking log on both sides

$$\log y = x\log x \quad [\because \log m^n = n\log m] \quad \textbf{(½ Mark)}$$

Differentiating both sides w.r.t. x $\qquad$ **(½ Mark)**

$$\frac{1}{y}\frac{dy}{dx} = x \cdot \frac{1}{x} + \log x$$

$$\frac{dy}{dx} = y(1 + \log x) \qquad\qquad ...(1) \quad \textbf{(1 Mark)}$$

Again differentiating w.r.t. x

$$\frac{d^2y}{dx^2} = \frac{dy}{dx}(1 + \log x) + y \cdot \frac{1}{x}$$

$$= \frac{dy}{dx}\left(\frac{1}{y}\frac{dy}{dx}\right) + \frac{y}{x} \ \text{(from (1))} \qquad \textbf{(1 Mark)}$$

$$\frac{d^2y}{dx^2} - \frac{1}{y}\left(\frac{dy}{dx}\right)^2 - \frac{y}{x} = 0$$

Hence proved. $\qquad\qquad\qquad\qquad$ **(1 Mark)**

 *Note*

For function in the form of variable to the power variable, always take logarithm of it and then find derivative.

16. $f(x) = 3x^4 - 4x^3 - 12x^2 + 5$

Differentiating w.r.t. x

$f'(x) = 12x^3 - 12x^2 - 24x$ **(1 Mark)**

$= 12x(x^2 - x - 2)$

$= 12x(x^2 - 2x + 1x - 2)$

$= 12x(x - 2)(x + 1)$

Critical values for f are $0, 2, -1$ **(1 Mark)**

$$\xleftarrow{\qquad \underset{-\infty}{\ } \quad \overset{-}{\ } \quad \underset{-1}{|} \quad \overset{+}{\ } \quad \underset{0}{|} \quad \overset{-}{\ } \quad \underset{2}{|} \quad \overset{+}{\ } \quad \underset{\infty}{\ } \qquad}\rightarrow$$

(1 Mark)

For $-\infty < x < -1$, $f'(x) = (-)(-)(-) < 0$

$\therefore$ Function is strictly decreasing

For $-1 < x < 0$, $f'(x) = (-)(+)(-) = + > 0$

$\therefore$ Function is strictly increasing

For $0 < x < 2$, $f'(x) = (+)(+)(-) = - < 0$

$\therefore$ Function is strictly decreasing

For $2 < x < \infty$, $f'(x) = (+)(+)(+) = + > 0$

Function is strictly increasing **(1 Mark)**

OR

$x = a \sin^3 \theta$

$\Rightarrow \dfrac{dx}{d\theta} = 3a \sin^2 \theta \cos \theta$ ...(1) **(½ Mark)**

$y = a \cos^3 \theta$

$\Rightarrow \dfrac{dy}{d\theta} = -3a \cos^2 \theta \sin \theta$ ...(2) **(½ Mark)**

Dividing (2)/(1)

$\dfrac{dy}{dx} = \dfrac{dy/d\theta}{\dfrac{dx}{d\theta}} = \dfrac{-3a \cos^2 \theta \sin \theta}{3a \sin^2 \theta \cdot \cos \theta} = -\cot \theta$

$\Rightarrow \left.\dfrac{dy}{dx}\right|_{\theta = \frac{\pi}{4}} = -\cot \dfrac{\pi}{4} = -1$ **(½ Mark)**

Slope of tangent at $\left(\theta = \dfrac{\pi}{4}\right) = -1$

Slope of normal $= \dfrac{-1}{\text{Slope of tangent}}$

Slope of normal $= 1$ **(½ Mark)**

$x = a \sin^3 \theta$, at $\theta = \dfrac{\pi}{4}$

$x = a \sin^3 \dfrac{\pi}{4} = a\left(\dfrac{1}{\sqrt{2}}\right)^3 = \dfrac{a}{2\sqrt{2}}$

$y = a \cos^3 \theta$, at $\theta = \dfrac{\pi}{4}$ $\therefore y = \dfrac{a}{2\sqrt{2}}$

Point $P\left(\dfrac{a}{2\sqrt{2}}, \dfrac{a}{2\sqrt{2}}\right)$ **(1 Mark)**

Equation of the tangent at P

$y - \dfrac{a}{2\sqrt{2}} = -1\left(x - \dfrac{a}{2\sqrt{2}}\right)$

$\Rightarrow x + y = \dfrac{a}{\sqrt{2}}$ **(½ Mark)**

Equation of the normal at P

$y - \dfrac{a}{2\sqrt{2}} = 1\left(x - \dfrac{a}{2\sqrt{2}}\right)$

$\Rightarrow y = x$ **(½ Mark)**

17. Let $I = \displaystyle\int \dfrac{\sin^6 x + \cos^6 x}{\sin^2 x . \cos^2 x} \, dx$

$I = \displaystyle\int \dfrac{(\sin^2 x)^3 + (\cos^2 x)^3}{\sin^2 x . \cos^2 x} \, dx$

$I = \displaystyle\int \dfrac{(\sin^2 x + \cos^2 x)(\sin^4 x + \cos^4 x - \sin^2 x . \cos^2 x)}{\sin^2 x . \cos^2 x} \, dx$

(1 Mark)

$[\because a^3 + b^3 = (a + b)(a^2 + b^2 - ab)]$

$= \displaystyle\int \dfrac{\sin^4 x + \cos^4 x - \sin^2 x \cos^2 x}{\sin^2 x . \cos^2 x} \, dx$

$= \displaystyle\int \dfrac{(\sin^2 x)^2 + (\cos^2 x)^2 + 2\sin^2 x \cos^2 x - 2\sin^2 x \cos^2 x - \sin^2 x \cos^2 x}{\sin^2 x . \cos^2 x} \, dx$

$I = \displaystyle\int \dfrac{(\sin^2 x + \cos^2 x)^2 - 3\sin^2 x . \cos^2 x}{\sin^2 x . \cos^2 x} \, dx$ **(1 Mark)**

$I = \displaystyle\int \dfrac{1 - 3\sin^2 x . \cos^2 x}{\sin^2 x . \cos^2 x} \, dx$ $[\because \sin^2 x + \cos^2 x = 1]$

$I = \displaystyle\int \dfrac{1}{\sin^2 x . \cos^2 x} \, dx - 3\int 1 dx + c$

Multiply Num. & Den. by $\cos^2 x$

$I = \displaystyle\int \dfrac{\cos^2 x}{\sin^2 x \cdot \cos^4 x} \, dx - 3x + c = \int \dfrac{\sec^4 x}{\tan^2 x} \, dx - 3x + c$

$= \displaystyle\int \dfrac{\sec^2 x . \sec^2 x}{\tan^2 x} \, dx - 3x + c$

$= \displaystyle\int \dfrac{(1 + \tan^2 x) . \sec^2 x}{\tan^2 x} \, dx - 3x + c$ **(1 Mark)**

Let, $\tan x = t$

$\sec^2 x \, dx = dt$

$I = \displaystyle\int \dfrac{(1 + t^2)}{t^2} \, dt - 3x + c$

$I = \displaystyle\int \left(\dfrac{1}{t^2} + 1\right) dt - 3x + c$

$I = -\dfrac{1}{t} + t + t - 3x + c$

$I = \tan x - \dfrac{1}{\tan x} - 3x + c$ **(1 Mark)**

OR

Let $I = \int (x-3)\sqrt{x^2+3x-18}\,dx$

$I = \int \left[\frac{1}{2}(2x+3) - \frac{9}{2}\right]\sqrt{x^2+3x-18}\,dx$ **(1 Mark)**

$I = \frac{1}{2}\int (2x+3)\sqrt{x^2+3x-18}\,dx - \frac{9}{2}\int \sqrt{x^2+3x-18}\,dx$

Let $\quad x^2 + 3x - 18 = t$

$\qquad (2x+3)dx = dt$

$I = \frac{1}{2}\int \sqrt{t}\,dt - \frac{9}{2}\int \sqrt{x^2+3x-18+\left(\frac{3}{2}\right)^2-\left(\frac{3}{2}\right)^2}\,dx$

(1 Mark)

$I = \frac{1}{2}\frac{t^{3/2}}{3/2} - \frac{9}{2}\int \sqrt{\left(x+\frac{3}{2}\right)^2 - \left(\frac{9}{2}\right)^2}\,dx$

$I = \frac{1}{3}(x^2+3x-18)^{3/2} - \frac{9}{2}\left[\frac{1}{2}\left(x+\frac{3}{2}\right)\sqrt{\left(x+\frac{3}{2}\right)^2 - \left(\frac{9}{2}\right)^2}\right.$

$\left. -\frac{1}{2}\left(\frac{9}{2}\right)^2 \log\left|\left(x+\frac{3}{2}\right) + \sqrt{\left(x+\frac{3}{2}\right)^2 - \left(\frac{9}{2}\right)^2}\right|\right] + C$ **(1 Mark)**

$\left[\because \int \sqrt{x^2-a^2}\,dx = \frac{1}{2}x\sqrt{x^2-a^2} - \frac{a^2}{2}\log|x+\sqrt{x^2-a^2}|+c\right]$

$I = \frac{1}{3}(x^2+3x-18)^{3/2} - \frac{9}{4}\left[\left(x+\frac{3}{2}\right)\sqrt{x^2-3x-18}\right.$

$\left. -\frac{81}{4}\log\left|x+\frac{3}{2}+\sqrt{x^2-3x-18}\right|\right] + C$

(1 Mark)

Note

An integral of function in the form of $(px + q)\,\sqrt{ax^2+bx+c}$

then convert $px + q$ in the form $px + q = \dfrac{Ad(ax^2+bx+c)}{dx} + B.$

18. $e^x\sqrt{1-y^2}\,dx + \dfrac{y}{x}dy = 0$

$x\,e^x\,dx + \dfrac{y}{\sqrt{1-y^2}}\,dy = 0$

On integerating

$\int xe^x dx + \int \dfrac{y}{\sqrt{1-y^2}}\,dy = c$ **(1 Mark)**

Let $\quad 1 - y^2 = t$

$-2y\,dy = dt \Rightarrow y\,dy = -\dfrac{1}{2}dt$

$x\int e^x dx - \int 1.e^x dx - \dfrac{1}{2}\int \dfrac{dt}{\sqrt{t}} = c$

$\left[\because \int uv\,dx = u\int v\,dx - \int\left(\dfrac{du}{dx}\int v\,dx\right)dx\right]$ **(1 Mark)**

$x\,e^x - e^x - \dfrac{1}{2}\dfrac{t^{1/2}}{1/2} = c\left[\because \int x^n dx = \dfrac{x^{n+1}}{n+1}\right]$ **(½ Mark)**

$e^x(x-1) - \sqrt{t} = c \Rightarrow e^x(x-1) - \sqrt{1-y^2} = c$

Putting $\quad y = 1, x = 0$

$e^0(-1) - 0 = c$

$c = -1$ **(½ Mark)**

$e^x(x-1) - \sqrt{1-y^2} = -1$ **(1 Mark)**

Note

To solve differential equation shifting all terms containing dx in one side and terms containing dy in other side then separate variable by shifting all function of x to dx and all function of y to dy.

19. $(x^2 - 1)\dfrac{dy}{dx} + 2xy = \dfrac{2}{x^2-1}$

$\dfrac{dy}{dx} + \dfrac{2x}{x^2-1}y = \dfrac{2}{(x^2-1)^2}$ **(½ Mark)**

This is a linear differential equation of the form

$\dfrac{dy}{dx} + py = Q$

where $\quad P = \dfrac{2x}{x^2-1}\quad Q = \dfrac{2}{(x^2-1)^2}$ **(½ Mark)**

I.F. $= e^{\int p\,dx} = e^{\int \frac{2x}{x^2-1}dx}$ **(½ Mark)**

Let $x^2 - 1 = t \Rightarrow 2x\,dx = dt$

I.F. $= e^{\int \frac{1}{t}dt} = e^{\log t} = e^{\log(x^2-1)} = x^2 - 1$

I.F. $= x^2 - 1$ **(1 Mark)**

$y \cdot$ I.F. $= \int Q(IF)dx + c$ **(½ Mark)**

$y(x^2-1) = \int \dfrac{2}{(x^2-1)^2}\,(x^2-1)dx + c$

$y(x^2-1) = 2\int \dfrac{dx}{x^2-1} + c \Rightarrow y(x^2-1) = 2\int \dfrac{dx}{x^2-1} + c$

$\Rightarrow\quad y(x^2-1) = 2 \times \dfrac{1}{2}\log\left|\dfrac{x-1}{x+1}\right| + c$

$\left[\because \int \dfrac{1}{x^2-a^2}dx = \dfrac{1}{2a}\log\left|\dfrac{x-a}{x+a}\right|+c\right]$

$\Rightarrow\quad y(x^2-1) = \log\left|\dfrac{x-1}{x+1}\right| + c$ **(1 Mark)**

20. L.H.S. $[\vec{a}+\vec{b}, \vec{b}+\vec{c}, \vec{c}+\vec{a}]$

$= (\vec{a}+\vec{b})\cdot[(\vec{b}+\vec{c})\times(\vec{c}+\vec{a})]$ **(1 Mark)**

$= (\vec{a}+\vec{b}).[(\vec{b}\times\vec{c}+\vec{b}\times\vec{a}+\vec{c}\times\vec{c}+\vec{c}\times\vec{a}]$ **(1 Mark)**

$= (\vec{a}+\vec{b}).[\vec{b}\times\vec{c}-\vec{a}\times\vec{b}+\vec{o}+\vec{c}+\vec{a}]$ $[\because \vec{c}\times\vec{c}=0]$

$= \vec{a}.(\vec{b}\times\vec{c})-\vec{a}.(\vec{a}\times\vec{b})+\vec{a}.(\vec{c}\times\vec{a})+\vec{b}.(\vec{b}\times c)$
$\qquad +\vec{b}.(\vec{c}\times\vec{a})-\vec{b}.(\vec{a}\times\vec{b})$ **(1 Mark)**

$= \vec{a}.(\vec{b}\times\vec{c})+\vec{b}.(\vec{c}\times\vec{a})$ $\left[\because [\vec{a}\,\vec{a}\,\vec{b}]=0\right]$

$= [\vec{a}\,\vec{b}\,\vec{c}]+[\vec{b}\,\vec{c}\,\vec{a}]$

$\qquad [\because \vec{a}\,(\vec{b}\times\vec{c})=[\vec{a}\,\vec{b}\,\vec{c}],\vec{b}.(\vec{c}\times\vec{a})=[\vec{b}\,\vec{c}\,\vec{a}]]$

$= [\vec{a}\,\vec{b}\,\vec{c}]+[\vec{a}\,\vec{b}\,\vec{c}]$

$= 2[\vec{a}\,\vec{b}\,\vec{c}] = $ R.H.S. **(1 Mark)**

OR

Given: $|\vec{a}| = 3, |\vec{b}| = 5, |\vec{c}| = 7$

$\vec{a}+\vec{b}+\vec{c}=\vec{0} \Rightarrow \vec{a}+\vec{b} = -\vec{c}$

Squaring on both sides

$|\vec{a}+\vec{b}|^2 = |-\vec{c}|^2$ **(1 Mark)**

$\Rightarrow (\vec{a}+\vec{b}).(\vec{a}+\vec{b}) = 7^2 \Rightarrow \vec{a}.\vec{a}+\vec{a}.\vec{b}+\vec{b}.\vec{a}+\vec{b}.\vec{b} = 49$

$\Rightarrow |\vec{a}|^2 +2\vec{a}\cdot\vec{b}+|\vec{b}|^2 = 49$

$\Rightarrow |\vec{a}|^2 +2|\vec{a}||\vec{b}|\cos\theta+|\vec{b}|^2 = 49$ **(1 Mark)**

where θ is the angle between $\vec{a}$ and $\vec{b}$

$3^2 + 2\times 3\times 5\cos\theta + 5^2 = 49$

$\Rightarrow 30\cos\theta = 15$

$\Rightarrow \cos\theta = \dfrac{1}{2}$ **(1 Mark)**

$\Rightarrow \theta = \cos^{-1}\left(\dfrac{1}{2}\right)$

$\Rightarrow \theta = 60°$ **(1 Mark)**

21. Let $\dfrac{x+1}{3} = \dfrac{y+3}{5} = \dfrac{z+5}{7} = P$ ...(1)

Any point in this line is $(3p-1, 5p-3, 7p-5)$

Let $\dfrac{x-2}{1} = \dfrac{y-4}{3} = \dfrac{z-6}{5} = k$ ...(2)

Any point in this line is $(k+2, 3k+4, 5k+6)$ **(1 Mark)**

For lines (1) and (2) to intersect

$3p-1 = k+2 \Rightarrow 3p-k = 3$

$5p-3 = 3k+4 \Rightarrow 5p-3k = 7$

$7p-5 = 5k+6 \Rightarrow 7p-5k = 11$

Solving equations

$k = 3p-3; \quad 5p-3k = 7$

$\Rightarrow 5p-3(3p-3) = 7$

$\Rightarrow p = \dfrac{1}{2}$

$k = 3p-3 = 3\left(\dfrac{1}{2}\right)-3 \Rightarrow k = -\dfrac{3}{2}$

Putting $p = \dfrac{1}{2}, k = \dfrac{-3}{2}$ in $7p-5k = 11$ **(1 Mark)**

$7\left(\dfrac{1}{2}\right) - 5\left(\dfrac{-3}{2}\right) = 11 \Rightarrow \dfrac{7}{2}+\dfrac{15}{2} = 11 \Rightarrow 11 = 11$

Since, it satisfied third equation.

So, both lines intersect each other. **(1 Mark)**

$\therefore$ Lines (1) & and (2) intersect at point

$(3p-1, 5p-3, 7p-5) = \left(\dfrac{1}{2}, -\dfrac{1}{2}, -\dfrac{3}{2}\right)$ **(1 Mark)**

Note

If two lines are intersecting, then their point of intersection will lie on both lines.

22. Sample space of having two children in a family,

$S = [B_1B_2, B_1G_2, G_1G_2, G_1B_2]$

$n(S) = 4$ **(½ Mark)**

Let A be the event that both children are girls

$A = [G_1\,G_2], n(A) = 1$

$p(A) = \dfrac{1}{4}$ **(½ Mark)**

Let B be the event that the youngest child is a girl

$B = [G_1G_2, B_1G_2]; n(B) = 2$

$P(B) = \dfrac{2}{4}$ **(½ Mark)**

Let C be the event that at least one of the children is girl.

$C = [B_1G_2, G_1G_2, G_1B_2]$

$n(C) = 3, P(c) = \dfrac{3}{4}$ **(½ Mark)**

(i) $P(A/B) = \dfrac{P(A\cap B)}{P(B)}$

$A \cap B = \{G_1, G_2\}$

$P(A \cap B) = \dfrac{1}{4}$

$P(A/B) = \dfrac{\dfrac{1}{4}}{\dfrac{2}{4}} = \dfrac{1}{2}$ **(1 Mark)**

(ii) $P(A/C) = \dfrac{P(A\cap C)}{P(C)} = \dfrac{\dfrac{1}{4}}{\dfrac{3}{4}} = \dfrac{1}{3}$

$[\because A\cap C = \{G_1, G_2\}]$ **(1 Mark)**

SECTION - C

23. Let the awards for Discipline, Poltiteness and Punctuality be Rs x, Rs y and Rs z respectively.

$$3x + 2y + z = 1000$$
$$4x + y + 3z = 1500$$
$$x + y + z = 600 \qquad \textbf{(1 Mark)}$$

Matrix form of given equations is

$$AX = B$$

$$A\begin{bmatrix} 3 & 2 & 1 \\ 4 & 1 & 3 \\ 1 & 1 & 1 \end{bmatrix}, X = \begin{bmatrix} x \\ y \\ z \end{bmatrix}, B = \begin{bmatrix} 10 \\ 15 \\ 6 \end{bmatrix}$$

$$\begin{bmatrix} 3 & 2 & 1 \\ 4 & 1 & 3 \\ 1 & 1 & 1 \end{bmatrix} \begin{bmatrix} x \\ y \\ z \end{bmatrix} = \begin{bmatrix} 10 \\ 15 \\ 6 \end{bmatrix} \qquad \textbf{(½ Mark)}$$

$$|A| = \begin{vmatrix} 3 & 2 & 1 \\ 4 & 1 & 3 \\ 1 & 1 & 1 \end{vmatrix} = 3(1-3) - 2(4-3) + 1(4-1)$$

$$= -6 - 2 + 3 = -5 \neq 0 \quad \textbf{(½ Mark)}$$

$\therefore$ A^{-1} exists

$$A_{11} = (-1)^2 (1-3) = -2, A_{12} = (-1)^3 (4-3) = -1$$
$$A_{13} = (-1)^4 (4-1) = 3, A_{21} = (-1)^3 (2-1) = -1$$
$$A_{22} = (-1)^4 (3-1) = 2, A_{23} = (-1)^5 (3-2) = -1$$
$$A_{31} = (-1)^4 (6-1) = 5, A_{32} = (-1)^5 (9-4) = -5$$
$$A_{33} = (-1)^6 (3-8) = -5$$

$$\therefore \quad \text{adj } A = \begin{bmatrix} -2 & -1 & 3 \\ -1 & 2 & -1 \\ 5 & -5 & -5 \end{bmatrix}^T = \begin{bmatrix} -2 & -1 & 5 \\ -1 & 2 & -5 \\ 3 & -1 & -5 \end{bmatrix} \textbf{(2 Marks)}$$

$$A^{-1} = \frac{1}{|A|} \text{adj } A = -\frac{1}{5} \begin{bmatrix} -2 & -1 & 5 \\ -1 & 2 & -5 \\ 3 & -1 & -5 \end{bmatrix} \qquad \textbf{(1 Mark)}$$

$$AX = B$$
$$X = A^{-1} B$$

$$\begin{bmatrix} x \\ y \\ z \end{bmatrix} = -\frac{1}{5} \begin{bmatrix} -2 & -1 & 5 \\ -1 & 2 & -5 \\ 3 & -1 & -5 \end{bmatrix} \begin{bmatrix} 10 \\ 15 \\ 6 \end{bmatrix}$$

$$= -\frac{1}{5} \begin{bmatrix} -2000 & - & 1500 & + & 3000 \\ -1000 & + & 3000 & - & 3000 \\ 3000 & - & 1500 & - & 3000 \end{bmatrix} = -\frac{1}{5} \begin{bmatrix} -5 \\ -10 \\ -15 \end{bmatrix} = \begin{bmatrix} 1 \\ 2 \\ 3 \end{bmatrix}$$

$$\therefore \quad x = ₹100, y = ₹200, z = ₹300 \qquad \textbf{(1 Mark)}$$

A part from the three values, Discipline, Politeness and Punctuality, another value for award, should be hard work.

24. Let θ be the semi vertical angle, h is height, r base radius and l be slant height of a cone

In ΔOAB

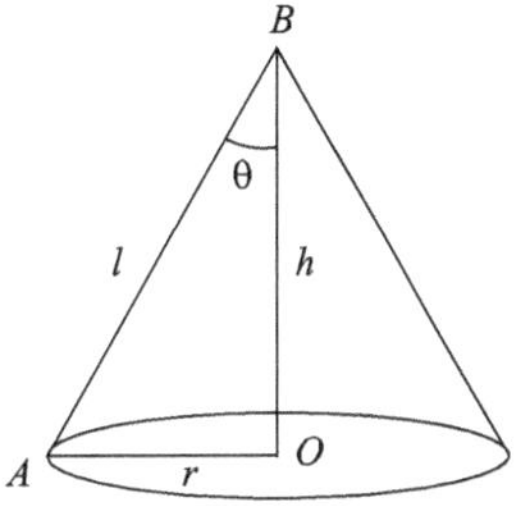

$$\sin \theta = \frac{r}{l} \qquad \left[\because \sin \theta = \frac{P}{H} \right]$$

$$r = l \sin \theta$$

$$\cos \theta = \frac{h}{l} \qquad \left[\because \cos \theta = \frac{B}{H} \right]$$

$$h = l \cos \theta \qquad \textbf{(1 Mark)}$$

Let V be the volume of cone

$$V = \frac{1}{3} \pi r^2 h \qquad \textbf{(1 Mark)}$$

$$V = \frac{1}{3} \pi (l \sin \theta)^2 (l \cos \theta)$$

$$V = \frac{1}{3} \pi l^3 \sin^2 \theta . \cos \theta \qquad \textbf{(½ Mark)}$$

Differentiating w.r.t. θ

$$\frac{dv}{d\theta} = \frac{1}{3} \pi l^3 (2 \sin \theta . \cos \theta \cos \theta - \sin^2 \theta \sin \theta)$$

$$= \frac{1}{3} \pi l^3 \sin \theta (2 \cos^2 \theta - \sin^2 \theta) \qquad \textbf{(1 Mark)}$$

For maxima or minima, $\quad \dfrac{dv}{d\theta} = 0$

$$\sin \theta (2 \cos^2 \theta - \sin^2 \theta) = 0$$
$$\Rightarrow \quad \sin \theta = 0 \text{ or } 2 \cos^2 \theta - \sin^2 \theta = 0$$
$$\Rightarrow \quad \sin \theta \neq 0 \qquad [\because \theta \text{ cannot be } 0]$$
$$\Rightarrow \quad 2 \cos^2 \theta - \sin^2 \theta = 0$$
$$\Rightarrow \quad 2 \cos^2 \theta - (1 - \cos^2 \theta) = 0$$
$$\Rightarrow \quad 3 \cos^2 \theta = 1 \Rightarrow \cos^2 \theta = \frac{1}{3}$$
$$\theta = \cos^{-1} \frac{1}{\sqrt{3}} \qquad \textbf{(1 Mark)}$$

Also, $\cos \theta = \dfrac{1}{\sqrt{3}} \Rightarrow \sin \theta = \dfrac{\sqrt{2}}{\sqrt{3}}$

Again differentiating $\dfrac{dv}{d\theta}$

$$\frac{d^2 v}{d\theta^2} = \frac{1}{3} \pi l^3$$

$[\cos \theta (2 \cos^2 \theta - \sin^2 \theta) + \sin \theta (-4 \cos \theta . \sin \theta - 2 \sin \theta . \cos \theta)]$ **(½ Mark)**

$$= \frac{1}{3} \pi l^3 \left[\frac{1}{\sqrt{3}} \left(2 . \frac{1}{3} - \frac{2}{3} \right) - 6 . \frac{2}{3} . \frac{1}{\sqrt{3}} \right] = \frac{1}{3} \pi l^3 \left(-\frac{4}{\sqrt{3}} \right) < 0$$

$\therefore$ V is maximum for $\theta = \cos^{-1} \left(\dfrac{1}{\sqrt{3}} \right)$

Hence proved.   **(1 Mark)**

25. Let $I = \displaystyle\int_{\frac{\pi}{6}}^{\frac{\pi}{3}} \frac{dx}{1+\sqrt{\cot x}}$

$I = \displaystyle\int_{\frac{\pi}{6}}^{\frac{\pi}{3}} \frac{dx}{1+\sqrt{\dfrac{\cos x}{\sin x}}}$ $\left[\because \cot x = \dfrac{\cos x}{\sin x}\right]$ **(1 Mark)**

$I = \displaystyle\int_{\frac{\pi}{6}}^{\frac{\pi}{3}} \frac{\sqrt{\sin x}}{\sqrt{\sin x}+\sqrt{\cos x}}\,dx$ ...(1) **(1 Mark)**

$I = \displaystyle\int_{\frac{\pi}{6}}^{\frac{\pi}{3}} \frac{\sqrt{\sin\left(\dfrac{\pi}{2}-x\right)}}{\sqrt{\sin\left(\dfrac{\pi}{2}-x\right)}+\sqrt{\cos\left(\dfrac{\pi}{2}-x\right)}}\,dx$

$\left[\because \displaystyle\int_a^b f(x)dx = \int_a^b f(a+b-x)\,dx\right.$

$\left.\text{where } a+b = \dfrac{\pi}{6}+\dfrac{\pi}{3} = \dfrac{\pi}{2}\right]$ **(1 Mark)**

$I = \displaystyle\int_{\frac{\pi}{6}}^{\frac{\pi}{3}} \frac{\sqrt{\cos x}}{\sqrt{\cos x}+\sqrt{\sin x}}\,dx$ ...(2) **(1 Mark)**

Adding (1) and (2)

$2I = \displaystyle\int_{\frac{\pi}{6}}^{\frac{\pi}{3}} \frac{\sqrt{\cos x}+\sqrt{\sin x}}{\sqrt{\cos x}+\sqrt{\sin x}}\,dx \;\Rightarrow\; 2I = \int_{\frac{\pi}{6}}^{\frac{\pi}{3}} 1\,dx$ **(1 Mark)**

$2I = (x)_{\frac{\pi}{6}}^{\frac{\pi}{3}} \;\Rightarrow\; 2I = \dfrac{\pi}{3}-\dfrac{\pi}{6} = \dfrac{\pi}{6}$ **(1 Mark)**

$I = \dfrac{\pi}{12}$

26. Equation of line: $y = x$ ...(1)

Equation of circle: $x^2 + y^2 = 32$ ...(2)

$y = \sqrt{32-x^2}$

$y^2 + y^2 = 32 \Rightarrow 2y^2 = 32$ [from (1) and (2)]

$\Rightarrow y = \pm 4;\; x = \pm 4$

$\therefore$ Point of intersection of circle and line is (4, 4) and (–4, –4). **(1 Mark)**

$x^2 + y^2 = 32$

$x^2 + y^2 = \left(4\sqrt{2}\right)^2$

Circle meets x axis at $p(4\sqrt{2}, 0)$ and $p'(-4\sqrt{2}, 0)$

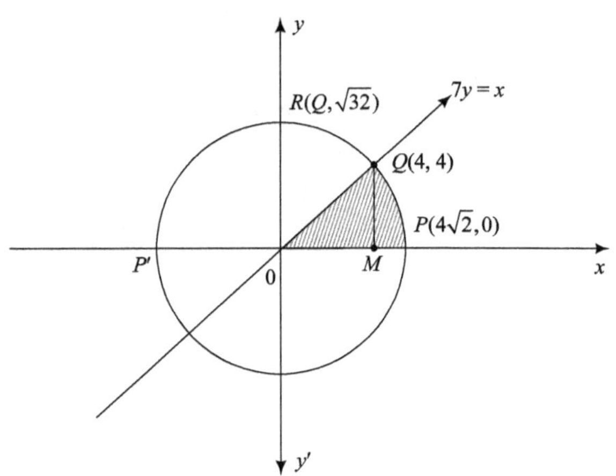

(1 Mark)

Required area = Area OPQ

$= \displaystyle\int_0^4 y_1\,dx + \int_4^{4\sqrt{2}} y_2\,dx = \int_0^4 x\,dx + \int_4^{4\sqrt{2}} \sqrt{32-x^2}\,dx$ **(1 Mark)**

Required area

$= \left[\dfrac{x^2}{2}\right]_0^4 + \left[\dfrac{x\sqrt{32-x^2}}{2} + \dfrac{32}{2}\sin^{-1}\left(\dfrac{x}{4\sqrt{2}}\right)\right]_4^{4\sqrt{2}}$ **(1 Mark)**

$\left[\because \displaystyle\int \sqrt{a^2-x^2}\,dx = \dfrac{x}{2}\sqrt{a^2-x^2} + \dfrac{a^2}{2}\sin^{-1}\dfrac{x}{a} + c\right]$

$= 8 + \left[0 + 16\sin^{-1}(1) - \dfrac{4.4}{2} - 16\sin^{-1}\left(\dfrac{1}{\sqrt{2}}\right)\right]$

$= 16\left(\dfrac{\pi}{2}-\dfrac{\pi}{4}\right) = 16 \times \dfrac{\pi}{4} = 4\pi$ sq. units **(2 Marks)**

27. The plane passing through $A(2, 5, -3)$ is
$a(x-2) + b(y-5) + c(z+3) = 0$ ...(1) **(1 Mark)**
It also passes through $B(-2, -3, 5)$ and $C(5, 3, -3)$
$-4a - 8b + 8c = 0$ ...(2) **(1 Mark)**
$3a - 2b + 0c = 0$ ...(3) **(1 Mark)**
On solving equation (2) and (3)

$\dfrac{a}{0+16} = \dfrac{b}{24-0} = \dfrac{c}{8+24}$

$\dfrac{a}{2} = \dfrac{b}{3} = \dfrac{c}{4}$ ...(4) **(1 Mark)**

From (1) & (4) equation of required plane is
$2(x-2) + 3(y-5) + 4(z+3) = 0$
$2x - 4 + 3y - 15 + 4z + 12 = 0$

$2x + 3y + 4z - 7 = 0$ **(1 Mark)**

$\therefore$ Distance of the point from plane is

$d = \left|\dfrac{ax_1 + by_1 + cz_1 - d}{\sqrt{a^2+b^2+c^2}}\right| = \left|\dfrac{2\times 7 + 3\times 2 + 4\times 4 - 7}{\sqrt{2^2+3^2+4^2}}\right|$

$d = \left|\dfrac{14+6+16-7}{\sqrt{4+9+16}}\right| = \dfrac{29}{\sqrt{29}} = \sqrt{29}$ **(1 Mark)**

 *Note*

Alternate method to find equation of plane by formula.

$$\begin{vmatrix} x-x_1 & y-y_1 & z-z_1 \\ x_2-x_1 & y_2-y_1 & z_2-z_1 \\ x_3-x_1 & y_3-y_1 & z_3-z_1 \end{vmatrix} = 0$$

OR

Given plane: $\vec{r}.(\hat{i} - \hat{j} + \hat{k}) = 5$

Cartesian form $x - y + z = 5$ ...(1)   **(1 Mark)**

The Given line is

$$\vec{r} = 2\hat{i} - \hat{j} + 2\hat{k} + \lambda(3\hat{i} + 4\hat{j} + 2\hat{k})$$

$$\frac{x-2}{3} = \frac{y+1}{4} = \frac{z-2}{2} = \lambda \qquad \textbf{(1 Mark)}$$

Point on the Given line is $(3\lambda + 2, 4\lambda - 1, 2\lambda + 2)$

(1 Mark)

As both of the plane and line are intersecting, point will also lie on plane

$3\lambda + 2 - 4\lambda + 1 + 2\lambda + 2 = 5$

$\lambda = 0$

$\therefore$ Point of intersection is $(2, -1, 2)$ **(1 Mark)**

Distance between $(2, -1, 2)$ and $(-1, -5, -10)$ is Given as

$$d = \sqrt{(x_2 - x_1)^2 + (y_2 - y_1)^2 + (z_2 - z_1)^2} \qquad \textbf{(1 Mark)}$$

$$d = \sqrt{9 + 16 + 144} = \sqrt{169} = 13$$

Distance = 13 units.   **(1 Mark)**

28. Let the electronic and manually operated sewing machine bought by dealer be x and y respectively

The LPP is

Maximize $z = 22x + 18y$ **(1 Mark)**

Subject to constraints

$x + y \leq 20$

$360x + 240y \leq 5760$

$3x + 2y \leq 48$

$x \geq 0, y \geq 0$ **(2 Marks)**

$x + y = 20$

x	20	0	8
y	0	20	12

$3x + 2y = 48$

x	16	0	8
y	0	24	12

Point of intersection of both the lines is $(8, 12)$

$\therefore$ The feasible region is $OCPAO$ which is shaded in the figure

The vertices of feasible region is $0(0, 0)$, $C(16, 0)$, $A(0, 20)$, $P(8, 12)$

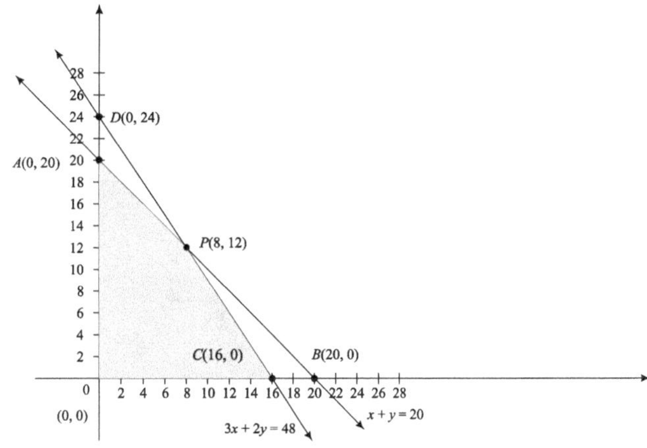

(2 Marks)

Corner Points	$Z = 22x + 18y$
$O(0, 0)$	$Z = 0$
$C(16, 0)$	$Z = 352$
$P(8, 12)$	$Z = 392$ (max)
$A(0, 20)$	$Z = 360$

$\therefore$ maximum profit is ₹392 when 8 electronic and 12 manually operated machines are purchases   **(1 Mark)**

29. Let the events be

E_1 = the missing card is a heart card

E_2 = the missing card is a spade card

E_3 = the missing card is a club card

E_4 = the missing card is a diamond card

A = drawing three spades card from the remaining card.

(1 Mark)

$$P(E_1) = \frac{13}{52} = \frac{1}{4} \quad \Rightarrow \quad P(E_2) = \frac{13}{52} = \frac{1}{4}$$

$$P(E_3) = \frac{13}{52} = \frac{1}{4}$$

$$P(E_4) = \frac{13}{52} = \frac{1}{4} \qquad \textbf{(1 Mark)}$$

$$P(A/E_1) = \frac{^{13}C_3}{^{51}C_3}, \ P(A/E_2) = \frac{^{12}C_3}{^{51}C_3}$$

$$P(A/E_3) = \frac{^{13}C_3}{^{51}C_3}, \ P(A/E_4) = \frac{^{13}C_3}{^{51}C_3} \qquad \textbf{(1 Mark)}$$

Required probability $= P\left(\dfrac{E_2}{A}\right)$

$$P\left(\frac{E_2}{A}\right)$$

$$= \frac{P(E_2)P\left(\dfrac{A}{E_2}\right)}{P\left(\dfrac{A}{E_1}\right)P(E_1) + P\left(\dfrac{A}{E_2}\right).P(E_2) + P\left(\dfrac{A}{E_3}\right)P(E_3) + P\left(\dfrac{A}{E_4}\right)P(E_4)}$$

(1 Mark)

$$= \dfrac{\dfrac{1}{4} \times \dfrac{^{12}C_3}{^{51}C_3}}{\dfrac{1}{4} \times \dfrac{^{13}C_3}{^{51}C_3} + \dfrac{1}{4} \times \dfrac{^{12}C_3}{^{51}C_3} + \dfrac{1}{4} \dfrac{^{13}C_3}{^{51}C_3} + \dfrac{1}{4} \times \dfrac{^{13}C_3}{^{51}C_3}}$$

$$= \dfrac{^{12}C_3}{^{12}C_3 + 3 \times {}^{13}C_3}$$

$$^{12}C_3 = \dfrac{12!}{(12-3)!\,3!} = \dfrac{12 \times 11 \times 10 \times 9!}{9! \times 3 \times 2 \times 1}$$

$$= 220 \quad \left[\because {}^nC_r = \dfrac{n!}{r!(n-r)!} \right]$$

$$^{13}C_3 = \dfrac{13!}{3!\,10!} = \dfrac{13 \times 12 \times 11 \times 10!}{3 \times 2 \times 1 \times 10!} = 286$$

$$\therefore \quad P\left(\dfrac{E_2}{A}\right) = \dfrac{220}{220 + 3 \times 286}$$

$$P\left(\dfrac{E_2}{A}\right) = \dfrac{110}{539} \qquad \textbf{(2 Marks)}$$

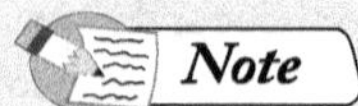 **Note**

An experiment is done in two steps, first step is done in two or more ways and second step gives final event. When we have to find the probability of final event occurs through any one event (way) of first step then use Bayes's theorem.

OR

Let D be the event of drawing a defective bulb and X denote the variable showing the number of defective bulbs in 4 draws.

$$P(D) = \dfrac{5}{15} = \dfrac{1}{3}$$

$$P(\bar{D}) = 1 - \dfrac{1}{3} = \dfrac{2}{3} \qquad \textbf{(1 Mark)}$$

The drawn bulb is replaced.

$\therefore$ X can take values 0, 1, 2, 3 and 4   **(½ Mark)**

$$P(X = 0) = P(\text{Getting no defective bulb})$$

$$= {}^4C_0 \left(\dfrac{1}{3}\right)^0 \left(\dfrac{2}{3}\right)^4$$

$$= \left(\dfrac{2}{3}\right)^4 = \dfrac{16}{81} \quad [\because P(X) = {}^nC_r\, P^r\, q^{n-r}] \quad \textbf{(½ Mark)}$$

$$P(X = 1) = {}^4C_1 \left(\dfrac{1}{3}\right)\left(\dfrac{2}{3}\right)^3 = \dfrac{32}{81}$$

$$P(X = 2) = {}^4C_2 \left(\dfrac{1}{3}\right)^2 \left(\dfrac{2}{3}\right)^2 = \dfrac{24}{81}$$

$$P(X = 3) = {}^4C_3 \left(\dfrac{1}{3}\right)^3 \left(\dfrac{2}{3}\right) = \dfrac{8}{81}$$

$$P(X = 4) = {}^4C_4 \left(\dfrac{1}{3}\right)^4 = \dfrac{1}{81} \qquad \textbf{(2 Marks)}$$

$\therefore$ The probability distribution is

X	0	1	2	3	4	Total
$P(X = x)$	$\dfrac{16}{81}$	$\dfrac{32}{81}$	$\dfrac{24}{81}$	$\dfrac{8}{81}$	$\dfrac{1}{81}$	1

(1 Mark)

Mean of the distribution $= \Sigma P_i X_i$

$$= \dfrac{16}{81} \times 0 + \dfrac{32}{81} \times 1 + \dfrac{24}{81} \times 2 + \dfrac{8}{81} \times 3 + \dfrac{1}{81} \times 4$$

$$= \dfrac{1}{81}(0 + 32 + 48 + 24 + 4) = \dfrac{108}{81} = \dfrac{4}{3} \quad \textbf{(1 Mark)}$$

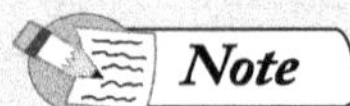 **Note**

In case of with replacement, number of trial is finite and probability of success is large then use binomial distribution.

All India *2013*
CBSE Board Solved Paper

Time Allowed : 3 Hours   *Maximum Marks : 100*

General Instructions:
- (i) **All** questions are compulsory.
- (ii) The question paper contains of **29** questions divided into three sections A, B and C. Section A comprises of **10** questions of **one** mark each, section B comprises of **12** questions of **four** marks each and section C comprises of **07** questions of **six** marks each.
- (iii) All questions in Section A are to be answered in one word, one sentence or as per the exact requirement of the question.
- (iv) There is no overall choice. However, internal choice has been provided in **04** questions of **four** marks each and **02** questions of **six** marks each. You have to attempt only one of the alternatives in all such questions.
- (v) Use of calculator is not permitted. You may ask for logarithmic tables, if required.

SECTION - A

1. Write the principal value of $\tan^{-1}\left(\sqrt{3}\right) - \cot^{-1}\left(-\sqrt{3}\right)$

2. Write the value of $\tan^{-1}\left[2\sin\left(2\cos^{-1}\dfrac{\sqrt{3}}{2}\right)\right]$

3. For what value of x, is the matrix $A = \begin{bmatrix} 0 & 1 & -2 \\ -1 & 0 & 3 \\ x & -3 & 0 \end{bmatrix}$ a skew-symmetric matrix?

4. If matrix $A = \begin{bmatrix} 1 & -1 \\ -1 & 1 \end{bmatrix}$ and $A^2 = kA$, then write the value of k.

5. Write the differential equation representing the family of curves $y = mx$, where m is an arbitrary constant.

6. If A_{ij} is the cofactor of the element a_{ij} of the determinant $\begin{vmatrix} 2 & -3 & 5 \\ 6 & 0 & 4 \\ 1 & 5 & -7 \end{vmatrix}$, then write the value of $a_{32}.A_{32}$.

7. P and Q are two points with position vectors $3\vec{a} - 2\vec{b}$ and $\vec{a} + \vec{b}$ respectively. Write the position vector of a point R which divides the line segment PQ in the ratio 2 : 1 externally.

8. Find $\left|\vec{x}\right|$, if for a unit vector $\vec{a}$, $\left(\vec{x} - \vec{a}\right).\left(\vec{x} + \vec{a}\right) = 15$

9. Find the length of the perpendicular drawn from the origin to the plane $2x - 3y + 6z + 21 = 0$

10. The money to be spent for the welfare of the employees of a firm is proportional to the rate of change of its total revenue (marginal revenue). If the total revenue (in rupees) received from the sale of x units of a product is given by $R(x) = 3x^2 + 36x + 5$, find the marginal revenue, when $x = 5$, and write which value does the question indicate.

SECTION - B

11. Consider $f : R^+ \to [4, \infty)$ given by $f(x) = x^2 + 4$. Show that f is invertible with the inverse f^{-1} of f given by $f^{-1}(y) = \sqrt{y - 4}$, where R^+ is the set of all non-negative real numbers.

12. Show that $\tan\left(\dfrac{1}{2}\sin^{-1}\dfrac{3}{4}\right) = \dfrac{4 - \sqrt{7}}{3}$

OR

Solve the following equation: $\cos(\tan^{-1} x) = \sin\left(\cot^{-1}\dfrac{3}{4}\right)$

13. Using properties of determinants, prove the following:
$$\begin{vmatrix} x & x+y & x+2y \\ x+2y & x & x+y \\ x+y & x+2y & x \end{vmatrix} = 9y^2(x+y)$$

14. If $y^x = e^{y-x}$, prove that $\dfrac{dy}{dx} = \dfrac{(1+\log y)^2}{\log y}$

15. Differentiate the following with respect to x:
$$\sin^{-1}\left(\dfrac{2^{x+1}.3^x}{1 + (36)^x}\right)$$

16. Find the value of k, for which

$$f(x) = \begin{cases} \dfrac{\sqrt{1+kx} - \sqrt{1-kx}}{x}, & \text{if } -1 \le x < 0 \\ \dfrac{2x+1}{x-1}, & \text{if } 0 \le x < 1 \end{cases}$$

is continuous at $x = 0$

OR

If $x = a\cos^3\theta$ and $y = a\sin^3\theta$, then find the value of $\dfrac{d^2y}{dx^2}$ at $\theta = \dfrac{\pi}{6}$.

17. Evaluate : $\displaystyle\int \dfrac{\cos 2x - \cos 2\alpha}{\cos x - \cos \alpha}\, dx$

OR

Evaluate: $\displaystyle\int \dfrac{x+2}{\sqrt{x^2 + 2x + 3}}\, dx$

18. Evaluate : $\displaystyle\int \dfrac{dx}{x(x^5 + 3)}$

19. Evaluate: $\displaystyle\int_0^{2\pi} \dfrac{1}{1 + e^{\sin x}}\, dx$

20. If $\vec{a} = \hat{i} - \hat{j} + 7\hat{k}$ and $\vec{b} = 5\hat{i} - \hat{j} + \lambda\hat{k}$, then find the value of λ, so that $\vec{a} + \vec{b}$ and $\vec{a} - \vec{b}$ are perpendicular vectors.

21. Show that the lines $\vec{r} = 3\hat{i} + 2j - 4\hat{k} + \lambda(\hat{i} + 2\hat{j} + 2\hat{k})$; $\vec{r} = 5\hat{i} - 2j + \mu(3\hat{i} + 2\hat{j} + 6\hat{k})$ are intersecting. Hence, find their point of intersection

OR

Find the vector equation of the plane through the points $(2, 1, -1)$ and $(-1, 3, 4)$ and perpendicular to the plane $x - 2y + 4z = 10$.

22. The probabilities of two students A and B coming to the school in time are $\dfrac{3}{7}$ and $\dfrac{5}{7}$ respectively. Assuming that the events, 'A coming in time' and 'B coming in time' are independent, find the probability of only one of them coming to the school in time. Write at least one advantage of coming to school in time.

SECTION - C

23. Find the area of greatest rectangle that can be inscribed in an ellipse $\dfrac{x^2}{a^2} + \dfrac{y^2}{b^2} = 1$.

OR

Find the equation of tangent to the curve $3x^2 - y^2 = 8$, which pass through the point $\left(\dfrac{4}{3}, 0\right)$.

24. Find the area of the region bounded by the parabola $y = x^2$ and $y = |x|$.

25. Find the particular solution of the differential equation $(\tan^{-1} y - x)\, dy = (1 + y^2)dx$, given that when $x = 0$, $y = 0$.

26. Find the equation of the plane passing through the line of intersection of the planes $\vec{r}.(\hat{i} + 3\hat{j}) - 6 = 0$ and $\vec{r}.(3\hat{i} - \hat{j} - 4\hat{k}) = 0$, whose perpendicular distance from origin is unity.

OR

Find the vector equation of the line passing through the point $(1, 2, 3)$ and parallel to the plane $\vec{r}.(\hat{i} - \hat{j} + 2\hat{k}) = 5$ and $\vec{r}.(3\hat{i} + \hat{j} + \hat{k}) = 6$

27. In a hockey match, both teams A and B scored same number of goals up to the end of the game, so to decide the winner, the referee asked both the captains to throw a die alternatively and decided that the team, whose captain gets a six first, will be declared the winner. If the captain of team A was asked to start, find their respective probabilities of winning the match and state whether the decision of the referee was fair or not.

28. A manufacturer considers that men and women workers are equally efficient and so he pays them at the same rate. He has 30 and 17 units of workers (male and female) and capital respectively, which he uses to produce two types of goods A and B. To produce one unit of A, 2 workers and 3 units of capital are required while 3 workers and 1 unit of capital is required to produce one unit of B. If A and B are prices at ₹ 100 and ₹ 120 per unit respectively, how should he use his resources to maximise the total revenue? Form the above as a LPP and solve graphically.

Do you agree with this view of the manufacturer that men and women workers are equally efficient and so should be paid at the same rate?

29. The management committee of a residential colony decided to award some of its members (say x) for honesty, some (say y) for helping others and some others (say z) for supervising the workers to keep the colony neat and clean. The sum of all the awardees is 12. Three times the sum of awardees for cooperation and supervision added to two times the number of awardees for honesty is 33. If the sum of the number of awardees for honesty and supervision is twice the number of awardees for helping others, using matrix method, find the number of awardees of each category. Apart from these values, namely, honesty, cooperation and supervision, suggest one more value which the management of the colony must include for awards.

Solutions

SECTION - A

1. Cocsider $\tan^{-1}\sqrt{3} - \cot^{-1}\left(-\sqrt{3}\right)$

$= \tan^{-1}\left(\tan\dfrac{\pi}{3}\right) - \cot^{-1}\left(-\cot\dfrac{\pi}{6}\right)$ **(½ Mark)**

$= \dfrac{\pi}{3} - \cot^{-1}\left(\cot\left(\pi - \dfrac{\pi}{6}\right)\right)$

$= \dfrac{\pi}{3} - \dfrac{5\pi}{6} = -\dfrac{\pi}{2}$ **(½ Mark)**

> **Note**
>
> *The value of an inverse trigonometric function which lies in the range of principal branch is the principal value of that inverse trigonometric function.*

2. Consider $\tan^{-1}\left[2\sin\left(2\cos^{-1}\dfrac{\sqrt{3}}{2}\right)\right]$

$= \tan^{-1}\left[2\sin\left(2\cos^{-1}\left(\cos\dfrac{\pi}{6}\right)\right)\right]$

$= \tan^{-1}\left[2\sin\left(2\times\dfrac{\pi}{6}\right)\right] = \tan^{-1}\left[2\sin\dfrac{\pi}{3}\right] = \tan^{-1}\left[2.\dfrac{\sqrt{3}}{2}\right]$

$= \tan^{-1}\sqrt{3} = \tan^{-1}\left(\tan\dfrac{\pi}{3}\right) = \dfrac{\pi}{3}$ **(1 Mark)**

3. $A = \begin{bmatrix} 0 & 1 & -2 \\ -1 & 0 & 3 \\ x & -3 & 0 \end{bmatrix}$, $A' = \begin{bmatrix} 0 & -1 & x \\ 1 & 0 & -3 \\ -2 & 3 & 0 \end{bmatrix}$

We know that A is skew-symmetric, if $A' = -A$ **(½ Mark)**

$\Rightarrow \begin{bmatrix} 0 & -1 & x \\ 1 & 0 & -3 \\ -2 & 3 & 0 \end{bmatrix} = -\begin{bmatrix} 0 & 1 & -2 \\ -1 & 0 & 3 \\ x & -3 & 0 \end{bmatrix} = \begin{bmatrix} 0 & -1 & 2 \\ 1 & 0 & -3 \\ -x & 3 & 0 \end{bmatrix}$

On comparing values of elements of matrices

$\Rightarrow \quad x = 2 \text{ or} -x = -2$ **(½ Mark)**

$\Rightarrow \quad x = 2$

4. Let $A = \begin{bmatrix} 1 & -1 \\ -1 & 1 \end{bmatrix}$

$\Rightarrow \quad A^2 = \begin{bmatrix} 1 & -1 \\ -1 & 1 \end{bmatrix}\begin{bmatrix} 1 & -1 \\ -1 & 1 \end{bmatrix} = \begin{bmatrix} 2 & -2 \\ -2 & 2 \end{bmatrix}$

Given $A^2 = kA$

$\Rightarrow \begin{bmatrix} 2 & -2 \\ -2 & 2 \end{bmatrix} = k\begin{bmatrix} 1 & -1 \\ -1 & 1 \end{bmatrix} = \begin{bmatrix} k & -k \\ -k & k \end{bmatrix}$

$\Rightarrow \quad k = 2$ **(1 Mark)**

5. Consider $y = mx$ ...(i)

$\Rightarrow \dfrac{dy}{dx} = m$

From (i), we have $y = \dfrac{dy}{dx}x \Rightarrow x\dfrac{dy}{dx} - y = 0$ **(1 Mark)**

which is the required differential equation.

> **Note**
>
> *Differentiate the given equation as many number of times as the number of arbitrary constants present in the equation.*

6. $\Delta = \begin{vmatrix} 2 & -3 & 5 \\ 6 & 0 & 4 \\ 1 & 5 & -7 \end{vmatrix}$

$A_{32} = $ Cofactor of element a_{32} **(½ Mark)**

$= -\begin{vmatrix} 2 & 5 \\ 6 & 4 \end{vmatrix} = -(8-30) = 22$

$\therefore a_{32}.A_{32} = 5(22) = 110$ $[\because a_{32} = 5]$ **(½ Mark)**

7. Let $P\left(3\vec{a} - 2\vec{b}\right)$ and $Q\left(\vec{a} + \vec{b}\right)$ be the given points

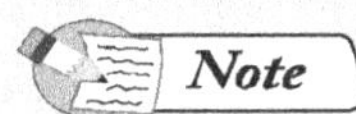

   (½ Mark)

The position vector of point R dividing PQ externally in the ratio 2 : 1 is

$\dfrac{2\left(\vec{a} + \vec{b}\right) - 1\left(3\vec{a} - 2\vec{b}\right)}{2 - 1} = -\vec{a} + 4\vec{b}$ **(½ Mark)**

> **Note**
>
> *If ratios are given externaly, then take ratios as m : −n in the farmula to get position vector of a point.*

8. Given, $\vec{a}$ is a unit vector $\therefore |\vec{a}| = 1$

Now, consider $(\vec{x} - \vec{a}).(\vec{x} + \vec{a}) = 15$

$\Rightarrow \quad |\vec{x}|^2 - |\vec{a}|^2 = 15$

$\Rightarrow \quad |\vec{x}|^2 - 1 = 15 \Rightarrow |\vec{x}|^2 = 16 \Rightarrow |\vec{x}| = 4$ **(1 Mark)**

9. Required length of the perpendicular from origin $(0, 0, 0)$ to the given plane

$$= \frac{|2(0) - 3(0) + 6(0) + 21|}{\sqrt{2^2 + (-3)^2 + (6)^2}} = \frac{21}{7} = 3 \text{ units.} \quad \textbf{(1 Mark)}$$

10. Here, total revenue (in ₹) received from sale of x units of a product is given by
$R(x) = 3x^2 + 36x + 5$
Differentiate w.r.t. 'x'

$$\Rightarrow \quad \frac{d}{dx} R(x) = 6x + 36$$

$$\Rightarrow \quad \frac{d}{dx} R(x) \bigg]_{x=5} = 6 \times 5 + 36 = ₹66 \quad \textbf{(1 Mark)}$$

Welfare of the employees indicate social and moral values.

SECTION - B

11. Here, $f : R^+ \rightarrow [4, \infty)$ is given by $f(x) = x^2 + 4$

If f is one-one and onto then it is also invertible
To show one-one
Let $x_1, x_2 \in R^+$, such that
$f(x_1) = f(x_2)$

$\Rightarrow x_1^2 + 4 = x_2^2 + 4$

$\Rightarrow \quad x_1^2 = x_2^2 \Rightarrow x_1 = x_2 \qquad [\because x_1, x_2 \geq 0]$

Thus, f is one-one.   **(1 Mark)**
For onto

Let $y \in R_f$, then $y = f(x)$, for all $x \in D_f = R^+$
$\Rightarrow \quad y = x^2 + 4$

$\Rightarrow \quad x = \sqrt{y - 4} \qquad [\because x \geq 0]$

As x is real, $y - 4 \geq 0 \Rightarrow R_f = [4, \infty)$

$R_f =$ Co-domain $\Rightarrow$ f is onto.   **(1 Mark)**
Now, f is one-one and onto
$\therefore f^{-1}$ exists.
For f^{-1}, we have

$\qquad fof^{-1}(x) = x$, for all $x \in R_f$

$\Rightarrow f(f^{-1}(x)) = x$
$\Rightarrow \{f^{-1}(x)\}^2 + 4 = x \qquad$ (By defn of f(x))
$\Rightarrow \{f^{-1}(x)\}^2 = x - 4$
$\Rightarrow f^{-1}(x) = \sqrt{x - 4}$ **(2 Marks)**

12. Let $\sin^{-1} \frac{3}{4} = \theta \Rightarrow \sin\theta = \frac{3}{4}$

$$\cos\theta = \sqrt{1 - \sin^2\theta} = \sqrt{1 - \left(\frac{3}{4}\right)^2} = \frac{\sqrt{7}}{4}$$

Now, L.H.S : $\tan\left(\frac{1}{2} \sin^{-1} \frac{3}{4}\right) = \tan\frac{\theta}{2}$ **(2 Marks)**

As $\tan\theta = \sqrt{\dfrac{1 - \cos 2\theta}{1 + \cos 2\theta}}$

$$\therefore \tan\frac{\theta}{2} = \sqrt{\frac{1 - \cos\theta}{1 + \cos\theta}} = \sqrt{\frac{1 - \frac{\sqrt{7}}{4}}{1 + \frac{\sqrt{7}}{4}}}$$

$$= \sqrt{\frac{4 - \sqrt{7}}{4 + \sqrt{7}} \times \frac{4 - \sqrt{7}}{4 - \sqrt{7}}}$$

$$= \frac{4 - \sqrt{7}}{\sqrt{16 - 7}} = \frac{4 - \sqrt{7}}{3} = \text{R.H.S.} \quad \textbf{(2 Marks)}$$

OR

Let $\cot^{-1} \frac{3}{4} = \theta \Rightarrow \cot\theta = \frac{3}{4}$

$$\Rightarrow \quad \tan\theta = \frac{4}{3} \Rightarrow \sin\theta = \frac{4}{5}$$

$$\Rightarrow \quad \theta = \sin^{-1} \frac{4}{5}, \therefore \cot^{-1} \frac{3}{4} = \sin^{-1} \frac{4}{5} \quad ...(i) \quad \textbf{(1 Mark)}$$

and let $\tan^{-1} x = \phi$

$\Rightarrow \quad \tan\phi = x \Rightarrow \sec\phi = \sqrt{1 + \tan^2\phi}$

$\Rightarrow \quad \sec\phi = \sqrt{1 + x^2}$

$$\Rightarrow \quad \cos\phi = \frac{1}{\sqrt{1 + x^2}}$$

$$\Rightarrow \quad \phi = \cos^{-1} \frac{1}{\sqrt{1 + x^2}}, \quad \textbf{(2 Marks)}$$

$$\therefore \quad \tan^{-1} x = \cos^{-1} \frac{1}{\sqrt{1 + x^2}} \quad ...(ii)$$

Now, consider $\cos(\tan^{-1} x) = \sin\left(\cot^{-1}\dfrac{3}{4}\right)$

$\Rightarrow \quad \cos\left(\cos^{-1}\dfrac{1}{\sqrt{1+x^2}}\right) = \sin\left(\sin^{-1}\dfrac{4}{5}\right)$

[From equations (i) & (ii)]

$\Rightarrow \quad \dfrac{1}{\sqrt{1+x^2}} = \dfrac{4}{5} \Rightarrow x = \pm\dfrac{3}{4}$ **(1 Mark)**

13. Let $\Delta = \begin{vmatrix} x & x+y & x+2y \\ x+2y & x & x+y \\ x+y & x+2y & x \end{vmatrix}$

Operating $C_1 \to C_1 + C_2 + C_3$

$\Delta = \begin{vmatrix} 3(x+y) & x+y & x+2y \\ 3(x+y) & x & x+y \\ 3(x+y) & x+2y & x \end{vmatrix}$ **(1 Mark)**

Taking $3(x+y)$ common from C_1

$\Delta = 3(x+y)\begin{vmatrix} 1 & x+y & x+2y \\ 1 & x & x+y \\ 1 & x+2y & x \end{vmatrix}$

Operating $R_2 \to R_2 - R_1$ and $R_3 \to R_3 - R_1$

$\Delta = 3(x+y)\begin{vmatrix} 1 & x+y & x+2y \\ 0 & -y & -y \\ 0 & y & -2y \end{vmatrix}$ **(1 Mark)**

Taking y common from R_2 and R_3

$\Delta = 3y^2(x+y)\begin{vmatrix} 1 & x+y & x+2y \\ 0 & -1 & -1 \\ 0 & 1 & -2 \end{vmatrix}$

Expanding by C_1, we get
$\Delta = 3y^2(x+y)\{1(2+1)\} = 9y^2(x+y)$
Hence Proved. **(2 Marks)**

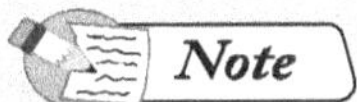 **Note**

For evaluation of determinant, use properties of determinant to obtain maximum number of zeroes in a row or a column.

14. Given $y^x = e^{y-x}$
Taking log on both sides, we get
$\qquad x \log y = (y - x) \log e$

$\Rightarrow \quad x \log y = y - x \Rightarrow x(1 + \log y) = y$

$\Rightarrow \quad x = \dfrac{y}{1 + \log y}$ **(1 Mark)**

Differentiate both sides w.r.t, y, we get

$\dfrac{dx}{dy} = \dfrac{(1+\log y).1 - y\left(0 + \dfrac{1}{y}\right)}{(1+\log y)^2}$

$\left[\because \ \dfrac{d}{dx}\left(\dfrac{u}{v}\right) = \dfrac{v\dfrac{du}{dx} - u\dfrac{dv}{dx}}{v^2}\right]$

$\dfrac{dx}{dy} = \dfrac{1+\log y - 1}{(1+\log y)^2} = \dfrac{\log y}{(1+\log y)^2}$ **(1 Mark)**

$\Rightarrow \quad \dfrac{dy}{dx} = \dfrac{(1+\log y)^2}{\log y}$ **(2 Marks)**

15. Let $y = \sin^{-1}\left(\dfrac{2^{x+1}.3^x}{1+(36)^x}\right)$

$= \sin^{-1}\left(\dfrac{2^x.2.3^x}{1+(6)^{2x}}\right) = \sin^{-1}\left(\dfrac{2.6^x}{1+(6)^{2x}}\right)$ **(1 Mark)**

Put $6^x = \tan\theta$
$\Rightarrow 1 + (6)^{2x} = 1 + \tan^2\theta = \sec^2\theta$

Now, $y = \sin^{-1}\left(\dfrac{2\tan\theta}{\sec^2\theta}\right)$ **(1 Mark)**

$= \sin^{-1}\left(2\dfrac{\sin\theta}{\cos\theta}.\cos^2\theta\right) = \sin^{-1}(\sin 2\theta)$

$y = 2\theta$
$\Rightarrow y = 2\tan^{-1}(6^x)$ **(1 Mark)**
Differentiate both sides w.r.t. x, we have

$\dfrac{dy}{dx} = 2.\dfrac{1}{1+\left(6^x\right)^2}.6^x \log 6$

$\left[\because \ \dfrac{d}{dx}\tan^{-1}x = \dfrac{1}{1+x^2}\right.$
$\left.\dfrac{d}{dx}a^x = a^x \log a\right]$

$= \dfrac{2.6^x \log 6}{1+(6)^{2x}}$ **(1 Mark)**

16. $\displaystyle\lim_{x\to 0^-} f(x) = \lim_{x\to 0^-}\left(\dfrac{\sqrt{1+kx} - \sqrt{1-kx}}{x}\right)$

$$= \lim_{x \to 0^-} \left(\frac{\sqrt{1+kx} - \sqrt{1-kx}}{x} \times \frac{\sqrt{1+kx} + \sqrt{1-kx}}{\sqrt{1+kx} + \sqrt{1-kx}} \right)$$

$$= \lim_{x \to 0^-} \left(\frac{1+kx-1+kx}{x\left(\sqrt{1+kx} + \sqrt{1-kx}\right)} \right)$$

$$= \lim_{x \to 0^-} \left(\frac{2kx}{x\left(\sqrt{1+kx} + \sqrt{1-kx}\right)} \right)$$

$$= \lim_{x \to 0^-} \left(\frac{2k}{\left(\sqrt{1+kx} + \sqrt{1-kx}\right)} \right) = \frac{2k}{2} = k \qquad \textbf{(1 Mark)}$$

$$\lim_{x \to 0^+} f(x) = \lim_{x \to 0^+} \frac{2x+1}{x-1} = \frac{0+1}{0-1} = -1 \qquad \textbf{(1 Mark)}$$

Since f(x) is continuous at x = 0

$$\Rightarrow \lim_{x \to 0^-} f(x) = \lim_{x \to 0^+} f(x) \Rightarrow k = -1 \qquad \textbf{(2 Marks)}$$

OR

Let $x = a\cos^3\theta$

Diff. w.r.t., 'θ'

$$\Rightarrow \frac{dx}{d\theta} = -3a\cos^2\theta\sin\theta \qquad \text{...(i)}$$

and $y = a\sin^3\theta$

Diff. w.r.t., 'θ'

$$\Rightarrow \frac{dy}{d\theta} = 3a\sin^2\theta\cos\theta \qquad \text{...(ii)} \qquad \textbf{(1 Mark)}$$

From (i) and (ii), we have

$$\frac{dy}{dx} = \frac{3a\sin^2\theta\cos\theta}{-3a\cos^2\theta\sin\theta}$$

$$\Rightarrow \frac{dy}{dx} = -\tan\theta \qquad \textbf{(1 Mark)}$$

$$\Rightarrow \frac{d^2y}{dx^2} = -\sec^2\theta\frac{d\theta}{dx}$$

$$\Rightarrow \frac{d^2y}{dx^2} = -\sec^2\theta . \frac{1}{-3a\cos^2\theta\sin\theta}$$

$$= \frac{1}{3a}\sec^4\theta . \csc\theta \qquad \textbf{(1 Mark)}$$

Now, $\dfrac{d^2y}{dx^2}\bigg]_{\theta=\frac{\pi}{6}} = \dfrac{1}{3a} . \sec^4\dfrac{\pi}{6} . \csc\dfrac{\pi}{6}$

$$= \frac{1}{3a} . \left(\frac{2}{\sqrt{3}}\right)^4 . 2 = \frac{32}{27a} \qquad \textbf{(1 Mark)}$$

17. Let $I = \displaystyle\int \frac{\cos 2x - \cos 2\alpha}{\cos x - \cos \alpha} dx$

$$= \int \frac{2\cos^2 x - 1 - \left(2\cos^2\alpha - 1\right)}{\cos x - \cos\alpha} dx \qquad \textbf{(2 Marks)}$$

$$= \int \frac{2\left(\cos^2 x - \cos^2\alpha\right)}{\cos x - \cos\alpha} dx$$

$$= 2\int (\cos x + \cos\alpha) dx = 2\sin x + 2x\cos\alpha + C$$

$$= 2(\sin x + x\cos\alpha) + C \qquad \textbf{(2 Marks)}$$

OR

Let $I = \displaystyle\int \frac{x+2}{\sqrt{x^2 + 2x + 3}} dx$

$$= \int \frac{\frac{1}{2}(2x+2-2)+2}{\sqrt{x^2+2x+3}} dx = \int \frac{\frac{1}{2}(2x+2)+1}{\sqrt{x^2+2x+3}} dx \qquad \textbf{(1 Mark)}$$

$$= \frac{1}{2}\int \frac{2x+2}{\sqrt{x^2+2x+3}} dx + \int \frac{1}{\sqrt{x^2+2x+3}} dx$$

$$= \int \frac{2x+2}{\sqrt{x^2+2x+3}} dx \qquad \textbf{(1 Mark)}$$

Let $x^2 + 2x + 3 = t$

$(2x+2)dx = dt$

$$\int \frac{dt}{\sqrt{t}} = \frac{t^{1/2}}{\frac{1}{2}} = \frac{(x^2+2x+3)^{1/2}}{\frac{1}{2}}$$

$$\because \quad \int \frac{1}{\sqrt{x^2+2x+3}} dx = \int \frac{1}{\sqrt{x^2+2x+3+1^2-1^2}}$$

$$= \int \frac{1}{\sqrt{(x+1)^2 + (\sqrt{2})^2}}$$

$$= \log\left|x+1+\sqrt{x^2+2x+3}\right| + C \qquad \textbf{(1 Mark)}$$

$$I = \frac{1}{2}\frac{\left(x^2+2x+3\right)^{\frac{1}{2}}}{\frac{1}{2}} + \log\left|x+1+\sqrt{(x+1)^2+\left(\sqrt{2}\right)^2}\right| + C$$

$$= \sqrt{x^2+2x+3} + \log\left|x+1+\sqrt{x^2+2x+3}\right| + C \qquad \textbf{(1 Mark)}$$

18. Here, Let $I = \int \dfrac{dx}{x(x^5+3)}$

Put $x^5 = t \Rightarrow 5x^4\,dx = dt \Rightarrow dx = \dfrac{dt}{5x^4}$

Now, $I = \int \dfrac{1}{x(t+3)}\cdot\dfrac{dt}{5x^4} = \int \dfrac{dt}{5x^5(t+3)} = \int \dfrac{dt}{5t(t+3)}$

$$\textbf{(2 Marks)}$$

$$= \frac{1}{5}\int \left(\frac{\frac{1}{3}}{t} - \frac{\frac{1}{3}}{t+3}\right) dt \quad \text{(By using partial fraction)}$$

$$= \frac{1}{5}\left[\frac{1}{3}\int\frac{1}{t}\,dt - \frac{1}{3}\int\frac{1}{t+3}\,dt\right] = \frac{1}{15}\log|t| - \frac{1}{15}\log|t+3| + C$$

$$= \frac{1}{15}\log x^5 - \frac{1}{15}\log\left|x^5+3\right| + C = \frac{1}{15}\log\left|\frac{x^5}{x^5+3}\right| + C$$

$$\textbf{(2 Marks)}$$

19. Let $I = \displaystyle\int_0^{2\pi} \dfrac{1}{1+e^{\sin x}}\,dx$ $\qquad$ ...(i)

Also, $I = \displaystyle\int_0^{2\pi} \dfrac{1}{1+e^{\sin(2\pi-x)}}\,dx \quad \left[\because \displaystyle\int_0^a f(x)dx = \int_0^a f(a-x)dx\right]$

$$= \int_0^{2\pi} \frac{1}{1+e^{-\sin x}}\,dx$$

$$= \int_0^{2\pi} \frac{e^{\sin x}}{e^{\sin x}+1}\,dx \qquad \text{...(ii)} \qquad \textbf{(2 Marks)}$$

Adding (i) and (ii), we get

$$2I = \int_0^{2\pi} \frac{1+e^{\sin x}}{e^{\sin x}+1}\,dx = \int_0^{2\pi} 1\,dx \Rightarrow 2I = |x|_0^{2\pi} = 2\pi$$

$$I = \pi \qquad \textbf{(2 Marks)}$$

20. $\vec{a} + \vec{b} = \hat{i} - \hat{j} + 7\hat{k} + 5\hat{i} - \hat{j} + \lambda\hat{k}$

$$= 6\hat{i} - 2\hat{j} + (7+\lambda)\hat{k}$$

$$\vec{a} - \vec{b} = \hat{i} - \hat{j} + 7\hat{k} - \left(5\hat{i} - \hat{j} + \lambda\hat{k}\right) = \hat{i} - \hat{j} + 7\hat{k} - 5\hat{i} + \hat{j} - \lambda\hat{k}$$

$$= -4\hat{i} + (7-\lambda)\hat{k} \qquad \textbf{(2 Marks)}$$

Since $\left(\vec{a}+\vec{b}\right)$ is perpendicular to $\left(\vec{a}-\vec{b}\right)$

$$\Rightarrow \quad \left(\vec{a}+\vec{b}\right)\cdot\left(\vec{a}-\vec{b}\right) = 0$$

$$\Rightarrow \quad \left(6\hat{i} - 2\hat{j} + (7+\lambda)\hat{k}\right)\cdot\left(-4\hat{i} + (7-\lambda)\hat{k}\right) = 0$$

$$\Rightarrow \quad -24 - 2(0) + (7+\lambda)\cdot(7-\lambda) = 0$$

$$\Rightarrow \quad -24 + 49 - \lambda^2 = 0$$

$$\Rightarrow \quad \lambda^2 = 25 \Rightarrow \lambda = \pm 5 \qquad \textbf{(2 Marks)}$$

> **Note**
>
> *If two vectors are perpendicular, then their dot product will always be zero.*

21. Position vector of arbitrary points on the given lines are given by

$$(3+\lambda)\hat{i} + (2+2\lambda)\hat{j} + (-4+2\lambda)\hat{k} \qquad \text{...(i)}$$

$$(5+3\mu)\hat{i} + (-2+2\mu)\hat{j} + 6\mu\hat{k} \qquad \text{...(ii)}$$

If the given lines intersect, then given lines have one common point.

$\therefore$ For some values of λ and μ, we have

$$(3+\lambda)\hat{i} + (2+2\lambda)\hat{j} + (-4+2\lambda)\hat{k} = (5+3\mu)\hat{i}$$

$$+ (-2+2\mu)\hat{j} + 6\mu\hat{k}. \qquad \textbf{(1 Mark)}$$

Equating coefficients of $\hat{i}, \hat{j}$ and $\hat{k}$, we have $3 + \lambda = 5 + 3\mu$;

$2 + 2\lambda = -2 + 2\mu$ and $-4 + 2\lambda = 6\mu$

which implies $\lambda = 2 + 3\mu$

$\qquad \lambda = -2 + \mu$

$\Rightarrow \quad 2 + 3\mu = -2 + \mu \Rightarrow 2\mu = -4$

$\Rightarrow \quad \mu = -2$ and $\lambda = 3(-2) + 2 = -6 + 2 = -4$

Thus, $\lambda = -4$ and $\mu = -2$

Now, $\lambda = 3\mu + 2$

$\Rightarrow \quad -4 = 3(-2) + 2$

$\Rightarrow \quad -4 = -4$

which is true. $\qquad \textbf{(1 Mark)}$

Thus, given lines intersect.

From (i), by putting $\lambda = -4$, we have

Position vector of point of intersection is given by

$$\vec{r} = (3-4)\hat{i} + (2+2(-4))\hat{j} + (-4+2(-4))\hat{k}$$

$$= -\hat{i} - 6\hat{j} - 12\hat{k} \qquad \textbf{(2 Marks)}$$

Note

If two lines are intersecting then try to find the point of intersection of that lines by equating the coefficient of $\hat{i}$, $\hat{j}$ and $\hat{k}$.

OR

Let equation of plane through $(2, 1, -1)$ be
$$a(x-2)+b(y-1)+c(z+1)=0 \quad ...(i)$$
It passes through $(-1, 3, 4)$
$$\Rightarrow \quad a(-1-2)+b(3-1)+c(4+1)=0$$
$$\Rightarrow \quad -3a+2b+5c=0 \qquad ...(ii) \quad \textbf{(1 Mark)}$$
Also, (i) is perpendicular to
$$x-2y+4z=10$$
$$\Rightarrow \quad a-2b+4c=0 \qquad ...(iii)$$
From equations (ii) and (iii)

Now, $\dfrac{a}{\begin{vmatrix} 2 & 5 \\ -2 & 4 \end{vmatrix}} = \dfrac{b}{\begin{vmatrix} 5 & -3 \\ 4 & 1 \end{vmatrix}} = \dfrac{c}{\begin{vmatrix} -3 & 2 \\ 1 & -2 \end{vmatrix}}$

$$\Rightarrow \quad \frac{a}{8+10} = \frac{b}{5+12} = \frac{c}{6-2} = k(\text{say})$$
$$\Rightarrow \quad a=18k, b=17k \text{ and } c=4k \qquad \textbf{(2 Marks)}$$
From (i), we have
$$18k(x-2)+17k(y-1)+4k(z+1)=0$$
$$\Rightarrow \quad 18x-36k+17y-17k+4z+4k=0$$
$$\Rightarrow \quad 18x+17y+4z-49=0 \qquad \textbf{(1 Mark)}$$

22. $P(A)$ = Probability of student A coming to school in time = $\dfrac{3}{7}$

$P(B)$ = Probability of student B coming to school in time = $\dfrac{5}{7}$

Given, events A and B are independent.

$\therefore$ Probability that only one of them will come in time

$$= P(A).P\left(\overline{B}\right)+P(B)P\left(\overline{A}\right) \qquad \textbf{(2 Marks)}$$

$$= P(A).\left(1-P(B)\right)+P(B)\left(1-P(A)\right)$$

$$= \frac{3}{7}\left(1-\frac{5}{7}\right)+\frac{5}{7}\left(1-\frac{3}{7}\right)=\frac{3}{7}.\frac{2}{7}+\frac{5}{7}.\frac{4}{7}$$

$$= \frac{6}{49}+\frac{20}{49}=\frac{26}{49} \qquad \textbf{(1 Mark)}$$

Advantages of coming to school in time are:
(i)   developing habit of being punctual in everything.
(ii) never misses any class. **(1 Mark)**

Note

Two events A and B are independent, if $P(A \cap B) = P(A).P(B)$

SECTION - C

23. Let the coordinates of the vertices of rectangle ABCD be A $(a\cos\theta, b\sin\theta)$, B $(-a\cos\theta, b\sin\theta)$, C $(-a\cos\theta, -b\sin\theta)$ and D $(a\cos\theta, -b\sin\theta)$
Length of rectangle, AB = $2a\cos\theta$
Breadth of rectangle, AD = $2b\sin\theta$
Area of rectangle ABCD = AB × AD
$$= 2a\cos\theta \times 2b\sin\theta \qquad \textbf{(2 Marks)}$$

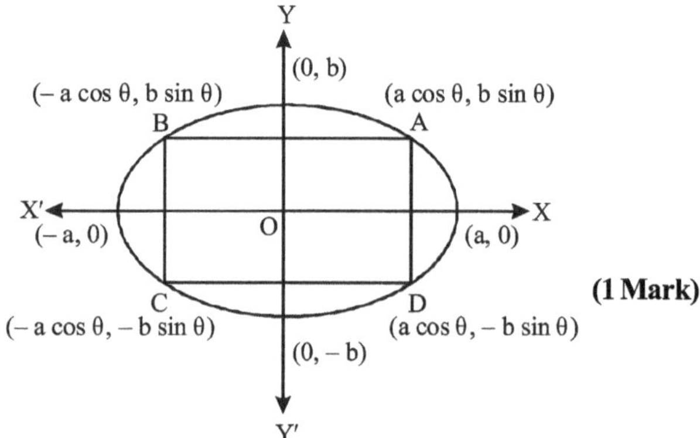

(1 Mark)

Area of rectangle (A) = $2ab\sin2\theta$
Differentiate w.r.t. 'θ'

$$\frac{dA}{d\theta} = 2ab\cos 2\theta.(2)$$

For maximum or minimum,

put $\dfrac{dA}{d\theta} = 0 \Rightarrow 4ab\cos 2\theta = 0 \Rightarrow \cos2\theta = 0$

$$\Rightarrow \quad 2\theta = \frac{\pi}{2} \Rightarrow \theta = \frac{\pi}{4} \qquad \textbf{(1 Mark)}$$

Also, $\dfrac{d^2A}{d\theta^2} = -8ab\sin 2\theta < 0$

$\therefore$ Area is maximum at $\theta = \dfrac{\pi}{4}$ **(1 Mark)**

Hence, maximum area of rectangle ABCD

$$= 2ab\sin\left(2.\frac{\pi}{4}\right) = 2ab\sin\frac{\pi}{2}$$

$$= 2ab \text{ sq. units} \qquad \textbf{(1 Mark)}$$

OR

The equation of the curve is $3x^2 - y^2 = 8$

On differentiating

$$6x - 2y\frac{dy}{dx} = 0$$

$$\frac{dy}{dx} = \frac{3x}{y} \qquad \text{(1 Mark)}$$

Let (x, y) be the point on the curve at which tangent passes

through the point $\left(\frac{4}{3}, 0\right)$

$$\therefore \quad 3x_1^2 - y_1^2 = 8$$

$$y_1^2 = 3x_1^2 - 8 \qquad \text{...(i)}$$

Slope of tangent

$$\left(\frac{dy}{dx}\right)_{(x_1, y_1)} = \frac{3x_1}{y_1} \qquad \text{(1 Mark)}$$

Equation of the tangent passing through the point (x_1, y_1)

with slope $\dfrac{3x_1}{y_1}$ is

$$y - y_1 = \frac{3x_1}{y_1}(x - x_1) \qquad \text{(1 Mark)}$$

Point $\left(\frac{4}{3}, 0\right)$ lies on the above tangent.

$$\therefore \quad 0 - y_1 = \frac{3x_1}{y_1}\left(\frac{4}{3} - x_1\right) \Rightarrow y_1^2 - 3x_1^2 + 4x_1 = 0$$

$$\Rightarrow \quad y_1^2 = 3x_1^2 - 4x_1 \qquad \text{...(ii)}$$

From (i) and (ii)

$$3x_1^2 - 8 = 3x_1^2 - 4x_1 \Rightarrow 4x_1 = 8$$

$$\Rightarrow \quad x_1 = 2$$

From (ii)

$$y_1^2 = 3(2)^2 - 4(2) \Rightarrow y_1^2 = 4$$

$$y_1 = \pm 2 \qquad \text{(1 Mark)}$$

Equation of tangent at $(2, 2)$

$$y - 2 = \frac{3 \times 2}{2}(x - 2)$$

$$\Rightarrow \quad y - 3x + 4 = 0$$

Equation of tangent at $(2, -2)$

$$y + 2 = \frac{3 \times 2}{(-2)}(x - 2)$$

$$\Rightarrow \quad y + 3x - 4 = 0 \qquad \text{(2 Marks)}$$

24. Given curves are

$y = x^2$ and $y = |x|$

$$\Rightarrow \quad x^2 - |x| = 0$$

$$\Rightarrow \quad |x|(|x| - 1) = 0$$

$$\Rightarrow \quad |x| = 0 \text{ or } |x| - 1 = 0$$

$$\Rightarrow \quad x = 0 \text{ or } x = \pm 1 \qquad \text{(2 Marks)}$$

Thus, points of intersection are $(0, 0)$ and $(\pm 1, 1)$

Since $y = x^2$ is an upward parabola with vertex $(0, 0)$ and symmetric about y-axis. **(1 Mark)**

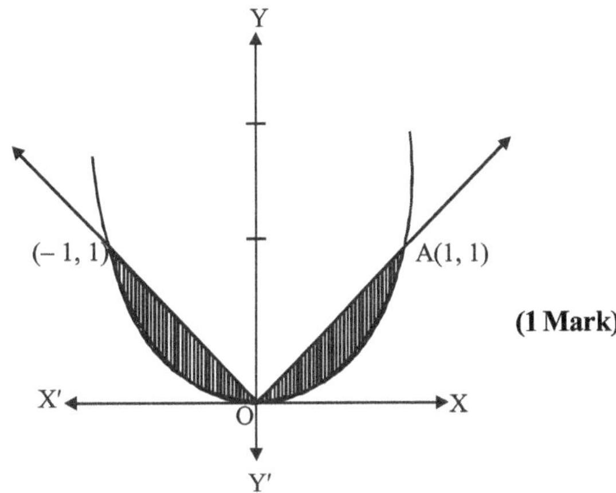

(1 Mark)

$$\therefore \text{ Required area} = 2\int_0^1 \left(|x| - x^2\right)dx$$

$$= 2\left|\frac{x^2}{2} - \frac{x^3}{3}\right|_0^1 = 2\left(\frac{1}{2} - \frac{1}{3}\right) - 0$$

$$= \frac{1}{3} \text{ sq. units.} \qquad \text{(2 Marks)}$$

25. Given differential equation is

$(\tan^{-1} y - x)dy = (1 + y^2)dx$

$$\Rightarrow \frac{dx}{dy} + \frac{x}{1 + y^2} = \frac{\tan^{-1} y}{1 + y^2} \qquad \text{...(i)} \qquad \text{(1 Mark)}$$

Which is of the form $\dfrac{dx}{dy} + Px = Q$

where $P = \dfrac{1}{1 + y^2}$ and $Q = \dfrac{\tan^{-1} y}{1 + y^2}$

$$\text{I.F.} = e^{\int \frac{1}{1+y^2}dy} = e^{\tan^{-1} y} \qquad \text{(1 Mark)}$$

Now, required solution is

$$xe^{\tan^{-1} y} = \int \frac{\tan^{-1} y}{1 + y^2}.e^{\tan^{-1} y}dy + C \qquad \text{...(ii)}$$

Put $\tan^{-1} y = t \Rightarrow \dfrac{1}{1+y^2} dy = dt$

$\therefore \quad xe^t = \int t.e^t dt + C = t.e^t - \int 1.e^t dt + C$

$\because \quad \int uv\,dx = u\int v\,dx - \int\left[\int \dfrac{du}{dx}\int v\,dx\right]dx$

$= t.e^t - e^t + C$ **(2 Marks)**

$xe^t = e^t(t-1) + C$

$\therefore \ xe^{\tan^{-1} y} = e^{\tan^{-1} y}\left(\tan^{-1} y - 1\right) + C$

$x = \tan^{-1} y - 1 + C.e^{-\tan^{-1} y}$ `**(1 Mark)**

when $x = 0, y = 0$

$\Rightarrow \quad 0 = \tan^{-1} 0 - 1 + C.e^{-\tan^{-1} 0}$

$\Rightarrow \quad 0 = 0 - 1 + C \Rightarrow C = 1$

Hence, the required solution is

$x = \tan^{-1} y - 1 + e^{-\tan^{-1} y}$ **(1 Mark)**

Note

Perticular solution of a differential equation does not contain any arbitrary constant.

26. Let the equation of the plane through the intersection of given planes be

$\vec{r}.(\hat{i} + 3\hat{j}) - 6 + \lambda\left[\vec{r}.(3\hat{i} - \hat{j} - 4\hat{k})\right] = 0$

$\Rightarrow \vec{r}.\left[(1+3\lambda)\hat{i} + (3-\lambda)\hat{j} - 4\lambda\hat{k}\right] - 6 = 0$ ...(i)   **(1 Mark)**

Since plane (i) is at a unit distance from origin.

$\therefore \ \dfrac{|-6|}{\sqrt{(1+3\lambda)^2 + (3-\lambda)^2 + (-4\lambda)^2}} = 1$

$\Rightarrow \quad 36 = 1 + 9\lambda^2 + 6\lambda + 9 + \lambda^2 - 6\lambda + 16\lambda^2$

$\Rightarrow \quad \lambda^2 = 1 \Rightarrow \lambda = \pm 1$ **(2 Marks)**

Now, from (i), we have

$\vec{r}.\left[(1\pm 3)\hat{i} + (3\mp 1)\hat{j} \mp 4(1)\hat{k}\right] - 6 = 0$

or $\vec{r}.\left[-2\hat{i} + 4\hat{j} + 4\hat{k}\right] - 6 = 0$ **(1 Mark)**

Hence, the equation of the plane is

$\vec{r}.(4\hat{i} + 2\hat{j} - 4\hat{k}) = 6$ or $\vec{r}.(-2\hat{i} + 4\hat{j} + 4\hat{k}) = 6$

    (2 Marks)

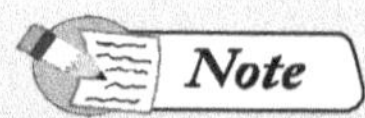
Note

Equation of plane passes through the intersection of given plane

1st plane + l(2nd plane) = 0

OR

Let the vector equation of the line passing through the point $(1, 2, 3)$ and having $< a, b, c >$ as direction ratios be

$\vec{r} = \hat{i} + 2\hat{j} + 3\hat{k} + \lambda\left(a\hat{i} + b\hat{j} + c\hat{k}\right)$

$\vec{r} = (1+a\lambda)\hat{i} + (2+b\lambda)\hat{j} + (3+c\lambda)\hat{k}$ ...(i)   **(1 Mark)**

Line (i) is parallel to plane

$\vec{r}.(\hat{i} - \hat{j} + 2\hat{k}) = 5$

$\Rightarrow \quad a - b + 2c = 0$ **(1 Mark)**

Also, line (i) is parallel to plane

$\vec{r}.(3\hat{i} + \hat{j} + \hat{k}) = 6$

$\Rightarrow \quad 3a + b + c = 0$ **(1 Mark)**

$\Rightarrow \quad \dfrac{a}{\begin{vmatrix} -1 & 2 \\ 1 & 1 \end{vmatrix}} = \dfrac{b}{\begin{vmatrix} 2 & 1 \\ 1 & 3 \end{vmatrix}} = \dfrac{c}{\begin{vmatrix} 1 & -1 \\ 3 & 1 \end{vmatrix}}$

$\Rightarrow \quad \dfrac{a}{-1-2} = \dfrac{b}{6-1} = \dfrac{c}{1+3} = s \, (\text{say})$

$\Rightarrow \quad \dfrac{a}{-3} = \dfrac{b}{5} = \dfrac{c}{4} = s$

$\Rightarrow \quad a = -3s, b = 5s$ and $c = 4s$ **(1 Mark)**

Now, from (i), we have

$\vec{r} = \hat{i} + 2\hat{j} + 3\hat{k} + \lambda s\left(-3\hat{i} + 5j + 4\hat{k}\right)$

$\vec{r} = \hat{i} + 2\hat{j} + 3\hat{k} + \mu\left(-3\hat{i} + 5j + 4\hat{k}\right)$

where $\mu = \lambda s$.   **(2 Marks)**

Note

When line is parallel to plane means line is perpendicular to the normal of plane.

27. Let S denotes the success (getting 6) and F denotes the failure (not getting 6).

Thus, $P(S) = \dfrac{1}{6}$ and $P(F) = \dfrac{5}{6}$

$P(A \text{ wins in first throw}) = P(S) = \dfrac{1}{6}$

A gets the third throw when the first throw by A and second throw by B results into failures.

$\therefore \ P(A \text{ wins in the 3rd throw}) = P(FFS) = P(F).\ P(F).\ P(S)$

$= \dfrac{5}{6} \times \dfrac{5}{6} \times \dfrac{1}{6} = \left(\dfrac{5}{6}\right)^2 .\dfrac{1}{6}$ **(2 Marks)**

Similarly, $P(A \text{ wins in the 5th throw}) = P(FFFFS)$

$= P(F).\ P(F).\ P(F).\ P(F).\ P(S)$

$$= \frac{5}{6} \times \frac{5}{6} \times \frac{5}{6} \times \frac{5}{6} \times \frac{1}{6} = \left(\frac{5}{6}\right)^4 \cdot \frac{1}{6}$$ **(1 Mark)**

Thus, P(A wins)

$$= \frac{1}{6} + \left(\frac{5}{6}\right)^2 \cdot \frac{1}{6} + \left(\frac{5}{6}\right)^4 \cdot \frac{1}{6} + \dots \text{ to } \infty$$

$$= \frac{\dfrac{1}{6}}{1 - \dfrac{25}{36}} \quad \left[\because S_\infty = \frac{a}{1-r}\right]$$

$$= \frac{1}{6} \times \frac{36}{11} = \frac{6}{11}$$

$$P(B \text{ wins}) = 1 - P(A \text{ wins}) = 1 - \frac{6}{11} = \frac{5}{11}$$ **(2 Marks)**

Yes, the decision of the referee was fair. For the result of the game, refree has to call one of the captain of team A or team B. So, by taking alphabetical consideration, referee call captain of team A first. **(1 Mark)**

28. Let x and y be the number of goods of type A and of type B respectively.

$\therefore$ No. of units of labour $= 2x + 3y$

As 30 units of labour are available.

$\therefore$ $2x + 3y \le 30$

Similarly, constraint for capital is

$3x + y \le 17$

and non-zero constraints are

$x \ge 0, y \ge 0$

Objective function **(1 Mark)**

$Z = 100x + 120y$

Consider

$2x + 3y = 30$

When $x = 0$, then $y = 10$

When $x = 15$, then $y = 0$

$\therefore$ $2x + 3y = 30$

passes through A $(0, 10)$ and B $(15, 0)$

Consider

$3x + y = 17$

When $x = 0$, then $y = 17$,

When $y = 0$ then $x = \dfrac{17}{3} = 5.7$

$\therefore 3x + y = 17$ passes through C$(0, 17)$ and D$\left(\dfrac{17}{3}, 0\right)$

Further above two equations intersect at E$(3, 8)$, vertices of

the feasible region are A$(0, 10)$, O$(0, 0)$, D$\left(\dfrac{17}{3}, 0\right)$ and E$(3, 8)$.

(1 Mark)

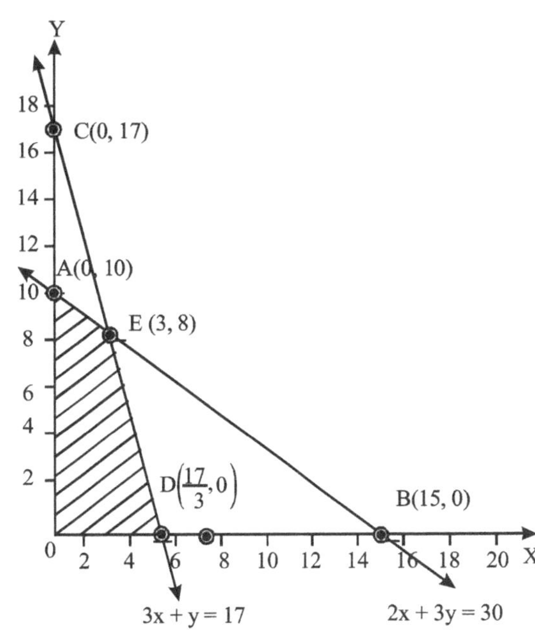

(1 Mark)

At A $(0, 10)$, $Z = 100(0) + 120(10) = ₹ 1200$

At O $(0, 0)$, $Z = 100(0) + 120(0) = ₹ 0$

At D $\left(\dfrac{17}{3}, 0\right)$, $Z = 100\left(\dfrac{17}{3}\right) + 120(0) = ₹ 566.67$

At E $(3, 8)$, $Z = 100(3) + 120(8) = ₹ 1260$

Thus, maximum value of $Z = ₹ 1260$ at $x = 3$ and $y = 8$

(2 Marks)

Yes, the view of manufacturer that men and women workers are equally efficient is correct and so they should be paid at the same rate. **(1 Mark)**

29. Let award for honesty be denoted by x, for helping others by y and for supervising the workers by z, we have

$x + y + z = 12$

$2x + 3y + 3z = 33$

$x + z = 2y$

$\Rightarrow$ $x - 2y + z = 0$ **(1 Mark)**

Its matrix form is

$$\begin{bmatrix} 1 & 1 & 1 \\ 2 & 3 & 3 \\ 1 & -2 & 1 \end{bmatrix} \begin{bmatrix} x \\ y \\ z \end{bmatrix} = \begin{bmatrix} 12 \\ 33 \\ 0 \end{bmatrix}$$

i.e., $AX = B$ **(1 Mark)**

Now, $|A| = \begin{vmatrix} 1 & 1 & 1 \\ 2 & 3 & 3 \\ 1 & -2 & 1 \end{vmatrix}$

$= 1(3 + 6) - 1(2 - 3) + 1(-4 - 3)$

$= 9 + 1 - 7 = 3 \ne 0$

$\therefore A^{-1}$ exists

$$A_{11} = 9, \quad A_{12} = 1, \quad A_{13} = -7$$
$$A_{21} = -3, \quad A_{22} = 0, \quad A_{23} = 3$$
$$A_{31} = 0, \quad A_{32} = -1, \quad A_{33} = 1$$

$$\text{adj.A} = \begin{bmatrix} 9 & 1 & -7 \\ -3 & 0 & 3 \\ 0 & -1 & 1 \end{bmatrix}' = \begin{bmatrix} 9 & -3 & 0 \\ 1 & 0 & -1 \\ -7 & 3 & 1 \end{bmatrix}$$

$$A^{-1} = \frac{\text{adj.A}}{|A|} = \frac{1}{3}\begin{bmatrix} 9 & -3 & 0 \\ 1 & 0 & -1 \\ -7 & 3 & 1 \end{bmatrix}$$

Now, $AX = B$

$\Rightarrow \quad X = A^{-1}B$

(2 Marks)

$$= \frac{1}{3}\begin{bmatrix} 9 & -3 & 0 \\ 1 & 0 & -1 \\ -7 & 3 & 1 \end{bmatrix}\begin{bmatrix} 12 \\ 33 \\ 0 \end{bmatrix}$$

$$= \frac{1}{3}\begin{bmatrix} 108-99+0 \\ 12+0+0 \\ -84+99+0 \end{bmatrix} = \frac{1}{3}\begin{bmatrix} 9 \\ 12 \\ 15 \end{bmatrix} = \begin{bmatrix} 3 \\ 4 \\ 5 \end{bmatrix}$$

Hence, $x = 3$, $y = 4$ and $z = 5$.

The management of the colony must include the award for those who help the committee financially. **(2 Marks)**

Delhi *2013*

CBSE Board Solved Paper

Time Allowed : 3 Hours   *Maximum Marks : 100*

General Instructions:

(i) All questions are compulsory.

(ii) The question paper consists of **29** questions divided into three Sections **A**, **B** and **C**. Section **A** comprises of **10** questions of **one** mark each, Section **B** comprises of **12** questions of **four** marks each and Section **C** comprises of **07** questions of **six** marks each.

(iii) All questions in Section **A** are to be answered is **one** word, **one** sentence or as per the exact requirement of the question.

(iv) There is no overall choice. However, internal choice has been provided in **04** questions of **four** marks each and **02** questions of **six** marks each. You have to attempt only one of the alternatives in all such questions.

(v) Use of calculators is **not** permitted. You may ask for logarithmic tables, if required.

Question numbers 1 to 10 carry 1 mark each.

1. Write the principal value of $\tan^{-1}(1) + \cos^{-1}\left(-\dfrac{1}{2}\right)$.

2. Write the value of $\tan\left(2\tan^{-1}\dfrac{1}{5}\right)$.

3. Find the value of a if $\begin{bmatrix} a-b & 2a+c \\ 2a-b & 3c+d \end{bmatrix} = \begin{bmatrix} -1 & 5 \\ 0 & 13 \end{bmatrix}$

4. If $\begin{vmatrix} x+1 & x-1 \\ x-3 & x+2 \end{vmatrix} = \begin{vmatrix} 4 & -1 \\ 1 & 3 \end{vmatrix}$, then write the value of x.

5. If $\begin{bmatrix} 9 & -1 & 4 \\ -2 & 1 & 3 \end{bmatrix} = A + \begin{bmatrix} 1 & 2 & -1 \\ 0 & 4 & 9 \end{bmatrix}$, then find the matrix A.

6. Write the degree of the differential equation $x^3\left(\dfrac{d^2 y}{dx^2}\right)^2 + x\left(\dfrac{dy}{dx}\right)^4 = 0.$

7. If $\vec{a} = x\hat{i} + 2\hat{j} - z\hat{k}$ and $\vec{b} = 3\hat{i} - y\hat{j} + \hat{k}$ are two equal vectors, then write the value of $x + y + z$.

8. If a unit vector $\vec{a}$ makes angles $\dfrac{\pi}{3}$ with $\hat{i}$, $\dfrac{\pi}{4}$ with $\hat{j}$ and an acute angle θ with $\hat{k}$, then find the value of θ.

9. Find the Cartesian equation of the line which passes through the point $(-2, 4, -5)$ and is parallel to the line $\dfrac{x+3}{3} = \dfrac{4-y}{5} = \dfrac{z+8}{6}$.

10. The amount of pollution content added in air in a city due to x-diesel vehicles is given by $P(x) = 0.005x^3 + 0.02x^2 + 30x$. Find the marginal increase in pollution content when 3 diesel vehicles are added and write which value is indicated in the above question.

Question numbers 11 to 22 carry 4 marks each.

11. Show that the function f in $A = \mathbb{R} - \left\{\dfrac{2}{3}\right\}$ defined as $f(x) = \dfrac{4x+3}{6x-4}$ is one-one and onto. Hence find f^{-1}.

12. Find the value of the following:

$$\tan\dfrac{1}{2}\left[\sin^{-1}\dfrac{2x}{1+x^2} + \cos^{-1}\dfrac{1-y^2}{1+y^2}\right], |x| < 1, y > 0 \text{ and } xy < 1.$$

OR

Prove that: $\tan^{-1}\left(\dfrac{1}{2}\right) + \tan^{-1}\left(\dfrac{1}{5}\right) + \tan^{-1}\left(\dfrac{1}{8}\right) = \dfrac{\pi}{4}$

13. Using properties of determinants, prove the following :

$$\begin{vmatrix} 1 & x & x^2 \\ x^2 & 1 & x \\ x & x^2 & 1 \end{vmatrix} = (1 - x^3)^2$$

14. Differentiate the following function with respect to x : $(\log x)^x + x^{\log x}$

15. If $y = \log\left[x + \sqrt{x^2 + a^2}\right]$, show that $(x^2 + a^2)\dfrac{d^2 y}{dx^2} + x\dfrac{dy}{dx} = 0.$

16. Show that the function $f(x) = |x - 3|, x \in \mathbb{R}$, is continuous but not differentiable at $x = 3$.

OR

If $x = a \sin t$ and $y = a\left(\cos t + \log \tan \dfrac{t}{2}\right)$, find $\dfrac{d^2y}{dx^2}$.

17. Evaluate: $\displaystyle\int \dfrac{\sin(x-a)}{\sin(x+a)}\,dx$

OR

Evaluate: $\displaystyle\int \dfrac{5x-2}{1+2x+3x^2}\,dx$

18. Evaluate: $\displaystyle\int \dfrac{x^2}{(x^2+4)(x^2+9)}\,dx$

19. Evaluate: $\displaystyle\int_0^4 \big(|x| + |x-2| + |x-4|\big)\,dx$

20. If $\vec{a}$ and $\vec{b}$ are two vectors such that $|\vec{a}+\vec{b}| = |\vec{a}|$, then prove that vector $2\vec{a}+\vec{b}$ is perpendicular to vector $\vec{b}$.

21. Find the coordinates of the point, where the line $\dfrac{x-2}{3} = \dfrac{y+1}{4} = \dfrac{z-2}{2}$ intersects the plane $x - y + z - 5 = 0$. Also find the angle between the line and the plane.

OR

Find the vector equation of the plane which contains the line of intersection of the planes $\vec{r}.(\hat{i}+2\hat{j}+3\hat{k}) - 4 = 0$ and $\vec{r}.(2\hat{i}+\hat{j}-\hat{k}) + 5 = 0$ and which is perpendicular to the plane $\vec{r}.(5\hat{i}+3\hat{j}-6\hat{k}) + 8 = 0$.

22. A speaks truth in 60% of the cases, while B in 90% of the cases. In what percent of cases are they likely to contradict each other in stating the same fact? In the cases of contradiction do you think, the statement of B will carry more weight as he speaks truth in more number of cases than A?

SECTION - C

Question numbers 23 to 29 carry 6 marks each.

23. A school wants to award its students for the values of honesty, regularity and hardwork with a total cash award of ₹ 6,000. Three times the award money for hardwork added to that given for honesty amounts to ₹ 11,000. The award money given for honesty and hardwork together is double the one given for regularity. Represent the above situation algebraically and find the award money for each value using matrix method. Apart from these values, namely, honesty, regularity and hardwork, suggest one more value which the school must include for awards.

24. Show that the height of the cylinder of maximum volume, that can be inscribed in a sphere of radius R is $\dfrac{2R}{\sqrt{3}}$. Also find the maximum volume.

OR

Find the equation of the normal at a point on the curve $x^2 = 4y$ which passes through the point $(1, 2)$. Also find the equation of the corresponding tangent.

25. Using integration, find the area bounded by the curve $x^2 = 4y$ and the line $x = 4y - 2$.

OR

Using integration, find the area of the region enclosed between the two circles $x^2 + y^2 = 4$ and $(x-2)^2 + y^2 = 4$.

26. Show that the differential equation $2ye^{x/y}dx + (y - 2x\,e^{x/y})\,dy = 0$ is homogeneous. Find the particular solution of this differential equation, given that $x = 0$ when $y = 1$.

27. Find the vector equation of the plane passing through three points with position vectors $\hat{i}+\hat{j}-2\hat{k}$, $2\hat{i}-\hat{j}+\hat{k}$ and $\hat{i}+2\hat{j}+\hat{k}$. Also find the coordinates of the point of intersection of this plane and the line $\vec{r} = 3\hat{i} - \hat{j} - \hat{k} + \lambda(2\hat{i} - 2\hat{j} + \hat{k})$.

28. A cooperative society of farmers has 50 hectares of land to grow two crops A and B. The profits from crops A and B per hectare are estimated as ₹ 10,500 and ₹ 9,000 respectively. To control weeds, a liquid herbicide has to be used for crops A and B at the rate of 20 litres and 10 litres per hectare, respectively. Further not more than 800 litres of herbicide should be used in order to protect fish and wildlife using a pond which collects drainage from this land. Keeping in mind that the protection of fish and other wildlife is more important than earning profit, how much land should be allocated to each crop so as to maximize the total profit? Form an LPP from the above and solve it graphically. Do you agree with the message the protection of wildlife is utmost necessary to preserve the balance in environment?

29. Assume that the chances of a patient having a heart attack is 40%. Assuming that a meditation and yoga course reduces the risk of heart attack by 30% and prescription of certain drug reduces its chance by 25%. At a time a patient can choose any one of the two options with equal probabilities. It is given that after going through one of the two options, the patient selected at random suffers a heart attack. Find the probability that the patient followed a course of meditation and yoga. Interpret the result and state which of the above stated methods is more beneficial for the patient.

Solutions

SECTION - A

1. $\tan^{-1}(1) + \cos^{-1}\left(-\dfrac{1}{2}\right)$

$= \tan^{-1}\left(\tan\dfrac{\pi}{4}\right) + \cos^{-1}\cos\left(\pi - \dfrac{\pi}{3}\right)$ **(½ Mark)**

$= \tan^{-1}\tan\dfrac{\pi}{4} + \cos^{-1}\cos\dfrac{2\pi}{3}$

$$\left[\because \dfrac{\pi}{4} \in \left(-\dfrac{\pi}{2}, \dfrac{\pi}{2}\right) \text{ and } \dfrac{2\pi}{3} \in [0, \pi]\right]$$

$= \dfrac{\pi}{4} + \dfrac{2\pi}{3} = \dfrac{3\pi + 8\pi}{12} = \dfrac{11\pi}{12}$ **(½ Mark)**

> **Note**
>
> *It can be solved by using formula $\cos^{-1}(-x) = \pi - \cos^{-1}x$*

2. Let $2\tan^{-1}\dfrac{1}{5} = \theta$

$\tan^{-1}\dfrac{1}{5} = \dfrac{\theta}{2} \Rightarrow \tan\dfrac{\theta}{2} = \dfrac{1}{5}$

$\tan\left(2\tan^{-1}\dfrac{1}{5}\right) = \tan\theta = \dfrac{2\tan\dfrac{\theta}{2}}{1 - \tan^2\dfrac{\theta}{2}}$

$$\left[\because \tan 2\theta = \dfrac{2\tan\theta}{1 - \tan^2\theta}\right] \text{ (½ Mark)}$$

$= \dfrac{2 \times \dfrac{1}{5}}{1 - \left(\dfrac{1}{5}\right)^2} = \dfrac{2}{5} \times \dfrac{25}{24} = \dfrac{5}{12}$ **(½ Mark)**

3. $\begin{bmatrix} a-b & 2a+c \\ 2a-b & 3c+d \end{bmatrix} = \begin{bmatrix} -1 & 5 \\ 0 & 13 \end{bmatrix}$

On comparing elements of both the sides

$a - b = -1$ ...(i)

$2a + c = 5$ ...(ii)

$2a - b = 0$ ...(iii)

$3c + d = 13$ ...(iv)   **(½ Mark)**

From (iii)

$b = 2a \Rightarrow a = \dfrac{b}{2}$

Putting value of a in (i)

$\dfrac{b}{2} - b = -1 \Rightarrow b = 2 \;\;\Rightarrow\;\; a = \dfrac{2}{2} = 1 \;\;\Rightarrow\;\; a = 1$

From (ii)

$2a + c = 5 \Rightarrow c = 5 - 2(1) \;\;\Rightarrow\;\; c = 3$

From (iv)

$d = 13 - 3c \Rightarrow d = 13 - 3(3) \;\;\Rightarrow\;\; d = 4$ **(½ Mark)**

4. $\begin{vmatrix} x+1 & x-1 \\ x-3 & x+2 \end{vmatrix} = \begin{vmatrix} 4 & -1 \\ 1 & 3 \end{vmatrix}$

$(x+1)(x+2) - (x-1)(x-3) = 12 + 1$ **(½ Mark)**

$x^2 + 2x + x + 2 - (x^2 - 3x - x + 3) = 13$

$7x - 1 = 13 \;\;\Rightarrow\;\; 7x = 14 \;\;\Rightarrow\;\; x = 2$ **(½ Mark)**

5. $\begin{bmatrix} 9 & -1 & 4 \\ -2 & 1 & 3 \end{bmatrix} = A + \begin{bmatrix} 1 & 2 & -1 \\ 0 & 4 & 9 \end{bmatrix}$

$A = \begin{bmatrix} 9 & -1 & 4 \\ -2 & 1 & 3 \end{bmatrix} - \begin{bmatrix} 1 & 2 & -1 \\ 0 & 4 & 9 \end{bmatrix}$ **(½ Mark)**

$= \begin{bmatrix} 8 & -3 & 5 \\ -2 & -3 & -6 \end{bmatrix}$ **(½ Mark)**

6. $x^3\left(\dfrac{d^2y}{dx^2}\right)^2 + x\left(\dfrac{dy}{dx}\right)^4 = 0$

Degree $= 2$ **(1 Mark)**

> **Note**
>
> *The degree of differential equation is represented by the power of the highest order derivative in the given differential equation.*

7. As $\vec{a} = \vec{b}$

$x\hat{i} + 2\hat{j} - z\hat{k} = 3\hat{i} - y\hat{j} + \hat{k}$

On equating both of the sides

$x = 3;\ y = -2;\ z = -1$ **(½ Mark)**

$\therefore x + y + z = 3 - 2 - 1 = 0$ **(½ Mark)**

8. Let l, m, n be direction cosines of $\vec{a}$

$l = \cos\dfrac{\pi}{3} \;\;\Rightarrow\;\; l = \dfrac{1}{2}$

$\Rightarrow m = \cos\dfrac{\pi}{4} = \dfrac{1}{\sqrt{2}}$

$\Rightarrow n = \cos\theta$

$\Rightarrow l^2 + m^2 + n^2 = 1$ **(½ Mark)**

$\Rightarrow \left(\dfrac{1}{2}\right)^2 + \left(\dfrac{1}{\sqrt{2}}\right)^2 + \cos^2\theta = 1$

$\Rightarrow \cos^2\theta = 1 - \dfrac{1}{4} - \dfrac{1}{2} = 1 - \dfrac{3}{4} = \dfrac{1}{4}$

$\cos\theta = \dfrac{1}{2} \Rightarrow \theta = \dfrac{\pi}{3}$ **(½ Mark)**

9. Given line:

$$\dfrac{x+3}{3} = \dfrac{4-y}{5} = \dfrac{z+8}{6}$$

$$\Rightarrow \dfrac{x-(-3)}{3} = \dfrac{y-4}{-5} = \dfrac{z-(-8)}{6}$$

Direction ratios are (3, –5, 6)   **(½ Mark)**

Required line passes through (–2, 4, –5) and parallel to given line equation of required line is given as

$$\dfrac{x-(-2)}{3} = \dfrac{y-4}{-5} = \dfrac{z-(-5)}{6}$$

$$\Rightarrow \dfrac{x+2}{3} = \dfrac{4-y}{5} = \dfrac{z+5}{6}$$ **(½ Mark)**

10. $P(x) = 0.005x^3 + 0.02x^2 + 30x$

On differentiating

$P'(x) = 0.005\,(3x^2) + 0.02\,(2x) + 30$

$\qquad = 0.015x^2 + 0.04x + 30$

$[P'(x)]_{x=3} = 0.015(9) + 0.04(3) + 30 = 30.255$ **(½ Mark)**

This question indicates "how increase in number of diesel vehicle increase the air pollution, which is harmful for living body.   **(½ Mark)**

<hr>

Note

Marginal means rate of change of function with respect to quantity (Independent variable). So, marginal means differentiate p(x) with respect to x.

<hr>

SECTION - B

11. Let $x_1, x_2 \in A$

Now $f(x_1) = f(x_2)$

$$\dfrac{4x_1 + 3}{6x_1 - 4} = \dfrac{4x_2 + 3}{6x_2 - 4}$$

$24x_1 x_2 + 18x_2 - 16x_1 - 12 = 24x_1 x_2 + 18x_1 - 16x_2 - 12$

$-34x_1 = -34x_2 \Rightarrow x_1 = x_2$

Hence f is one–one function.   **(1 Mark)**

For onto,

Let $y = \dfrac{4x+3}{6x-4} \Rightarrow 6xy - 4y = 4x + 3$

$$x = \dfrac{4y+3}{6y-4}$$ **(1 Mark)**

$\Rightarrow \forall\, y \in$ codomain $\exists\, x \in$ domain $\left[\because x \neq \dfrac{2}{3}\right]$

$\Rightarrow f$ is onto function.

Thus f is one-one onto function.   **(1 Mark)**

Also $f^{-1}(x) = \dfrac{4x+3}{6x-4}$ **(1 Mark)**

<hr>

Note

If f(x) is bijective function then it is invertable also.

12. $\tan\dfrac{1}{2}\left[\sin^{-1}\dfrac{2x}{1+x^2} + \cos^{-1}\dfrac{1-y^2}{1+y^2}\right]$

$= \tan\dfrac{1}{2}[2\tan^{-1}x + 2\tan^{-1}y]$

$\left[\because 2\tan^{-1}x = \sin^{-1}\dfrac{2x}{1+x^2}\text{ and }2\tan^{-1}x = \cos^{-1}\dfrac{1-x^2}{1+x^2}\right]$ **(2 Marks)**

$= \tan(\tan^{-1}x + \tan^{-1}y) = \tan\left(\tan^{-1}\dfrac{x+y}{1-xy}\right)$

$= \dfrac{x+y}{1-xy}$ **(2 Marks)**

OR

L.H.S. $= \tan^{-1}\left(\dfrac{1}{2}\right) + \tan^{-1}\left(\dfrac{1}{5}\right) + \tan^{-1}\left(\dfrac{1}{8}\right)$

$= \tan^{-1}\left(\dfrac{\frac{1}{2}+\frac{1}{5}}{1-\frac{1}{2}\times\frac{1}{5}}\right) + \tan^{-1}\left(\dfrac{1}{8}\right)$ $[\because xy < 1]$ **(1 Mark)**

$= \tan^{-1}\dfrac{7}{9} + \tan^{-1}\dfrac{1}{8} = \tan^{-1}\left(\dfrac{\frac{7}{9}+\frac{1}{8}}{1-\frac{7}{9}\times\frac{1}{8}}\right)$ **(1 Mark)**

$= \tan^{-1}\left(\dfrac{65}{65}\right) = \tan^{-1}(1) = \tan^{-1}\tan\dfrac{\pi}{4} = \dfrac{\pi}{4}$ **(2 Marks)**

13. L.H.S.

Let $\Delta = \begin{vmatrix} 1 & x & x^2 \\ x^2 & 1 & x \\ x & x^2 & 1 \end{vmatrix}$

Applying $C_1 \to C_1 + C_2 + C_3$

$$\Delta = \begin{vmatrix} 1+x+x^2 & x & x^2 \\ 1+x+x^2 & 1 & x \\ 1+x+x^2 & x^2 & 1 \end{vmatrix}$$ **(1 Mark)**

Taking $(1 + x + x^2)$ common from C_1.

$$\Delta = (1 + x + x^2)\begin{vmatrix} 1 & x & x^2 \\ 1 & 1 & x \\ 1 & x^2 & 1 \end{vmatrix}$$ **(1 Mark)**

Applying $R_2 \to R_2 - R_1$ and $R_3 \to R_3 - R_1$

$$\Delta = (1 + x + x^2)\begin{vmatrix} 1 & x & x^2 \\ 0 & 1-x & x(1-x) \\ 0 & x(x-1) & 1-x^2 \end{vmatrix}$$ **(1 Mark)**

$$= (1 + x + x^2)(1-x)^2\begin{vmatrix} 1 & x & x^2 \\ 0 & 1 & x \\ 0 & -x & 1+x \end{vmatrix}$$

Expanding by C_1

$\Delta = (1 + x + x^2)(1 - x)^2(1 + x + x^2)$

$\Delta = [(1 - x)(1 + x^2 + x)]^2$

$\Delta = (1 - x^3)^2$ **(1 Mark)**

14. Let $y = (\log x)^x + x^{\log x}$

$\quad\quad y = u + v$ ...(i)

$\quad\quad u = (\log x)^x$

Taking log on both sides

$\log u = x \log(\log x)$ **(½ Mark)**

Differentiating on both sides w.r.t. x

$\dfrac{1}{u}\dfrac{du}{dx} = x.\dfrac{1}{\log x}\ .\ \dfrac{1}{x} + \log(\log x)$

$\Rightarrow \dfrac{du}{dx} = u\left[\dfrac{1}{\log x} + \log(\log x)\right]$

$\Rightarrow \dfrac{du}{dx} = (\log x)^x\left[\dfrac{1}{\log x} + \log(\log x)\right]$ ...(ii) **(1 Mark)**

$v = x^{\log x}$

Taking log on both sides

$\log v = \log x^{\log x}$

$\Rightarrow \log v = \log x\ .\ \log x$

$\Rightarrow \log v = (\log x)^2$ **(½ Mark)**

Differentiating on both sides w.r.t. x

$\dfrac{d}{dx}(\log v) = \dfrac{d}{dx}(\log x)^2$

$\Rightarrow \dfrac{1}{v}\dfrac{dv}{dx} = 2\log x.\dfrac{1}{x}$

$\Rightarrow \dfrac{dv}{dx} = 2x^{\log x}\dfrac{\log x}{x}$ ...(iii) **(1 Mark)**

From (i)

$y = u + v$

Differentiating on both sides w.r.t. x

$\dfrac{dy}{dx} = \dfrac{du}{dx} + \dfrac{dv}{dx}$

from (ii) & (iii)

$\dfrac{dy}{dx} = (\log x)^x\left[\dfrac{1}{\log x} + \log(\log x)\right] + \dfrac{2\log x.x^{\log x}}{x}$

(1 Mark)

15. $y = \log\left[x + \sqrt{x^2 + a^2}\right]$

Differentiating w.r.t. x

$\dfrac{dy}{dx} = \dfrac{1}{x + \sqrt{x^2 + a^2}} \times \left[1 + \dfrac{1}{2}(x^2 + a^2)^{-1/2}.2x\right]$ **(1 Mark)**

$= \dfrac{1}{x + \sqrt{x^2 + a^2}} \times \left[1 + \dfrac{x}{\sqrt{x^2 + a^2}}\right]$

$\Rightarrow \dfrac{dy}{dx} = \dfrac{1}{x + \sqrt{x^2 + a^2}} \times \left[\dfrac{\sqrt{x^2 + a^2} + x}{\sqrt{x^2 + a^2}}\right]$

$\Rightarrow \dfrac{dy}{dx} = \dfrac{1}{\sqrt{x^2 + a^2}}$ **(1 Mark)**

$\Rightarrow \sqrt{x^2 + a^2}\ \dfrac{dy}{dx} = 1$

Again differentiating both sides w.r.t. x

$\sqrt{x^2 + a^2}\ \dfrac{d^2y}{dx^2} + \dfrac{1}{2}(x^2 + a^2)^{-1/2}(2x)\dfrac{dy}{dx} = 0$ **(1 Mark)**

$\Rightarrow (x^2 + a^2)\dfrac{d^2y}{dx^2} + x\dfrac{dy}{dx} = 0$ **(1 Mark)**

16. $f(x) = |x - 3|,\ x \in R$

$$f(x) = \begin{cases} -(x-3) & ;\quad x < 3 \\ 0 & ;\quad x = 3 \\ x-3 & ;\quad x > 3 \end{cases}$$ **(½ Mark)**

Now, $\lim\limits_{x \to 3^+} f(x) = \lim\limits_{h \to 0} f(3+h)$

$$[\text{Let } x = 3 + h \text{ and } x \to 3^+ \Rightarrow h \to 0]$$

$$= \lim\limits_{h \to 0}(3 + h - 3) = \lim\limits_{h \to 0} h = 0$$

$\therefore \lim\limits_{x \to 3^+} f(x) = 0$ ...(i)   **(½ Mark)**

$$\lim\limits_{x \to 3^-} f(x) = \lim\limits_{h \to 0} f(3-h)$$

$$[\text{Let } x = 3 - h \text{ and } x \to 3^- \Rightarrow h \to 0]$$

$$= \lim\limits_{h \to 0} -(3 - h - 3) = \lim\limits_{h \to 0} h = 0$$

$\therefore \lim\limits_{x \to 3^-} f(x) = 0$ ...(ii)   **(½ Mark)**

Also $f(3) = 0$ ...(iii)

From equations (i), (ii) and (iii)

$$\lim\limits_{x \to 3^+} f(x) = \lim\limits_{x \to 3^-} f(x) = f(3)$$

Hence, $f(x)$ is continuous at $x = 3$ **(½ Mark)**

At $x = 3$

$$\text{R.H.D.} = \lim\limits_{h \to 0} \frac{f(3+h) - f(3)}{h} = \lim\limits_{h \to 0} \frac{(3+h-3) - 0}{h}$$

$$= \lim\limits_{h \to 0} \frac{h}{h} = 1 \qquad [\because |h| = h, |0| = 0]$$

R.H.D. $= 1$ ...(iv)

$$\text{L.H.D.} = \lim\limits_{h \to 0} \frac{f(3-h) - f(3)}{-h} = \lim\limits_{h \to 0} \frac{-(3-h-3) - 0}{-h}$$

$$= \lim\limits_{h \to 0} \frac{h}{-h} = \lim\limits_{h \to 0}(-1) \; [\because |h| = h] = -1$$

L.H.D. $= -1$ ...(v)

Equations (iv) & (v) $\Rightarrow$ L.H.D. $\ne$ R.H.D at $x = 3$ **(1 Mark)**

$\therefore f(x)$ is not differentiable at $x = 3$

$\therefore f(x) = |x - 3|, x \in R$ is continuous but not differentiable at $x = 3$ **(1 Mark)**

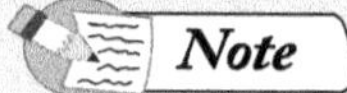

Note

The function of the form $f(x) = |x - a|$ is not differentiable at $x = a$.

17. Let $I = \int \dfrac{\sin(x-a)}{\sin(x+a)} dx = \int \dfrac{\sin(x+a-2a)}{\sin(x+a)} dx$ **(1 Mark)**

$$= \int \frac{\sin(x+a)\cos 2a - \sin 2a \cos(x+a)}{\sin(x+a)} dx \quad \textbf{(1 Mark)}$$

$$[\because \sin(A - B) = \sin A \cos B - \cos A \sin B]$$

$$I = \int \left[\frac{\sin(x+a)\cos 2a}{\sin(x+a)} - \frac{\sin 2a \cdot \cos(x+a)}{\sin(x+a)}\right] dx$$

$$I = \int \cos 2a \, dx - \int \sin 2a \cdot \cot(x+a) dx$$

$$I = x \cos 2a - \sin 2a \log \sin(x + a) + C$$

$$\left[\because \int \cot x \, dx = \log \sin x + C\right] \quad \textbf{(2 Marks)}$$

OR

Let $I = \displaystyle\int \dfrac{5x-2}{1+2x+3x^2} dx$

Let $5x - 2 = A + B \dfrac{d}{dx}(1 + 2x + 3x^2)$

$5x - 2 = A + B(6x + 2)$

$5x - 2 = (6B)x + A + 2B$

$A = -\dfrac{11}{3}$ and $B = \dfrac{5}{6}$

$$I = \int \frac{A\,dx}{3x^2 + 2x + 1} + B\int \frac{(6x+2)}{3x^2 + 2x + 1} dx$$

$$I = -\frac{11}{3}\int \frac{dx}{3x^2 + 2x + 1} + \frac{5}{6}\int \frac{6x+2}{3x^2 + 2x + 1} dx \quad \textbf{(1 Mark)}$$

$I = I_1 + I_2$

$$I_2 = \frac{5}{6}\int \frac{6x+2}{3x^2 + 2x + 1} dx$$

Let $3x^2 + 2x + 1 = t$

$(6x + 2) dx = dt$

$$I_2 = \frac{5}{6}\int \frac{dt}{t} = \frac{5}{6} \log t + C_1$$

$$= \frac{5}{6} \log |3x^2 + 2x + 1| + C_1 \quad \textbf{(1 Mark)}$$

$$I_1 = -\frac{11}{3}\int \frac{dx}{3x^2 + 2x + 1} = -\frac{11}{9}\int \frac{dx}{x^2 + \frac{2}{3}x + \frac{1}{3}}$$

$$= -\frac{11}{9}\int \frac{dx}{x^2 + \frac{2}{3}x + \frac{1}{3} - \left(\frac{1}{3}\right)^2 + \left(\frac{1}{3}\right)^2}$$

$$= -\frac{11}{9}\int \frac{dx}{\left(x + \frac{1}{3}\right)^2 + \left(\frac{\sqrt{2}}{3}\right)^2}$$

$$= -\frac{11}{9}\left(\frac{1}{\frac{\sqrt{2}}{3}}\right) \tan^{-1}\left(\frac{x + \frac{1}{3}}{\frac{\sqrt{2}}{3}}\right) + C_2$$

$$= -\frac{11}{3\sqrt{2}} \tan^{-1}\left(\frac{3x+1}{\sqrt{2}}\right) + C_2 \quad \textbf{(1½ Marks)}$$

Putting values of I_1 and I_2 in I

$I = \dfrac{5}{6} \log |3x^2 + 2x + 1| - \dfrac{11}{3\sqrt{2}} \tan^{-1}\left[\dfrac{3x+1}{\sqrt{2}}\right] + C$

$$[\text{where } C = C_1 + C_2] \quad \textbf{(½ Mark)}$$

18. Let $I = \displaystyle\int \dfrac{x^2}{(x^2+4)(x^2+9)}\,dx$

Let $x^2 = t$

$\dfrac{x^2}{(x^2+4)(x^2+9)} = \dfrac{t}{(t+4)(t+9)}$

$\Rightarrow \dfrac{t}{(t+4)(t+9)} = \dfrac{A}{t+4} + \dfrac{B}{t+9}$

$t = A(t+9) + B(t+4)$

Put $t = -9$, $B = \dfrac{9}{5}$

Put $t = -4$, $A = -\dfrac{4}{5}$

$\therefore \dfrac{x^2}{(x^2+4)(x^2+9)} = -\dfrac{4}{5(x^2+4)} + \dfrac{9}{5(x^2+9)}$ **(2 Marks)**

$I = -\dfrac{4}{5}\displaystyle\int \dfrac{dx}{x^2+4} + \dfrac{9}{5}\displaystyle\int \dfrac{dx}{x^2+9}$

$= -\dfrac{4}{5}\displaystyle\int \dfrac{dx}{x^2+2^2} + \dfrac{9}{5}\displaystyle\int \dfrac{dx}{x^2+3^2}$

$= -\dfrac{4}{5}\times\dfrac{1}{2}\tan^{-1}\dfrac{x}{2} + \dfrac{9}{5}\times\dfrac{1}{3}\tan^{-1}\dfrac{x}{3} + C$

$= -\dfrac{2}{5}\tan^{-1}\dfrac{x}{2} + \dfrac{3}{5}\tan^{-1}\dfrac{x}{3} + C$ **(2 Marks)**

19. Let $I = \displaystyle\int_0^4 (|x| + |x-2| + |x-4|)\,dx$

$I = \displaystyle\int_0^4 |x|\,dx + \int_0^4 |x-2|\,dx + \int_0^4 |x-4|\,dx$

$= \displaystyle\int_0^4 x\,dx + \int_0^4 |x-2|\,dx + \int_0^4 -(x-4)\,dx$ **(½ Mark)**

$|x-2| = \begin{cases} -(x-2) & ;\text{if } 0 \le x < 2 \\ x-2 & ;\text{if } 2 \le x \le 4 \end{cases}$

$|x| = x$ if $0 \le x \le 4$

$|x-4| = -(x-4)$ if $0 \le x \le 4$ **(1 Mark)**

$I = \displaystyle\int_0^4 x\,dx - \int_0^2 (x-2)\,dx + \int_2^4 (x-2)\,dx - \int_0^4 (x-4)\,dx$

$= \dfrac{1}{2}[x^2]_0^4 - \left[\dfrac{x^2}{2} - 2x\right]_0^2 + \left[\dfrac{x^2}{2} - 2x\right]_2^4 - \left[\dfrac{x^2}{2} - 4x\right]_0^4$

(1 Mark)

$= \dfrac{1}{2}(16) - \left(\dfrac{1}{2}\times 4 - 4\right) + \left[\dfrac{1}{2}\times 16 - 8 - \dfrac{4}{2} + 4\right] - \left[\dfrac{16}{2} - 16\right]$

(1½ Marks)

$= 8 + 2 + 2 + 8 = 20$

20. Given: $|\vec{a}+\vec{b}| = |\vec{a}|$

Squaring on both sides

$|\vec{a}+\vec{b}|^2 = |\vec{a}|^2$ **(1 Mark)**

$\Rightarrow (\vec{a}+\vec{b}).(\vec{a}+\vec{b}) = |\vec{a}|^2$

$\Rightarrow \vec{a}.\vec{a} + \vec{a}.\vec{b} + \vec{b}.\vec{a} + \vec{b}.\vec{b} = |\vec{a}|^2$

$\Rightarrow |\vec{a}|^2 + 2\vec{a}.\vec{b} + |\vec{b}|^2 = |\vec{a}|^2 \left[\because \vec{a}.\vec{b} = \vec{b}.\vec{a}\right]$ **(1 Mark)**

$\Rightarrow 2\vec{a}.\vec{b} + \vec{b}.\vec{b} = 0$

$\Rightarrow (2\vec{a}+\vec{b}).\vec{b} = 0$

Hence $(2\vec{a}+\vec{b})$ is perpendicular to $\vec{b}$ **(2 Marks)**

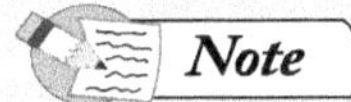

Note

Two vectors are perpendicular if their dot product is zero.

21. Let the given line

$\dfrac{x-2}{3} = \dfrac{y+1}{4} = \dfrac{z-2}{2}$ ...(i)

intersect the plane $x - y + z - 5 = 0$ at point $P(\alpha, \beta, \gamma)$

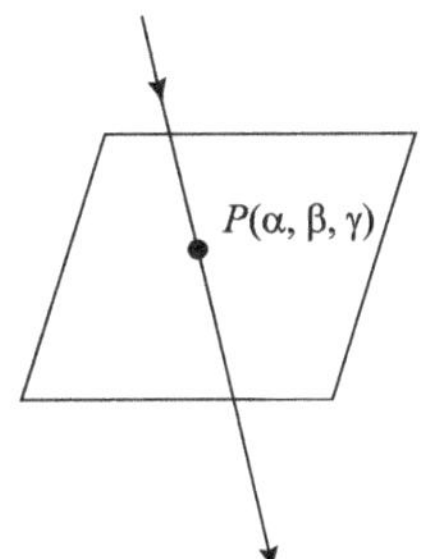

$\therefore P(\alpha, \beta, \gamma,)$ lie on line (i)

$\dfrac{\alpha-2}{3} = \dfrac{\beta+1}{4} = \dfrac{\gamma-2}{2}$

Let $\dfrac{\alpha-2}{3} = \dfrac{\beta+1}{4} = \dfrac{\gamma-2}{2} = \lambda$

$\alpha = 3\lambda + 2$, $\beta = 4\lambda - 1$, $\gamma = 2\lambda + 2$ **(1 Mark)**

Also $P(\alpha, \beta, \gamma)$ lie on plane

$(3\lambda + 2) - (4\lambda - 1) + (2\lambda + 2) - 5 = 0$

$3\lambda + 2 - 4\lambda + 1 + 2\lambda + 2 - 5 = 0 \Rightarrow \lambda = 0$

$\therefore \alpha = 2$, $\beta = -1$, $\gamma = 2$

Hence, coordinate of required point $(2, -1, 2)$ **(1½ Marks)**

Angle between line and plane is given as

$$\sin \theta = \left| \frac{\vec{b}.\vec{n}}{|\vec{b}|.|\vec{n}|} \right|$$

where θ is required angle

$$\sin\theta = \left| \frac{1}{\sqrt{9+16+4}\sqrt{1^2+(-1)^2+1^2}} \right| \qquad \begin{bmatrix} \because \vec{b} = 3\hat{i}+4\hat{j}+2\hat{k} \\ \vec{n} = \hat{i}-\hat{j}+\hat{k} \\ \therefore \vec{b}.\vec{n} = 3-4+2 = 1 \end{bmatrix}$$

$$\Rightarrow \sin \theta = \left| \frac{1}{\sqrt{29}\sqrt{3}} \right| = \frac{1}{\sqrt{87}}$$

$$\Rightarrow \theta = \sin^{-1} \frac{1}{\sqrt{87}} \qquad \text{(1½ Marks)}$$

OR

Equations of the given planes are

$$\vec{r}.(\hat{i}+2\hat{j}+3\hat{k})-4 = 0 \qquad \text{...(i)}$$

and $\vec{r}.(2\hat{i}+\hat{j}-\hat{k})+5 = 0 \qquad \text{...(ii)}$

Let equation of the required plane be

$$\vec{r}.(\hat{i}+2\hat{j}+3\hat{k})-4+\lambda\left[\vec{r}.(2\hat{i}+\hat{j}-\hat{k})+5\right] = 0 \quad \text{(1 Mark)}$$

$$\vec{r}.\left[(1+2\lambda)\hat{i}+(2+\lambda)\hat{j}+(3-\lambda)\hat{k}\right]-4+5\lambda = 0 \qquad \text{...(iii)}$$

Now, plane (3) is perpendicular to plane

$$\vec{r}.(5\hat{i}+3\hat{j}-6\hat{k})+8 = 0$$

$$5(1+2\lambda)+3(2+\lambda)-6(3-\lambda) = 0 \Rightarrow \lambda = \frac{7}{19} \quad \text{(2 Marks)}$$

From (iii), we have

$$\vec{r}.\left[\left(1+\frac{14}{19}\right)\hat{i}+\left(2+\frac{7}{19}\right)\hat{j}+\left(3-\frac{7}{19}\right)\hat{k}\right]-4+\frac{35}{19} = 0$$

$$\Rightarrow \vec{r}.[33\hat{i}+45\hat{j}+50\hat{k}]-41 = 0$$

Which is required equation of plane.   **(1 Mark)**

22. Let E be the event of A speaking truth and F be the event of B speaking truth

$$\therefore P(E) = \frac{60}{100} = \frac{3}{5}$$

$$P(F) = \frac{90}{100} = \frac{9}{10} \qquad \text{(1 Mark)}$$

Probability of A and B likely to contradict each other in stating the same fact

$$= P(E\bar{F})+P(\bar{E}F)$$

$$= P(E).P(\bar{F})+P(\bar{E}).P(F) \qquad \text{(1 Mark)}$$

$$= \frac{3}{5}\left(1-\frac{9}{10}\right)+\left(1-\frac{3}{5}\right)\frac{9}{10}$$

$$= \frac{3}{5}\times\frac{1}{10}+\frac{2}{5}\times\frac{9}{10} \Rightarrow \frac{21}{50} \qquad \text{(1 Mark)}$$

Thus, A and B likely to contradict each other in stating the same fact in 42% cases.

Yes, statement of B will carry more weight.   **(1 Mark)**

SECTION - C

23. Let x, y and z be the awarded money for honesty, regularity and hardwork.

$$x + y + z = 6000 \qquad \text{...(i)}$$

$$x + 3z = 11000 \qquad \text{...(ii)}$$

$$x + z = 2y \Rightarrow x - 2y + z = 0 \qquad \text{...(iii)} \quad \text{(1 Mark)}$$

The above system of three equations may be written in matrix form as

$$AX = B$$

where $A = \begin{bmatrix} 1 & 1 & 1 \\ 1 & 0 & 3 \\ 1 & -2 & 1 \end{bmatrix}, X = \begin{bmatrix} x \\ y \\ z \end{bmatrix}, B = \begin{bmatrix} 6000 \\ 11000 \\ 0 \end{bmatrix}$

$$|A| = \begin{vmatrix} 1 & 1 & 1 \\ 1 & 0 & 3 \\ 1 & -2 & 1 \end{vmatrix} = 1(0+6)-1(1-3)+1(-2-0)$$

$$= 6+2-2 = 6 \neq 0, \text{ Hence } A^{-1} \text{ exist} \qquad \text{(1 Mark)}$$

$$A_{11} = (-1)^{1+1}\begin{vmatrix} 0 & 3 \\ -2 & 1 \end{vmatrix} = 0+6 = 6$$

$$A_{12} = (-1)^3 (1-3) = 2, \ A_{13} = (-1)^4 (-2-0) = -2$$

$$A_{21} = (-1)^3 (1+2) = -3, \ A_{22} = (-1)^4 (1-1) = 0$$

$$A_{23} = (-1)^5 (-2-1) = 3, \ A_{31} = (-1)^4 (3-0) = 3$$

$$A_{32} = (-1)^5 (3-1) = -2, \ A_{33} = (-1)^6 (0-1) = -1$$

$$\text{adj } A = \begin{bmatrix} 6 & 2 & -2 \\ -3 & 0 & 3 \\ 3 & -2 & -1 \end{bmatrix}^T = \begin{bmatrix} 6 & -3 & 3 \\ 2 & 0 & -2 \\ -2 & 3 & -1 \end{bmatrix}$$

$$\therefore A^{-1} = \frac{1}{|A|}.\text{adj}A = \frac{1}{6}\begin{bmatrix} 6 & -3 & 3 \\ 2 & 0 & -2 \\ -2 & 3 & -1 \end{bmatrix} \qquad \text{(2 Marks)}$$

$$\because AX = B \Rightarrow X = A^{-1}B$$

$$\begin{bmatrix} x \\ y \\ z \end{bmatrix} = \frac{1}{6}\begin{bmatrix} 6 & -3 & 3 \\ 2 & 0 & -2 \\ -2 & 3 & -1 \end{bmatrix}\begin{bmatrix} 6000 \\ 11000 \\ 0 \end{bmatrix}$$

$$= \frac{1}{6}\begin{bmatrix} 36000-33000+0 \\ 12000+0+0 \\ -12000+33000+0 \end{bmatrix} = \frac{1}{6}\begin{bmatrix} 3000 \\ 12000 \\ 21000 \end{bmatrix} = \begin{bmatrix} 500 \\ 2000 \\ 3500 \end{bmatrix}$$

$\Rightarrow x = 500,\ y = 2000,\ z = 3500$ **(1 Mark)**

Except above three values, school must include discipline for award as discipline has great importance in student's life.   **(1 Mark)**

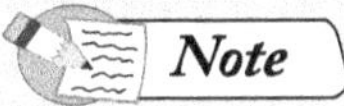

Note

For ony matrix A, A^{-1} exist if $|A| \neq 0$.

24. Let r be the radius and $2h$ be the height of cylinder

$\therefore OC = h$

In $\triangle OBC$

$r^2 + h^2 = R^2 \Rightarrow r^2 = R^2 - h^2 ...(i)$ **(½ Mark)**

Let V be the volume of cylinder

$V = \pi r^2(2h)$

$V = 2\pi h(R^2 - h^2) \Rightarrow V = 2\pi(R^2 h - h^3)$

$\dfrac{dV}{dh} = 2\pi(R^2 - 3h^2)$ **(1 Mark)**

For maxima or minima $\dfrac{dV}{dh} = 0$

$2\pi(R^2 - 3h^2) = 0 \Rightarrow R^2 = 3h^2$

$\Rightarrow R = \sqrt{3}\,h \Rightarrow h = \dfrac{R}{\sqrt{3}}$ **(1 Mark)**

$\Rightarrow \dfrac{d^2V}{dh^2} = 2\pi(0 - 6h)$

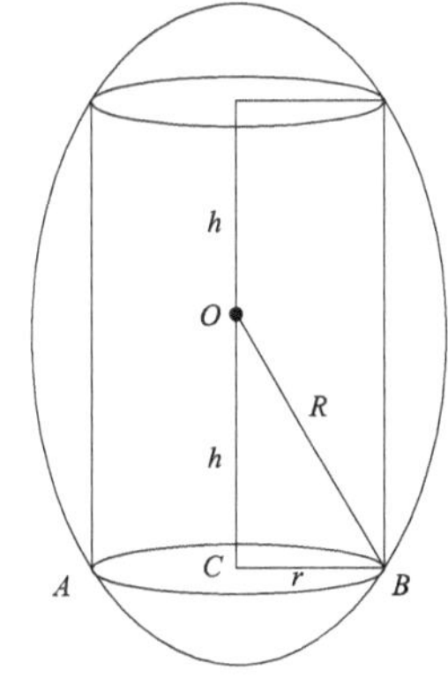

   (1½ Marks)

At $h = \dfrac{R}{\sqrt{3}},\ \dfrac{d^2V}{dh^2} = -12\pi\,\dfrac{R}{\sqrt{3}} < 0$

$\therefore V$ is maximum when $h = \dfrac{R}{\sqrt{3}}$ **(1 Mark)**

Height of cylinder, $2h = \dfrac{2R}{\sqrt{3}}$

From (i)

$r^2 = R^2 - \dfrac{R^2}{3} = \dfrac{2R^2}{3}$

$\therefore$ Maximum volume $= \pi\,r^2\,(2h)$

$= \pi \dfrac{2R^2}{3} \times \dfrac{2R}{\sqrt{3}} = \dfrac{4\pi}{3\sqrt{3}}R^3$ **(1 Mark)**

OR

Let the point of contact of tangent to the given curve be (x_0, y_0)

Now the given curve is $x^2 = 4y$

Differentiating on both side w.r.t. x

$2x = 4\dfrac{dy}{dx} \Rightarrow \dfrac{dy}{dx} = \dfrac{x}{2}$ **(1 Mark)**

Now slope of tangent to the given curve at (x_0, y_0)

$= \left[\dfrac{dy}{dx}\right]_{(x_0, y_0)} = \dfrac{x_0}{2}$ **(½ Mark)**

$\therefore$ Slope of normal to the given curve at (x_0, y_0)

$= -\dfrac{1}{\text{Slope of tangent at}(x_0, y_0)} = \dfrac{-1}{x_0/2} = \dfrac{-2}{x_0}$ **(1 Mark)**

Hence equation of required normal is

$(y - y_0) = \dfrac{-2}{x_0}(x - x_0)$ ...(i)   **(½ Mark)**

$\because$ (i) passes through $(1, 2)$

$(2 - y_0) = \dfrac{-2}{x_0}(1 - x_0)$

$\Rightarrow 2x_0 - x_0 y_0 = -2 + 2x_0$

$\Rightarrow x_0 y_0 = 2$ ...(ii)   **(½ Mark)**

Also, $\because (x_0, y_0)$ lie on given curve $x^2 = 4y$

$\Rightarrow x_0^2 = 4y_0 \Rightarrow y_0 = \dfrac{x_0^2}{4}$ ...(iii)   **(½ Mark)**

Putting value of y_0 in (ii)

$x_0 \cdot \dfrac{x_0^2}{4} = 2 \Rightarrow x_0^3 = 8 \Rightarrow x_0 = 2$

$\Rightarrow y_0 = \dfrac{x_0^2}{4} = \dfrac{2^2}{4} = 1$ **(1 Mark)**

Equation of normal

$(y - 1) = \dfrac{-2}{2}(x - 2) \Rightarrow y - 1 = -x + 2$

$x + y - 3 = 0$ **(½ Mark)**

Also, equation of required tangent is

$$(y - 1) = \frac{2}{2}(x - 2) \Rightarrow y - 1 = x - 2$$

$$x - y - 1 = 0 \qquad \textbf{(½ Mark)}$$

25. The equation $x^2 = 4y$ ...(1) represents an upward parabola with vertex at $(0, 0)$

The equation $x = 4y - 2$ ...(2) represents a straight line

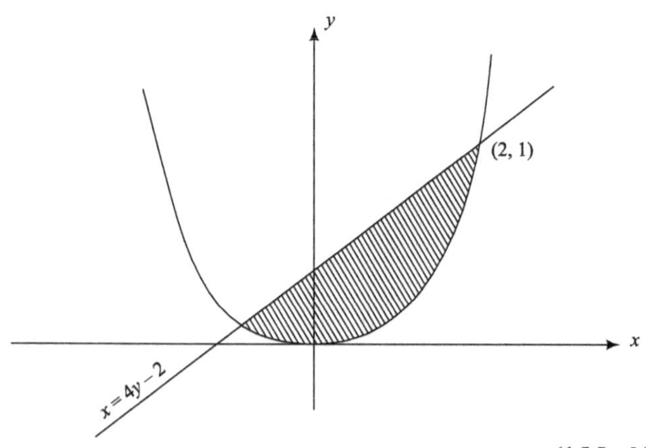

(1 Mark)

Intersection of parabola and line

$$x^2 = 4y,\ x = 4y - 2$$

$$x = x^2 - 2,\ x^2 - x - 2 = 0$$

$$x = 2, -1$$

When $x = 2$, $y = \dfrac{x^2}{4} = \dfrac{4}{4} = 1$

When $x = -1$, $y = \dfrac{1}{4}$

Intersection points are $(2, 1)$ and $\left(-1, \dfrac{1}{4}\right)$ **(1 Mark)**

Required area $= \displaystyle\int_{-1}^{2} (\text{Line})dx - \int_{-1}^{2} (\text{Parabola})dx$

$$= \int_{-1}^{2}\left(\frac{x+2}{4}\right)dx - \int_{-1}^{2}\frac{x^2}{4}dx \qquad \textbf{(1 Mark)}$$

$$= \frac{1}{4}\left[\frac{x^2}{2} + 2x\right]_{-1}^{2} - \frac{1}{4}\left[\frac{x^3}{3}\right]_{-1}^{2} \qquad \textbf{(1 Mark)}$$

$$= \frac{1}{4}\left[\frac{2^2}{2} + 4 - \left(\frac{1}{2} - 2\right)\right] - \frac{1}{12}\left[2^3 - (-1)^3\right]$$

$$= \frac{1}{4}\left(6 + \frac{3}{2}\right) - \frac{1}{12}\times 9 = \frac{15}{8} - \frac{3}{4}$$

$$= \frac{9}{8}\ \text{square units} \qquad \textbf{(2 Marks)}$$

OR

Given: Equation of two circles are

$$x^2 + y^2 = 4 \qquad\qquad\qquad ...(1)$$

$$(x - 2)^2 + y^2 = 4 \qquad\qquad ...(2)$$

Circle in eq. (1), Centre $(0, 0)$, $r = 2$

Circle in eq. (2), Centre $(2, 0)$, $r = 2$

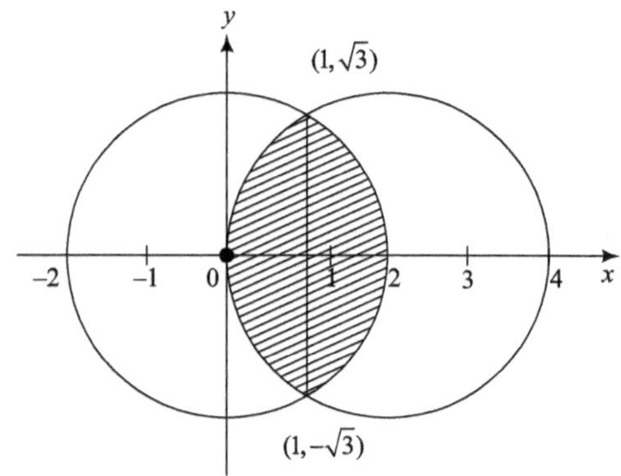

(1 Mark)

Now, we find the point of intersection of the two circles.

Subtracting (2) – (1)

$$(x - 2)^2 - x^2 = 0 \Rightarrow x^2 + 4 - 4x - x^2 = 0$$

$$4 - 4x = 0 \Rightarrow x = 1$$

$$1 + y^2 = 4 \Rightarrow y = \pm\sqrt{3}$$

Point of intersection $(1, \sqrt{3})$ and $(1, -\sqrt{3})$ **(1 Mark)**

Area of shaded region $= 2\left[\displaystyle\int_{0}^{1} y\,dx + \int_{1}^{2} y\,dx\right]$

Area $= 2\left[\displaystyle\int_{0}^{1}\sqrt{4-(x-2)^2}\,dx + \int_{1}^{2}\sqrt{4-x^2}\,dx\right]$ **(1 Mark)**

As $\left[\displaystyle\int\sqrt{a^2 - x^2}\,dx = \frac{x}{2}\sqrt{a^2 - x^2} + \frac{a^2}{2}\sin^{-1}\frac{x}{a}\right]$

Area $= 2\left[\left(\dfrac{x-2}{2}\sqrt{4-(x-2)^2} + \dfrac{4}{2}\sin^{-1}\left(\dfrac{x-2}{2}\right)\right)_{0}^{1}\right.$

$$\left. + \left(\dfrac{x}{2}\sqrt{4-x^2} + \dfrac{4}{2}\sin^{-1}\dfrac{x}{2}\right)_{1}^{2}\right]$$

(1 Mark)

$$= 2\left[\left(\dfrac{x-2}{2}\sqrt{4-(x-2)^2} + 2\sin^{-1}\left(\dfrac{x-2}{2}\right)\right)_{0}^{1}\right.$$

$$\left. + \left(\dfrac{x}{2}\sqrt{4-x^2} + 2\sin^{-1}\dfrac{x}{2}\right)_{1}^{2}\right]$$

$$= 2\left[\left[\frac{-1}{2}\sqrt{3}+2\sin^{-1}\left(\frac{-1}{2}\right)-2\sin^{-1}(-1)\right]\right.$$

$$\left.+\left[2\sin^{-1}1\right]-\frac{1}{2}\sqrt{3}-2\sin^{-1}\frac{1}{2}\right]$$

$$= 2\left[-\frac{\sqrt{3}}{2}+2\sin^{-1}\sin\left(-\frac{\pi}{6}\right)-2\sin^{-1}\sin\left(-\frac{\pi}{2}\right)+\right.$$

$$\left. 2\sin^{-1}\sin\frac{\pi}{2}-\frac{\sqrt{3}}{2}-2\sin^{-1}\sin\frac{\pi}{6}\right]$$

$$= 2\left[-\frac{\sqrt{3}}{2}+2\left(-\frac{\pi}{6}\right)-2\left(-\frac{\pi}{2}\right)+2\left(\frac{\pi}{2}\right)-\frac{\sqrt{3}}{2}-2\left(\frac{\pi}{6}\right)\right]$$

$$= 2\left[-\frac{\sqrt{3}}{2}-\frac{\pi}{3}+\pi+\pi-\frac{\sqrt{3}}{2}-\frac{\pi}{3}\right]$$

$$= 2\left[\frac{-2\sqrt{3}}{2}-\frac{\pi}{3}+2\pi-\frac{\pi}{3}\right] = \left[\frac{8\pi}{3}-2\sqrt{3}\right] \text{ sq. units}$$

Hence required area $= \left[\dfrac{8\pi}{3}-2\sqrt{3}\right]$ sq. units. **(2 Marks)**

26. Given:

$$2y \cdot e^{x/y}\,dx + (y - 2x\,e^{x/y})\,dy = 0$$

$$\frac{dx}{dy} = -\frac{(y-2xe^{x/y})}{2ye^{x/y}}=\frac{2xe^{x/y}-y}{2ye^{x/y}}$$

Let $F(x, y) = \dfrac{2xe^{x/y}-y}{2ye^{x/y}}$

$$\therefore\ F(\lambda x, \lambda y) = \frac{2\lambda xe^{\lambda x/\lambda y}-\lambda y}{2\lambda ye^{\lambda x/\lambda y}}$$

$$= \lambda^0\frac{2xe^{x/y}-y}{2ye^{x/y}} = \lambda^0\,F(x, y)$$

Hence, given differential equation is homogeneous.

(1 Mark)

Now, $\dfrac{dx}{dy} = \dfrac{2xe^{x/y}-y}{2ye^{x/y}}$ ...(1)

Let $x = vy \Rightarrow \dfrac{dx}{dy} = v+y\,\dfrac{dv}{dy}$ **(1 Mark)**

From (1)

$$\Rightarrow v+y\frac{dv}{dy} = \frac{2vye^{\frac{vy}{y}}-y}{2ye^{\frac{vy}{y}}}$$

$$\Rightarrow y\frac{dv}{dy} = \frac{y(2ve^v-1)}{2ye^v}-v = \frac{2ve^v-1}{2e^v}-v = -\frac{1}{2e^v}$$

$$\Rightarrow 2ye^v\,dv = -dy$$

$$\Rightarrow 2\int e^v\,dv = -\int\frac{dy}{y}$$ **(2 Marks)**

$$\Rightarrow 2e^v = -\log y + C$$

$$\Rightarrow 2e^{x/y} + \log y = C$$ **(½ Mark)**

When $x = 0$, $y = 1$

$$\Rightarrow 2e^0 + \log 1 = C$$

$$\Rightarrow C = 2$$ **(1 Mark)**

Hence required solution is

$$2e^{x/y} + \log y = 2$$ **(½ Mark)**

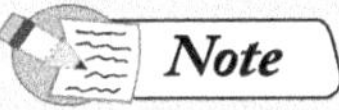

For a homogenous differential equation of form $\dfrac{dx}{dy}$, always assume $x = vy$

27. Plane passes through three points
$(1, 1, -2)$ $(2, -1, 1)$ and $(1, 2, 1)$

Equation of plane is given as

$$\begin{vmatrix} x-1 & y-1 & z+2 \\ 2-1 & -1-1 & 1+2 \\ 1-1 & 2-1 & 1+2 \end{vmatrix} = 0$$ **(1 Mark)**

$$\begin{vmatrix} x-1 & y-1 & z+2 \\ 1 & -2 & 3 \\ 0 & 1 & 3 \end{vmatrix} = 0$$

$(x - 1)(-6 - 3) - (y - 1)(3 - 0) + (z + 2)(1 + 0) = 0$

$$\Rightarrow -9x + 9 - 3y + 3 + z + 2 = 0$$

$$\Rightarrow 9x + 3y - z = 14$$

Vector form: $\vec{r}\cdot(9\hat{i}+3\hat{j}-\hat{k}) = 14$ **(2 Marks)**

The given line is

$$\vec{r} = (3\hat{i}-\hat{j}+\hat{k})+\lambda(2\hat{i}-2\hat{j}+\hat{k})$$

Cartesian form of line

$$\frac{x-3}{2}=\frac{y+1}{-2}=\frac{z+1}{1}=\lambda$$

$$\Rightarrow \alpha = 2\lambda + 3,\ \beta = -2\lambda - 1,\ v = \lambda - 1$$ **(1 Mark)**

Let line intersect plane at (α, β, γ)

$\therefore\ (\alpha, \beta, \gamma)$ lie on plane

$$9\alpha + 3\beta - \gamma = 14$$

$$\Rightarrow 9(2\lambda + 3) + 3(-2\lambda - 1) - (\lambda - 1) = 14$$

$$\Rightarrow 18\lambda + 27 - 6\lambda - 3 - \lambda + 1 = 14$$

$$\Rightarrow 11\lambda = 14 - 25 \Rightarrow 11\lambda = -11 \Rightarrow \lambda = -1$$

$\therefore$ Point of intersection is $(1, 1, -2)$ **(2 Marks)**

Write the equation of plane form cartisian to vector form by replacing x, y, z by $\hat{i}, \hat{j}, \hat{k}$ respectively with dot product r and constant remains same.

28. Let x and y hectare of land be allocated to crop A and B respectively

If Z is profit

Maximize $Z = 10500x + 9000y$

Subject to constraints

$x + y \leq 50$

$20x + 10y \leq 800 \Rightarrow 2x + y \leq 80$

$x \geq 0, y \leq 0$ **(2 Marks)**

$x + y = 50$

x	0	50
y	50	0

$2x + y = 80$

x	0	40
y	80	0

Intersection point $y = 50 - x$

$2x + y = 80 \Rightarrow 2x + 90 - x = 80$

$y = 50 - 30 = 20$, Point (30, 20) **(1 Mark)**

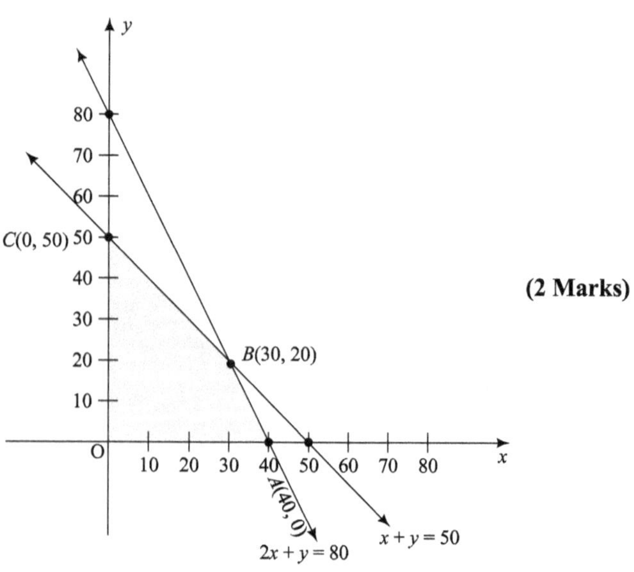

(2 Marks)

$OABC$ is feasible region with corner points O(0, 0), A(40, 0), B(30, 20), C(0, 50)

Corner Point	$Z = 10500x + 9000y$	
O(0, 0)	0	
A(40, 0)	420000	
B(30, 20)	495000	← **Maximum**
C(0, 50)	450000	

Hence co-operative society of farmers will get the maximum profit of ₹4,95,000 by allocating 30 hectares for crop A and 20 hectares for crop B. **(½ Mark)**

Yes, because excess use of herbicide can make drainage water poisonous and thus it harm the life of water living creature and wildlife. **(½ Mark)**

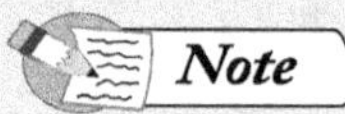 *Note*

In order to get feasible region in LPP, always check inequality and shade the region with the inequality sign.

29. Let E_1, E_2, A be events defined as

E_1 = treatment of heart attack with yoga and meditation.

E_2 = treatment of heart attack with certain drugs **(1 Mark)**

A = Person getting heart attack.

$$P(E_1) = \frac{1}{2}, \; P(E_2) = \frac{1}{2}$$

Now $P\left(\dfrac{A}{E_1}\right) = 40\% - 40 \times \dfrac{30}{100}$

$= 40\% - 12\% = 28\% = \dfrac{28}{100}$

$P\left(\dfrac{A}{E_2}\right) = 40\% - \left(40 \times \dfrac{25}{100}\right)$

$= 40\% - 10\% = 30\% = \dfrac{30}{100}$ **(1 Mark)**

$P(E_1/A)$ = Person getting heart attack treated with yoga and meditation

By Bayes' theorem

$$P\left(\frac{E_1}{A}\right) = \frac{P(E_1).P\left(\dfrac{A}{E_1}\right)}{P(E_1).P\left(\dfrac{A}{E_1}\right) + P(E_2).P\left(\dfrac{A}{E_2}\right)}$$ **(1 Mark)**

$$= \frac{\dfrac{1}{2} \times \dfrac{28}{100}}{\dfrac{1}{2} \times \dfrac{28}{100} + \dfrac{1}{2} \times \dfrac{30}{100}} = \frac{28}{100} \times \frac{100}{58} = \frac{14}{29}$$ **(2 Marks)**

The problem emphasises the importance of yoga and meditation.

Treatment with yoga and meditation is more beneficial for the heart patient. **(1 Mark)**

www.ingramcontent.com/pod-product-compliance
Lightning Source LLC
LaVergne TN
LVHW060511070726
842759LV00029BA/940